core JAVA ™ 1.2

Volume I – Fundamentals

D0817559

THE SUN MICROSYSTEMS PRESS
JAVA SERIES

▼ **Core Java 1.2, Volume 1 - Fundamentals**
Cay S. Horstmann & Gary Cornell

▼ **Core Java 1.2, Volume 2 - Advanced Features**
Cay S. Horstmann & Gary Cornell

▼ **Graphic Java 1.2, Volume I: AWT**
David M. Geary

▼ **Graphic Java 1.2, Volume II: Swing**
David M. Geary

▼ **Graphic Java 1.2, Volume III: Advanced Swing**
David M. Geary

▼ **Graphic Java 1.2, Volume IV: 2D API**
David M. Geary

▼ **Inside Java Workshop 2.0**
Lynn Weaver

▼ **Instant Java, Third Edition**
John A. Pew & Stephen G. Pew

▼ **Java by Example 1.2**
Jerry R. Jackson & Alan L. McClellan

▼ **Java Studio by Example**
Lynn Weaver & Leslie Robertson

▼ **Jumping JavaScript**
Janice Winsor & Brian Freeman

▼ **Just Java 1.2**
Peter van der Linden

▼ **More Jumping JavaScript**
Janice Winsor, Brian Freeman, & Bill Anderson

▼ **Not Just Java, Second Edition**
Peter van der Linden

core JAVA™ 1.2

Volume I – Fundamentals

CAY S. HORSTMANN • GARY CORNELL

Sun Microsystems Press
A Prentice Hall Title

The publisher offers discounts on this book when ordered in bulk quantities.
For more information, contact Corporate Sales Department, Prentice Hall PTR ,
One Lake Street, Upper Saddle River, NJ 07458. Phone: 800-382-3419; FAX: 201- 236-7141.
E-mail: corpsales@prenhall.com.

Editorial/production supervision: *Navta Associates*
Cover design director: *Jerry Votta*
Cover designer: *Anthony Gemmellaro*
Cover illustration: *Karen Strelecki*
Manufacturing manager: *Alexis R. Heydt*
Marketing manager: *Kaylie Smith*
Acquisitions editor: *Gregory G. Doench*
Sun Microsystems Press publisher: *Rachel Borden*

10 9

ISBN 0-13-081933-6

Sun Microsystems Press
A Prentice Hall Title

Contents

Chapter 10

Chapter 11

List of Tables
Code Examples
and Figures

Tables

Code Examples

Preface

To the Reader

In late 1995, the Java programming language burst onto the Internet scene and gained instant celebrity status. The promise of Java is that it will become the *universal glue* that connects users with information, whether that information comes from Web servers, databases, information providers, and any other imaginable source. Indeed Java is in a unique position to fulfill this promise. It is an extremely solidly engineered language that has gained acceptance by all major vendors. Its built-in security and safety features are reassuring both to programmers and to the users of Java programs. Java even has built-in support that makes advanced programming tasks, such as network programming, database connectivity, and multithreading, straightforward.

Since then, Sun Microsystems has released three major revisions of the language. Version 1.02, released in 1996, supported database connectivity and distributed objects. Version 1.1, released in 1997, added a robust event model, internationalization, and the Java Beans component model. Version 1.2, released at the end of 1998, has numerous enhancements, but one major improvement stands out: the "Swing" user interface toolkit that finally allows programmers to write truly portable GUI applications.

The book you have in your hand is the fourth edition of our *Core Java* book. Each time, the book followed the release of the Java development kit as quickly as possible, and each time, we rewrote the book to take advantage of the newest Java features. This time is no exception. In particular, all examples are updated to use the Swing toolkit and other 1.2 features.

As with the previous editions of this book, we *still target serious programmers who want to put Java to work on real projects.* We still guarantee no nervous text or dancing tooth-shaped characters. We think of you, our reader, as a programmer with a solid background in a programming language. *But you do not need to know C++ or object-oriented programming.* Based on the responses we have received to the earlier editions of this book, we remain confident that experienced Visual Basic, C, COBOL, Delphi, or PowerBuilder programmers will have no trouble with this book. (You don't even need any experience in building graphical user interfaces in Windows, Unix, or the Macintosh.)

What we do is assume you want to:

- Write real code to solve real problems

and

- Don't like books filled with toy examples (such as kitchen appliances or fruit trees).

You will find lots of sample code on the accompanying CD that demonstrates almost every language and library feature that we discuss. We kept the sample programs purposefully simple to focus on the major points, but, for the most part, they aren't fake and they don't cut corners. They should make good starting points for your own code.

We assume you are willing, even eager, to learn about all the advanced features that Java puts at your disposal. For example, we give you a detailed treatment of:

- Object-oriented programming
- The Java reflection mechanism
- Inner classes
- Java event listener model
- Graphical user interface design with the Swing UI toolkit
- Exception handling (Java's error handling mechanism)
- Stream input/output and object serialization

We *still* don't spend much time on the fun but less serious kind of Java programs whose sole purpose is to liven up your Web page. There are quite a few sources for this kind of material already—we recommend John Pew's book *Instant Java*, also published by Sun Microsystems Press/Prentice Hall.

Finally, with the explosive growth of the Java class library, a one-volume treatment of all the features of Java that serious programmers need to know is no longer possible. Hence, we decided to break the book up into two volumes. The first volume, which you hold in your hands, concentrates on the fundamental concepts of the Java language, along with the basics of user-interface programming. The second volume goes further into the enterprise features and advanced user-interface programming. It includes detailed discussions of:

- Multithreading
- Network programming
- Distributed objects
- Container classes
- Databases
- Advanced graphics
- Advanced GUI components
- Internationalization
- Native methods
- JavaBeans

When writing a book, errors and inaccuracies are inevitable. We'd very much like to know about them. But, of course, we'd prefer to learn about each of them only once. We have put up a list of frequently asked questions, bugs fixes, and workarounds in a Web page at http://www.horstmann.com. Strategically placed at the end of the FAQ (to encourage you to read through it first) is a form you can use to report bugs and problems.

We hope that you find this book enjoyable and helpful in your Java programming.

About This Book

Chapter 1 gives an overview of the capabilities of Java that set it apart from other programming languages. We explain what the designers of the language set out to do and to what extent they succeeded. Then, we give a short history of how Java came into being and how it has evolved.

In Chapter 2, we tell you how to install Java and the companion software for this book from the CD-ROM onto your computer. Then we guide you through compiling and running three typical Java programs, a console application, a graphical application, and an applet.

Chapter 3 starts the discussion of the Java language. In this chapter, we cover the basics: variables, loops, and simple functions. If you are a C or C++ programmer, this is smooth sailing because the syntax for these language features is essentially the same as in C. If you come from a non-C background such as Visual Basic or Pascal/Delphi, you will want to read this chapter carefully.

Object-oriented programming (OOP) is now in the mainstream of programming practice, and Java is completely object oriented. Chapter 4 introduces *encapsulation*, the first of two fundamental building blocks of object orientation, and the Java language mechanism to implement it, that is, classes and methods. In addition to the rules of the Java language, we also give advice on sound OOP design. If you are familiar with C++, then you can browse through this chapter quickly. Programmers coming from a non-object-oriented background should expect to spend some time mastering OOP concepts before going further with Java.

Classes and encapsulation are only one part of the OOP story, and Chapter 5 introduces the other, namely, *inheritance*. Inheritance lets you take an existing class and modify it according to your needs. This is a fundamental technique for programming in Java. The inheritance mechanism in Java is quite similar to that in C++. Once again, C++ programmers can focus on the differences between the languages.

Chapter 6 shows you how to use Java's notion of an *interface*. Interfaces let you go beyond the simple inheritance model of Chapter 5. Mastering interfaces allows you full access to the power of Java's completely object-oriented approach to programming. We also cover a useful technical feature of Java here. These are called *inner classes*. Inner classes help make your code cleaner and more concise.

In Chapter 7, we begin application programming in earnest. We show how you can make windows, how to paint on them, how to draw with geometric shapes, how to format text in multiple fonts, and how to display images.

Chapter 8 is a detailed discussion of the event model of the AWT, the *abstract windows toolkit*. (We discuss the event model that was added to Java 1.1, not the obsolete and simplistic 1.0 event model.) You'll see how to write the code that responds to events like mouse clicks or key presses. Along the way you'll see how to handle basic GUI elements like buttons and panels.

Chapter 9 discusses the Swing GUI toolkit in great detail. The Swing toolkit is how you can use Java to build a cross-platform graphical user interface. You'll learn all about the various kinds of buttons, text components, borders, scroll bars, list boxes, menus, and dialog boxes. However, some of the more advanced components are discussed in Volume 2.

After you finish Chapter 9, you finally have all mechanisms in place to write *applets*, those mini-programs that can live inside a Web page, and so applets are the topic of Chapter 10. We show you a number of useful and fun applets, but more importantly, we show you what goes on behind the scenes. And we show you how to use the Java Plug-in that enables you to roll out applets that take advantage of all the newest Java features, even if your users use old browsers or browsers made by hostile vendors.

Chapter 11 discusses *exception handling*, Java's robust mechanism to deal with the fact that bad things can happen to good programs. For example, a network connection can become unavailable in the middle of a file download, a disk can fill up, and so on. Exceptions give you an efficient way of separating the normal processing code from the error handling. Of course, even after hardening your program by handling all exceptional conditions, it still might fail to work as expected. In the second half of this chapter, we give you some debugging tips. Finally, we guide you through a sample debugging session with the JDB debugger to show you the basics of Java debugging. While the JDB is not useful for serious work, understanding the JDB will help you when you move to a debugger from a professional development environment.

We finish the book with input and output handling. In Java, all I/O is handled through so-called *streams*. Streams let you deal in a uniform manner with communicating with any source of data, such as files, network connections, or memory blocks. We include detailed coverage of the reader and writer classes, which make it easy to deal with Unicode; and we show you what goes on under the hood when you use object serialization mechanism, which makes saving and loading objects easy and convenient.

The appendices cover the Java keywords, the automatic Java documentation (javadoc) facility, and installation instructions for the CD-ROM.

Conventions

As is common in many computer books, we use `courier type` to represent computer code.

There are many C++ and Visual Basic (VB) notes that explain the difference between Java and these languages. You can skip over them if you don't have a background in either of those languages.

Notes and tips are tagged with "note" and "tip" icons that look like these.

When there is danger ahead, we warn you with a "Caution" icon.

Java comes with a large programming library or Application Programming Interface (API). When using an API call for the first time, we add a short summary description tagged with an API icon at the end of the section. These descriptions are a bit more informal, but we hope also a little more informative than those in the official on-line API documentation.

Programs whose source code is on the CD-ROM are listed as examples, for instance **Example 2–4: WelcomeApplet.java**.

CD-ROM

The CD-ROM on the back of the book contains the latest version of the Java development kit. At the time we are writing this, these materials are available only for Windows 95/NT or Solaris 2.

Of course, the CD-ROM contains all sample code from the book, compressed as a ZIP file. You can expand the file either with one of the familiar unzipping programs or simply with the jar utility that is part of the Java Development Kit.

The CD-ROM also contains shareware programs that you may find helpful for your development. Please read Appendix 3 for detailed installation instructions for the Java Development Kit, the sample code, and the other CD ROM materials.

NOTE: People have often asked what the licensing requirements for using the sample code in a commercial situation are. You can freely use any code from this book for non-commercial use. However, if you do want to use the code as a basis for a commercial product, we simply require that every person on the development team for that project own a copy of *Core Java*.

Acknowledgments

Cay's love and gratitude go once again to his wife Hui-Chen and his children Tommy and Nina for their patience and support for this never-ending book project. He also appreciates the support and understanding from Vincent Pluvinage and his colleagues at Preview Systems.

Gary wants to thank his friends and his co-workers for their patience as he too slowly extricated himself from the quagmire of his own overcommitments.

The *heroes* of this book production were our long-suffering editor, Greg Doench at Prentice-Hall, who once again managed to fight the odds and kept this project on track, always being the gentleman in the process; our copyeditor Mary Lou Nohr for bringing the manuscript into publishable shape; and our production coordinator Kathi Beste from Navta Associates, who did a superb job organizing the editing and typesetting of the manuscript. You three were instrumental in getting this book out on time—a big "Thank you" for your tremendous efforts! This time around, there were also a number of *villains* who were trying to torpedo this project—you know who you are.

We also would like to thank Mary Treacy and Yvette Raven from Prentice-Hall, for their work with the errata reports and the Web site, Hui-Chen Hung and Blake Connell from Sun Microsystems, for help with API notes and the Java Plug-in, and Bert and Marilyn Stutz at Navta Associates for the typesetting work. Thanks also to all the folks at Prentice-Hall, and Sun Microsystems who worked behind the scenes to get the book produced and into the bookstores. Finally, a big thanks to our reviewers who greatly contributed into making this a better book: Buzzy Brown from IBM, Alexander Day Chaffee, CEO of Purple Technology, Judah Diament from New York University, John Gray from the University of Hartford, John Mannino and Vipin Agrawal from Sun Microsystems, and our fellow Prentice-Hall authors Marty Hall, Tim Kimmet, Chris Taylor, and Kim Topley.

Chapter 1

An Introduction to Java

For a long time, to open a computer magazine that did not have a feature article on Java seemed impossible. Even mainstream newspapers and magazines like *The New York Times*, *The Washington Post*, and *Business Week* have run numerous articles on Java. It gets better (or worse, depending on your perspective): can you remember the last time National Public Radio ran a 10-minute story on a computer language? Or, a $100,000,000 venture capital fund is set up solely for products produced using a *specific* computer language? CNN, CNBC, you name the mass medium, it seems everyone was and to a certain extent is still talking about how Java will do this or Java will do that.

However, we decided to write this book for serious programmers, and because Java is a serious programming language, there's a lot to tell. So, rather than immediately getting caught up in an analysis of the Java hype and trying to deal with the limited (if still interesting) truth behind the hype, we will write, in some detail, about Java as a programming language (including, of course, the features added for its use on the Internet that started the hype). After that, we will try to separate current fact from fancy by explaining what Java can and cannot do.

In the early days of Java, there was a huge disconnect between the hype and the actual abilities of Java. As Java is maturing, the technology is becoming a lot more stable and reliable, and expectations are coming down to reasonable levels. As we write this, Java is being increasingly used for "middleware" to communicate between clients and databases and other server resources. While not glitzy, this is an important area where Java, primarily due to its portability and multi-threading and networking capabilities, can add real value. Java is making great inroads in embedded systems, where it is well positioned to become a standard for hand-held devices, Internet kiosks, car computers, and so on. However, early attempts to rewrite familiar PC programs in Java were not encouraging—the applications were underpowered and slow. With the current version of Java, some of these problems could be overcome, but still, users don't generally care what programming language was used to write their applications. We think that the benefits of Java will come from new kinds of devices and applications, not from rewriting existing ones.

Java as a Programming Tool

As a computer language, Java's hype is overdone: Java is certainly a *good* programming language. There is no doubt that it is one of the better languages available to serious programmers. We think it could *potentially* have been a great programming language, but it is probably too late for that. Once a language is out in the field, the ugly reality of compatibility with existing code sets in. Moreover, even in cases where changes are possible without breaking existing code, it is hard for the creators of a language as acclaimed as Java to sit back and say, "Well, maybe we were wrong about X, and Y would be better." In sum, while we expect there to be some improvements over time, basically, the structure of the Java language tomorrow will be much the same as it is today.

Having said that, the obvious question is, Where did the dramatic improvements of Java come from? The answer is that they didn't come from changes to the underlying Java programming language, they came from *major changes in the Java libraries*. Over time, Sun Microsystems changed everything from the names of many of the library functions (to make them more consistent), to how graphics worked (by changing the event handling model and rewriting parts from scratch), to adding important features like printing that were not part of Java 1.0. The result is a far more useful programming tool, a tool moreover that, while not yet completely robust, is far less flaky than were earlier versions of Java.

But *every* version of Java has made major changes to the libraries of its predecessor, and the current version is no exception. In fact, the changes made in the libraries are by far the most extensive in Java 1.2—there is roughly a *doubling of the number of library functions* over Java 1.1.

> NOTE: Microsoft is producing a product called J++ that shares a family relationship with Java. Like Java, J++ is interpreted by a virtual machine that is compatible with the Java Virtual Machine for executing Java bytecodes, but there are substantial differences when interfacing with external code. The basic language syntax is almost identical to Java. However, Microsoft added language constructs that are of doubtful utility except for interfacing with the Windows API. In addition to Java and J++ sharing a common syntax, their foundational libraries (strings, utilities, networking, multithreading, math, and so on) are essentially identical. However, the libraries for graphics, user interfaces, and remote object access are completely different. Beyond the common syntax that is discussed in Chapters 3–6, we do not cover J++ in this book.

Advantages of Java

One obvious advantage is a run-time library that hopes to provide platform independence: you are supposed to be able to use the same code on Windows 95/98/NT, Solaris, Unix, Macintosh, and so on. This is certainly necessary for Internet programming. (However, implementations on other platforms usually lag behind those on Windows and Solaris. For example, as we write this, Java 1.2 is not even in beta for the Mac.)

Another programming advantage is that Java has a syntax similar to that of C++, which makes it economical without being absurd. Then again, Visual Basic (VB) programmers will probably find the syntax annoying and miss some of the nicer syntactic VB constructs like Select Case.

> NOTE: If you are coming from a language other than C++, some of the terms used in this section will be less familiar—just skip those sections. You will be comfortable with all of these terms by the end of Chapter 6.

Java also is fully object oriented—even more so than C++. Everything in Java, except for a few basic types like numbers, is an object. (Object-oriented design has replaced earlier structured techniques because it has many advantages for dealing with sophisticated projects. If you are not familiar with Object-Oriented Programming (OOP), Chapters 4 through 6 provide what you need to know.)

However, having yet another, somewhat improved, dialect of C++ would not be enough. The key point is this: *It is far easier to turn out bug-free code using Java than using C++.*

Why? The designers of Java thought hard about what makes C++ code so buggy. They added features to Java that eliminate the *possibility* of creating code with the most common kinds of bugs. (Some estimates say that roughly every 50 lines of C++ code have at least one bug.)

- The Java designers eliminated manual memory allocation and deallocation.

  Memory in Java is automatically garbage collected. You *never* have to worry about memory leaks.

- They introduced true arrays and eliminated pointer arithmetic.

  You *never* have to worry about overwriting a key area of memory because of an off-by-one error when working with a pointer.

- They eliminated the possibility of confusing an assignment with a test for equality in a conditional.

  You cannot even compile if (ntries = 3) . . . . (VB programmers may not see the problem, but, trust us, this is a common source of confusion in C/C++ code.)

- They eliminated multiple inheritance, replacing it with a new notion of *interface* that they derived from Objective C.

  Interfaces give you what you want from multiple inheritance, without the complexity that comes with managing multiple inheritance hierarchies. (If inheritance is a new concept for you, Chapter 5 will explain it.)

NOTE: The Java language specification is public. You can find it on the Web by going to the Java home page and following the links given there. (The Java home page is at http://java.sun.com.)

The Java "White Paper" Buzzwords

The authors of Java have written an influential White Paper that explains their design goals and accomplishments. Their paper is organized along the following eleven buzzwords:

Simple	Portable
Object Oriented	Interpreted
Distributed	High Performance
Robust	Multithreaded
Secure	Dynamic
Architecture Neutral	

We touched on some of these points in the last section. In this section, we will:

- Summarize via excerpts from the White Paper what the Java designers say about each buzzword, and

- Tell you what we think of that particular buzzword, based on our experiences with the current version of Java.

NOTE: As we write this, the White Paper can be found at `http://java.sun.com/doc/language_environment`. (If it has moved, you can find it by marching through the links at the Java home page.)

Simple

> *We wanted to build a system that could be programmed easily without a lot of esoteric training and which leveraged today's standard practice. So even though we found that C++ was unsuitable, we designed Java as closely to C++ as possible in order to make the system more comprehensible. Java omits many rarely used, poorly understood, confusing features of C++ that, in our experience, bring more grief than benefit.*

The syntax for Java is, indeed, a cleaned-up version of the syntax for C++. There is no need for header files, pointer arithmetic (or even a pointer syntax), structures, unions, operator overloading, virtual base classes, and so on. (See the C++ notes interspersed throughout the text for more on the differences between Java and C++.) The designers did not, however, *improve* on some stupid features in C++, like the `switch` statement. If you know C++, you will find the transition to Java's syntax easy.

If you are a VB programmer, you will not find Java simple. There is much strange syntax (though it does not take long to get the hang of it). More importantly, you must do a lot more programming in Java. The beauty of VB is that its visual design environment provides a lot of the infrastructure for an application almost automatically. The equivalent functionality must be programmed manually, usually with a fair bit of code, in Java. (See the following description of how Sun Microsystems is bringing the component-based, "glue" model to Java programming via "JavaBeans," a specification for developing plug-and-play components.)

At this point, the Java language is pretty simple, as object-oriented languages go. But there are many subtle points that you need to know to solve real-world problems. As time goes by, more and more of these details will be farmed off to libraries and development environments. Products like Sun's Java WorkShop, Symantec's Visual Café, and Inprise JBuilder have form designers that can make designing the interface of your programs easier. They are far from perfect but are a step forward. (Designing forms with nothing but the JDK is tedious at best and unbearable at worst.) An ever-increasing supply of third-party class libraries and a lot of code samples (including many libraries) are actually freely available on the Net.

> *Another aspect of being simple is being small. One of the goals of Java is to enable the construction of software that can run stand-alone in small machines. The size of the basic interpreter and class support is about 40K bytes; adding the basic standard libraries and thread support (essentially a self-contained microkernel) adds an additional 175K.*

This is a great achievement. Note, however, that the GUI libraries are significantly larger.

Object Oriented

> *Simply stated, object-oriented design is a technique for programming that focuses on the data (= objects) and on the interfaces to that object. To make an analogy with carpentry, an "object-oriented" carpenter would be mostly concerned with the chair he was building, and secondarily with the tools used to make it; a "non-object-oriented" carpenter would think primarily of his tools. The object-oriented facilities of Java are essentially those of C++.*

Object orientation has proven its worth in the last 30 years, and it is inconceivable that a modern programming language would not use it. Indeed, the object-oriented features of Java are comparable to C++. The major difference between Java and C++ lies in multiple inheritance, for which Java has found a better solution, and in the Java metaclass model. The reflection mechanism (see Chapter 5) and object serialization feature (see Volume 2) make it much easier to implement persistent objects and GUI builders that can integrate off-the-shelf-components.

> NOTE: If you do not have any experience with OOP languages, you will want to carefully read Chapters 4 through 6. These chapters explain what OOP is and why it is more useful for programming sophisticated projects than traditional, procedure-oriented languages like BASIC or C.

Distributed

> *Java has an extensive library of routines for coping with TCP/IP protocols like HTTP and FTP. Java applications can open and access objects across the Net via URLs with the same ease as when accessing a local file system.*

We have found the networking capabilities of Java to be both strong and easy to use. Anyone who has tried to do Internet programming using another language will revel in how simple Java makes onerous tasks like opening a socket connection. Java even makes common gateway interface (CGI) scripting easier, and an elegant mechanism, called servlets, makes server-side processing in Java extremely efficient. Many popular web servers support servlets. (We will cover networking in Volume 2 of this book.) The remote method invocation mechanism enables communication between distributed objects (also covered in Volume 2).

Robust

Java is intended for writing programs that must be reliable in a variety of ways. Java puts a lot of emphasis on early checking for possible problems, later dynamic (run-time) checking, and eliminating situations that are error-prone.... The single biggest difference between Java and C/C++ is that Java has a pointer model that eliminates the possibility of overwriting memory and corrupting data.

This feature is also very useful. The Java compiler (in both its original incarnation and in the various improved versions in third-party implementations) detects many problems that, in other languages, would only show up at run time (or, perhaps, not even then). As for the second point, anyone who has spent hours chasing memory corruption caused by a pointer bug will be very happy with this feature of Java.

If you are coming from a language like VB that doesn't explicitly use pointers, you are probably wondering why this is so important. C programmers are not so lucky. They need pointers to access strings, arrays, objects, even files. In VB, you do not use pointers for any of these entities, nor do you need to worry about memory allocation for them. On the other hand, if you implement some of the fancier data structures in VB that require pointers using class modules, you need to manage the memory yourself. Java gives you the best of both worlds. You do not need pointers for everyday constructs like strings and arrays. You have the power of pointers if you need it, for example, for linked lists. And you always have complete safety, since you can never access a bad pointer, make memory allocation errors, or have to protect against memory leaking away.

Secure

Java is intended to be used in networked/distributed environments. Toward that end, a lot of emphasis has been placed on security. Java enables the construction of virus-free, tamper-free systems.

In the first edition of *Core Java* we said: "Well, one should 'never say never again,'" and we turned out to be right. A group of security experts at Princeton University found the first bugs in the security features of Java 1.0—not long after the JDK 1.0 was shipped. Moreover, they and various other people have continued to find other bugs in the security mechanisms of all subsequent versions of Java. All we can suggest is that you check

1.   The URL for the Princeton group:
      http://www.cs.princeton.edu/sip/

2.   The `comp.risks` newsgroup

for opinions from outside experts on the current status of Java's security mechanisms.

The good side is that the Java team has said that they will have a "zero tolerance" for security bugs and will immediately go to work on fixing any bugs found in the applet security mechanism (the browser companies go to work immediately as well). In particular, by making public the internal specifications of how the Java interpreter works, Sun is making it far easier for people to find any bugs in Java's security features—essentially enlisting the outside community in the ever-so-subtle security bug detection. This makes one more confident that security bugs will be found as soon as possible. In any case, Java makes it extremely difficult to outwit its security mechanisms. The bugs found so far have been very subtle and (relatively) few in number.

NOTE: Sun's URL for security-related issues is currently at:
`http://java.sun.com/sfaq/`

Here is a sample of what Java's security features are supposed to keep a Java program from doing:

1.   Overrunning the run-time stack, like the infamous Internet worm did

2.   Corrupting memory outside its own process space

3.   Reading or writing local files when invoked through a security-conscious class loader, like a Web browser that has been programmed to forbid this kind of access

All of these features are in place and for the most part seem to work as intended. Java is certainly the most secure programming language to date. But, caution is always in order: though the bugs found in the security mechanism to date were not trivial to find and full details are often kept secret, still it may be impossible to *prove* that Java is secure. So, all we can do is repeat what we said before with even more force attached to it:

　　"*Never say never again.*"

Regardless of whether Java can ever be proved secure, Java 1.1 now has the notion of signed classes (see Volume 2). With a signed class, you can be sure of who wrote it. Once a signing mechanism is in place, any time you trust the author of the class, the class can be allowed more privileges on your machine.

> NOTE: A competing code delivery mechanism from Microsoft based on its ActiveX technology relies on digital signatures alone for security. Clearly this is not sufficient—as any user of Microsoft's own products can confirm, programs from well-known vendors do crash and in so doing, create damage. Java has a far stronger security model than ActiveX since it controls the application as it runs and stops it from wreaking havoc. (For example, you can ensure that local file input and output is forbidden even for signed classes.)

Architecture Neutral

The compiler generates an architecture neutral object file format—the compiled code is executable on many processors, given the presence of the Java run time system. The Java compiler does this by generating bytecode instructions which have nothing to do with a particular computer architecture. Rather, they are designed to be both easy to interpret on any machine and easily translated into native machine code on the fly.

This is not a new idea. More than twenty years ago, the UCSD Pascal system did the same thing in a commercial product, and even before that, Niklaus Wirth's original implementation of Pascal used the same approach. With the use of bytecodes, performance takes a major hit (but just-in-time compilers mitigate this, in many cases). The designers of Java did an excellent job developing a bytecode instruction set that works well on today's most common computer architectures. And the codes have been designed to translate easily into actual machine instructions.

Portable

Unlike C and C++, there are no "implementation-dependent" aspects of the specification. The sizes of the primitive data types are specified, as is the behavior of arithmetic on them.

For example, an int in Java is always a 32-bit integer. In C/C++, int can mean a 16-bit integer, a 32-bit integer, or any other size that the compiler vendor likes. The only restriction is that the int type must have at least as many bytes as a short int and cannot have more bytes than a long int. Having a fixed size of number types eliminates a major porting headache. Binary data is stored in a fixed format, eliminating the "big endian/little endian" confusion. Strings are saved in a standard Unicode format.

The libraries that are a part of the system define portable interfaces. For example, there is an abstract Window class and implementations of it for Unix, Windows, and the Macintosh.

As anyone who has ever tried knows, it is an effort of heroic proportions to write a program that looks good on Windows, the Macintosh, and 10 flavors of Unix. Java 1.0 made the heroic effort, delivering a simple toolkit that mapped common user-interface elements to a number of platforms. Unfortunately, the result was a library that, with a lot of work, could give barely acceptable results on different systems. (And there were often *different* bugs on the different platform graphics implementations.) But it was a start. There are many applications in which portability is more important than the nth degree of slickness, and these applications did benefit from early versions of Java. By now, the user interface toolkit has been completely rewritten so that it no longer relies on the host user interface. The result is far more consistent and, we think, more attractive than in earlier versions of Java.

Interpreted

The Java interpreter can execute Java bytecodes directly on any machine to which the interpreter has been ported. Since linking is a more incremental and lightweight process, the development process can be much more rapid and exploratory.

Perhaps this is an advantage while developing an application, but it is clearly overstated. In any case, we have found the Java compiler to be quite slow. If you are used to the speed of VB's or Delphi's development cycle, you will likely be disappointed.

High Performance

While the performance of interpreted bytecodes is usually more than adequate, there are situations where higher performance is required. The bytecodes can be translated on the fly (at run time) into machine code for the particular CPU the application is running on.

If you use the standard Java interpreter to translate the bytecodes, "high performance" is not the term that we would use ("middling to poor" is probably more accurate). While it is certainly true that the speed of the interpreted bytecodes can be acceptable, it isn't fast. (At best, Java is only slightly faster than VB4, according to our tests, and is not as fast as later versions of VB.) On the other hand, you will want to run many Java programs through a true compiler and not restrict yourself to interpreting the bytecodes. For example, you will almost certainly want to do so for any program that is designed to be a stand-alone application on a specific machine. Ultimately, you will want compilers for every platform.

Some native code compilers for Java are available, for example, from Asymetrix, Symantec and IBM. There is also another form of compilation, the *just-in-time* (JIT) compilers. These work by compiling the bytecodes into native code once, caching the results, and then calling them again if needed. This approach speeds up loops tremendously since one has to do the interpretation only once. Although still slightly slower than a true native code compiler, a just-in-time compiler can give you a 10- or even 20-fold speedup for some programs and will almost always be significantly faster than the Java interpreter. This technology is being improved continuously and may eventually yield results that cannot be matched by traditional compilation systems. For example, a just-in-time compiler can monitor which code is executed frequently and optimize just that code for speed.

Multithreaded

[The] benefits of multithreading are better interactive responsiveness and real-time behavior.

If you have ever tried to do multithreading in another language, you will be pleasantly surprised at how easy it is in Java. Threads in Java also have the capacity to take advantage of multiprocessor systems if the base operating system does so. On the downside, thread implementations on the major platforms differ widely, and Java makes no effort to be platform independent in this regard. Only the code for calling multithreading remains the same across machines; Java offloads the implementation of multithreading to the underlying operating system. (Threading will be covered in Volume 2.) Nonetheless, the ease of multithreading is one of the main reasons why Java is such an appealing language for server-side development.

Dynamic

In a number of ways, Java is a more dynamic language than C or C++. It was designed to adapt to an evolving environment. Libraries can freely add new methods and instance variables without any effect on their clients. In Java, finding out run time type information is straightforward.

This is an important feature in those situations where code needs to be added to a running program. A prime example is code that is downloaded from the Internet to run in a browser. In Java 1.0, finding out run-time type information was anything but straightforward, but current versions of Java give the programmer full insight into both the structure and behavior of its objects. This is extremely useful for systems that need to analyze objects at run time such as Java GUI builders, smart debuggers, pluggable components, and object databases.

Java and the Internet

The idea here is simple: users will download Java bytecodes from the Internet and run them on their own machines. Java programs that work on Web pages are called *applets*. (Actually, it is the bytecodes, rather than the source file, that you download and then run.) To use an applet, you need a Java-enabled Web browser, which will interpret the bytecodes for you. Because Sun is licensing the Java source code and insisting that there be no changes in the language and basic library structure, you can be sure that a Java applet will run on any browser that is advertised as Java enabled. Note that Netscape 2.x and Netscape 3.x are only *Java 1.02 enabled*, as is Internet Explorer 3.0. Netscape 4 and Internet Explorer 4 run different subsets of Java 1.1. This sorry situation made it increasingly difficult to develop applets that take advantage of the most current Java version. To remedy this problem, Sun has developed the *Java Plug-in*, a tool that makes the newest Java run-time environment available to both Netscape and Internet Explorer (see Chapter 10).

We suspect that, ultimately, most of the initial hype around Java stemmed from the lure of making money from special-purpose software. You have a nifty "Will Writer" program. Convert it to an applet, and charge people per use—presumably, most people would be using this kind of program infrequently. Some people predict a time when everyone downloads software from the Net on a per-use basis. This might be great for software companies, but we think it is absurd, for example, to expect people to download and pay for a spell-checker applet each time they send an e-mail message.

Another early suggested use for applets was so-called content and protocol handlers that allow a Java-enabled Web browser to deal with new types of information dynamically. Suppose you invent a nifty fractal compression algorithm for dealing with humongous graphics files and want to let someone sample your technology before you charge them big bucks for it. Write a Java content handler that does the decompression and send it along with the compressed files. The HotJava browser by Sun Microsystems supports this feature, but neither Netscape nor Internet Explorer ever did.

Applets can also be used to add buttons and input fields to a Web page. But downloading those applets over a dialup line is slow, and you can do much of the same with Dynamic HTML, HTML forms, and a scripting language such as JavaScript. And, of course, early applets were used for animation: the familiar spinning globes, dancing cartoon characters, nervous text, and so on. But animated GIFs can do much of this and Dynamic HTML combined with scripting can do even more of what Java applets were first used for.

As a result of the browser incompatibilities and the inconvenience of downloading applet code through slow net connections, applets on Internet Web pages have not become a huge success. The situation is entirely different on *intranets*. There are typically no bandwidth problems, so the download time for applets is no issue. And in an intranet, it is possible to control which browser is being used or to use the Java Plug-in consistently. Employees can't misplace or misconfigure programs that are delivered through the Web with each use, and the system administrator never needs to walk around and upgrade code on client machines. Many corporations have rolled out programs such as inventory checking, vacation planning, travel reimbursement, and so on, as applets that use the browser as the delivery platform.

Applets at Work

This book includes a few sample applets; ultimately, the best source for applets is the Web itself. Some applets on the Web can only be seen at work; many others include the source code. When you become more familiar with Java, these applets can be a great way to learn more about Java. A good Web site to check for Java applets is Gamelan—it is now hosted as part of the developer.com site, but you can still reach it through the URL http://www.gamelan.com. (By the way, *gamelan* also stands for a special type of Javanese musical orchestra. Attend a gamelan performance if you have a chance—it is gorgeous music.)

To place an applet onto a Web page, you need to know or work with someone who knows hypertext markup language (HTML). The number of HTML tags needed for a Java applet are few and easy to master (see Chapter 10). Using general HTML tags to design a Web page is a design issue—it is not a programming problem.

As you can see in Figure 1-1, when the user downloads an applet, it works much like embedding an image in a Web page. (For those who know HTML, we mean one set with an IMG tag.) The applet becomes a part of the page, and the text flows around the space used for the applet. The point is, the image is *alive*. It reacts to user commands, changes its appearance, and sends data between the computer viewing the applet and the computer serving it.

Figure 1-1 shows a good example of a dynamic web page that carries out sophisticated calculations, an applet to simulate genetic variations in the fruit fly

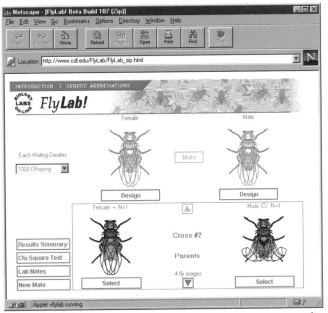

Figure 1-1: FlyLab Applet (http://www.cdl.edu/FlyLab)

species Drosophila Melanogaster. This is part of the Center for Distributed Learning of the California State University. Students design parent flies by setting features such as eye color or wing shape, and the Java program determines the possible features of their offspring.

A Short History of Java

This section gives a short history of Java's evolution. It is based on various published sources (most importantly, on an interview with Java's creators in the July 1995 issue of *SunWorld's* on-line magazine).

Java goes back to 1991, when a group of Sun engineers, led by Patrick Naughton and Sun Fellow (and all-around computer wizard) James Gosling, wanted to design a small computer language that could be used for consumer devices like cable TV switchboxes. Since these devices do not have a lot of power or memory, the language had to be small and generate very tight code. Also, because different manufacturers may choose different central processing units (CPUs), it was important not to be tied down to any single architecture. The project got the code name "Green."

The requirements for small, tight code led the team to resurrect the model that a language, called UCSD Pascal, tried in the early days of PCs and that Niklaus Wirth had pioneered earlier. What Wirth pioneered and UCSD Pascal did commercially, and the Green project engineers did as well, was to design a portable language that generated intermediate code for a hypothetical machine. (These are often called *virtual machines*—hence, the Java Virtual Machine or JVM.) This intermediate code could then be used on any machine that had the correct interpreter. Intermediate code generated with this model is always small, and the interpreters for intermediate code can also be quite small, so this solved their main problem.

The Sun people, however, come from a UNIX background, so they based their language on C++ rather than Pascal. In particular, they made the language object oriented rather than procedure oriented. But, as Gosling says in the interview, "All along, the language was a tool, not the end." Gosling decided to call his language "Oak." (Presumably because he liked the look of an oak tree that was right outside his window at Sun.) The people at Sun later realized that Oak was the name of an existing computer language, so they changed the name to Java.

In 1992, the Green project delivered its first product, called "*7." It was an extremely intelligent remote control. (It had the power of a SPARCstation in a box that was 6" by 4" by 4".) Unfortunately, no one was interested in producing this at Sun, and the Green people had to find other ways to market their technology. However, none of the standard consumer electronics companies were interested. The group then bid on a project to design a cable TV box that could deal with new cable services such as video on demand. They did not get the contract. (Amusingly, the company that did was led by the same Jim Clark who started Netscape—a company that did much to make Java successful.)

The Green Project (with a new name of "First Person Inc.") spent all of 1993 and half of 1994 looking for people to buy its technology—no one was found. (Patrick Naughton, one of the founders of the group and the person who ended up doing most of the marketing, claims to have accumulated 300,000 air miles in trying to sell the technology.) First Person was dissolved in 1994.

While all of this was going on at Sun, the World Wide Web part of the Internet was growing bigger and bigger. The key to the Web is the browser that translates the hypertext page to the screen. In 1994, most people were using Mosaic, a noncommercial Web browser that came out of the supercomputing center at the University of Illinois in 1993. (Mosaic was partially written by Marc Andreessen for $6.85 an hour as an undergraduate student on a work-study project. He moved on to fame and fortune as one of the cofounders and the chief of technology at Netscape.)

In a *SunWorld* interview, Gosling says that in mid-1994, the language developers realized that "We could build a real cool browser. It was one of the few things in the client/server mainstream that needed some of the weird things we'd done: architecture neutral, real-time, reliable, secure—issues that weren't terribly important in the workstation world. So we built a browser."

The actual browser was built by Patrick Naughton and Jonathan Payne and evolved into the HotJava browser that we have today. The HotJava browser was written in Java to show off the power of Java. But the builders also had in mind the power of what are now called applets, so they made the browser capable of interpreting the intermediate bytecodes. This "proof of technology" was shown at SunWorld '95 on May 23, 1995, and inspired the Java craze that continues unabated today.

The big breakthrough for widespread Java use came in the fall of 1995, when Netscape decided to make the next release of Netscape (Netscape 2.0) Java enabled. Netscape 2.0 came out in January of 1996, and it has been (as have all subsequent releases) Java enabled. Other licensees include IBM, Symantec, Inprise, and many others. Even Microsoft has licensed and supports Java. Internet Explorer is Java enabled, and Windows ships with a Java virtual machine. (Note that Microsoft does not support the most current version of Java, however, and that its implementation differs from the Java standard.)

Sun released the first version of Java in early 1996. It was followed by Java 1.02 a couple of months later. People quickly realized that Java 1.02 was not going to cut it for serious application development. Sure, you could use Java 1.02 to make a nervous text applet. (It moves text randomly around in a canvas.) But you couldn't even *print* in Java 1.02. To be blunt, Java 1.02 was not ready for prime time.

The big announcements about Java's future features trickled out over the first few months of 1996. Only at the JavaOne conference held in San Francisco in May of 1996 did the bigger picture of where Java was going become clearer. At JavaOne the people at Sun Microsystems outlined their vision of the future of Java with a seemingly endless stream of improvements and new libraries. We were, to say the least, suspicious that all this would take *years* to come to pass. We are happy to report that while not everything they have outlined has come to pass, surprisingly much was incorporated into Java 1.1 in an equally surprisingly short amount of time.

The big news of the 1998 JavaOne conference was the upcoming release of Java 1.2, which replaces the early toy-like GUI and graphics toolkits with sophisticated and scalable versions that come a lot closer to the promise of "write once, run anywhere" than their predecessors. Three days after its release in December 1998, the name was changed to Java 2. Again we were, to say the least, suspicious that all this would take *years* to come to pass. We are happy to report again that while not everything they have outlined has come to pass, surprisingly much was incorporated into Java 2 in an equally surprisingly short amount of time.

Common Misconceptions About Java

In summary, what follows is a list of some common misconceptions about Java, along with commentary.

Java is an extension of HTML.

Java is a programming language; HTML is a way to describe the structure of a Web page. They have nothing in common except that there are HTML extensions for placing Java applets on a Web page.

Java is an easy programming language to learn.

No programming language as powerful as Java is easy. You always have to distinguish between how easy it is to write toy programs and how hard it is to do serious work. Also, consider that only four chapters in this book discuss the Java language. The remaining chapters of both volumes show how to put the language to work, using the Java *library*. The Java library contains over 1500 classes and interfaces. Just listing every possible function and constant in the library takes more than 600 pages in the Java Developers Almanac. (The annotated listing of all the Java 1.02 library, which is quite a bit smaller than the Java 1.1 library, included a reasonable number of code snippets, but it took more than 1500 printed pages!) Luckily, you do not need to know every one of the 20,000 + entries in the Java Developers Almanac, but you do need to know surprisingly many of them in order to use Java for anything realistic.

Java is an easy environment in which to program.

The native Java development environment is not an easy environment to use—except for people who swear by 1970s command-line tools. There are integrated development environments that bring Java development into the modern era of VB-style drag-and-drop form designers combined with decent debugging facilities, but they can be somewhat complex and daunting for the newcomer. They also work by generating what is often hundreds of lines of code. We don't think you are well served when first learning Java by starting with hundreds of lines of computer-generated UI code filled with comments that say DO NOT MODIFY or the equivalent. We have found in teaching Java that using your favorite text editor is still the best way to learn Java, and that is what we will do.

Java will become a universal programming language for all platforms.

This is possible, in theory, and it is certainly the case that every vendor but Microsoft seems to want this to happen. However, there are many applications, already working perfectly well on desktops, that would not work well on other devices or inside a browser. Also, these applications have been written to take advantage of the speed of the processor and the native user-interface library and have been ported to all of the important platforms anyway. Among these kinds of applications are word processors, photo editors, and Web browsers. They are typically written in C or C++, and we see no benefit to the end user in rewriting them in Java. And, at least in the short run, there would be significant disadvantages since the Java version is likely to be slower, less powerful, and to use incompatible file formats.

Java is just another programming language.

Java is a nice programming language; most programmers prefer it to C or C++. But there have been hundreds of nice programming languages that never gained widespread popularity, whereas languages with obvious flaws, such as C++ and VB, have been wildly successful.

Why? Well we feel that the success of a programming language is determined more by the utility of the *support system* surrounding it, not by the elegance of its syntax. Are there useful, convenient, and standard libraries for the features that you need to implement? Are there tools vendors that build great programming and debugging environments? Does the language and the tool set integrate with the rest of the computing infrastructure? Java is successful on the server because its class library lets you easily do things that were hard before, such as networking and multithreading. The fact that Java reduces pointer errors is a bonus and so programmers seem to be more productive with Java, but these are not the source of its success. Whether Java's ability to make portable user interfaces will be important remains to be seen—the necessary support libraries were not there in versions of Java before Java 2.

This is an important point that one vendor in particular—who sees portable user interfaces as a threat—tries to ignore, by labeling Java "just a programming language" and by supplying a system that uses a derivative of the Java syntax and a proprietary and nonportable library. The result may well be a very nice language that is a direct competitor to VB but has little to do with Java.

Java is interpreted, so it is too slow for serious applications on a specific platform.

Many programs spend most of their time on things like user-interface interactions. All programs, no matter what language they are written in, will detect a mouse click in adequate time. It is true that we would not do CPU-intensive tasks with the interpreter supplied with the Java development kit. However, on platforms where a just-in-time compiler is available, all you need to do is run the bytecodes through it and most performance issues simply go away. Finally, Java is great for network-bound programs. Experience has shown that Java can comfortably keep up with the data rate of a network connection, even when doing computationally intensive work such as encryption. As long as Java is faster than the data that it processes, it does not matter that C++ might be faster still. Java is easier to program, and it is portable. This makes Java a great language for implementing network services.

All Java programs run inside a Web page.

All Java *applets* run inside a Web browser. That is the definition of an applet—a Java program running inside a browser. But it is entirely possible, and quite useful, to write stand-alone Java programs that run independently of a Web browser. These programs (usually called *applications*) are completely portable. Just take the code and run it on another machine! And because Java is more convenient and less error-prone than raw C++, it is a good choice for writing programs. It is an even more compelling choice when it is combined with database access tools like Sun's JDBC (see Volume 2). It is certainly the obvious choice for a first language in which to learn programming.

Most of the programs in this book are stand-alone programs. Sure, applets are interesting, and right now most useful Java programs are applets. But we believe that stand-alone Java programs will become extremely important, very quickly.

Java applets are a major security risk.

There have been some well-publicized reports of failures in the Java security system. Most have been in the implementation of Java in a specific browser. Researchers viewed it as a challenge to try to find chinks in the Java armor and to defy the strength and sophistication of the applet security model. The technical failures that they found have all been quickly corrected, and to our knowledge, no actual systems were ever compromised. To keep this in perspective, consider the literally millions of virus attacks in Windows executable files and Word macros that cause real grief but, generally, little publicity. Also, the ActiveX mechanism in Internet Explorer would be a fertile ground for abuse, but it so boringly obvious how to circumvent it that few have bothered to publicize their findings.

Some system administrators have even deactivated Java in company browsers, while continuing to permit their users to download executable files, ActiveX controls, and Word documents. That is pretty ridiculous—currently, the risk of being attacked by a hostile Java applet is perhaps comparable to the risk of dying from a plane crash; the risk of the latter activities is comparable to the risk of dying while crossing a busy freeway on foot.

JavaScript is a simpler version of Java.

JavaScript, a scripting language that can be used inside Web pages, was invented by Netscape and originally called LiveScript. JavaScript has a syntax that is reminiscent of Java, but otherwise there are no relationships (except for the name, of course). A subset of JavaScript is standardized as ECMA-262, but the extensions that you need for real work have not been standardized, and as a result, writing JavaScript code that runs both in Netscape and Internet Explorer is an exercise in frustration.

Java eliminates the need for CGI scripting.

Not yet. With today's technology, CGI is still the most common mechanism for server-side processing. However, there are technologies on the horizon that greatly reduce the need for CGI scripts. Servlets give you the same execution environment on the server that applets have on the client. JDBC (see Volume 2) permits direct database manipulations by the client of information lying on the server.

Java will revolutionize client-server computing.

This is possible and it is where much of the best work in Java is being done. There are quite a few application servers such as Weblogic's Tengah that are built entirely in Java. The JDBC discussed in Volume 2 certainly makes using Java for client-server development easier. As third-party tools continue to be developed, we expect database development with Java to be as easy as the Net library makes network programming. Accessing remote objects is significantly easier in Java than in C++ (see Volume 2).

With Java, I can replace my computer with a $500 "Internet appliance."

Some people are betting big that this is going to happen. We believe it is pretty absurd to think that people are going to give up a powerful and convenient desktop for a limited machine with no local storage. However, if your Java-powered computer has enough local storage for the inevitable situation when your local intranet goes down, a Java-powered network computer is a viable option for a "zero administration initiative" to cut the costs of computer ownership in a business.

We also see an Internet appliance as a portable *adjunct* to a desktop. Provided the price is right, wouldn't you rather have an Internet-enabled *device* with a screen on which to read your e-mail or see the news? Because the Java kernel is so small, Java is the obvious choice for such a telephone or other Internet "appliance."

Java will allow the component-based model of computing to take off.

No two people mean the same thing when they talk about components. Regarding visual controls, like ActiveX components that can be dropped into a graphical user interface (GUI) program, Java 1.1 includes the JavaBeans initiative (see Volume 2). Java beans can potentially do the same sorts of things as ActiveX components *except* they are *automatically* cross-platform and *automatically* come with a security manager. All this shows that the success of the JavaBeans initiative will go far toward making Java successful.

Chapter 2

The Java Programming Environment

▼ INSTALLING THE JAVA COMPILER

▼ NAVIGATING THE JAVA DIRECTORIES

▼ WINDOWS 95/98/NT AS A PROGRAMMING ENVIRONMENT

▼ COMPILING AND RUNNING JAVA PROGRAMS

▼ USING TEXTPAD

▼ GRAPHICAL APPLICATIONS

▼ APPLETS

This chapter is about getting Java to work in various environments, concentrating on Windows 95/98/NT since that seems to be the most common platform. It is somewhat unusual for a book at this level to provide so many tips for various platforms; experienced programmers do not usually need to be told how to work with most software. However, at this point, the setup of Java is somewhat complex, and "gotchas" abound.

NOTE: A good, general source of information on Java can be found via the links on the Java frequently asked questions (FAQ) page: http://www.`www-net.com/java/faq/`.

Installing the Java Compiler and Tools

The most complete versions of Java are available for Sun's Solaris 2.x, Windows NT, or Windows 95/98. (We will usually refer to these platforms collectively as

"Windows" (Java is identical for all these versions of Windows). Versions of Java in various states of development exist for Linux, OS/2, Macintosh, Windows 3.1, and many other platforms. In particular, if you use a PC and you want to use the Java features described in this book, you must have Windows 95/98 or NT to run Java. (Linux users on a PC should check out the Linux newsgroups for the status of the JDK port to Linux.) Realistically, you also need either a Pentium, a minimum of 32 MB of memory, and at least 50 MB of free hard disk space.

> TIP: For one of the big three—Solaris, Windows, or the Mac—you will want to periodically visit the Java home page to see if a more recent release is available for your platform. Point your browser to `java.sun.com`. For other platforms, you will need to cruise the Web or contact the vendor. A good place to turn to is the `comp.lang.java.programmer` newsgroup.

The CD that accompanies this book contains a version of the Java Development Kit (JDK) for Windows 95/98/NT and Solaris. See Appendix 3 for detailed installation instructions. The CD-ROM does *not* contain support for the Macintosh. Once a Macintosh version of Java is available, you can download it from `java.sun.com` and install it by following the directions given there.

> NOTE: Only the installation instructions for Java are system dependent. If a full version of Java exists for your operating system, then, once you get Java up and running, everything else in this book should apply to you. System independence is a major benefit of Java. (Occasionally there are minor problems in practice, especially on Macs where command-line tools don't fit the Mac model very well.)

Development Environments for Windows Users

If your programming experience comes from VB, Delphi, or a modern PC or Macintosh version of C or C++, you are accustomed to a development environment with a built-in text editor and menus to compile and launch a program along with an integrated debugger. The basic JDK contains nothing even remotely similar. *Everything* is done from the command line. We will tell you how to install and use the basic JDK, because we have found that the full-fledged development environments can be somewhat complex and don't make it easy to learn Java.

The CD-ROM also contains TextPad, an excellent shareware programming editor for Windows. It can make developing Java programs easier, and we used it for developing and testing most of the programs in this book. Since you can compile and execute source code from within the editor, it can become your de facto IDE as you work through this book. (We hope, of course, if you choose to use it beyond the trial period, you will pay the vendor the small fee asked.)

NOTE: Some other shareware editors such as Kawa (http://www.tek-tools.com/) and JPad Pro (http://www.modelworks.com/) are specially adapted to Java development; they are certainly worth checking out. These two products also have integrated debuggers. Many professional programming editors, such as the well known CodeWright editor (http://www.premia.com/), are also set up for Java development.

However, if you have a Java IDE such as Java WorkShop, Inprise JBuilder, or Symantec Café that supports the current version of Java, then you can continue using it and manually add the special files that we use in this book. We will give you general instructions, but of course the details depend on the particular environment that you are using. Fair warning: If you add the Core Java code package to a commercial environment but the environment doesn't seem to find it, please contact the vendor, not us, for technical assistance.

In sum, you have at this time three choices for a development environment under Windows:

1. Install the JDK and TextPad from the CD-ROM.

2. Install the JDK from the CD-ROM and use your favorite ASCII editor (it must support long file names).

3. Install just the Core Java code, not the JDK, and use it with the Java development environment that you already own.

If you hate choices, just pick the first option. It will work fine. You simply write the source code for your program in the editor. When you are happy with it, you can use the various TextPad menu items to compile, execute, or see the frequent syntax error messages that you will encounter for the first few weeks of working with Java.

Commercial development environments tend to be more cumbersome to use for a simple program since you have often have to set up a separate project for each program you write. These environments have the edge if you write larger Java programs consisting of many source files. (And usually their bytecode compilers are so much faster than the one in the JDK as to often make the extra work, even for a small program, worthwhile!) And these commercial environments also supply debuggers, which are certainly necessary for serious development—the command-line debugger that comes for free with the JDK is rather awkward to use.

Adding Core Java Files to an Integrated Development Environment

If you already have another development environment such as Java WorkShop, Inprise JBuilder, or Symantec Café, and your IDE supports the most current version of Java , then installing the JDK may interfere with your existing installation. You will want to contact your vendor to see exactly what they suggest doing. (Some vendors' IDE coexists nicely with Sun's JDK; others get *very* confused.) In any case, you should install the Core Java files.

Note that you still may not be able to use the Core Java files easily. The reason is that once the Core Java files are installed into the \CoreJavaBook directory, you need to add that directory to the *class path* of your development environment. This may be as simple as locating the CLASSPATH environment variable in your AUTOEXEC.BAT file. Or, you may need to set an option in your development environment or edit another file such as SC.INI for Symantec's Café. Be careful—in some environments a new setting *overrides* all others, whereas in others the additional setting gets *appended* to the regular settings. Consult the documentation of your environment and contact the vendor for assistance if necessary.

Navigating the Java Directories

In your explorations of Java, you will occasionally want to peek inside the Java source files. And, of course, you will need to work extensively with our *Core Java* files. Table 2–1 shows the Java directory tree. The layout will be different if you have an integrated development environment, and the root will be different depending on the JDK version that you installed. Also, the source files are delivered in the JDK as a compressed file, and you must unpack that file to get access to the source code. We highly recommend that you do that.

Table 2–1: Java directory tree

\jdk	*(the name may be different, e.g.,* jdk1.2*)*
docs	*library documentation in HTML format is here*
bin	*the compiler and tools are here*
demo	*look here for demos*
include	*files for native methods (see Volume 2)*
lib	*library files*
src	*look in the various subdirectories for the library source*

The two most important subdirectories in this tree are docs and src. The docs directory contains the Java library documentation in HTML format. You can view it with any Web browser, such as Netscape.

TIP: Set a bookmark in your browser to the local version of docs\api\index.html. You will be referring to this page a lot as you go further with Java!

The src directory contains the source code for the public part of the Java libraries. As you become more comfortable with Java, you may find yourself in situations for which this book and the on-line information do not provide what you need to know. At this point, the source code for Java is a good place to begin digging. It is occasionally reassuring to know that you can always dig into the source to find out what a library function really does. For example, if you are curious about the inner workings of the Hashtable class, you can look inside src\java\util\Hashtable.java.

Windows 95/98/NT as a Programming Environment

If you have done all your programming in the various version of Windows, using a comfortable programming environment such as VB, Delphi, or one of the C++-integrated environments, you may find the JDK primitive. ("Quaint" may be a more charitable word for it.) In this section, we give a few tips for working with Windows 95/98/NT. If you are a seasoned veteran or if you do not use one of these versions of Windows , just skip this section.

Long File Names

Even if you are an experienced programmer under previous versions of DOS or Windows 3.1, Windows now has one major new feature—*long file names.* If you are coming from DOS or Windows 3.1, you know that a DOS file can have, at most, eight characters in the name and three characters in the extension, such as WLCMAPPL.HTM. These are the so-called 8.3 file names. With Windows , you can now use essentially as many characters as you like (the limit is 255 characters). For example, you can call a file WelcomeApplet.html. This is welcome news, indeed. In fact, you *do not* have a choice when dealing with Java; all Java source files use long file names. They *must* have the four-letter extension .java. Luckily, most of the new versions of the traditional DOS utility functions included in Windows NT or Windows 95 understand long file names. For example, you can type

```
del WelcomeApplet.html
```

or

```
copy *.java a:
```

Of course, if you prefer, you can delete and copy the files through the Explorer, but many programmers type faster than they mouse and therefore prefer the command line.

To let you use programs that were written before long file names were invented, Microsoft gives each long file name an 8.3 file name *alias.* These aliases contain a ~ character, for example, WELCOM~1.HTM. If there are two files in the same directory whose names start with WELCOM and have HTM in the extension, then their aliases are WELCOM~1.HTM and WELCOM~2.HTM. In the event that there are 8.3 aliases for some files in the directory (which will always be the case when you use long file names), be careful when deleting files, especially when you use wild cards. For example, the command

```
del *.HTM
```

will delete all files with the extension HTM and all files whose extension *starts with* HTM. In particular, all *.html files will also be deleted.

Windows Explorer gives you access to the long file names. But if you are working with a DOS shell, how do you find the long file name?

• The DIR command shows the 8.3 alias on the left and the long file name on the right.

After a few weeks, you will get into the habit of looking at the right-hand side and ignoring the left-hand side.

CAUTION: You can make a real hash out of a collection of Java files by using the DOS version of PKZIP. If you use the venerable PKZIP 2.04g to bundle and compress files, you will find that it only packs and unpacks the 8.3 file names. You can safely use PKZIP 2.50 and above.

We suggest that you use a modern zipping tool like WinZip. We include a shareware copy of WinZip on the CD-ROM. For example, you can use WinZip to peek inside the rt.jar file in the \jdk\jre\lib directory.

Long file names can even contain spaces. You may have noticed that some programs are installed in a directory with the name Program Files. As you can imagine, this can be confusing for some DOS commands that traditionally expect spaces to separate the file names and command options and can confuse the tools supplied with

```
MS-DOS Prompt

D:\CoreJavaBook\ch2>dir

 Volume in drive D is DISK2_VOL1
 Volume Serial Number is 15DD-1D24
 Directory of D:\CoreJavaBook\ch2

.              <DIR>        02-18-96   2:45p .
..             <DIR>        02-18-96   2:45p ..
WELCOME        <DIR>        02-18-96   2:45p Welcome
WELCOM~1       <DIR>        02-18-96   2:45p WelcomeApplet
IMAGEV~1       <DIR>        02-18-96   2:45p ImageViewer
         0 file(s)              0 bytes
         5 dir(s)      264,044,544 bytes free

D:\CoreJavaBook\ch2>_
```

Figure 2–1: The DIR command with long file names

with the JDK. We suggest not putting files that are used for Java development in a directory whose name contains spaces. In any case, you need to enclose any file or directory name that contains spaces in quotation marks, for example,

```
del "The first applet in the Core Java book.java"
```

Don't worry. We will not use file names like this one in our examples.

Long file names are not case sensitive *for DOS commands.* For example,

```
del WelcomeApplet.java
```

and

```
del welcomeapplet.JAVA
```

both have the same effect. But Windows 95/98/NT *retains the case* that you used when you first created the file. For example, if you named the file `WelcomeApplet.java`, then Windows will use the uppercase `W` and `A` in the directory display and all directory dialog boxes.

NOTE: Java, on the other hand, *is* case sensitive and does care about the case that was retained for the file name. As you will soon see, a file like `WelcomeApplet.java` contains a class with the same name, `WelcomeApplet`. If you compile this file with the command

```
javac welcomeapplet.java
```

then the compiler will ask DOS to open the file. DOS has no problem opening the `welcomeapplet.java` file, but the compiler will insist that it cannot find a `welcomeapplet` class. You will get some strange error message that relates to the file not being found. The moral is that anytime you cannot compile a file that you know is there, check the case of the file name with the DIR command or with Explorer. If you notice the problem and regret your decision, you can use the `ren` command to change the look of the file name.

```
ren welcomeapplet.java WelcomeApplet.java
```

Multiple Windows

When you use the JDK, multiple DOS windows are a way of life. You often run the editor in one DOS window and the compiler in another. (The Textpad editor we supply is configured to spawn these DOS shells transparently to you.) Graphical applications, applets, and the browser run in other windows. Windows has a nifty *task bar* at the bottom of the screen that lets you easily switch between windows.

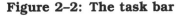

Figure 2–2: The task bar

If you use a computer with a small screen (such as a laptop computer), you may find that the task bar takes up valuable screen real estate. You can *hide* the task bar. (Click on an empty area of the task bar with the right mouse button, then select Properties and Auto Hide.) This tells Windows to display the task bar only when you move the mouse toward the bottom of the screen. (You can also drag the task bar to another corner of your screen if you like.)

Keyboard Shortcuts

The mouse was originally designed by researchers in the prestigious SRI International lab. One of their unstated goals seems to have been to slow you down so the computer can keep up with you. Programmers do not like to be slowed down, and their programmer comrades at Microsoft have fought the mouse maniacs and kept a number of *keyboard shortcuts* in the operating system. Here are a few of these keystroke combinations that we have found helpful.

ALT+TAB: This key combination displays a small window with icons, one for each running task.

Figure 2–3: The ALT+TAB task switcher

Keep your thumb on the ALT key and hold down TAB. Different icons will be selected. Let go of both keys, and you switch to the selected window.

CTRL+ESC: This key combination pops up the Start menu in the task bar. (Some keyboards have a "Windows" key that has the same effect.) If you arrange your most-used program icons into the first level of the Start menu, then you can run them with a couple of keystrokes.

TIP: Put the MS-DOS prompt, TextPad, and your browser in the first level of the Start menu. (To edit the Start menu, right-click on an empty area of the task bar, then select Properties and Start Menu Programs.)

SHIFT+F10: This key combination pops up a *context menu*, just as if you had clicked the right mouse button.

Under Windows 95, the CTRL+ALT+DEL key combination does not reboot the computer. Instead, it pops up a window of all active applications, like this:

Figure 2–4: The CTRL+ALT+DEL Close Program dialog

If you have a nonresponsive program:

1. Pop up this box.
2. Select the program from the given list.
3. Click on the End Task button. (You may need to wait a few seconds before this has any effect.)

CAUTION: Hitting CTRL+ALT+DEL *twice* does reboot the computer, so you want to have a steady hand when using this key combination.

More on DOS Shells

The humble MS-DOS shell has come a long way from that in earlier versions of Windows. In fact, the DOS shell in Windows is now, in many ways, a better DOS than DOS. For starters, as you have seen, you can run multiple DOS shells and toggle between them. You can also launch Windows applications directly from the DOS shell. For example, if you type

```
notepad
```

into a DOS prompt and hit ENTER, the Notepad program starts up. This is certainly faster than clicking on Start Menu | Programs | Accessories | Notepad.

TIP: If you use the DOS shell, you should use the DOSKEY program. The DOSKEY utility keeps a *command history*. Type the up and down arrow keys to cycle through the previously typed commands. Use the left and right arrow keys to edit the current command. Type the beginning of a command and hit F8 to complete it. For example, if you have typed

```
appletviewer WelcomeApplet.html
```

once, then you just type

```
ap
```

then type the F8 key to instantly retype the command. You get a chance to edit it, in case you want to issue a slightly different command.

To install DOSKEY automatically, simply add the line

```
DOSKEY /INSERT
```

into your AUTOEXEC.BAT file and reboot.

The EDIT Program

If you need to do a quick edit and you do not want to wait for your regular editor to start, try the EDIT program that comes with Windows 95/98. You will be pleasantly surprised. This is not the QuickBasic editor that came with DOS 5 and 6 and still comes with Windows NT, but a completely different program. In particular, this editor handles long file names, *and* it can edit up to 10 files at a time. You switch between the files by hitting ALT+1, ALT+2, and so on. You can even launch the editor with a wild card:

```
edit *.java
```

Unfortunately, EDIT is still a DOS program, which means that it is difficult to cut and paste between it and other Windows programs. (It can be done, but you need to use the Mark, Copy, and Paste icons on the top of the DOS shell, not the usual editor commands.) Of course, you can cut and paste between different files that are loaded into the editor. (You can use TextPad if you want a more efficient way to cut and paste text between Windows programs.)

Compiling and Running Java Programs

There are two methods for compiling and launching a Java program: from the command line and from an editor. Let us do it the hard way first: from the command line. Go to the \CoreJavaBook\v1ch2\Welcome directory. Then enter the following commands:

```
javac Welcome.java
java Welcome
```

You should see the message shown in Figure 2–5 on the screen:

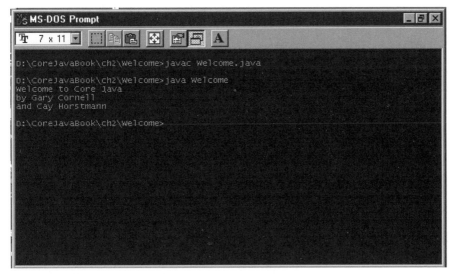

Figure 2–5: Running the first Java program

Congratulations! You have just compiled and run your first Java program.

What happened? The javac program is the Java compiler. It compiles the file Welcome.java into the file Welcome.class. The java program is the Java interpreter. It interprets the bytecodes that the compiler placed in the class file.

The Welcome program is extremely simple. It simply prints a message to the console. You may enjoy looking inside the program shown in Example 2–1—we will explain how it works in the next chapter.

Example 2–1: Welcome.java

```
public class Welcome
{  public static void main(String[] args)
    {  String[] greeting = new String[3];
       greeting[0] = "Welcome to Core Java";
       greeting[1] = "by Cay Horstmann";
```

```
        greeting[2] = "and Gary Cornell";

        int i;
        for (i = 0; i < greeting.length; i++)
            System.out.println(greeting[i]);
    }
}
```

NOTE: Every integrated environment has commands for compiling and running programs. If you do not use TextPad, read your documentation to find out how to compile and run programs. If you want to use TextPad, read the next section.

Using TextPad
Compiling and Running Programs

We grew quite comfortable with TextPad in the course of writing this book. The editors use the normal editing commands that most Windows programs expect. (The keystrokes for most tasks are customizable as well.) It comes with a complete help system, so we will not go into the details of using the editor. (It should take an experienced programmer maybe 15 minutes to master the product.)

In this section, we will show you the steps needed to run the `Welcome` program from inside the editing environment. Then, we will explain the advantages of using the editor for the situations when you make a typo or three.

To compile and run the `Welcome` program from the customized version of TextPad:

1. Start up TextPad.
2. Choose File | Open and work with the dialog box to find and then load the `Welcome.java` source code.
3. Select Tools | Compile Java (or the keyboard shortcut CTRL+1) to run the Java compiler.
4. Select Tools | Run Java (or the keyboard shortcut CTRL+2) to execute the compiled program.

Figure 2–6 shows a Java program launched from TextPad.

Locating Compilation Errors

Presumably, our program did not have typos or bugs. (It was only a few lines of code, after all.) Let us suppose, for the sake of argument, that you occasionally have a typo (perhaps even a bug) in your code. Try it out—ruin our file, for example, by changing the capitalization in the first few lines like this:

```
Public class Welcome
{  Public Static void main(String[] args)
```

```
{   String[] Greeting = new String[3];
    greeting[0] = "Welcome to Core Java";
    greeting[1] = "by Cay Horstmann Gary Cornell";
    greeting[2] = "and Gary Cornell Cay Horstmann";

    int i;
    for (i = 0; i < greeting.length; i++)
        System.out.println(greeting[i]);
}
}
```

Figure 2–6: Running a Java program from TextPad

Now, run the Java compiler again. Now TextPad will show all error messages in the compilation window.

Figure 2–7: Locating compiler errors in TextPad

Double-click on the first line of an error message to move to the matching location in the file. Use the Search | Jump Next command (or the F4 key) to walk through the remaining error messages.

Graphical Applications

The `Welcome` program was not terribly exciting. Next, let us run a graphical application. This program is a very simple GIF file-viewer. It simply loads and displays a GIF file. Again, let us first compile and run it from the command line.

1. Open a DOS shell window.

2. Change to the directory `\CoreJavaBook\v1ch2\ImageViewer`.

3. Enter

```
javac ImageViewer.java
java ImageViewer
```

A new program window pops up with our ImageViewer application.

Now select File | Open and look for a GIF file to open. (We supplied a couple of sample files in the directory.)

Figure 2–8: Running the ImageViewer application

To close the program, click on the Close box in the title bar or pull down the system menu and close the program. (To compile and run this program inside TextPad or a development environment, do the same as before. For example, for TextPad, choose Tools | Compile Java, then choose Tools | Run Java.)

We hope that you find this program interesting and useful. Have a quick look at the source code. The program is substantially longer than the first program, but it is not terribly complex if you consider how much code it would take in C or C++ to write a similar application. In VB, of course, it is easy to write or, rather, drag and drop, such a program—you need only add about two lines of code to make it functional. The JDK does not have a visual interface builder, so you need to write code for everything, as shown in Example 2–2. You will learn how to write graphical programs like this in Chapters 7–9.

Example 2–2: ImageViewer.java

```java
import javax.swing.*;
import java.awt.*;
import java.awt.event.*;
import java.awt.image.*;
import java.io.*;

public class ImageViewer extends JFrame
    implements ActionListener
{  public ImageViewer()
   {  setTitle("ImageViewer");
      setSize(300, 400);

      JMenuBar mbar = new JMenuBar();
      JMenu m = new JMenu("File");
      JMenuItem m1 = new JMenuItem("Open");
      m1.addActionListener(this);
      m.add(m1);
      JMenuItem m2 = new JMenuItem("Exit");
      m2.addActionListener(this);
      m.add(m2);
      mbar.add(m);
      setJMenuBar(mbar);

      label = new JLabel();
      Container contentPane = getContentPane();
      contentPane.add(label, "Center");
   }

   public void actionPerformed(ActionEvent evt)
   {  String arg = evt.getActionCommand();
      if (arg.equals("Open"))
      {  JFileChooser chooser = new JFileChooser();
```

```
            chooser.setCurrentDirectory(new File("."));

            chooser.setFileFilter(new
                javax.swing.filechooser.FileFilter()
                {   public boolean accept(File f)
                    {   return f.getName().toLowerCase()
                            .endsWith(".gif");
                    }
                    public String getDescription()
                    {   return "GIF Images";
                    }
                });

            int r = chooser.showOpenDialog(this);
            if(r == JFileChooser.APPROVE_OPTION)
            {   String name
                    = chooser.getSelectedFile().getName();
                label.setIcon(new ImageIcon(name));
            }
        }
        else if(arg.equals("Exit")) System.exit(0);
    }

    public static void main(String[] args)
    {   JFrame frame = new ImageViewer();
        frame.show();
    }

    private JLabel label;
}
```

Applets

The first two programs presented in this book are Java *applications,* stand-alone programs like any native programs. On the other hand, as we mentioned in the last chapter, most of the hype about Java comes from its ability to run *applets* inside a Web browser. We want to show you how to build and run an applet from the command line. Finally, we will load the applet into the applet viewer that comes with the JDK and into a web browser.

First, go to the directory `\CoreJavaBook\v1ch2\WelcomeApplet`, then enter the following commands:

```
javac WelcomeApplet.java
appletviewer WelcomeApplet.html
```

Here is what you see in the applet viewer window.

Figure 2–9: The WelcomeApplet applet as viewed by the applet viewer

The first command is the now-familiar command to invoke the Java compiler. This compiles the `WelcomeApplet.java` source into the bytecode file `WelcomeApplet.class`.

This time, however, we do not run the Java interpreter; we use the `appletviewer` program instead. This program is a special tool included with the JDK that lets you quickly test an applet. You need to give it an HTML file, rather than the name of a Java class file. The contents of the `WelcomeApplet.html` file are shown below in Example 2–3.

Example 2–3: WelcomeApplet.html

```
<HTML>
<TITLE>WelcomeApplet</TITLE>
<BODY>
<HR>
This applet is from the book
<A HREF="http://www.horstmann.com/corejava.html">
Core Java</A> by <I>Cay Horstmann</I> and <I>Gary Cornell</I>,
published by Sun Microsystems Press.

<!--"CONVERTED_APPLET"-->
<!-- CONVERTER VERSION 1.0 -->
<SCRIPT LANGUAGE="JavaScript"><!--
    var _info = navigator.userAgent; var _ns = false;
    var _ie = (_info.indexOf("MSIE") > 0 && _info.indexOf("Win") > 0
&& _info.indexOf("Windows 3.1") < 0);
//--></SCRIPT>
<COMMENT><SCRIPT LANGUAGE="JavaScript1.1"><!--
    var _ns = (navigator.appName.indexOf("Netscape") >= 0 &&
((_info.indexOf("Win") > 0 && _info.indexOf("Win16") < 0 &&
java.lang.System.getProperty("os.version").indexOf("3.5") < 0) ||
```

```
(_info.indexOf("Sun") > 0) || (_info.indexOf("Linux") > 0)));
//--></SCRIPT></COMMENT>

<SCRIPT LANGUAGE="JavaScript"><!--
    if (_ie == true) document.writeln('<OBJECT
classid="clsid:8AD9C840-044E-11D1-B3E9-00805F499D93" WIDTH = 400
HEIGHT = 200  codebase="http://java.sun.com/products/plugin
  /1.1.1/jinstall-111-win32.cab#Version=1,1,1,0"><NOEMBED><XMP>');
    else if (_ns == true) document.writeln('<EMBED type=
      "application/x-java-applet;version=1.1" java_CODE =
WelcomeApplet.class WIDTH = 400 HEIGHT = 200  greeting = "Welcome
to Core Java!"  pluginspage="http://java.sun.com/products
  /plugin/1.1.1/plugin-install.html"><NOEMBED><XMP>');
//--></SCRIPT>
<APPLET CODE = WelcomeApplet.class WIDTH = 400 HEIGHT = 200
></XMP>
<PARAM NAME = CODE VALUE = WelcomeApplet.class >

<PARAM NAME="type" VALUE="application/x-java-applet;version=1.1">
<PARAM NAME = greeting VALUE ="Welcome to Core Java!">

</APPLET>

</NOEMBED></EMBED></OBJECT>

<!--
<APPLET  CODE = WelcomeApplet.class WIDTH = 400 HEIGHT = 200 >
<PARAM NAME = greeting VALUE ="Welcome to Core Java!">

</APPLET>
-->
<!--"END_CONVERTED_APPLET"-->

<HR>
<A href="WelcomeApplet.java">The source.</A>
</BODY>
</HTML>
```

If you are familiar with HTML, you will notice some standard HTML instructions and the APPLET tag, telling the applet viewer to load the applet whose code is stored in `WelcomeApplet.class`. The applet viewer ignores all other tags in this file. Furthermore, there is a mess of other tags that enable a browser to load in the Java Plug-in and display the HTML text together with the applet as an embedded object. Provided you have the Java Plug-in installed, you can view the Web page in either Netscape or Internet Explorer.

Try it out.

1.   Start your browser.

2.   Select <u>F</u>ile | Open <u>F</u>ile (or the equivalent).

3.   Go to the `\CoreJavaBook\v1ch2\WelcomeApplet` directory.

You should see the `WelcomeApplet.html` file in the file dialog. Load that file. Your browser now loads the applet, including the surrounding text. It will look something like Figure 2–10.

NOTE: If you are familiar with Java applets, you may be surprised to see the OBJECT and EMBED tags to load the applet, instead of the APPLET tag. Unfortunately, browsers have not kept up with the rapid evolution of Java, and at the time of this writing, no browser can display applets that use features that are specific to Java 2. However, the two major browsers have mechanisms to embed objects. Sun developed such an object, the *Java Plug-in*. The Java Plug-in locates the current Java run-time environment and uses it to load and display the applet. Unfortunately, embedding objects is handled differently by Netscape and Internet Explorer. To display the applet in both browsers, the Web page contains JavaScript code that detects the browser and generates the appropriate tags. This code has been automatically generated by the Java Plug-in HTML converter.

Figure 2–10: Running the WelcomeApplet applet in a browser

You can see that this application is actually alive and willing to interact with the Internet. Click on the Gary Cornell button. The applet directs the browser to pop up a mail window, with Gary's e-mail address already filled in. Click on the Cay Horstmann button. The applet directs the browser to display Cay's Web page.

Notice that neither of these two buttons works in the applet viewer. The applet viewer has no capabilities to send mail or display a Web page, so it ignores your requests. The applet viewer is good for testing applets in isolation, but you need to put applets inside a browser to see how they interact with the browser and the Internet.

TIP: You can also compile and run applets from inside TextPad. As always, select "compile," then "run." This time, the run command launches a batch file that realizes you are running an applet, not an application. It builds an HTML file on the fly and launches the applet viewer. If you use an integrated environment, it will have its own commands to launch an applet.

Finally, the code for the Welcome applet is shown in Example 2–4. At this point, do not give it more than a glance. We will come back to writing applets in Chapter 10.

Example 2–4: WelcomeApplet.java

```java
import javax.swing.*;
import java.applet.*;
import java.awt.*;
import java.awt.event.*;
import java.net.*;

public class WelcomeApplet extends JApplet
   implements ActionListener
{  public void init()
   {  Container contentPane = getContentPane();
      contentPane.setLayout(new BorderLayout());
      JLabel label = new JLabel(getParameter("greeting"),
         SwingConstants.CENTER);
      label.setFont(new Font("TimesRoman", Font.BOLD, 18));
      contentPane.add(label, "Center");
      JPanel panel = new JPanel();
      cayButton = new JButton("Cay Horstmann");
      cayButton.addActionListener(this);
      panel.add(cayButton);
      garyButton = new JButton("Gary Cornell");
      garyButton.addActionListener(this);
      panel.add(garyButton);
      contentPane.add(panel, "South");
```

```
   }

   public void actionPerformed(ActionEvent evt)
   {  Object source = evt.getSource();
      String urlName;
      if (source == cayButton)
         urlName = "http://www.horstmann.com";
      else if (source == garyButton)
         urlName = "mailto:gary@thecornells.com";
      else return;
      try
      {  URL u = new URL(urlName);
         getAppletContext().showDocument(u);
      }
      catch(Exception e)
      {  showStatus("Error " + e);
      }
   }

   private JButton cayButton;
   private JButton garyButton;
}
```

Chapter **3**

Fundamental Programming Structures in Java

At this point, we are assuming that you successfully installed Java and were able to run the sample programs that we showed you in Chapter 2. It's time to start programming. This chapter shows you how the basic programming concepts such as data types, loops, and user-defined functions (actually, in Java they are usually called *methods*) are implemented in Java.

Unfortunately, in Java you can't easily write a program that uses a graphical user interface—you need to learn a fair amount of machinery in order to put up windows, add text boxes and buttons that respond to them, and so on. Since introducing the techniques needed to write GUI-based Java programs would take us too far away from our goal of introducing the basic programming concepts, almost all the sample programs in this chapter will be "toy" programs, designed to illustrate a concept. All these examples will simply send output to the console. (For example, if you are using Windows, the console is an MS-DOS window.) When it comes to getting user input, we will stick to reading the information from the keyboard. In particular, we will be writing *applications* rather than *applets* in this chapter.

Unfortunately, getting input from the keyboard in Java is also somewhat cumbersome; there are no primitives supplied for numeric input. Since it is hard to write even toy programs without a decent method of getting input from the user, the CD contains sufficient code for doing simple (prompted) input. We suggest not worrying too much about how input works at first. We will explain some of the details later in this chapter and finish it off in Chapter 12.

Finally, if you are an experienced C++ programmer, you can get away with just skimming this chapter: concentrate on the C/C++ notes that are interspersed throughout the text. Programmers coming from another background, such as Visual Basic (VB), will find most of the concepts familiar and all of the syntax maddening—you will want to read this chapter very carefully.

A Simple Java Program

Let's look more closely at about the simplest Java program you can have—one that simply prints a message in the console:

```
public class FirstSample
{  public static void main(String[] args)
   {  System.out.println("We will not use 'Hello world!'");
   }
}
```

It is worth spending all the time that you need in order to become comfortable with the framework of this sample; the pieces will recur in all applications. First and foremost, *Java is case sensitive*. If you made any mistakes in capitalization (such as typing Main instead of main), the program will not run.

Now let's look at this source code line by line. The keyword public is called an *access modifier*; these modifiers control what other parts of a program can use this code. We will have more to say about access modifiers in Chapter 5. The keyword class is there to remind you that everything in a Java program lives inside a class. Although we will spend a lot more time on classes in the next chapter, for now think of a class as a blueprint for the data and methods (functions) that will make up part or all of an application. As mentioned in Chapter 1, classes are the building blocks with which all Java applications and applets are built. *Everything* in a Java program must be inside a class.

Following the keyword class is the name of the class. The rules for class names in Java are quite generous. They must begin with a letter and after that they can have any combination of letters and digits. The length is essentially unlimited. You cannot use a Java reserved word (such as public or if) for a class name. (See Appendix I for a list of reserved words.)

As you can see in the name FirstSample, the convention is that class names are nouns in initial caps.

You need to make the file name for the source code the same as the name of the public class, with the extension *.java* appended. Thus, we must store this code in a file called `FirstSample.java`. (Again, case is important, don't use `firstSample.java`.) If you don't do this, you'll get a pretty obvious error message when you try to run this source code through a Java compiler ("Public class FirstSample must be defined in a file called 'FirstSample.java'").

If you have named the file correctly and not made any typos in the source code, then when you compile this source code, you end up with a file containing the bytecodes for this class. The Java compiler automatically names the bytecode file `FirstSample.class` and stores it in the same directory as the source file. Finally, run the bytecode file through the Java interpreter by issuing the command:

```
java FirstSample
```

(Remember to leave off the `.class` extension.) When the program executes, it simply displays the string `We will not use 'Hello,World'!` on the console.

NOTE: Applets have a different structure—see Chapter 10 for information on applets.

Next, when you use

```
java NameOfClass
```

to run a compiled program, the Java interpreter always starts execution with the code in the `main` method in the class you indicate. Thus, you *must* have a `main` method in the source file for your class in order for your code to execute. You can, of course, add your own methods to a class and call them from the `main` method. (We cover writing your own methods later in this chapter.)

Next, notice the braces in the source code. In Java, as in C/C++ (but not in Pascal or VB), braces are used to delineate the parts (usually called *blocks*) in your program. A VB programmer can think of the outermost pair of braces as corresponding to a Sub/End Sub pair; a Pascal programmer can relate them to the first begin/end pair. In Java, the code for any method must be started by an opening brace { and so ended by a closing brace }.

Brace styles have inspired an inordinate amount of useless controversy. We use a style that lines up the braces that delineate each block. Since white space is irrelevant to the Java compiler, you can use whatever brace style you like. We will have more to say about the use of braces when we talk about the various kinds of loops.

If you are not a C++ programmer, don't worry about the keywords `static void`. For now, just think of them as part of what you need to get a Java program to compile. By the end of Chapter 4, you will understand this incantation completely. The point to remember for now is that every Java application must have a `main` method whose header is identical to the one shown here.

C++ NOTE: You know what a class is. Java classes are similar to C++ classes, but there are a few differences that can trap you. For example, in Java *all* functions are member functions of some class, and the standard terminology refers to them as *methods* rather than member functions. Thus, in Java you must have a shell class for the main method. You may also be familiar with the idea of *static member functions*. These are functions defined inside a class that do not operate on objects. The main method (function) in Java is always static. Finally, as in C/C++, the void keyword indicates that this method (function) does not return a value.

VB NOTE: The closest analogy in VB would be a program that uses a Sub Main rather than a startup form. Recall that if you choose to have a Sub Main, *everything* has to be explicitly called from Sub Main. Another way this analogy is a good one is that, as you know, if you use Sub Main to start a VB program, then it must start the process of creating any objects used by the rest of the program. As you will soon see, the same is true in Java. The main method is ultimately responsible for creating all the objects that the program uses either directly or indirectly.

Next, turn your attention to this fragment.

```
{   System.out.println("We will not use 'Hello world!'");
}
```

Braces mark the beginning and end of the *body* of the method. This method has only one statement in it. As with most programming languages, you can think of Java statements as being the sentences of the language. In Java, *every statement must end with a semicolon.* (For those coming from a Pascal background, the semicolon in Java is not the statement separator, but rather the statement terminator.)

In particular, neither white space nor carriage returns mark the end of a statement, so statements can span lines if need be. There are essentially no limits on the length of a statement.

The body of the main method contains a statement that outputs a single line of text to the console.

Here, we are using the System.out object and asking it to use its println method. Notice the periods used to invoke a method. Java uses the general syntax

object.method(parameters)

for its equivalent of function calls.

In this case, we are calling the println method, which works with a string and then displays it on the standard console. It then terminates the output line so that each call to println displays its output on a new line. Finally, notice that Java, like C/C++ and VB (but not Pascal), uses double quotes for strings. (See the section on strings later in this chapter for more information.)

Methods in Java, like functions in any programming languages, can use zero, one, or more *arguments* (some languages call them *parameters*). Even the `main` method in Java accepts what the user types on the command line as its argument. You will see how to use this information later in this chapter. (Even if a method takes zero arguments, you must still use empty parentheses.)

NOTE: There also is a `print` method in `System.out` that doesn't add a newline character to the string.

C++ NOTE: Although in Java, as in C/C++, the `main` method receives an array of command-line arguments, the array syntax in Java is different. A `String[]` is an array of strings, and so `args` denotes an array of strings. The name of the program is not stored in the `args` array, however. For example, when you start up the program `Bjarne.class` as

```
java Bjarne Stroustrup
```

from the command line, then `args[0]` will be `Stroustrup` and not `Bjarne` or `java`.

Comments

Comments in Java, like comments in most programming languages, do not show up in the executable program. Thus, you can add as many comments as needed without fear of bloating the code. Java has three ways of showing comments. The most common method is a `//`. You use this for a comment that will run from the `//` to the end of the line.

```
System.out.println("We will not use 'Hello world!'");
// is this too cute?
```

When longer comments are needed, you can mark each line with a `//`, but it is more common to use the `/*` and `*/` that let you block off a longer comment. This is shown in Example 3–1.

Example 3–1: FirstSample.java

```
/* This is the first sample program in Core Java Chapter 3
   Copyright (C) 1998 Cay Horstmann and Gary Cornell
*/

public class FirstSample
{  public static void main(String[] args)
   {  System.out.println("We will not use 'Hello, World!'");
   }
}
```

Since the `//` comment style is painful to modify when you need to extend comments over multiple lines, we suggest using it only when you are sure the comment will never grow.

Finally, there is a third kind of comment that can be used to generate documentation automatically. This comment uses a `/**` to start and a `*/` to end. For more on this type of comment and on automatic documentation generation, please see Appendix II.

CAUTION: `/* */` comments do not nest in Java. That is, you cannot deactivate code simply by surrounding it with `/*` and `*/` since the code that you want to deactivate might itself contain a `*/` delimiter.

Data Types

Java is a *strongly typed language*. This means that every variable must have a declared type. There are eight *primitive types* in Java. Six of them are number types (four integer and two floating-point types); one is the character type `char`, used for characters in Unicode encoding (see the section on the `char` type), and one is a `boolean` type for truth values.

NOTE: Java has an arbitrary precision arithmetic package. However, "Big numbers," as they are called, are Java *objects* and not a new Java type. You will see how to use them in Chapter 5.

VB NOTE: Java doesn't have any type analogous to the Variant data type, where you can store all possible basic types, nor is it as forgiving when you try assigning variables of one basic type to another (see below). It does have a way of converting all types to strings for display purposes analogous to using the & (ironically, it's the +) that you will see how to use later in this chapter.

Integers

The integer types are for numbers without fractional parts. Negative values are allowed. Java provides the four integer types shown in Table 3–1.

Table 3–1: Java integer types

Type	Storage Requirement	Range (inclusive)
int	4 bytes	–2,147,483,648 to 2,147,483, 647 (just over 2 billion)
short	2 bytes	–32,768 to 32,767
long	8 bytes	–9,223,372,036,854,775,808L to 9,223,372,036,854,775,807L
byte	1 byte	–128 to 127

In most situations, the int type is the most practical. If you want to represent the national debt in pennies, you'll need to resort to a long. The byte and short types are mainly intended for specialized applications, such as low-level file handling, or for large arrays when storage space is at a premium. The point is that, under Java, the ranges of the integer types do not depend on the machine on which you will be running the Java code. This alleviates a major pain for the programmer who wants to move software from one platform to another, or even between operating systems on the same platform. A C program that runs well on a SPARC may exhibit integer overflow under Windows 3.1. Since Java programs must run with the same results on all machines by its design, the ranges for the various types are fixed. Of course, having platform-independent integer types brings a small performance penalty, but in the case of Java, this is not a particular problem. (There are worse bottlenecks....)

Long integer numbers have a suffix L (for example, 4000000000L). Hexadecimal numbers have a prefix 0x (for example, 0xCAFE).

C++ NOTE: In C and C++, int denotes the integer type that depends on the target machine. On a 16-bit processor, like the 8086, integers are 2 bytes. On a 32-bit processor like the Sun SPARC, they are 4-byte quantities. On an Intel Pentium, the integer type depends on the operating system: for DOS and Windows 3.1, integers are 2 bytes. When using 32-bit mode for Windows 95 or Windows NT programs, integers are 4 bytes. In Java, the sizes of all numeric types are platform independent.

Note that Java does not have any unsigned types.

VB NOTE: Keep in mind that the ranges for the integer types are quite different in Java than they are in VB. An integer in VB corresponds to a short in Java. The int type in Java corresponds to the Longint type in VB, and so on.

Floating-Point Types

The floating-point types denote numbers with fractional parts. There are two floating-point types, as shown in Table 3–2.

Table 3–2: Floating-point types

Type	Storage Requirement	Range
float	4 bytes	approximately ±3.40282347E+38F (6–7 significant decimal digits)
double	8 bytes	approximately ±1.79769313486231570E+308 (15 significant digits)

The name double refers to the fact that these numbers have twice the precision of the float type. (Some people call these *double-precision* variables.) Here, the type to choose in most applications is double. The limited precision of float is simply not sufficient for many situations. Seven significant (decimal) digits may be enough to precisely express your annual salary in dollars and cents, but it won't be enough for your company president's salary. The only reason to use float is in the rare situations in which the slightly faster processing of single-precision numbers is important or when you need to store a large number of them.

Numbers of type float have a suffix F, for example, 3.402F. Floating-point numbers without an F suffix (such as 3.402) are always considered to be of type double. You can optionally supply the D suffix such as 3.402D. All the floating-point types follow the IEEE 754 specification. They will overflow on range errors and underflow on operations like a divide-by-zero.

VB

VB NOTE: That Java will merrily divide one floating-point number by 0 and not report an error is, of course, very strange behavior for a VB programmer. But of course even in VB you shouldn't be relying on error trapping to catch division by 0!

The Character Type (char)

First, single quotes are used to denote char constants. For example. 'H' is a character, "H" is a string containing a single character. Second, the char type denotes characters in the Unicode encoding scheme. You may not be familiar with Unicode, and, fortunately, you don't need to worry much about it if you don't program international applications. (Even if you do, you still won't have to worry about it too much because Unicode was designed to make the use of non-Roman characters easy to handle.) Because Unicode was designed to handle essentially all characters in all written languages in the world, it is a 2-byte code. This allows

65,536 characters (about 35,000 are currently in use). This is far richer than the ASCII/ANSI codeset, which is a 1-byte code—thus allowing only 255 characters. Note that the familiar ASCII/ANSI code that you use in Windows programming is a subset of Unicode. More precisely, it is the first 255 characters in the Unicode coding scheme. Thus, character codes like `'a'`, `'1'`, and `'['` are valid Unicode characters. Unicode characters are most often expressed in terms of a hexadecimal encoding scheme that runs from `'\u0000'` to `'\uFFFF'` (with `'\u0000'` to `'\u00FF'` being the ordinary ASCII/ANSI characters). The `\u` prefix indicates a Unicode value, and the four hexadecimal digits tell you what Unicode character. For example, `\u2122` is the trademark symbol (™). (For more on Unicode, you might want to check out the Web site at www.unicode.org.)

Besides the `\u` escape character that indicated the encoding of a Unicode character, Java allows you to use the escape sequences for the special characters shown in Table 3–3.

Table 3–3: Special characters

Escape Sequence	Name	Unicode Value
\b	backspace	\u0008
\t	tab	\u0009
\n	linefeed	\u000a
\r	carriage return	\u000d
\"	double quote	\u0022
\'	single quote	\u0027
\\	backslash	\u005c

NOTE: Although you can theoretically use any Unicode character in a Java application or applet, whether you can actually see it displayed depends on your browser (for applets) and (ultimately) on your operating system for both. For example, you cannot use Java to output Kanji on a machine running the U.S. version of Windows 95. For more on internationalization issues, please see Volume 2.

C++ NOTE: In C and C++, `char` denotes an *integral* type, namely, 1-byte integers. The standard is coy about the exact range. It can be either 0...255 or −128...127. In Java, `char` data are not numbers. Converting from numbers to characters requires an explicit cast in Java. (Values of the `char` type can be converted to the `int` type without an explicit cast.)

The Boolean Type

The `boolean` type has two values, `false` and `true`. It is used for logical testing, using the relational operators that Java, like any programming language, supports.

C++ NOTE: In C, there is no Boolean type. Instead, the convention is that any non-zero value denotes true, and zero denotes false. In C++, a Boolean type (called `bool`, not `boolean`) has recently been added to the language standard. It, too, has values `false` and `true`, but for historical reasons conversions between Boolean values and integers are allowed, and you can still use numbers or pointers in test conditions. In Java, you cannot convert between numbers and Boolean values—not even with a cast.

VB NOTE: In VB, as you know, any non-zero value is regarded as true and zero is regarded as false. This simply will not work in Java—you cannot use a number where a Boolean value is needed, nor can you convert a number to a Boolean via the equivalent of CBool.

Variables

Java, like C++ and Pascal-based languages, requires you to declare the type of a variable. (Of course, good programming practice in VB would require this as well.) You declare a variable by placing the type first, followed by the name of the variable. Here are some examples:

```
byte b; // for space-sensitive considerations
int anIntegerVariable;
long aLongVariable; // for the national debt in pennies
char ch;
```

Notice the semicolon at the end of each declaration (and the positioning of the comments in the first and third line). The semicolon is necessary because a declaration is a complete Java statement.

The rules for a variable name are as follows:

A variable name must begin with a letter and be a sequence of letters or digits. Note that the terms "letter" and "digit" are much broader in Java than in most languages. A letter is defined as `'A'-'Z'`, `'a'-'z'`, `'_'`, or *any* Unicode character that denotes a letter in a language. For example, German users can use umlauts such as `'ä'` in variable names; Greek speakers could use a μ. Similarly, digits are `'0'-'9'` and *any* Unicode characters that denote a digit in a language. Symbols like `'+'` or `'©'` cannot be used inside variable names, nor can spaces. *All* characters in the name of a variable are significant and *case is also significant.* The length of a variable name is essentially unlimited.

TIP: If you are really curious as to what Unicode characters are "letters" as far as Java is concerned, you can use the `isJavaIdentifierStart` and `isJavaIdentifierPart` methods in the `Character` class to check.

You also cannot use a Java reserved word for a variable name. (See Appendix I for a list of reserved words.)

You can have multiple declarations on a single line

```
int i, j; // both are integers (unlike in VB!)
```

but we generally comment and initialize each variable separately and so prefer putting declarations on separate lines.

Assignments and Initializations

After you declare a variable, you should explicitly initialize it by means of an assignment statement—you should never have uninitialized variables. (And the compiler will usually prevent you from having them anyway.) You assign to a previously declared variable using the variable name on the left, an equal sign (=), and then some Java expression that has an appropriate value on the right.

```
int foo; // this is a declaration
foo = 37; // this is an assignment
```

Here's an example of an assignment to a character variable:

```
char yesChar;
yesChar = 'Y';
```

One nice feature of Java is the ability to both declare and initialize a variable on the same line. For example:

```
int i = 10; // this is an initialization
```

Finally, in Java you can put declarations anywhere in your code, but you can only declare a variable once in any block in a method. (See the section on Control Flow in this chapter for more on blocks.)

NOTE: C and C++ distinguish between the *declaration* and *definition* of variables. For example,

```
        int i = 10;
```

is a definition, whereas

```
        extern int i;
```

is a declaration. In Java, there are no declarations that are separate from definitions.

Conversions Between Numeric Types

Java does not have any trouble multiplying, say, an integer by a double—it will treat the result as a double. More generally, any binary operations on numeric values of different types will be acceptable and be treated in the following fashion:

- If any of the operands is of type `double`, the other one will be converted to a `double`.

- Otherwise, if any of the operands is of type `float`, the other one will be converted to a `float`.

- Otherwise, if any of the operands is of type `long`, the other one will be converted to a `long`.

This works similarly down the line of the integer types: `int`, `short`, and `byte`.

On the other hand, there are obviously times when you want to consider a `double` as an integer. Numeric conversions are possible in Java, but, of course, information may be lost. Conversions where loss of information is possible are done by means of *casts*. The syntax for casting is to give the target type in parentheses, followed by the variable name. For example:

```
double x = 9.997;
int nx = (int)x;
```

Then, the variable nx has the value 9, as casting a floating-point value to an integer discards the fractional part (and does not round as in VB).

If you want to *round* a floating-point number to the *nearest* integer (which is the more useful operation in most cases), use the `Math.round` method:

```
double x = 9.997;
int nx = (int)Math.round(x);
```

Now the variable nx has the value 10. You still need to use the cast (int) when you call round. The reason is that the return value of the round method is a `long`, and a `long` can only be assigned to an `int` with an explicit cast since there is the possibility of information loss.

NOTE: Java does not complain ("throw an exception" in Java-speak—see Chapter 11) if you try to cast a number of one type to another that is out of the range for the target type. The result will be a truncated number that has a different value. It is, therefore, a good idea to explicitly test that the value is in the correct range before you perform a cast.

C++ NOTE: You cannot cast between Boolean values and any numeric type.

Finally, Java allows you to make certain assignment conversions by assigning the value of a variable of one type to another without an explicit cast. Those that are permitted are

`byte→short→int→long→float→double` and `char→int`

where you can always assign a variable of a type that is to the left to the type on its right in the list above.

Constants

In Java, you use the keyword `final` to denote a constant. For example,

```java
public class UsesConstants
{   public static void main(String[] args)
    {   final double CM_PER_INCH = 2.54;
        double paperWidth = 8.5;
        double paperHeight = 11;
        System.out.println("Paper size in centimeter: "
            + paperWidth * CM_PER_INCH + " by "
            + paperHeight * CM_PER_INCH);
    }
}
```

The keyword `final` indicates that you can assign to the variable once, then its value is set once and for all. It is customary to name constants in all upper case.

It is probably more common in Java to want a constant that is available to multiple methods inside a single class. These are usually called *class constants.* You set up a class constant with the keywords `static final`. Here is an example of using a class constant:

```java
public class UsesConstants2
{   public static final double G = 9.81;
    // gravitation in meters/second squared;
    public static void main(String[] args)
    {   System.out.println(G + " meters per second squared");
    }
}
```

Note that the definition of the class constant appears *outside* the `main` method. The use of the access specifier `public` here means that other Java methods outside the class can use the constant.

C++ NOTE: `const` is a reserved Java keyword, but it is not currently used for anything. You must use `final` for a constant.

Operators

The usual arithmetic operators + − * / are used in Java for addition, subtraction, multiplication, and division. The / operator denotes integer division if both arguments are integers, and floating-point division otherwise. Integer remainder (i.e., the mod function) is denoted by %. For example, 15 / 4 is 3, 15 % 2 is 1, and 11.0 / 4 is 2.75. You can use the arithmetic operators in your variable initializations:

```
int n = 5;
int a = 2 * n; // a is 10
```

As in C and C++, there is actually a shortcut for using binary arithmetic operators in an assignment. For example,

```
x += 4;
```

is equivalent to

```
x = x + 4;
```

(In general, place the operator to the left of the = sign, such as *= or %=.)

Exponentiation

Unlike languages like VB, Java has no operator for raising a quantity to a power: you must use the pow method. The pow method is part of the Math class in java.lang. The usual way of doing exponentiation is via the statement:

```
double y = Math.pow(x, a);
```

which sets y to be x raised to the power a (x^a). The pow method takes arguments that are both of type double and returns a double as well.

NOTE: The Math class in Java has a large number of functions a scientist or engineer would need. For example, there are constants for π and e (as doubles, so they are very accurate). You also have the square root, natural log, exponential and trig functions. However, even people who would never use any of these scientific functions will occasionally need the Math class because it also contains methods for rounding off floating-point numbers, taking the maximum and minimum of two numbers of the same type, the absolute value function, and the greatest integer function.

Increment and Decrement Operators

Programmers, of course, know that one of the most common operations with a numeric variable is to add or subtract 1. Java, following in the footsteps of C and C++, has both increment and decrement operators: x++ adds 1 to the current value of the variable x, and x-- subtracts 1 from it. For example, the code

```
int n = 12;
n++;
```

changes n to 13. Because these operators change the value of a variable, they cannot be applied to numbers themselves. For example, 4++ is not a legal statement.

There are actually two forms of these operators; you have seen the "postfix," i.e., after the variable form. There is also a prefix form, ++n. Both change the value of the variable by 1. The difference between the two only appears when they are used inside expressions. The prefix form does the addition first; the postfix form evaluates to the old value of the variable.

```
int m = 7;
int n = 7;
int a = 2 * ++m; // now a is 16, m is 8
int b = 2 * n++; // now b is 14, n is 8
```

We recommend against using ++ inside other expressions as this often leads to annoying bugs that are hard to track down.

(Of course, while it is true that the ++ operator gives the C++ language its name, it also led to the first joke about the language. The joke is credited to anti-C++ programmers who point out that even the name of the language contains a bug: "After all, it should really be called ++C, since we only want to use a language after it has been improved." Continuing the joke, you can argue that the correct name for Java is ++C. This is because Java really does make it easier to produce bug-free code. It does this by eliminating many of C++ more bug-prone features such as pointer arithmetic, manual memory allocation, and null-terminated arrays of chars. Of course, it does retain the murky side effects of prefix and postfix ++.)

Relational and Boolean Operators

Java has the full complement of relational operators. To test for equality you use a double equal sign, ==. For example, the value of

```
(3 == 7)
```

is false.

VB NOTE: It is important to remember that Java uses different symbols for assignment and equality testing.

C++ NOTE: Java eliminates the possibility of bugs resulting from the use of the = sign when you meant the ==. A line that begins if (k=0) won't even compile since the condition evaluates to the integer 0, which doesn't convert to a Boolean value in Java.

Use a != for inequality. For example, the value of

```
(3 != 7)
```

is true.

Finally, you have the usual < (less than), > (greater than), <= (less than or equal), and >= (greater than or equal) operators.

Java, following C++, uses && for the logical "and" operator and || for the logical "or" operator. As you can easily remember from the != operator, the exclamation point is the negation operator. The && and || operators are evaluated in "short circuit" fashion. This means that when you have an expression like:

```
(A && B)
```

once the truth value of the expression A has been determined to be false, the value for the expression B is *not* calculated. (See the sections on conditionals for an example of where this is useful.)

Bitwise Operators

When working with any of the integer types, you have operators that can work directly with the bits that make up the integers. This means that you can use masking techniques to get at individual bits in a number. The bitwise operators are:

& ("and") | ("or")   ^ ("xor")   ~ ("not")

VB NOTE: Remember that ^ is the xor operator and not the power operator.

These operators work on bit patterns. For example, if foo is an integer variable, then

```
int fourthBitFromRight = (foo & 8) / 8;
```

gives you a one if the fourth bit from the right in the binary representation of foo is one, and a zero if not. Using & with the appropriate power of 2 lets you mask out all but a single bit when need be.

There are also >> and << operators, which shift a bit pattern to the right or left. These operators are often convenient when you need to build up bit patterns to do bit masking:

```
int fourthBitFromRight = (foo & (1 << 3)) >> 3;
```

Note that whether you use these operators to divide and multiply by powers of two is matter of taste. Java compilers are almost certainly smart enough to change multiplication by powers of 2 into the appropriate shift operators.

Finally, there is even a >>> operator that fills the top bits with zero, whereas >> extends the sign bit into the top bits. There is no <<< operator.

C++ NOTE: In C/C++, there is no guarantee as to whether >> performs an arithmetic shift (extending the sign bit) or a logical shift (filling in with zeroes). Implementors are free to choose whatever is more efficient. That means the C/C++ >> operator is really only defined for non-negative numbers. Java removes that ambiguity.

Parentheses and Operator Hierarchy

As in all programming languages, you are best off using parentheses to indicate the order in which you want operations to be carried out. However, in Java the hierarchy of operations is as shown in Table 3–4.

Table 3–4: Operator precedence

Operators	Associativity
[] . () (method call)	left to right
! ~ ++ -- + (unary) – (unary) () (cast) new	right to left
* / %	left to right
+ -	left to right
<< >> >>>	left to right
< <= > >= instanceof	left to right
== !=	left to right
&	left to right
^	left to right
|	left to right
&&	left to right
||	left to right
?:	left to right
= += -= *= /= %= &= |= ^= <<= >>= >>>=	right to left

If no parentheses are used, operations are performed in the hierarchical order indicated. Operators on the same level are processed from left to right, except for those that are right associative, as indicated in the table.

C++ NOTE: Unlike C or C++, Java does not have a comma operator. However, you can use a *comma-separated list of expressions* in the first and third slot of a `for` statement.

Strings

Strings are sequences of characters, such as `"hello"`. Java does not have a built-in string type. Instead, the standard Java library contains a predefined class called, naturally enough, `String`. Each quoted string is an instance of the `String` class:

```
String e = ""; // an empty string
String greeting = "Hello";
```

Concatenation

Java, like most programming languages, allows you to use the + sign to join (concatenate) two strings together.

```
String expletive = "Expletive";
String PG13 = "deleted";
String message = expletive + PG13;
```

The above code makes the value of the string variable `message` `"Expletivedeleted"`. (Note the lack of a space between the words: the + sign joins two strings together in the order received, *exactly* as they are given.)

When you concatenate a string with a value that is not a string, the latter is converted to a string. (As we will see in Chapter 5, every Java object can be converted to a string.) For example:

```
String rating = "PG" + 13;
```

sets `rating` to the string `"PG13"`.

This feature is commonly used in output statements; for example,

```
System.out.println("The answer is " + answer);
```

is perfectly acceptable and will print what one would want (and with the correct spacing because of the space after the word `is`).

VB NOTE: Although Java will convert a number to a string when concatenating using the + (in analogy to the &) with another string, it does not add a space in front of a positive number.

Substrings

You extract a substring from a larger string with the `substring` method of the `String` class. For example,

```
String greeting = "Hello";
String s = greeting.substring(0, 4);
```

creates a string consisting of the characters `"Hell"`. Java counts the characters in strings in a peculiar fashion: the first character in a string has position 0, just like in C and C++. (In C, there was a technical reason for counting positions starting at 0, but that reason has long gone away, and only the nuisance remains.)

For example, the character `'H'` has position 0 in the string `"Hello"`, and the character `'o'` has position 4. The second argument of `substring` is the first position that you *do not* want to copy. In our case, we want to copy the characters in positions 0, 1, 2, and 3 (from position 0 to position 3 inclusive). As `substring` counts it, this means from position 0 inclusive to position 4 *exclusive*.

There is one advantage to the way `substring` works: it is easy to compute the length of the substring. The string `s.substring(a, b)` always has b – a characters. For example, the substring `"Hell"` has length 4 – 0 = 4.

String Editing

To find out the length of a string, use the `length` method. For example:

```
String greeting = "Hello";
int n = greeting.length(); // is 5.
```

Just as `char` denotes a Unicode character, `String` denotes a sequence of Unicode characters. It is possible to get at individual characters of a string. For example, `s.charAt(n)` returns the Unicode character at position n, where n is between 0 and `s.length()` – 1.

However, the `String` class gives no methods that let you *change* a character in an existing string. If you want to turn `greeting` into `"Help!"`, you cannot directly change the third position of `greeting` into a `'p'` and the fourth position into a `'!'`. If you are a C programmer, this will make you feel pretty helpless. How are you going to modify the string? In Java, it is quite easy: take the substring that you want to keep and then concatenate it with the characters that you want to replace.

```
greeting = greeting.substring(0, 3) + "p!";
```

This changes the current value of the `greeting` variable to `"Help!"`.

Since you cannot change the individual characters in a Java string, the documentation refers to the objects of the `String` class as being *immutable*. Just as the number 3 is always 3, the string `"Hello"` will always contain the character sequence `'H'`, `'e'`, `'l'`, `'l'`, `'o'`. You cannot change these values. You can, as you just saw however, change the contents of the string *variable* `greeting` and make it refer to a different string, just as you can make a numeric variable currently holding the value 3 hold the value 4.

Isn't that a lot less efficient? It would seem simpler to change the characters than to build up a whole new string from scratch. Well, yes and no. Indeed, it isn't efficient to generate a new string that holds the concatenation of `"Hel"` and `"p!"`. But immutable strings have one great advantage: The compiler can arrange that strings are *shared*.

To understand how this works, think of the various strings as sitting on the heap. (For non-C/C++ programmers, think of them as just being located in memory somewhere.) String variables then point to locations on the heap. For example, the substring `greeting.substring(0, 3)` is just a pointer to the existing `"Hello"` string, together with the range of characters that are used in the substring. Overall, the designers of Java decided that the efficiency of string-sharing outweighs the inefficiency of immutability.

Look at your own programs; we suspect that most of the time, you don't change strings—you just compare them. Of course, there are some cases in which direct manipulation of strings is more efficient. (One example is when assembling strings from individual characters that come from a file or the keyboard.) For these situations, Java provides a separate `StringBuffer` class that we describe in Chapter 12. If you are not concerned with the efficiency of string handling (which is not a bottleneck in many Java applications anyway), you can ignore `StringBuffer` and just use `String`.

C++ NOTE: C programmers generally are bewildered when they see Java strings for the first time, because they think of strings as arrays of characters:

```
char greeting[] = "Hello";
```

That is the wrong analogy: a Java string is roughly analogous to a `char*` pointer,

```
char* greeting = "Hello";
```

When you replace `greeting` with another string, the Java code does roughly the following:

```
char* temp = malloc(6);
strncpy(temp, greeting, 3);
strcpy(temp + 3, "p!");
greeting = temp;
```

Sure, now `greeting` points to the string `"Help!"`. And even the most hardened C programmer must admit that the Java syntax is more pleasant than a sequence of `strncpy` calls. But what if we make another assignment to `greeting`?

```
greeting = "Howdy";
```

Don't we have a memory leak? After all, the original string was allocated on the heap. C and C++ programmers must change their way of thinking because Java does automatic garbage collection. Java automatically reclaims any unused memory. If a string is no longer needed, its memory will eventually be recycled.

If you are a C++ programmer and use the `string` class defined by ANSI C++, you will be much more comfortable with the Java `String` type. C++ `string` objects also perform automatic allocation and deallocation of memory. The memory management is performed explicitly by constructors, assignment operators, and destructors. However, C++ strings are mutable—you can modify individual characters in a string.

Testing Strings for Equality

To test whether or not two strings are equal, use the `equals` method; the expression

```
s.equals(t)
```

returns `true` if the strings s and t are equal, `false` otherwise. For the `equals` method, s and t can be string variables or string constants. For example,

```
"Hello".equals(command)
```

is perfectly legal. To test if two strings are identical except for the upper/lower-case letter distinction, use the `equalsIgnoreCase` method.

```
"Hello".equalsIgnoreCase("hello")
```

Do *not* use the `==` operator to test if two strings are equal! It only determines whether or not the strings are stored in the same location. Sure, if strings are in the same location, they must be equal. But it is entirely possible to store multiple copies of identical strings in different places.

```
String greeting = "Hello"; //initialize greeting to a string
if (greeting == "Hello") . . . // probably true
if (greeting.substring(0, 4) == "Hell") . . .
    // probably false
```

If the compiler would always arrange for equal strings to be shared, then you could use `==` for testing equality. But string storage is implementation dependent. The standard implementation only shares string constants, not strings that are the result of operations like `+` or `substring`. Therefore, *never* use `==` to compare strings or you will have a program with the worst kind of bug—an intermittent one that seems to occur randomly.

C++ NOTE: If you are used to the C++ `string` class, you have to be particularly careful about equality testing. The C++ `string` class does overload the `==` operator to test for equality of the string contents. It is pretty silly that Java goes out of its way to give strings the same "look and feel" as numeric values but then makes strings behave like pointers for equality testing. The language designers could have redefined `==` for strings, just as they made a special arrangement for `+`. Oh well, every language has its share of inconsistencies.

C programmers never use `==` to compare strings but use `strcmp` instead. The Java method `compareTo` is the exact analog to `strcmp`. You can use

```
if (greeting.compareTo("Help") == 0) . . .
```

but it seems clearer to use `equals` instead.

The `String` class in Java contains more than 50 methods. A surprisingly large number of them are sufficiently useful so that we can imagine using them on a day-to-day basis. The following API note summarizes the ones we found most useful.

NOTE: You will find these API notes throughout the book to help you understand the Java Application Programming Interface or API. Each API note lists the name of a class (such as `java.lang.String`—the significance of the so-called *package* name `java.lang` will be explained in Chapter 5), followed by the names, explanations, and parameter descriptions of one or more methods. We typically do not list all methods of a particular class but instead select those that are most commonly used. For a full listing, consult the on-line documentation. See Chapter 4 for more information on the organization of the on-line documentation.

`java.lang.String`

- `char charAt(int index)`

  returns the character at the specified location.

- `int compareTo(String other)`

  returns a negative value if the string comes before `other` in dictionary order, a positive value if the string comes after `other` in dictionary order, or 0 if the strings are equal.

- `boolean endsWith(String suffix)`

  returns `true` if the string ends with `suffix`.

- `boolean equals(Object other)`

  returns `true` if the string equals `other`.

- `boolean equalsIgnoreCase(String other)`

  returns `true` if the string equals `other`, except for upper/lowercase distinction.

- `int indexOf(String str)`
- `int indexOf(String str, int fromIndex)`

  return the start of the first substring equal to `str`, starting at index 0 or at `fromIndex`.

- `int lastIndexOf(String str)`
- `int lastIndexOf(String str, int fromIndex)`

  return the start of the last substring equal to `str`, starting at index 0 or at `fromIndex`.

- `int length()`

  returns the length of the string.

- `String replace(char oldChar, char newChar)`

  returns a new string that is obtained by replacing all characters `oldChar` in the string with `newChar`.

- `boolean startsWith(String prefix)`

  returns `true` if the string begins with `prefix`.

- `String substring(int beginIndex)`
- `String substring(int beginIndex, int endIndex)`

  return a new string consisting of all characters from `beginIndex` until the end of the string or until `endIndex` (exclusive).

- `String toLowerCase()`

  returns a new string containing all characters in the original string, with uppercase characters converted to lower case.

- `String toUpperCase()`

  returns a new string containing all characters in the original string, with lowercase characters converted to upper case.

- `String trim()`

  returns a new string by eliminating all leading and trailing spaces in the original string.

Reading Input

Reading input from the keyboard is unbelievably difficult in plain Java. Naturally, that is not a problem for graphical programs that collect user input from a dialog box. But it is a problem for anyone who wants to write simple programs to learn the language. Consider a common task—reading a floating-point number that the user is trying to enter from the keyboard. This turns out to be a nightmare of epic proportions. Before you look at the code, relax—the code library for this book gives you a simpler method for achieving this task. Example 3–2 shows what you have to do in plain Java. Don't worry about the details of streams—they will be covered in Chapter 12.

Example 3–2: ReadDoubleTest.java

```java
import java.io.*;
import java.text.*;

public class ReadDoubleTest
   // shows how to read a double the hard way
{  public static void main(String[] args)
   {  System.out.println
         ("Enter a number, I'll add two to it.");
      double x; // the number we wish to read
      try
      {  InputStreamReader isr
            = new InputStreamReader(System.in);
         BufferedReader br
            = new BufferedReader(isr);
         String s = br.readLine();
         DecimalFormat df = new DecimalFormat();
         Number n = df.parse(s);
         x = n.doubleValue();
      }
      catch(IOException e)
      {  x = 0;
      }
      catch(ParseException e)
      {  x = 0;
      }
      System.out.println(x + 2);
   }
}
```

That is great if you get paid by the number of lines of code that you write. For the rest of us, we decided to write a class that we call `Console`, with methods to prompt a user for input and to convert the user input to a numeric value that can be used in a Java program. If you use the `Console` class, then you can rewrite the above monstrosity simply as follows:

```java
import corejava.*; // important--imports corejava package

public class ConsoleTest
{  public static void main(String[] args)
   {  double x = Console.readDouble
         ("Enter a number, I'll add two to it.");
      System.out.println(x + 2);
   }
}
```

Directions for Using our `Console` Class

Before we go on (so that we can give you some examples that are at least somewhat nontrivial!), this sidebar shows you what is needed in order to use the `Console` class to get various kinds of prompted input from the keyboard. The `Console` class has three methods. These methods let you:

- Capture an integer by a prompted input
- Capture a floating-point number with a prompted input
- Capture a string or word by a prompted input

The `Console` class can be found in the `corejava` subdirectory of the `CoreJavaBook` directory that contains the sample code from the CD. To use the `Console` class, it is important that you set up your `CLASSPATH` environment variable as described in Appendix III.

Be sure to add the line: `import corejava.*;` above the class definitions to each program that uses the `Console` class. Here's another example of using the `Console` class:

```
import corejava.*;
public class StringPromptSample
{   public static void main(String[] args)
    {   String yourName;
        yourName = Console.readLine
          ("Please enter your name.");
        System.out.println("Hello " + yourName);
    }
}
```

If you compile and run this program, you will see that the `readLine` method displays the string prompt and then grabs the text the user enters before he or she hits the ENTER key.

Besides the `readLine` and `readDouble` methods that you have already seen, the `Console` class supplies a `readInt` method to get an integer. Here are the signatures of all the methods in the `Console` class with short descriptions:

`readLine(String prompt)` reads a string (until the end of the line).

`readInt(String prompt)` reads an integer. If you do not enter an integer, it reprompts you to enter the integer correctly.

`readDouble(String prompt)` reads a floating-point number in the `double` range. If you do not enter a floating-point number, it reprompts you to do so.

Formatting Output

You can print a number to the console (a DOS window, for example) by the statement `System.out.print(x)`. That command will print x with the maximum number of non-zero digits for that type. For example,

```
x = 10000.0 / 3.0;
System.out.print(x);
```

prints

```
3333.3333333333335
```

That is a problem if you want to display, for example, dollars and cents.

You can control the display format in order to arrange your output neatly. The `NumberFormat` class in the `java.text` package has three methods that yield standard *formatters* for

- *numbers*

- *currency values*

- *percentage values*

Suppose that the United States locale is your default locale. (A *locale* is a set of specifications for country-specific properties of strings and numbers, such as collation order, currency symbol, and so on. Locales are an important concept for writing *internationalized* applications—programs that are acceptable to users from countries around the world. We will discuss internationalization in Volume 2.) Then, the value `10000.0 / 3.0` will print as

```
3,333.333
$3,333.33
333,333%
```

in these three formats. As you can see, the formatter adds the commas that separate the thousands, currency symbols ($), and percent signs.

To obtain a formatter for the default locale, use one of the three methods

```
NumberFormat.getNumberInstance()
NumberFormat.getCurrencyInstance()
NumberFormat.getPercentInstance()
```

Each of these methods returns an object of type `NumberFormat`. You can use that object to format one or more numbers. You then apply the `format` method to the `NumberFormat` object to get a string that contains the formatted number. Once you have the formatted string, you will probably simply display the newly formatted number by printing the string:

```
double x = 10000.0 / 3.0;
NumberFormat nf = NumberFormat.getNumberInstance();
String fx = nf.format(x); // the string "3,333.33"
System.out.println(fx);
```

You also may want to set the minimum and maximum number of integer digits or fractional digits to display. You can do this with the `setMinimumIntegerDigits`, `setMinimumFractionDigits`, `setMaximumIntegerDigits`, `setMaximumFractionDigits` methods in the `NumberFormat` class. For example,

```
double x = 10000.0 / 3.0;
NumberFormat nf = NumberFormat.getNumberInstance();
nf.setMaximumFractionDigits(4);
nf.setMinimumIntegerDigits(6);
String fx = nf.format(x); // the string "003,333.3333"
```

Setting the maximum number of fractional digits is often useful. The last displayed digit is rounded up if the first discarded digit is 5 or above. If you want to show trailing zeroes, set the minimum number of fractional digits to the same value as the maximum. Otherwise, you should leave the minimum number of fractional digits at the default value, 0.

Setting the number of integer digits is much less common. By specifying a minimum number, you force leading zeroes for smaller values. Specifying a maximum number is downright dangerous—the displayed value is silently truncated, yielding a nicely formatted but very wrong result.

You can also obtain number formats that are appropriate for different locales. For example, let us look up the number formats that are used by the German locale and use them to print our test output. There is a predefined object named `Locale.GERMANY` of a new type called `Locale` that knows about German number formatting rules. When we pass that `Locale` object to the `getNumberInstance` method, we obtain a formatter that follows those German rules.

```
double x = 10000.0 / 3.0;
NumberFormat nf =
NumberFormat.getNumberInstance(Locale.GERMANY);
System.out.println(nf.format(x));
NumberFormat nf = NumberFormat.getCurrencyInstance(Locale.GERMANY);
```

This code prints the numbers

```
3.333,333
3.333,33 DM
```

Note that the German convention for periods and commas in numbers is the exact opposite of the U.S. convention: a comma is used as the decimal separator, and a period is used to separate thousands. Also, the formatter knows that the currency symbol (DM) is placed *after* the number.

Finally, you can create your own format. For example, you may want to show the number with six digits after the decimal point, but no thousands separator. To do this, you must define a `DecimalFormat` object that indicates the form you want your numbers to take. You indicate your formatting requirements in a format string that shows what the number should look like. For example:

```
DecimalFormat df = new DecimalFormat("0.######");
System.out.println(df.format(x));
```

This code prints the number in the following form:

```
3333.333333
```

As you can see, you no longer see a thousands separator, and there are six digits after the decimal point.

You can use the characters shown in Table 3–5 in the format string.

Table 3–5: Formatting characters for the `DecimalFormat` class

Symbol	Meaning
0	A digit
#	A digit; don't show if it is a leading or trailing zero
.	Location of decimal separator
,	Location of grouping separator
;	Separates formats for positive and negative numbers
−	Negative prefix
%	Multiply by 100 and show as percentage
any other symbol	Include symbol in output string

Table 3–6 shows a few examples.

Table 3–6: Sample format strings for the `DecimalFormat` class

Format String	Sample Number	Explanation
`,##0.00`	1,234.50	Two digits after the decimal point; show trailing zeroes
		Separate groups of thousands with commas
		If number is < 1, print leading zero (e.g., 0.123)
`$,##0.00;($,##0.00)`	($1,234.50)	Enclose negative numbers in parentheses instead of using a minus sign; also prepend the $ symbol
`0.######`	1234.5	If number is between −1 and 1, print leading zero (e.g., 0.123)
		Don't show trailing zeroes

The `DecimalFormat` mechanism works well for formatting numbers such as currency values. However, it is not suitable for scientific notation, tables with fixed column widths, or numbers in octal or hexadecimal format. For those applications, you can use the `Format` class that we provide as part of the `corejava` package.

`java.text.NumberFormat`

- `static NumberFormat getCurrencyInstance()`

  returns a `NumberFormat` object to convert currency values to strings using the conventions of the current locale.

- `static NumberFormat getNumberInstance()`

  returns a `NumberFormat` object to format numbers using the conventions of the current locale.

- `static NumberFormat getPercentInstance()`

  returns a `NumberFormat` object to convert percentages to strings.

- `void setMaximumFractionDigits(int digits)`

  Parameters: `digits`   the number of digits to display

  sets the maximum number of digits after the decimal point for the format object. The last displayed digit is rounded.

- `void setMaximumIntegerDigits(int digits)`

  Parameters: `digits`   the number of digits to display

  sets the maximum number of digits before the decimal point for the format object. *Use this method with extreme caution.* If you specify too few digits, then the number is simply truncated, displaying a dramatically wrong result!

- `void setMinimumFractionDigits(int digits)`

  Parameters: `digits`   the number of digits to display

  sets the minimum number of digits after the decimal point for the format object. If the number has fewer fractional digits than the minimum, then trailing zeroes are supplied.

- `void setMinimumIntegerDigits(int digits)`

  Parameters: `digits`   the number of digits to display

  sets the minimum number of digits before the decimal point for the format object. If the number has fewer digits than the minimum, then leading zeroes are supplied.

`java.text.DecimalFormat`

- `void DecimalFormat(String pattern)`

  Parameters: `pattern`   the format string

  returns a `DecimalFormat` object that follows the given pattern (see Table 3–5) for converting numbers to strings.

Directions for Using the CoreJava `Format` Class

Not only did we give you a `Console` class to easily read numbers from the screen, we also supply you with a class that can format numbers with less hassle than the `NumberFormat` class. Rather than reinvent the wheel, we simply reimplemented the C `printf` function that has a good set of formatting options and is, for the most part, easy to use. For example, to format a floating-point number with a field width of 10 and two digits after the decimal point, you use

```
Format.printf("Your monthly payment is %10.2f\n",
    payment);
```

That sends a string like

```
"Your monthly payment is     1141.30\n"
```

to `System.out`. If you'd rather capture that string in a string variable, use

```
String s = new Format
  ("Your monthly payment is %10.2f\n").format(payment);
```

The output string contains all characters of the format string, except that the format specification (starting with a `%`) is replaced by the formatted value. However, a `%%` denotes a percent sign.

Unlike the `printf` statement in C, you can have only one formatted value at a time. If you need to print two values, use two calls.

```
Format.printf("With rate %6.3f", 100 * y);
Format.printf("%%, your monthly payment is
    %10.2f\n", payment);
```

Apart from the `%m.nf` format, the most common format is `%nd`, to print an integer in a field with width n. Those two will get you a long way, and you may never need to learn more about the formatting codes.

Here are the rules for the formatting specifiers. The code starts with `%` and ends with one of the letters c, d, e, E, f, g, G, i, o, s, x, X. They have the following meanings:

f	Floating-point number in fixed format
e, E	Floating-point number in exponential notation (scientific format). The E format results in an uppercase E for the exponent (`1.14130E+003`), the e format in a lowercase e.
g, G	Floating-point number in general format (fixed format for small numbers, exponential format for large numbers). Trailing zeroes are suppressed. The G format results in an uppercase E for the exponent (if any), the g format in a lowercase e.
d, i	Integer in decimal
x, X	Integer in hexadecimal (with lower- or uppercase letters)
o	Integer in octal
s	String
c	Character

In between the `%` and the format code are the following fields. They are all optional.

+	Force display of + for positive numbers
0	Show leading zeroes
–	Align left in the field
space	Prepend a space in front of positive numbers
#	Use "alternate" format. Add 0 or 0x for octal or hexadecimal numbers. Don't suppress trailing zeroes in general floating point format.

Finally, remember that to use our `Format` class, you *must* add the `import corejava.*;` at the top of any file that defines any class that will use it.

A Mortgage Calculator

As our first semiserious application for Java, let's write a program that calculates the cost of a mortgage. We will use our `Console` class to prompt the user to enter the principal amount, the term in years, and the interest rate. The program will then display the monthly mortgage.

NOTE: We use the following standard formula to calculate the mortgage payment.

$$payment = \frac{principal \cdot monthlyInterest}{1 - (1 / (1 + monthlyInterest))^{years \cdot 12}}$$

Example 3–3 shows the code.

Example 3–3: Mortgage.java

```java
import corejava.*;
import java.text.*;

public class Mortgage
{  public static void main(String[] args)
   {  double principal;
      double yearlyInterest;
      int years;

      principal = Console.readDouble
         ("Loan amount (no commas):");
      yearlyInterest = Console.readDouble
         ("Interest rate in % (ex: use 7.5 for 7.5%):")/100;
      years = Console.readInt("The number of years:");

      double monthlyInterest = yearlyInterest / 12;
      double payment = principal * monthlyInterest
         / (1 - (Math.pow(1/(1 + monthlyInterest),
            years * 12)));
      System.out.println("Your payment is ");
      NumberFormat nf = NumberFormat.getCurrencyInstance();
```

```
        System.out.println(nf.format(payment));
    }
}
```

Control Flow

Java, like any programming language, supports both conditional statements and loops to determine control flow. We start with the conditional statements and then move on to loops. We end with the somewhat cumbersome `switch` statement that can be used when you have many values of a single expression to test for.

C++ NOTE: The Java control flow constructs are identical to those in C and C++, with one exception. There is no `goto`, but there is a "labeled" version of `break` that you can use to break out of a nested loop (where you perhaps would have used a `goto` in C).

Block Scope

Before we get into the actual control structures, you need to know more about *blocks*.

A block or compound statement is any number of simple Java statements that are surrounded by a pair of braces. Blocks define the scope of your variables. Blocks can be *nested* inside another. Here is a block that is nested inside the block of the `main` method.

```
public static void main(String[] args)
{   int n;
    . . .
    {   int k;
        . . .
    } // k local to block and defined
      // only until the end of the block
}
```

However, it is not possible to declare identically named variables in two nested blocks. For example, the following is an error and will not compile:

```
public static void main(String[] args)
{   int n;
    . . .
    {   int k;
        int n; // error--can't redefine n in inner block
        . . .
    }
}
```

C++ NOTE: In C++, it is possible to redefine a variable inside a nested block. The inner definition then shadows the outer one. This can be a source of programming errors; hence Java does not allow it.

Conditional Statements

The simplest conditional statement in Java has the form

```
if (condition) statement;
```

but in Java, as in most programming languages, you will often want to execute multiple statements when a single condition is true. In this case, the conditional takes the form:

```
if (condition) { block }
```

The condition must be surrounded by parentheses, and here the "block" is, as indicated before, any number of statements that are surrounded by a pair of braces. For example:

```
if (yourSales >= target)
{   performance = "Satisfactory";
    bonus = 100;
}
```

In this code all the statements surrounded by the braces will be executed when `yourSales` is greater than or equal to `target`. (See Figure 3–1.)

NOTE: A block (sometimes called a *compound statement*) allows you to have more than one (simple) statement in any Java programming structure that might otherwise have a single (simple) statement.

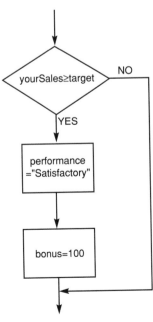

Figure 3–1: Flowchart for the `if` statement

The more general conditional in Java looks like this (see Figure 3–2):

```
if (condition) statement₁ else statement₂;
```

or, more likely,

```
if (condition) {block₁}    else {block₂}
```

For example:

```
if (yourSales >= target)
{   performance = "Satisfactory";
    bonus = 100 + 0.01 * (yourSales - target);
}
else
{   performance = "Unsatisfactory";
    bonus = 0;
}
```

The `else` part is always optional (see Figure 3–3). An `else` groups with the closest `if`. For example:

```
if (yourSales >= 2 * target)
{   performance = "Excellent";
    bonus = 1000;
}
```

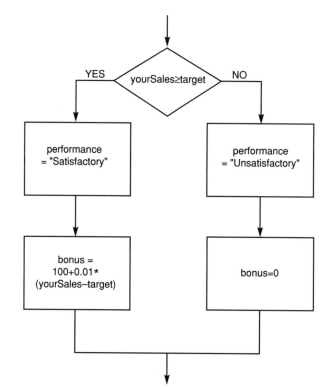

Figure 3–2: Flowchart for the `if/else` statement

```
else if {yourSales >= 1.5 * target)
{   performance = "Fine";
    bonus = 500;
}
else if (yourSales >= target)
{   performance = "Satisfactory";
    bonus = 100;
}
else
{   System.out.println("You're fired");
}
```

NOTE: Because of the short-circuit evaluation built into Java,

```
    if (x != 0 && 1 / x + y > x) // no division by 0
```

does not evaluate 1 / x if x is zero, and so cannot lead to a divide-by-zero error.

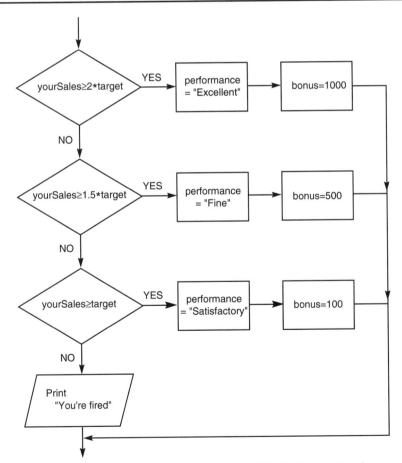

Figure 3–3: Flowchart for `if/else if` **(multiple branches)**

Finally, Java supports the ternary ? operator that is occasionally useful. The expression `condition ? e1 : e2` evaluates to `e1` if the `condition` is true, to `e2` otherwise. For example, `(x < y) ? x : y` gives the smaller of x and y.

Indeterminate Loops

In Java, as in all programming languages, there are control structures that let you repeat statements. There are two forms for repeating loops that are best when you do not know how many times a loop should be processed (these are "indeterminate loops").

First, there is the `while` loop that only executes the body of the loop while a condition is `true`. The general form is:

```
while (condition) { block }
```

The `while` loop will never execute if the condition is `false` at the outset (see Figure 3–4).

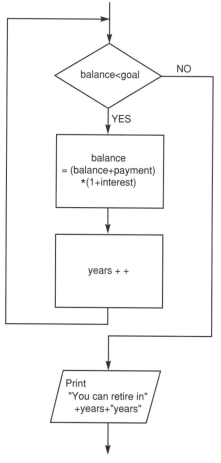

Figure 3–4: Flowchart for `while` statement

In Example 3–4, let's use our Console class to determine how long it will take to save a specific amount of money, assuming you get a specified interest rate per year and deposit the same amount of money per year.

Example 3–4: Retirement.java

```
import corejava.*;

public class Retirement
{  public static void main(String[] args)
   {  double goal;
      double interest;
      double payment;
      int years = 0;
      double balance = 0;

      goal = Console.readDouble
         ("How much money do you need to retire?");
      payment = Console.readDouble
         ("How much money will you contribute every year?");
      interest = Console.readDouble
         ("Interest rate in % (ex: use 7.5 for 7.5%):") / 100;

      while (balance < goal)
      {  balance = (balance + payment) * (1 + interest);
         years++;
      }

      System.out.println
         ("You can retire in " + years + " years.");
   }
}
```

In the example above, we are incrementing a counter and updating the amount currently accumulated in the body of the loop until the total exceeds the targeted amount. (Don't rely on this program to plan for your retirement. We left out a few niceties such as inflation and your life expectancy. We also made the assumption that you are putting in the money at the beginning of the year and so will get interest on it for the whole year—few people do that.)

A while loop tests at the top. Therefore, the code in the block may never be executed. If you want to make sure a block is executed at least once, you will need to move the test to the bottom. This is done with the do version of a while loop. Its syntax looks like this:

```
do { block } while (condition);
```

This executes the block and only then tests the condition. It then repeats the block and retests the condition, and so on. For instance, the code in Example 3–5 computes an approximation to the square root of any positive number, using an iterative process by continuing the process until the absolute value of the current and previous iterations are very close. Figure 3–5 illustrates this.

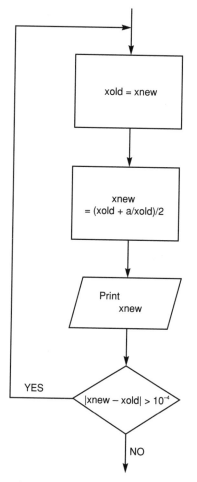

Figure 3–5: Flowchart for do/while **statement**

Example 3–5: SquareRoot.java

```
import corejava.*;

public class SquareRoot
{  public static void main(String[] args)
   {  double a = Console.readDouble("Please enter a number:");
```

```
double xnew = a / 2;
double xold;

do
{   xold = xnew;
    xnew = (xold + a / xold) / 2;
    System.out.println(xnew);
}
while (Math.abs(xnew - xold) > 1E-4);

}
}
```

Finally, since a block may contain *any* Java statements, you can nest loops as deeply as you want.

Determinate Loops

Java, like C++, has a very general construct to support iteration. As Figure 3–6 shows, the following prints the numbers from 1 to 10 on the screen.

```
for (int i = 1; i <= 10; i++)
    System.out.println(i);
```

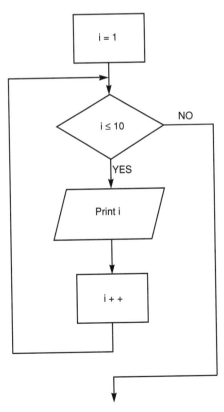

Figure 3–6: Flowchart for `for` statement

The idea is that the first slot of the `for` statement will (usually) hold the counter initialization. (The counter is occasionally declared and initialized there, as in this example). The second slot gives the condition which will be tested before each new pass through the loop, and the third slot explains how to change the state of the counter. What follows the initialization can be a simple Java statement or a block. (Thus, nested `for` loops are possible in Java.)

Although Java, like C++, allows almost any expression in the various slots of a `for` loop, it is an unwritten rule of good taste that the three slots of a `for` statement should only initialize, test, and update a counter variable. One can write very obscure loops by disregarding this rule.

Even within the bounds of good taste, much is possible. This is because you can have variables of any type and use any method of updating them, so you can have loops that count down:

```
for (int i = 10; i > 0; i--)
    System.out.println("Counting down " + i);
System.out.println("Blastoff!");
```

Or, you can have loops in which the variables and increments are of one of the floating-point types.

> NOTE: Again, be careful about testing for equality of floating-point numbers. A `for` loop that looks like this:
>
> ```
> for (x = 0; x != 10; x += 0.01)
> ```
>
> may never end. Due to roundoff errors, the value 10.0 is not reached exactly.

When you declare a variable in the first slot of the `for` statement, the scope of that variable extends until the end of the body of the `for` loop. In particular, if you do this, you cannot use that value of this variable outside the loop. Therefore, if you wish to use the end value of a loop counter outside the `for` loop, be sure to declare it outside the header for the loop!

Of course, a `for` loop is equivalent to a `while` loop; choose the one that fits your picture of the situation. More precisely,

```
for (statement₁; expression₁; expression₂) { block };
```

is completely equivalent to:

```
{   statement₁;
    while (expression₁)
    {   block;
        expression₂;
    }
}
```

Example 3–6 shows a reasonable use of floating-point numbers in a loop by extending the mortgage program. The program prints out the monthly payments for a range of interest rates around the entered value that go up and down by .125% by surrounding the core of the previous Mortgage program in a `for` loop.

Example 3–6: MortgageLoop.java

```java
import corejava.*;

public class MortgageLoop
{  public static void main(String[] args)
   {  double principal;
      double yearlyInterest;
      int years;

      principal = Console.readDouble
         ("Loan amount (no commas):");
      yearlyInterest = Console.readDouble
         ("Interest rate in % (ex: use 7.5 for 7.5%):") / 100;
      years = Console.readInt
         ("The number of years:");

      double y;
      for (y = yearlyInterest - 0.01;
         y <= yearlyInterest + 0.01; y += 0.00125)
      {  double monthlyInterest = y / 12;
         double payment = principal * monthlyInterest
            / (1 - (Math.pow(1/(1 + monthlyInterest),
              years * 12)));
         Format.printf("With rate %6.3f", 100 * y);
         Format.printf
            ("%%, your monthly payment is $%10.2f\n",
             payment);
      }
   }
}
```

Multiple Selections—the `switch` *Statement*

The `if`/`else` construct can be cumbersome when you have to deal with multiple selections with many alternatives. Unfortunately, the only alternative available in Java is almost as cumbersome—it is not nearly as neat as VB's Select Case statement, which allows you to test for ranges or for values in any type. Java, following the lead of C/C++, calls the device for multiple selection a `switch` statement. Unfortunately, the designers didn't improve on C/C++'s `switch` statement. You still can select only against a `char` or against all the integer types but `long`; you still cannot use a range of values.

For example, if you set up a menuing system with four alternatives like that in Figure 3–7, you could use code that looks like this:

```
int choice = Console.readInt("Select an option (1 to 4)");
// reads one keypress
switch(choice)
{   case 1:
        . . .
        break;
    case 2:
        . . .
        break;
    case 3:
        . . .
        break;
    case 4:
        . . .
        break;
    default:
        // bad input
        break;
}
```

In general, execution starts at the `case` label, matching the value on which the selection is performed, and continues until the next `break` or the end of the switch. The `default` clause is optional.

CAUTION: Unlike in languages like VB, it is possible for multiple switches to be triggered. This is because execution falls through to another case *unless* a `break` keyword gets you out of the whole `switch` statement. (It is extremely unusual to use a `switch` statement without a `break` keyword in every case. In the extremely rare situation where you want the "fall through" behavior, you ought to clearly comment it.)

Labeled Breaks

Although the designers of Java kept the `goto` as a reserved word, they decided not to include it in the language. In general, `goto` statements are considered poor style. Some programmers feel the anti-goto forces have gone too far (see, for example, the famous article of Donald Knuth called "Structured Programming with goto's"). They argue that unrestricted use of `goto` is error-prone, but that an occasional jump *out of a loop* is beneficial. The Java designers agreed and even added a new statement to support this programming style, the labeled break.

Let us first look at the unlabeled `break` statement. The same `break` statement that you use to exit a `switch` can also be used to break out of a loop. For example,

```
while (years <= 100)
{   balance = (balance + payment) * (1 + interest);
    if (balance > goal) break;
```

```
    years++;
}
```

Now the loop is exited if either `years > 100` occurs on the top of the loop or `balance > goal` occurs in the middle of the loop. Of course, you could have achieved the same effect without a break. You would need an `if/else` inside the loop and another termination condition in the loop test.

Unlike C/C++, Java also offers a *labeled break* statement that lets you break out of multiple nested loops. The reason for this is simple: occasionally something weird happens inside a deeply nested loop. In that case, you may want to break completely out of all the nested loops. It is inconvenient to program that simply by adding extra conditions to the various loop tests.

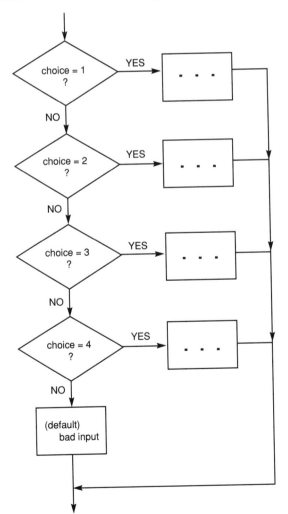

Figure 3–7: Flowchart for `switch` statement

Here's an example that shows this at work. Notice that the label must precede the outermost loop out of which you want to break. It also must be followed by a colon (:).

```
int n;
read_data:
while (. . .)
{   . . .
    for (. . .)
    {   n = Console.readInt(. . .);
        if (n < 0) // should never happen—can't go on
            break read_data;
        // break out of read_data loop
        . . .
    }
}
// check for success or failure here
if (n < 0)
{   // deal with bad situation
}
else
{   // got here normally
}
```

If there was a bad input, the labeled break moves past the end of the labeled block. As with any use of the break statement, you then need to test if the loop exited normally or as a result of a break.

Class Methods (User-Defined Functions)

Like any programming language, Java lets a programmer break down complex tasks into simpler units (traditionally called *functions*). Of course, modern programming languages take great pride in introducing a new terminology for these units. As mentioned previously, in Java the name for such a unit is *method* instead of function. (Well, most of the time; the designers and documenters are somewhat inconsistent. They occasionally slip and use the C/C++ function terminology.) We will follow in the footsteps of the designers of Java and use the term *method* with an occasional slip when it seems appropriate. (In the next chapter, we will survey the ideas behind object-oriented programming that led to the multitude of possible terminologies.)

A method definition must occur inside a class. It can occur anywhere inside the class, although custom places all the other methods of a class before the main method. There are many types of methods possible in Java, but in this chapter we will use only those that, like main, are public static. For now, don't worry about what this means—it has to do with which other methods can use a method—we will explain the terminology in the next chapter.

C++ NOTE: Java does not have "global" functions. All functions must be defined inside a class. The functions we study in this chapter don't yet operate on objects and are, therefore, defined as `static`. Except for visibility issues, there is no difference between a C function and a static Java method.

For example, suppose we want to write a program that computes the odds on winning any lottery that requires bettors to choose a certain number of numbers from the range 1 to n. For example, if you must match six numbers from the numbers 1 to 50, then there are $(50 \cdot 49 \cdot 48 \cdot 47 \cdot 46 \cdot 45)/(1 \cdot 2 \cdot 3 \cdot 4 \cdot 5 \cdot 6)$ possible outcomes, so your chance is 1 in 15,890,700. Good luck!

Just in case someone asks you to participate in a "pick 7 out of 38" lottery, you will want a method that computes the odds. Later, we'll put it together with a `main` method that asks you for how many numbers you need to choose and then asks for the highest number from which to draw.

Here's the method:

```
public static long lotteryOdds(int high, int number)
{   long r = 1;
    int i;
    for (i = 1; i <= number; i++)
    {   r = r * high / i;
        high--;
    }
    return r;
}
```

Notice the header for the `lotteryOdds` method:

```
public static long lotteryOdds(int high, int number)
```

The header for a method starts with keywords—in our case, `public static`—that explain the scope of the method. In general, `public` methods can be called from other classes. (An example of this is our use of the `println` method, which is a `public` method in a Java class called `PrintStream`.)

Next, the method header lists the type of the returned value. In our case, a `long`. Methods in Java can return values of any Java type. In particular, they can be arrays (see the next section) or classes (see the next chapter). Next comes the name of the method, and finally the types and names of its arguments. The rules for the names of methods are the same as those for classes and variables. Note that in Java, methods need not take any arguments. In the case of methods that take zero arguments, you still need to use the parentheses when calling the method. For example, the `getCurrencyInstance` method takes no arguments but the method call still contains parentheses:

```
NumberFormat.getCurrencyInstance()
```

After the header of the method comes the code that implements the method. Notice the brace structure in the example above: the outermost braces (that start after the method header) mark off what is traditionally called the *body of the method*. Variables declared inside a method (like the `int i` for the loop counter in our `lotteryOdds`) are *local* to the method. They can neither be accessed nor contaminate any similarly named variables in the other methods of the class. More precisely, when a method is executed, its local variables are initialized as indicated in the body of the method. Within a method the scope of a local variable is determined by the block in which it is declared. (Note that you *must* initialize them: local variables in a method are not given default values.) When the method exits, the memory allocated for local variables will automatically be reclaimed.

When Java processes a `return` statement, it immediately exits from the method. The expression following the `return` keyword is the method's return value. If you don't need the return value, make the header indicate that by using `void` as the return type.

VB

VB NOTE: Java methods are analogous to the functions that you define in class modules. Of course, since VB5 you have had the choice in VB of throwing away the return value of a function instead of using a procedure. Still, Sub procedures are probably the closest analogy to Java methods that return void.

Example 3–7 is an application whose code is distributed over two methods. Notice how we call the `lotteryOdds` method from the `main` method via the line:

```
long oddsAre = lotteryOdds(topNumber, numbers);
```

We do not have to specify a class name since both the `main` method and the `lotteryOdds` method belong to the `LotteryOdds` class. You can always call another method of the same class by simply giving the method name followed by the parameters needed. This should be contrasted with the method call in the statement:

```
NumberFormat.getCurrencyInstance();
```

The `getCurrencyInstance` method is defined in the `NumberFormat` class, and therefore the class name must be specified.

The `main`, `lotteryOdds`, and `getCurrencyInstance` methods do not operate on objects. However, other methods, such as the `println` method, require an object:

```
System.out.println("Hello"); // operates on the System.out object
```

You will learn more about these *instance methods* in the next chapter.

Next, when the statement `lotteryOdds(topNumber, numbers)` is processed, the current values of the `topNumber` and `numbers` variables are passed to the `lotteryOdds` method. In this example, the argument `high` is initialized with the current value of topNumber and the argument number is initialized with the current value of numbers. Also note that argument variables truly are variables; for example, the lotteryOdds method modifies the contents of high inside of itself. But again, this only changes the high variable inside the method and has no effect on the topNumber variable that was defined in the main method and then used as a parameter to this method call.

It is important that you keep in mind that *all arguments to methods in Java are passed by value and not by reference.* It is, therefore, *impossible* to change variables by means of method calls. (See Chapter 4 for more on this important point.) Argument variables (such as high and number in the lotteryOdds method) are simply local variables that are initialized with the values passed to them as arguments when the method is called. They are tossed away when the method terminates.

NOTE: On the other hand, if you are familiar with the notion of a pointer or a reference, since arrays and objects in Java are actually references (pointers), methods can modify the *contents* of arrays or the state of an object. They just can't modify the actual parameters.

Example 3–7: LotteryOdds.java

```java
import corejava.*;

public class LotteryOdds
{   public static long lotteryOdds(int high, int number)
    {   long r = 1;
        int i;
        for (i = 1; i <= number; i++)
        {   r = r * high / i;
            high--;
        }
        return r;
    }

    public static void main(String[] args)
    {   int numbers = Console.readInt
            ("How many numbers do you need to draw?");
        int topNumber = Console.readInt
            ("What is the highest number you can draw?");
        long oddsAre = lotteryOdds(topNumber, numbers);

        System.out.println
            ("Your odds are 1 in " + oddsAre + ". Good luck!");
    }
}
```

C++ NOTE: Methods in Java are similar but not identical to functions in C++. For example, there is no analog to function prototypes in Java. They are not required because functions can be defined after they are used—the compiler makes multiple passes through the code. More significantly, pointer and reference arguments do not exist in Java: you cannot pass the location of a variable. Overloading function names is always possible, just like in C++.

Class Variables

Occasionally, you need to declare a variable that will be accessible by all the methods in the class. (It is possible but not recommended to declare a variable that can be seen outside its class—i.e., a true global variable.) Usually these are called *class variables* because the scope of such a variable is potentially the whole class. The syntax is similar to the *class constants* that you saw earlier. Class variables are simply declared outside any method, as in the following example:

```
public class Employee
{   private static double socialSecurityRate = 7.62;
    public static void main(String[] args)
    {  . . .}
}
```

In this case, the variable `socialSecurityRate` is a class variable that we initialized to a value of `7.62`. Note that class variables, unlike local variables, are given default values automatically. (Objects are initialized to `null`, boolean variables to `false`, and numeric variables to `0`.)

CAUTION: Class variables can be shadowed by variables of the same name declared inside a method of the class (although this is a rather strange way to program).

Finally, although it completely defeats the premises behind object-oriented programming, by replacing the keyword `private` with the keyword `public`, one can have true global variables accessible by all methods in an application.

C++ NOTE: Except for visibility issues, there is no difference between a global variable in C/C++ and a static variable in Java.

Recursion

Recursion is a general method of solving problems by reducing them to simpler problems of a similar type. The general framework for a recursive solution to a problem looks like this:

```
solve recursively(Problem p)
{  if (the problem is trivial) return the obvious answer;
```

```
// Simplify the problem
p1 = simpler problem(p)
s1 = solve recursively(p1)
// Turn solution of simpler problem into
// solution of original problem
s = solution of original problem(s1)
return s;
}
```

A recursive method repeatedly calls itself, each time in a simpler situation, until it gets to the trivial case, at which point it stops. For the experienced programmer, thinking recursively presents a unique perspective on certain problems, often leading to particularly elegant solutions and, therefore, equally elegant programs. (For example, most of the very fast sorts, such as QuickSort, are recursive.)

There are actually two types of recursion possible. The first is where the subprogram calls only itself. This is called *direct recursion.* The second type is called, naturally enough, *indirect recursion.* This occurs, for example, when a method calls another method that, in turn, calls the first one. Both types of recursion are possible with Java methods and (unlike Pascal, say) no special incantations are needed for the indirect situation.

Let's look at a recursive way to compute the lottery odds. If you draw 1 number out of 50, your chances are plainly 1 in 50. In general, we can write

```
public static long lotteryOdds(int high, int number)
{   if (number == 1) return high;
    . . .
}
```

That wasn't too bad. Now let's look at the number of possible ways of drawing 6 numbers out of 50. Let's just grab one number. There are 50 chances. That leaves us with 5 numbers out of 49. Aha! A simpler problem. There are lotteryOdds(49, 5) ways to pick those five numbers. That gives a total of 50 * lotteryOdds(49, 5) possibilities to pick the six numbers. Actually, we have to fudge a little and divide that result by six because our process counts each combination six times, depending on which number we choose first.

Replacing the 50 and 6 with the general parameters high and number, we get the recursive solution

```
public static long lotteryOdds(int high, int number)
{   if (number <= 0) return 0; // just in case
    else if (number == 1) return high;
    else return high
        * lotteryOdds(high - 1, number - 1) / number;
}
```

Note that the number argument gets decremented in each recursive call and, therefore, must eventually reach 1 and end. This is vital when writing a recursive method: you must be sure the recursion ends!

> NOTE: In this case, the recursive solution is actually somewhat less efficient than the loop that we used previously, but it clearly shows the syntax (or rather the absence of any special syntax) of the recursive call. This is actually a general principle: recursive solutions have more overhead and are usually slower than an iterative solution. To quote Niklaus Wirth (the inventor of Pascal) from his *Algorithms + Data Structures = Programs* (Englewood Cliffs, NJ: Prentice Hall, 1976), "...the lesson to be drawn is to avoid the use of recursion when there is an *obvious* solution by iteration" (italics in original).

Arrays

In Java, arrays are first-class objects. You are better off not thinking about how arrays are implemented in Java—accept them as objects that exist in and of themselves. For example, you can assign one array of integers to another, just as you can assign one integer variable to another. If you assign one array to another, then both refer to the same set of values. Any change to one will affect the other.

Once you create an array, you cannot change its size easily (although you can, of course, easily change an individual array element). If you need to expand the size of an array while a program is running, you will generally need to use a different Java object called a *vector*. (See Chapter 5 for more on vectors and expanding arrays.)

You have already seen some examples of Java arrays. The `String[] args` argument in the `main` method indicates that the `main` method receives an array of strings, namely, the arguments specified on the command line.

Arrays are the first example of objects whose creation the programmer must explicitly handle. This is most commonly done through the `new` operator. For example:

```
int[] arrayOfInt = new int[100];
```

sets up an array that can hold 100 integers. The array entries are *numbered from 0 to 99* (and not 1 to 100). Once the array is created, you can fill the entries in an array, for example, by using a loop:

```
int[] arrayOfInt = new int[100];
for (int i = 0; i < 100; i++)
    arrayOfInt[i] = i;   // fills the array with 0 to 99
```

If you try to access, say, the 101st element of an array declared as having 100 elements, your source code will compile without an error or warning, and you will be able to run your program. However, your program will stop when it attempts to access any array element that goes outside the declared bounds of the array.

Java has a shorthand to create an array object and supply inital values at the same time. Here's an example of the syntax at work:

```
int[] smallPrimes = { 2, 3, 5, 7, 11, 13 };
```

Notice that you do not use a call to new when you use this syntax.

You can even initialize an *anonymous array:*

```
new int[] { 2, 3, 5, 7, 11, 13 }
```

This expression allocates a new array and fills it with the values inside the braces. It counts the number of initial values and sets the array size accordingly. You use this syntax if you want to pass an array to a method and you don't want to create a local variable for it. For example,

```
printLabels(new String[] { "Region", "Sales" });
```

is a shorthand for

```
String[] titles = { "Region", "Sales" };
printLabels(titles);
```

To find the number of elements of an array, use *arrayName*.length. For example,

```
for (int i = 0; i < smallPrimes.length; i++)
    System.out.println(smallPrimes[i]);
```

Copying Arrays

You can copy one array variable into another, but then *both variables refer to the same array:*

```
int[] luckyNumbers = smallPrimes;
luckyNumbers[5] = 12; // now smallPrimes[5] is also 12
```

Figure 3–8 shows the result. If you actually want to copy all values of one array into another, you have to use the arraycopy method in its System class. The syntax for this is

```
System.arraycopy(from, fromIndex, to, toIndex, count);
```

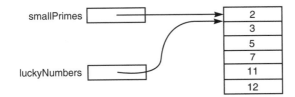

Figure 3–8: Copying an array variable

For example, the following program, whose result is illustrated in Figure 3–9, sets up two arrays and then copies the last four entries of the first array to the second array. The copy starts at position 2 in the source array and copies 4 entries, starting at position 3 of the target.

```
public class ArrayExample
{   public static void main(String args[])
    {   int[] smallPrimes = {2, 3, 5, 7, 11, 13};
        int[] luckyNumbers =
            {1001, 1002, 1003, 1004, 1005, 1006, 1007};
        System.arraycopy(smallPrimes, 2, luckyNumbers, 3, 4);
        for (int i = 0; i < luckyNumbers.length; i++)
        {   System.out.println(i +
            " entry after copy is " + luckyNumbers[i]);
        }
    }
}
```

The output of this program is

```
0 entry after copy is 1001
1 entry after copy is 1002
2 entry after copy is 1003
3 entry after copy is 5
4 entry after copy is 7
5 entry after copy is 11
6 entry after copy is 13
```

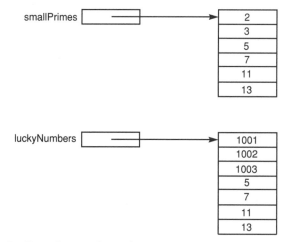

Figure 3–9: Copying values between arrays

C++ NOTE: You can define an array variable either as `int[] arrayOfInt` or as `int arrayOfInt[]`. Most Java programmers prefer the former style because it neatly separates the type `int[]` (integer array) from the variable name.

A Java array is quite different from a C/C++ array on the stack. It is, however, essentially the same as a pointer to an array allocated on the *heap*. The `[]` operator is predefined to perform *bounds checking*. There is no pointer arithmetic—you can't increment `arrayOfInt` to point to the second element in the array.

You can tell that arrays are pointers because their contents can be modified when you pass an array to a method and because arrays can be assigned.

VB NOTE: There is no way to use index ranges in a Java array.

Arrays as Arguments

Arrays can be used as arguments of a user-defined method exactly as any other type. However, since arrays in Java are actually hidden references, the method can change the elements in the array. Example 3–8 is a Shell sort that sorts whatever integer array is passed to it.

Example 3–8: ShellSort.java

```java
public class ShellSort
{  public static void sort(int[] a)
   {  int n = a.length;
      int incr = n / 2;
      while (incr >= 1)
      {  for (int i = incr; i < n; i++)
         {  int temp = a[i];
            int j = i;
            while (j >= incr && temp < a[j - incr])
            {  a[j] = a[j - incr];
               j -= incr;
            }
            a[j] = temp;
         }
         incr /= 2;
      }
   }

   public static void print(int[] a)
   {  for (int i = 0; i < a.length; i++)
         System.out.print(a[i] + " ");
      System.out.println();
   }
```

```
public static void main(String[] args)
{   // make an array of ten integers
    int[] a = new int[10];
    int i;
    // fill the array with random values
    for (i = 0; i < a.length; i++)
        a[i] = (int)(Math.random() * 100);
    print(a);
    sort(a);
    print(a);
}
}
```

Actually, ShellSort is not the best sorting algorithm for large arrays (although it works quite well for small arrays). We used it here only because it is easy to program. If you really want to sort an array of numbers, you should use one of the sort methods in the Arrays class:

```
int[] a = new int[10000];
. . .
Arrays.sort(a)
```

This method uses a tuned version of the QuickSort algorithm that is claimed to be very efficient on most data sets. The Arrays class provides several other convenience methods for arrays that are included in the API notes at the end of this section.

Arrays as Return Values

The return type of a method can also be an array. This is really useful when a method computes a sequence of values. For example, let's write a method that draws a sequence of numbers in a simulated lottery and then returns the sequence. The header of the method is

```
public static int[] drawing(int high, int number)
```

In Example 3–9, the method makes two arrays, one that holds the numbers 1, 2, 3, ..., high from which the lucky combination is drawn, and one to hold the numbers that are drawn. The first array is abandoned when the method exits and will eventually be garbage collected. The method returns the second array as its result.

Example 3–9: LotteryDrawing.java

```
import java.util.*;
import corejava.*;

public class LotteryDrawing
{   public static int[] drawing(int high, int number)
```

```
{   int i;
    int numbers[] = new int[high];
    int result[] = new int[number];
    // fill an array with numbers 1 2 3 . . . high
    for (i = 0; i < high; i++) numbers[i] = i + 1;
    for (i = 0; i < number; i++)
    {   int j = (int)(Math.random() * (high - i));
        result[i] = numbers[j];
        numbers[j] = numbers[high - 1 - i];
    }
    return result;
}

public static void main(String[] args)
{   int numbers = Console.readInt
        ("How many numbers do you need to draw?");
    int topNumber = Console.readInt
        ("What is the highest number you can draw?");

    int[] a = drawing(topNumber, numbers);
    Arrays.sort(a);
    System.out.println("Bet the following combination."
        + "It'll make you rich!");
    int i;
    for (i = 0; i < a.length; i++)
        System.out.println(a[i]);
}
}
```

`java.lang.System`

- `static void arraycopy(Object from, int fromIndex, Object to, int toIndex, int count)`

Parameters:	from	an array of any type (Chapter 5 explains why this is a parameter of type `Object`)
	fromIndex	the starting index from which to copy elements
	to	an array of the same type as `from`
	toIndex	the starting index to which to copy elements
	count	the number of elements to copy

  copies elements from the first array to the second array.

java.util.Arrays

- `static void sort(Xxx[] a)`

  Parameters: a   an array of type `int`, `long`, `short`, `char`, `byte`, `boolean`, `float` or `double`

  sorts the array, using a tuned QuickSort algorithm.

- `static int binarySearch(Xxx[] a, Xxx v)`

  Parameters: a   a *sorted* array of type `int`, `long`, `short`, `char`, `byte`, `boolean`, `float` or `double`

                 v   a value of the same type as the elements of a

  uses the BinarySearch algorithm to search for the value v. If it is found, its index is returned. Otherwise, a negative value r is returned; $-r + 1$ is the spot at which v should be inserted to keep a sorted.

- `static void fill(Xxx[] a, Xxx v)`

  Parameters: a   an array of type `int`, `long`, `short`, `char`, `byte`, `boolean`, `float` or `double`

                 v   a value of the same type as the elements of a

  sets all elements of the array to v.

- `static boolean equals(Xxx[] a, Object other)`

  Parameters: a   an array of type `int`, `long`, `short`, `char`, `byte`, `boolean`, `float` or `double`

              other   an object

  returns `true` if `other` is an array of the same type, if it has the same length, and if the elements in corresponding indexes match.

Multidimensional Arrays

Suppose you want to make a table of numbers that shows how much an investment of $10,000 will grow after a number of years under different interest rate scenarios in which interest is paid monthly and reinvested. Table 3–7 illustrates this scenario.

Table 3–7: Interest rates for different investment time periods

| Years | Interest Rate | | | | | |
	5.00%	5.50%	6.00%	6.50%	7.00%	7.50%
10	16470.09	17310.76	18193.97	19121.84	20096.61	21120.65
20	27126.40	29966.26	33102.04	36564.47	40387.39	44608.17
30	44677.44	51873.88	60225.75	69917.98	81164.97	94215.34
40	73584.17	89797.65	109574.54	133696.02	163114.11	198988.89
50	121193.83	155446.59	199359.55	255651.37	327804.14	420277.39

The obvious way to store this information is in a two-dimensional array (or matrix), which we will call `balance`.

Declaring a matrix in Java is simple enough. For example:

```
double[][] balance;
```

As always in Java, you cannot use an object (an array, in this case) until you initialize it with a call to `new`. In this case, you can do the initialization as follows:

```
balance = new double[5][6];
```

Once the array is initialized, you can access individual elements:

```
balance[i][j] = futureValue(10000, 10 + 10 * i, 5 + 0.5 * j);
```

Example 3–10 shows the full program that computes the table.

Example 3–10: CompoundInterest.java

```
import corejava.*;

public class CompoundInterest
{  public static double futureValue(double initialBalance,
      double nyear, double p)
   {  return initialBalance * Math.pow(1 + p / 12 / 100,
      12 * nyear);
   }

   public static void main(String[] args)
   {  double[][] balance;
      balance = new double[5][6];
      int i;
      int j;
      for (i = 0; i < 5; i++)
         for (j = 0; j < 6; j++)
            balance[i][j] = futureValue(10000, 10 + 10 * i,
               5 + 0.5 * j);
      System.out.print("    ");
      for (j = 0; j < 6; j++)
```

```
        Format.printf("%9.2f%", 5 + 0.5 * j);
      System.out.println("");
      for (i = 0; i < 5; i++)
      {  Format.printf("%3d", 10 + 10 * i);
         for (j = 0; j < 6; j++)
            Format.printf("%10.2f", balance[i][j]);
         System.out.println("");
      }
   }
}
```

So far, what you have seen is not too different from other programming languages. But there is actually something subtle going on behind the scenes that you can sometimes turn to your advantage: Java has *no* multidimensional arrays at all, only one-dimensional arrays. Multidimensional arrays are faked as "arrays of arrays."

For example, the `balance` array in the preceding example is actually an array that contains five elements, each of which is an array of six floating-point numbers (see Figure 3–10).

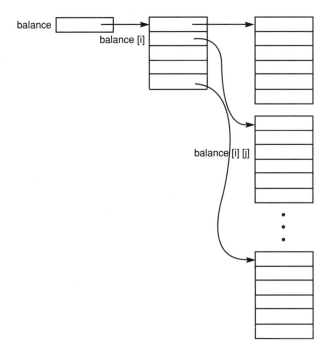

Figure 3–10: A two-dimensional array

The expression `balance[i]` refers to the i'th subarray, that is, the i'th row of the table. It is, itself, an array, and `balance[i][j]` refers to the j'th entry of that array.

Because rows of arrays are individually accessible, you can actually swap them!

```
double[] temp = balance[i];
balance[i] = balance[i + 1];
balance[i + 1] = temp;
```

Another consequence of multidimensional arrays being "arrays of arrays" is that you can use the shorthand notion for initializing multidimensional arrays without needing a call to new. For example;

```
int[][] lastTwoYearSales = { {1997, 1998}, {100000, 200000} };
```

It is also easy to make "ragged" arrays, that is, arrays in which different rows have different lengths. Here is the standard example. Let us make an array in which the entry at row i and column j equals the number of possible outcomes of a "choose j numbers from i numbers" lottery.

```
1
1    1
1    2    1
1    3    3    1
1    4    6    4    1
1    5    10   10   5    1
1    6    15   20   15   6    1
```

Because j can never be larger than i, the matrix is triangular. The i'th row has i + 1 elements. (We allow choosing 0 elements; there is one way to make such a choice.) To build this ragged array, first allocate the array holding the rows.

```
int[][] odds = new int[n + 1][];
```

Next, allocate the rows.

```
for (i = 0; i <= n; i++)
    odds[i] = new int[i + 1];
```

Now that the array is allocated, we can access the elements in the normal way, provided we do not overstep the bounds.

```
for (i = 0; i < odds.length; i++)
    for (j = 0; j < odds[i].length; j++)
        odds[i][j] = lotteryOdds(i, j);
```

Example 3–11 gives the complete program.

C++ NOTE: Recall that a one-dimensional array in Java really corresponds to a C++ pointer to a heap array. That is,

```
int[] numbers = new int[50]; // Java
```
is not the same as
```
int numbers[50]; // C++
```
but rather
```
int* numbers = new int[50]; // C++
```
Similarly,
```
double[][] balance = new double[5][6]; // Java
```
is not the same as
```
double balance[5][6]; // C++
```
or even
```
double (*balance)[6] = new double[5][6]; // C++
```
Instead, an array of five pointers is allocated:
```
double** balance = new double*[5];
```
Then, each element in the pointer array is filled with an array of 6 numbers:
```
for (i = 0; i < 5; i++) balance[i] = new double[6];
```
Mercifully, this loop is automatic when you ask for a new `double[5][6]`. When you want ragged arrays, you allocate the row arrays separately.

Example 3–11: LotteryArray.java

```java
import corejava.*;

public class LotteryArray
{   public static long lotteryOdds(int high, int number)
    {   long r = 1;
        int i;
        for (i = 1; i <= number; i++)
        {   r = r * high / i;
            high--;
        }
        return r;
    }

    public static void main(String[] args)
    {   int i;
        int j;

        final int MAX_HIGH = 10;

        // allocate triangular array
        long[][] odds = new long[MAX_HIGH + 1][];
        for (i = 0; i <= MAX_HIGH; i++)
            odds[i] = new long[i + 1];

        // fill triangular array
```

```
    for (i = 0; i < odds.length; i++)
        for (j = 0; j < odds[i].length; j++)
            odds[i][j] = lotteryOdds(i, j);

    // print triangular array
    for (i = 0; i < odds.length; i++)
    {   for (j = 0; j < odds[i].length; j++)
            Format.printf("%4d", odds[i][j]);
        System.out.println();
    }
  }
}
```

Chapter **4**

Objects
and Classes

▼ INTRODUCTION TO OBJECT-ORIENTED PROGRAMMING

▼ USING EXISTING CLASSES

▼ STARTING TO BUILD YOUR OWN CLASSES

▼ PACKAGES

▼ CLASS DESIGN HINTS

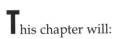

This chapter will:

- Introduce you to Object-Oriented Programming (OOP)

- Show you how Java implements OOP by going further into its notion of a *class* and how you can use existing classes supplied by Java or by third parties

- Show you how to write your own *reusable* classes that can perform non-trivial tasks

If you are coming from an object-based language like early versions of VB or a procedure-oriented language like BASIC, COBOL, or C, you will want to read this chapter carefully. You may also need to spend a fair amount of time on the introductory sections. OOP requires a different way of thinking than for procedure-oriented languages (or even object-based languages like older versions of VB). The transition is not always easy, but you do need some familiarity with OOP to go further with Java. (We are, however, assuming you are comfortable with a procedural-oriented language or VB.)

For experienced C++ programmers, this chapter, like the previous chapter, will present familiar information; however, there are enough differences between how OOP is implemented in Java and how it is done in C++ to warrant your reading the later sections of this chapter (concentrating on the C++ notes).

Because you need to understand a fair amount of terminology in order to make sense of OOP, we'll start with some concepts and definitions. Then, we'll show you the basics of how Java implements OOP. We should note, however, that it is possible to write endlessly about the ideas behind OOP. A quick survey of *Books in Print* shows that there are more than 150 books with "Object Oriented Programming" in the title, and more seem to appear each week. (We do make references to the literature, if you need more information on the ideas behind OOP and object-oriented design.)

Introduction to Object-Oriented Programming

OOP is the dominant programming paradigm these days, having replaced the "structured," procedure-based programming techniques that were developed in the early '70s. Java is totally object oriented, and it is impossible to program it in the procedural style that you may be most comfortable with. We hope this section—especially when combined with the example code supplied in the text and on the CD—will give you enough information about OOP to become productive with Java.

Let's begin with a question that, on the surface, seems to have nothing to do with programming: How did companies like Compaq, Dell, Gateway, Micron Technologies, and the other major personal computer manufacturers get so big, so fast? Most people would probably say they made generally good computers and sold them at rock-bottom prices in an era when computer demand was skyrocketing. But go further—how were they able to manufacture so many models so fast and respond to the changes that were happening so quickly?

Well, a big part of the answer is that these companies farmed out a lot of the work. They bought components from reputable vendors and then assembled them. They often didn't invest time and money in designing and building power supplies, disk drives, motherboards, and other components. This made it possible for the companies to produce a product and make changes quickly for less money than if they had done the engineering themselves.

What the personal computer manufacturers were buying was "prepackaged functionality." For example, when they bought a power supply, they were buying something with certain properties (size, shape, and so on) and a certain functionality (smooth power output, amount of power available, and so on). Compaq provides a good example of how effective this operating procedure is. When Compaq moved from engineering all of the parts in their machines to buying many of the parts, they dramatically improved their bottom line.

OOP springs from the same idea. Your program is made of objects, with certain properties and operations that the objects can perform. The current state may change over time, but you always depend on objects not interacting with each other in undocumented ways. Whether you build an object or buy it might depend on your budget or on time. But, basically, as long as objects satisfy your specifications, you don't care how the functionality was implemented. In OOP, you only care about what the objects *expose*. So, just as clone manufacturers don't care about the internals of a power supply as long as it does what they want, most Java programmers don't care how the audio clip component in Figure 4–1 is implemented as long as it does what *they* want.

Figure 4–1: An audio clip object

Traditional structured programming consists of designing a set of functions to solve a problem. (These functions are usually called *algorithms*.) The traditional next step is to find appropriate ways to store the data. This is why the designer of the original Pascal, Niklaus Wirth, called his famous book on programming *Algorithms + Data Structures = Programs* (Prentice Hall, 1975). Notice that in Wirth's title, algorithms come first, and data structures come second. This mimics the way programmers worked at that time. First, you decided how to manipulate the data; then, you decided what structure to impose on the data in order to make the manipulations easier. OOP reverses the order and puts data structures first, then looks at the algorithms that operate on the data.

The key to being most productive in OOP is to make each object responsible for carrying out a set of related tasks. If an object relies on a task that isn't its responsibility, it needs to have access to an object whose responsibilities include that task. The first object then asks the second object to carry out the task. This is done with a more generalized version of the function call that you are familiar with in procedural programming. (Recall that in Java these function calls are usually called *method calls*.) In OOP jargon, you *have clients send messages to server objects*.

In particular, an object should never directly manipulate the internal data of another object. All communication should be via messages, that is, method calls. By designing your objects to handle all appropriate messages and manipulate their data internally, you maximize reusability, reduce data dependency and minimize debugging time.

Of course, just as with modules in a procedure-oriented language, you will not want an individual object to do *too* much. Both design and debugging are simplified when you build small objects that perform a few tasks, rather than humongous objects with internal data that are extremely complex, with hundreds of functions to manipulate the data.

The Vocabulary of OOP

You need to understand some of the terminology of OOP to go further. The most important term is `class`, which you have already seen in the code in Chapter 3. A class is usually described as the template or blueprint from which the object is actually made. This leads to the standard way of thinking about classes: as cookie cutters. Objects are the cookies themselves. The "dough," in the form of memory, will need to be allocated as well. Java is pretty good about hiding this "dough preparation" step from you. You simply use the new keyword to obtain memory, and the built-in garbage collector will eat the cookies when nobody uses them any more. (Oh well, no analogy is perfect.) When you create an object from a class, you are said to have *created an instance* of the class. When you have a statement like

```
AudioClip meow = new AudioClip();
```

you are using the new operator to create a *new instance* of the `AudioClip` class as shown in Figure 4–2. (Actually, it turns out that you must work harder in Java to create real audio clips. We just want to show the syntax here.)

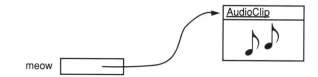

Figure 4–2: Creating a new object

As you have seen, everything you write in Java is inside a class. The standard Java library supplies several thousand classes for such diverse purposes as user interface design and network programming. Nonetheless, you still have to create your own classes in Java, to describe the objects of the problem domains of your applications and to adapt the classes that are supplied by the standard library to your own purposes.

When you do start writing your own classes in Java, another tenet of OOP makes this easier: classes can be (and in Java always are) built on other classes. We say that a class that builds on another class *extends* it. Java, in fact, comes with a "cosmic base class," that is, a class from which all other classes are built. In Java, all classes extend this cosmic base class called, naturally enough, `Object`. You will see more about the `Object` base class in the next chapter.

When you extend a base class, the new class initially has all the properties and methods of its parent. You can choose whether you want to modify or simply keep any method of the parent, and you can also supply new methods that apply to the child class only. The general concept of extending a base class is called *inheritance*. (See the next chapter for more on inheritance.)

Encapsulation (sometimes called data hiding) is another key concept in working with objects. Formally, encapsulation is nothing more than combining data and behavior in one package and hiding the implementation of the data from the user of the object. The data in an object are usually called its *instance variables* or *fields,* and the functions and procedures in a Java class are called its *methods* (see Figure 4–3). A specific object that is an instance of a class will have specific values for its fields that define its current *state.*

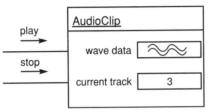

Figure 4–3: Encapsulation of data in an object

It cannot be stressed enough that the key to making encapsulation work is to have programs that *never* directly access instance variables (fields) in a class. Programs should interact with this data *only* through the object's methods. Encapsulation is the way to give the object its "black box" behavior, which is the key to reuse and reliability. This means an object may totally change how it stores its data but, as long as it continues to use the same methods to manipulate the data, no other object will know or care.

Objects

To work with OOP, you should be able to identify three key characteristics of objects. (For those who can remember back to high school, think of them as analogous to the "Who, What, and Where" that teachers told you characterize an event.) The three key questions are:

- What is the object's behavior?
- What is the object's state?
- What is the object's identity?

All objects that are instances of the same class share a family resemblance by supporting similar *behavior.* The behavior of an object is defined by the messages it accepts.

Next, each object stores information about what it currently looks like and how it got to be the way it currently is. This is what is usually called the object's *state.* An object's state may change over time, but not spontaneously. A change in the state of an object must be a consequence of messages sent to the object (otherwise you break encapsulation).

However, the state of an object does not completely describe it, since each object has a distinct *identity.* For example, in an order-processing system, two orders are distinct even if they request identical items. Notice that the individual objects that are instances of a class *always* differ in their identity and *usually* differ in their state.

These key characteristics can influence each other. For example, the state of an object can influence its behavior. (If an order is "shipped" or "paid," it may reject a message that asks it to add or remove items. Conversely, if an order is "empty," that is, no items have yet been ordered, it should not allow itself to be shipped.)

In a traditional procedure-oriented program, you start the process at the top, with the `main` function. When designing an object-oriented system, there is no "top," and newcomers to OOP often wonder where to begin. The answer is: You first find classes and then you add methods to each class.

TIP: A simple rule of thumb in identifying classes is to look for nouns in the problem analysis. Methods, on the other hand, correspond to verbs.

For example, in an order-processing system, some of these nouns are:
- item
- order
- shipping address
- payment
- account

These nouns may lead to the classes `Item`, `Order`, and so on.

Next, one looks for verbs. Items are *added* to orders. Orders are *shipped* or *canceled.* Payments are *applied* to orders. With each verb, such as "add," "ship," "cancel," and "apply," you have to identify the one object that has the major responsibility for carrying it out. For example, when a new item is added to an order, the order object should be the one in charge since it knows how it stores and sorts items. That is, `add` should be a method of the `Order` class that takes an `Item` object as a parameter.

Of course, the "noun and verb" rule is only a rule of thumb, and only experience can help you decide which nouns and verbs are the important ones when building your classes.

Relationships between Classes

The most common relationships between classes are:
- *use*
- *containment* ("has–a")
- *inheritance* ("is–a")

The *use* relationship is the most obvious and also the most general. For example, the `Order` class uses the `Account` class, since `Order` objects need to access `account` objects to check for credit status. But the `Item` class does not use the `Account` class, since `Item` objects never need to worry about customer accounts. Thus, a class uses another class if it manipulates objects of that class.

In general, a class `A` uses a class `B` if:

- a method of `A` sends a message to an object of class `B`, or
- a method of `A` creates, receives, or returns objects of class `B`.

TIP: Try to minimize the number of classes that use each other. The point is, if a class A is unaware of the existence of a class B, it is also unconcerned about any changes to B! (And this means that changes to B do not introduce bugs into A.)

The *containment* relationship is easy to understand because it is concrete; for example, an `Order` object contains `Item` objects. Containment means that objects of class `A` contain objects of class `B`. Of course, containment is a special case of use; if an `A` object contains a `B` object, then at least one method of the class `A` will make use of that object of class `B`.

The *inheritance* relationship denotes specialization. For example, a `RushOrder` class inherits from an `Order` class, as shown in Figure 4–4. The specialized `RushOrder` class has special methods for priority handling and a different method for computing shipping charges, but its other methods, such as adding items and billing, are inherited from the `Order` class. In general, if class `A` extends class `B`, class `A` inherits methods from class `B` but has more capabilities. (Inheritance will be more fully described in the next chapter, in which we discuss this important notion at some length.)

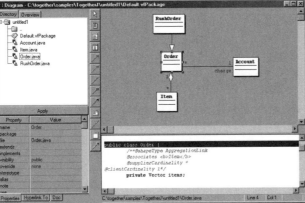

Figure 4–4: A class diagram

NOTE: These three essential relationships between classes form the foundation of object-oriented design. *Class diagrams* show the classes (usually denoted with boxes or clouds) and their relationships (denoted with lines with various decorations that are maddeningly different from one methodologist to the next). Figure 4–4 shows an example, using the UML (Unified Modeling Language) notation. This diagram was created using the whiteboard edition of Together/J, a Java application to keep design diagrams and Java code synchronized. You can find the program on the book's CD ROM.

Contrasting OOP with Traditional Procedural Programming Techniques

We want to end this short introduction to OOP by contrasting OOP with the procedural model that you may be more familiar with. In procedure-oriented programming, you identify the tasks to be performed and then:

- By a stepwise refinement process, break the task to be performed into sub-tasks, and these into smaller subtasks, until the subtasks are simple enough to be implemented directly (this is the top-down approach).

- Write procedures to solve simple tasks and combine them into more sophisticated procedures, until you have the functionality you want (this is the bottom-up approach).

Most programmers, of course, use a mixture of the top-down and bottom-up strategies to solve a programming problem. The rule of thumb for discovering procedures is the same as the rule for finding methods in OOP: look for verbs, or actions, in the problem description. The important difference is that in OOP, you *first* isolate the classes in the project. Only then do you look for the methods of the class. And there is another important difference between traditional procedures and OOP methods: each method is associated with the class that is responsible for carrying out the operation.

For small problems, the breakdown into procedures works very well. But for larger problems, classes and methods have two advantages. Classes provide a convenient clustering mechanism for methods. A simple Web browser may require 2,000 functions for its implementation, or it may require 100 classes with an average of 20 methods per class. The latter structure is much easier to grasp by the programmer or to handle by teams of programmers. The encapsulation built into classes helps you here as well: classes hide their data representations from all code except their own methods. As Figure 4–5 shows, this means that if a programming bug messes up data, it is easier to search for the culprit among the 20 methods that had access to that data item than among 2,000 procedures.

You may say that this doesn't sound much different than *modularization.* You have certainly written programs by breaking the program up into modules that communicate with each other through procedure calls only, not by sharing data. This (if well done) goes far in accomplishing encapsulation. However, in many programming languages (such as C and VB), the slightest sloppiness in programming allows you to get at the data in another module—encapsulation is easy to defeat.

There is a more serious problem: while classes are factories for multiple objects with the same behavior, you cannot get multiple copies of a useful module. Suppose you have a module encapsulating a collection of orders, together with a spiffy balanced binary tree module to access them quickly. Now it turns out that you actually need

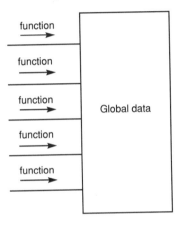

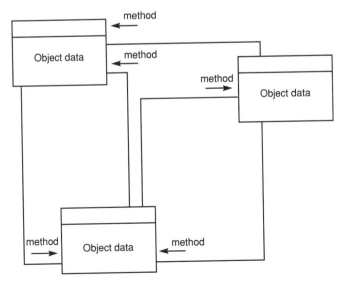

Figure 4–5: Procedural vs. OO programming

two such collections, one for the pending orders and one for the completed orders. You cannot simply link the order tree module twice. And you don't really want to make a copy and rename all procedures in order for the linker to work!

Classes do not have this limitation. Once a class has been defined, it is easy to construct any number of instances of that class type (whereas a module can have only one instance).

We have only scratched a very large surface. The end of this chapter has a short section on "Class Design Hints," but for more information on understanding the OOP design process, here are some book recommendations.

NOTE: The definitive book on object-oriented design with the Booch methodology is

Object-Oriented Analysis and Design, 2nd Edition, by Grady Booch, (Benjamin Cummings, 1994).

There are now many books on UML and you can also check out Rational's Web site for lots of free information about it (http://www.rational.com/uml/index.shtml) You can find a lighter version of the methodology adapted to both C++ and Java in

Practical Object-Oriented Development in C++ and Java, by Cay S. Horstmann, (John Wiley & Sons, 1997).

VB NOTE: If you are used to VB, the best book to read to get a sense of object-oriented design is the latest version of *Doing Objects in Microsoft Visual Basic,* by Deborah Kurota (Ziff-Davis Press). For a briefer treatment try "Core VB" by Gary Cornell and David Jezak.

Using Existing Classes

Since you can't do anything in Java without classes, we have shown you many classes at work. Unfortunately, many of these are quite anomalous in the Java scheme of things. A good example of this is our `Console` class. You have seen that you can use our `Console` class without needing to know how it is implemented—all you need to know is the syntax for its methods. That is the point of encapsulation and will certainly be true of all classes. Unfortunately, the `Console` class *only* encapsulates functionality; it neither needs nor hides data. Since there is no data, you do not need to worry about making objects and initializing their instance fields—there aren't any!

Object Variables

For most classes in Java, you create objects, specify their initial state, and then work with the objects.

To access objects, you define object variables. For example, the statement

```
AudioClip meow; // meow doesn't refer to any object
```

defines an object variable, meow, that can refer to objects of type AudioClip. It is important to realize that the variable meow *is not an object* and, in fact, does not yet even refer to an object. You cannot use any AudioClip methods on this variable at this time. The statement

```
meow.play(); // not yet.
```

would cause a runtime error.

Use the new operator to create an object.

```
meow = new AudioClip();
    // does create an instance of AudioClip
```

Now you can start applying AudioClip methods to meow. (Again, it is a little harder in Java to obtain a real audio clip. Here we just use audio clips to introduce the typical object notation.)

Most of the time, you will need to create multiple instances of a single class.

```
AudioClip chirp = new AudioClip();
```

Now there are two objects of type AudioClip, one attached to the object variable meow and one to the object variable chirp.

If you assign one variable to another variable using the assignment operator,

```
AudioClip wakeUp = meow;
```

then both variables refer to the *same* object. This can lead to surprising behavior in your programs if you are not careful. For example, if you call

```
meow.play();
wakeUp.stop();
```

the audio clip object will play and then stop, since the *same* audio clip is referred to by the wakeUp and meow variables. (See Figure 4–6)

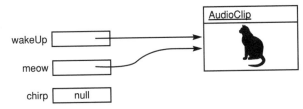

Figure 4–6: Object variables

But suppose you want meow and wakeUp to refer to different objects, so you can change one of them without changing the other. As it turns out, there is no method available to change audio clips, and there isn't a method available to make a copy of one.

> NOTE: Many classes have a method called `clone` that makes a true copy. When you clone an existing object, you get a copy that reflects the current state of the object. The two objects exist independently, so they can diverge over time. We will discuss the `clone` method further in the next chapter.

You can explicitly set an object variable to `null` to indicate that it currently refers to no objects.

```
chirp = null;
. . .
if (chirp != null) chirp.play();
```

If you call a method through a `null` variable then a run-time error occurs.

Local object variables are not automatically initialized to `null`. You must initialize them, either by calling `new` or by setting them to `null`.

> C++ NOTE: Many people mistakenly believe that Java object variables behave like C++ references. But in C++ there are no null references, and references cannot be assigned. You should think of Java object variables as analogous to *object pointers* in C++. For example,
>
> ```
> AudioClip meow; // Java
> ```
>
> is really the same as
>
> ```
> AudioClip* meow; // C++
> ```
>
> Once you make this association, everything falls into place. Of course, an `AudioClip*` pointer isn't initialized until you initialize it with a call to `new`. The syntax is almost the same in C++ and Java.
>
> ```
> AudioClip* meow = new AudioClip(); // C++
> ```
>
> If you copy one variable to another, then both variables refer to the same audio clip—they are pointers to the same object. The equivalent of the Java `null` object is the C++ `NULL` pointer.
>
> All Java objects live on the heap. When an object contains another object variable, that variable still contains just a pointer to yet another heap object.
>
> In C++, pointers make you nervous because they are so error-prone. It is easy to create bad pointers or to mess up memory management. In Java, these problems simply go away. If you use an uninitialized pointer, the run-time system will reliably generate a run-time error, instead of producing random results. You don't worry about memory management because the garbage collector takes care of it.
>
> C++ makes quite an effort, with its support for copy constructors and assignment operators, to allow the implementation of objects that copy themselves automatically. For example, a copy of a linked list is a new linked list with the same contents but with an independent set of links. This makes it possible to design classes with the same copy behavior as the built-in types. In Java, you must use the `clone` method to get a complete copy of an object.

VB NOTE: Object variables in VB are actually quite close to object variables in Java—both have the capacity to point (refer) to objects; you even have an analogous use of new. The difference, of course, is that, in VB you use set rather than the equal sign to make one object variable point to another object and you must reclaim the memory yourself by setting the object variable to Nothing!

The GregorianCalendar *Class of the Java Library*

It is time to go further into the ways of working with Java and third-party classes that are more typical than our Console class. Let's start with a class to represent dates, such as December 31, 1999. There is a class called Date that comes with Java. An instance of the Date class has a state, namely *a particular point in time,* counted in both positive and negative milliseconds from a fixed point, the so-called *epoch,* which is 00:00:00 GMT, January 1, 1970 (perhaps Time would have been a better name for this class). But as it turns out, the Date class is not very useful for manipulating dates. Java takes the point of view that a description of a point in time such as "December 31, 1999, 23:59:59" is an arbitrary convention, governed by a *calendar,* in this case the Gregorian calendar, which is the 365-day (with occasional leap year) calendar used in most places of the world. The same point in time would be described quite differently in the Chinese or Hebrew Lunar calendars, not to mention the calendar used by your customers from Mars.

To manipulate dates in the Gregorian calendar, you can use the GregorianCalendar class in Java. For example,

```
GregorianCalendar todaysDate = new GregorianCalendar();
```

does the following:

1. It creates a new instance of the GregorianCalendar class called todaysDate.

2. At the same time, it initializes the state of the todaysDate object to be the current date (as maintained by the host operating system).

You can also create an instance of the GregorianCalendar class with a specific date:

```
GregorianCalendar preMillenium = new GregorianCalendar(1999, 11, 31);
```

This creates a GregorianCalendar instance called preMillenium, with the initial state of December 31, 1999. Somewhat curiously, the months are counted from 0. Therefore, 11 is December. For greater clarity, there are constants like Calendar.DECEMBER.

Note that the GregorianCalendar class is actually a Date/Time class, so you can also set the time. (If you don't set it, it defaults to midnight at the beginning of the new day.) For example:

```
GregorianCalendar preMillenium
    = new GregorianCalendar(1999, Calendar.DECEMBER, 31,
        23, 59, 59);
```

would give you a GregorianCalendar object whose instance fields are set at one second to midnight on December 31, 1999. (When you use GregorianCalendar(), you get a date instance with the time set at the time maintained in the operating system.)

Now you may be wondering: Why use classes to represent dates rather than (as in some languages) a built-in type? The reason is simple: language developers are reluctant to add too many basic types. For example, suppose Java had a notation like #6/1/1995#, which is used in VB to denote an example of Date type. Since the ordering for year, month, and day is different in different locales, the *language designers* would need to foresee all the issues of internationalization. If they do a poor job, the language becomes an unpleasant muddle, but unhappy programmers are powerless to do anything about it. By making GregorianCalendar into a class, the design task is offloaded to a library designer. If the class is not perfect, other programmers can easily write their own class. (In fact, we will do just this in the next section.)

Unlike our Console class, the GregorianCalendar class must have encapsulated data (instance fields) to maintain the date to which it is set. Without looking at the source code, *it is impossible to know the representation used internally by these classes*. But, of course, the whole point is that this doesn't matter, and this is what makes it possible to use the GregorianCalendar class in a system-independent way.

What *matters* are the methods that a class exposes. If you look at the documentation for the GregorianCalendar class, you will find that it has 28 public methods, most of which are not of general interest.

In this book, we present a method in the following format, which is essentially the same as the on-line documentation.

Here are the most useful methods of the GregorianCalendar class, together with a couple of not so useful ones.

`java.util.GregorianCalendar`

- `GregorianCalendar()`

  constructs a calendar object that represents the current time in the default time zone with the default locale.

- `GregorianCalendar(int year, int month, int date)`

  constructs a Gregorian calendar with the given date.

Parameters:	`year`	the year of the date
	`month`	the month of the date. This value is 0-based; e.g., 0 for January.
	`date`	the day of the month

- `GregorianCalendar(int year, int month, int date, int hour, int minutes, int seconds)`

  constructs a Gregorian calendar with the given date and time.

Parameters:	`year`	the year of the date
	`month`	the month of the date. This value is 0-based; e.g., 0 for January.
	`date`	the day of the month
	`hour`	the hour (between 0 and 23)
	`minutes`	the minutes (between 0 and 59)
	`seconds`	the seconds (between 0 and 59)

- `boolean equals(Object when)`

  compares this calendar object with `when` and returns `true` if the objects represent the same point in time.

- `boolean before(Object when)`

  compares this calendar object with `when` and returns `true` if it comes before `when`.

- `boolean after(Object when)`

  compares this calendar object with `when` and returns `true` if it comes after `when`.

- `int get(int field)`

  gets the value of a particular field.

  Parameters: `field`   one of

                               `Calendar.ERA`

                               `Calendar.YEAR`

                               `Calendar.MONTH`

                               `Calendar.WEEK_OF_YEAR`

                               `Calendar.WEEK_OF_MONTH`

                               `Calendar.DATE`

                               `Calendar.DAY_OF_MONTH`

                               `Calendar.DAY_OF_YEAR`

                               `Calendar.DAY_OF_WEEK`

                               `Calendar.DAY_OF_WEEK_IN_MONTH`

                               `Calendar.AM_PM`

                               `Calendar.HOUR`

                               `Calendar.HOUR_OF_DAY`

                               `Calendar.MINUTE`

                               `Calendar.SECOND`

                               `Calendar.MILLISECOND`

                               `Calendar.ZONE_OFFSET`

                               `Calendar.DST_OFFSET`

- `void set(int field, int value)`

  sets the value of a particular field. Use this method with caution—you can create impossible dates.

  Parameters: `field`   one of the constants accepted by `get`

                        `value`   the new value

- `void set(int year, int month, int date)`

  sets the date fields to a new date.

  Parameters: `year`   the year of the date

                        `month`   the month of the date. This value is 0-based; e.g., 0 for January.

                        `date`   the day of the month

- void set(int year, int month, int date, int hour, int minutes, int seconds)

  sets the date and time fields to new values.

Parameters:	year	the year of the date
	month	the month of the date. This value is 0-based; e.g., 0 for January.
	date	the day of the month
	hour	the hour (between 0 and 23)
	minutes	the minutes (between 0 and 59)
	seconds	the seconds (between 0 and 59)

- void add(int field, int amount)

  is a date arithmetic function. Adds the specified amount of time to the given time field. For example, to add 7 days to the current calendar date, call c.add(Calendar.DATE, 7).

Parameters:	field	the field to modify (using one of the constants documented in the get method)
	amount	the amount by which the field should be changed (can be negative)

- void setGregorianChange(Date date)

  sets the date at which the Julian calendar ends and the Gregorian calendar (with a more precise leap year correction) starts. The default is 00:00:00 local time, October 15, 1582.

Parameters:	date	the desired Gregorian cutover date

- Date getGregorianChange()

  gets the date at which the calendar switches from Julian to Gregorian.

Mutator and Accessor Methods

At this point, you are probably asking yourself: How do I get at the current day or month or year for the date encapsulated in a specific GregorianCalendar object? And how do I change the values if I am unhappy with them? You can find out how to carry out these tasks by looking at the API reference of the preceding section.

The GregorianCalendar class has a rather atypical way of accessing the information stored in a calendar object. Most classes would have methods such as getYear, getMonth, and so on, to access the object state. However, the GregorianCalendar class has a single catch-all get method that can be used to query the state of a large number of settings, not just the year, month, and so on, but also information such as the weekday. To select the item that you want to get, you pass a constant defined in the `Calendar` class, such as `Calendar.MONTH` or `Calendar.DAY_OF_WEEK`:

```
GregorianCalendar todaysDate = new GregorianCalendar();
System.out.println(todaysDate.get(Calendar.MONTH));
System.out.println(todaysDate.get(Calendar.DAY_OF_WEEK));
```

You can change a date with one of the `set` methods or with the `add` method. For example,

```
dueDate.set(1999,11,31);
```

There is a conceptual difference between the `get` method on the one hand and the `set` and `add` methods on the other hand. The `get` method only looks up the state of the object and reports on it. The `set` and `add` methods modify the state of the object. Methods that change instance fields are called *mutator methods* and those that only access instance fields without modifying them are called *accessor methods*. The convention in Java is to use the lowercase prefix `get` for accessor methods and `set` for mutator methods. For example, the `GregorianCalendar` class has methods `getGregorianChange` and `setGregorianChange`. Actually, as already noted, the `GregorianCalendar` class is a little strange—to access year, month, day, hour, minute, and second fields, you don't use separate `get` accessors but a single `get` method. The `getGregorianChange` and `setGregorianChange` methods, even though they are of no practical interest except to calendar enthusiasts, are more characteristic of typical Java methods. In the next section, we will introduce a `Day` class that is easier to understand than the `GregorianCalendar` and whose methods are similar to those of typical Java classes.

C++ NOTE: In C++, it is important to make a formal distinction between mutator operations that change an object and accessor operations that merely read its data fields. The latter need to be declared as `const` operations. This is not needed in Java.

VB NOTE: The analogous situation (in VB4 or VB5) is that mutator methods correspond to a Property Let or Property Set procedure, and accessor methods correspond to a Property Get procedure.

Using Our Day *Class*

Unfortunately, even if you look at *all* the methods in the `GregorianCalendar` class to see if your idea of what is important corresponds to ours, you will quickly discover that this class is not only unintuitive to use but is also missing certain types of functionality. There are instances in which you want to find the difference between two dates. For example, a retirement calculator certainly needs to compute the difference between today's date and the user's retirement date. The question then arises, What is the best way to add this functionality to the GregorianCalendar class? Could we build on the GregorianCalendar class (i.e., use *inheritance*—to be described in the next chapter)?

When we tried this, we discovered that the GregorianCalendar class did not let us easily access the information we needed to do date calculations. There is a method for finding out if the current date comes before the retirement date, but that doesn't do us a lot of good—we know we aren't retired yet. The method won't tell us how many days will elapse until our well-deserved retirement. Just out of curiosity, we examined the source code for the GregorianCalendar class and discovered that in principle we could use the getTimeinMillis method to obtain the time in milliseconds that have elapsed since January 1, 1970. We could then divide the difference by 1000*60*60*24 = 86,400,000 to get the number of days since January 1, 1970, but this is hardly convenient.

NOTE: The CD includes the source code for all of the publicly available parts of Java. As you become more experienced with Java, you will find the source code extremely useful for getting ideas about and (occasional) insights into Java programming.

We, therefore, decided to write our own Day class to give you a better example of a class with cleanly designed accessor and mutator functions. The source code (it's around 150 lines of code) has been installed in the corejava package inside the \CoreJavaBook directory of your hard disk during the installation described in Chapter 2. (When you finish this chapter, you may want to glance through the source code to see the basic ideas. Fair warning: some of the code is fairly obscure because of the algorithms needed to work with a year that is, in reality, slightly more than 365 days long.)

We allow two ways to create an instance of our Day class that are similar to the two methods for Java's Date class:

```
Day todaysDate = new Day();
Day preMillenium = new Day(1999, 12, 31);
```

Unlike Java's GregorianCalendar class, our class does not do anything with the time of day and will also prevent you from creating an illegal date. Furthermore, we specify the month in a more natural way, starting at 1 = January and going up to 12 = December.

To create an object of our Day class, you need to make sure that Java knows where the Day class is. Do this by setting the class path appropriately to include the CoreJavaBook directory as was described in Chapter 2. Because the Day class is contained in a package named corejava, you also need to use the statement import corejava.* at the beginning of the source file. What we want to stress here is that once you know how to create an instance of the Day class, then all you need to use our class is the following list that tells you how our methods affect the current state of an instance of the Day class.

corejava.Day

- void advance(int n)

  advances the date currently set by a specified number of days. For example, d.advance(100) changes d to a date 100 days later.

- int getDay(), int getMonth(), int getYear()

  returns the day, month, or year of this day object. Days are between 1 and 31, months between 1 and 12, and years can be any year (such as 1996 or −333). The class knows about the switch from the Julian to the Gregorian calendar in 1582.

- int weekday()

  returns an integer between Day.SUNDAY and Day.SATURDAY, corresponding to the day of the week.

- int daysBetween(Day b)

  This method is one of the main reasons we created the Day class. It calculates the number of days between the current instance of the Day class and instance b of the Day class.

Notice that our Day class has no method for changing the date other than to use the advance method.

The following code combines the Console class with our Day class in order to calculate how many days you have been alive.

```
import corejava.*;
public class DaysAlive
{  public static void main(String[] args)
   {  int year;
      int month;
      int day;

      month = Console.readInt
         ("Please enter the month you were born",
            + "1 for January and so on");
      day = Console.readInt
         ("Please enter the day you were born.");
      year = Console.readInt
```

```
                    ("Please enter the year you were born" +
                    "(starting with 19..)");

        Day birthday = new Day(year, month, day);
        Day today = new Day();
        System.out.println("You have been alive "
            + today.daysBetween(birthday) + " days.");
    }
}
```

NOTE: If you try to enter invalid data, the program will terminate with an exception.
See Chapter 11 for more on exceptions.

A Calendar Program

As a more serious example of putting it all together, here is the code for an
application that prints out a calendar for the month and year specified in the
command-line arguments. For example, if you compile this class (make sure our
Day class is available, of course) and then run

```
java Calendar 12 1999
```

you will see the calendar for December 1999. (December 31 is rather conveniently
on a Friday that year, by the way.)

```
12   1999
Sun   Mon   Tue   Wed   Thu   Fri   Sat
                    1     2     3     4
 5     6     7     8     9    10    11
12    13    14    15    16    17    18
19    20    21    22    23    24    25
26    27    28    29    30    31
```

There are two issues in writing a calendar program like this: you have to know
the weekday of the first day of the month, and you have to know how many
days the month has. We sidestep the latter problem with the following trick:
we make a Day object that starts out with the first of the month.

```
Day d = new Day(y, m, 1); // start date of the month
```

After printing each day, we advance d by one day:

```
d.advance(1);
```

In Example 4–1 we check the month (d.getMonth()) and see if it is still the same as m. If not, we are done.

Example 4–1: Calendar.java

```java
import corejava.*;

public class Calendar
{  public static void main(String[] args)
   {  int m;
      int y;
      if (args.length == 2)
      {  m = Integer.parseInt(args[0]);
         y = Integer.parseInt(args[1]);
      }
      else
      {  Day today = new Day(); // today's date
         m = today.getMonth();
         y = today.getYear();
      }

      Day d = new Day(y, m, 1); // start date of the month

      System.out.println(m + " " + y);
      System.out.println("Sun Mon Tue Wed Thu Fri Sat");
      for (int i = Day.SUNDAY; i < d.weekday(); i++ )
          System.out.print("    ");
      while (d.getMonth() == m)
      {  if (d.getDay() < 10) System.out.print(" ");
         System.out.print(d.getDay());
         if (d.weekday() == Day.SATURDAY)
            System.out.println();
         else
            System.out.print("  ");
         d.advance(1);
      }
      if (d.weekday() != Day.SUNDAY) System.out.println();
   }
}
```

Objects as Function Arguments

There is a tendency for programmers coming from languages that have both call by value and call by reference to assume that since objects are references, they are passed by reference. Unfortunately, that is wrong in Java!

First, consider trying to write a swap method for days. Because you got tired of writing the three lines of code that are needed, you decide to write once and for all:

```java
static void swapDays(Day a, Day b)
```

```
{  Day temp = b;
   b = a;
   a = temp;
}
```

Unfortunately, the call `swapDays(foo, bar)` (as opposed to writing the three lines of code) still does nothing; `foo` and `bar` still refer to whatever they did before the call—*because* they were passed by value to the `swapDays` method (see Figure 4–7).

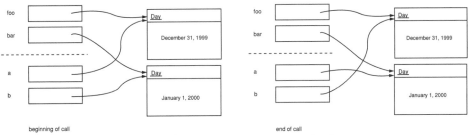

Figure 4–7: Parameters of the `swapDays` method

As another example of this phenomenon, consider the following method that *tries* to change the delivery date for a software product:

```
static void changeDeliveryDay(Day d, int yearsDelayed)
// won't work
{  int month = d.getMonth();
   int day = d.getDay();
   int year = d.getYear();
   d = new Day(year + yearsDelayed, month, day);
}
```

Suppose you call this function as follows:

```
target = new Day(1996, 10, 15);
changeDeliveryDay(target, 2);
```

in order to change the delivery date to be two years later. Does `target` now have the correct state?

What we are doing seems natural at first glance. It *looks* like the `target` object is changed inside the method so that it refers to a new `Day` object since the parameter certainly is being changed to a new `day` object. However, *this code will also not work.* The point is that Java never passes method parameters by reference. The variable d in the `changeDeliveryDay` method is a *copy* of the `target` variable. Now, it is true that both of these variables are references and they do both point to the same `Day` object right after the method is called. It is also true that the assignment

```
d = new Day(year + yearsDelayed, month, day);
```

changes the value of the d object variable inside the method. It now refers (points) to a new Day object. The original target variable, however, has not changed; it *still* refers to the original Day object (see Figure 4–8). Thus, the method call does not change what the target refers to at all. (The d object variable is abandoned when Java finishes executing the method, and the memory allocated for it will eventually be garbage collected.)

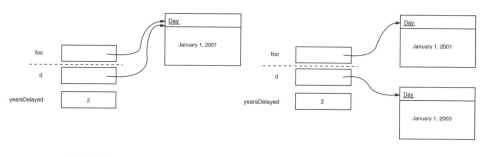

Figure 4–8: Parameters of the incorrect changeDeliveryDay **method**

To sum up: *In Java, methods can never change the values of their parameters.* Both object references and base types such as numbers are *always* passed by value.

On the other hand, as you have seen repeatedly, methods can change the *state* of an object used as a parameter. They can do this since they have access to the mutator methods and data of the object the parameter points to. Here's a version of a method to change the delivery day that will do the job.

```
static void changeDeliveryDay(Day d, int yearsDelayed)
// works
{    int ndays = 365 * yearsDelayed;
     d.advance(ndays);
}
```

This method changes the state of d by using the advance method of the Day class. It doesn't try to attach a different object to d; it simply uses the fact that it can access and change the data of d via its mutator methods. When you call this method with a parameter equal to target, the advance method updates target when it is called by the line d.advance(ndays). This changes the state of the target object as we wanted to do.

Starting to Build Your Own Classes

You saw how to write simple classes in Chapter 3. In that chapter, the classes were all designed to run as stand-alone programs and depended only on the classes built into Java and our little Console class. When you said

```
java Mortgage
```

for example, the Java interpreter looked for the `main` method in the `Mortgage` class and ran it. The `main` method, in turn, called other methods of the class as needed. Although you will see more about methods like `main` later in this chapter, this kind of class is not what we are concerned with in this chapter. In more sophisticated Java programs, the class you choose to run from the interpreter will usually have very little functionality other than creating the various objects that do the actual work of your program.

What we want to do in the rest of this chapter (and in the next chapter) is show you how to write the kind of "workhorse classes" that are needed for more sophisticated applications. These classes do not (and often cannot) stand alone: they are the building blocks for *constructing* stand-alone programs.

The simplest syntax for a class in Java is:

```
accessSpecifier class NameOfClass
{  // definitions of the class's features
   // includes methods and instance fields
}
```

The outermost pair of braces (block) defines the code that will make up the class. (You will find more information on the various possible access specifiers later in this chapter.) The most common convention (and thus our convention) is to use initial caps for class names. Just as with the classes from Chapter 3, individual method definitions define the operations of the class. The difference is that we want to allow other classes to use our classes while still maintaining encapsulation of the data. This means that we now want to allow for (encapsulated) instance fields that will hold the private data for these classes.

NOTE: We adopt the policy that the methods for the class come first and the instance fields come at the end. (Perhaps this, in a small way, encourages the notion of leaving instance fields alone.)

An `Employee` *Class*

Consider the following, very simplified version of an `Employee` class that might be used by a business in writing a payroll system.

```
class Employee
{  public Employee(String n, double s, Day d)
   {  name = n;
      salary = s;
      hireDay = d;
   }

   public void print()
   {  System.out.println(name + " " + salary + " "
```

```
          + hireYear());
    }

    public void raiseSalary(double byPercent)
    {   salary *= 1 + byPercent / 100;
    }

    public int hireYear()
    {   return hireDay.getYear();
    }

    private String name;
    private double salary;
    private Day hireDay;
}
```

We will break down the code in this class in some detail in the sections that follow. First, though, Example 4–2 shows some code that lets you see how to use the Employee class. On the CD ROM, we placed both classes into a single source file. This file contains the source code for *two* classes: the Employee class and a class EmployeeTest with the public access specifier. We had to give this file the name EmployeeTest.java since the name of the file must match the name of the public class. Next, when you compile this source code, Java will create two classes in the directory: EmployeeTest.class and Employee.class. Finally, when you go to run this code via

```
    java EmployeeTest
```

the Java bytecode interpreter starts running the code in the main method in the EmployeeTest class. This code in turn creates some new Employee objects and shows you their state.

Example 4–2: EmployeeTest.java

```
import java.util.*;
import corejava.*;

public class EmployeeTest
{   public static void main(String[] args)
    {   Employee[] staff = new Employee[3];

        staff[0] = new Employee("Harry Hacker", 35000,
            new Day(1989,10,1));
        staff[1] = new Employee("Carl Cracker", 75000,
            new Day(1987,12,15));
        staff[2] = new Employee("Tony Tester", 38000,
            new Day(1990,3,15));
```

```
      int i;
      for (i = 0; i < 3; i++) staff[i].raiseSalary(5);
      for (i = 0; i < 3; i++) staff[i].print();
   }
}
```

C++ NOTE: In Java, all functions are defined inside the class itself. This does not auto-matically make them inline functions. There is no analog to the C++ syntax:

```
class Employee
{  //...
};
void Employee::raiseSalary(double byPercent) // C++, not Java
{  salary *= 1 + byPercent / 100;
}
```

Analyzing the `Employee` *Class*

In the sections that follow, we want to dissect the `Employee` class. Let's start with the methods in this class. As you can see by examining the source code, this class has four methods, whose headers look like this:

```
public Employee(String n, double s, Day d)
public void print()
public void raiseSalary(double byPercent)
public int hireYear()
```

As you can see, you may also use access modifiers with methods. In Java, method access modifiers describe who can use the method or who can use the class if a modifier is used in the name of the class. The keyword `public` means that any method in any class that has access to an instance of the `Employee` class can call the method. (There are four possible access levels; they are covered in this and the next chapter.)

Next, notice that there are three *instance fields* that will hold the data we will manipulate inside an instance of the `Employee` class.

```
private String name;
private double salary;
private Day hireDay;
```

The `private` keyword makes sure that no outside agency can access the instance fields *except* through the methods of our class. In this book, instance fields will almost always be private. (Exceptions occur only when we have to implement very closely collaborating classes, for example, a `List` and a `Link` class in a linked list data structure.)

NOTE: It is possible to use the `public` keyword with your instance variables, but it would be a very bad idea. Having `public` data fields would allow any part of the program to read and modify the instance variables. That completely ruins encapsulation and, at the risk of repeating ourselves too often, we strongly urge against using public instance fields.

Finally, notice that we use an instance field that is itself an instance of our Day class. This is quite usual: classes will often contain instance fields that are themselves class instances.

NOTE: Please see the section *Packages* later in this chapter if you want to use all of our classes in the simplest fashion without worrying about the location of the source files, and if you want more information on access modifiers for classes.

First Steps with Constructors

Let's look at the first method listed in our Employee class.

```
public Employee(String n, double s, Day d)
{   name = n;
    salary = s;
    hireDay = d;
}
```

This is an example of a *constructor method*. It is used to initialize objects of a class—giving the instance variables the initial state you want them to have. You didn't see any methods like this in Chapter 3 because we didn't initialize any objects in that chapter.

For example, when you create an instance of the Employee class with code like this:

```
hireDate = new Day(1950, 1, 1);
Employee number007 = new Employee
    ("James Bond", 100000, hireDate);
```

you have set the instance fields as follows:

```
name = "James Bond";
salary = 100000;
hireDay = January 1, 1950 // actually a Day object with this
                          // data encapsulated
```

The new method is always used together with a constructor to create an object of the class. This forces you to set the initial state of your objects. In Java, you cannot create an instance of a class without initializing the instance variables (either explicitly or implicitly). The reason for this design decision is simple: an object created without a correct initialization is always useless and occasionally dangerous. In many languages, like Delphi, you can create uninitialized objects; the result is almost always the platform equivalent of a general protection fault (GPF) or segmentation fault, which means memory is being corrupted.

While we will have more to say about constructor methods later in this chapter, for now, always keep the following in mind:

1. A constructor has the same name as the class.

2. A constructor may (as in this example) take one or more (or even no) parameters.

3. A constructor is always called with the new keyword.

4. A constructor has no return value.

Remember, too, the following important difference between constructors and other methods:

•   A constructor can only be called with new. You can't apply a constructor to an existing object to reset the instance fields. For example, d.Day(1950, 1, 1) is an error.

Of course, if resetting all fields of a class is an important and recurring operation, the designers of the class can provide a mutator method such as empty or reset for that purpose. We want to stress that only the supplied mutator methods will let you revise the state of the instance variables in an already constructed class (assuming, of course, that all data are private).

It is possible to have more than one constructor in a class. You have already seen this both in Java's GregorianCalendar class and in our Day class. (You saw two of the three constructors available in the GregorianCalendar class and both of the constructors available in our Day class.)

C++ NOTE: Constructors work the same way in Java as they do in C++. But keep in mind that all Java objects are constructed on the heap and that a constructor must be combined with new. It is a common C++ programmer error to forget the new operator:

```
Employee number007("James Bond", 100000, hireDate);
    // C++, not Java
```

That works in C++ but does not work in Java.

```
public Employee(String n, double s, Day d)
{   name = n;
    hireDay = d;
    double salary = s; // ERROR
}
```

The last line declares a local variable `salary` that is only accessible inside the constructor and that *shadows* the instance field `salary`. This is a nasty error that can be hard to track down. You just have to be careful in all of your methods that you don't use variable names that equal the names of instance fields.

The Methods of the Employee Class

The first three methods in our `Employee` class should not pose many problems. They are much like the methods you saw in the previous chapter. Notice, however, that all of these methods can access the private instance fields by name. This is a key point: instance fields are always accessible by the methods of their own class.

For example,

```
public void raiseSalary(double byPercent)
{   salary *= 1 + byPercent / 100;
}
```

sets a new value for the `salary` instance field in the object that executes this method. (This particular method does not return a value.) For example, the call

```
number007.raiseSalary(5);
```

raises number007's salary by increasing the `number007.salary` variable by 5%.

The `raiseSalary` method is a function with two arguments. The first argument, called the *implicit* argument is the object of type `Employee` that appears before the method name. The second argument, the number inside the parentheses after the method name, is an *explicit* argument. As you can see, the explicit arguments are listed in the function declaration. For example, `double byPercent` is explicitly listed. The implicit parameter does not appear in the function declaration.

Of the remaining methods in this class, the most interesting is the one that returns the year hired. Recall that it looks like this:

```
public int hireYear()
{   return hireDay.getYear();
}
```

Notice that this method returns an integer value, and it does this by applying a method to the `hireDay` instance variable. This makes perfect sense because `hireDay` is an instance of our `Day` class, which indeed has a `getYear` method.

Finally, let's look more closely at the rather simple `getName` method.

```
public String getName()
{   return name;
}
```

This is an obvious example of an accessor method. Because it works directly with a field in the class, it is sometimes called a *field accessor method*. It simply returns the current state of the `name` field.

For the class implementor, it is obviously more trouble to write both a private field and a public accessor method than to simply write a public data field. But programmers using the class are not inconvenienced—if `number007` is the name of the instance of the `Employee` class, they simply write `number007.getName()`, rather than `number007.name`.

The point is that the `name` field has become "read only" to the outside world. Only operations of the class can modify it. In particular, should the value ever be wrong, only the class operations need to be debugged.

By the way, the function is called `getName()` because it would be confusing to call it `name()`—that is already taken by the instance variable itself, and it would be confusing to have a variable and a method with the same name. (In any case, the convention in Java is that accessor methods begin with a lowercase `get`.)

Now, because secret agents come and go, one might want to modify the class at some later point to allow for a field mutator that resets the name of the current "007." This would be done by the maintainers of the class as the need arises.

The point to keep in mind is that, in most classes, private data fields are of a technical nature and of no interest to anyone but the implementor of the operations. When the user of a class has a legitimate interest in both reading and setting a field, the class implementors need to supply *three* items:

- a private data field
- a public field accessor method
- a public field mutator method

This is a lot more tedious than supplying a single public data field, but there are considerable benefits:

1. The internal implementation can be changed without affecting any code other than the operations of the class.

Of course, the accessor and mutator methods may need to do a lot of work—especially when the data representation of the instance fields is changed. But that leads us to our second benefit.

2. Mutator methods can perform error-checking, whereas code that simply assigns to a field cannot.

Our Day class is a good example of a class that should *not* have mutators for each field. Suppose we had methods called setDay, setMonth, and setYear that do the obvious things. Suppose d was an instance of our Day class. Now consider the code:

```
d.setDay(31);
d.setMonth(3);
d.setYear(1996);
```

If the date encapsulated in d was currently at February 1, then the setDay operation described above would set it to an invalid date of February 31. What do you think setDay should do in this case? At first glance, this appears to be only a nuisance, but if you think this through carefully, you will find that there is no good answer.

Should an invalid setDay abort the program? Well, how *would* you then safely set the date from February 1 to March 31? Of course, you could set the month first:

```
d.setMonth(3);
d.setDay(31);
```

That will work. Now, how do you change it back to February 1? This time, you can't set the month first. These functions would be a real hassle to use.

So perhaps setDay should just quietly adjust the date? If you set the date to February 31, then maybe the date should be adjusted to March 2 or 3, depending on whether the year is a leap year or not. The Java GregorianCalendar class does exactly that when the "lenient" flag is turned on. We think this is a lousy idea. Consider again our effort to set the date from February 1 to March 31.

```
d.setDay(31); // now it is March 2 or 3
d.setMonth(3); // still March 2 or 3
```

Or perhaps setDay should temporarily make an invalid date and count on the fact that the programmer won't forget to adjust the month. Then we lose a major benefit of encapsulation: the guarantee that the object state is never corrupted.

We hope we have convinced you that a mutator that sets only the day field is not worth the trouble. It is obviously better to supply a single setDate(int, int, int) function that does the error-checking needed. (This also fits one's mental model better—after all, one sets a date and not a day, month, and year.)

CAUTION: Be careful not to write accessor methods that return references to mutable objects. Consider the following example.

```
class Employee
{   . . .
    public String getName() { return name; }
    public Day getHireDay() { return hireDay; }
    private String name;
    private double salary;
    private Day hireDay;
}
```

This breaks the encapsulation! Consider the following rogue code:

```
Employee harry = . . .;
Day d = harry.getHireDay();
d.advance(-3650);
// let's give Harry ten years added seniority
```

The reason is subtle. Both d and `harry.hireDay` refer to the same object (see Figure 4–9). Changing d automatically changes the private state of the employee object!

Why didn't the `getName` method suffer from the same problem? Couldn't someone get the name and change it? No. The name is a string, and strings are *immutable*. There is no method that can change a string. In contrast, Day objects are mutable. There is exactly one mutator, namely, `advance`.

The remedy is to *clone* the `hireDay` field before returning it in the accessor method. A clone is an exact copy of an object that is stored in a new location. We will discuss cloning in detail in Chapter 5. Here is the corrected code:

```
class Employee
{   . . .
    public Day getHireDay() { return (Day)hireDay.clone(); }
}
```

As a rule of thumb, always use `clone` whenever you need to return a copy of a mutable data field.

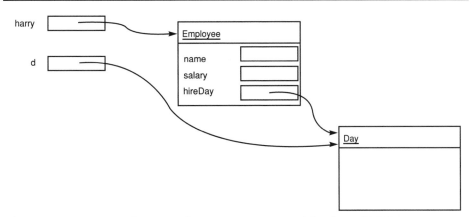

Figure 4–9: Returning a reference to a mutable data field

Method Access to Private Data

You know that a method can access the private data of the object on which it is invoked. What many people find surprising is that a method can access the private data of *all objects of its class*. For example, consider a method `equals` that compares two dates.

```
class Day
{   . . .
    boolean equals(Day b)
    {   return year == b.year && month == b.month
            && day == b.day;
    }
}
```

A typical call is

```
if (hireday.equals(d)) . . .
```

This method accesses the private fields of `hireday`, which is not surprising. It also accesses the private fields of `d`. This is legal because `d` is an object of type `Day`, and a method of the `Day` class is permitted to access the private fields of *any* object of type `Day`.

C++ NOTE: C++ has the same rule. A member function can access the private features of any object of its class, not just the implicit argument.

Private Methods

When implementing a class, we make all data fields private, since `public` data are dangerous. But what about the methods? While most methods are `public`, `private` methods occur quite frequently. These methods can be called only from other methods of the same class. The reason is simple: to implement operations, you may wish to break up the code into many separate methods. Many of these methods are not particularly useful to the public. (For example, they may be too close to the current implementation or require a special protocol or calling order.) Such methods are best implemented as `private` operations.

To implement a private method in Java, simply change the `public` keyword to `private`.

As an example, consider how our `Day` class might require a method to test whether or not a year is a leap year. By making the method private, we are under no obligation to keep it available if we change to another implementation. The method may well be *harder* to implement or *unnecessary* if the data representation changes: this is irrelevant. The point is that as long as the operation is private, the designers of the class can be assured that it is never used outside the other class operations and can simply drop it. Had the method been public, we would be forced to reimplement it if we changed the representation, because other code might have relied on it.

In sum, choose private methods:

- For those methods that are of no concern to the class user
- For those methods that could not easily be supported if the class implementation were to change

More on Object Construction

You have seen how to write simple constructors that define the initial state of your objects. However, because object construction is so important, Java offers quite a variety of mechanisms for writing constructors. We will go over these mechanisms in the sections that follow.

Overloading

Recall that both Java's GregorianCalendar class and our Day class had more than one constructor. We could use:

```
Day today = new Day();
```

or

```
Day preMillenium =  new Day(1999,12,31);
```

This capability is called *overloading*. Overloading occurs if several methods have the same name (in this case, the Day constructor method) but different arguments. The Java interpreter must sort out which method to call. (This is usually called *overloading resolution*.) It picks the correct method by matching the argument types in the headers of the various methods with the types of the values used in the specific method call. (Even if there are no arguments, you must use the empty parentheses.) A compile-time error occurs if the compiler cannot match the arguments or if more than one match is possible.

NOTE: Java allows you to overload any method—not just constructor methods.

Instance Field Initialization

Since you can overload the constructor methods in a class, you can obviously build in many ways to set the initial state of the instance fields of your classes. It is always a good idea to make sure that, regardless of the constructor call, every instance field is set to something meaningful. Actually, Java does set all instance fields to a default value (numbers to zero, objects to null, booleans to false), if you don't set them explicitly. But it is considered poor programming practice to rely on this. Certainly, it makes it harder for someone to use your code if variables are being initialized invisibly.

NOTE: In this regard, instance variables differ from local variables in a method. Local variables must be initialized explicitly.

For example, if our Day class did not have any constructors, then the day, month, and year fields would be initialized with zero whenever you made a new Day object. (That wouldn't be a good idea. In the Julian/Gregorian calendar, there is no year 0—the year 1 B.C. is immediately followed by 1 A.D. For that reason, we supply explicit constructors.)

If all constructors of a class need to set a particular instance variable to the same value, there is a convenient syntax for doing the initialization. You simply assign to the field in the class definition. For example, when you initialize a Customer object, you would want to set the nextOrder instance variable to 1 all the time. This can be done as in the following code:

```
class Customer
{   public Customer(String n)
    {   name = n;
        accountNumber = Account.getNewNumber();
    }
    public Customer(String n, int a)
    {   name = n;
        accountNumber = a;
    }
    . . .
    private String name;
    private int accountNumber = 1;
    private int nextOrder = 1;
}
```

Now the nextOrder field is set to 1 in all Customer objects.

We recommend that you use this convenient syntax whenever you want to set a field to the same constant value in all the constructors. However, it is not an intuitive notation if the initialization expression is not a constant. For example, consider this modification of the Customer class:

```
class Customer
{   public Customer(String n)
    {   name = n;
    }
    . . .
    private String name;
    private int accountNumber = Account.getNewNumber();
}
```

Each Customer object is initialized with a separate call to Account.getNewNumber(). In this situation, we suggest performing the initialization *inside* the constructor.

Default Constructors

A *default constructor* is a constructor with no arguments. If you write the code for your class with no constructors whatsoever, Java provides a default constructor for you. This default constructor sets *all* the instance variables to their default values. So, all numeric data contained in the instance fields would be zeroed out, and all object variables would point to `null` and all booleans would be `false`.

CAUTION: Please keep in mind that Java creates a default constructor for you *only* when your class has no other constructors. If you write your class with even a single constructor of your own, and you want the users of your class to have the ability to create an instance via a call to:

```
new ClassName()
```

then Java insists that you provide a default constructor (with no arguments).

For example, the `Customer` class didn't define constructors that use no arguments, so it is illegal for the users of the class to use

```
c = new Customer(); // ERROR—no default constructor
```

C++ NOTE: In C++, you cannot directly initialize data members of a class. All data must be set in a constructor.

Java has no analog for the C++ initializer list syntax, such as:

```
Customer::Customer(String n)
:   name(n),
    accountNumber(Account::getNewNumber())
{}
```

C++ uses this special syntax to call the constructor for member objects. In Java, there is no need for it because objects have no member objects, only pointers to other objects.

The `this` Object Reference

Occasionally, you want to access the current object in its entirety and not a particular instance variable. Java has a convenient shortcut for this—the `this` keyword. In a method, the keyword `this` refers to the object on which the method operates.

For example, many Java classes have a method called `toString()` that returns a string describing the object. (For example, Java's `Date` class has this method.) If you pass any object to the `System.out.println` method, that method invokes the `toString` method on the object and prints the resulting string. Therefore, you can print out the current state of the implicit argument of any method as

```
System.out.println(this);
```

This is a useful strategy for debugging. We will later see other uses for the `this` object reference.

There is a second meaning for the `this` keyword. If *the first statement of a constructor* has the form `this(. . .)`, then the constructor calls another constructor of the same class. Here is a typical example:

```
class Customer
{   public Customer(String n)
    {   this(n, Account.getNewNumber());
    }
    public Customer(String n, int a)
    {   name = n;
        accountNumber = a;
    }
    . . .
}
```

When you call `new Customer("James Bond")`, then the `Customer(String)` constructor calls the `Customer(String, int)` constructor.

Using the `this` keyword in this manner is a useful device to factor out (combine) common code between constructors.

In sum, as you have seen, constructors are somewhat complex in Java. Before a constructor is called, all instance fields are initialized to the value you specified in the class or to their default values (zero for numbers, `null` for objects, `false` for booleans). The first statement of your constructor may call another constructor.

C++ NOTE: The `this` object in Java is identical to the `this` pointer in C++. However, in C++ it is not possible for one constructor to call another. If you want to factor out common initialization code in C++, you must write a separate member function.

Initialization Blocks

You have already seen two ways to initialize a data field:

1.   by setting a value in a constructor

2.   by assigning a value in the declaration

There is a actually a *third* mechanism in Java; it's called an *initialization block*. Class declarations can contain arbitrary blocks of code. These blocks are executed whenever an object of that class is constructed. For example,

```
class Customer
{   public Customer(String n)
    {   name = n;
```

```
        }
        // an initialization block
        {   accountNumber = Account.getNewNumber();
        }
        . . .
    }
```

This mechanism is never necessary and it is not common. It usually is clearer to place the initialization code inside a constructor. However, for initializing static variables, a static initialization block can be useful, as you will see in the `RandomIntGenerator` class a little later on in this chapter.

With so many ways of initializing data fields, it can be quite confusing to give all possible pathways for the construction process. Here is what happens in detail, when a constructor is called.

1. All data fields are initialized, in the order in which they are declared. The values are set, either to their default value (0, `false`, or `null`) or to the specified initial values.

2. All initialization blocks are executed, in the order in which they occur in the class declaration.

3. If the first line of the constructor calls another constructor, then that constructor is executed.

4. The body of the constructor is executed.

Naturally, it is always a good idea to organize your initialization code so that it is easy to understand without having to be a language lawyer. For example, it would be quite strange and somewhat error-prone to have a class whose constructors depend on the order in which the data fields are declared.

Object Destruction and the `finalize()` Method

Many languages, such as C++ and Delphi, have explicit destructor methods for any cleanup code that may be needed. The most common activity in a destructor is reclaiming the memory set aside for objects. Since Java does automatic garbage collection, manual memory reclamation is not needed, and Java does not support destructors.

NOTE: Objects are not garbage collected as long as there is at least one reference to them. However, in some situations, it is desirable to have objects that stay around when there is sufficient memory but that are collected to make more memory available for more important objects. A typical application is a cache. This is a specialized mechanism that we will not discuss in detail. You will find more information in the documentation of the `java.lang.ref` package.

Of course, some objects utilize a resource other than memory, such as a file or a handle to another object that uses system resources. In this case, it is important that the resource be reclaimed and recycled when it is no longer needed.

Java does allow you to add a `finalize()` method to any class. The `finalize()` method will be called before the garbage collector sweeps away the object. In practice, *do not rely on the* `finalize` *method* for recycling any resources that are in short supply—you simply cannot know when this method will be called.

> NOTE: There is a method `System.runFinalizersOnExit(true)` to guarantee that finalizer methods are called before Java shuts down. However, this method is inherently unsafe and has been deprecated in Java 2.

If a resource needs to be closed as soon as you have finished using it, you need to manage it manually. Add a `dispose` method that *you* call to clean up what needs cleaning. Just as importantly, if a class you use has a `dispose` method, you will want to call it to reclaim what the designers of the class thought was important to reclaim. In particular, if your class has an instance field that has a `dispose` method, provide a `dispose` method that invokes that field's dispose.

Static Methods and Fields

The last method modifier we want to talk about in this chapter is the `static` modifier. You saw the `static` modifier used to create class constants in Chapter 3. Classes can have both static fields and static methods. Static fields do not change from one instance of a class to another, so you should think of them as belonging to a class. Similarly, static methods belong to a class and do not operate on any instance of a class. This means that you can use them without creating an instance of a class. For example, all of the methods in the `Console` class are static methods, as are all the methods in the `Math` class built into Java.

```
double x = Console.readDouble();
double x = Math.pow(3, 0.1);
```

You have also seen the use of static data fields, for example

```
Math.PI
System.out
```

are static data fields in the `Math` and `System` class.

You can have both static and nonstatic fields and methods in any class.

The general syntax for using a static method from a class is:

```
ClassName.staticMethod(parameters);
```

and the general syntax for using a static field is:

```
ClassName.staticFieldName;
```

> NOTE: Because static methods do not work with an instance of the class, they can only access static fields. In other words, static methods don't have a `this` argument. If a method needs to access a nonstatic instance field of an object, it cannot be a static method.

You initialize a static field either by supplying an initial value or by using a static initialization block. You have already seen the first mechanism:

```
public static final double CM_PER_INCH = 2.54;
```

The second mechanism is used when the initialization does not fit into one expression. You place the initialization code inside a block and tag it with the keyword `static`. For example, later in this section, you will see a random number generator that initializes a static buffer with random numbers:

```
static double[] buffer = new double[BUFFER_SIZE];
static
{   int i;
    for (i = 0; i < buffer.length; i++)
        buffer[i] = java.lang.Math.random();
}
```

The `for` loop does not fit inside an initialization expression, hence we use a static initialization block. Of course, just like static methods, static initialization blocks can only access the static variables and methods of the class and not the instance variables and methods.

Static initialization occurs when the class is first loaded. First, all static variables are initialized in the order in which they are declared. Then, all static initialization blocks are executed in the order in which they occur in the class declaration.

> NOTE: Here is a Java trivia fact to amaze your fellow Java coders: You can write a "Hello, World" program in Java without ever writing a `main` function.
>
> ```
> public class Hello
> {   static
>     {   System.out.println("Hello, World");
>     }
> }
> ```
>
> When you invoke the class with `java Hello`, the class is loaded, the static initialization block prints `"Hello, World"`, and only then do you get an ugly error message that `main` is not defined.

C++ NOTE: Static variables and methods in Java are the same as static data members and member functions in C++. However, the syntax is slightly different. In C++, you use the : : operator to access a static variable or method outside its scope, such as `Math::PI`.

The term "static" makes no sense in C++ or Java when applied to class variables and class methods. The original purpose of `static` in C/C++ was to denote local variables that don't go away when the local scope is exited. In that context, the term "static" indicates that the variable stays around and is still there when the block is entered again. Then `static` got a second meaning in C/C++, to denote, with file scope, functions and global variables that could not be accessed from other files. Finally, C++ reused the keyword for a third, unrelated interpretation, to denote variables and functions that belong to a class but not to any particular object of the class. That is the same meaning that the keyword has in Java.

Of course, C++ does not have static initialization blocks.

As another example, consider the header for the `main` method in a class:

```
public static void main(String[] args)
```

Since `main` is `static`, you don't need to create an instance of the class in order to call it—and the Java interpreter doesn't either. For example, if your `main` method is contained in the class `Mortgage` and you start the Java interpreter with

```
java Mortgage
```

then the interpreter simply starts the `main` method without creating an object of the `Mortgage` class. Because of this, `main` can only access static instance fields in the class. It is actually not uncommon for `main` to create an object of its own class in a sort of "bootstrap process"!

```
public class Application
{   . . .
    public static void main(String[] args)
    {   Application a = new Application();
        // can now call methods a.foo() etc. . .
    }
}
```

When the program starts, the `main` method executes. It creates an object of type `Application`. The `main` method then invokes instance methods on that object.

As a more serious example of a class that combines both static and instance methods, the following class provides a random-number generator that is a significant improvement over the one supplied with Java. (Java uses a simple "linear congruential generator" that can be nonrandom in certain situations by displaying undesirable regularities. This is especially true when it is used to plot random points in space or for certain kinds of simulations.) The idea for the improvement is simple (we found it in Donald E. Knuth's *Semi-Numerical Algorithms,* which is Volume 2 of his *Art of Computer Programming* [Addison-Wesley, 1981]). Instead of using the random number supplied by a call to

```
java.lang.Math.random();
```

we created a class that:

1. adds the convenience of generating random integers in a specific range and

2. is more "random" than the one supplied with Java (but takes about twice as long to generate a random number).

The class works in the following way:

1. It fills up a small array with random numbers, using the built-in random number generator. The size of the array and the array itself are made class constants (i.e., declared with `private static final`). This way, all instances of the `RandomIntGenerator` class can share this information. (This is obviously more efficient than storing a separate set of numbers for each instance of the random number generator class.)

2. It has a public method, called `draw`, for drawing a random integer in the specified range. (You will need to create an instance of our `RandomIntGenerator` class in order to use this method.)

3. The `draw` method, in turn, uses a static method called `nextRandom` that actually implements the algorithm described in Knuth's *Semi-Numerical Algorithms,* p. 32. The method calls the built-in random number generator twice: the first time tells us which random array element to take, and the second time, we use the resulting random number to replace the "used up" element in the array. The `nextRandom` method is static because it only accesses the static data. The `draw` method, however, is not static since it accesses the instance variables `low` and `high`.

4. We use static initialization blocks because the `RandomIntGenerator` class needs to initialize the buffer entries before you can call the `nextRandom` method for the first time. You need a loop to initialize the buffer array, and a loop cannot be coded with a simple initializer.

5. The class constructor defines the range of integers.

The code is shown in Example 4–3 below. Note that the test program is simply included as the `main` method in the `RandomIntGenerator` class.

Example 4–3: RandomIntGenerator.java

```java
public class RandomIntGenerator
{ /**
    * Constructs the class that encapsulates the random integer
    * @param l the lowest integer in the range
    * @param h the highest integer in the range
    */

   public RandomIntGenerator(int l, int h)
   {  low = l;
      high = h;
   }

   /**
    * Used to return a random integer in the range constructed
    */

   public int draw()
   {  int r = low
         + (int)((high - low + 1) * nextRandom());
      return r;
   }

   /**
    * test stub for the class
    */

   public static void main(String[] args)
   {  RandomIntGenerator r1
         = new RandomIntGenerator(1, 10);
      RandomIntGenerator r2
         = new RandomIntGenerator(0, 1);
      int i;
      for (i = 1; i <= 100; i++)
         System.out.println(r1.draw() + " " + r2.draw());
   }

   private static double nextRandom()
   {  int pos =
         (int)(java.lang.Math.random() * BUFFER_SIZE);
      double r = buffer[pos];
      buffer[pos] = java.lang.Math.random();
      return r;
   }

   private static final int BUFFER_SIZE = 101;
   private static double[] buffer
```

```
    = new double[BUFFER_SIZE];
  static
  {  int i;
     for (i = 0; i < BUFFER_SIZE; i++)
        buffer[i] = java.lang.Math.random();
  }

  private int low;
  private int high;
}
```

NOTE: If you look at the code for the `RandomIntGenerator` class in the `corejava` directory, you'll see that we have the test code as part of the `main` method. Having the test code as part of the class in the `main` method is quite a common way of testing your classes.

A `CardDeck` *Class*

To put together the information in this chapter, we want to show you the code needed for the simplest card game of all. The program chooses two cards at random, one for you and one for the computer. The highest card wins.

The underlying object structure in this example is this: a class called `Card` is used to build up a class called `CardDeck`. A card stores its value (a number between 1 and 13 to denote ace, 2, . . . 10, jack, queen, or king) and its suit (a number between 1 and 4 to denote clubs, diamonds, hearts, or spades).

```
class Card
{  public static final int ACE = 1;
   public static final int JACK = 11;
   public static final int QUEEN = 12;
   public static final int KING  = 13;
   public static final int CLUBS = 1;
   public static final int DIAMONDS = 2;
   public static final int HEARTS = 3;
   public static final int SPADES = 4;


     .  .  .


   private int value;
   private int suit;
}
```

Here's the constructor for the `Card` object. As you might expect, it takes two integers, one for the value and one for the suit.

```
public Card(int v, int s)
{  value = v;
   suit = s;
}
```

The card deck stores an array of cards.

```
class CardDeck
{   . . .
    private Card[] deck;
    private int cards;
}
```

The cards field counts how many cards are still in the deck. At the beginning, there are 52 cards, and the count will go down as we draw cards from the deck.

Here's the constructor for the CardDeck class:

```
public CardDeck()
{   deck = new Card[52];
    fill();
    shuffle();
}
```

Notice that this constructor initializes the array of Card objects. After the array of cards is allocated, it will automatically be filled with cards and shuffled. The fill method fills the card deck with 52 cards.

The idea of the shuffle method is to choose randomly which of the cards becomes the last one. We then swap the last card with the chosen card and repeat the process with the remainder of the pile.

The full code for the CardDeck class is shown in Example 4–4. Note the code for the game in the play method and how the main method creates a new CardDeck object.

Example 4–4: CardDeck.java

```
import corejava.*;

public class CardDeck
{   public CardDeck()
    {   deck = new Card[52];
        fill();
        shuffle();
    }

    public void fill()
    {   int i;
        int j;

        for (i = 1; i <= 13; i++)
            for (j = 1; j <= 4; j++)
                deck[4 * (i - 1) + j - 1] = new Card(i, j);
        cards = 52;
```

```
   }

   public void shuffle()
   {  int next;
      for (next = 0; next < cards - 1; next++)
      {  int r = new
             RandomIntGenerator(next, cards - 1).draw();
         Card temp = deck[next];
         deck[next] = deck[r];
         deck[r] = temp;
      }
   }

   public Card draw()
   {  if (cards == 0) return null;
      cards--;
      return deck[cards];
   }

   public void play(int rounds)
   {  int i;
      int wins = 0;

      for (i = 1; i <= rounds; i++)
      {  Card yours = draw();
         System.out.print("Your draw: " + yours + " ");
         Card mine = draw();
         System.out.print("My draw: " + mine + " ");
         if (yours.rank() > mine.rank())
         {  System.out.println("You win");
            wins++;
         }
         else
            System.out.println("I win");
      }
      System.out.println("Your wins: " + wins
         + " My wins: " + (rounds - wins));
   }

   public static void main(String[] args)
   {  CardDeck d = new CardDeck();
      d.play(10); // play ten rounds
   }

   private Card[] deck;
   private int cards;
}
```

Example 4–5 is the complete code for the Card class. Note how we encapsulate the integers that represent the card's suit and value and only return information about them. Also note that once a Card object is constructed, its contents can never change.

Example 4–5: Card.java

```
public class Card
{   public static final int ACE = 1;
    public static final int JACK = 11;
    public static final int QUEEN = 12;
    public static final int KING  = 13;
    public static final int CLUBS = 1;
    public static final int DIAMONDS = 2;
    public static final int HEARTS = 3;
    public static final int SPADES = 4;

    public Card(int v, int s)
    {   value = v;
        suit = s;
    }

    public int getValue()
    {   return value;
    }

    public int getSuit()
    {   return suit;
    }

    public int rank()
    {   if (value == ACE)
            return 4 * 13 + suit;
        else
            return 4 * (value - 1) + suit;
    }

    public String toString()
    {   String v;
        String s;
        if (value == ACE) v = "Ace";
        else if (value == JACK) v = "Jack";
        else if (value == QUEEN) v = "Queen";
        else if (value == KING) v = "King";
        else v = String.valueOf(value);
        if (suit == DIAMONDS) s = "Diamonds";
        else if (suit == HEARTS) s = "Hearts";
        else if (suit == SPADES) s = "Spades";
```

153

```
        else /* suit == CLUBS */ s = "Clubs";
        return v + " of " + s;
    }

    private int value;
    private int suit;
}
```

Please note that if you look in the Chapter 4 directory, you can see that this is the first sample program we distributed with two source files. To compile this program, you have two choices:

1. You can invoke the Java compiler with a wildcard:

    ```
    javac Card*.java
    ```

Then, all source files will be compiled into class files. Or

2. You can simply type

    ```
    javac CardDeck.java
    ```

You may find it surprising that the second choice works since the `Card.java` file is never explicitly compiled. However, when the Java compiler sees the `Card` class being used inside `CardDeck.java`, it will look for a `Card.class` file. If it does not find that file, it automatically searches for `Card.java` (using the class path to determine the potential source directories) and then compiles it. Even more is true: if the time stamp of the version of `Card.java` that it finds is newer than that of the existing `Card.class` file, the Java compiler will *automatically* recompile the file.

In general then, the Java compiler always compiles the class files of the classes it needs to translate the source files that you specify on the command line.

NOTE: If you are familiar with the "make" facility of Unix (or one of its Windows cousins such as "nmake"), then you can think of the Java compiler as having the "make" functionality already built in.

Packages

Java allows you to group classes in a collection called a *package*. Packages are convenient for organizing your work and for separating your work from code libraries provided by others.

For example, we give you what we think of as a number of useful classes in a package we called `corejava`. The standard Java library is distributed over a number of packages, including `java.lang`, `java.util`, `java.net`, and so on. The standard Java packages are examples of a hierarchical package. Just as you have nested subdirectories on your hard disk, you can organize packages by using levels of nesting. All standard Java packages are inside the `java` package hierarchy.

One reason for nesting packages is to guarantee the uniqueness of package names. If we supplied more utility classes with our packages, we could place them inside a package called `corejava.util`. That is better than simply naming the package `util`—someone else might have the same bright idea, causing a conflict. You can have as many levels of nesting as you like. In fact, to absolutely guarantee a unique package name, Sun recommends that you use your company's Internet domain name (which presumably is unique) written in reverse order as a package prefix. For example, `corebooks.com` is a domain that we registered, so we might have called the `corejava` package

```
com.corebooks.corejava
```

When you write a package, you must put the name of the package at the top of your source file, *before* the code that defines the classes in the package. For example, if you look into the `GregorianCalendar.java` file of the Java library, you will see the line:

```
package java.util;
```

This means that the `GregorianCalendar.java` file is part of the `java.util` package. The `package` statement must be the first statement in the file after any comments.

Thus, the files in our `corejava` package start like this:

```
package corejava;
```

If you don't put a `package` statement in the source file, then Java adds the classes in that source file to what is called the *default package*. The default package has no package path, but if the current directory `(.)` is part of the class path, then the classes with no package declaration in the current directory automatically become part of the default package. Excluding the files in the `corejava` package, our sample programs will always be located in the default package since they contain no package statement. To use them successfully, therefore, you must make sure that you have the ". " set in your class path. Obviously, for more complex projects, you should use packages to organize your code clearly.

Using Packages

You can use the public classes in a package in two ways. The first is simply to give the full name of the package. For example:

```
int i = corejava.Console.readInt();
java.util.GregorianCalendar today
    = new java.util.GregorianCalendar();
```

That is obviously tedious. The simpler, and more common, approach is to use the `import` keyword that we have been using with our `corejava` package in many of the examples you have already seen. The point of the `import` statement is simply to give you a shorthand to refer to the classes in the package. Once you use `import`, you no longer have to give the classes their full names.

You can import a specific class or the whole package. As you have seen with the examples that use our `corejava` package, you place the `import` statement before the source code of the class that will use it. For example:

```
import corejava.*; // imports all the classes in the
                   // corejava package
import java.util.*; //imports all the classes in the
                    // Java utility package
```

then you can use:

```
int i = Console.readInt();
GregorianCalendar today = new GregorianCalendar();
```

You can also import a specific class inside a package. To do this, adjust the `import` statement as in the following:

```
import corejava.Console; // imports only the Console class
import java.util.GregorianCalendar;
```

Normally, importing all classes in a package is simpler. It has no negative effect on compile time or code size, so there is generally no reason not to do it. However, if two packages each have classes with the same name, then you can't import them both.

Finally, you can only use the * to import a single package. You cannot use `import java.*` or `import java.*.*` to import all packages with the `java` prefix.

How the Compiler Locates Packages

How the designers of a compiler or IDE choose to organize source code is, unfortunately, completely up to the designers of the product. There are no standards. Some products (such as IBM's VisualAge family) choose to put all the files in a rather sophisticated database. However, the JDK compiler and most other Java compilers store packages in subdirectories of the file system or inside archives such as ZIP or JAR files. Note that all files in a package must be located in a subdirectory that matches the full package name. For example, all files in our `corejava` package must be in the subdirectory *named* `corejava`. All files in the `java.util` package are in a subdirectory `java\util` (`java/util` on Unix).

These subdirectories need not branch off directly from the root directory; they can branch off from any directory named in the class path. If you use the JDK with Windows or Unix, the class path is set by the CLASSPATH environment variable. Suppose your Windows CLASSPATH is as follows:

```
CLASSPATH=c:\CoreJavaBook;.
```

Suppose your code contains the lines:

```
import java.util.*;
import corejava.*;
```

Let's assume that the source file that uses the Console class has no package declaration so that it is in the default package. Then, if your code uses the Console class, the compiler first looks inside *all* files in the default package to see if any contain a class named Console. The file locations for the default package are determined by the class path, so there are three directories to search in our example. Thus, the Java compiler searches:

> all files in c:\CoreJavaBook
> all files in the current directory (.)

At this point, the compiler has exhausted the search through the classes in the current package (the default package). If it did not find a class named Console, then the compiler looks for a file named Console.class in one of the imported packages. It searches for the following files:

```
java\util\Console.class  inside c:\jdk\jre\lib\rt.jar
corejava\Console.class  inside c:\jdk\jre\lib\rt.jar
c:\CoreJavaBook\java\util\Console.class
c:\CoreJavaBook\corejava\Console.class
.\java\util\Console.class
.\corejava\Console.class
```

In other words, the Java compiler concatenates all possible directories listed in the class path with the file name Console.class. If it finds a matching file, it checks that the package name matches the path and that the file contains a public class named Console.

Finally, the compiler always searches the java.lang package. You never need to specify it, nor do you need to import it.

When you make a package, it is your responsibility to place the object files in the correct subdirectory. For example, if you compile a file that starts with the line

```
package acme.util;
```

then you must put the resulting class file into the subdirectory acme\util. The compiler won't do it for you.

C++ NOTE: C++ programmers usually confuse `import` with `#include`. The two have nothing in common. In C++, you must use `#include` to include the declarations of external features because the C++ compiler does not look inside any files except the one that it is compiling and explicitly included header files. The Java compiler will happily look inside other files provided you tell it where to look.

In Java, you can entirely avoid the `import` mechanism by explicitly naming all packages, such as `java.util.GregorianCalendar`. In C++, you cannot avoid the `#include` directives.

The only benefit of the `import` statement is convenience. You can refer to a class by a name shorter than the full package name. For example, after an `import java.util.*` (or `import java.util.GregorianCalendar`) statement, you can refer to the `java.util.GregorianCalendar` class simply as `GregorianCalendar`.

The analogous construction to the package mechanism in C++ is the *namespace* feature. Think of the `package` and `import` keywords in Java as the analogs of the `namespace` and `using` directives in C++.

Package Scope

We have already encountered the access modifiers `public` and `private`. Features tagged as `public` can be used by any class. Private features can only be used by the class that defines them. If you don't specify either `public` or `private`, then the feature (that is, the class, method, or variable) can be accessed by all methods in the same *package.*

NOTE: Every source file can contain, at most, one public class, which must have the same name as the file.

For example, if the class `Card` in the `CardDeck` example you saw earlier was not defined as a public class, then only other classes in the same package—the default package in this case—such as `CardDeck` can access it. For classes, this is a reasonable default. However, for variables this default was an unfortunate choice. Variables now must explicitly be marked private or they will default to being package-visible. This, of course, breaks encapsulation. The problem when you don't make instance fields private by default is that it is awfully easy to forget to type the `private` keyword. Here is an example from the `Window` class in the `java.awt` package, which is part of the source code supplied with the JDK:

```
public class Window extends Container
{  String warningString;

   . . .
   private FocusManager focusMgr;
   private static int nameCounter = 0;

   . . .
}
```

In spite of having two programmers (whose names we won't mention to protect the guilty—you can look into the source file yourself) work on this file, the source code still omits the `private` modifier for the `warningString` variable. That means, the methods of all classes in the `java.awt` package can access this variable and set it to whatever they like (such as `"Trust me!"`). Actually, the only methods that do access this variable are in the `Window` class, so it would have been entirely appropriate to make the variable private. We suspect that the programmer typed the code in a hurry and simply forgot the `private` modifier.

Is this really a problem? Since no other class in the package took advantage of the privilege to access the `warningString` variable, no great harm was done. But in Java, packages are not closed entities. Anyone can add to any package. You can author a class `SetWarning` in a file that starts out with

```
package java.awt;
```

That class can access all items in the `java.awt` package that have package scope. In particular, you can write a static method

```
public class SetWarning
{   public static void trustMe(Window w)
    {   w.warningString = "Trust me!";
    }
}
```

Put the `SetWarning.class` file inside a subdirectory `java\awt` some-where onto the class path, and you have gained access to the internals of the `java.awt` package. You can easily use that access to set the warning border (see Figure 4–10).

Fig. 4–10: Changing the warning string in an applet window

Actually, the security manager watches for additions to the system packages (such as `java.awt`), so if you try this in an applet that is loaded from the

Internet, the security manager will refuse to load the class. But your own packages do not enjoy the same protection by the security manager, so you should be very careful to avoid variables with package visibility in your own code.

Class Design Hints

Without trying to be comprehensive or tedious, we want to end this chapter with some hints that may make your classes more acceptable in well-mannered OOP circles.

1. *Always keep data private.*

   This is first and foremost: doing anything else violates encapsulation. You may need to write an accessor or mutator method occasionally, but you are still better off keeping the instance fields private. Bitter experience has shown that how the data are represented may change, but how they are used will change much less frequently. When data are kept private, changes in their representation do not affect the user of the class, and bugs are easier to detect.

2. *Always initialize data.*

   Java won't initialize local variables for you, but it will initialize instance variables of objects. Don't rely on the defaults, but initialize the variables explicitly, either by supplying a default or by setting defaults in all constructors.

3. *Don't use too many basic types in a class.*

   The idea is to replace multiple *related* uses of basic types with other classes. This keeps your classes easier to understand and to change. For example, replace the following instance fields in a Customer class

   ```
   private String street;
   private String city;
   private String state;
   private int zip;
   ```

   with a new class called Address. This way, you can easily cope with changes to addresses, such as the need to deal with international addresses.

4. *Not all fields need individual field accessors and mutators.*

   You may need to get and set a person's salary. You certainly won't need to change his or her hiring date once the object is constructed. And, quite often, objects have instance variables that you don't want others to get or set, for example, the array of cards in the card deck.

5. *Use a standard form for class definitions.*

We always list the contents of classes in the following order:

> public features
> package scope features
> private features

Within each section, we list:

> constants
> constructors
> methods
> static methods
> instance variables
> static variables

After all, the users of your class are more interested in the public interface than in the details of the private implementation. And they are more interested in methods than in data.

Whether you use this order or not, the most important thing is to be consistent.

6. *Break up classes with too many responsibilities.*

This hint is, of course, vague: "too many" is obviously in the eye of the beholder. However, if there is an obvious way to make one complicated class into two classes that are conceptually simpler, seize the opportunity. (On the other hand, don't go overboard; 10 classes, each with only one method, is usually overkill.)

Here is an example of a bad design. In our card game, we could do without the Card class by having the deck store two arrays: one for the suits and one for the values. That would make it hard to draw and return a card, so we would need to fake it with functions that can look up the properties of the top card on the deck.

```
class CardDeck // bad design
{   public CardDeck() {  .  .  .  }
    public void shuffle() {  .  .  .  }
    public int getTopValue() {  .  .  .  }
    public int getTopSuit() {  .  .  .  }
    public int topRank() {  .  .  .  }
    public void draw() {  .  .  .  }

    private int[] value;
    private int[] suit;
    private int cards;
}
```

As you can see, this is implementable, but it is clumsy. It makes sense to introduce the `Card` class because the cards are meaningful objects in this context.

7. *Make the names of your classes and methods reflect their responsibilities.*

    Just as variables should have meaningful names that reflect what they represent, so should classes. (The standard library certainly contains some dubious examples, such as the `Date` class that describes time.)

    A good convention is that a class name should be a noun (`Order`) or a noun preceded by an adjective (`RushOrder`) or a gerund (an "ing" word—`BillingAddress`). As for methods, follow the standard convention that accessor methods begin with a lowercase `get` (`getDay`), and mutator methods use a lowercase `set` (`setSalary`). The implementors of Java 1.1 actually made a concerted effort to improve the method names from Java 1.0, so that now most of the accessor methods begin with `get` and most of the mutator methods begin with `set`.

Chapter 5

Inheritance

The last chapter introduced OOP. This chapter explains most of the remaining OOP concepts that you'll need to know. In particular we'll concentrate in this chapter on the techniques needed to derive new classes from existing classes. This concept, introduced in the last chapter, is usually called *inheritance*.

Recall that the idea behind inheritance is that you can reuse or change the methods of existing classes, as well as add new instance fields and new methods in order to adapt them to new situations. This technique is essential in Java programming. (For example, as you will see in Chapter 7, you cannot even show text or graphics in a window without using inheritance!)

As with the previous chapter, if you are coming from a procedure-oriented language like C or COBOL, you will want to read this chapter carefully. The same holds true for *all* users of VB (even those using the latest version of VB—the more limited object model used in VB does not have inheritance).

For experienced C++ programmers or those coming from another object-oriented language like Smalltalk, this chapter will seem largely familiar, but there are *many* differences between how inheritance is implemented in Java and how it is done in C++ or in other object-oriented languages. You will probably want to read the later sections of this chapter carefully.

First Steps with Inheritance

Let's return to the `Employee` class that we discussed in the previous chapter. Suppose (alas) you work for a company at which managers are treated substantially differently than other employees. Their raises are computed differently; they have access to a secretary; and so on. This is the kind of situation that in OOP cries out for inheritance. Why? Well, you need to define a new class, `Manager`, and add functionality. But you can retain some of what you have already programmed in the `Employee` class, and *all* the instance fields of the original class can be preserved. More abstractly, there is an obvious "is–a" relationship between `Manager` and `Employee`. Every manager *is an* employee: this "is–a" relationship is the hallmark of inheritance.

Here is some code for extending the `Employee` class to be a `Manager` class.

```
class Manager extends Employee
{  public Manager(String n, double s, Day d)
   {  super(n, s, d);
      secretaryName = "";
   }

   public void raiseSalary(double byPercent)
   {  // add 1/2% bonus for every year of service
      Day today = new Day();
      double bonus = 0.5 * (today.getYear() - hireYear());
      super.raiseSalary(byPercent + bonus);
   }

   public String getSecretaryName()
   {  return secretaryName;
   }

   public void setSecretaryName(String name)
   {  secretaryName = name;
   }

   private String secretaryName;
}
```

Let's go over the new features of this class, line by line. First, notice that the header for this class is a little different:

```
class Manager extends Employee
```

The keyword `extends` indicates that you are making a new class that derives from an existing class. The existing class is called the *superclass*, *base class*, or parent class. The new class is called the *subclass, derived class,* or *child class.* The terms superclass and subclass are those most commonly used by Java programmers, although we prefer the parent/child analogy, which also ties in nicely with the "inheritance" theme.

The Employee class is a superclass, but not because it is superior to its subclass or contains more functionality. *In fact, the opposite is true:* subclasses have *more* functionality than their superclasses. For example, as you will see when we go over the rest of the Manager class code, the Manager class encapsulates more data and has more functionality than its superclass Employee. As another example, as you will see when we cover user interface programming in Java, Java has a superclass JComponent, which is extended to many useful subclasses, such as the JDialog class that can be used to create dialog boxes or the JTextField class for text input fields.

NOTE: The prefixes *super* and *sub* come from the language of sets used in theoretical computer science and mathematics. The set of all employees *contains* the set of all managers, and this is described by saying it is a *superset* of the set of managers. Similarly, the set of all file dialog windows is *contained* by the set of all windows, so it is a *subset* of the set of all windows.

Next, notice the constructor for the Manager class:

```
public Manager(String n, double s, Day d)
{   super(n, s, d);
    secretaryName = "";
}
```

The keyword super always refers to the superclass (in this case, Employee). So the line

```
super(n, s, d);
```

is shorthand for "call the constructor of the Employee class with n, s, and d as parameters." The reason for this line is that every constructor of a subclass must also invoke a constructor for the data fields of the superclass. If the subclass constructor does not call a superclass constructor explicitly, then the superclass uses its default (no-argument) constructor. If the superclass has no default constructor and the subclass constructor does not call another superclass constructor explicitly, then the Java compiler reports an error. Unless the subclass constructor is happy with the default constructor of the superclass, it must explicitly use the super keyword with the appropriate parameters so as to call the constructor it wants. Finally, the Java compiler insists that the call using super must be the first statement in the constructor for the subclass.

Next, as this example shows, subclasses can have more instance fields than the parent class. Following good programming practices, we set the secretaryName instance field to the empty string in order to initialize it. (By default, it would have been initialized to null.)

If you compare the Manager class with the Employee class, you will see that many of the methods in the Employee class are not repeated in the Manager class. This is because, unless otherwise specified, a subclass always uses the methods of the superclass. In particular, when building the subclass by inheriting from the superclass, you only need to indicate the *differences* between the subclass and superclass. The ability to reuse methods in the superclass is automatic. In our situation for example, we do not need to give a new definition of the getName method, since the one in the superclass does what we need. This *factoring* out of common functionality by moving it to a superclass is essential to the proper use of inheritance in object-oriented programming.

However, do note that we are giving a new definition of the raiseSalary method:

```
public void raiseSalary(double byPercent)
{   // add 1/2% bonus for every year of service
    Day today = new Day();
    double bonus = 0.5 * (today.getYear() - hireYear());
    super.raiseSalary(byPercent + bonus);
}
```

because, as we mentioned previously, we want this method to work differently for managers and (ordinary) employees.

The need to redefine methods is one of the main reasons to use inheritance; this is a good example. Life being the way it is, raises for managers are calculated differently than those for nonmanagers. In this case, suppose you give a company-wide raise of five percent. For managers, the raiseSalary method, however, does the following:

1. It calculates a bonus percentage increase based on time employed.

2. Then, because of the use of super in the line

    ```
    super.raiseSalary(byPercent + bonus);
    ```

    the method looks to the raiseSalary method of the superclass and passes it a parameter that adds the original parameter and a bonus of half a percent for each year the managers have been employed since they were hired.

Next, notice that the raiseSalary method of the Manager class *has no direct access to the private instance fields of the superclass.* This means that the raiseSalary method of the Manager class cannot directly change the salary field, even though every Manager object has a salary field. Only the methods of the Employee class have access to the private instance fields. If the Manager methods want to access those private instance fields, they have to do what every other method does—use the public interface of the superclass, in this case, the public raiseSalary method of the Employee class.

The result of our redefining the raiseSalary method for Manager objects in this way is that when you give all employees a raise of five percent, managers will *automatically* be given a larger raise.

Here's an example of this at work: we make a new manager and set the manager's secretary's name:

```
Manager boss = new Manager("Carl Cracker", 75000,
    new Day(1987,12,15));
boss.setSecretaryName("Harry Hacker");
```

We make an array of three employees:

```
Employee[] staff = new Employee[3];
```

We populate the array with a mix of employees and managers:

```
staff[0] = boss;
staff[1] = new Employee("Harry Hacker", 35000,
    new Day(1989,10,1));
staff[2] = new Employee("Tony Tester", 38000,
    new Day(1990,3,15));
```

We raise everyone's salary by five percent:

```
for (i = 0; i < 3; i++) staff[i].raiseSalary(5);
```

Now staff[1] and staff[2] each get a raise of five percent because they are Employee objects. However, staff[0] is a Manager object and gets a higher raise. Finally, let's print out all employee records and the name of the secretary.

```
for (i = 0; i < 3; i++) staff[i].print();
System.out.println("The department secretary is "
    + boss.getSecretaryName());
```

Because we didn't define a special print method for managers, all three objects are printed with the Employee print method. (We could have changed the print method in the Manager class in order to print out the current name of a manager's secretary.) Example 5–1 shows you how objects of the subclass Manager can be used in place of objects of the superclass Employee.

Example 5–1: ManagerTest.java

```
import java.util.*;
import corejava.*;

public class ManagerTest
{  public static void main(String[] args)
   {  Manager boss = new Manager("Carl Cracker", 75000,
      new Day(1987,12,15));

      boss.setSecretaryName("Harry Hacker");

      Employee[] staff = new Employee[3];
```

```
        staff[0] = boss;
        staff[1] = new Employee("Harry Hacker", 35000,
            new Day(1989,10,1));
        staff[2] = new Employee("Tony Tester", 38000,
            new Day(1990,3,15));

        int i;
        for (i = 0; i < 3; i++) staff[i].raiseSalary(5);
        for (i = 0; i < 3; i++) staff[i].print();
        System.out.println("The department secretary is "
            + boss.getSecretaryName());
    }
}

class Employee
{   public Employee(String n, double s, Day d)
    {   name = n;
        salary = s;
        hireDay = d;
    }

    public void print()
    {   System.out.println(name + " " + salary + " "
            + hireYear());
    }

    public void raiseSalary(double byPercent)
    {   salary *= 1 + byPercent / 100;
    }

    public int hireYear()
    {   return hireDay.getYear();
    }

    private String name;
    private double salary;
    private Day hireDay;
}

class Manager extends Employee
{   public Manager(String n, double s, Day d)
    {   super(n, s, d);
        secretaryName = "";
    }

    public void raiseSalary(double byPercent)
    {   // add 1/2% bonus for every year of service
        Day today = new Day();
        double bonus = 0.5 * (today.getYear() - hireYear());
        super.raiseSalary(byPercent + bonus);
    }

    public void setSecretaryName(String n)
```

```
{   secretaryName = n;
}

public String getSecretaryName()
{   return secretaryName;
}

private String secretaryName;
}
```

C++ NOTE: Inheritance is similar in Java and C++. Java uses the `extends` keyword instead of the `":"` token. All inheritance in Java is public inheritance; there is no analog to the C++ features of private and protected inheritance.

Java uses the keyword `super` to refer to the base class. In C++, you would use the name of the base class with the `::` operator instead. For example, the `raiseSalary` function of the `Manager` class would call `Employee::raiseSalary` instead of `super.raiseSalary`. In a C++ constructor, you do not call `super`, but you use the initializer list syntax to construct the base class. The `Manager` constructor looks like this in C++:

```
Manager::Manager(String n, double s, Day d) // C++
: Employee(n, s, d)
{
}
```

Inheritance Hierarchies

Inheritance need not stop at deriving one layer of classes. We could have an `Executive` class that derives from `Manager`, for example. The collection of all classes extending from a common parent is called an *inheritance hierarchy,* as shown in Figure 5–1. The path from a particular class to its ancestors in the inheritance hierarchy is its *inheritance chain.*

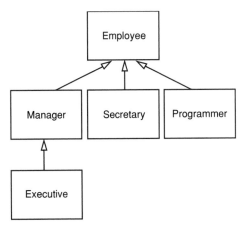

Figure 5–1: Employee inheritance hierarchy

There is usually more than one chain of descent from a distant ancestor class. You could derive a `Programmer` class from `Employee` class or a `Secretary` class from `Employee`, and they would have nothing to do with the `Manager` class (or with each other). This process can continue as long as is necessary.

Working with Subclasses

One way to know whether or not inheritance is right for your program is to keep in mind that any object that is an instance of a subclass must be useable in place of an object that is an instance of the superclass. If this is not true, do not use inheritance. (This is a more concrete way of thinking of the "is–a" relationship that is the hallmark of inheritance.) In particular, subclass objects are useable in any code that uses the superclass.

For example, you can assign a subclass object to a superclass variable.

```
Employee[] staff = new Employee[3];
Manager boss = new Manager("Carl Cracker", 75000,
   new Day(1987,12,15));
staff[0] = boss;
```

In this case, the variables `staff[0]` and `boss` refer to the same area of memory. However, `staff[0]` is considered to be only an `Employee` object by the compiler.

Similarly, a subclass object can be passed as an argument to any method that expects a superclass parameter.

The converse is false in general: a superclass object cannot usually be assigned to a subclass object. For example, it is not legal to make the assignment:

```
boss = staff[i]; // ERROR
```

The reason is clear: the subclass object may have more fields than the superclass object (as it does in this case), and the subclass methods have to be able to access those fields. If the fields are not accessible, run-time errors will result. Always keep in mind that because fields can only be added, not taken away, in inheritance subclass objects have at least as many data fields as superclass objects.

C++ NOTE: Java does not support multiple inheritance. (For ways to recover much of the functionality of multiple inheritance, see the section on Interfaces in the next chapter.)

Objects Know How to Do Their Work: Polymorphism

It is important to understand what happens when a method call is applied to objects of various types in an inheritance hierarchy. Remember that in OOP, you are sending messages to objects, asking them to perform actions. When you send a message that asks a subclass to apply a method using certain parameters, here is what happens:

- The subclass checks whether or not it has a method with that name and with *exactly* the same parameters. If so, it uses it.

If not,

- the parent class becomes responsible for handling the message and looks for a method with that name and those parameters. If so, it calls that method.

Since the message handling can continue moving up the inheritance chain, parent classes are checked until the chain of inheritance stops or until a matching method is found. (If there is no matching method anywhere in the inheritance chain, you get a compile-time error.) Notice that methods with the same name can exist on many levels of the chain. This leads to one of the fundamental rules of inheritance:

- A method defined in a subclass with the same name and parameter list as a method in one of its ancestor classes hides the method of the ancestor class from the subclass.

For example, the `raiseSalary` method of the `Manager` class is called instead of the `raiseSalary` method of the `Employee` class when you send a `raiseSalary` message to a `Manager` object.

NOTE: The name and parameter list for a method is usually called the method's *signature*. For example, `raiseSalary(double)` and `raiseSalary(boolean)` are two methods with the same name but different signatures. However, the return type is not part of the signature. In Java, having methods in a class or in a superclass and a subclass with the same signature but differing return types will give you a compile-time error. For instance, you cannot have a method `void raiseSalary(double)` in the `Employee` class and a method `int raiseSalary(double)` in the `Manager` class.

An object's ability to decide what method to apply to itself, depending on where it is in the inheritance hierarchy, is usually called *polymorphism*. The idea behind polymorphism is that while the message may be the same, objects may respond differently. Polymorphism can apply to any method that is inherited from a superclass.

The key to making polymorphism work is called *late binding*. This means that the compiler does not generate the code to call a method at compile time. Instead, every time you apply a method to an object, the compiler generates code to calculate which method to call, using type information from the object.

(This process is also called *dynamic binding* or *dynamic dispatch*.) The traditional method call mechanism is called *static binding,* since the operation to be executed is completely determined at compile time. Static binding depends on the type of the object variable alone; dynamic binding depends on the type of the actual object at run-time.

> NOTE: Many Java users follow C++ terminology and refer to functions that are dynamically bound as *virtual functions.*

> C++ NOTE: In Java, you do not need to declare a method as virtual. This is the default behavior. If you do *not* want a function to be virtual, you tag it as `final`. (We discuss this in the next section.)

To sum up, inheritance and polymorphism let the application spell out the general way to proceed. The individual classes in the inheritance hierarchy are responsible for carrying out the details—using polymorphism to determine which methods to call. Polymorphism in an inheritance hierarchy is sometimes called *true polymorphism.* The idea is to distinguish it from the more limited kind of name overloading that is not resolved dynamically but is resolved statically at compile time.

Preventing Inheritance: Final Classes and Methods

Occasionally, you want to prevent someone from deriving a class from one of your classes. Classes that cannot be parent classes are called `final` classes, and you use the `final` modifier in the definition of the class to indicate this. For example, let us suppose we want to prevent others from subclassing the `Card` class from the last chapter. Then, we simply declare the class using the `final` modifier as follows:

```
final class Card
{  . . .
}
```

You can also make a specific method in a class `final`. If you do this, then no subclass can override that method. (All methods in a `final` class are automatically `final`.) You will want to make a class or method `final` for one of two reasons:

1. Efficiency

    Dynamic binding has more overhead than static binding—thus, virtual methods run slower. The dynamic dispatching mechanism is slightly less efficient than a straight procedure call. More importantly, the compiler cannot replace a trivial method with inline code because it is possible that a derived class would override that trivial code. The compiler can put `final` methods inline. For example, if `e.getName()` is `final`, the compiler can replace it with `e.name`. (So, you get all the benefits of direct access to instance fields *without violating encapsulation*.)

Microprocessors hate procedure calls because procedure calls interfere with their strategy of getting and decoding the next instructions while processing the current one. Replacing calls to trivial procedures with inline code is a big win. This is more important for a true compiler than for a bytecode interpreter, but just-in-time compilers can take advantage of this, and true Java compilers for all platforms are in the works.

2. Safety

The flexibility of the dynamic dispatch mechanism means that you have no control over what happens when you call a method. When you send a message, such as `e.getName()`, it is possible that `e` is an object of a derived class that redefined the `getName` method to return an entirely different string. By making the method `final`, you avoid this possible ambiguity.

Since it is reasonable to assume that nobody would derive a new class from the `Card` class, it makes sense to declare it `final` for efficiency reasons. The `String` class in the Java library is `final` probably for the same reasons.

C++ NOTE: In C++, a member function is not virtual by default, and you can tag it as inline in order to have function calls replaced with the function source code. However, there is no mechanism that would prevent a derived class from overriding a member function. In C++, it is possible to write classes from which no other class can derive, but it requires an obscure trick, and there are few reasons to do so.

Casting

Recall from Chapter 3 that the process of converting from one basic type to another was called casting and Java has a special notation for casts. For example:

```
double x = 3.405;
int nx = (int)x;
```

converts the variable `x` into an integer, discarding the fractional part.

Just as you occasionally need to convert a floating-point number to an integer, you also need to convert an object reference from one class to another. As with converting basic types, this process is also called *casting*. To actually make a cast, you use a syntax similar to what you used for casting between variables of the basic types. Surround the target type with parentheses and place it before the object reference you want to cast. For example:

```
Manager boss = (Manager)staff[0];
```

There is only one reason why you would want to make a cast—to use an object in its full capacity after its actual type has been downplayed. For example, in the Manager class, the staff array had to be an array of Employee objects since *some* of its entries were regular employees. We would need to cast the managerial elements of the array back to Manager in order to access any of its new fields. (Note that in the sample code for the first section, we made a special effort to avoid the cast. We initialized the boss variable with a Manager object before storing it in the array. We needed the correct type in order to set the secretary of the manager.)

As you know, in Java, every object variable has a type. The type describes the kind of object the variable refers to and what it can do. For example, staff[i] refers to an Employee object (so it can also refer to a Manager object).

You rely on these descriptions in your code, and the compiler checks that you do not promise too much when you describe a variable. If you assign a subclass object to a superclass variable, you are promising less, and the compiler will simply let you do it. If you assign a superclass object to a subclass variable, you are promising more, and you must confirm that you mean what you say to the compiler with the (Subclass) cast notation.

What happens if you try to cast down an inheritance chain and you are "lying" about what an object contains?

```
Manager boss = (Manager)staff[1]; // Error
```

When the program runs, the Java run-time system notices the broken promise, generates an exception (see the sidebar later on in this chapter and Chapter 11), and the program will usually die. It is good programming practice to find out whether or not your object is an instance of another class before doing a cast. This is accomplished with the instanceof operator. For example:

```
if (staff[1] instanceof Manager)
{  boss = (Manager)staff[1];
    . . .
}
```

Finally, the compiler will not let you make a cast if there is no chance for the cast to succeed. For example, the cast

```
Window w = (Window)staff[1];
```

is a compile-time error because Window is not a subclass of Employee.

To sum up:

- You can cast only within an inheritance hierarchy.

- Use `instanceof` to check a hierarchy before casting from a parent to a child class.

Actually, converting the type of an object by performing a cast is not usually a good idea. In our example, you do not need to cast an `Employee` object to a `Manager` object for most purposes. The `raiseSalary` method will work correctly on both types because the dynamic binding that makes polymorphism work locates the correct method automatically.

The only reason to make the cast is to use a method that is unique to managers, such as `getSecretaryName`. If it is important to get the name of a secretary for an object of type `Employee`, you could redesign that class and add a `getSecretaryName` method, which simply returns an empty string. This makes more sense than trying to remember which array locations stored which type or making tedious type inquiries. Remember, it takes only one bad cast to terminate your program. In general, it is best to minimize the use of the `instanceof` operator.

Casts are commonly used with containers such as the `Vector` class, which will be introduced later in this chapter. When retrieving a value from a container, its type is only known as the generic type `Object`, and you must use a cast to cast it back to the type of the object that you inserted into the container.

C++ NOTE: Java uses the cast syntax from the "bad old days" of C, but it works like the safe `dynamic_cast` operation of C++. For example,

```
Manager boss = (Manager)staff[1]; // Java
```

is the same as

```
Manager* boss = dynamic_cast<Manager*>(staff[1]); // C++
```

with one important difference. If the cast fails, it does not yield a `null` object, but throws an exception. In this sense, it is like a C++ cast of *references*. This is a pain in the neck. In C++, you can take care of the type test and type conversion in one operation.

```
Manager* boss = dynamic_cast<Manager*>(staff[1]); // C++
if (boss != NULL) . . .
```

In Java, you use a combination of the `instanceof` operator and a cast.

```
if (staff[1] instanceof Manager)
{   Manager boss = (Manager)staff[1];
    . . .
}
```

Abstract Classes

As you move up the inheritance hierarchy, classes become more general and probably more abstract. At some point, the ancestor class becomes *so* general that you think of it more as a framework for other classes than as a class with specific instances you want to use. Consider, for example, an electronic messaging system that integrates your e-mail, faxes, and voice mail. It must be able to handle text messages, fax messages, and voice messages.

Following the principles of OOP, the program will need classes called `TextMessage`, `VoiceMessage`, and `FaxMessage`. Of course, a mailbox needs to store a mixture of these messages types, so it will access them through references to the common parent class `Message`. The inheritance hierarchy is shown in Figure 5–2.

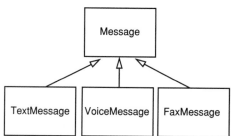

Figure 5–2: Inheritance diagram for message classes

Why bother with so high a level of abstraction? The answer is that it makes the design of your classes cleaner. (Well, it does once you are familiar with OOP.) Ultimately, one of the keys to OOP is to understand how to factor out common operations to a higher level in the inheritance hierarchy. In our case, all messages have a common method, namely, `play()`. It is easy to figure out how to play a voice message—you send it to the loudspeaker. You play a text message by showing it in a text window and a fax message by showing it in a graphics window. But how do you implement `play()` in the parent class `Message`?

The answer is that you can't. In Java, you use the `abstract` keyword to indicate that a method cannot be specified in this class. For added clarity, a class with one or more abstract methods must itself be declared abstract.

```
public abstract class Message
{  . . .
   public abstract void play();
}
```

In addition to abstract methods, abstract classes can have concrete data and methods. For example, the `Message` class can store the sender of the mail message and have a concrete method that returns the sender's name.

```
abstract class Message
{   public Message(String from) { sender = from; }

    public abstract void play();
    public String getSender() { return sender; }

    private String sender;
}
```

An abstract method promises that all nonabstract descendants of this abstract class will implement that abstract method. Abstract methods act as placeholder methods that are implemented in the subclasses.

A class can even be declared as `abstract` even though it has no abstract methods.

Abstract classes cannot be instantiated. That is, if a class is declared as `abstract`, no objects of that class can be created. You will have to extend that class in order to create an instance of the class. Note that you can still create *object variables* of an abstract class, but these variables must refer to an object of a nonabstract subclass. For example,

```
Message msg = new VoiceMessage("greeting.au");
```

Here `msg` is a variable of the abstract type `Message` that refers to an instance of the nonabstract subclass `VoiceMessage`.

TIP: While it is common to think that abstract classes should have only abstract methods, this is not true. It always makes sense to move as much functionality as possible into a superclass, whether or not it is abstract. In particular, move common instance fields and *nonabstract* operations to the abstract superclass. Only those operations that cannot be implemented in the superclass should be given to the subclasses. For example, the designers of many of the GUI classes in Java use this technique.

C++ NOTE: In C++, an abstract method is called a *pure virtual function* and is tagged with a trailing = 0 , such as in

```
class Message // C++
{   public:virtual void play() = 0;

    . . .
}
```

A C++ class is abstract if it has at least one pure virtual function. In C++, there is no special keyword to denote abstract classes.

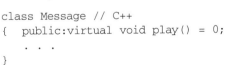

To see a concrete realization of this abstract class and also of the play method, try this code for the TextMessage class:

```
class TextMessage extends Message
{   public TextMessage(String from, String t)
    {  super(from); text = t;  }

    public void play() {  System.out.println(text);  }

    private String text;
}
```

Notice that we need only give a concrete definition of the abstract play method in the TextMessage class.

Here's the code for the sample messaging program. Don't worry too much about the code for playing the wave file in this example; it uses a few language features, such as exceptions and streams, that we will discuss in Chapters 11 and 12. This is a teaching example, so we kept the user interface simple and ugly to allow you to focus on the OOP aspects instead of being distracted by GUI code. When you run the program, you can leave a text message by typing it in or leave a voice message by typing in the name of an audio file. We supply you with two sample audio files on the CD, or you can use your own. They must be in .au format. Example 5–2 shows the code.

Example 5–2: MailboxTest.java

```
import java.net.*;
import java.applet.*;
import corejava.*;

public class MailboxTest
{   public static void main(String[] args)
    {   Mailbox mbox = new Mailbox();
        while (true)
        {   System.out.println(mbox.status());
            String cmd = Console.readLine
                    ("play, text, voice, quit> ");
            if (cmd.equals("play"))
            {   Message m = mbox.remove();
                if (m != null)
                {   System.out.println("From: " + m.getSender());
                    m.play();
                }
            }
            else if (cmd.equals("text"))
            {   String from = Console.readLine("Your name: ");
                boolean more = true;
```

```
            String msg = "";
            System.out.println
               ("Enter message, 'exit' when done");

            while (more)
            {  String line = Console.readLine();
               if (line.equals("exit"))
                  more = false;
               else msg = msg + line + "\n";
            }
            mbox.insert(new TextMessage(from, msg));
         }
         else if (cmd.equals("voice"))
         {  String from = Console.readLine("Your name: ");
            String msg
               = Console.readLine("Audio file name: ");
            mbox.insert(new VoiceMessage(from, msg));
         }
         else if (cmd.equals("quit"))
            System.exit(0);
      }
   }
}


abstract class Message
{  public Message(String from) { sender = from; }

   public abstract void play();
   public String getSender() { return sender; }

   private String sender;
}

class TextMessage extends Message
{  public TextMessage(String from, String t)
   { super(from); text = t; }

   public void play() { System.out.println(text); }

   private String text;
}

class VoiceMessage extends Message
{  public VoiceMessage(String from, String f)
   { super(from); filename = f; }

   public void play()
```

```
{   try
    {   URL u = new URL("file", "localhost", filename);
        AudioClip clip = Applet.newAudioClip(u);
        clip.play();
    }
    catch(Exception e)
    {
        System.out.println("Can't open " + filename);
    }
}

    private String filename;
}


class Mailbox
{   public Message remove()
    {   if (nmsg == 0) return null;
        Message r = messages[out];
        nmsg--;
        out = (out + 1) % MAXMSG;
        return r;
    }

    public void insert(Message m)
    {   if (nmsg == MAXMSG) return;
        messages[in] = m;
        nmsg++;
        in = (in + 1) % MAXMSG;
    }

    public String status()
    {   if (nmsg == 0) return "Mailbox empty";
        else if (nmsg == 1) return "1 message";
        else if (nmsg < MAXMSG) return nmsg + " messages";
        else return "Mailbox full";
    }

    private static final int MAXMSG = 10;
    private int in = 0;
    private int out = 0;
    private int nmsg = 0;
    private Message[] messages = new Message[MAXMSG];
}
```

Catching Exceptions

We will cover exception handling fully in Chapter 11, but once in a while you will encounter code that involves exceptions. Here is a quick introduction on what exceptions are and how to handle them.

When an error occurs at run time, a Java program can "throw an exception." For example, code that attempts to open a file can throw an exception if the file unexpectedly cannot be opened. Throwing an exception is less violent and less fatal than terminating the program because it provides the option of "catching" the exception and dealing with it.

If an exception is not caught anywhere, the program will terminate and a message will be printed to the console, giving the type of the exception.

Without going into too much detail, here is the basic syntax. To run code that might throw an exception, you have to place it inside a "try" block. Then, you have to provide an emergency action to deal with the exception, in the unlikely case that one actually occurs.

```
try
{   code that might
    throw exceptions
}   catch(ExceptionType e)
{   emergency action
}
```

We used that mechanism in the code that plays an audio clip.

```
try
{   URL u = new URL("file", "localhost", filename);
    AudioClip clip = Applet.newAudioClip(u);
    clip.play();
}
catch(Exception e)
{
    System.out.println("Can't open " + filename);
}
```

The above says, in effect, "Do not end the program if you encounter an error condition—just display an error message and do not play the clip."

The compiler is somewhat selective as to which exceptions *must* be handled (see Chapter 12). For example, when you access an array or perform a cast, you need not supply an exception handler, even though the array index or the cast might be invalid, causing the code to throw an exception. However, for other operations, such as input and output, you must specify what you want to happen when there is a problem.

C++ NOTE: The Java and C++ exception mechanisms are similar. Chapter 11 explains the differences.

Protected Access

As you know, instance fields in a class are best tagged as `private`, and methods are usually tagged as `public`. Any features declared `private` won't be visible to other classes. As we said at the beginning of this chapter, this is also true for subclasses: a subclass cannot access the private data members of its superclass.

There are, however, times when you want a subclass to have access to a method or to data from a parent class. In that case, you declare that feature as `protected`. For example, if the base class `Employee` declares the `hireDay` object as `protected` instead of `private`, then the `Manager` methods can access it directly.

In practice, use the `protected` attribute with caution. Suppose your class is used by other programmers and you designed it with protected data. Unbeknownst to you, other programmers may derive classes from your class and then start accessing your protected instance fields. In this case, you can no longer change the implementation of your class without upsetting the other programmers. That is against the spirit of OOP, which encourages data encapsulation.

Protected methods make more sense. A class may declare a method as `protected` if it is tricky to use. This indicates that the subclasses (which, presumably, know their ancestors well) can be trusted to use the method correctly, but other classes cannot. (For a good example of this kind of method, please see the section on "Cloning" in Chapter 6.)

C++ NOTE: As it happens, `protected` features in Java are visible to all subclasses as well as all other classes in the same package. This is slightly different from the C++ meaning of `protected`.

Here is a summary of the four access modifiers in Java that control visibility:

1. Visible to the class only (`private`)
2. Visible to the world (`public`)
3. Visible to the package and all subclasses (`protected`)
4. Visible to the package (the default—no modifier needed)

`Object`: **The Cosmic Superclass**

The `Object` class is the ultimate ancestor—every class in Java extends `Object`. However, you never have to write:

```
class Employee extends Object
```

since the ultimate parent class `Object` is taken for granted if no parent is explicitly mentioned. Because *every* class in Java extends `Object`, it is important to be familiar with the services provided by the Object class. We will go over the basic ones in this chapter and refer you to later chapters or to the on-line documentation for what is not covered here. (Several methods of Object come up only when dealing with threads—see Volume 2 for more on threads.)

You can use a variable of type Object to refer to objects of any type:

```
Object obj = new Employee("Harry Hacker", 35000);
```

Of course, a variable of type Object is only useful as a generic holder for arbitrary values. To do anything specific with the value, you need to have some knowledge about the original type and then apply a cast:

```
Employee e = (Employee)obj;
```

C++ NOTE: In C++, there is no cosmic root class. Of course, in C++, every pointer can be converted to a void* pointer. Java programmers often use Object references for generic programming, to implement data structures and algorithms that support a variety of data types. In C++, templates are commonly used for generic programming. But Java has no templates, so Java programmers often have to give up compile-time typing and make do with code that manipulates Object references.

The equals method in Object tests whether or not one object is equal to another. The equals method, as it is implemented in the Object parent class, determines whether or not two objects point to the same area of memory. This is not a useful test. If you want to test objects for equality, you will need to override equals for a more meaningful comparison. For example,

```
class Employee
{  // . . .
    public boolean equals(Object obj)
    {   if (!(obj instanceof Employee))
            return false;
        Employee b = (Employee)obj;
        return name.equals(b.name)
            && salary == b.salary
            && hireDay.equals(b.hireDay);
    }
}
```

Another important method in Object is the toString method that returns a string that represents the value of this object. Almost any class will override this method in order to give you a printed representation of the object's current state. For example, the toString method of the Day class to give a string representation of the date.

The toString method is ubiquitous for an important reason: whenever an object is concatenated with a string, using the "+" operator, the Java compiler automatically invokes the `toString` method to obtain a string representation of the object. For example,

```
Day d = new Day(1999, 12, 31);
String last = "The last day of the millennium is " + d;
   // automatically invokes d.toString()
```

TIP: Instead of writing `x.toString()`, you can write `" " + x`. This concatenates the empty string with the string representation of `x` that is exactly `x.toString()`.

Finally, all values of any class type can be held in variables of type `Object`. In particular, `String` values are objects:

```
Object obj = "Hello"; // OK
```

However, numbers, characters, and **boolean** values are *not* objects.

```
obj = 5; // ERROR
obj = false; // ERROR
```

You will see later in this chapter how you can turn these types into objects by using *wrapper classes* such as `Integer` and `Boolean`.

Furthermore, all array types are class types that derive from `Object`.

```
Employee[] staff = new Employee[10];
Object arr = staff; // OK
arr = new int[10]; // OK
```

An array of objects of class type can be converted to an array of objects. For example, an `Employee[]` array can be passed to a function that expects an `Object[]` array. That conversion is useful for *generic programming*.

Here is a simple example that illustrates the concept of generic programming. Suppose you want to find the index of an element in an array. This is a generic situation, and by writing the code for objects, you can reuse it for employees, dates, or whatever.

```
static int find(Object[] a, Object key)
{  int i;
   for (i = 0; i < a.length; i++)
      if (a[i].equals(key)) return i;
   return -1; // not found
}
```

For example,

```
Employee[] staff = new Employee[10];
Employee harry;
. . .
int n = find(staff, harry);
```

Note that you can only convert an array of objects into an Object[] array. You cannot convert an int[] array into an Object[] array. (However, as previously pointed out, both can be converted to Object.)

If you convert an array of objects to an Object[] array, the generic array still remembers its original type at run time. You cannot store a foreign object into the array.

```
Employee[] staff = new Employee[10];
Object[] arr = staff;
arr[0] = new AudioClip();
    // not legal, but suppose it was
for (i = 0; i < n; i++) arr[i].raiseSalary(3);
    // ouch, now the audio clip gets a raise!
```

Of course, this must be checked at run time. The code above compiles without error—it is legal to store an AudioClip value in arr[0], which has type Object. But when the code executes, the array remembers its original type and it monitors the type of all objects that are stored in it. If you store an incompatible type into an array, an exception is thrown.

C++ NOTE: C++ programmers may be surprised that the cast from Employee[] to Object[] is legal. Even if Object was a base class of Employee in C++, the equivalent cast from Employee** to Object** would not be legal. (Of course, the cast from Employee* to Object* is legal in C++.)

There is a security reason behind this restriction. If the cast "Derived** → Base**" were permitted, you could corrupt the contents of an array. Consider this code:

```
Employee** staff; // C++
Object** arr = staff;
    // not legal, but suppose it was
arr[0] = new AudioClip();
    // legal, AudioClip also inherits from Object
for (i = 0; i < n; i++) arr[i]→raiseSalary(3);
    // ouch, now the audio clip gets a raise!
```

In Java, this problem is averted by remembering the original type of all arrays and by monitoring all array stores for type compatibility at run time.

`java.lang.Object`

• `Class getClass()`

returns a Class object that contains information about the object. As you will see later in this chapter, Java has a run-time representation for classes that is encapsulated in the Class class that you can often use to your advantage.

- `boolean equals(Object obj)`

  compares two objects for equality; returns `true` if the objects point to the same area of memory, and `false` otherwise.

- `Object clone()`

  creates a clone of the object. The Java run-time system allocates memory for the new instance and copies the memory allocated for the current object.

NOTE: Cloning an object is important, but it also turns out to be a fairly subtle process filled with potential pitfalls for the unwary. We will have a lot more to say about the `clone` method in Chapter 6.

- `String toString()`

  returns a string that represents the value of this object.

Vectors

In many programming languages—in particular in C—you have to fix the sizes of all arrays at compile time. Programmers hate this because it forces them into uncomfortable trade-offs. How many items will a customer order at one time? Surely no more than 10. What if one customer needs 15 items? Do we want to waste 14 entries if the majority of customers want only one item?

In Java, the situation is much better. You can set the size of an array at run time.

```
int n;
. . .
Item[] itemsOrdered = new Item[n + 1];
```

Of course, this code does not completely solve the problem of dynamically modifying arrays at run time. Once you set the array size, you cannot change it easily. Instead, the easiest way in Java to deal with this common situation is to use another Java object that works much like an array that will shrink and grow automatically. This object is called a *vector*. Thus, in Java, vectors are arraylike objects that can grow and shrink automatically without you needing to write any code.

NOTE: The name "vector" is a bit of a misnomer. Vectors in Java have nothing to do with the vectors used in mathematics and physics. (There, vectors are arrays of floating-point numbers, but their dimensions are fixed.)

VBNOTE: You can think of Java vectors as being analogous to using an unkeyed collection class in VB. Even the fact that collections hold variants and Vectors will hold Objects is similar.

There is an important difference between a vector and an array. Arrays are a feature of the Java language, and there is an array type T[] for each element type T. However, the Vector class is a library class, defined in the java.util package, and there is a single "one size fits all" type Vector which holds elements of type Object. In particular, you will need a cast whenever you want to take an item out of a vector.

You make a new vector by specifying its initial *capacity* in the Vector constructor.

```
Vector itemsOrdered = new Vector(3);
    // start out with space for one order item,
    // plus two items for tax and shipping charges
```

There is an important distinction between the capacity of a vector and the size of an array. If you allocate an array with three entries, then the array has three slots, ready for use. A vector with a capacity of three elements has the potential of holding three elements (and, in fact, more than three), but at the beginning, even after its initial construction, a vector holds no elements at all.

Use the add method to add new elements to a vector. For example, suppose you have a class called Item and use the following code to create three item objects.

```
Item nextItem = new Item(...);
Item stateTax = new Item(...);
Item shipping = new Item(...);
```

Then, you use the following code to add these items to a vector called itemsOrdered (that started out with a capacity of three objects, as indicated in the above code).

```
itemsOrdered.add(nextItem);
itemsOrdered.add(stateTax);
itemsOrdered.add(shipping);
```

Let's suppose you created the vector so that it had an original capacity of three items. If you insert another item, then you have exceeded the capacity of the vector in our example. This is where vectors work their magic: the vector *relocates and resizes itself* automatically. The vector finds a bigger home and automatically copies all the objects it is currently storing to its new home.

How much more space is allocated? By default, the space allocated doubles each time the vector relocates. Because of the problem of exponential growth, you may not want to rely on this for potentially massive memory reallocation for large vectors. Instead, you can specify a *capacity increment* as the second constructor argument when you create the vector. For example:

```
Vector itemsOrdered = new Vector(3, 10);
```

Now the vector grows in increments of 10 at each relocation.

On the other hand, if Java has to reallocate the space for the vector often, it slows down your program, so it pays to set reasonable estimates for the initial capacity and the capacity increment—so 10 may turn out to be too small an increment.

NOTE: For simple programs, you may not want to worry about the capacity and capacity increment for your vectors at all. If you use the default constructor

```
Vector itemsOrdered = new Vector();
```

the vector has an initial capacity of 10 and doubles in size every time the capacity is exceeded. This works fine for situations in which the items to be handled are few, and it frees you from micromanaging the vector allocations.

C++ NOTE: The Java `Vector` class differs in a number of important ways from the C++ `vector` template. Most noticeably, since `vector` is a template, only elements of the correct type can be inserted, and no casting is required to retrieve elements from the vector. For example, the compiler will simply refuse to insert a `Rectangle` object into a `vector<Employee>`. The C++ `vector` template overloads the `[ ]` operator for convenient element access. Since Java does not have operator over-loading, it must use explicit method calls instead. C++ vectors are copied by value. If a and b are two vectors, then the assignment a = b; makes a into a new vector with the same length as b, and all elements are copied from b to a. The same assignment in Java makes both a and b refer to the same vector.

VB NOTE: If you don't mind the extra syntax and occasionally casting a basic type to its wrapper class (and casting the retrieved objects), vectors in Java give you all the convenience of Redim Preserve (and quite a bit more).

Working with an Existing Vector

The `size` method returns the current number of elements in the vector. Thus,

```
v.size()
```

is the vector equivalent of

```
a.length
```

for an array a. Of course, the size of a vector is always less than or equal to its capacity.

Once you are reasonably sure that the vector is at its permanent size, you can call the `trimToSize` method. This method adjusts the size of the memory block to use exactly as much storage space as is required to hold the current number of elements. The garbage collector will reclaim any excess memory.

NOTE: Once you trim a vector's size, adding new elements will move the block again, which takes time. You should only use `trimToSize` when you are sure you won't add any more elements to the vector.

`java.util.Vector`

- `Vector()`

  constructs an empty vector (initial capacity is 10, and the capacity doubles whenever current capacity is exceeded).

- `Vector(int initialCapacity)`

  constructs an empty vector with the specified capacity.

  Parameters: `initialCapacity`   the initial storage capacity of the vector

- `Vector(int initialCapacity, int capacityIncrement)`

  constructs an empty vector with the specified capacity and the specified increment.

  Parameters: `initialCapacity`   the initial storage capacity of the vector

                 `capacityIncrement`   the amount by which the capacity is increased when the vector outgrows its current capacity

- `boolean add(Object obj)`

  appends an element at the end of the vector so that it becomes the last element of the vector. Always returns `true`.

  Parameters: `obj`   the element to be added

- `int size()`

  returns the number of elements currently stored in the vector. (This is different from, and, of course, never larger than, the vector's capacity.)

- `void setSize(int n)`

  sets the size of the vector to exactly n elements. If n is larger than the current size, null elements are added to the end of the vector. If n is less than the current size, all elements from index n on are removed.

  Parameters: `n`   the new size of the vector

- `void trimToSize()`

  reduces the capacity of the vector to its current size.

Accessing Vector Elements

Unfortunately, nothing comes for free; the extra convenience that vectors give requires a more complicated syntax for accessing the elements of the vector. The reason is that the Vector class is not a part of the Java language; it is just a utility class programmed by someone and supplied in the standard library.

NOTE: Vectors, like arrays, are zero-based.

The two most important differences in working with vectors, as opposed to arrays, are as follows:

1. Instead of using the pleasant [] syntax to access or change the element of an array, you must use the get and set methods.

Array	**Vector**
`x = a[i];`	`x = v.elementAt(i);` or `x = v.get(i);`
`a[i] = x;`	`v.setElementAt(x, i);` or `v.set(i, x);`

NOTE: The convenient get and set methods were added in Java 2.

TIP: You can sometimes get the best of both worlds—flexible growth and convenient element access—with the following trick. First, make a vector and add all the elements.
```
Vector v = new Vector();
while (. . .)
{   String s = . . .
    v.add(s);
}
```
When you are done, make an array and copy the elements into it. There is even a special method, copyInto, for this purpose.
```
String[] a = new String[v.size()];
v.copyInto(a);
```

CAUTION: Do not call `v.setElementAt(x, i)` until the *size* of the vector is larger than `i`. For example, the following code is wrong:
```
Vector v = new Vector(10); // capacity 10, size 0
v.set(0, x); // no element 0 yet
```
There are two remedies. You can use addElement instead of setElementAt. Or, you can call setSize after the vector is created.
```
Vector v = new Vector(10);
v.setSize(10);
```

2. As we said earlier, there is a single Vector class and that class holds elements of any type: a vector stores a sequence of *objects*.

That is not a problem when inserting elements into a vector—all classes implicitly inherit from Object. (Actually, there is a problem if you want to build a vector of numbers. Then, you must use a wrapper class like Integer or Double—see the next section.) But since the items are stored as objects, you can run into problems when retrieving data from a vector.

For example, consider

```
Item nextItem = new Item();
itemsOrdered.set(n, nextItem);
```

The variable nextItem is automatically cast from type Item to type Object when it is inserted into the vector. *But,* when you read an item from the vector, you get an Object and then you must cast it back to the type that you really want to work with.

```
Item currentItem = (Item)itemsOrdered.get(n);
```

If you forget the (Item) cast, the compiler generates an error message.

Vectors are inherently somewhat *unsafe*. It is possible to accidentally add an element of the wrong type to a vector.

```
Rectangle r = new Rectangle();
itemsOrdered.set(n, r);
```

The compiler won't complain. It is perfectly willing to convert a Rectangle to an Object, but when the accidental rectangle is later retrieved out of the vector container, it will probably be cast into an Item. This is an invalid cast that will cause the program to abort. That *is* a problem! The problem arises because vectors store values of type Object . Had itemsOrdered been an array of Item values, then the compiler would not have allowed a rectangle inside of it.

```
Rectangle r = new Rectangle();
itemsOrdered[n] = r; // ERROR
```

How serious is this problem? It depends. In practice, you can often guarantee that the elements inserted into a vector are of the correct type, simply because there are only one or two locations in the code where the insertion into the vector takes place. You can then write code that checks the type before you store it in the vector.

Consider the example of a PurchaseOrder class.

```
class PurchaseOrder
{   . . .
    public void add(Item i)
    {   itemsOrdered.add(i);
    }
    . . .
    private Vector itemsOrdered;
}
```

The `itemsOrdered` vector is a private field of the `PurchaseOrder` class.

The only method that adds objects into that vector is `PurchaseOrder.add`. Plainly, since the argument of `PurchaseOrder.add` is an `Item`, only items can be added into the vector. The compiler can check the type at that level—a call to `order.add(new Rectangle())` will give an error message. Thus, we can safely remove elements from that vector and cast them as `Item` objects.

On very rare occasions, vectors are useful for *heterogeneous collections*. Objects of completely unrelated classes are inserted into the vector on purpose. When a vector entry is retrieved, the type of every retrieved object must be tested, as in the following code:

```
Vector purchaseOrder;
purchaseOrder.add(new Name(. . .));
purchaseOrder.add(new Address(. . .));
purchaseOrder.add(new Item(. . .));
  . . .
Object obj = purchaseOrder.get(n);
if (obj instanceof Item)
{  Item i = (Item)obj;
    sum += i.price();
}
```

Actually, this is a crummy way to write code. It is not a good idea to throw away type information and laboriously try to retrieve it later.

VB NOTE: You may be wondering about arrays of variants. Well, we think using variants, except for OLE automation or where their special properties are really needed, is also a crummy way to write code. For example, copying arrays is faster if you turn them into variants, so they are great for that. Using them for numbers, on the other hand, is a sure way to slow down your program.

`java.util.Vector`

- `void set(int index, Object obj)`

  puts a value in the vector at the specified index, overwriting the previous contents.

Parameters:	index	the position (must be between 0 and `size()` - 1)
	obj	the new value

- `Object get(int index)`

  gets the value stored at a specified index.

Parameters:	index	the index of the element to get (must be between 0 and `size()` - 1)

Inserting and Removing Elements in the Middle of a Vector

Instead of appending elements at the end of a vector, you can also insert them in the middle.

```
int n = itemsOrdered.size() - 2;
itemsOrdered.add(n, nextItem);
```

The elements at locations n and above are shifted up to make room for the new entry. After the insertion, if the new size of the vector after the insertion exceeds the vector's current capacity, then Java reallocates its storage.

Similarly, you can remove an element from the middle of a vector.

```
Item i = (Item)itemsOrdered.remove(n);
```

The elements located above it are copied down, and the size of the array is reduced by one.

Inserting and removing elements is not terribly efficient. It is probably not worth worrying about for small vectors. But if you store many elements and frequently insert and remove in the middle of the sequence, consider using a linked list instead. We will explain how to program with linked lists in Volume 2.

`java.util.Vector`

- `void add(int index, Object obj)`

  shifts up elements in order to insert an element.

Parameters:	index	the insertion position (must be between 0 and `size()`)
	obj	the new element

- `void remove(int index)`

  removes an element and shifts down all elements above it.

Parameters:	index	the position of the element to be removed (must be between 0 and `size() - 1`)

Running a Vector Benchmark

The dynamic growth of vectors makes them more convenient to use than arrays in many circumstances. Given their extra convenience, it is reasonable to ask what price, if any, one pays in terms of efficiency for using them. To answer this question, we ran two benchmark tests to measure the cost of relocating arrays and vectors and the cost of accessing array and vector elements. When running the benchmark program (see Example 5–3) on a 200-MHz Pentium with 96 Mbytes of memory and the Windows 95 operating system, we obtained the following data.

```
Allocating vector elements: 17910 milliseconds
Allocating array elements:   4220 milliseconds
Accessing vector elements: 18130 milliseconds
Accessing array elements:  10110 milliseconds
```

As you can see, vectors are significantly slower than raw arrays. There are two reasons. It takes longer to call a method than it takes to access an array directly. And the vector methods are *synchronized*. When two threads access the same vector, the method calls are queued so that only one thread updates the vector at one time. Synchronization is a performance bottleneck. (We will discuss threads and synchronized methods in the multithreading chapter in Volume 2.)

Vectors are undeniably convenient. They grow dynamically and they manage the distinction between size and capacity for you, but element access is both cumbersome and slow. We prefer vectors over arrays to collect small data sets of variable size. They are also useful in multithreaded programs. Otherwise, it makes sense to use raw arrays.

Example 5–3: VectorBenchmark.java

```java
import java.util.*;

class VectorBenchmark
{  public static void main(String[] args)
   {  Vector v = new Vector();

      long start = new Date().getTime();
      for (int i = 0; i < MAXSIZE; i++)
         v.add(new Integer(i));
      long end = new Date().getTime();
      System.out.println("Allocating vector elements: "
         + (end - start) + " milliseconds");

      Integer[] a = new Integer[1];
      start = new Date().getTime();
      for (int i = 0; i < MAXSIZE; i++)
      {  if (i >= a.length)
         {  Integer[] b = new Integer[i * 2];
```

```
         System.arraycopy(a, 0, b, 0, a.length);
         a = b;
      }
      a[i] = new Integer(i);
   }
   end = new Date().getTime();
   System.out.println("Allocating array elements:   "
      + (end - start) + " milliseconds");

   start = new Date().getTime();
   for (int j = 0; j < NTRIES; j++)
      for (int i = 0; i < MAXSIZE; i++)
      {  Integer r = (Integer)v.get(i);
         v.set(i, new Integer(r.intValue() + 1));
      }
   end = new Date().getTime();
   System.out.println("Accessing vector elements:   "
      + (end - start) + " milliseconds");

   start = new Date().getTime();
   for (int j = 0; j < NTRIES; j++)
      for (int i = 0; i < MAXSIZE; i++)
      {  Integer r = a[i];
         a[i] = new Integer(r.intValue() + 1);
      }
   end = new Date().getTime();
   System.out.println("Accessing array elements:   "
      + (end - start) + " milliseconds");
   }

   public static final int MAXSIZE = 100000;
   public static final int NTRIES = 10;
}
```

Object Wrappers

Occasionally, you need to convert a basic type like `int` to an object. All basic types have class counterparts. For example, there is a class `Integer` corresponding to the basic type `int`. These kinds of classes are usually called *object wrappers*. The wrapper classes have obvious names: `Integer`, `Long`, `Float`, `Double`, `Short`, `Byte`, `Character`, `Void`, and `Boolean`. (The first six inherit from the common parent wrapper `Number`.) The wrapper classes are `final`. (So you can't override the `toString` method in `Integer` in order to display numbers using Roman numerals, sorry.) You also cannot change the values you store in the object wrapper.

Suppose we want a vector of floating-point numbers. As mentioned previously, simply adding numbers won't work.

```
Vector v = new Vector();
v.add(3.14); // ERROR
```

The floating-point number 3.14 is not an `Object`. Here, the `Double` wrapper class comes in. An instance of `Double` is an object that wraps the `double` type.

```
v.add(new Double(3.14));
```

Of course, to retrieve a number from a vector of `Double` objects, we need to extract the actual value from the wrapper by using the `doubleValue()` method in `Double`.

```
double x = ((Double)v.get(n)).doubleValue();
```

Ugh. Here it really pays off to define a class we will call `DoubleVector` that hides all this ugliness once and for all.

```
class DoubleVector
{  public void set(int n, double x)
   {  v.set(n, new Double(x));
   }

   public void add(double x)
   {  v.add(new Double(x));
   }

   public double get(int n)
   {  return ((Double)v.get(n)).doubleValue();
   }

   public int size()
   {  return v.size();
   }

   private Vector v = new Vector();
}
```

CAUTION: Some people think that the wrapper classes can be used to implement methods that can modify numeric arguments. However, that is not correct. Recall from Chapter 4 that it is impossible to write a Java function that increments an integer because arguments to Java methods are always passed by value.

```java
static void increment(int x) // won't work
{  x++; // increments local copy
}
static void main(String[] args)
{  int a = 3;
   increment(a);
   . . .
}
```

Changing x has no effect on a. Could we overcome this by using an Integer instead of an int?

```java
static void increment(Integer x) // won't work
{  . . .
}

static void main(String[] args)
{  Integer a = new Integer(3);
   increment(a);
   . . .
}
```

After all, now a and x are references to the same object. If we managed to update x, then a would also be updated. The problem is that Integer objects are *immutable*: the information contained inside the wrapper can't change. In particular, there is no analog to the statement x++ for Integer objects. Thus, you cannot use these wrapper classes to create a method that modifies numeric arguments.

NOTE: If you do want to write a method to change numeric arguments, you can use one of the *holder* types defined in the org.omg.CORBA package. There are types IntHolder, BooleanHolder, and so on. Each holder type has a public (!) data field value through which you can access the stored value.

```java
static void increment(IntegerHolder x)
{  x.value++;
}

static void main(String[] args)
{  IntegerHolder a = new IntegerHolder(3);
   increment(a);
   int result = a.value;
   . . .
}
```

You will often see the number wrappers for another reason. The designers of Java found the wrappers a convenient place to put certain basic methods, like the ones for converting strings of digits to numbers. The place is convenient, but the functionality, unfortunately, isn't.

To convert a string to an integer, you need to use the following statement:

```
int x = Integer.parseInt(s);
```

This has nothing to do with `Integer` objects—`parseInt` is a static method. But the `Integer` class was a good place to put it. Until Java 2, there was no corresponding `parseDouble` in the `Double` class. Instead, you had to use the cumbersome

```
double x = new Double(s).doubleValue();
```

What this does is:

1. Uses a constructor in the `Double` class that accepts a string of digits in the form of a double and gives you a `Double` object,

2. Uses the `doubleValue` method in the `Double` class that returns an actual double.

(VB users are probably longing for a simple CDb function.)

Actually, in real life it is even worse: you have to contend with the possibility that the string has leading or trailing spaces or that it may contain nondigits. So, a correct version would be as follows:

```
x = new Double(s.trim()).doubleValue();
```

You will see this kind of long-winded code in many Java programs.

There is another method for parsing numbers, although it isn't any simpler. You can use the `parse` method of the `DecimalFormat` class. When s is a string and df is an object of type `DecimalFormat`, then the method call `df.parse(s)` returns an object of type `Number`.

```
DecimalFormat df = new DecimalFormat(); // uses default locale
Number n = df.parse(s);
```

Actually, `Number` is an abstract class, and the returned object is an object of either type `Long` or `Double`, depending on the contents of the string s. You can use the `instanceof` operator to find out the return type of the object:

```
if (n instanceof Double) Double d = (Double)n;
```

But in practice, you don't usually care about the return type. The `doubleValue` method is defined for the `Number` class, and it returns the floating-point equivalent of the number object, whether it is a Long or a Double. That is, you can use the following code:

```
try
{   x = new DecimalFormat().parse(s.trim()).doubleValue();
}
catch(ParseException e)
{   x = 0;
}
```

Using the DecimalFormat has one advantage: the string can contain group separators for thousands such as "12,301.4".

The API notes show some of the more important methods of the Integer class. The other number classes implement corresponding methods.

---

java.lang.Integer

- int intValue()

  returns the value of this Integer object as an int (overrides the intValue method in the Number class).

- static String toString(int i)

  returns a new String object representing the specified integer in base 10.

- static String toString(int i, int radix)

  lets you return a representation of the number i in the base specified by the radix parameter.

- static int parseInt(String s)

  returns the integer's value, assuming the specified String represents an integer in base 10.

- static int parseInt(String s, int radix)

  returns the integer's value, assuming the specified String represents an integer in the base specified by the radix parameter.

- static Integer valueOf(String s)

  returns a new Integer object initialized to the integer's value, assuming the specified String represents an integer in base 10.

- static Integer valueOf(String s, int radix)

  returns a new Integer object initialized to the integer's value, assuming the specified String represents an integer in the base specified by the radix parameter.

java.text.NumberFormat

- Number parse(String s)

  returns the numeric value, assuming the specified String represents a number.

Big Numbers

If the precision of the basic integer and floating-point types is not sufficient, you can turn to a couple of handy classes in the java.math package, called BigInteger and BigDecimal. These are classes for manipulating numbers with an arbitrarily long sequence of digits. The BigInteger class implements arbitrary precision integer arithmetic, and BigDecimal does the same for floating-point numbers. You usually construct big numbers out of strings by using one of the BigInteger or BigDecimal constructors that takes a string.

```
BigInteger b =
    new BigInteger("1234567890123456789012345678901234567890");
```

There are no constructors that take ordinary numbers, but you can use the static valueOf method:

```
BigInteger a = BigInteger.valueOf(100);
```

Unfortunately, you cannot use the familiar mathematical operators such as + and * to combine big numbers. Instead, you must use the appropriate methods in the correct big number class.

```
BigInteger c = a.add(b); // c = a + b
BigInteger d = c.multiply(b.add(BigInteger.valueOf(2)));
    // d = c * (b + 2)
```

C++ NOTE: Unlike C++, Java has no programmable operator overloading. There was no way for the programmer of the BigInteger class to redefine the + and * operators to give the add and multiply operations of the BigInteger classes. The language designers did overload the + operator to denote concatenation of strings. They chose not to overload other operators, and they did not give Java programmers the opportunity to overload operators themselves.

Example 5–4 shows a version of the lottery odds program that we introduced in Chapter 3, modified to work with big numbers. For example, if you are invited to participate in a lottery in which you need to pick 60 numbers out of a possible 490 numbers, then this program will tell you that your odds are 1 in 716395843461995557415116222540092933411717612789263493493351013459481104 668848. Good luck!

Example 5–4: BigIntegerTest.java

```
import corejava.*;
import java.math.*;

public class BigIntegerTest
{  public static BigInteger lotteryOdds(int high, int number)
   {  BigInteger r = new BigInteger("1");
      int i;
      for (i = 1; i <= number; i++)
      {  r = r.multiply(BigInteger.valueOf(high))
            .divide(BigInteger.valueOf(i));
         high--;
      }
      return r;
   }

   public static void main(String[] args)
   {  int numbers = Console.readInt
         ("How many numbers do you need to draw?");
      int topNumber = Console.readInt
         ("What is the highest number you can draw?");
      BigInteger oddsAre = lotteryOdds(topNumber, numbers);

      System.out.println("Your odds are 1 in " + oddsAre +
         ". Good luck!");
   }
}
```

Reading a Page in the HTML Documents

At this point, you have seen all the basic terms that Java uses to describe its methods, classes, and interfaces. Once you are comfortable with this information, you will often consult the API documentation. The API documentation is part of the JDK. It is in HTML format. Point your web browser to \jdk\docs\api\index.html. Figures 5–3 through 5–6 show the pages of API documentation for the Double class. As you can see, the API documentation pages are always organized in the same way:

1. The screen is organized into three windows. A small window on the top left shows all available packages. Click on any package, and all classes on that window are displayed in the small window below it. Click on any class name, and the API documentation for the class is displayed in the large window to the right (see Figure 5–3).

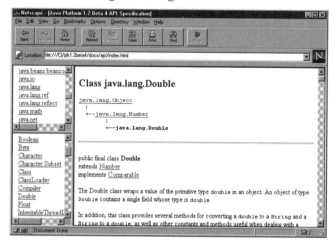

Figure 5–3: The three panes of the API documentation

2. The top of the documentation page of each class shows the name of the class and the inheritance chain for this class (starting from `java.lang.Object`), followed by a (more or less useful) discussion of the class (occasionally, this includes some sample code).

3. Next follows a summary of all public and protected fields, constructors and methods. (see Figure 5–4).

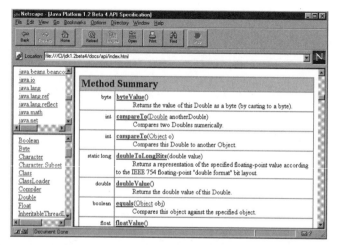

Figure 5–4: Method summary for the `Double` class

4. Click on any field or method name for a detailed description (see Figure 5-5).

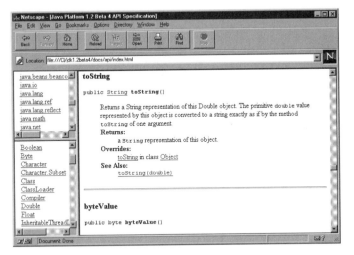

Figure 5–5: Detailed method description for the `Double` class

5. The top of each page has a convenient set of links. Click on "Tree" to get a tree view of all classes in this package (see Figure 5–6). Click again on "All packages" to get a humongous tree view of all classes in the library.

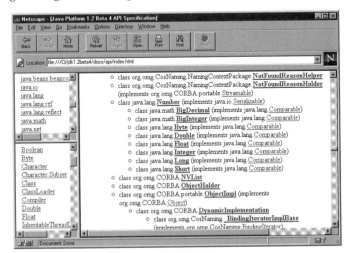

Figure 5–6: Tree view

The `Class` Class (Run-Time Type Identification)

While your program is running, the Java run-time system always maintains what is called run-time type identification on all objects. This information keeps track of the class to which each object belongs. Run-time type information is used by Java to select the correct methods to execute at run time.

However, you can also access this information by working with a special Java class. The class that holds this information is called, somewhat confusingly, `Class`. The `getClass()` method in the `Object` class returns an instance of `Class` type.

```
Employee e ;
   . . .
Class cl = e.getClass();
```

Probably the most commonly used method of `Class` is `getName`. This returns the name of the class. You can use it in a simple `println`; for example, the code

```
System.out.println(e.getClass().getName() + " " + e.getName());
```

prints

```
Employee Harry Hacker
```

if `e` is an employee; the code prints

```
Manager Harry Hacker
```

if `e` is a manager.

You can obtain a `Class` object in two ways: by asking an object for its corresponding class object, and by requesting the class object corresponding to a string by using the static `forName` method.

```
String className = "Manager";
Class cl = Class.forName(className);
```

You would use this method if the class name is stored in a string that varies at run time. This works if `className` is the name of a class or interface. Otherwise, it throws an exception.

A third method for obtaining an object of type `Class` is a convenient shorthand. If `T` is any Java type, then `T.class` is the matching class object. For example:

```
Class cl1 = Manager.class;
Class cl2 = int.class;
Class cl3 = Double[].class;
```

Note that `Class` really describes a *type*, which may or may not be a class.

NOTE: For historical reasons, the `getName` method returns somewhat strange names for array types:

```
System.out.println(Double[].class.getName());
   // prints [Ljava.lang.Double;
System.out.println(int[].class.getName());
   // prints [I
```

Another example of a useful method is one that lets you create an instance of a class on the fly. This method is called, naturally enough, `newInstance()`. For example, when combined with a bit of code needed to catch certain exceptions,

```
e.getClass().newInstance();
```

would create a new instance of the same class type as e. The `newInstance` method calls the default constructor (the one that takes no arguments) to initialize the newly created object.

Using a combination of `forName` and `newInstance` lets you create an object from a class name stored in a string.

```
String s = "Manager";
Object m = Class.forName(s).newInstance();
```

NOTE: If you need to provide parameters for the constructor of a class you want to create by name in this manner, then you can't use statements like the above, instead, you must use the `newInstance` method in the `Constructor` class. (This is one of several classes in the `java.lang.reflect` package. We will discuss reflection in the next section.)

C++ NOTE: The `newInstance` method corresponds to the idiom of a *virtual constructor* in C++. However, virtual constructors in C++ are not a language feature but just an idiom that needs to be supported by a specialized library. The `Class` class is similar to the `type_info` class in C++, and the `getClass` method is equivalent to the `typeid` operator. The Java `Class` is quite a bit more versatile than `type_info`, though. The C++ `type_info` can only reveal a string with the name of the type, not create new objects of that type.

java.lang.Class

- `String getName()`

  returns the name of this class.

- `Class getSuperclass()`

  returns the superclass of this class as a `Class` object.

- `Class[] getInterfaces()`

  returns an array of `Class` objects that give the interfaces implemented by this class; returns an array of length 0 if this class implements no interfaces. Somewhat confusingly, interface descriptions are also stored in `Class` objects. Interfaces are discussed in Chapter 6.

- `boolean isInterface()`

  returns `true` if this class is an interface, and `false` if not.

- `String toString()`

  returns the name of this class or this interface. The word *class* precedes the name if it is a class; the word *interface* precedes the name if it is an interface. (See the next chapter for more on interfaces.) This method overrides the `toString` method in `Object`.

- `static Class forName(String className)`

  returns the `Class` object representing the class with name `className`.

- `Object newInstance()`

  returns a new instance of this class.

java.lang.reflect.Constructor

- `Object newInstance(Object[] args)`

  constructs a new instance of the constructor's declaring class.

  Parameters: args   the parameters supplied to the constructor

Reflection

The class `Class` gives you a very rich and elaborate toolset to write programs that manipulate Java code dynamically. This feature is heavily used in *JavaBeans*, the component architecture for Java (see Volume 2 for more on JavaBeans). Using reflection, Java is able to support tools like the ones users of Visual Basic or Delphi have grown accustomed to. In particular, when new classes are added at design or run time, rapid application development tools that are JavaBeans enabled need to be able to inquire about the capabilities of the classes (beans) that were added. (This is equivalent to the process that occurs when you add controls in Visual Basic to the toolbox.)

A program that can analyze the capabilities of classes is called *reflective*. The package that brings this functionality to Java is therefore called, naturally enough, `java.lang.reflect`. The reflection mechanism is extremely powerful. As the next four sections show, you can use it to:

- Analyze the capabilities of classes at run time

- Inspect objects at run time, for example, to write a single `toString` method that works for *all* classes

- Implement generic array manipulation code

- Take advantage of `Method` objects that work just like function pointers in languages such as C++

(Please note that the section on JavaBeans in Volume 2 will have a discussion of the parts of the reflection mechanism relevant to JavaBeans.)

Using Reflection to Analyze the Capabilities of Classes

Here is a brief overview of the most important parts of the reflection mechanism for letting you examine the structure of a class.

The three classes `Field`, `Method`, and `Constructor` in `java.lang.reflect` package describe the data fields, the operations, and the constructors of a class, respectively. All three classes have a method called `getName` that returns the name of the item. The `Field` class has a method `getType` that returns an object, again of type `Class`, that describes the field type. The `Method` and `Constructor` classes have methods to report the return type and the types of the parameters used for these functions. All three of these classes also have a method called `getModifiers` that returns an integer, with various bits turned on and off, that describe the modifiers used, such as `public` and `static`. You can then use the static methods in the `Modifier` class in `java.lang.reflect` to analyze the integer that `getModifiers` returns. For example, there are methods like `isPublic`, `isPrivate`, or `isFinal` in the `Modifier` class that you could use to tell whether a method or constructor was `public`, `private`, or `final`. All you have to do is have the appropriate method in the `Modifier` class work on the integer that `getModifiers` returns. You can also use the `Modifier.toString` method to print the modifiers.

The `getFields()`, `getMethods()`, and `getConstructors()` methods of the `Class` class return arrays of the *public* fields, operations, and constructors that the class supports as arrays of objects of the appropriate class from `java.lang.reflect`. The `getDeclaredFields()`, `getDeclaredMethods()`, and `getDeclaredConstructors()` methods of the `Class` class return arrays consisting of all fields, operations, and constructors in the class.

Example 5–5 shows you how to print out all information about a class. The program prompts you for the name of a class and then writes out the signatures of all methods and constructors as well as the names of all data fields of a class. For example, if you enter

```
java.lang.Double
```

then Example 5–5 prints

```
class java.lang.Double extends java.lang.Number
{
public java.lang.Double(double);
public java.lang.Double(java.lang.String);

public byte byteValue();
public int compareTo(java.lang.Double);
public int compareTo(java.lang.Object);
public static native long doubleToLongBits(double);
public double doubleValue();
public boolean equals(java.lang.Object);
public float floatValue();
public int hashCode();
public int intValue();
public boolean isInfinite();
public static boolean isInfinite(double);
public boolean isNaN();
public static boolean isNaN(double);
public static native double longBitsToDouble(long);
public long longValue();
public short shortValue();
public java.lang.String toString();
public static java.lang.String toString(double);
public static java.lang.Double valueOf(java.lang.String);
static native double valueOf0(java.lang.String);

public static final double POSITIVE_INFINITY;
public static final double NEGATIVE_INFINITY;
public static final double NaN;
public static final double MAX_VALUE;
public static final double MIN_VALUE;
public static final java.lang.Class TYPE;
private double value;
private static final long serialVersionUID;
}
```

Example 5–5: ReflectionTest.java

```java
import java.lang.reflect.*;
import corejava.*;

public class ReflectionTest
{  public static void main(String[] args)
   {  String name = Console.readLine
         ("Please enter a class name (e.g. java.util.Date): ");
      try
      {  Class cl = Class.forName(name);
         Class supercl = cl.getSuperclass();
         System.out.print("class " + name);
         if (supercl != null && !supercl.equals(Object.class))
            System.out.print(" extends " + supercl.getName());
         System.out.print("\n{\n");
         printConstructors(cl);
         System.out.println();
         printMethods(cl);
         System.out.println();
         printFields(cl);
         System.out.println("}");
      }
      catch(ClassNotFoundException e)
      {  System.out.println("Class not found.");
      }
   }

   public static void printConstructors(Class cl)
   {  Constructor[] constructors = cl.getDeclaredConstructors();

      for (int i = 0; i < constructors.length; i++)
      {  Constructor c = constructors[i];
         Class[] paramTypes = c.getParameterTypes();
         String name = c.getName();
         System.out.print(Modifier.toString(c.getModifiers()));
         System.out.print(" " + name + "(");
         for (int j = 0; j < paramTypes.length; j++)
         {  if (j > 0) System.out.print(", ");
            System.out.print(paramTypes[j].getName());
         }
         System.out.println(");");
      }
   }

   public static void printMethods(Class cl)
```

```
{  Method[] methods = cl.getDeclaredMethods();

    for (int i = 0; i < methods.length; i++)
    {  Method m = methods[i];
        Class retType = m.getReturnType();
        Class[] paramTypes = m.getParameterTypes();
        String name = m.getName();
        System.out.print(Modifier.toString(m.getModifiers()));
        System.out.print(" " + retType.getName() + " " + name
            + "(");
        for (int j = 0; j < paramTypes.length; j++)
        {  if (j > 0) System.out.print(", ");
            System.out.print(paramTypes[j].getName());
        }
        System.out.println(");");
    }
}

public static void printFields(Class cl)
{  Field[] fields = cl.getDeclaredFields();

    for (int i = 0; i < fields.length; i++)
    {  Field f = fields[i];
        Class type = f.getType();
        String name = f.getName();
        System.out.print(Modifier.toString(f.getModifiers()));
        System.out.println(" " + type.getName() + " " + name
            + ";");
    }
}
}
```

What is remarkable about this program is that it can analyze any class that the
Java interpreter can load, not just the classes that were available when the program was compiled. We will use this program in the next chapter to peek inside
the new inner classes that the Java compiler generates automatically.

 java.lang.Class

- `Field[] getFields()`

- `Field[] getDeclaredFields()`

    The `getFields` method returns an array containing `Field` objects for the
    public fields. The `getDeclaredField` method returns an array of `Field`
    objects for all fields. The methods return an array of length 0 if there are no
    such fields or the `Class` object represents a primitive or array type.

- `Method[] getMethods()`
- `Method[] getDeclaredMethods()`

  return an array containing `Method` objects that give you all the public methods (for `getMethods`) or all methods (for `getDeclaredMethods`) of the class or interface. This includes those inherited from classes or interfaces above it in the inheritance chain.

- `Constructor[] getConstructors()`
- `Constructor[] getDeclaredConstructors()`

  return an array containing `Constructor` objects that give you all the public constructors (for `getConstructors`) or all constructors (for `getDeclaredConstructors`) of the class represented by this `Class` object.

`java.lang.reflect.Field`

`java.lang.reflect.Method`

`java.lang.reflect.Constructor`

- `Class getDeclaringClass()`

  returns the `Class` object for the class that defines this constructor, method, or field.

- `Class[] getExceptionTypes()`

  (in `Constructor` and `Method` classes). Returns an array of `Class` objects that represent the types of the exceptions thrown by the method.

- `int getModifiers()`

  returns an integer that describes the modifiers of this constructor, method, or field. Use the methods in the `Modifier` class to analyze the return value.

- `String getName()`

  returns a string that is the name of the constructor, method, or field.

- `Class[] getParameterTypes()`

  (in `Constructor` and `Method` classes). Returns an array of `Class` objects that represent the types of the parameters.

Using Reflection to Analyze Objects at Run Time

In the preceding section, we saw how we can find out the *names* and *types* of the data fields of any object:

- Get the corresponding `Class` object.

- Call `getDeclaredFields` on the `Class` object.

In this section, we go one step further and actually look at the *contents* of the data fields. Of course, it is easy to look at the contents of a specific field of an object whose name and type are known when you write a program. But reflection lets us look at fields of objects that were not known at compile time.

The key method to achieve this is the `get` method in the `Field` class. If f is an object of type `Field` (for example, one obtained from `getDeclaredFields`) and `obj` is an object of the class of which f is a field, then `f.get(obj)` returns an object whose value is the current value of the field of `obj`. This is all a bit abstract, so let's run through an example.

```
Employee harry = new Employee("Harry Hacker", 35000,
    new Day(10, 1, 1989));
Class cl = harry.getClass();
    // the class object representing Employee
Field f = cl.getField("name");
    // the name field of the Employee class
Object v = f.get(harry);
    // the value of the name field of the harry object
    // i.e. the String object "Harry Hacker"
```

Actually, there is a problem with this code. Since the `name` field is a private field, the `get` method will throw an `IllegalAccessException`. You can only use the `get` method to get the values of accessible fields. The security mechanism of Java lets you find out what fields any object has, but it won't let you read the values of those fields unless you have access permission.

The default behavior of the reflection mechanism is to respect Java access control. However, if a Java program is not controlled by a security manager that disallows it, it is possible to override access control. To do this, invoke the `setAccessible` method on a `Field`, `Method`, or `Constructor` object, for example:

```
f.setAccessible(true);
    // now OK to call f.get(harry);
```

The `setAccessible` method is a method of the `AccessibleObject` class, the common superclass of the `Field`, `Method`, and `Constructor`. This feature is provided for debuggers, persistent storage, and similar mechanisms. We will use it for a generic `toString` method later in this section.

There is another issue with the `get` method that we need to deal with. The `name` field is a `String`, and so it is not a problem to return the value as an `Object`.

But suppose we want to look at the salary field. That is a double, and in Java, number types are not objects. To handle this, you can either use the getDouble method of the Field class, or you can call get, where Java's reflection mechanism automatically wraps the field value into the appropriate wrapper class, in this case, Double.

Of course, you can also set the values that you can get. The call f.set(obj, value) sets the field represented by f of the object obj to the new value.

Example 5–6 shows how to write a generic toString method that works for *any* class. It uses getDeclaredFields to obtain all data fields. It then uses the setAccessible convenience method to make all fields accessible. For each field, it obtains the name and the value. Each value is turned into a string by invoking *its* toString method.

```
class ObjectAnalyzer
{   public static String toString(Object obj)
    {   Class cl = obj.getClass();
        String r;
            . . .
        Field[] fields = cl.getDeclaredFields();
        AccessibleObject.setAccessible(fields, true);
        for (int i = 0; i < fields.length; i++)
        {   Field f = fields[i];
            r += f.getName() + "=";
            Object val = f.get(obj);
            r += val.toString();
            . . .
        }
        return r;
    }
}
```

You can use this toString method to peek inside any object. For example, here is what you get when you look inside the System.out object:

```
java.io.PrintStream[classjava.io.FilterOutputStream,autoFlush=tr
ue,trouble=false,textOut=java.io.BufferedWriter@115c2454,charOut
=java.io.OutputStreamWriter@33902454,closing=false]
```

In Example 5–6, the generic toString method is used to implement the toString of the Employee class:.

```
public String toString()
{   return ObjectAnalyzer.toString(this);
}
```

This is a hassle-free method for supplying a toString method, and it is highly recommended, especially for debugging. The same recursive approach can also be used to define a generic equals method. See the code in the example program for details.

Example 5–6: ObjectAnalyzerTest.java

```
import java.lang.reflect.*;
import corejava.*;

public class ObjectAnalyzerTest
{  public static void main(String[] args)
   {  Employee harry  = new Employee("Harry Hacker", 35000,
         new Day(1996,12, 1));
      System.out.println(harry);
      Employee coder  = new Employee("Harry Hacker", 35000,
         new Day(1996,12, 1));
      System.out.println(harry.equals(coder));
      harry.raiseSalary(5);
      System.out.println(harry.equals(coder));

      System.out.println(ObjectAnalyzer.toString(System.out));
   }
}

class ObjectAnalyzer
{  public static String toString(Object obj)
   {  Class cl = obj.getClass();
      String r = cl.getName() + "[";
      Class sc = cl.getSuperclass();
      if (!sc.equals(Object.class)) r += sc + ",";
      Field[] fields = cl.getDeclaredFields();
      try
      {  AccessibleObject.setAccessible(fields, true);
      }
      catch(SecurityException e) {}
      for (int i = 0; i < fields.length; i++)
      {  Field f = fields[i];
         r += f.getName() + "=";
         try
         {  Object val = f.get(obj);
            r += val.toString();
         } catch (IllegalAccessException e)
         {  r += "???";
         }
         if (i < fields.length - 1)
            r += ",";
         else
            r += "]";
      }
      return r;
   }

   public static boolean equals(Object a, Object b)
```

```
    {   Class cl = a.getClass();
        if (!cl.equals(b.getClass())) return false;
        Field[] fields = cl.getDeclaredFields();
        AccessibleObject.setAccessible(fields, true);
        for (int i = 0; i < fields.length; i++)
        {   Field f = fields[i];
            try
            {   if (!f.get(a).equals(f.get(b)))
                    return false;
            }
            catch(IllegalAccessException e)
            {   return false;
            }
        }
        return true;
    }
}

class Employee
{   public Employee(String n, double s, Day d)
    {   name = n;
        salary = s;
        hireDay = d;
    }

    public String toString()
    {   return ObjectAnalyzer.toString(this);
    }

    public boolean equals(Object b)
    {   return ObjectAnalyzer.equals(this, b);
    }

    public void print()
    {   System.out.println(name + " " + salary + " "
            + hireYear());
    }

    public void raiseSalary(double byPercent)
    {   salary *= 1 + byPercent / 100;
    }

    public int hireYear()
    {   return hireDay.getYear();
    }

    private String name;
    private double salary;
    private Day hireDay;
}
```

`java.lang.reflect.AccessibleObject.`

- `void setAccessible(boolean flag)`

  sets the accessibility flag for this reflection object. A value of `true` indicates that Java language access checking is suppressed, and that the private properties of the object can be queried and set.

- `boolean isAccessible()`

  gets the value of the accessibility flag for this reflection object.

- `static void setAccessible(AccessibleObject[] array,boolean flag)`

  is a convenience method to set the accessibility flag for an array of objects.

Using Reflection to Write Generic Array Code

The `Array` class in `java.lang.reflect` allows you to create arrays dynamically. For example, when you use this feature with the `arrayCopy` method from Chapter 3, you can dynamically expand an existing array while preserving the current contents.

> **VB NOTE:** Although not as convenient as Redim Preserve, this technique is sure to be welcome to VB programmers who have long since grown accustomed to the convenience the Redim Preserve command provides.

The problem we want to solve is pretty typical. Suppose you have an array of some type that is full and you want to grow it. And suppose you are sick of writing the grow-and-copy code by hand. You want to write a generic method to grow an array.

```
Employee[] a = new Employee[100];
. . .
// array is full
a = (Employee[])arrayGrow(a);
```

How can we write such a generic method? It helps that an `Employee[]` array can be converted to an `Object[]` array. That sounds promising. Here is a first attempt to write a generic method. We simply grow the array by 10% + 10 elements (since the 10% growth is not substantial enough for small arrays).

```
static Object[] arrayGrow(Object[] a) // not useful
{  int newLength = a.length * 11 / 10 + 10;
   Object[] newArray = new Object[newLength];
   System.arraycopy(a, 0, newArray, 0, a.length);
   return newArray;
}
```

However, there is a problem with actually *using* the resulting array. The type of the array that this code returns is an array of *objects* (Object []) because we created the array using the line of code:

```
new Object [newLength]
```

An array of objects *cannot* be cast to an array of employees (Employee []). Java would generate a ClassCast exception at run time. The point is, as we mentioned earlier, that a Java array remembers the type of its entries, that is, the element type used in the new expression that created it. It is legal to cast an Employee [] temporarily to an Object [] array and then cast it back, but an array that started its life as an Object [] array can never be cast into an Employee [] array. To write this kind of generic array code, we need to be able to make a new array of the *same* type as the original array. For this, we need the methods of the Array class in the java.lang.reflect package. The key is the static newInstance method of the Array class that constructs a new array. You must supply the type for the entries and the desired length as parameters to this method.

```
Object newArray = Array.newInstance(componentType, newLength);
```

To actually carry this out, we need to get the length and component type of the new array.

The length is obtained by calling Array.getLength(a). The static getLength method of the Array class returns the length of any array. To get the component type of the new array,

- First, get the class object of a.
- Confirm that it is indeed an array.
- Then, use the getComponentType method of the Class class (which is defined for only class objects that represent arrays) in order to find the right type for the array.

Why is getLength a method of Array but getComponentType a method of Class? We don't know—the distribution of the reflection methods seems a bit ad hoc at times.

Here's the code:

```
static Object arrayGrow(Object a) // useful
{  Class cl = a.getClass();
   if (!cl.isArray()) return null;
   Class componentType = a.getClass().getComponentType();
   int length = Array.getLength(a);
   int newLength = length * 11 / 10 + 10;

   Object newArray = Array.newInstance(componentType,
      newLength);
   System.arraycopy(a, 0, newArray, 0, length);
   return newArray;
}
```

Note that this `arrayGrow` method can be used to grow arrays of any type, not just arrays of objects.

```
int[] ia = { 1, 2, 3, 4 };
ia = (int[])arrayGrow(ia);
```

To make this possible, the parameter of `arrayGrow` is declared to be of type `Object`, *not an array of objects* (`Object[]`). The integer array type `int[]` can be converted to an `Object`, but not to an array of objects!

Example 5–7 shows both array grow methods in action. Note that the cast of the return value of `badArrayGrow` will throw an exception.

Example 5–7: ArrayGrowTest.java

```
import java.lang.reflect.*;
import corejava.*;

public class ArrayGrowTest
{  public static void main(String[] args)
   {  int[] a = { 1, 2, 3 };
      Day[] b = { new Day(1996, 1, 1), new Day(1997, 3, 26) };
      a = (int[])goodArrayGrow(a);
      arrayPrint(a);
      b = (Day[])goodArrayGrow(b);
      arrayPrint(b);
      System.out.println
         ("The following cast will generate an exception.");
      b = (Day[])badArrayGrow(b);
   }

   static Object[] badArrayGrow(Object[] a)
   {  int newLength = a.length * 11 / 10 + 10;
      Object[] newArray = new Object[newLength];
      System.arraycopy(a, 0, newArray, 0, a.length);
      return newArray;
   }

   static Object goodArrayGrow(Object a)
   {  Class cl = a.getClass();
      if (!cl.isArray()) return null;
      Class componentType = a.getClass().getComponentType();
      int length = Array.getLength(a);
      int newLength = length * 11 / 10 + 10;

      Object newArray = Array.newInstance(componentType,
         newLength);
      System.arraycopy(a, 0, newArray, 0, length);
      return newArray;
```

```
    }

    static void arrayPrint(Object a)
    {   Class cl = a.getClass();
        if (!cl.isArray()) return;
        Class componentType = a.getClass().getComponentType();
        int length = Array.getLength(a);
        System.out.println(componentType.getName()
            + "[" + length + "]");
        for (int i = 0; i < Array.getLength(a); i++)
            System.out.println(Array.get(a, i));
    }
}
```

Method Pointers!
On the surface, Java does not have method pointers—ways of giving the location of a method to another method in order that the second method can invoke it later. In fact, the designers of Java have said that method pointers are dangerous and error-prone and that Java *interfaces* (discussed in the next chapter) are a superior solution. However, it turns out that Java now does have method pointers, as a (perhaps accidental) byproduct of the reflection package.

NOTE: Some Java tool vendors provide nonstandard language extensions that purport to implement method pointers in a more efficient or convenient fashion. We recommend against using these nonstandard language extensions unless you absolutely have to use a feature in their tool that is available in no other way. We suggest that you either use the method pointers described in this section or inner classes, described in Chapter 6.

To see method pointers at work, recall that you can inspect a field of an object with the get method of the Field class. Similarly, the Method class has an invoke method that lets you call the method that is wrapped in the current Method object. The signature for the invoke method is:

```
    Object invoke(Object obj, Object[] args)
```

The first parameter is the implicit parameter, and the array of objects provides the explicit parameters. For a static method, the first parameter is ignored—you can set it to null. If the method has no explicit parameters, you pass null for the args parameter. For example, if m1 represents the getName method of the Employee class, the following code shows how you can call it:

```
    String n = (String)m1.invoke(harry, null);
```

As with the get and set methods of the Field type, there's a problem if the parameter or return type is not a class but a basic type. You must wrap any of the basic types into their corresponding wrappers before inserting them into the args array. Conversely, the invoke method will return the wrapped type and not the basic type. For example, suppose that m2 represents the raiseSalary method of the Employee class. Then, you need to wrap the double parameter into a Double object.

```
Object[] args = { new Double(5.5) };
m2.invoke(harry, args);
```

How do you obtain a Method object? You can, of course, call getDeclaredMethods and search through the returned array of Method objects until you find the method that you want. Or, you can call the getMethod method of the Class class. This is similar to the getField(String) method that takes a string with the field name and returns a Field object. However, there may be several methods with the same name, so you need to be careful that you get the right one. For that reason, you must also supply an array that gives the correct parameter types. For example, here is how you can get method pointers to the getName and raiseSalary methods of the Employee class.

```
Method m1 = Employee.class.getMethod("getName", null);
Method m2 = Employee.class.getMethod("raiseSalary",
    new Class[] { double.class } );
```

The second parameter of the getMethod method is an array of Class objects. Since the raiseSalary method has one argument of type double, we must supply an array with a single element, double.class. It is usually easiest to make that array on the fly, as we did in the example above. The expression

```
new Class[] { double.class }
```

denotes an array of Class objects, filled with one element, namely, the class object double.class.

Now that we have seen the syntax of Method objects, let's put them to work. Example 5–8 is a program that prints a table of values for a function such as Math.sqrt or Math.sin. The printout looks like this:

```
public static native double java.lang.Math.sqrt(double)
    1.0000 |       1.0000
    2.0000 |       1.4142
    3.0000 |       1.7321
    4.0000 |       2.0000
    5.0000 |       2.2361
    6.0000 |       2.4495
    7.0000 |       2.6458
    8.0000 |       2.8284
    9.0000 |       3.0000
   10.0000 |       3.1623
```

The code for printing a table is, of course, independent of the actual function that is being tabulated.

```
double dx = (to - from) / (n - 1);
```

```
for (double x = from; x <= to; x += dx)
{   double y = f(x); // where f is the function to be tabulated
    Format.printf(System.out, "%12.4f |", x);
    Format.printf(System.out, "%12.4f\n", y);
}
```

We want to write a generic `printTable` method that can tabulate any function. We will pass the function as a parameter of type `Method`.

```
static void printTable(double from, double to, int n, Method f)
```

Of course, `f` is not actually a function, so we cannot simply write `f(x)` to evaluate it. Instead, we must supply `x` in the parameter array (suitably wrapped as a `Double`), use the `invoke` method, and unwrap the return value.

```
Object[] args = { new Double(x) };
Double d = (Double)f.invoke(null, args);
double y = d.doubleValue();
```

The first parameter of `invoke` is `null` because we are calling a static function.

Here is a sample call to `printTable` that tabulates the `Math.sqrt` function.

```
printTable(1, 10, 10,
    java.lang.Math.class.getMethod("sqrt",
    new Class[] { double.class }));
```

The hardest part is to get the method object. Here, we get the method of the `java.lang.Math` class that has the name `sqrt` and whose parameter list contains just one type, `double`.

Example 5–8 shows the complete code of the `printTable` method and a couple of test runs.

Example 5–8: MethodPointerTest

```
import java.lang.reflect.*;
import corejava.*;

public class MethodPointerTest
{   public static void main(String[] args) throws Exception
    {   printTable(1, 10, 10,
            MethodPointerTest.class.getMethod("square",
                new Class[] { double.class }));
        printTable(1, 10, 10, java.lang.Math.class.getMethod("sqrt",
            new Class[] { double.class }));
    }

    public static double square(double x) { return x * x; }

    public static void printTable(double from, double to,
        int n, Method f)
    {   System.out.println(f);
```

```
        double dx = (to - from) / (n - 1);
        for (double x = from; x <= to; x += dx)
        {  Format.printf("%12.4f |", x);
           try
           {  Object[] args = { new Double(x) };
              Double d = (Double)f.invoke(null, args);
              double y = d.doubleValue();
              Format.printf("%12.4f\n", y);
           } catch (Exception e)
           {  System.out.println("???");
           }
        }
     }
  }
}
```

As this example shows clearly, you can do anything with Method objects that you can do with function pointers in C. Just as in C, this style of programming is usually quite inconvenient and always error-prone. What happens if you invoke a method with the wrong parameters? The invoke method throws an exception.

Also, the parameters and return values of invoke are necessarily of type Object. That means you must cast back and forth a lot. As a result, the compiler is deprived of the chance to check your code. That means that errors surface only during testing, when they are more tedious to find and fix. Moreover, code that uses reflection to get at method pointers is significantly slower than simply calling methods directly.

For that reason, we suggest that you use Method objects in your own programs only when absolutely necessary. Using interfaces and inner classes (the subject of the next chapter) is almost always a better idea. In particular, we echo the developers of Java and suggest not using Method objects for callback functions. Using interfaces for the callbacks (see the next chapter as well) leads to code that runs faster and is a lot more maintainable.

Design Hints for Inheritance

We want to end this chapter with some hints for using inheritance that we have found useful.

1. *Place common operations and fields in the superclass.*

   This is why we put the sender field into the Message class, rather than replicating it in TextMessage and VoiceMessage.

2. *Use inheritance to model the "is–a" relationship.*

   Inheritance is a handy code-saver, and sometimes people overuse it. For example, suppose we need a Contractor class. Contractors have names and hire dates, but they do not have salaries. Instead, they are paid by the hour, and they do not stay around long enough to get a raise. There is the temptation to derive `Contractor` from `Employee` and add an `hourlyWage` field.

```
class Contractor extends Employee
{   public Contractor(String name, double wage, Day hireDay)
    {   super(name, 0, hireDay);
        hourlyWage = wage;
    }
    private double hourlyWage;
}
```

This is *not* a good idea, however, because now each contractor object has both a salary and hourly wage instance variable. It will cause you no end of grief when you implement methods for printing paychecks or tax forms. You will end up writing more code than you would have by not inheriting in the first place.

The contractor/employee relationship fails the "is–a" test. A contractor is not a special case of an employee (although the IRS is pushing to make this true).

3. *Don't use inheritance unless* all *inherited methods make sense.*

   Suppose we want to write a `Holiday` class. Surely every holiday is a day, so we can use inheritance.

   ```
   class Holiday extends Day { . . . }
   ```

   Unfortunately, this is somewhat subtle. When we say that `Holiday` extends `Day`, we have to consider that we are talking about the *class* `Day`, as specified by its public methods. One of the public methods of `Day` is advance. And advance can turn holidays into nonholidays, so it is not an appropriate operation for holidays.

   ```
   Holiday xmas;
   xmas.advance(10);
   ```

   In that sense, a holiday is a day *but* not a Day.

4. *Use polymorphism, not type information.*

   Whenever you find code of the form

   ```
   if (x is of type 1)
       action1(x);
   else if (x is of type 2)
       action2(x);
   ```

   think polymorphism.

   Do *action1* and *action2* represent a common concept? If so, make the concept a method of a common parent class or interface of both types.

Then, you can simply call

```
x.action();
```

and have the dynamic dispatch mechanism inherent in polymorphism launch the correct action.

The point is that code using polymorphic methods or interface implementations is much easier to maintain and extend than code that uses multiple type tests.

Chapter 6

Interfaces and
Inner Classes

- ▼ INTERFACES
- ▼ CLONING
- ▼ INNER CLASSES

You have now seen all the basic tools for doing object-oriented programming in Java. This chapter shows you two advanced techniques that are quite a bit more complex. Despite their less obvious nature, you will need to master them in order to complete your Java tool chest.

The first, called an *interface,* is Java's way of dealing with the common situation of wanting a class to reflect the behavior of two (or even more) parents. (This is often called multiple inheritance.) After we cover interfaces, we take up cloning an object (or deep copying as it is sometimes called), which we briefly discussed in the last chapter. Finally, we move on to the mechanism of *inner classes.* Inner classes are more of a convenience than a necessity; there will often be workarounds if you decide that using them is not to your taste. However, as we will show you in this chapter, there are a few situations where there are no convenient alternatives, and so inner classes are commonly used in these specialized circumstances. In particular, inner classes are important to write concise, professional-looking code to handle graphical user interface events.

Interfaces

Using an Abstract Superclass

Suppose you wanted to write a general sorting routine that would work on many different kinds of Java objects. You now know how to organize this in an object-oriented fashion. You start with an abstract class Sortable with a method compareTo that determines whether or not one sortable object is less than, equal to, or greater than another.

Now you can implement a generic sorting algorithm. Here is an implementation of a Shell sort variant, for sorting an array of Sortable objects. Don't be concerned with the inner workings of this algorithm. We simply chose it because it is simple to implement. Just observe that the algorithm visits array elements, compares them with the compareTo method and rearranges them.

```
abstract class Sortable
{   public abstract int compareTo(Sortable b);
}

class ArrayAlg
{   public static void shellSort(Sortable[] a)
    {   int n = a.length;
        int incr = n / 2;
        while (incr >= 1)
        {   for (int i = incr; i < n; i++)
            {   Sortable temp = a[i];
                int j = i;
                while (j >= incr
                    && temp.compareTo(a[j - incr]) < 0)
                {   a[j] = a[j - incr];
                    j -= incr;
                }
                a[j] = temp;
            }
            incr /= 2;
        }
    }
}
```

You can use this sorting routine with all subclasses of the Sortable abstract class (by overriding the compareTo method in the subclass).

For example, to sort an array of employees (ordering them by—what else—their salary), we

1.   derive Employee from Sortable,
2.   implement the compareTo method for employees,
3.   call ArrayAlg.shellSort on the employee array.

Here's an example of the extra code needed to do this in our Employee class:

```
class Employee extends Sortable
```

```
{   . . .
    public int compareTo(Sortable b)
    {   Employee eb = (Employee)b;
        if (salary < eb.salary) return -1;
        if (salary > eb.salary) return 1;
        return 0;
    }

    public static void main(String[] args)
    {   Employee[] staff = new Employee[3];
        . . .
        Sort.shellSort(staff);
        . . .
    }
}
```

See Example 6–1 for the full code for the generic sorting algorithm and the sorting of the employee array.

Example 6–1: EmployeeSortTest.java

```java
import java.util.*;
import corejava.*;

public class EmployeeSortTest
{   public static void main(String[] args)
    {   Employee[] staff = new Employee[3];

        staff[0] = new Employee("Harry Hacker", 35000,
            new Day(1989,10,1));
        staff[1] = new Employee("Carl Cracker", 75000,
            new Day(1987,12,15));
        staff[2] = new Employee("Tony Tester", 38000,
            new Day(1990,3,15));

        ArrayAlg.shellSort(staff);

        int i;
        for (i = 0; i < staff.length; i++)
            System.out.println(staff[i]);

    }
}

abstract class Sortable
{   public abstract int compareTo(Sortable b);
}

class ArrayAlg
{   public static void shellSort(Sortable[] a)
```

```
    {   int n = a.length;
        int incr = n / 2;
        while (incr >= 1)
        {   for (int i = incr; i < n; i++)
            {   Sortable temp = a[i];
                int j = i;
                while (j >= incr
                    && temp.compareTo(a[j - incr]) < 0)
                {   a[j] = a[j - incr];
                    j -= incr;
                }
                a[j] = temp;
            }
            incr /= 2;
        }
    }
}

class Employee extends Sortable
{   public Employee(String n, double s, Day d)
    {   name = n;
        salary = s;
        hireDate = d;
    }

    public void raiseSalary(double byPercent)
    {   salary *= 1 + byPercent / 100;
    }

    public String getName() { return name; }

    public double getSalary() { return salary; }

    public String toString()
    {   return name + " " + salary + " " + hireYear();
    }

    public int hireYear()
    {   return hireDate.getYear();
    }

    public int compareTo(Sortable b)
    {   Employee eb = (Employee)b;
        if (salary < eb.salary) return -1;
        if (salary > eb.salary) return 1;
        return 0;
    }

    private String name;
    private double salary;
```

```
    private Day hireDate;
}
```

Using an Interface

There is, unfortunately, a major problem with using an abstract base class to express a generic property. Here's an example of where this problem arises: consider a `Tile` class that models tiled windows on a screen desktop. Tiled windows are rectangles plus a "z-order." Windows with a larger z-order are displayed in front of those with a smaller z-order. To reuse code, we inherit `Tile` from `Rectangle`, a class that is already defined in the `java.awt` package.

```
class Tile extends Rectangle
{   public Tile(int x, int y, int w, int h, int zz)
    {   super(x, y, w, h);
        z = zz;
    }

    private int z;
}
```

Now we would like to sort an array of tiles by comparing z-orders. If we try to apply the procedure for making tiles sortable, we get stuck at step (1). We cannot derive `Tile` from `Sortable`—it already derives from `Rectangle`!

The problem is that, in Java, a class can have only *one* superclass. Other programming languages, in particular C++, allow a class to have more than one superclass. This feature is called *multiple inheritance*.

Instead, Java introduces the notion of *interfaces* to recover much of the functionality that multiple inheritance gives you. The designers of Java chose this road because multiple inheritance makes compilers either very complex (as in C++) or very inefficient (as in Eiffel). Interfaces are also the preferred method of implementing "callback functions" in Java—see the section on callbacks later in this chapter for more on this important topic.

So, what is an interface? Essentially, it is a promise that your class will implement certain methods with certain signatures. You even use the keyword `implements` to indicate that your class will keep these promises. The way in which these methods are implemented is up to the class, of course. The important point, as far as the compiler is concerned, is that the methods have the right signature.

For example, the standard library defines an interface called `Comparable` that could be used by any class whose elements can be compared. The code for the `Comparable` interface looks like this:

```
public interface Comparable
{   public int compareTo(Object b);
}
```

This code promises that any class that implements the `Comparable` interface will have a `compareTo` method. Of course, the way in which the `compareTo` method works (or even whether or not it works as one would expect) in a specific class depends on the class that is implementing the `Comparable` interface. The key point is that any class can promise to implement `Comparable`—regardless of whether or not its superclass promises the same. All descendants of such a class would automatically implement `Comparable`, since they all would have access to a `compareTo` method with the right signature.

To tell Java that your class implements `Comparable`, you define it as follows:

```
class Tile extends Rectangle implements Comparable
```

Then, all you need to do is implement a `compareTo` method inside the class.

```
class Tile extends Rectangle implements Comparable
{   public int compareTo(Object b)
    {   Tile tb = (Tile)b;
        return z - tb.z;
    }
    . . .

    private int z;
}
```

NOTE: If the parent class already implements an interface, its subclasses do not need to explicitly use the `implements` keyword.

Conveniently, the `Arrays` class in Java supplies a sorting algorithm for an array of `Comparable` objects. We can use it to sort an array of tiles:

```
Tile[] a = new Tile[20];
. . .
Arrays.sort(a);
```

Example 6–2 is the complete code for the tile example.

Example 6–2: TileTest.java

```
import java.awt.*;
import java.util.*;

public class TileTest
{   public static void main(String[] args)
    {   Tile[] a = new Tile[20];

        int i;
        for (i = 0; i < a.length; i++)
            a[i] = new Tile(i, i, 10, 20,
```

```
                (int)(100 * Math.random())));

        Arrays.sort(a);

        for (i = 0; i < a.length; i++)
            System.out.println(a[i]);
    }
}

class Tile extends Rectangle implements Comparable
{   public Tile(int x, int y, int w, int h, int zz)
    {   super(x, y, w, h);
        z = zz;
    }

    public int compareTo(Object b)
    {   Tile tb = (Tile)b;
        return z - tb.z;
    }

    public String toString()
    {   return super.toString() + "[z=" + z + "]";
    }

    private int z;
}
```

C++ NOTE: C++ has multiple inheritance and all the complications that come with it, such as virtual base classes, dominance rules, and transverse pointer casts. Few C++ programmers use multiple inheritance, and some say it should never be used. Other programmers recommend using multiple inheritance only for "mix in" style inheritance. In the "mixin" style, a primary base class describes the parent object, and additional base classes (the so-called mixins) may supply auxiliary characteristics. That style is similar to a Java class with a single base class and additional interfaces. However, in C++, mixins can add default behavior, whereas Java interfaces cannot.

VB NOTE: The Java notion of Interface and the VB notion of Interface (VB5 and later) are essentially equivalent.

NOTE: Microsoft has long been a proponent of using interfaces instead of using multiple inheritance. Somewhat ironically as a result of this, the Java notion of an interface is essentially equivalent to how Microsoft used interfaces in the definition of their COM/OLE specification. As a result of this unlikely convergence of minds, it is relatively easy to use Java to build COM/OLE objects like ActiveX controls. This is done (pretty much transparently to the coder) in, for example, Microsoft's J++ product and is also the basis for Sun's JavaBeans-to-ActiveX bridge.

`java.lang.Comparable`

- `int compareTo(Object b)`

    compares this object with b and returns zero if they are identical, a negative integer if this object is less than b, a positive integer otherwise.

`java.util.Arrays`

- `static void sort(Object[] a)`

    sorts the elements in the array a, using a tuned mergesort algorithm. All elements in the array must implement the `Comparable` interface, and they must all be comparable to each other.

Properties of Interfaces

Although interfaces are not instantiated with new, they have certain properties similar to ordinary classes. For example, once you set up an interface, you can declare that an object variable will be of that interface type.

```
Comparable x = new Tile(. . .);
Tile y = new Tile(. . .);

if (x.compareTo(y) < 0) . . .
```

As you can see, you can always assign an object variable of a type that implements an interface to an object variable declared to be of that interface type.

Next, just as you use `instanceof` to check if a object is of a specific class, you can use `instanceof` to check if an object implements an interface:

```
if (anObject instanceof Comparable) { . . . }
```

Also, nothing prevents you from extending one interface in order to create another. This allows for multiple chains of interfaces that go from a greater degree of generality to a greater degree of specialization. For example, suppose you had an interface called `Moveable`.

```
public interface Moveable
{  public void move(double x, double y);
}
```

Then, you could imagine an interface called `Powered` that extends it:

```
public interface Powered extends Moveable
{  public String powerSource();
}
```

> NOTE: Unfortunately, the Java documentation often refers to *classes* when it means *classes* or *interfaces*. You have to use contextual clues to decide whether the reference is only to classes or to both classes and interfaces.

Although you cannot put instance fields or static methods in an interface, you can supply constants in them. For example:

```
public interface Powered extends Moveable
{    public String powerSource(PoweredVehicle);
     public static final int SPEED_LIMIT = 95;
}
```

Classes can implement multiple interfaces. This gives you the maximum amount of flexibility in defining a class's behavior. For example, Java has an important interface built into it, called `Cloneable`. (We will discuss this interface in detail in the next section.) If your class implements `Cloneable`, the `clone` method in the `Object` class will make a bitwise copy of your class's objects. Suppose, therefore, you want cloneability and comparability. Then you simply implement both interfaces.

```
class Tile extends Rectangle implements Cloneable, Comparable
```

Use commas to separate the interfaces that describe the characteristics that you want to supply.

The `Cloneable` *Interface*

When you make a copy of a variable, the original and the copy are references to the same object. (See Figure 6-1). This means a change to either variable also affects the other.

```
Day bday = new Day(1959, 6, 16);
Day d = bday;
d.advance(100); // oops--also changed bday
```

If you would like d to be a new object that begins its life being identical to bday but whose state can diverge over time, then you use the clone() method.

```
Day bday = new Day(1959, 6, 16);
Day d = (Day)bday.clone();
     // must cast—clone returns an Object
d.advance(100); // ok—bday unchanged
```

But it isn't quite so simple. The clone method is a protected method of Object, which means that your code cannot simply call it. Only the Day class can clone Day objects. There is a reason for this. Think about the way in which the Object class can implement clone. It knows nothing about the object at all, so it can make only a bit-by-bit copy. If all data fields in the object are numbers or other basic types, a bitwise copy is just fine. It is simply another object with the same base types and fields. But if the object contains references to other objects in one or more of its instance fields, then a bitwise copy contains exact

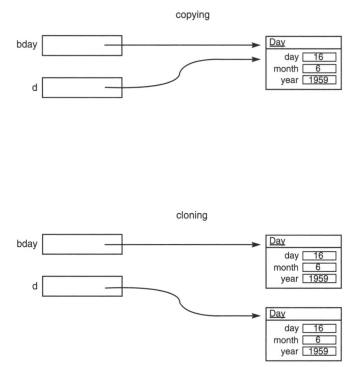

Figure 6–1: Copying and cloning

copies of the reference fields, so the original and the cloned objects still share some information. This is shown in Figure 6–2.

It is up to the derived class designer to judge whether or not

1. the default `clone` method is good enough,
2. the default `clone` method can be patched up by calling `clone` on the object instance variables,
3. the situation is hopeless and `clone` should not be attempted.

The third option is actually the default. To choose either the first or the second option, a class must

1. implement the `Cloneable` *interface* and
2. redefine the `clone` method with the public access modifier.

NOTE: Users of your public `clone` method still have to cast the result. The `clone` method always has return type `Object`.

In this case, the appearance of the `Cloneable` interface has nothing to do with the normal use of interfaces. The interfaces merely serve as a tag, indicating that

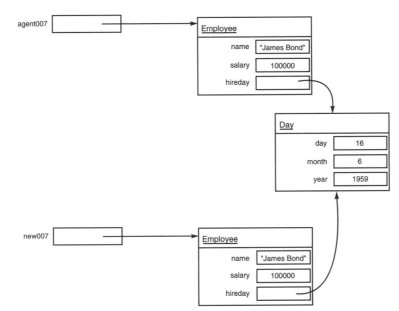

Figure 6–2: Original and cloned objects sharing information

the class designer understands the cloning process. Objects are so paranoid about cloning that they generate a run-time exception if an object requests cloning but does not implement that interface.

NOTE: The Cloneable interface is one of a handful of *tagging interfaces* that Java provides. Recall that the usual purpose of an interface such as Comparable is to ensure that a class implements a particular method or set of methods. A tagging interface has no methods; its only purpose is to allow you to use instanceof in a type inquiry:

```
if (obj instanceof Cloneable) . . .
```

Here is the drudgery that the Day class has to do to redefine clone.

```
public class Day implements Cloneable
{  . . .
   public Object clone()
   {  try
      {  return super.clone(); // calls Object.clone()
      } catch (CloneNotSupportedException e)
      {  // this shouldn't happen, since we are Cloneable
         return null;
      }
   }
}
```

And this is the easy case!

If we want to clone `Employee`, we:

1. call the `clone` method in `Object` to make a bitwise copy,
2. cast the result to `Employee` so that we can change its `hireDay` instance field to be a clone of the original `Day` object,
3. then return the result.

Here's the code:

```
public class Employee implements Cloneable
{   . . .
    public Object clone()
    {   try
        {   Employee e = (Employee)super.clone();
            e.hireDay = (Day)hireDay.clone();
            return e;
        }   catch (CloneNotSupportedException e)
        {   // this shouldn't happen, since we are Cloneable
            return null;
        }
    }
}
```

As you can see, cloning is a subtle business, and it makes sense that it is defined as `protected` in the `Object` class. (See Chapter 12 for an elegant method for cloning objects, using the object serialization feature of Java.)

Interfaces and Callbacks

Suppose you want to implement a `Timer` class in Java. You want to be able to program your class to:

*   start the timer,
*   have the timer measure some time delay,
*   then carry out some action when the correct time has elapsed.

For this to be practical, the `Timer` class needs a way of communicating with the calling class. This is usually called a *callback function*. Interfaces are the preferred way to implement callback functions in Java. To see why, let's peek inside the `Timer` class.

```
class Timer extends Thread
{   . . .
    public void run()
    {   while (true)
        {   sleep(delay);
            // now what?
        }
    }
}
```

(Don't worry about the fact that this class has to extend Java's built-in Thread class. Threads have many uses—one of the simplest is to sleep until some time has elapsed. See the multithreading chapter in Volume 2 for more about threads.)

The object constructing a Timer object must somehow tell the timer what to do when the time is up. In C++, the code creating the timer gives it a pointer to a function, and the timer calls that function at the end of every interval. Java has no function pointers. It uses interfaces instead. So the //now what? comment in the preceding code is replaced by a method call that was declared inside an interface.

Thus, in addition to the Timer class, we need the interface TimerListener. It has a single method called timeElapsed.

```
interface TimerListener
{   public void timeElapsed(Timer t);
}
```

Any class wanting to be called from a timer must implement that interface. The constructor of the Timer object is given a reference to an object that implements the TimerListener interface. That object is notified, via its timeElapsed method, whenever the time has progressed to the next interval.

In the following example, an AlarmClock class both constructs a Timer object and implements the TimerListener interface. In the constructor of the Timer object, it passes the this reference, a reference to itself, to be notified at every timer tick. The timeElapsed method simply checks whether it is time to play the wakeUp audio clip.

```
class AlarmClock implements TimerListener
{   AlarmClock()
    {   Timer t = new Timer(this);
        t.setDelay(1000); // 1000 milliseconds
    }

    public void timeElapsed(Timer t)
    {   if(t.getTime() >= wakeUpTime)
            wakeUp.play();
    }
}
```

Here's the code for the Timer class. Notice how the constructor of the Timer class receives the reference to the object that needs to be notified and stores it in the listener variable. Whenever the timing interval has elapsed, its timeElapsed() method is called. Because the listener object implements the TimerListener interface, the compiler knows that it supports a timeElapsed method.

```
class Timer extends Thread
{   Timer(TimerListener t) { listener = t; }
```

```
   . . .
   public void run()
   {   while (true)
       {   sleep(interval);
           listener.timeElapsed(this);
       }
   }
   TimerListener listener;
}
```

NOTE: We have only explained the part of this code that shows how an interface can supply a notification mechanism and, hence, allow callback functions. The Java library has a `Timer` class in the `javax.swing` package. It works almost like the `Timer` class that we sketched out here. However, instead of the `TimerListener` interface and the `timeElapsed` method, a class that is interested in timer notifications must implement the `ActionListener` interface and its `actionPerformed` method. That is a catch-all interface that is also used for button clicks and list selections.

C++ NOTE: As you saw in Chapter 5, Java does have the equivalent of function pointers, namely, `Method` objects. However, they are difficult to use, slower, and cannot be checked for type safety at compile time. Whenever you would use a function pointer in C++, you should use polymorphism in Java, either by deriving from a base class or by implementing an interface. You can derive from only one base class, but you can implement any number of interfaces. It is quite common in Java to have trivial interfaces for callback protocols.

Inner Classes

An *inner class* is a class that is defined inside another class. Why would you want to do that? There are four reasons:

- An object of an inner class can access the implementation of the object that created it—including data that would otherwise be private.

- Inner classes can be hidden from other classes in the same package.

- *Anonymous* inner classes are handy when you want to define callbacks on the fly.

- Inner classes are very convenient when you are writing event-driven programs.

You will soon see examples that demonstrate the first three benefits. (For more information on the event model, please turn to Chapter 8.)

C++ NOTE: C++ has *nested classes*. A nested class is contained inside the scope of the enclosing class. Here is a typical example: a linked list class defines a class to hold the links, and a class to define an iterator position.

```
class LinkedList
{
public:
    class Iterator
    {
    public:
        void insert(int x);
        int erase();
        . . .
    };
    . . .
private:
    class Link
    {
    public:
        Link* next;
        int data;
    };
    . . .
};
```

The nesting is a relationship between *classes,* not *objects.* A LinkedList object does *not* have subobjects of type Iterator or Link.

There are two benefits: *name control* and *access control.* Because the name Iterator is nested inside the LinkedList class, it is externally known as LinkedList::Iterator and cannot conflict with another class called Iterator. In Java, this benefit is not as important since Java *packages* give the same kind of name control. Note that the Link class is in the *private* part of the LinkedList class. It is completely hidden from all other code. For that reason, it is safe to make its data fields public. They can be accessed by the methods of the LinkedList class (which has a legitimate need to access them), and they are not visible elsewhere. In Java, this kind of control was not possible until inner classes were introduced.

However, the Java inner classes have an additional feature that makes them richer and therefore potentially more useful than nested classes in C++. An object that comes from an inner class has an implicit reference to the outer class object that instantiated it. Through this pointer, it gains access to the total state of the outer object. You will see the details of the Java mechanism later in this chapter.

Only static inner classes do not have this added pointer. They are the exact Java analog to nested classes in C++.

A Property *Interface*

We now want to develop a more realistic example to show where inner classes are useful. We will build a *property editor*. This is a sheet that shows properties of various objects and lets you modify them. What is a property? It is something that has a name, a value, and that can be set to a new value. At the beginning of this chapter, you have learned that such a collection of methods can be expressed as an *interface*:

```
interface Property
{   public String get();
    public void set(String s);
    public String name();
}
```

Since we haven't yet covered how to write a graphical program, we will implement our property editor in a way that is much more mundane. Our editor simply displays the properties on the screen, numbers them, and asks the user which one should be modified. Then it asks for the new value of the property. Here is a sample interaction:

```
1:Harry Hacker's salary=35000.0
2:Carl Cracker's salary=75000.0
3:Carl Cracker's years on the job=9
Change which property? (0 to quit) 2
New value: 94000
```

Here is the code for the PropertyEditor class. Note that the property editor does not need to know anything about properties, except that it can get and set them.

```
class PropertyEditor
{   public PropertyEditor(Property[] p)
    {   properties = p;
    }

    public void editProperties()
    {   while (true)
        {   for (int i = 0; i < properties.length; i++)
                System.out.println((i + 1) + ":"
                    + properties[i].name()
                    + "=" + properties[i].get());
            int n = Console.readInt
                ("Change which property? (0 to quit)");
            if (n == 0) return;
            if (0 < n && n <= properties.length)
            {   String value
                    = Console.readString("New value:");
                properties[n - 1].set(value);
            }
        }
    }
```

```
    }

    private Property[] properties;
}
```

Using an Inner Class to Implement the `Property` Interface

Now let us add a property to the `Employee` class in order to put the class in a position to work with our property editor. An employee object will now expose a `SalaryProperty` object that can be given to a property editor.

```
Employee carl = new Employee("Carl Cracker",
    75000, new Day(1987, 12, 15));

Property carlsSalary = carl.getSalaryProperty();
```

Of course, `Property` is just an interface. The object returned by the `getSalaryProperty` method must be an object of a class implementing that interface. In fact, in our example, it will be an instance of the class `SalaryProperty`—which will be an *inner class inside of* `Employee` implementing the `Property` interface.

```
class Employee
{   . . .

    private class SalaryProperty implements Property
    {   public String get() { . . . }
        public void set(String s) { . . . }
        public String name() { . . . }
    }

    public Property getSalaryProperty()
    {   return new SalaryProperty();
    }
}
```

The `SalaryProperty` class is a *private inner class* inside `Employee`. This is a safety mechanism—since only `Employee` methods can generate `SalaryProperty` objects, we don't have to worry about breaking encapsulation. Note that only inner classes can be private. Regular classes always have either package or public visibility.

Let us implement the `get` method. For this, the `SalaryProperty` object must report the *salary of the employee that instantiated it.* For example, in the code

```
Property carlsSalary = carl.getSalaryProperty();
String s = carlsSalary.get();
```

the `get` method must return Carl's salary.

In Java, an object created by an inner class can automatically access *all* data fields of the *object that created it*. This allows the code for the get method to be extremely simple:

```
private class SalaryProperty implements Property
{   public String get()
    {   return "" + salary;
    }
        .  .  .
}
```

The name salary in the code above refers to the salary field of the outer class object that created this SalaryProperty. This is quite innovative. Traditionally, a method could refer to the data fields of the object invoking the method. An inner class method gets to access both its own data fields *and* those of the outer object creating it.

For this to work, of course, an object of an inner class always gets an implicit reference to the object that created it. (See Figure 6–3.)

This reference is invisible in the Java code—it is a detail of the implementation of the inner class.

Next, let us see an example of an inner class method that accesses both its own data fields and that of the outer object. We will define the set method in the SalaryProperty object so that it can change the employee's salary, but it can do so only *once*. If you want to change the salary twice, then you must obtain two SalaryProperty objects. Here is the code for the method:

```
private class SalaryProperty implements Property
{   .  .  .
    public void set(String s)
    {   if (isSet) return; // can set once
        double sal = Double.parseDouble(s);
        if (sal > 0)
        {   salary = sal;
            isSet = true;
        }
    }
    private boolean isSet = false;
}
```

![Figure showing SalaryProperty object with isSet field set to false, and an arrow pointing to an Employee object with name "Carl Cracker", salary 75000, and hireDay.]

Figure 6–3: An object of an inner class

The name `isSet` refers to the `isSet` field of the inner object; the name `salary` refers to the `salary` field of the outer object.

Let us assume that the reference to the outer object is called `outer`. (It actually is called something different internally.) Then, the code of the `set` method can be visualized as follows:

```
public void set(String s)
{  if (this.isSet) return; // can set once
   double sal = Double.parseDouble(s);
   if (sal > 0)
   {  outer.salary = sal;
      this.isSet = true;
   }
}
```

The `outer` reference is set in the constructor.

```
private class SalaryProperty implements Property
{  SalaryProperty(Employee o) { outer = o; }

   private Employee outer; // this is what happens internally
}
```

Again, please note, `outer` is not a Java keyword. We just use it to indicate the mechanism involved in an inner class.

The proper syntax for the outer object is `Employee.this`. For example, you can write the `set` method of the `SalaryProperty` inner class as

```
public void set(String s)
{  if (this.isSet) return; // can set once
   double sal = Double.parseDouble(s);
   if (sal > 0)
   {  Employee.this.salary = sal;
      this.isSet = true;
   }
}
```

In our example, the inner class object is always generated in a method of the outer class:

```
public Property getSalaryProperty()
{  return new SalaryProperty();
}
```

Here, the outer class reference is set to the `this` reference of the method that creates the inner class object. This is the most common case. However, it is also possible to set the outer class reference to another object by explicitly naming it. For example, the following expression creates a `SalaryProperty` object that sets the outer class reference to the `Employee` object harry:

```
Property p = harry.new SalaryProperty();
```

Example 6–3 shows the complete program that tests inner classes implementing the `Property` interface. There are two instances of the `SalaryProperty` for the same employee object, allowing us to change the salary twice. We also added a second property, called the `SeniorityProperty`, that reports how many years an employee has been with the company. The `set` method of this property does nothing—you can update a salary but you can't change history. The `PropertyEditor` just treats this class as yet another property.

Example 6–3: PropertyTest.java

```java
import corejava.*;

public class PropertyTest
{  public static void main(String[] args)
   {  Employee harry = new Employee("Harry Hacker",
          35000, new Day(1989, 10, 1));
      Employee carl = new Employee("Carl Cracker",
          75000, new Day(1987, 12, 15));

      PropertyEditor editor = new PropertyEditor(
          new Property[]
          {  harry.getSalaryProperty(),
             harry.getSalaryProperty(),
             carl.getSalaryProperty(),
             carl.getSeniorityProperty()
          });

      System.out.println("Before:");
      harry.print();
      carl.print();
      System.out.println("Edit properties:");
      editor.editProperties();
      System.out.println("After:");
      harry.print();
      carl.print();
   }
}

interface Property
{  public String get();
   public void set(String s);
   public String name();
}

class PropertyEditor
{  public PropertyEditor(Property[] p)
   {  properties = p;
```

```
    }

    public void editProperties()
    {   while (true)
        {   for (int i = 0; i < properties.length; i++)
                System.out.println((i + 1) + ":"
                    + properties[i].name()
                    + "=" + properties[i].get());
            int n = Console.readInt
                ("Change which property? (0 to quit)");
            if (n == 0) return;
            if (0 < n && n <= properties.length)
            {   String value
                    = Console.readLine("New value:");
                properties[n - 1].set(value);
            }
        }
    }

    private Property[] properties;
}

class Employee
{   public Employee(String n, double s, Day d)
    {   name = n;
        salary = s;
        hireDay = d;
    }
    public void print()
    {   System.out.println(name + " " + salary + " "
            + hireYear());
    }
    public void raiseSalary(double byPercent)
    {   salary *= 1 + byPercent / 100;
    }
    public int hireYear()
    {   return hireDay.getYear();
    }

    private class SalaryProperty implements Property
    {   public String name()
        {   return name + "'s salary";
        }
        public String get()
        {   return "" + salary;
        }

        public void set(String s)
```

```
    {   if (isSet) return; // can set once
        double sal = Double.parseDouble(s);
        if (sal > 0)
        {   salary = sal;
            isSet = true;
        }
    }
    private boolean isSet = false;
}

public Property getSalaryProperty()
{   return new SalaryProperty();
}

private class SeniorityProperty implements Property
{   public String name()
    {   return name + "'s years on the job";
    }
    public String get()
    {   Day today = new Day();
        int years = today.daysBetween(hireDay) / 365;
        return "" + years;
    }
    public void set(String s)
    {} // can't set seniority
}

public Property getSeniorityProperty()
{   return new SeniorityProperty();
}

private String name;
private double salary;
private Day hireDay;
}
```

Are Inner Classes Useful? Are They Actually Necessary? Are They Secure?

Inner classes are a major addition to the language. Java started out with the goal of being simpler than C++. But inner classes are anything but simple. The syntax is complex. (It will get more complex as we study anonymous inner classes later in this chapter.) It is not obvious how inner classes interact with other features of the language, such as access control and security.

Has Java started down the road to ruin that has afflicted so many other languages, by adding a feature that was elegant and interesting rather than needed?

While we won't try to answer this question completely, it is worth noting that inner classes are a phenomenon of the *compiler,* not the virtual machine. Inner classes are translated into regular class files (with $ signs delimiting outer and inner class names), and the virtual machine does not have any special knowledge about them.

For example, the `SalaryProperty` class inside the `Employee` class is translated to a class file `Employee$SalaryProperty.class`. To see this at work, try out the following experiment: run the `ReflectionTest` program of Chapter 5, and give it the class `Employee$SalaryProperty` to reflect upon. You will get the following printout:

```
class Employee$SalaryProperty
{
Employee$SalaryProperty(Employee);

public java.lang.String name();
public java.lang.String get();
public void set(java.lang.String);

private final Employee this$0;
private boolean isSet;
}
```

You can plainly see that the compiler has generated an additional data field, `this$0`, for the reference to the outer class. (The name `this$0` is synthesized by the compiler—you cannot refer to it in your code.)

If the compiler can do this transformation, couldn't you simply program the same mechanism by hand? Let's try it. We would make `SalaryProperty` a regular class, outside the `Employee` class. When constructing a `SalaryProperty` object, we pass it the `this` reference of the object that is creating it.

```
class Employee
{   . . .

    public Property getSalaryProperty()
    {   return new SalaryProperty(this);
    }
}

class SalaryProperty implements Property
{   String get() { . . . }
    public void set(String s) { . . . }
    public String name() { . . . }
    SalaryProperty(Employee o) { outer = o; }

    private Employee outer;
}
```

Now let us look at the `get` method. It needs to return `outer.salary`.

```
class SalaryProperty implements Property
{  public String get()
   { return "" + outer.salary; // ERROR
   }
   . . .
}
```

Here we run into a problem. The inner class can access the private data of the outer class, but our external `SalaryProperty` class cannot. We can use a public accessor `getSalary()` in this case. But look at the `set` method. We need to set the salary, and the `Employee` class has no `setSalary` mutator. Maybe we don't want to add one. After all, the `SalaryProperty` object had a built-in protection: the salary can be set only by the recipient of the property object, and it can be set only *once*. A public `setSalary` mutator would have no such restriction.

Thus, inner classes are genuinely more powerful than regular classes, since they have more access privileges.

You may well wonder how inner classes manage to acquire those added access privileges, since inner classes are translated to regular classes with funny names—the virtual machine knows nothing at all about them. To solve this mystery, let's again use the `ReflectionTest` program to spy on the version of the `Employee` class that has an inner class:

```
class Employee
{
public Employee(java.lang.String, double, corejava.Day);

static java.lang.String access$0(Employee);
static double access$1(Employee);
static void access$2(Employee, double);
static corejava.Day access$3(Employee);
public Property getSalaryProperty();
public Property getSeniorityProperty();
public int hireYear();
public void print();
public void raiseSalary(double);

private java.lang.String name;
private double salary;
private corejava.Day hireDay;
}
```

Notice the static `access$0...access$3` methods that the compiler added to the outer class. The inner class methods call those methods. For example, the method of the `SalaryProperty` effectively makes the following call:

```
public String get()
{   return "" + access$1(this$0);
}
```

Is this a security risk? You bet it is. It is an easy matter for someone else to invoke the access$1 method to read the private salary field or, even worse, to call the access$2 method to set it. The Java language standard reserves $ characters in variable and method names for system usage. However, for those hackers who are familiar with the structure of class files, it is an easy (if tedious) matter to produce a class file with virtual machine instructions to call that method. Of course, such a class file would need to be generated manually (for example, with a hex editor) and placed inside the same package as the class under attack.

To summarize, if an inner class accesses a private data field, then it is possible to access that data field through other classes that are added to the package of the outer class, but to do so requires skill and determination. A programmer cannot accidentally obtain access but must intentionally build or modify a class file for that purpose.

Could we have done away with the inner class entirely and simply have `Employee` implement the `Property` interface? Unfortunately, that would not work, either. There are two separate properties that the `Employee` class spawns: the `SalaryProperty` and the `SeniorityProperty`. Had `Employee` simply implemented the `get` and `set` methods itself, rather than delegating them to other classes, it could have implemented only one or the other behavior. And even if there was only a single behavior to implement, the property objects need to have their own independent *state*. Each `SalaryProperty` object has a separate flag to indicate whether it has already used up its opportunity to set the salary. If `Employee` had implemented the `get` and `set` methods itself, there would not be a separate state.

To summarize. Inner classes are useful in all of the following circumstances:

- A helper object needs to control the private implementation of a class, but you don't want to grant that access to others.
- A class needs to spawn helper objects with the same protocol but different implementations of the protocol.
- A class needs to spawn helper objects that have their own state.

Local and Anonymous Inner Classes

If you look carefully at the code of the `PropertyTest` example, you will find that you need the name of the types `SalaryProperty` and

SeniorityProperty only once: when you create an object of those types in the getSalaryProperty and getSeniorityProperty methods.

When you have a situation like this, Java lets you define the classes *locally in a single method*. Let us look at the getSeniorityProperty method in order to illustrate this concept.

```
public Property getSeniorityProperty()
{   class SeniorityProperty implements Property
    {   public String name()
        {   return name + "'s years on the job";
        }
        public String get()
        {   Day today = new Day();
            int years = today.daysBetween(hireDay) / 365;
            return "" + years;
        }
        public void set(String s)
        {} // can't set seniority
    }

    return new SeniorityProperty();
}
```

Local classes have a great advantage—they are completely hidden from the outside world—not even other code in the Employee class can access them. No method except getSeniorityProperty has any knowledge of the SeniorityProperty class.

You can go even a step further. Since you want to make only a single object of this class, you don't even need to give it a name. You can return an object inside the method that is without a name—hence the term *anonymous inner class*.

```
public Property getSeniorityProperty()
{   return new Property()
    {   public String name()
        {   return name + "'s years on the job";
        }
        public String get()
        {   Day today = new Day();
            int years = today.daysBetween(hireDay) / 365;
            return "" + years;
        }
        public void set(String s)
        {} // can't set seniority
    }
}
```

This is a very cryptic syntax indeed. What it means is:

Create a new object of a class that implements the Property interface, where the required three methods name, get, and set are the ones defined inside the braces { }. The parameters used to construct the object are given inside the parentheses ( ) following the supertype name. In general, the syntax is

```
new SuperType(construction parameters)
{   inner class methods and data
}
```

Here, `SuperType` can be an interface, such as `Property`; then, the inner class *implements* that interface. Or, `SuperType` can be a class; then, the inner class *extends* that class.

An anonymous inner class cannot have constructors because the name of a constructor must be the same as the name of a class, and the class has no name. Instead, the construction parameters are given to the *superclass* constructor. In particular, whenever an inner class implements an interface, it cannot have any construction parameters. Nevertheless, you must supply a set of parentheses as in:

```
new InterfaceType() { methods and data }
```

You have to look very carefully to see the difference between the construction of a new object of a class and the construction of an object of an anonymous inner class extending that class. If the closing parenthesis of the construction parameter list is followed by an opening brace, then an anonymous inner class is being defined.

```
Button b = new Button("Ok");
    // a Button object
Button b = new Button("Help") { ... };
    // an object of an inner class extending Button
```

Are anonymous inner classes a great idea or are they a great way of writing obfuscated code? Probably a bit of both. When the code for an inner class is short, just a few lines of simple code, then they can save typing time, but it is exactly timesaving features like this that lead you down the slippery slope to "Obfuscated Java Code contests."

It is a shame that the designers of Java did not try to improve the syntax of anonymous classes, since, generally, Java syntax is a great improvement over C++. The designers of the inner class feature could have helped the human reader with a syntax such as

```
Button b = new class extends Button("Help") { ... };
    // not the actual Java syntax
```

But they didn't. We recommend great restraint when thinking of using anonymous inner classes.

Local Classes That Access Local Variables

Local classes have a few other peculiarities. For example, they can not only access the fields of their outer classes, they can even access local variables! Here is a rather dramatic illustration of this capability. Rather than allowing the `SalaryProperty` a single chance to change the salary, we give it a counter setCount that is incremented whenever the salary is set. Once it has reached a value maxSetCount, then the salary cannot be set further. However, maxSetCount is a *local* variable of the getSalaryProperty method; in fact, it is a parameter variable.

```java
public Property getSalaryProperty(final int maxSetCount)
{  class SalaryProperty implements Property
   {  public String name()
      {  return name + "'s salary";
      }
      public String get()
      {  return "" + salary;
      }
      public void set(String s)
      {  if (setCount >= maxSetCount) return;
         double sal = Double.parseDouble(s);
         if (sal > 0)
         {  salary = sal;
            setCount++;
         }
      }

      private int setCount = 0;
   }
   Property p = new SalaryProperty();
   return p;
}
```

Maybe this should not be so surprising. The line

```java
if (setCount >= maxSetCount) return;
```

is, after all, ultimately inside the getSalaryProperty method, so why shouldn't it have access to the value of the maxSetCount variable?

To see why there is a subtle issue here, let's consider the flow of control more closely.

- The getSalaryProperty method is called.

- The object variable p of type SalaryProperty is initialized via a call to the constructor of the inner class SalaryProperty.

- The method returns p as its value and then the method exits. At this point, the maxSetCount variable no longer exists.

- Much later, some other code calls p.set(value).

For the code in the set method to work, the SalaryProperty class must have made a copy of the maxSetCount field before it went away as a local variable of the getSalaryProperty method. That is indeed exactly what happened. For example, the compiler synthesized the name Employee1SalaryProperty for the local inner class. If you use the `ReflectionTest` program again to spy on the `Employee$1$SalaryProperty` class, you get the following output:

```
class Employee$1$SalaryProperty
{
Employee$1$SalaryProperty(int, Employee);

public java.lang.String name();
public java.lang.String get();
public void set(java.lang.String);

private final int val$maxSetCount;
private final Employee this$0;
int setCount;
}
```

Note the extra `int` parameter to the constructor and the `val$maxSetCount` data field. When an object is created, the value `maxSetCount` is passed into the constructor and stored in the `val$maxSetCount` field. This sounds like an extraordinary amount of trouble for the implementors of the compiler. The compiler must detect access of local variables, make matching data fields for each one of them, and copy the local variables into the constructor so that the data fields can be initialized as copies of them.

The methods of a local class can refer only to local variables that are declared `final`. For that reason, the `maxSetCount` parameter was declared `final` in our example. A local variable that is declared `final` cannot be modified. Thus, it is guaranteed that the local variable and the copy that is made inside the local class always have the same value.

NOTE: You have seen `final` variables used for constants, such as

```
public static final double SPEED_LIMIT = 55;
```

The `final` keyword can be applied to local variables, instance variables, and static variables. In all cases it means the same thing: You can assign to this variable *once*. Afterwards, you cannot change the value—it is final.

However, you don't have to initialize a `final` variable when you define it. For example, the `final` parameter variable max is initialized once, when the `getSalaryProperty` method is called. The `val$maxSetCount` instance variable that you can see in the `Employee$1$SalaryProperty` inner class is set once, in the inner class constructor. A final variable that isn't initialized when it is defined is often called a *blank final* variable.

Why go through all this confusion? Wouldn't it have been just as simple to define a data field in the `SalaryProperty` class and set it in the constructor?

```
public Property getSalaryProperty(final int max)
{ class SalaryProperty implements Property
```

```
{   public SalaryProperty(int max)
    {   maxSetCount = max;
    }
    public String name()
    {   return name + "'s salary";
    }
    public String get()
    {   return "" + salary;
    }
    public void set(String s)
    {   if (setCount >= maxSetCount) return;
        double sal = Double.parseDouble(s);
        if (sal > 0)
        {   salary = sal;
            setCount++;
        }
    }
    private int maxSetCount;
    private int setCount = 0;
}
Property p = new SalaryProperty(max);
return p;
}
```

Indeed, that would have been easier to understand, but there is one situation when you cannot do that. *Anonymous* inner classes cannot have construction parameters that set the data fields of the class.

```
public Property getSalaryProperty(final int maxSetCount)
{   return new Property()
// can't supply construction parameters
    {   public String name()
        {   return name + "'s salary";
        }
        public String get()
        {   return "" + salary;
        }
        public void set(String s)
        {   if (setCount >= maxSetCount) return;
            double sal = Double.parseDouble(s);
            if (sal > 0)
            {   salary = sal;
                setCount++;
            }
        }

        private int setCount = 0;
    }
}
```

Static Inner Classes

Occasionally, you want to use an inner class simply to hide one class inside another, but you don't need the inner class to have a reference to the outer class object. You can suppress the generation of that reference by declaring the inner class `static`.

Here is a typical example of where you would want to do this. Consider the task of computing the minimum and maximum value in an array. Of course, you write one function to compute the minimum and another function to compute the maximum. When you call both functions, then the array is traversed twice. It would be more efficient to traverse the array only once, computing both the minimum and the maximum simultaneously.

```
double min = d[0];
double max = d[0];
for (int i = 1; i < d.length; i++)
{  if (min > d[i]) min = d[i];
   if (max < d[i]) max = d[i];
}
```

However, the function must return two numbers. We can achieve that by defining a class `Pair` that holds two values:

```
class Pair
{  public Pair(double f, double s)
   {  first = f;
      second = s;
   }
   public double getFirst()
   {  return first;
   }
   public double getSecond()
   {  return second;
   }

   private double first;
   private double second;
}
```

The `minmax` function can then return an object of type `Pair`.

```
class ArrayAlg
{  public static Pair minmax(double[] d)
   {  . . .
      return new Pair(min, max);
   }
}
```

The caller of the function then uses the `getFirst` and `getSecond` methods to retrieve the answers:

```
Pair p = ArrayAlg.minmax(d);
System.out.println("min = " + p.getFirst());
System.out.println("max = " + p.getSecond());
```

Of course, the name `Pair` is an exceedingly common name, and in a large project, it is quite possible that some other programmer had the same bright idea, except that the other programmer made a `Pair` class that contains a pair of strings. We can solve this potential name clash by making `Pair` a public inner class inside `ArrayAlg`. Then the class will be known to the public as `ArrayAlg.Pair`:

```
ArrayAlg.Pair p = ArrayAlg.minmax(d);
```

However, unlike the inner classes that we used in previous examples, we do not want to have a reference to any other object inside a `Pair` object. That reference can be suppressed by declaring the inner class `static`:

```
class ArrayAlg
{  public static class Pair
   {  . . .
   }
   . . .
}
```

Of course, only inner classes can be declared static. A static inner class is exactly like any other inner class, except that an object of a static inner class does not have a reference to the outer class object that generated it. In our example, we must use a static inner class because the inner class object is constructed inside a static method:

```
public static Pair minmax(double[] d)
{  . . .
   return new Pair(min, max);
}
```

Had the `Pair` class not been declared as `static`, the compiler would have complained that there was no implicit object of type `ArrayAlg` available to initialize the inner class object.

NOTE: You use a static inner class whenever the inner class does not need to access an outer class object. Some programmers use the term *nested class* to describe static inner classes.

Example 6–4 contains the complete source code of the `ArrayAlg` class and the nested `Pair` class.

Example 6–4: StaticInnerClassTest.java

```java
public class StaticInnerClassTest
{   public static void main(String[] args)
    {   double[] d = new double[20];
        for (int i = 0; i < d.length; i++)
            d[i] = 100 * Math.random();
        ArrayAlg.Pair p = ArrayAlg.minmax(d);
        System.out.println("min = " + p.getFirst());
        System.out.println("max = " + p.getSecond());
    }
}

class ArrayAlg
{   public static class Pair
    {   public Pair(double f, double s)
        {   first = f;
            second = s;
        }
        public double getFirst()
        {   return first;
        }
        public double getSecond()
        {   return second;
        }

        private double first;
        private double second;
    }

    public static Pair minmax(double[] d)
    {   if (d.length == 0) return new Pair(0, 0);
        double min = d[0];
        double max = d[0];
        for (int i = 1; i < d.length; i++)
        {   if (min > d[i]) min = d[i];
            if (max < d[i]) max = d[i];
        }
        return new Pair(min, max);
    }
}
```

Graphics Programming

To this point, you have only seen how to write programs that take input from the keyboard, fuss with it, and then display the results on a console screen. This is not what most users want now. Modern programs don't work this way and neither do Web pages. This chapter starts you on the road to writing Java programs that use a graphical user interface (GUI). In particular, you will learn how to write programs that size and locate windows on the screen, display text with multiple fonts in a window, display images, and so on. The next two chapters show you how to process events such as keystrokes and mouse clicks, and how to add interface elements, such as menus and buttons, to your applications. When you finish these three chapters, you will know the essentials for writing *stand-alone* graphical applications. Chapter 10 shows how to program applets that use these features and are embedded in Web pages. For more sophisticated graphics programming techniques, we refer you to Volume 2.

Introduction

When Java 1.0 was introduced, it contained a class library, which Sun called the Abstract Window Toolkit or AWT, for basic GUI programming. The way the basic AWT library deals with user interface elements is to delegate their creation and behavior to the native GUI toolkit on each target platform (Windows, Solaris, Mac, and so on). For example, if you used the original AWT to put a text box on a Java window, an underlying "peer" text box lurking in the background actually handled the text input. When writing these kinds of AWT programs, the idea was that you simply specify the location and behavior of your user interface elements, and Java would create the peers. The resulting program could then, in theory, run on any of these platforms, with the "look and feel" of the target platform—hence Sun's trademarked slogan "write once, run everywhere."

The peer-based approach worked well for simple applications, but it soon became apparent that it was fiendishly difficult to write a high-quality portable graphics library that depended on native user interface elements. User interface elements such as menus, scrollbars, and text fields can have subtle differences in behavior on different platforms. It was hard, therefore, to give users a consistent and predictable experience with this approach. Moreover, some graphical environments (such as X11/Motif) do not have as rich a collection of user interface components as does Windows or the Mac. This in turn further limits a portable library based on peers to a "lowest common denominator" approach. As a result, GUI applications built with the AWT simply did not look as nice as native Windows or Macintosh applications, nor did they (usually) have the kind of functionality that users of those platforms had come to expect. More depressingly, there were *different* bugs in the AWT UI library on the different platforms. Developers complained that they needed to test their applications on each platform, a practice derisively called "write once, debug everywhere."

In 1996, Netscape created a GUI library they called the *IFC* (Internet Foundation Classes) that used an entirely different approach. User interface elements, such as buttons, menus, and so on, were *painted* onto blank windows. The only peer functionality needed was a way to put up windows and to paint on the window. Thus, Netscape's IFC widgets looked and behaved the same no matter which platform the program ran on. Sun worked with Netscape to perfect this approach, creating a user interface library with the code name "Swing" (sometimes called the "Swing set").

Since, as Duke Ellington said, "It Don't Mean a Thing If It Ain't Got That Swing," Swing is now the official name for the non-peer-based GUI toolkit that is part of the Java Foundation Classes (JFC). The full JFC is vast and is far more than the Swing GUI toolkit. JFC features not only include the Swing components but also an accessibility API, a 2D API, and a drag-and-drop API.

NOTE: Swing is not a complete replacement for the AWT. Swing simply gives you more-capable user interface components. The basic architecture of the AWT, in particular, event handling, remains the same as it was in Java 1.1. (AWT event handling underwent a significant change between Java 1.0 and Java 1.1.) Swing uses the 1.1 event handling model, and a version of Swing can even be downloaded from Sun's Web site for use in Java 1.1 programs. Therefore, you will find the next three chapters useful even if you don't use Java 2. And, although the AWT peer-based user interface components are still available, you will rarely, if ever, want to use them. From now on, we'll say "Swing" when we mean the lightweight user interface classes, and we'll say "AWT" when we mean the underlying mechanisms of the windowing toolkit, such as event handling.

Of course, Swing-based user interface elements will be somewhat slower to appear on the user's screen than the peer-based components used by the AWT. Our experience is that on any reasonably modern machine, the speed difference shouldn't be a problem. On the other hand, the reasons to choose Swing are overwhelming:

- Swing has a much richer and more convenient set of user interface elements.

- Swing depends far less on the underlying platform; it is therefore less prone to platform-specific bugs.

- Swing will give a consistent user experience across platforms.

All this means Swing has the potential of finally fulfilling the promise of Sun's "Write once, run anywhere" slogan.

Still, the third plus is also a potential drawback: if the user interface elements look the same on all platforms, then they will look *different* from the native controls on at least some platforms, and thus users will be less familiar with them.

Swing solves this problem in a very elegant way. Programmers writing Swing programs can give the program a specific "look and feel." For example, Figures 7–1 and 7–2 show the same program running with the Windows[1] and the Motif look and feel.

![SwingSet application window showing the Windows look and feel with RadioButtons tab selected, displaying Text RadioButtons, Image RadioButtons, Image & Text RadioButtons, Display Options, and Pad Amount controls]

Figure 7–1: The Windows look and feel of Swing

![SwingSet application window showing the Motif look and feel with RadioButtons tab selected, displaying Text RadioButtons, Image RadioButtons, Image & Text RadioButtons, Display Options, and Pad Amount controls]

Figure 7–2: The Motif look and feel of Swing

---

1 For what are apparently copyright reasons, the Windows look and feel is available only for Java programs running on Windows platforms.

> NOTE: While we won't have space in this book to tell you how to do it, it is possible for Java programmers to extend an existing look and feel or even design a totally new look and feel. This is a tedious process that involves specifying how various Swing components need to be painted, but some developers have done just that, especially when porting Java to nontraditional platforms such as kiosk terminals or handheld terminals. See the "Swing Connection" at `http://java.sun.com/products/jfc/tsc/` for more on this process.

Furthermore, Sun developed a platform-independent look and feel that they call "Metal," which we think looks very nice (see Figure 7–3). In this book, we will use Swing, with the Metal look and feel, for all our graphical programs.

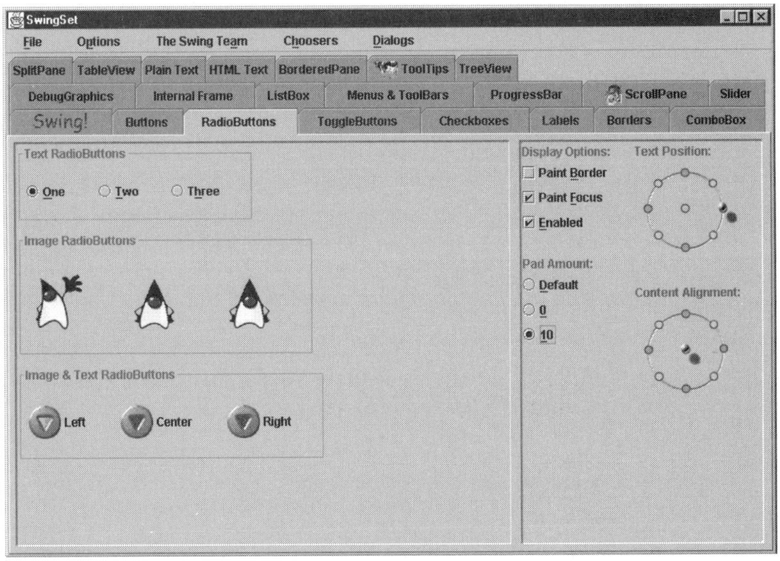

Figure 7–3: The Metal look and feel of Swing

In sum, Swing is more robust, has more features, is more portable, and is easier to use than the peer-based AWT user interface components. We feel strongly that Swing is the future of UI programming in Java, and we think that you will want to use it for all your new Java programming projects.

Finally, we do have to warn you that if you have programmed Microsoft Windows applications using VB, Delphi, or Visual C++, you know about the ease of use that comes with the graphical layout tools and resource editors these products provide. These tools let you design the visual appearance of your application, and then they generate much (often all) of the GUI code for you.

Although some GUI builders are now available for Java programming, these products are not as mature as the corresponding tools for Windows. In any case, to fully understand graphical user interface programming (or even, we feel, to use these tools effectively), you need to know how to build a user interface manually. Naturally, this often requires writing *a lot of code*.

Creating a Closeable Frame

A top-level window (that is, a window that is not contained inside another window) is called a *frame* in Java. The AWT library has a peer-based class, called Frame, for this top level. The Swing version of this class is called JFrame; JFrame extends the Frame class and is one of the few Swing components that is not drawn on a canvas. Thus, the decorations (buttons, title bar, icons, and so on) are drawn by the user's windowing system, not by Swing.

> TIP: For users coming from an earlier version of Java, most of the AWT components have Swing equivalents whose class names simply add a "J"; hence, JButton, JPanel etc. JFrame is one of the few peer-based-only components in the Swing set.

Frames are examples of *containers*. This means that a frame can contain other user interface components such as buttons and text fields. In this section, we want to go over the most common methods for working with a Swing JFrame.

Example 7–1 lists a simple program that displays an empty frame on the screen, as illustrated in Figure 7–4.

Figure 7–4: The simplest visible frame

Example 7–1: FirstTest.java

```
import javax.swing.*;

class FirstFrame extends JFrame
{  public FirstFrame()
   {  setTitle("FirstFrame");
      setSize(300, 200);
   }
}

public class FirstTest
{  public static void main(String[] args)
   {  JFrame frame = new FirstFrame();
      frame.show();
   }
}
```

Let's work through this program, line by line.

The Swing classes are placed in the `javax.swing` package. The package name `javax` indicates a Java extension package, not a core package. The Swing classes are indeed an extension to Java 1.1. Because the Swing classes were not made a part of the core hierarchy, it is possible to load the Swing classes into a Java 1.1-compatible browser. (The security manager of the browser does not allow adding any packages that start with "`java.`") In Java 2, the Swing package is no longer an extension, but it is part of the core hierarchy. Any Java implementation that is compatible with Java 2 must supply the Swing classes. Nevertheless, the `javax` name remains, for compatibility with Java 1.1 code. (Actually, the Swing package started out as `com.sun.java.swing`, then briefly got moved to `java.awt.swing` during early Java 2 beta versions, then went back to `com.sun.java.swing` in late Java 2 beta versions, and after howls of protest by Java programmers, found its final resting place in `javax.swing`.)

In our program, we define a class, `FirstFrame`, that behaves exactly like the class `JFrame` in the `javax.swing` package, with two exceptions. The constructor of `FirstFrame` sets the title bar to the string `"FirstFrame"` and the size of the frame to 300 × 200 pixels. (By default, a frame has width and height 0.) In this simple example, our `FirstFrame` class has no other methods. Of course, frames with more interesting behavior must have additional methods.

The `main` method shows the frame and exits. Note that does not terminate the program, just the main thread. Showing the window activates a user interface thread that keeps the program alive.

To actually show a frame, you perform the following steps:

- Create the frame object by a call to new.

- Optionally, position it on the user's screen, using the setLocation method. (By default, the frame will be in the top-left corner.)

- Call the show method to make the frame visible and to bring it to the front if it is behind another window.

NOTE: The JFrame class inherits the show method from the superclass Window. The Window class has a superclass Component that also has a show method. The Component.show method is deprecated, and you are supposed to call setVisible(true) instead. However, the Window.show method is *not* deprecated, and for windows and frames it makes sense to call show, not setVisible, because show makes the window visible *and* brings it to the front.

The key line in the main method in Example 7–1 is:

```
JFrame = new FirstFrame();
```

This line makes a new FirstFrame by giving all the necessary information for the underlying windowing system to display a window. The call to new does not display the frame; as we just mentioned, you must call either the show or setVisible methods to actually make the frame appear on the screen.

However, you aren't done. The default is that visible frames are 0 × 0 pixels, so before you can see a frame, you also need to set its size. In Example 7–1, we make it 300 pixels wide by 200 pixels high by using the setSize method in the constructor of the frame. Finally, the frame will appear in the top-left corner since we didn't use the setLocation method in order to reposition it. (Actually, if you want to both size and position a window, it saves a little typing to use the setBounds method instead of using calls to both setSize and setLocation—see the API notes.) The running program is shown in Figure 7–4—it is a truly boring top-level window.

NOTE: In the above example we wrote two classes, one to define the frame and one that creates and then shows it. Frequently, you will see programs in which the code for creating and showing the frame is actually placed in the main method of the class itself. Here's an example of how this code would look for our FirstFrame class:

```
public class FirstFrame extends JFrame
{  public FirstFrame()
   {  setTitle("FirstFrame");
      setSize(300, 200);
   }

   public static void main(String[] args)
```

```
  {  JFrame frame = new FirstFrame();
     frame.show();
  }
}
```

Using the `main` method of your frame class for the code that both instantiates and shows the frame is simpler in the sense that you do not have to introduce another auxiliary class for this. Quite a few programmers find this code style a bit confusing and prefer to separate out the class that launches the program from the class that controls the look and behavior of the frame. We agree, and we will use separate classes in this book.

Terminating Graphics Programs

There is, unfortunately, one problem with the FirstFrame program. If you run the program, you may find that you have a hard time quitting it. If you look carefully at the window shown in Figure 7–4, you will find it has a close box in its upper, right-hand corner. Clicking on this close box merely *hides* the window, but it does *not close the application*. Clicking on the upper, left-hand corner reveals a menu (see Figure 7–5), but selecting Close from the menu doesn't work either. (Under Solaris, you can terminate the program by selecting Destroy from the system menu, but under Windows you don't have this option.)

You can change this behavior with the setDefaultCloseOperation method. But your only three choices are to do nothing, to hide the frame (the default), or to destroy the frame. There is no choice to terminate the program.

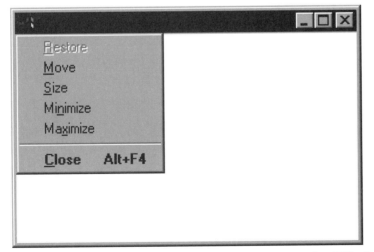

Figure 7–5: The system menu of a Java program under Windows 95/98

Nothing obvious will get this application to terminate although the window is long gone. You will soon see how to write Swing programs that can be terminated properly, but right now you need a way to kill a wayward, windowed Java application.

If you launched the program from a console window by typing

```
java FirstTest
```

then you can tell easily that the program is still running—there is no shell prompt (i.e., a string such as `C:\CoreJavaBook\v1ch7\FirstTest>` in Windows). You can terminate the Java program by pressing CTRL+C or by clicking on the Close button in the top right of the shell window. Alternatively, under Windows 95/98, you can carefully press CTRL+ALT+DEL.

You have to be careful when pressing CTRL+ALT+DEL. If you press the key combination twice, your computer reboots immediately and you lose all work in all open applications. If you do it right (that is, hit the key combination only once), you get a dialog box similar to the one shown in Figure 7–6. This dialog box lists all running programs. Select the Java program you want to shut down and click on the End Task button. If a dialog box comes up that alerts you that the program isn't responding, confirm that you do want to end it.

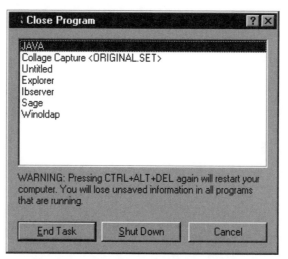

Figure 7–6: The Windows Close program dialog

Obviously, you can't very well tell a user of your program that the natural way to end your program is via something like a CTRL+ALT+DEL "three-finger salute" or a CTRL+C. However, in Java the default behavior for a frame is to simply hide itself when the user closes it. Moreover, the frame is not aware of the program that started it, and so it will not tell that program to exit either.

We need to have a way of being notified when the frame is being closed. In general, getting a notification whenever something interesting happens is the job of the Java AWT event model. You will learn all about AWT event handling in Chapter 8. Right now, we'll just consider how to get a notification when a window is being closed. Unfortunately, as it happens, this is an event that is relatively complex to handle.

In the AWT event model, we need to tell the frame "here's an object that wants to know when you are being closed." The object must be an instance of a class that implements the `WindowListener` interface. We will implement a class, `Terminator`, that implements that interface. Then, we need to add an object of that class to the frame as the *window listener*:

```
class MyFrame extends JFrame
{   public MyFrame()
    {   WindowListener exitOnClose = new Terminator();
        addWindowListener(exitOnClose);
        . . .
    }
    . . .
}
```

Unfortunately, to implement the `WindowListener` interface, a class must implement seven (!) methods, namely:

```
public void windowActivated(WindowEvent e)
public void windowClosed(WindowEvent e)
public void windowClosing(WindowEvent e)
public void windowDeactivated(WindowEvent e)
public void windowDeiconified(WindowEvent e)
public void windowIconified(WindowEvent e)
public void windowOpened(WindowEvent e)
```

We don't care about six of these events, so we do nothing for six of the methods. But for the `windowClosing` call, we exit the program and shut down the Java Virtual Machine.

Having to code six do-nothing methods is pretty tedious, and the AWT provides a class `WindowAdapter` that implements all seven methods of the `WindowListener` interface to do nothing. Using that class, we only need to override one method:

```
class Terminator extends WindowAdapter
{   public void windowClosing(WindowEvent e) { System.exit(0); }
}
```

To further simplify the program, note that we don't need to give a name to the `Terminator` object. Let's drop the `exitOnClose` variable from the frame constructor:

```
addWindowListener(new Terminator());
```

And, using the magic of anonymous classes, we can even avoid giving a name to the `Terminator` class:

```
addWindowListener(new WindowAdapter()
    {  public void windowClosing(WindowEvent e)
        {  System.exit(0);
        }
    } );
```

If you did not follow the intricacies of anonymous inner classes in Chapter 6, you may simply want to take this incantation on faith, as the simplest way of convincing a frame to terminate an application when it is closed. (See the next chapter for more on the AWT event model.)

Example 7–2 shows the complete code for a program that displays a blank frame and that properly terminates when the user closes the frame.

Example 7–2: CloseableTest.java

```
import java.awt.event.*;
import javax.swing.*;

class CloseableFrame extends JFrame
{  public CloseableFrame()
    {  setTitle("CloseableFrame");
        setSize(300, 200);
        addWindowListener(new WindowAdapter()
            {  public void windowClosing(WindowEvent e)
                {  System.exit(0);
                }
            } );
    }
}

public class CloseableTest
{  public static void main(String[] args)
    {  JFrame frame = new CloseableFrame();
        frame.show();
    }
}
```

Frame Layout

The `JFrame` class itself has only a few methods for changing how frames look. Of course, through the magic of inheritance, most of the methods for working with the size and position of a frame come from the various superclasses of `JFrame`. Probably the most important methods, inherited from the base class `Frame`, are the following ones:

- The dispose method that closes the window down and reclaims any system resources used in creating it.

- The setIconImage method, which takes an Image object to use as the icon when the window is minimized (often called *iconized* in Javaspeak). Under Windows, this icon will also appear as the control box icon.

- The setTitle method for changing the text in the title bar.

- The setResizable method, which takes a boolean to determine if a frame will be resizeable by the user.

Figure 7–7 illustrates the inheritance chain for the JFrame class.

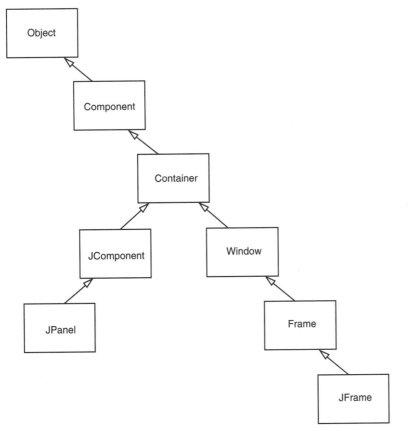

Figure 7–7: Inheritance hierarchy for the JFrame and JPanel classes

As the API notes indicate, the Component class (which is the ancestor of all GUI objects) and the Window class (which is the Frame's class parent) are where you usually need to look to find the methods to resize and reshape frames. For example, the Window class is where the show method lives that you use to display the component. As another example, the `setLocation` method in the `Component` class is one way to reposition a component. If you make the call

```
setLocation(int x, int y)
```

the top-left corner is located x pixels across and y pixels down (where (0, 0) is the top-left corner). Similarly, the `setBounds` method in `Component` lets you resize and relocate a component (in particular, a `JFrame`) in one step. Note that for a frame, the coordinates are taken relative to the whole screen. (As you will see in the next chapter, for other components inside a container, the measurements are taken relative to the container.)

VB NOTE: The `setBounds` method is completely analogous to the Move method in that you can use it to move and resize any component, but, of course, you only have pixels as the scale mode.

Remember: if you don't explicitly size a frame, all frames will default to being 0 by 0 pixels. To keep our example programs simple, we resize the frames to a size that we hope works acceptably on most displays. However, in a professional application, you should check the resolution of the user's screen and write code that resizes the frames accordingly: a window that looks nice on a laptop screen will look like a postage stamp on a high-resolution screen. As you will soon see, you can obtain the screen dimensions in pixels on the user's system. You can then use information to compute the optimal window size for your program.

TIP: The API notes for this section give what we think are the most important methods for giving frames the proper look and feel. Some of these methods are defined in the `JFrame` class. Others come from the various parent classes of `JFrame`. At some point, you may need to search the API docs to see if there are methods for some special purpose. Unfortunately, that is a bit tedious to do with the JDK documentation. For subclasses, the API docs only explain *overridden* methods. For example, `show` is applicable to objects of type `JFrame`, but because it is simply inherited from the `Window` class, the `JFrame` documentation doesn't explain it. If you feel that there should be a method to do something and it isn't explained in the documentation for the class you are working with, try looking at the API docs for the methods of the *superclasses* of that class. The top of each API page has hyperlinks to the superclasses, and there is a list of inherited methods below the method summary for the new and overridden methods.

To give you an idea of what you can do with a window, we end this section by showing you a sample program that positions one of our closeable frames so that:

• Its area is one-fourth that of the whole screen.

For example, if the screen was 800×600 pixels, we need a frame that is 400×300 pixels and we need to move it so the top left-hand corner is at (200,150).

To do this, we need a method to find out the screen resolution. This method obviously requires interacting with the underlying operating system since this is the only place where this information is likely to be stored. In Java, you usually get at system-dependent information via what is called a *toolkit*. The Toolkit class has a method called getScreenSize that returns the screen size as a Dimension object. (A Dimension object d simultaneously stores a height and a width, in public (!) instance variables d.height and d.width.)

Here's a fragment you use to get the screen size:

```
Toolkit tk = Toolkit.getDefaultToolkit();
Dimension d = tk.getScreenSize();
int screenHeight = d.height;
int screenWidth = d.width;
```

We also supply an icon. Because the representation of images is also system dependent, we again need to use the toolkit to load an image. Then, we set the image as the icon for the frame.

```
Image img = tk.getImage("icon.gif");
setIconImage(img);
```

Depending on your operating system, you can see the icon in various places. For example, in Windows, the icon is displayed in the top-left corner of the window, and you can see it in the list of active tasks when you hit ALT + TAB.

Example 7–3 is the complete program.

Example 7–3: CenteredTest.java

```
import java.awt.*;
import java.awt.event.*;
import javax.swing.*;

class CenteredFrame extends JFrame
{  public CenteredFrame()
    {  setTitle("CenteredFrame");
       addWindowListener(new WindowAdapter()
           {  public void windowClosing(WindowEvent e)
               {  System.exit(0);
               }
           } );
       Toolkit tk = Toolkit.getDefaultToolkit();
       Dimension d = tk.getScreenSize();
       int screenHeight = d.height;
       int screenWidth = d.width;
       setSize(screenWidth / 2, screenHeight / 2);
```

```
        setLocation(screenWidth / 4, screenHeight / 4);
        Image img = tk.getImage("icon.gif");
        setIconImage(img);
    }
}

public class CenteredTest
{   public static void main(String[] args)
    {   JFrame frame = new CenteredFrame();
        frame.show();
    }
}
```

java.awt.Component

- `boolean isVisible()`

  checks if this component is set to be visible. Components are initially visible, with the exception of top-level components such as `JFrame`.

- `void setVisible(boolean b)`

  shows or hides the component depending on whether b is `true` or `false`.

- `boolean isShowing()`

  checks if this component is showing on the screen. For this, it must be visible and be inside a container that is showing.

- `boolean isEnabled()`

  checks if this component is enabled. An enabled component can receive keyboard input. Components are initially enabled.

- `void setEnabled(boolean b)`

  enables or disables a component.

- `Point getLocation()`

  returns the location of the top-left corner of this component, relative to the top-left corner of the surrounding container. (A `Point` object p encapsulates an x and a y coordinate which are accessible by `p.x` and `p.y`)

- `Point getLocationOnScreen()`

  returns the location of the top-left corner of this component, using the screen's coordinates.

- `void setBounds(int x, int y, int width, int height)`

  moves and resizes this component. The location of the top-left corner is given by x and y, and the new size is given by the width and height parameters.

- void setLocation(int x, int y)

- void setLocation(Point p)

  moves the component to a new location. The x and y coordinates (or p.x and p.y) use the coordinates of the container if the component is not a top-level component, or the coordinates of the screen if the component is top level (for example, a JFrame).

- Dimension getSize()

  gets the current size of this component.

- void setSize(int width, int height)

- void setSize(Dimension d)

  resizes the component to the specified width and height.

`java.awt.Window`

- void toFront()

  shows this window on top of any other windows.

- void toBack()

  moves this window to the back of the stack of windows on the desktop and rearranges all other visible windows accordingly.

`java.awt.Frame`

- void setResizable(boolean b)

  determines whether the user can resize the frame.

- void setTitle(String s)

  sets the text in the title bar for the frame to the string s.

- void setIconImage(Image image)

  Parameters: image the image you want to appear as the icon for the frame

---

`java.awt.Toolkit`

- Dimension getScreenSize()

  gets the size of the user's screen.

- Image getImage(String filename)

  loads an image from the file with name filename.

Displaying Information in a Frame

In this section, we'll show you how to display information in a frame. For example, rather than displaying "Not a Hello, World program" in text mode in a console window as we did in Chapter 3, we will display the message in a frame, as shown in Figure 7–8.

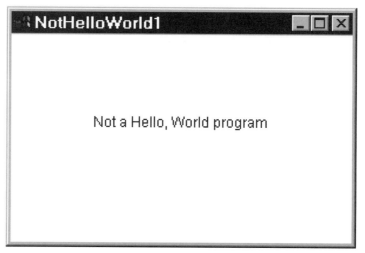

Figure 7–8: A simple graphical program

It would be possible to draw the message string directly onto a frame, but that is not considered good programming practice. In Java, frames are really designed only to be containers for components such as a menu bar and other user interface elements. You normally draw on another component, called a *panel*, which you add to the frame.

The structure of a JFrame is surprisingly complex. Look at Figure 7–9 which shows the makeup of a JFrame. As you can see, four panes are layered in a JFrame. The root pane, layered pane, and the glass pane are of no interest to us; they are required to organize the menu bar and content pane and to implement the look and feel. The part that most concerns Swing programmers is the *content pane*. When designing a frame, you add components into the content pane, using code such as the following:

```
Container contentPane = frame.getContentPane();
Component c = . . .;
contentPane.add(c);
```

NOTE: If you are familiar with AWT programming, you know that you used to call the add method to add components directly into an AWT Frame. In Swing, that is not possible. You must add all components into the content pane.

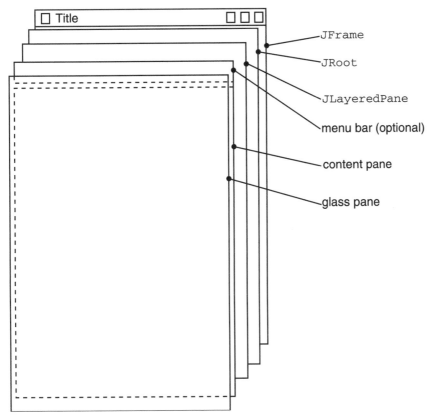

Figure 7–9: The internal structure of a JFrame

In our case, we want to add a single *panel* to the content pane onto which we will draw our message. Panels are implemented by the JPanel class. They are user interface elements with two useful properties:

- They have a surface onto which you can draw.
- They themselves are containers.

Thus, they can hold other user interface components such as buttons, sliders, and so on.

The complete code to add a panel into a frame is thus:

```
Container contentPane = frame.getContentPane();
JPanel p = new JPanel();
contentPane.add(p);
```

`javax.swing.JFrame`

- `Container getContentPane()`

    returns the content pane object for this JFrame.

Graphics Objects and the `paintComponent` Method

Every time you need a user interface component that is similar to one of the basic Swing components, you use inheritance to create a new class and then override or add methods to get the extra functionality you want. For example, our `FirstFrame` and `CloseableFrame` classes inherited from the Swing `JFrame` class.

To draw on a panel, you will need to:

- Define a class that extends `JPanel`

- Override the `paintComponent` method in that class

The `paintComponent` method is actually in `JComponent`—the parent class for all nonwindow Swing components. It takes one parameter of type `Graphics`. The `Graphics` parameter is similar to a device context in Windows or a graphics context in X11 programming. It has methods to draw patterns, images, and text. Here's how to make a panel onto which you can draw:

```
class MyPanel extends JPanel
{   public void paintComponent(Graphics g)
    {  . . . // code for drawing will go here
    }
}
```

In general, anytime you want to put text messages or graphics into a panel, you need to define a new class and override the `paintComponent` method.

> **VB NOTE:** VB programmers rarely need a device context, but it is there just the same. For now, think of a `Graphics` object as being like a Picture box that fills the Form (which actually encapsulates a graphics context). On a `Graphics` object, like a Picture box, you have certain methods for drawing, changing colors, fonts, and pen styles. Also, there is no way to make graphics persistent in Java by setting a property analogous to AutoRedraw; you will always need to write the code in, for example, the `paintComponent` method to do the redrawing (as you would in the Paint and Resize event procedures when AutoRedraw is off).

Each time a window needs to be redrawn, no matter what the reason, the Java event handler notifies the window. This causes the `paintComponent` methods of all components to be executed.

Never call the `paintComponent` method yourself. It is called automatically whenever a part of your application needs to be redrawn, and you should not interfere with this automatic process.

What sorts of actions trigger this automatic response? For example, painting occurs because the user increased the size of the window or minimized and then restored the window. If the user popped up another window and it covered an existing window and then made the overlaid window disappear, the application window that was covered is now corrupted and will need to be repainted. (The graphics system in Java does not save the pixels underneath.) And, of course, when the window is displayed for the first time, it needs to process the code that specifies how (and where) it should draw the initial elements.

TIP: If you need to force repainting of the screen, call the `repaint` method instead of `paintComponent`. The `repaint` method will cause `paintComponent` to be called for all components, with properly configured `Graphics` arguments.

As you saw in the code framework above, the `paintComponent` method takes a single parameter of type `Graphics`. A `Graphics` object remembers a collection of settings for drawing images and text, such as the font you set or the current color. All drawing in Java must go through a `Graphics` object. Measurement on a `Graphics` object for screen display is done in pixels. The (0, 0) coordinate denotes the top-left corner of the component on whose surface you are drawing.

NOTE: Actually, the argument of `paintComponent` is an object of type `Graphics2D`, a subclass of the `Graphics` class. the `Graphics2D` class has additional methods for more sophisticated drawing; we will discuss these methods in Volume 2. The conceptually simpler `Graphics` class is sufficient for simple line drawings.

Displaying text (usually called *rendering text*) is considered a special kind of drawing. For example, a `Graphics` object has a `drawString` method that has the following syntax:

```
g.drawString(text, xCoord, yCoord)
```

In our case, we want to draw the string `"Not a Hello, World Program"` in our original window, roughly one-quarter of the way across and halfway down. Although we don't yet know how to measure the size of the string, we'll start the string at coordinates (75, 100). This means the first character in the string will start at a position 75 pixels to the right and 100 pixels down. (Actually, it is the baseline for the text that is 100 pixels down—see below for more on how text is measured.) Thus, our `paintComponent` method looks like this:

```
class NotHelloWorldPanel extends JPanel
{  public void paintComponent(Graphics g)
   {  . . . // routine code—see below
      g.drawString("Not a Hello, World program", 75, 100);
   }
}
```

However, this `paintComponent` method is not complete. The `NotHelloWorldPanel` class extends the `JPanel` class, which has its own idea how to draw the panel, namely, to fill it with the background color. To make sure that the superclass does its part of the job, we must call `super.paintComponent` before doing any painting on our own.

```
class NotHelloWorldPanel extends JPanel
{   public void paintComponent(Graphics g)
    {   super.paintComponent(g);

        g.drawString("Not a Hello, World program", 75, 100);
    }
}
```

> NOTE: If you have programmed for the old AWT, you will have noticed quite a few differences. In the old AWT, you drew onto a `Canvas`, a subclass of `Component` just for drawing. In Swing, there is no special canvas class. You can draw onto any Swing component, but if you want to separate a drawing area from the remainder of your user interface, you should just render it on the surface of a `JPanel`.
>
> More importantly, you no longer use the `paint` method for drawing. In fact, if you override `paint`, then your program will not work correctly. You then interfere with the `JComponent.paint` method which carries out a number of complex actions, such as setting up the graphics context and image buffering. In Swing, you should always use the `paintComponent` method.
>
> In the old AWT, you may have defined the `update` method to call `paint` without erasing the window in order to avoid screen flicker. This is no longer necessary in Swing. The Swing components use buffering for flicker-free painting.

Example 7–4 shows the complete code.

Example 7–4: NotHelloWorld.java

```
import java.awt.*;
import java.awt.event.*;
import javax.swing.*;

class NotHelloWorldPanel extends JPanel
{   public void paintComponent(Graphics g)
    {   super.paintComponent(g);
        g.drawString("Not a Hello, World program", 75, 100);
    }
}

class NotHelloWorldFrame extends JFrame
{   public NotHelloWorldFrame()
    {   setTitle("NotHelloWorld");
```

```
        setSize(300, 200);
        addWindowListener(new WindowAdapter()
            {   public void windowClosing(WindowEvent e)
                {   System.exit(0);
                }
            } );

        Container contentPane = getContentPane();
        contentPane.add(new NotHelloWorldPanel());
    }
}

public class NotHelloWorld
{   public static void main(String[] args)
    {   JFrame frame = new NotHelloWorldFrame();
        frame.show();
    }
}
```

`java.awt.Component`

- `void repaint()`

  causes a repaint of the component by calling update "as soon as possible."

- `public void repaint(int x, int y, int width, int height)`

  causes a repaint of a part of the component by calling update "as soon as possible."

Parameters:	x	the *x*-coordinate of the top-left corner of the area to be repainted
	y	the *y*-coordinate of the top-left corner of the area to be repainted
	width	the width of the area to be repainted
	height	the height of the area to be repainted

`javax.swing.JComponent`

- `void paintComponent(Graphics g)`

  Override this method to describe how your component needs to be painted.

Text and Fonts

To display text, you must first select a font. To select a font, you must first create an object of the class Font. You specify a font by its *font face name* (or font name for short) and its point size. A font face name is composed of a *font family name*, such as

"Helvetica," and an optional suffix, such as "Bold" or "Italic." In other words, font faces such as "Helvetica," "Helvetica Bold," "Helvetica Italic," "Helvetica Ultra Condensed" are all considered to be part of the Helvetica family.

Here is how you construct a `Font` object:

```
Font helvb14 = new Font("Helvetica", Font.BOLD, 14)
```

The third argument is the point size.

To find out which fonts are available on a particular computer, call the `getAvailableFontFamilyNames` method of the `GraphicsEnvironment` class. The method returns an array of strings that contains the names of all available fonts. To obtain an instance of the `GraphicsEnvironment` class that describes the graphics environment of the user's system, use the static `getLocalGraphicsEnvironment` method. Thus, the following call gives you an array of the names of all fonts on the user's system:

```
String[] fontNames = GraphicsEnvironment
    .getLocalGraphicsEnvironment()
    .getAvailableFontFamilyNames();
```

Unfortunately, there is no absolute way of knowing what fonts a particular user might have installed. Particular font designs are copyrighted, and their distribution usually involves royalty payments to the copyright holder. Of course, just as there are inexpensive imitations of famous perfumes, there are lookalikes for name-brand fonts. Since the names of the fonts themselves (such as Helvetica) are often trademarked by a font foundry, the lookalikes often have other names. For example, the Helvetica and Times Roman imitations that are shipped with Windows are called Arial and Times New Roman.

To establish a common baseline, the AWT defines five *logical* font names:

SansSerif

Serif

`Monospaced`

Dialog

`DialogInput`

These font names are always mapped to fonts that actually exist on the client machine. For example, on a Windows system, SansSerif is mapped to Arial. You can use a logical font name in the place of a font face name in the `Font` constructor. You then specify the style (plain, **bold**, *italic*, or ***bold italic***) by setting the second `Font` constructor argument to one of the following values:

```
Font.PLAIN
Font.BOLD
Font.ITALIC
Font.BOLD + Font.ITALIC
```

Here is an example:

```
Font sansb14 = new Font("SansSerif", Font.BOLD, 14)
```

> NOTE: Prior versions of Java used the names Helvetica, TimesRoman, Courier, and
> ZapfDingbats as logical font names. For backward compatibility, these font names are
> still treated as logical font names even though Helvetica is really a font face name
> and TimesRoman and ZapfDingbats are not font names at all—the actual font face
> names are "Times Roman" and "Zapf Dingbats."

The Java fonts contain the usual ASCII characters as well as symbols. For example, if you print the character `'\u2297'` in the Dialog font, then you get a ⊗ character. Only those symbols that are defined in the Unicode character set are available. (See the sidebar at the end of this section for more information about available symbols and adding more fonts.)

Here's the code that displays the string "Not a Hello, World program" in the standard sans serif font on your system, using 14-point bold type:

```
Font f = new Font("SansSerif", Font.BOLD, 14);
g.setFont(f);
g.drawString("Not a Hello, World program", 75, 100);
```

Actually, since we now have the freedom to choose fonts and font styles, let's display the text with a mixture of Roman and italic letters:

> Not a *Hello, World* program

We need two fonts, the base font, `f`, and its italicized version:

```
Font f = new Font("SansSerif", Font.BOLD, 14);
Font fi = new Font("SansSerif", Font.BOLD + Font.ITALIC, 14);
```

Now we have a problem. We need to know the length—in *pixels on the user's machine*—of the string "Not a" in sans serif, bold, 14-point so that we can tack the "Hello, World" string right after it.

To measure a string in a specific font, you use the `FontMetrics` class. This class encapsulates a lot of information about a font, such as global size properties of the font. It also has methods that let you measure the sizes of strings rendered in the font. For example, the `stringWidth` method of the `FontMetrics` class takes a string and returns its current width in pixels.

VB NOTE: You cannot paint a mixture of fonts on a panel without carefully positioning the strings yourself. There is no notion of a last point referenced that is accessed by CurrentX and CurrentY methods. The `stringWidth` method in the `FontMetrics` class works much like `GetTextWidth`, however.

To use the `FontMetrics` class in Java, you need to become familiar with basic terminology taken from typesetting (see Figure 7–10). Many of the properties used in typesetting correspond to methods of the `FontMetrics` class.

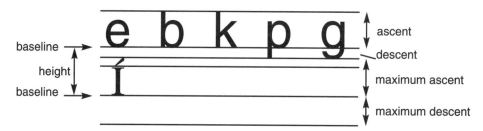

Figure 7–10: Typesetting terms illustrated

Here is a short explanation of the terms shown in Figure 7–10. The *baseline* is the imaginary line where, for example, characters like a basic "e" would rest. The *ascent* is the distance from the baseline to the top of an *ascender,* which is the upper part of a letter like "b" or "k," or an uppercase character. The *descent* is the distance from the baseline to a *descender,* which is the lower portion of a letter like "p" or "g." These correspond to the `getAscent` and `getDescent` methods of the `FontMetrics` class.

You also need the `getLeading` and `getHeight` methods of the `FontMetrics` class, which correspond to what typesetters call *leading* and *height.* Leading is the space between the descent of one line and the ascent of the next line. (The term has its origin from the strips of lead that typesetters used to separate lines.) The height of a font is the distance between successive baselines, which is the same as descent + leading + ascent.

Some characters, typically those with diacritical marks such as "Í," extend above the normal ascent. (There is, in fact, a slight chance that such characters may overlap with descenders from the preceding line.) The *maximum ascent* is the largest height of such a character. Similarly, the *maximum descent* is the largest depth of a descender. You would use the ascent and descent measurements for line spacing and the maximum ascent and descent if you need to determine the maximum screen area occupied by a font.

These vertical measurements are properties of the font. In contrast, horizontal measurements are properties of the individual characters. In a proportionally spaced font such as Serif or SansSerif, different characters have different sizes. For example, a "w" is much wider than an "l." In fact, the size of a word may not even equal the sum of the sizes of its characters because some fonts move certain character pairs closer together. (This process is called *kerning*.) For example, the pair "Av" is often kerned. The stringWidth method of the FontMetrics object of a font computes the width of any string and thus takes into account any kerning that may have occurred.

The following code uses all this information to display the mixed font text "Not a *Hello, World* program" and uses the FontMetric class to position the various pieces of the text correctly:

```
public void paintComponent(Graphics g)
{   super.paintComponent(g);
    Font f = new Font("SansSerif", Font.BOLD, 14);
    Font fi = new Font("SansSerif", Font.BOLD + Font.ITALIC, 14);
    FontMetrics fm = g.getFontMetrics(f);
    FontMetrics fim = g.getFontMetrics(fi);
    String s1 = "Not a ";
    String s2 = "Hello, World";
    String s3 = " Program";
    int cx = 75;
    int cy = 100;
    g.setFont(f);
    g.drawString(s1, cx, cy);
    cx += fm.stringWidth(s1);
    g.setFont(fi);
    g.drawString(s2, cx, cy);
    cx += fim.stringWidth(s2);
    g.setFont(f);
    g.drawString(s3, cx, cy);
}
```

Actually, this code is unrealistic because allocating fonts and font metrics is time consuming; it is usually best to do this allocation only once. We'll do that in the code for Example 7–5 by:

- Making the fonts and font metrics into variables of our frame class

- Setting them once in a setFonts method

We then call the setFonts method in the paintComponent method. (Note that it would have been more logical to set the fonts in the constructor for the panel, but this is not possible since the graphics context did not yet exist when we first constructed the panel.)

Figure 7–11 shows the screen display; Example 7–5 is the program listing.

NotHelloWorld2

Not a *Hello, World* Program

Figure 7–11: Using multiple fonts

Example 7–5: NotHelloWorld2.java

```java
import java.awt.*;
import java.awt.event.*;
import javax.swing.*;

class NotHelloWorld2Panel extends JPanel
{   public void setFonts(Graphics g)
    {   if (f != null) return;
        f = new Font("SansSerif", Font.BOLD, 14);
        fi = new Font("SansSerif",
            Font.BOLD + Font.ITALIC, 14);
        fm = g.getFontMetrics(f);
        fim = g.getFontMetrics(fi);
    }

    public void paintComponent(Graphics g)
    {   super.paintComponent(g);

        setFonts(g);
        String s1 = "Not a ";
        String s2 = "Hello, World";
        String s3 = " Program";
        int w1 = fm.stringWidth(s1);
```

```
        int w2 = fim.stringWidth(s2);
        int w3 = fm.stringWidth(s3);

        Dimension d = getSize();
        int cx = (d.width - w1 - w2 - w3) / 2;
        int cy = (d.height - fm.getHeight()) / 2
            + fm.getAscent();

        g.setFont(f);
        g.drawString(s1, cx, cy);
        cx += w1;
        g.setFont(fi);
        g.drawString(s2, cx, cy);
        cx += w2;
        g.setFont(f);
        g.drawString(s3, cx, cy);
    }

    private Font f;
    private Font fi;
    private FontMetrics fm;
    private FontMetrics fim;
}

class NotHelloWorld2Frame extends JFrame
{  public NotHelloWorld2Frame()
    {   setTitle("NotHelloWorld2");
        setSize(300, 200);
        addWindowListener(new WindowAdapter()
            {  public void windowClosing(WindowEvent e)
                {   System.exit(0);
                }
            } );
        Container contentPane = getContentPane();
        contentPane.add(new NotHelloWorld2Panel());
    }
}

public class NotHelloWorld2
{  public static void main(String[] args)
    {  JFrame frame = new NotHelloWorld2Frame();
        frame.show();
    }
}
```

›

java.awt.Font

- `Font(String name, int style, int size)`

  creates a new font object.

Parameters:	name	the font name. This is either a font face name (such as "Helvetica Bold") or a logical font name (such as "Serif", "SansSerif")
	style	the style (`Font.PLAIN`, `Font.BOLD`, `Font.ITALIC` or `Font.BOLD + Font.ITALIC`)
	size	the point size (e.g., 12)

- `String getFontName()`

  gets the font face name (such as "Helvetica Bold").

- `String getFamily()`

  gets the font family name (such as "Helvetica").

- `String getName()`

  gets the logical name (such as "SansSerif") if the font was created with a logical font name; otherwise gets the font face name.

java.awt.FontMetrics

- `int getAscent()`

  gets the font ascent—the distance from the baseline to the tops of uppercase characters.

- `int getDescent()`

  gets the font descent—the distance from the baseline to the bottoms of descenders.

- `int getLeading()`

  gets the font leading—the space between the bottom of one line of text and the top of the next line.

- `int getHeight()`

  gets the total height of the font—the distance between the two baselines of text (descent + leading + ascent).

- `int getMaxAscent()`

  gets the maximum height of all characters in this font.
- `int getMaxDescent()`

  gets the maximum descent of all characters in this font.
- `int stringWidth(String str)`

  computes the width of a string.

  Parameters: `str`   the string to be measured

`java.awt.Graphics`

- `void setFont(Font font)`

  selects a font for the graphics context. That font will be used for subsequent text-drawing operations.

  Parameters: `font`   a font
- `FontMetrics getFontMetrics()`

  gets the metrics of the current font.
- `void drawString(String str, int x, int y)`

  draws a string in the current font and color.

  Parameters: `str`   the string to be drawn

  `x`   the *x*-coordinate of the start of the string

  `y`   the *y*-coordinate of the baseline of the string

Fonts and the `font.properties` file

Sun's Java runtime looks at the `font.properties` file in the `\jdk\jre\lib` directory to find out which logical fonts are available and which symbol sets are contained in a specific font. To be able to use more logical fonts in Java than the default ones, you need to modify this file. Let us look at a typical entry in this file:

```
serif.0=Times New Roman,ANSI_CHARSET
serif.1=WingDings,SYMBOL_CHARSET,NEED_CONVERTED
serif.2=Symbol,SYMBOL_CHARSET,NEED_CONVERTED
exclusion.serif.0=0100-ffff
fontcharset.serif.1=sun.awt.windows.CharToByteWingDings
fontcharset.serif.2=sun.awt.CharToByteSymbol
```

This means: To render a character in the serif font, first check if it is in the "0" range, that is, it is not in the excluded area `0100-ffff`. If it is not excluded, use the Times New Roman font to render it. Next, check if the class `sun.awt.windows.CharToByteWingDings` will accept the character. This (undocumented) class extends the (equally undocumented) class `sun.io.CharToByteConverter`. There are two key methods in these classes that you work with. The method call:

```
boolean canConvert(char)
```

tests whether Java can convert a character. To actually perform the conversion, you need to supply two arrays: one for source characters and one for the target bytes. Then you call:

```
int convert(char[] input, int inStart, int inPastEnd,
    byte[] output, int outStart, int outPastEnd)
```

This method converts the `inPastEnd-inStart` characters in the array `input`, starting from `inStart`, and places them into the byte array `output`, starting at `outStart`. It also fills out at most `outPastEnd - outStart` bytes. (You may wonder why the `convert` method uses arrays instead of simply converting one character into a byte. The reason is that in some encoding schemes, such as the Japanese JIS code, some characters are encoded as single bytes, others as multiple bytes, with control codes switching between character sets.)

If the `canConvert` method returns `true`, then Java will render the character in the `WingDings` font. Otherwise, Java tries the `Symbol` font. If this fails as well, Java renders the character as a `'?'`.

Note that font descriptions are dependent on the operating system. The lines in these examples describe fonts for Windows. In other operating systems, the font descriptions will be different. For example, in Solaris the description of the Times font looks like this:

```
serif.plain.0=
    -linotype-times-medium-r-normal—*-%d-*-*-p-*-iso8859-1
```

You can add your own fonts to the `font.properties` file. For example, if you run Java under Windows, add the following lines:

```
oldstyle.0=Bookman Old Style,ANSI_CHARSET
exclusion.oldstyle.0=0100-ffff
```

You can then make a font:

```
new Font("Oldstyle", Font.PLAIN, 12)
```

You can even add your own font maps. Let us consider the most common case, that is, when characters in your font are described by single bytes. To add your own font map:

- Extend the (undocumented and poorly named) class `sun.io.CharToByte8859_1`. (ISO 8859-1 is the Latin-1 8-bit character set, one of ten 8-bit character sets in the ISO 8859 standard. This Java class can be used as the base class for *any* Unicode to 8-bit code conversion, not just Latin-1.)
- Override two methods: `canConvert`, which returns `true` for those Unicode characters that are part of your font, and `convert`, which converts a character array into the equivalent byte arrays.

Here is a practical example. Suppose that you have a Russian font in ISO 8859-5 format. Omitting a couple of technical exceptions, the mapping from Unicode to ISO 8859-5 is simple:

```
'\u0021'...'\u007E': ch -> ch
'\u0401'...'\u045F': ch -> ch - 0x0360
```

Here is a converter class that does the conversion.

```
public class CharToByteRussian extends sun.io.CharToByte8859_1
{   public boolean canConvert(char ch)
    {   return 0x0021 <= ch && ch <= 0x007E
        || 0x0401 <= ch && ch <= 0x45F;
    }

    public int convert(char[] input, int inStart, int inPastEnd,
        byte[] output, int outStart, int outPastEnd)

    throws ConversionBufferFullException;
    {   int outIndex = outStart;
        for (int i = inStart; i < inPastEnd; i++)
        {   char ch = input[i];
            byte b = 0;
            if (0x0021 <= ch && ch <= 0x007E)
                b = (byte)ch;
            if (0x0401 <= ch && ch <= 0x45F)
                b = (byte)(ch - 0x0360);
            if (b != 0)
            {   if (outIndex >= outPastEnd)
                throw new ConversionBufferFullException();
                output[outIndex] = b;
                outIndex++;
            }
        }
        return outIndex - outStart;
    }
}
```

To add the Russian font to Java, you need to place the class `CharToByteRussian` somewhere on your class path. Then, add the following lines to `font.properties`:

```
russian.0=RUSSIAN,SYMBOL_CHARSET,NEED_CONVERTED
fontcharset.russian.0=CharToByteRussian
```

Colors

The `setColor` method of the `java.awt.Graphics` class lets you select a color that is used for all subsequent drawing operations on the graphics context or component. To draw in multiple colors, you select a color, draw, then select another color and draw again.

The `setColor` method takes a parameter of type `Color`. The `java.awt.Color` class offers predefined constants for the 13 standard colors listed in Table 7–1. Alternatively, you can specify a color by creating a `Color` object by its red, green, and blue components. Using a scale of 0–255 (that is, one byte) for the redness, blueness, and greenness, the most general `Color` constructor is:

```
Color(int redness, int  greenness, int blueness)
```

Here are some examples of setting colors:

```
g.setColor(Color.pink);
g.drawString("Hello", 75, 100);
g.setColor(new Color(0, 128, 128)); // a dull blue-green
g.drawString("World", 75, 125);
```

Table 7–1: Standard colors

black	green	red
blue	lightGray	white
cyan	magenta	yellow
darkGray	orange	
gray	pink	

To set the *background color,* you use the `setBackground` method of the `Component` class, an ancestor of `JFrame`. In fact, you should set the background before displaying the frame for the first time.

```
JFrame f = new MyFrame();
f.setBackground(Color.white);
f.show();
```

Similarly, if you want to change the color Java uses to display information such as text on a frame, use the `setForeground` method on the frame.

TIP: Occasionally useful and often amusing special effects can be obtained by using the `brighter()` and `darker()` methods of the `Color` class, which, as their names suggest, return either brighter or darker versions of the current color. Using the `brighter` method is also a good way to highlight an item. Actually, `brighter()` is just a little bit brighter. To make a color really stand out, apply it three times: `c.brighter().brighter().brighter()`.

Java gives you predefined names for many more colors in its `SystemColor` class. The constants in this class encapsulate the colors used for various elements of the user's system. For example,

```
f.setBackground(SystemColor.window)
```

sets the background color of the frame `f` to the default used by all windows on the user's desktop. (The background is filled in whenever the window is repainted.) Using the colors in the `SystemColor` class is particularly useful when you want to draw user interface elements so that the colors match those already found on the user's desktop. Table 7–2 lists the system color names and their meanings.

Table 7–2: System colors

`desktop`	Background color of desktop
`activeCaption`	Background color for captions
`activeCaptionText`	Text color for captions
`activeCaptionBorder`	Border color for caption text
`inactiveCaption`	Background color for inactive captions
`inactiveCaptionText`	Text color for inactive captions
`inactiveCaptionBorder`	Border color for inactive captions
`window`	Background for windows
`windowBorder`	Color of window border frame
`windowText`	Text color inside windows
`menu`	Background for menus
`menuText`	Text color for menus
`text`	Background color for text
`textText`	Text color for text
`textHighlight`	Background color for highlighted text
`textHighlightText`	Text color for highlighted text
`control`	Background color for controls
`controlText`	Text color for controls
`controlLtHighlight`	Light highlight color for controls
`controlHighlight`	Highlight color for controls
`controlShadow`	Shadow color for controls
`controlDkShadow`	Dark shadow color for controls
`inactiveControlText`	Text color for inactive controls
`scrollbar`	Background color for scrollbars
`info`	Background color for spot-help text
`infoText`	Text color for spot-help text

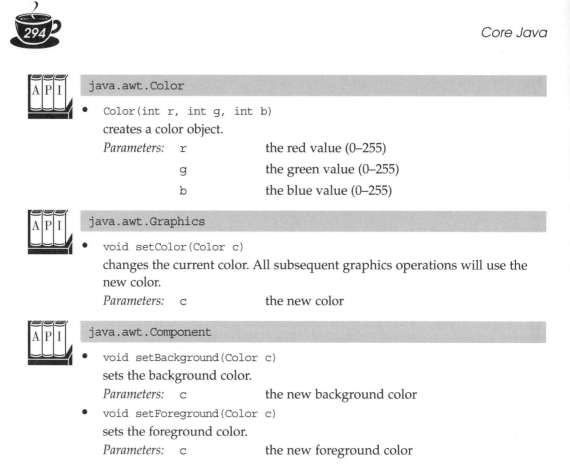

java.awt.Color

- Color(int r, int g, int b)
  creates a color object.
  Parameters: r   the red value (0–255)
                              g   the green value (0–255)
                              b   the blue value (0–255)

java.awt.Graphics

- void setColor(Color c)
  changes the current color. All subsequent graphics operations will use the new color.
  Parameters: c   the new color

java.awt.Component

- void setBackground(Color c)
  sets the background color.
  Parameters: c   the new background color
- void setForeground(Color c)
  sets the foreground color.
  Parameters: c   the new foreground color

Drawing Shapes from Lines

You use the drawLine, drawArc, drawPolyline, and drawPolygon methods in java.awt.Graphics to draw straight and curved lines on a graphics object. For example, in Java, a *polygon* is a closed sequence of line segments. The easiest way to create a polygon in Java is:

- create a polygon object, and
- add points to the object

Then, use the drawPolygon method to draw the polygon. For example, here is how to draw a triangle:

```
Polygon p = new Polygon();
p.addPoint(10, 10);
p.addPoint(10, 30);
p.addPoint(20, 20);
g.drawPolygon(p);
```

There is another version of the drawPolygon method that takes two arrays, one for each of the *x*- and *y*-coordinates of the end points of the line segments, but it is less convenient to use.

If you want a sequence of line segments that is not closed (that is, the first and the last point are not automatically joined), then use the `drawPolyline` method instead.

TIP: Polygons with very closely spaced points are useful to render curved shapes. For more precise drawing of curves, you can use the `QuadCurve2D` and `CubicCurve2D` classes—see the chapter on 2D graphics in Volume 2.

Now let's draw these figures. In Figure 7–12 we have drawn a Pac Man® shape (by using an arc and two line segments), a pentagon, and a spiral (actually, a polygon with many closely spaced points). Example 7–6 is the code for drawing the shapes.

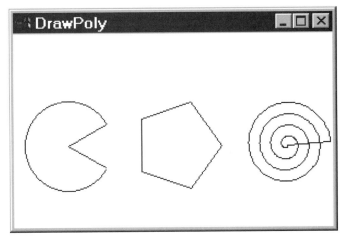

Figure 7–12: Drawing arcs and polygons

Example 7-6: DrawPoly.java

```java
import java.awt.*;
import java.awt.event.*;
import javax.swing.*;

class DrawPolyPanel extends JPanel
{  public void paintComponent(Graphics g)
   {  super.paintComponent(g);

      int r = 40; // radius of circle bounding PacMan(R)
      int cx = 50; // center of that circle
      int cy = 100;
      int angle = 30; // opening angle of mouth

      int dx = (int)(r * Math.cos(angle * Math.PI / 180));
      int dy = (int)(r * Math.sin(angle * Math.PI / 180));

      g.drawLine(cx, cy, cx + dx, cy + dy); // lower jaw
```

```
        g.drawLine(cx, cy, cx + dx, cy - dy); // upper jaw
        g.drawArc(cx - r, cy - r, 2 * r, 2 * r, angle,
            360 - 2 * angle);

        Polygon p = new Polygon();
        cx = 150;
        int i;
        for (i = 0; i < 5; i++)
            p.addPoint(
                (int)(cx + r * Math.cos(i * 2 * Math.PI / 5)),
                (int)(cy + r * Math.sin(i * 2 * Math.PI / 5)));

        g.drawPolygon(p);

        Polygon s = new Polygon();
        cx = 250;
        for (i = 0; i < 360; i++)
        {   double t = i / 360.0;
            s.addPoint(
                (int)(cx + r * t * Math.cos(8 * t * Math.PI)),
                (int)(cy + r * t * Math.sin(8 * t * Math.PI)));
        }
        g.drawPolygon(s);
    }
}

class DrawPolyFrame extends JFrame
{   public DrawPolyFrame()
    {   setTitle("DrawPoly");
        setSize(300, 200);
        addWindowListener(new WindowAdapter()
            {   public void windowClosing(WindowEvent e)
                {   System.exit(0);
                }
            } );
        Container contentPane = getContentPane();
        contentPane.add(new DrawPolyPanel());
    }
}

public class DrawPoly
{   public static void main(String[] args)
    {   JFrame frame = new DrawPolyFrame();
        frame.show();
    }
}
```

java.awt.Graphics

- void drawLine(int x1, int y1, int x2, int y2)

  draws a line between the points with coordinates (x1,y1) and (x2,y2).

Parameters:	x1	the first point's *x*-coordinate
	y1	the first point's *y*-coordinate
	x2	the second point's *x*-coordinate
	y2	the second point's *y*-coordinate

- `void drawArc(int x, int y, int width, int height, int startAngle, int arcAngle)`

  draws an arc bounded by the rectangle with the upper-left corner (x, y) and the given width and height. The arc starts at `startAngle` and spans the `arcAngle`. (That is, the end angle is `startAngle + arcAngle`.) Angles are measured in degrees and follow the usual mathematical conventions: 0 degrees is at the three o'clock position, and positive angles indicate counter-clockwise rotation. The Pac Man figure in Figure 7–12 illustrates how to use these parameters

Parameters:	x	the *x*-coordinate of the top-left corner
	y	the *y*-coordinate of the top-left corner
	width	the width of the bounding rectangle
	height	the height of the bounding rectangle
	startAngle	the beginning angle
	arcAngle	the angle of the arc (relative to `startAngle`)

- `void drawPolygon(Polygon p)`

  draws a path joining the points in the `Polygon` object.

| *Parameters:* | p | a polygon |

- `void drawPolygon(int[] xPoints, int[] yPoints, int nPoints)`

  draws a polygon joining a sequence of points.

Parameters:	xPoints	an array of *x*-coordinates of the corner points
	yPoints	an array of *y*-coordinates of the corner points
	nPoints	the number of corner points

- `void drawPolyline(int[] xPoints, int[] yPoints, int nPoints)`

  draws a path joining a sequence of points. The path is not closed unless the first and last point are identical.

Parameters:	xPoints	an array of *x*-coordinates of the corner points
	yPoints	an array of *y*-coordinates of the corner points
	nPoints	the number of corner points

- `void translate(int x, int y)`

  sets the point with coordinates (x, y) in the usual coordinates (i.e., the one with (0, 0) at the top left) to be the new origin.

Drawing Rectangles and Ovals

The drawRect, drawRoundRect, draw3DRect, and drawOval functions render the outlines of rectangles and ellipses (called ovals in the AWT). Figure 7–13 shows the various rectangle styles and the oval. Example 7–7 is the code that drew Figure 7–13. The 3D effect of the draw3DRect call is not very easy to see because the 3D border is only one pixel thick. For a better effect, you can thicken the border, drawing several 3D rectangles as follows:

```
for (int i = 0; i < thickness; i++)
    g.draw3DRect(x - i, y - i,
        width + 2 * i - 1, height + 2 * i - 1, true);
```

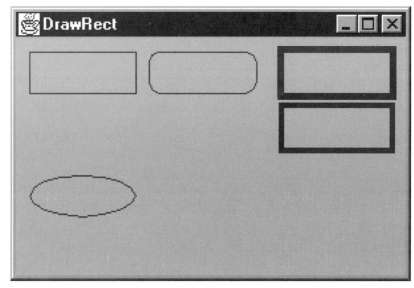

Figure 7–13: Rectangles and ovals

Example 7–7: DrawRect.java

```
import java.awt.*;
import java.awt.event.*;
import javax.swing.*;

class DrawRectPanel extends JPanel
{  public void paintComponent(Graphics g)
   {  super.paintComponent(g);
      g.setColor(Color.blue);
      g.drawRect(10, 10, 80, 30);
      g.drawRoundRect(100, 10, 80, 30, 15, 15);
```

```
    int thickness = 4;

    for (int i = 0; i <= thickness; i++)
        g.draw3DRect(200 - i, 10 - i,
            80 + 2 * i, 30 + 2 * i, true);
    for (int i = 0; i < thickness; i++)
        g.draw3DRect(200 - i, 50 - i,
            80 + 2 * i, 30 + 2 * i, false);

    g.drawOval(10, 100, 80, 30);
    }
}

class DrawRectFrame extends JFrame
{   public DrawRectFrame()
    {   setTitle("DrawRect");
        setSize(300, 200);
        addWindowListener(new WindowAdapter()
            {   public void windowClosing(WindowEvent e)
                {   System.exit(0);
                }
            } );
        Container contentPane = getContentPane();
        contentPane.add(new DrawRectPanel());
    }
}

public class DrawRect
{   public static void main(String[] args)
    {   JFrame frame = new DrawRectFrame();
        frame.show();
    }
}
```

`java.awt.Graphics`

- `void drawRect(int x, int y, int width, int height)`

   draws the outline of the rectangle. Note that the third and fourth parameters are *not* the opposite corner points.

Parameters:	x	the *x*-coordinate of the top-left corner
	y	the *y*-coordinate of the top-left corner
	width	the width of the rectangle
	height	the height of the rectangle

- `void drawRoundRect(int x, int y, int width, int height, int arcWidth, int arcHeight)`

  draws the outline of the rectangle, using curved arcs for the corners.

Parameters:		
	x	the x-coordinate of the top-left corner
	y	the y-coordinate of the top-left corner
	width	the width of the rectangle
	height	the height of the rectangle
	arcWidth	the horizontal diameter of the arcs at the corners
	arcHeight	the vertical diameter of the arcs at the corners

- `void draw3DRect(int x, int y, int width, int height, boolean raised)`

  draws the outline of a raised (3D) rectangle. Note that the third and fourth parameters are *not* the opposite corner points.

Parameters:		
	x	the x-coordinate of the top-left corner
	y	the y-coordinate of the top-left corner
	width	the width of the rectangle
	height	the height of the rectangle
	raised	`true` to have the rectangle appear above the window; `false` to have it appear "pushed in"

- `void drawOval(int x, int y, int width, int height)`

  draws the outline of an ellipse. The parameters specify the bounding rectangle.

Parameters:		
	x	the x-coordinate of the top-left corner of the bounding rectangle
	y	the y-coordinate of the top-left corner of the bounding rectangle
	width	the width of the bounding rectangle
	height	the height of the bounding rectangle

Filling Shapes

You can tell the AWT to fill the interiors of closed shapes (rectangles, ellipses, polygons, and pie chart segments) with a color. The method calls are similar to the ones used for the `draw` calls of the preceding section, except that `draw` is replaced by `fill`.

- void fillRect(int x, int y, int width, int height)
- void fillRoundRect(int x, int y, int width, int height, int arcWidth, int arcHeight)
- void fill3DRect(int x, int y, int width, int height, boolean raised)
- void fillOval(int x, int y, int width, int height)
- void fillArc(int x, int y, int width, int height, int startAngle, int arcAngle)
- void fillPolygon(Polygon p)
- void fillPolygon(int[]xPoints, int[]yPoints, int nPoints)

To *fill* rectangles and ovals simply means to color the inside of the shape with the current color. However, there is one minor point to be aware of, as Figure 7–14 illustrates: When you *fill* a rectangle, you get one pixel less on the right and on the bottom of the rectangle than when you *draw* it. When you look closely at the output of the test program (Example 7–8), you can see that the top and left line segments of the drawn rectangles are covered by the subsequent fills, but the right and bottom line segments are not. This is different from the Windows API, where the end points of lines and rectangles are neither drawn nor filled.

The 3D effect of the fill3DRect call is not very easy to see because the 3D border is only one pixel thick. For a better effect, you can thicken the border by calling draw3DRect a few times, just as described in the preceding section.

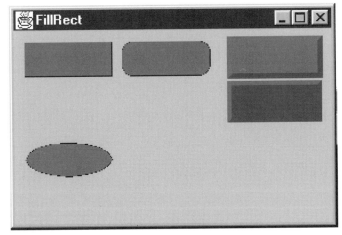

Figure 7–14: Filled rectangles and ovals

Example 7-8: FillRect.java

```java
import java.awt.*;
import java.awt.event.*;
import javax.swing.*;

class FillRectPanel extends JPanel
{  public void paintComponent(Graphics g)
    {  super.paintComponent(g);
       g.drawRect(10, 10, 80, 30);
       g.drawRoundRect(100, 10, 80, 30, 15, 15);
       g.drawOval(10, 100, 80, 30);
       g.setColor(Color.red);
       g.fillRect(10, 10, 80, 30);
       g.fillRoundRect(100, 10, 80, 30, 15, 15);

       int thickness = 4;

       g.fill3DRect(200, 10, 80, 30, true);
       for (int i = 1; i <= thickness; i++)
          g.draw3DRect(200 - i, 10 - i,
             80 + 2 * i - 1, 30 + 2 * i - 1, true);

       g.fill3DRect(200, 50, 80, 30, false);
       for (int i = 1; i <= thickness; i++)
          g.draw3DRect(200 - i, 50 - i,
             80 + 2 * i - 1, 30 + 2 * i - 1, true);

       g.fillOval(10, 100, 80, 30);
    }
}

class FillRectFrame extends JFrame
{  public FillRectFrame()
    {  setTitle("FillRect");
       setSize(300, 200);
       addWindowListener(new WindowAdapter()
          {  public void windowClosing(WindowEvent e)
             {  System.exit(0);
             }
          } );
       Container contentPane = getContentPane();
       contentPane.add(new FillRectPanel());
    }
}

public class FillRect
{  public static void main(String[] args)
```

```
    {   JFrame frame = new FillRectFrame();
        frame.show();
    }
}
```

Note that filling arcs and polygons is quite different from drawing them. Arcs are filled as pie segments by joining the center of the enclosing rectangle with the two end points of the arc and filling the interior. To see this, look at the filled Pac Man in the screen picture in Figure 7–15.

Polygons, on the other hand, are filled according to the "alternating" rule. For the alternating rule, a point is inside if an infinite ray with the point as origin crosses the path an odd number of times. The effect shows up nicely in the filled spiral in Example 7–9.

Figure 7–15: Filled shapes

Example 7–9: FillPoly.java

```
import java.awt.*;
import java.awt.event.*;
import javax.swing.*;

class FillPolyPanel extends JPanel
{   public void paintComponent(Graphics g)
    {   super.paintComponent(g);
        int r = 40; // radius of circle bounding PacMan(R)
        int cx = 50; // center of that circle
        int cy = 100;
        int angle = 30; // opening angle of mouth
```

```
          g.fillArc(cx - r, cy - r, 2 * r, 2 * r, angle,
             360 - 2 * angle);

          Polygon p = new Polygon();
          cx = 150;
          int i;
          for (i = 0; i < 5; i++)
             p.addPoint(
                (int)(cx + r * Math.cos(i * 2 * Math.PI / 5)),
                (int)(cy + r * Math.sin(i * 2 * Math.PI / 5)));

          g.fillPolygon(p);

          Polygon s = new Polygon();
          cx = 250;
          for (i = 0; i < 360; i++)
          {  double t = i / 360.0;
             s.addPoint(
                (int)(cx + r * t * Math.cos(8 * t * Math.PI)),
                (int)(cy + r * t * Math.sin(8 * t * Math.PI)));
          }
          g.fillPolygon(s);
       }
}

class FillPolyFrame extends JFrame
{  public FillPolyFrame()
   {  setTitle("FillPoly");
      setSize(300, 200);
      addWindowListener(new WindowAdapter()
          {  public void windowClosing(WindowEvent e)
             {  System.exit(0);
             }
          } );
      Container contentPane = getContentPane();
      contentPane.add(new FillPolyPanel());
   }
}

public class FillPoly
{  public static void main(String[] args)
   {  JFrame frame = new FillPolyFrame();
      frame.show();
   }
}
```

Paint Mode

When you paint shapes on top of one another, the AWT draws the last drawn shape on top of everything under it. In addition to this *overwrite* paint mode, the AWT also has a second method of combining new shapes with the old window contents; this is usually called *XOR* paint mode. You select XOR paint mode with the call

```
g.setXORMode(xorColor);
```

XOR paint mode is used for highlighting a portion of the screen. Suppose you draw a filled rectangle over a part of the screen. If you draw on top of pixels that are already in the current color, then the AWT changes them to the color specified in the setXORMode call. If you draw on top of pixels in the color of the setXORMode parameter, the AWT changes them to the current color. Any other colors under the highlighted area are also changed by the AWT in some way. The key point is that XOR is a *toggle.* If you draw the same shape twice in XOR mode, the second drawing erases the first, and the screen looks just as it did at the outset. Example 7–10 provides some sample code.

Usually, you use the background color (as in Figure 7–16) as the argument to setXORMode.

Example 7–10: XOR.java

```
import java.awt.*;
import java.awt.event.*;
import javax.swing.*;

class XORPanel extends JPanel
{   XORPanel()
    {   setBackground(Color.black);
    }

    public void paintComponent(Graphics g)
    {   super.paintComponent(g);
        g.setColor(Color.red);
        g.fillRect(10, 10, 80, 30);
        g.setColor(Color.green);
        g.fillRect(50, 20, 80, 30);
        g.setColor(Color.blue);
        g.fillRect(130, 40, 80, 30);
        g.setXORMode(Color.green);
        g.fillRect(90, 30, 80, 30);
    }
}

class XORFrame extends JFrame
{   public XORFrame()
```

```
    {   setTitle("XOR");
        setSize(300, 200);
        addWindowListener(new WindowAdapter()
            {   public void windowClosing(WindowEvent e)
                {   System.exit(0);
                }
            } );
        Container contentPane = getContentPane();
        contentPane.add(new XORPanel());
    }
}

public class XOR
{   public static void main(String[] args)
    {   JFrame frame = new XORFrame();
        frame.show();
    }
}
```

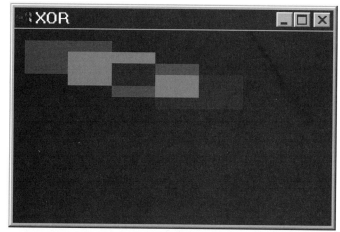

Figure 7–16: Combining colors in XOR mode

java.awt.Graphics

- void setPaintMode()

  sets the graphics context to use paint mode, in which new pixels replace old ones.

- void setXORMode(Color xorColor)

  sets the graphics context to use XOR mode. The color of a pixel is determined as oldColor ^ newColor ^ xorColor. If you draw the same shape twice, then it is erased and the screen is restored to its original appearance.

  Parameters: xorColor   the color to which the current color should change during drawing

Images

You have already seen how to build up simple images by drawing lines and shapes. Complex images, such as photographs, are usually generated externally, for example, with a scanner or special image-manipulation software. (As you will see in Volume 2, it is also possible to produce an image, pixel by pixel, and store the result in a Java array. This procedure is common for fractal images, for example.)

Once images are stored in local files or someplace on the Net, you can then read them into a Java application and display them on `Graphics` objects. To read a graphics file into an application, you use a `Toolkit` object. A `Toolkit` object can read in GIF and JPEG files.

TIP: Most image-manipulation programs can convert image formats (such as Windows bitmaps or icon files) to one of the formats that Java can use. This conversion will be necessary when you want, for example, to use standard Windows icons in the `setIconImage` method to set the icon for your frames.)

To get a `Toolkit` object, use the static `getDefaultToolkit` method of the `Toolkit` class. Here is the code to get a local image file from the current user's directory (supply a full pathname if the image file isn't in the current user's directory):

```
String name = "blue-ball.gif";
Image image = Toolkit.getDefaultToolkit().getImage(name);
```

To get an image file from the Net, you must supply the URL. For example,

```
URL u = new URL("http://www.someplace.com/anImage.gif");
Image image = Toolkit.getDefaultToolkit().getImage(u);
```

Now the variable `image` contains a reference to an object that encapsulates the GIF file image. You can display it with the `drawImage` method of the `Graphics` class.

```
public void paintComponent(Graphics g)
{   . . .
    g.drawImage(image, x, y, null);
}
```

Example 7–11 takes this a little bit further and *tiles* the window with the graphics image. The result looks like the screen shown in Figure 7–17. We do the tiling in the `paintComponent` method. We first draw one copy of the image in the top-left corner and then use the `copyArea` call to copy it into the entire window.

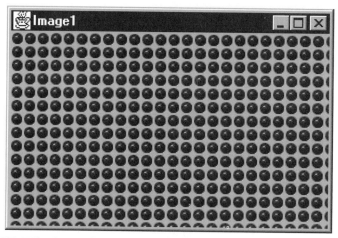

Figure 7–17: Window with tiled graphics image

However, there is a catch. The AWT was written with the assumption that an image may arrive slowly over a network connection. The *first* call to the `drawImage` function recognizes that the GIF file has not yet been loaded. Instead of loading the file and returning to the caller when the image is actually loaded, Java spawns a new thread of execution to load the image *and then returns to the caller without actually having completed that task.* (See Volume 2 for more on threads.)

This is—to say the least—surprising to anyone who expects that a function won't return until it has done its job. But here, the multithreaded aspect of Java works against your assumptions. What will happen is that the code in your program runs in parallel with the code to load the image. Eventually, the image will be loaded and available. Of course, in the meantime, our code has tiled the entire buffer with copies of a blank image.

There is a mechanism for tracking the image acquisition process. Using this mechanism, you can be notified when the image size is known, each time that a chunk of the image is ready, and, finally, when the entire image is complete. When you use an Internet browser and look at a Web page that contains an image, you can see how these notifications are translated into actions. An Internet browser lays out a Web page as soon as it knows the sizes of the images in the page. Then it gradually fills in the images, as more detailed information becomes available. The fourth parameter of the `drawImage` call, which we set to `null`, can optionally point to an `ImageObserver` object that receives these notifications.

However, we are not interested in incremental rendering. We just want to find out when the GIF image is completely loaded and *then* tile the buffer. A special class, called `MediaTracker`, makes it easy to program this delay. A media tracker can track the acquisition of one or more images. (The name "media" suggests that the class should also be able to track audio files or other media. While such an extension may be available in the future, the current implementation tracks images only.)

You add an image to a tracker object with the following command:

```
MediaTracker tracker = new MediaTracker();
Image img = Toolkit.getDefaultToolkit().getImage(name);
int id = 1; // the ID used to track the image loading process
tracker.addImage(img, id);
```

You can add as many images as you like to a single media tracker. Each of the images should have a different ID number, but you can choose any numbering that is convenient. To wait for an image to be loaded completely, you use code like this:

```
try { tracker.waitForID(id); }
catch (InterruptedException e) {}
```

The `try`/`catch` statements are necessary for a technical reason; we will discuss the general topic of exception handling in Chapter 12 and the `InterruptedException` in the multithreading chapter of Volume 2. In our sample program, we just insert this code into the constructor as shown here:

```
public ImagePanel()
{   image = Toolkit.getDefaultToolkit().getImage
        ("blue-ball.gif");
    MediaTracker tracker = new MediaTracker(this);
    tracker.addImage(image, 0);
    try { tracker.waitForID(0); }
    catch (InterruptedException e) {}
}
```

This code causes the effect of waiting until the image is loaded completely before more code will be processed.

If you want to acquire multiple images, then you can add them all to the media tracker object and wait until they are all loaded. You can achieve this with the following code:

```
try { tracker.waitForAll(); }
catch (InterruptedException e) {}
```

NOTE: When programming with the basic AWT, you need to work harder to produce flicker-free images: you need to use *buffering*. With Swing, buffering is automatically done for you by default. (You can turn it off but there is never any reason to do so.) If you need to acquire an image for an AWT component, first assemble your drawing in a background image, then draw the background image.

```
Image buffered_image = createImage(client_width,
    client_height);
Graphics bg = buffered_image.getGraphics();
// all drawing commands that use bg fill the buffered_image
// . . .
// finally, draw the buffer
g.drawImage(buffered_image, 0, 0, null);
bg.dispose();
buffered_image.flush();
```

Example 7–11 shows the full source code of the image display program. This concludes our introduction into Java graphics programming. For more advanced techniques, you will want to turn to the discussion about 2D graphics and image manipulation in Volume 2.

Example 7–11: ImageTest.java

```
import java.awt.*;
import java.awt.event.*;
import javax.swing.*;

class ImagePanel extends JPanel
{  public ImagePanel()
    {  image = Toolkit.getDefaultToolkit().getImage
            ("blue-ball.gif");
        MediaTracker tracker = new MediaTracker(this);
        tracker.addImage(image, 0);
        try { tracker.waitForID(0); }
        catch (InterruptedException e) {}
    }

    public void paintComponent(Graphics g)
    {  super.paintComponent(g);
        Dimension d = getSize();
```

```
          int clientWidth = d.width;
          int clientHeight = d.height;

          int imageWidth = image.getWidth(this);
          int imageHeight = image.getHeight(this);

          g.drawImage(image, 0, 0, this);
          for (int i = 0; i * imageWidth <= clientWidth; i++)
            for (int j = 0;
                    j * imageHeight <= clientHeight; j++)
              if (i + j > 0)
                 g.copyArea(0, 0, imageWidth, imageHeight,
                    i * imageWidth, j * imageHeight);
      }

      private Image image;
}

class ImageFrame extends JFrame
{   public ImageFrame()
    {   setTitle("ImageTest");
        setSize(300, 200);
        addWindowListener(new WindowAdapter()
            {   public void windowClosing(WindowEvent e)
                {   System.exit(0);
                }
            } );
        Container contentPane = getContentPane();
        contentPane.add(new ImagePanel());
    }
}

public class ImageTest
{   public static void main(String[] args)
    {   JFrame frame = new ImageFrame();
        frame.show();
    }
}
```

`java.awt.Toolkit`

- `Toolkit getDefaultToolkit()`

  returns the default toolkit.

- `Image getImage(String filename)`

  returns an image that will read its pixel data from a file.

  Parameters: `filename`   the file containing the image (e.g., a GIF or
  JPEG file)

A P I `java.awt.Graphics`

- `boolean drawImage(Image img, int x, int y, ImageObserver observer)`

  draws a scaled image. Note: This call may return before the image is drawn.

Parameters:	img	the image to be drawn
	x	the *x*-coordinate of the upper-left corner
	y	the *y*-coordinate of the upper-left corner
	observer	the object to notify of the progress of the rendering process (may be `null`)

- `boolean drawImage(Image img, int x, int y, int width, int height, ImageObserver observer)`

  draws a scaled image. The system scales the image to fit in a region with the given width and height. Note: This call may return before the image is drawn.

Parameters:	img	the image to be drawn
	x	the *x*-coordinate of the upper-left corner
	y	the *y*-coordinate of the upper-left corner
	width	the desired width of image
	height	the desired height of image
	observer	the object to notify of the progress of the rendering process (may be `null`)

- `void copyArea(int x, int y, int width, int height, int dx, int dy)`

  copies an area of the screen.

Parameters:	x	the *x*-coordinate of the upper-left corner of the source area
	y	the *y*-coordinate of the upper-left corner of the source area
	width	the width of the source area
	height	the height of the source area
	dx	the horizontal distance from the source area to the target area
	dy	the vertical distance from the source area to the target area

- `void dispose()`

  disposes of this graphics context and releases operating system resources. You should always dispose of the graphics contexts that you receive from calls to methods such as `Image.getGraphics`, but not the ones handed to you by `paintComponent`.

`java.awt.Component`

- `Image createImage(int width, int height)`

  creates an off-screen image buffer to be used for double buffering.

  Parameters: `width`   the width of the image

                  `height`   the height of the image

`java.awt.Image`

- `Graphics getGraphics()`

  get a graphics context to draw into this image buffer.

- `void flush()`

  release all resources held by this image object.

`java.awt.MediaTracker`

- `void addImage(Image image, int id)`

  adds an image to the list of images being tracked. When the image is added, the image loading process is started.

  Parameters: `image`   the image to be tracked

                  `id`   the identifier used to later refer to this image

- `boolean waitForID(int id)`

  waits until all images with the specified ID are loaded.

- `void waitForAll()`

  waits until all images that are being tracked are loaded.

Chapter **8**

Event Handling

Event handling is of fundamental importance to programs with a graphical user interface. To go beyond the toy, console-based programs that you have seen so far, you must master how Java handles events. This chapter explains how the Java AWT event model works. This chapter also shows you how to use the simplest GUI elements, such as buttons. In particular, this chapter discusses how to work with the basic events generated by these components. The next chapter shows you how to put together the most common of the remaining components that Swing offers, along with a full coverage of the events they generate.

The current Java event model is different from the one used in Java 1.0. If you are already familiar with Java 1.0, you will need to learn a new way of coding: one that bears little, if any, relation to the way you used to do things. Note, however, that while Sun has said that code written following the older event model should still work in later versions of Java, moving to the new event model promises both performance improvements and a greater degree of flexibility. The older event model is only briefly discussed in this chapter. You can tell the compiler to flag all lines that use one of the older event handling methods by compiling your source code with the `-deprecation` switch. (There is some potential for incompatibility down the road. Sun has not said they will be supporting the older event model indefinitely. And, of course, if you use Swing components, then you must use the new event model.)

NOTE: If you need to write applets that can run under old browsers that are still using Java 1.0, such as Netscape Navigator 2 or 3 or Internet Explorer before version 4, then you must use the Java 1.0 event model.

Basics of Event Handling

Any operating system that supports graphical user interfaces must constantly be monitoring the environment for events such as keystrokes or mouse clicks. The operating system then reports these events to the programs that are running. Each program then decides what, if anything, to do in response to these events. In languages like Visual Basic, the correspondence between events and code is obvious. One writes code for each specific event of interest and places the code in what is usually called an *event procedure*. For example, a Visual Basic button named HelpButton would have a HelpButton_Click event procedure associated with it, and VB would activate the code in this procedure in response to that button being clicked. Each Visual Basic component (i.e., graphical user interface element) responds to a fixed set of events, and it is impossible to change the events a Visual Basic component responds to.

On the other hand, if you use a language like raw C to do event-driven programming, you need to write the code that checks the event queue constantly for what the operating system is reporting. (You usually do this by encasing your code in a giant loop with a massive switch statement!) This technique is obviously rather ugly, and, in any case, it is much more difficult to code. The advantage is that the events you can respond to are not as limited as in languages, like Visual Basic, that go to great lengths to hide the event queue from the programmer.

Java takes an approach somewhat between the Visual Basic approach and the raw C approach in terms of power and, therefore, in resulting complexity. Within the limits of the events that the AWT knows about, you completely control how events are transmitted from the *event sources* (such as buttons or scrollbars) to *event listeners*. You can designate *any* object to be an event listener—in practice, you pick an object that can conveniently carry out the desired response to the event. This *event delegation model* gives you much more flexibility than is possible with Visual Basic, where the listener is predetermined, but it requires more code and is more difficult to untangle (at least until you get used to it).

Event sources have methods that allow you to register event listeners with them. When an event happens to the source, the source sends a notification of that event to all the listener objects that were registered for that event. As one would expect in an object-oriented language like Java, the information about the event is encapsulated in an *event* object. In Java, all event objects ultimately derive from the class `java.util.EventObject`. Of course, there are subclasses for each event type, such as `ActionEvent` and `WindowEvent`.

Different event sources can produce different kinds of events. For example, a button can send `ActionEvent` objects, whereas a window can send `WindowEvent` objects.

To sum up, here's an overview of how event handling in the AWT works.

- A listener object is an instance of a class that implements a special interface called (naturally enough) a *listener interface*.
- An event source is an object that can register listener objects and send them event objects.
- The event source sends out event objects to all registered listeners when that event occurs.
- The listener objects will then use the information in the event object to determine their reaction to the event.

You register the listener object with the source object with lines of code that follow the model:

```
eventSourceObject.addEventListener(eventListenerObject);
```

For example,

```
MyPanel panel = new MyPanel();
JButton button = new JButton("Clear");
button.addActionListener(panel);
```

Now the `panel` object is notified whenever an "action event" occurs in the button. For buttons, as you might expect, an action event is a button click.

Code like the above requires that the class to which the `panel` listener object belongs must implement the appropriate interface (which in this case is called `ActionListener`). As with all interfaces in Java, implementing an interface means supplying methods with the right signatures. To implement the `ActionListener` interface, the listener class must have a method (called `actionPerformed`) that receives an `ActionEvent` object as a parameter.

```
public class MyPanel extends JPanel
    implements ActionListener
{   . . .
    public void actionPerformed(ActionEvent evt)
    {   // reaction to button click goes here
        . . .
    }
}
```

Whenever the user clicks the button, the `JButton` object creates an `ActionEvent` object and calls `panel.actionPerformed`, passing that event object. It is possible for other objects besides `panel` to be added as listeners to the button. In that case, their `actionPerformed` method is called as well.

Example: Which Button Was Clicked?

As a way of getting comfortable with the event delegation model, let's work through all details needed for the simple example of responding to a button click. For this example we will want

- A panel populated with buttons
- A listener object (namely, the panel itself) that registers itself with the buttons so that it can listen to them

With this scenario, each time a user clicks on any of the buttons on the panel, the panel (the listener object) then receives an `ActionEvent` that indicates a button click. Because the same panel object is the listener to multiple buttons, we will want to determine which button was clicked.

Before we can show you the program that listens to button clicks, we first need to explain how to create buttons and how to add them to a panel. (For more on GUI elements, please see Chapter 9.)

You create a button by specifying a label string, an icon, or both in the button constructor. Here are two examples:

```
JButton yellowButton = new JButton("Yellow");
JButton blueButton = new JButton(new ImageIcon("blue-ball.gif"));
```

Adding buttons to a panel occurs through a call to a method named (quite mnemonically) `add`. The `add` method takes as a parameter the specific component to be added to the container. For example,

```
class ButtonPanel extends JPanel
{  public ButtonPanel()
   {  yellowButton = new JButton("Yellow");
      blueButton = new JButton("Blue");
      redButton = new JButton("Red");

      add(yellowButton);
      add(blueButton);
      add(redButton);
   }

   private JButton yellowButton;
   private JButton blueButton;
   private JButton redButton;
}
```

Figure 8–1 shows the result.

Figure 8–1: A panel filled with buttons

Now that you know how to add buttons to a panel, you'll need to add code that lets the panel listen to these buttons. This requires having the panel implement the ActionListener interface, which, as we just mentioned, has one method: actionPerformed, whose signature looks like this:

```
public void actionPerformed(ActionEvent evt)
```

It turns out there are two ways to find out which button was clicked. The getSource method of the EventObject class, the superclass of all other event classes, will tell you the *source* of every event. The event source is the object that generated the event and notified the listener:

```
Object source = evt.getSource();
```

We can check which of the buttons was the source:

```
if (source == yellowButton) . . .
else if (source == blueButton) . . .
else if (source == redButton ) . . .
```

Of course, this approach requires that we keep references to the buttons as instance fields in the surrounding panel.

The other approach doesn't use the getSource method. Instead, it uses a method that is specific to the ActionEvent class, called getActionCommand. This method returns the *command string* associated with this action. For buttons, it turns out that the command string defaults to being the button label. If you take this approach, the actionPerformed method code for ButtonTest.java looks like this:

```
String command = evt.getActionCommand();
if (command.equals("Yellow")) . . .;
else if (command.equals("Blue")) . . .;
else if (command.equals("Red")) . . .;
```

Of course, relying on the button strings is a little dangerous. It is an easy mistake to label a button "Gray" and then to spell the string slightly differently in the test:

```
if (command.equals("Grey")) . . .
```

And button strings give you grief when the time comes to internationalize your application. To make the German version with button labels "Gelb,"

"Blau," and "Rot," you have to change *both* the button labels and the strings in the `actionPerformed` method. To overcome this problem, you can specify an action command string that is separate from the label, with the `setActionCommand` method of the `AbstractButton` super class of the `JButton` class:

```
yellowButton = new JButton("Gelb");
yellowButton.setActionCommand("Yellow");
```

Which approach should you use to identify event sources? Using object references is always safer, and we recommend it for that reason, but it requires that the event listener has access to instance variables that refer to the source objects. Using command strings is more flexible, but you must be careful about the command strings, and you must work harder to internationalize your application.

NOTE: The `ActionListener` interface we used in the button example is not restricted to button clicks. It is used in many separate situations such as:

- When an item is selected from a list box with a double click
- When a menu item is selected
- When the ENTER key is clicked in a text field
- When a certain amount of time has elapsed for a `Timer` component

You will see more details in this chapter and the next.

The way to use the `ActionListener` interface is the same in all situations: the `actionPerformed` method (which is the only method in `ActionListener`) takes an object of type `ActionEvent` as a parameter. This event object gives you information about the event that happened.

Now that you know how to analyze the action events, you still need to determine *which object* should carry out that analysis. The AWT event model gives you complete flexibility in this regard. You can add the `actionPerformed` method to any convenient object and then pass that object to the `addActionListener` methods of the buttons. In this example, we want to change the background color of the panel containing the buttons, and it is therefore convenient to place the `actionPerformed` method into the class implementing that panel. Therefore, you should make that panel class implement the `ActionListener` interface:

```
class ButtonPanel extends JPanel
    implements ActionListener
{  public ButtonPanel()
    {  . . .
    }

    public void actionPerformed(ActionEvent evt)
    {  Object source = evt.getSource();
        if (source == yellowButton) . . .
```

```
            else if (source == blueButton)  . . .
            else if (source == redButton )  . . .
    }

    private JButton yellowButton;
    private JButton blueButton;
    private JButton redButton;
}
```

Now that you have determined that the panel containing the buttons handles the events, you must let the buttons know to send the events to that panel. For each button, you call the `addActionListener` method with a reference to that panel. The most convenient place to make those calls seems to be in the constructor of the panel itself, where the buttons are created and added to the panel. Inside that method, the panel is accessed as the `this` pointer. Hence, the code for adding the panel as the action listener to the buttons is as follows:

```
public ButtonPanel()
{   yellowButton = new JButton("Yellow");
    blueButton = new JButton("Blue");
    redButton = new JButton("Red");

    add(yellowButton);
    add(blueButton);
    add(redButton);

    yellowButton.addActionListener(this);
    blueButton.addActionListener(this);
    redButton.addActionListener(this);
}
```

It is actually quite common that the event listener of a user interface component is the container of the component. However, we want to stress that you are free to designate any other object as the listener.

Figure 8–2 shows the interaction between the event source, event listener, and event object.

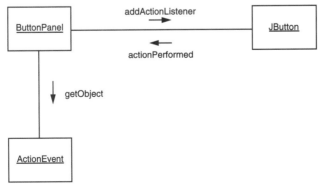

Figure 8–2: Event notification

The simple program in Example 8–1 extends the code above by changing the background color when the user clicks on a button. This change requires a call to the setBackground method, followed by a call to `repaint` to make the color of the panel actually change.

Example 8–1: ButtonTest.java

```java
import java.awt.*;
import java.awt.event.*;
import javax.swing.*;

class ButtonPanel extends JPanel
    implements ActionListener
{  public ButtonPanel()
   {  yellowButton = new JButton("Yellow");
      blueButton = new JButton("Blue");
      redButton = new JButton("Red");

      add(yellowButton);
      add(blueButton);
      add(redButton);

      yellowButton.addActionListener(this);
      blueButton.addActionListener(this);
      redButton.addActionListener(this);
   }

   public void actionPerformed(ActionEvent evt)
   {  Object source = evt.getSource();
      Color color = getBackground();
      if (source == yellowButton) color = Color.yellow;
      else if (source == blueButton) color = Color.blue;
      else if (source == redButton) color = Color.red;
      setBackground(color);
      repaint();
   }

   private JButton yellowButton;
   private JButton blueButton;
   private JButton redButton;
}


class ButtonFrame extends JFrame
{  public ButtonFrame()
   {  setTitle("ButtonTest");
      setSize(300, 200);
      addWindowListener(new WindowAdapter()
         {  public void windowClosing(WindowEvent e)
            {  System.exit(0);
            }
```

```
        } );

    Container contentPane = getContentPane();
    contentPane.add(new ButtonPanel());
    }
}

public class ButtonTest
{   public static void main(String[] args)
    {   JFrame frame = new ButtonFrame();
        frame.show();
    }
}
```

NOTE: If you have programmed graphical user interfaces in Java 1.0, then you may well be horribly confused after reading this section. In Java 1.0, life was simple: you didn't need to worry about listeners. Instead, you added code in methods like `action` and `handleEvent` to the classes that contained the user interface elements. For example, testing a button click would look like this:

```
public boolean action(Event evt, Object arg)
{   Color color = getBackground();
    if (arg.equals("Yellow")) color = Color.yellow;
    else if (arg.equals("Blue")) color = Color.blue;
    else if (arg.equals("Red")) color = Color.red;
    setBackground(color);
    repaint();
    return true;
}
```

There are two important differences between the new event model and the older one:

1. In Java 1.0, a button click is *always* received by the object that contains the button. Now, information about the button click is sent only to objects that were added as an `actionListener` for the button.

2. In Java 1.0, all events are caught in the `action` and `handleEvent` methods. Now, there are many separate methods (such as `actionPerformed` and `windowClosing`) that can react to events.

For simple programs, the old event model is easier to program (although whether it is conceptually as simple is another question). But for complex programs, the old event model has severe limitations. The new model, while initially more involved, is far more flexible and is potentially faster since events are sent only to the listeners that are actually interested in them.

java.util.EventObject

*   `Object getSource()`

    returns a reference to the object where the event initially occurred.

java.awt.event.ActionEvent

- String getActionCommand()

  returns the command string associated with this action event. If the action event originated from a button, the command string equals the button label, unless it has been changed with the setActionCommand method.

javax.swing.AbstractButton

- void setActionCommand(String s)

  sets the command string of the action command that is generated when this button is clicked to the string s.

javax.swing.JButton

- JButton(String label)

  constructs a button.

  Parameters: label   the text you want on the face of the button

- JButton(Icon icon)

  constructs a button.

  Parameters: icon   the icon you want on the face of the button

- JButton(String label, Icon icon)

  constructs a button.

  Parameters: label   the text you want on the face of the button

                  icon   the icon you want on the face of the button

java.awt.Container

- void add(Component c)

  adds a component to this container.

javax.swing.ImageIcon

- ImageIcon(String filename)

  constructs an icon whose image is stored in a file. The image is automatically loaded with a media tracker (see Chapter 7).

Changing the Look and Feel

By default, Swing programs use the Metal look and feel. There are two ways for changing to a different look and feel. You can supply a file `swing.proper-ties` in the `jdk\jre\lib` directories that sets the property `swing.default-laf` to the class name of the look and feel that you want. For example,

```
swing.defaultlaf=com.sun.java.swing.plaf.motif.MotifLookAndFeel
```

Note that the Metal look and feel is located in the `javax.swing` package. The other look and feel packages are located in the `com.sun.java` package and need not be present in every Java implementation. Currently, for copyright reasons, the Windows and Mac look and feel packages are only shipped with the Windows and Mac versions of the JDK.

Here is a useful tip for testing. Since lines starting with a # character are ignored in property files, you can supply several look and feel selections in the `swing.properties` file and move around the # to select one of them:

```
#swing.defaultlaf=javax.swing.plaf.metal.MetalLookAndFeel
swing.defaultlaf=com.sun.java.swing.plaf.motif.MotifLookAndFeel
#swing.defaultlaf=com.sun.java.swing.plaf.windows.WindowsLookAndFeel
```

You must restart your program to switch the look and feel in this way. A Swing program reads the `swing.properties` file only once, at startup.

You can also change the look and feel dynamically. Call the static `UIManager.setLookAndFeel` method and give it the name of the look and feel that you want. Then call the static method `SwingUtilities.updateComponentTreeUI` to refresh the entire set of components. You need to supply one component to that method; it will find all others. The `UIManager.setLookAndFeel` method may throw a number of exceptions, when it can't find the look and feel that you request, or when there is an error loading it. As always, we ask you to gloss over the exception handling code and wait until chapter 11 for a full explanation.

Here is an example how you can switch to the Motif look and feel in your program:

```
String plaf = "com.sun.java.swing.plaf.motif.MotifLookAndFeel";
try
{   UIManager.setLookAndFeel(plaf);
    SwingUtilities.updateComponentTreeUI(contentPane);
}
catch(Exception e) {}
```

Example 8–2 is a complete program that demonstrates how to switch the look and feel (see figure 8–3). The program is very similar to example 8–1. However, the `actionPerformed` method is changed so that clicking the buttons changes the look and feel, not the background color. Note that the "Windows" button will only work on Windows since Sun does not supply the Windows look and feel on other platforms.

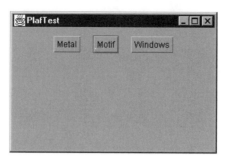

Figure 8–3: Switching the Look and Feel

Example 8–2: PlafTest.java

```java
import java.awt.*;
import java.awt.event.*;
import javax.swing.*;

class PlafPanel extends JPanel
    implements ActionListener
{  public PlafPanel()
   {  metalButton = new JButton("Metal");
      motifButton = new JButton("Motif");
      windowsButton = new JButton("Windows");

      add(metalButton);
      add(motifButton);
      add(windowsButton);

      metalButton.addActionListener(this);
      motifButton.addActionListener(this);
      windowsButton.addActionListener(this);
   }

   public void actionPerformed(ActionEvent evt)
   {  Object source = evt.getSource();
      String plaf = "";
      if (source == metalButton)
         plaf = "javax.swing.plaf.metal.MetalLookAndFeel";
      else if (source == motifButton)
         plaf = "com.sun.java.swing.plaf.motif.MotifLookAndFeel";
      else if (source == windowsButton)
         plaf =
"com.sun.java.swing.plaf.windows.WindowsLookAndFeel";
      try
      {  UIManager.setLookAndFeel(plaf);
         SwingUtilities.updateComponentTreeUI(this);
      }
      catch(Exception e) {}
```

```
      }

      private JButton metalButton;
      private JButton motifButton;
      private JButton windowsButton;
}


class PlafFrame extends JFrame
{   public PlafFrame()
    {   setTitle("PlafTest");
        setSize(300, 200);
        addWindowListener(new WindowAdapter()
            {   public void windowClosing(WindowEvent e)
                {   System.exit(0);
                }
            } );

        Container contentPane = getContentPane();
        contentPane.add(new PlafPanel());
    }
}

public class PlafTest
{   public static void main(String[] args)
    {   JFrame frame = new PlafFrame();
        frame.show();
    }
}
```

Example: Capturing Window Events

Not all events are as simple to handle as button clicks. Consider the problem
that we had at the beginning of Chapter 7. We wanted to know when the user
closed the frame window so that we could then terminate the application. When
the program user tries to close the window, a WindowEvent is generated by the
JFrame class that represents the window. We must now have an appropriate listener object and add it to the list of listeners.

```
    class MyFrame extends JFrame
    {   public MyFrame()
        {   addWindowListener(x); // what is x?
            . . .
        }
        . . .
    }
```

The window listener x must be an object of a class that implements the
WindowListener interface. There are actually seven methods in the
WindowListener interface. The frame calls them as the responses to seven
distinct events that could happen to a window. The names are self-explanatory

except that "iconified" is usually called "minimized" under Windows. The signatures for these methods are as follows.

```
public void windowClosed(WindowEvent e)
public void windowIconified(WindowEvent e)
public void windowOpened(WindowEvent e)
public void windowClosing(WindowEvent e)
public void windowDeiconified(WindowEvent e)
public void windowActivated(WindowEvent e)
public void windowDeactivated(WindowEvent e)
```

As is always the case in Java, any class that implements an interface must implement all its methods; in this case, this means implementing *seven* methods. Recall that we are only interested in one of these seven events: the user closing the window. In that case, we want to terminate the program. Thus, we can add a call to System.exit(0) in the windowClosing method and write do-nothing functions for the other six methods of the WindowListener interface:

```
class Terminator implements WindowListener
{   public void windowClosing(WindowEvent e){System.exit(0);}
    public void windowClosed(WindowEvent e){}
    public void windowIconified(WindowEvent e){}
    public void windowOpened(WindowEvent e){}
    public void windowDeiconified(WindowEvent e){}
    public void windowActivated(WindowEvent e){}
    public void windowDeactivated(WindowEvent e){}
}
```

Adapter Classes

Typing code for six methods that don't do anything is the kind of tedious busy-work that nobody likes. To simplify this task, each of the AWT listener interfaces that has more than one method comes with a companion *adapter* class that implements all the methods in the interface but does nothing with them. For example, the WindowAdapter class has seven do-nothing methods. This means the adapter class automatically satisfies the technical requirements that Java imposes for implementing the associated listener interface. You can extend the adapter class to specify the desired reactions to some, but not all, of the event types in the interface. (An interface such as ActionListener that has only a single method does not need an adapter class.)

Let us make use of the window adapter. We can extend the WindowAdapter class, inherit six of the do-nothing methods, and override the windowClosing method:

```
class Terminator extends WindowAdapter
{   public void windowClosing(WindowEvent e)
    {
        System.exit(0);
    }
}
```

> NOTE: You cannot make `MyFrame` into a subclass of `WindowAdapter` since `MyFrame` already extends `JFrame`. Therefore, you cannot simply set the window listener to `this`, and you must come up with a new class.

Now we can register an object of type `Terminator` as the event listener:

```
class MyFrame extends JFrame
{   public MyFrame()
    {   Terminator x = new Terminator();
        addWindowListener(x);
        . . .
    }
    . . .
}
```

Now, whenever the frame generates a window event, it passes it to the `x` object by calling one of its seven methods (See Figure 8–4). Six of those methods do nothing; the `windowClosing` method calls `System.exit(0)`, terminating the application.

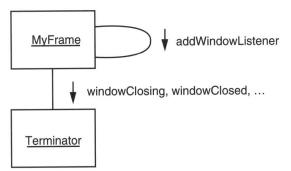

Figure 8–4: A window listener

Creating a listener class that extends the `WindowAdapter` is an improvement, but we can go even further. There is no need to give a name to the `x` object: Simply write

```
class MyFrame extends JFrame
{   public MyFrame()
    {   addWindowListener(new Terminator());
        . . .
    }
    . . .
}
```

But why stop there? We can make the listener class into an *anonymous inner class* of the frame by using the technique described in Chapter 6. This is the code that you have seen in all graphical example programs:

```
class MyFrame extends JFrame
{  public MyFrame()
     {  addWindowListener(new WindowAdapter()
          {   public void windowClosing(WindowEvent e)
              { System.exit(0); }
          } );
          . . .
     }
     . . .
}
```

This code does the following:

- Defines a class without a name that extends the `WindowAdapter` class.

- Adds a `windowClosing` method to that anonymous class. (As before, this method closes the window and exits the program.)

- Inherits the remaining six do-nothing methods from `WindowAdapter`.

- Creates an object of this class. That object does not have a name, either.

- Passes that object to the `addWindowListener` method.

Naturally, the syntax for using anonymous inner classes for event listeners takes some getting used to. The payoff is that the resulting code is as short as possible.

> NOTE: We want to stress that using an anonymous inner adapter class is purely techni-
> cal. Instead of using an anonymous inner class, you can always define a regular class
> with a name and then create an object of that named class.

The AWT Event Hierarchy

Having given you a taste of how event handling works, we want to turn to a more general discussion of event handling in Java. As we briefly mentioned earlier, event handling in Java is object oriented, with all events descending from the `EventObject` class in the `java.util` package. (The common superclass is not called `Event` since that is the name of the event class in the old event model. Although the old model is now deprecated, its classes are still a part of the current AWT.)

The `EventObject` class has a subclass `AWTEvent`, which is the parent of all AWT event classes. Figure 8–5 shows the inheritance diagram of the AWT events.

Some of the Swing components generate event objects of yet more event types; these directly extend `EventObject`, not `AWTEvent`.

You can even add your own custom events by subclassing `EventObject` or one of the other event classes, as you will see at the end of this chapter.

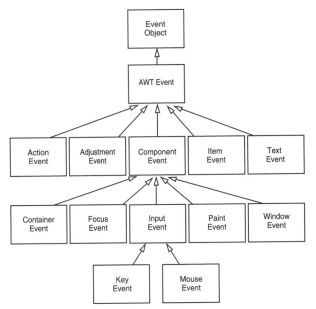

Figure 8–5: Inheritance diagram of the AWT event classes

The event objects encapsulate information about the event that the event source communicates to its listeners. When necessary, you can then analyze the event objects that were passed to the listener object, as we did in the button example with the getSource and getActionCommand methods.

Some of the AWT event classes are of no practical use for the Java programmer. For example, the AWT inserts PaintEvent objects into the event queue, but these objects are not delivered to listeners. Java programmers should override the paintComponent method to control repainting. Here is a list of those AWT event types that are actually passed to listeners.

```
ActionEvent              ItemEvent
AdjustmentEvent          KeyEvent
ComponentEvent           MouseEvent
ContainerEvent           TextEvent
FocusEvent               WindowEvent
```

You will see examples of all of these event types in this chapter and the next chapter.

The javax.swing.event package contains additional events that are specific to Swing components. We will cover some of them in the next chapter.

There are eleven listener interfaces altogether in the java.awt.event package:

```
ActionListener           KeyListener
AdjustmentListener       MouseListener
ComponentListener        MouseMotionListener
ContainerListener        TextListener
```

```
FocusListener          WindowListener
ItemListener
```

You have already seen the `ActionListener` and `WindowListener` interface.

Although the `javax.swing.event` package contains many more listener interfaces that are specific to Swing user interface components, it still uses the basic AWT listener interfaces extensively for general event processing.

Seven of the AWT listener interfaces, namely, those that have more than one method, come with a companion *adapter* class that implements all the methods in the interface to do nothing. (The remaining four interfaces have only a single method each, so there is no benefit in having adapter classes for these interfaces.) For example, the `WindowAdapter` class has seven do-nothing methods.

Here is a list of the names of these adapter classes:

```
ComponentAdapter       MouseAdapter
ContainerAdapter       MouseMotionAdapter
FocusAdapter           WindowAdapter
KeyAdapter
```

Obviously, there are a lot of classes and interfaces to keep track of—it can all be a bit overwhelming. Fortunately, the principle is simple. A class that is interested in receiving events must implement a listener interface. It registers itself with the event source. It then gets the events that it asked for and processes them through the methods of the listener interface.

NOTE: People coming from a C/C++ background may be wondering: why the proliferation of objects, methods, and interfaces that are needed for event handling? You are used to doing graphical user interface programming environments by writing callbacks with generic pointers or handles. This won't work in Java. The Java event model is *strongly typed:* the compiler watches out that events are sent only to objects that are capable of handling them.

Semantic and Low-Level Events in the AWT

The AWT makes a useful distinction between *low-level* and *semantic* events. A semantic event is one that expresses what the user is doing, such as "clicking that button"; hence, an `ActionEvent` is a semantic event. Low-level events are those events that make this possible. In the case of a button click, this is a mouse down, a series of mouse moves and a mouse up (but only if the mouse up is inside the button area). Or it might be a keystroke, which happens if the user selects the button with the TAB key and then activates it with the space bar. Similarly, adjusting a scrollbar is a semantic event, but dragging the mouse is a low-level event.

There are four semantic event classes in the `java.awt.event` package.

- `ActionEvent` (for a button click, a menu selection, selecting a list item, ENTER typed in a text field)

- `AdjustmentEvent` (the user adjusted a scroll bar)

- `ItemEvent` (the user made a selection from a set of checkbox or list items)

- `TextEvent` (the contents of a text field or text area were changed)

There are six low-level event classes.

- `ComponentEvent` (the component was resized, moved, shown, or hidden); also is the base class for all low-level events

- `KeyEvent` (a key was pressed or released)

- `MouseEvent` (the mouse button was depressed, released, moved, or dragged)

- `FocusEvent` (a component got focus, lost focus)

- `WindowEvent` (the window was activated, deactivated, iconified, deiconified, or closed)

- `ContainerEvent` (a component has been added or removed)

Event Handling Summary

Table 8–1 shows all AWT listener interfaces, events, and event sources. Notice that this table gives a number of events that track the *focus* of components and the *activation* of windows—these concepts are explained in the sections that follow.

Let's go over the event delegation mechanism one more time in order to make sure that you understand the relationship between event classes, listener interfaces, and adapter classes.

Event *sources* are user interface components, windows, and menus. The operating system notifies an event source about interesting activities, such as mouse moves and keystrokes. The event source describes the nature of the event in an *event object*. It also keeps a set of *listeners*—objects that want to be called when the event happens (See Figure 8–6). The event source then calls the appropriate method of the *listener interface* to deliver information about the event to the various listeners. The source does this by passing the appropriate event object to the method in the listener class. The listener analyzes the event object to find out more about the event. For example, you can use the `getSource` method to find out the source, or the `getX` and `getY` methods of the `MouseEvent` class to find out the current location of the mouse.

Table 8–1: Event handling summary

Interface	Methods	Parameter/Accessors	Events generated by
ActionListener	actionPerformed	ActionEvent getActionCommand getModifiers	Button List MenuItem TextField
AdjustmentListener	adjustmentValueChanged	AdjustmentEvent getAdjustable getAdjustmentType getValue	Scrollbar
ItemListener	itemStateChanged	ItemEvent getItem getItemSelectable getStateChange	Checkbox CheckboxMenuItem Choice List
TextListener	textValueChanged	TextEvent	TextComponent
ComponentListener	componentMoved componentHidden componentResized componentShown	ComponentEvent getComponent	Component
ContainerListener	componentAdded componentRemoved	ContainerEvent getChild getContainer	Container
FocusListener	focusGained focusLost	FocusEvent isTemporary	Component
KeyListener	keyPressed keyReleased keyTyped	KeyEvent getKeyChar getKeyCode getKeyModifiersText getKeyText isActionKey	Component
MouseListener	mousePressed mouseReleased mouseEntered mouseExited mouseClicked	MouseEvent getClickCount getX getY getPoint translatePoint isPopupTrigger	Component
MouseMotionListener	mouseDragged mouseMoved	MouseEvent	Component
WindowListener	windowClosing windowOpened windowIconified windowDeiconified windowClosed windowActivated windowDeactivated	WindowEvent getWindow	Window

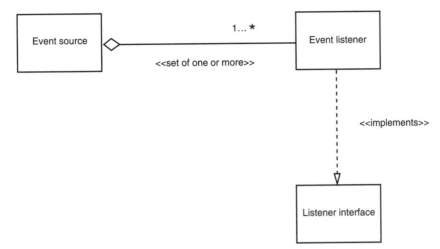

Figure 8–6: Relationship between event sources and listeners

With one exception, each AWT event type corresponds to a listener interface. The one exception is that both `MouseListener` and `MouseMotionListener` receive `MouseEvent` objects. This is done for efficiency—there are a lot of mouse events as the user moves the mouse around, and a listener that just cares about mouse *clicks* will not be bothered with unwanted mouse *moves*.

Furthermore, Java supplies a corresponding *adapter* class to all AWT listener interfaces with more than one method. The adapter class defines all the methods of the interface to do nothing. You use adapter classes as a time-saving tool: use them when you want to override just a few of the listener interface methods.

> NOTE: In the AWT 1.0 event mechanism, events originated in a particular component and were then propagated to all containers of the compontent. Starting with the AWT 1.1, events are only sent to listeners who registered their interest in receiving them.

The high-level semantic events are quite natural for GUI programming—they correspond to user input. To better understand the low-level events in Table 8–1, we will need to briefly review some terminology.

- A *component* is a user interface element such as a button, text field, or scrollbar.

- A *container* is a screen area or component that can contain components, such as a window or a panel.

All low-level events inherit from `ComponentEvent`. This class has a method, called `getComponent`, which reports the component that originated the event; you can use `getComponent` instead of `getSource`. The `getComponent` method returns the same value as `getSource`, but already cast as a `Component`. For example, if a key event was fired because of an input into a text field, then `getComponent` returns a reference to that text field.

A `ContainerEvent` is generated whenever a component is added or removed. This is quite different from the other events that we saw. Button clicks and keystrokes come from the user in a random fashion, but adding or removing components is a consequence of your programming. Therefore, you don't need an event notification mechanism—you could have programmed the notification yourself. This event was provided to make user interface generators simpler to program. Unless you have a dynamically changing user interface, you will not need to worry about it.

java.awt.event.ComponentEvent

- `Component getComponent()`

  returns a reference to the component that is the source for the event. This is the same as `(Component)getSource()`.

Individual Events

In the sections that follow, we will discuss in more detail the focus and window events that we have already briefly discussed. After that, we take up the events that are not linked to specific user interface components, in particular, events related to keystrokes and mouse activity. You can find a detailed discussion of events generated by user interface components, such as button clicks, list selections, and scrollbar adjustments, in the next chapter.

Focus Events

In Java, a component has the *focus* if it can receive keystrokes. For example, in Java, a text field has the focus when the cursor (caret) mark becomes visible. At that point, you can enter text into the text field. When a button has the focus, you can "click" it by pressing the space bar. Only one component can have the focus at a time. A component can *lose focus* if the user selects another component, which then *gains focus*. A component gains focus if the user clicks the mouse inside it. The user can also use the TAB key to give focus to each component in turn. This traverses all components that are able to receive input focus. In some windowing systems, just moving the mouse over a component moves the input focus. Some components, such as labels, do not get focus by default. By default, Swing components are traversed from left to right, then top to bottom, as they are shown in the ambient container. You can change the focus traversal order; see the next chapter for more on this subject.

Finally, you can use the `requestFocus` method to move the focus to any specific visible component at run time, or you can use the `transferFocus` method to move the focus to the next component in the traversal order.

TIP: You can prevent a Swing component from receiving the focus by overriding the `isFocusTraversable` method to return `false`.

Most Swing components give a visual clue if they currently have the focus. A text field has a blinking caret, a button has a colored rectangle around the label, and so on. Most components can receive the focus; however, by default, some components, such as labels and panels, do not.

VB NOTE: In VB, the concepts of "focus" and "being able to receive keystrokes" are not identical. A control can have focus, but if you set the KeyPreview property of the form to `true`, then the keystrokes go to the form.

A focus listener must implement two methods, `focusGained` and `focusLost`. These methods are triggered when the event *source* gains or loses the focus. Each of these methods has a `FocusEvent` parameter. There are two useful methods for this class. The `getComponent` method reports the component that gained or lost the focus, and the `isTemporary` method returns `true` if the focus change was *temporary*. (A temporary focus change occurs when a component loses control temporarily but will automatically get it back. This happens, for example, when the user selects a different active window. As soon as user selects the current window again, the same control regains the focus.)

One use for trapping focus events is error checking or data validation. Suppose you have a text field that contains a credit card number. When the user is done editing the field and moves to another field, you trap the lost focus event. If the credit card format was not formatted properly, you call `requestFocus()` to give the focus back to the credit card field.

```
public void focusLost(FocusEvent evt)
{  if (evt.getComponent() == ccField && !evt.isTemporary())
   {  if (!checkFormat(ccField.getText()))
          ccField.requestFocus();
   }
}
```

`java.awt.Component`

- `void requestFocus()`

    moves the focus to this component. The component must be visible for this to happen.

- `void transferFocus()`

    transfers the focus to the next component in the traversal order.

- `boolean isFocusTraversable()`

  tells whether a component can be reached by using TAB or SHIFT-TAB. Override this method to return `false` if you don't want the component to be reachable with TAB/SHIFT+TAB. (You can still set the focus explicitly by using `requestFocus`.)

Window Events

A (top-level) window is *active* if it can currently receive keystrokes from the operating system. The active window is usually indicated by a highlighted title bar. Only one window can be active at one time. As you saw earlier, you can be notified whenever one of the following events occurs in a window:

- The window has opened.
- The window has closed.
- The window becomes active.
- The window becomes inactive.
- The window becomes iconified (minimized).
- The window becomes deiconified (restored to its original size).
- The user wants to close the window.

For example, as you saw earlier, our `Frame` classes have an event handler that closes the application when the user wants to close the frame. This closure required trapping the "window closing" event.

Here is one obvious scenario where you will want to trap some of the other window events. Suppose your application displays an animation. You can stop the animation when the window is not active or when it is minimized (iconified). You would restart it only when the window becomes active or visible again.

Keyboard Events

When the user pushes a key, a `KEY_PRESSED` KeyEvent is generated. When the user releases the key, a `KEY_RELEASE` KeyEvent is triggered. You trap these events in the `keyPressed` and `keyReleased` methods of any class that implements the `KeyListener` interface. Use these methods to trap raw keystrokes. A third method, `keyTyped`, combines the two: it reports on the *characters* that were generated by the user's keystrokes.

The best way to see what happens is with an example. But before we can do that, we have to add a little more terminology. Java makes a distinction between characters and *virtual key codes.* Virtual key codes are indicated with a prefix of VK_, such as VK_A or VK_SHIFT. Virtual key codes correspond to keys on the keyboard. For example, VK_A denotes the key marked A. There is no separate lowercase virtual key code—the keyboard does not have separate lowercase keys.

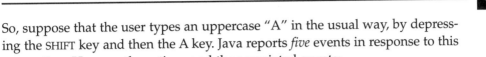

NOTE: Virtual key codes are similar (and related to) the *scan codes* of a PC keyboard.

So, suppose that the user types an uppercase "A" in the usual way, by depressing the SHIFT key and then the A key. Java reports *five* events in response to this user action. Here are the actions and the associated events:

Pressed the SHIFT key (keyPressed called for VK_SHIFT)

Pressed the A key (keyPressed called for VK_A)

Typed "A" (keyTyped called for an "A")

Released the A key (keyReleased called for VK_A)

Released the SHIFT key (keyReleased called for VK_SHIFT)

On the other hand, if the user typed a lowercase "a" by simply depressing the A key, then there are only three events:

Pressed the A key (keyPressed called for VK_A)

Typed "a" (keyTyped called for an "a")

Released the A key (keyReleased called for VK_A)

Thus, the keyTyped procedure reports the *character* that was typed ("A" or "a"), whereas the keyPressed and keyReleased methods report on the actual *keys* that the user pressed.

To work with the keyPressed and keyReleased methods, you want to first check the *key code*.

```
public void keyPressed(KeyEvent evt)
{   int keyCode = evt.getKeyCode();
    . . .
}
```

The key code will equal one of the following (reasonably mnemonic) constants. They are defined in the KeyEvent class.

```
VK_A . . . VK_Z
VK_0 . . . VK_9
VK_COMMA, VK_PERIOD, VK_SLASH, VK_SEMICOLON, VK_EQUALS
VK_OPEN_BRACKET, VK_BACK_SLASH, VK_CLOSE_BRACKET
VK_BACK_QUOTE, VK_QUOTE
VK_GREATER, VK_LESS, VK_UNDERSCORE, VK_MINUS
VK_AMPERSAND, VK_ASTERISK, VK_AT, VK_BRACELEFT, VK_BRACERIGHT
VK_LEFT_PARENTHESIS, VK_RIGHT_PARENTHESIS
VK_CIRCUMFLEX, VK_COLON, VK_NUMBER_SIGN, VK_QUOTEDBL
VK_EXCLAMATION_MARK, VK_INVERTED_EXCLAMATION_MARK
VK_DEAD_ABOVEDOT, VK_DEAD_ABOVERING, VK_DEAD_ACUTE
VK_DEAD_BREVE
VK_DEAD_CARON, VK_DEAD_CEDILLA, VK_DEAD_CIRCUMFLEX
VK_DEAD_DIAERESIS
```

```
VK_DEAD_DOUBLEACUTE, VK_DEAD_GRAVE, VK_DEAD_IOTA, VK_DEAD_MACRON
VK_DEAD_OGONEK, VK_DEAD_SEMIVOICED_SOUND, VK_DEAD_TILDE
VK_DEAD_VOICED_SOUND
VK_DOLLAR, VK_EURO_SIGN
VK_SPACE, VK_ENTER, VK_BACK_SPACE, VK_TAB, VK_ESCAPE
VK_SHIFT, VK_CONTROL, VK_ALT, VK_ALT_GRAPH, VK_META
VK_NUM_LOCK, VK_SCROLL_LOCK, VK_CAPS_LOCK
VK_PAUSE, VK_PRINTSCREEN
VK_PAGE_UP, VK_PAGE_DOWN, VK_END, VK_HOME, VK_LEFT, VK_UP VK_RIGHT
VK_DOWN
VK_F1 . . .VK_F24
VK_NUMPAD0 . . . VK_NUMPAD9
VK_KP_DOWN, VK_KP_LEFT, VK_KP_RIGHT, VK_KP_UP
VK_MULTIPLY, VK_ADD, VK_SEPARATER [sic], VK_SUBTRACT, VK_DECIMAL
VK_DIVIDE
VK_DELETE, VK_INSERT
VK_HELP, VK_CANCEL, VK_CLEAR, VK_FINAL
VK_CONVERT, VK_NONCONVERT, VK_ACCEPT, VK_MODECHANGE
VK_AGAIN, VK_ALPHANUMERIC, VK_CODE_INPUT, VK_COMPOSE, VK_PROPS
VK_STOP
VK_ALL_CANDIDATES, VK_PREVIOUS_CANDIDATE
VK_COPY, VK_CUT, VK_PASTE, VK_UNDO
VK_FULL_WIDTH, VK_HALF_WIDTH
VK_HIRAGANA, VK_KATAKANA, VK_ROMAN_CHARACTERS
VK_KANA, VK_KANJI
VK_JAPANESE_HIRAGANA, VK_JAPANESE_KATAKANA, VK_JAPANESE_ROMAN
VK_UNDEFINED
```

To find the current state of the SHIFT, CONTROL, ALT, and META keys, you can, of course, track the `VK_SHIFT`, `VK_CONTROL`, `VK_ALT`, and `VK_META` key presses, but that is tedious. Instead, simply use the `isShiftDown`, `isControlDown`, `isAltDown`, and `isMetaDown` methods.

For example, the following code tests whether the user presses SHIFT + RIGHT ARROW:

```
public void keyPressed(KeyEvent evt)
{   int keyCode = evt.getKeyCode();
    if (keyCode == keyEvent.VK_RIGHT && evt.isShiftDown())
    {   . . .
    }
}
```

In the `keyTyped` method, you call the `getKeyChar` method to obtain the actual character that was typed.

NOTE: Not all keystrokes result in a call to `keyTyped`. Only those keystrokes that generate a Unicode character can be captured in the `keyTyped` method. You need to use the `keyPressed` method to check for cursor keys and other command keys.

Example 8–3 shows how to handle keystrokes. The program is a simple implementation of the Etch-A-Sketch™ toy shown in Figure 8–7. You move a pen up,
down, left, and right with the cursor keys. If you hold down the SHIFT key, the
pen moves by a larger increment. Or, if you are used to the vi editor, you can
bypass the cursor keys and use the h, j, k, l keys to move the pen. The uppercase
H, J, K, L move the pen by a larger increment. We trap the cursor keys in the
`keyPressed` method and the characters in the `keyTyped` method.

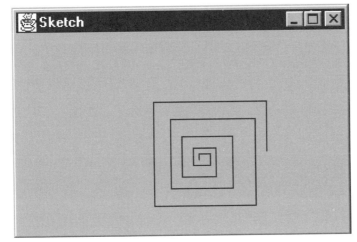

Figure 8–7: A sketch program

There is one technicality: Normally, a panel cannot get keyboard focus. That is,
it will not receive any key events. To allow it to gain focus, we override the
`isFocusTraversable` method of the `SketchPanel` class in order to return
`true`. When the focus manager decides which component should receive the
focus, it finds exactly one component that is willing to accept focus, namely, the
`SketchPanel`, and so all key events are sent to that panel.

Example 8–3: Sketch.java

```java
import java.awt.*;
import java.awt.event.*;
import javax.swing.*;

class SketchPanel extends JPanel
    implements KeyListener
{   public SketchPanel()
    {   addKeyListener(this);
    }

    public void keyPressed(KeyEvent evt)
    {   int keyCode = evt.getKeyCode();
```

```
        int d;
        if (evt.isShiftDown())
           d = 5;
        else
           d = 1;
        if (keyCode == KeyEvent.VK_LEFT) add(-d, 0);
        else if (keyCode == KeyEvent.VK_RIGHT) add(d, 0);
        else if (keyCode == KeyEvent.VK_UP) add(0, -d);
        else if (keyCode == KeyEvent.VK_DOWN) add(0, d);
     }

   public void keyReleased(KeyEvent evt)
   {}

   public void keyTyped(KeyEvent evt)
   {  char keyChar = evt.getKeyChar();
      int d;
      if (Character.isUpperCase(keyChar))
      {  d = 5;
         keyChar = Character.toLowerCase(keyChar);
      }
      else
         d = 1;
      if (keyChar == 'h') add(-d, 0);
      else if (keyChar == 'l') add(d, 0);
      else if (keyChar == 'k') add(0, -d);
      else if (keyChar == 'j') add(0, d);
   }

   public boolean isFocusTraversable() { return true; }

   public void add(int dx, int dy)
   {  end.x += dx;
      end.y += dy;
      Graphics g = getGraphics();
      g.drawLine(start.x, start.y, end.x, end.y);
      g.dispose();
      start.x = end.x;
      start.y = end.y;
   }

   private Point start = new Point(0, 0);
   private Point end = new Point(0, 0);
}

class SketchFrame extends JFrame
{  public SketchFrame()
   {  setTitle("Sketch");
      setSize(300, 200);
      addWindowListener(new WindowAdapter()
         {  public void windowClosing(WindowEvent e)
```

```
            {   System.exit(0);
            }
        } );

    Container contentPane = getContentPane();
    contentPane.add(new SketchPanel());
    }
}

public class Sketch
{  public static void main(String[] args)
    {   JFrame frame = new SketchFrame();
        frame.show();
    }
}
```

java.awt.event.KeyEvent

- `char getKeyChar()`

  returns the character that the user typed.

- `int getKeyCode()`

  returns the virtual key code of this key event.

- `boolean isActionKey()`

  returns `true` if the key in this event is an "action" key. The following keys are action keys: HOME, END, PAGE UP, PAGE DOWN, UP, DOWN, LEFT, RIGHT, F1 ... F24, PRINT SCREEN, SCROLL LOCK, CAPS LOCK, NUM LOCK, PAUSE, INSERT, DELETE, ENTER, BACKSPACE, DELETE, and TAB.

- `static String getKeyText(int keyCode)`

  returns a string describing the key code. For example, `getKeyText(KeyEvent.VK_END)` is the string `"End"`.

- `static String getKeyModifiersText(int modifiers)`

  returns a string describing the modifier keys, such as SHIFT or CTRL + SHIFT.

  Parameters: `modifiers`   the modifier state, as reported by `getModifiers`

java.awt.event.InputEvent

- `int getModifiers()`

  returns an integer whose bits describe the state of the modifiers SHIFT, CONTROL, ALT, and META. This method applies to both keyboard and mouse events. To see if a bit is set, test the return value against one of the bit masks SHIFT_MASK, CONTROL_MASK, ALT_MASK, META_MASK, or use one of the following methods.

- `boolean isAltDown()`
- `boolean isControlDown()`
- `boolean isMetaDown()`
- `boolean isShiftDown()`

The methods return `true` if the modifier key was held down when this event was generated.

Mouse Events

You do not need to handle mouse events explicitly if you just want the user to be able to click on a button or menu. These mouse operations are handled internally by the various components in the graphical user interface and then translated into the appropriate semantic event. You can react to that event in an `actionPerformed` or `itemStateChanged` method. However, if you want to enable the user to draw with the mouse, you will need to trap mouse move, click, and drag events.

In this section, we will show you a simple graphics editor application that allows the user to place, move, and erase squares on a canvas (see Figure 8–8).

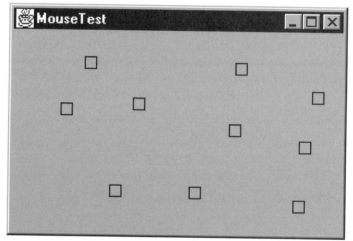

Figure 8–8: A mouse test program

When the user clicks a mouse button, three listener methods are called: `mousePressed` when the mouse is first pressed, `mouseReleased` when the mouse is released, and, finally, `mouseClicked`. If you are only interested in complete clicks, you can ignore the first two methods. By using the `getX` and `getY` methods on the `MouseEvent` argument, you can obtain the *x*- and *y*-coordinates of the mouse pointer when the mouse was clicked. If you want to distinguish between single and double clicks, use the `getClickCount` method.

You can even get triple clicks, but your users will hate you if you force them to exercise their fingers too much. Unless they come from an Emacs background, they will also hate you if you inflict keystroke + mouse click combinations, such as CONTROL + SHIFT + CLICK, on them. If you do want to check the state of the SHIFT, CONTROL, ALT, and META keys, you do it in the same way as you just saw for key events: use the `isShiftDown`, `isControlDown`, `isAltDown`, and `isMetaDown` methods.

For example, here is a handler for the CONTROL + SHIFT + triple click command.

```
public void mouseClicked(MouseEvent evt)
{   int x = evt.getX();
    int y = evt.getY();

    int clickCount = evt.getClickCount();
    if (evt.isShiftDown() && evt.isControlDown()
        && clickCount >= 3)
    {   Graphics g = getGraphics();
        g.drawString("Yikes", x, y);
        g.dispose();
    }
}
```

NOTE: In this example, we use the `Component.getGraphics` method to draw immediately when the mouse is clicked, rather than waiting for the next call to `paintComponent`. We must therefore call `g.dispose()` to recycle the resources that a `Graphics` object holds. You must always call `dispose` for the `Graphics` objects that you obtain yourself, but never for the ones that you receive as arguments of paint methods.

You can distinguish between the mouse buttons by testing the return value of `getModifiers` against the values BUTTON1_MASK, BUTTON2_MASK, BUTTON3_MASK. Note that BUTTON3_MASK tests for the right (nonprimary) mouse button under Windows. For example, you can use code like this to detect if the right mouse button is down:

```
if ((evt.getModifiers() & InputEvent.BUTTON3_MASK) != 0)
    // code for right click
```

In our sample program, we supply both a `mousePressed` and a `mouseClicked` method. When you click onto a pixel that is not inside any of the squares that have been drawn, a new square is added. We implemented this in the `mousePressed` method so that the user receives immediate feedback and does not have to wait until the mouse button is released. When a user double-clicks inside an existing square, it is erased. We implemented this in the `mouseClicked` method because we need the click count.

```
public void mousePressed(MouseEvent evt)
{   int x = evt.getX();
    int y = evt.getY();
    current = find(x, y);
    if (current < 0) // not inside a square
        add(x, y);
}

public void mouseClicked(MouseEvent evt)
{   int x = evt.getX();
    int y = evt.getY();
    current = find(x, y);
    if (evt.clickCount >= 2)
            remove(current);
}
```

As the mouse moves over a window, the window receives a steady stream of mouse movement events. These are ignored by most applications. However, our test application traps the events in order to change the cursor to a different shape (a cross hair) when it is over a square. This is done with the getPredefinedCursor method of the Cursor class. Table 8–2 lists the constants to use with this method along with what the cursors look like under Windows. (Note that several of these cursors look the same, but you should check how they look on your platform.)

```
public void mouseMoved(MouseEvent evt)
{   int x = evt.getX();
    int y = evt.getY();

    if (find(x, y) >= 0)
        setCursor(Cursor.getPredefinedCursor(
            Cursor.CROSSHAIR_CURSOR));
    else
        setCursor(Cursor.getDefaultCursor());
}
```

Table 8–2: Cursor shapes in Java under Windows

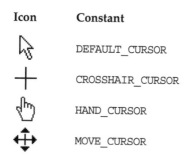

Icon	Constant
	DEFAULT_CURSOR
	CROSSHAIR_CURSOR
	HAND_CURSOR
	MOVE_CURSOR

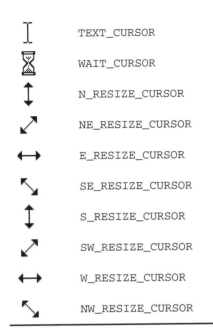

TEXT_CURSOR
WAIT_CURSOR
N_RESIZE_CURSOR
NE_RESIZE_CURSOR
E_RESIZE_CURSOR
SE_RESIZE_CURSOR
S_RESIZE_CURSOR
SW_RESIZE_CURSOR
W_RESIZE_CURSOR
NW_RESIZE_CURSOR

NOTE: You can also define your own cursor types through the use of the `createCustomCursor` method in the `Toolkit` class:

```
Toolkit tk = Toolkit.getDefaultToolkit();
Image img = tk.getImage("dynamite.gif");
Cursor dynamiteCursor = tk.createCustomCursor(img,
    new Point(10, 10), "dynamite stick");
```

The first parameter of the `createCustomCursor` points to the cursor image. The second parameter gives the offset of the "hot spot" of the cursor. This is the point that the user associates with the pointing action of the cursor. For example, if the cursor has the shape of a pointing hand, the hot spot would be the tip of the index finger. If the cursor has the shape of a magnifying glass, the hot spot would be the center of the lens. The third parameter is a string that describes the cursor. This string can be used for accessibility support, for example, to read the cursor shape to a user who is visually impaired or who simply is not facing the screen.

If the user presses a mouse button while the mouse is in motion, `mouseDragged` calls are generated instead of `mouseClicked` calls. Our test application lets you drag the square under the cursor. Before the square is moved, we erase the old location by drawing it over itself in XOR mode. Then, we set the new location for the square and draw it again.

```
public void mouseDragged(MouseEvent evt)
{   int x = evt.getX();
    int y = evt.getY();
```

```
       current = find(x, y);
       if (current >= 0)
       {  Graphics g = getGraphics();
          g.setXORMode(getBackground());
          draw(g, current);
          squares[current].x = x;
          squares[current].y = y;
          draw(g, current);
          g.dispose();
       }
    }
```

There are two other mouse event methods: mouseEntered and mouseExited. These methods are called when the mouse enters or exits a component.

Finally, we need to explain how to listen to mouse events. Mouse clicks are reported through the mouseClicked procedure, which is part of the MouseListener interface. Because many applications are interested only in mouse clicks and not in mouse moves and because mouse move events occur so frequently, the mouse move and drag events are in a separate interface called MouseMotionListener.

We capture mouse motion events, simply by having the MousePanel class implement the MouseMotionListener interface and by registering itself as a listener to its own mouse motion events.

```
    public class MousePanel extends JPanel
       implements MouseMotionListener
    {  public MousePanel()
       {  addMouseMotionListener(this);
          . . .
       }
       public void mouseMoved(MouseEvent evt)
       {  . . .
       }
       public void mouseDragged(MouseEvent evt)
       {  . . .
       }
       . . .
    }
```

NOTE: The mouseMoved method is only called as long as the mouse stays inside the component. However, the mouseDragged method keeps getting called even when the mouse is being dragged outside the component.

For the mousePressed and mouseClicked method, the situation is not as simple. The MouseListener interface has five methods, mouseClicked, mousePressed, mouseReleased, mouseEntered, and mouseExited. We have no interest in three

of them. Therefore, we use the `MouseAdapter` class that defines all these methods
to do nothing, and we build an inner class that overrides the `mousePressed` and
`mouseClicked` methods. Note that the outer class does *not* implement the
`MouseListener` interface.

```
public class MousePanel extends JPanel
    implements MouseMotionListener
{  public MousePanel()
    {  addMouseListener(new MouseAdapter()
            {  public void mousePressed(MouseEvent evt)
                {  . . .
                }
                public void mouseClicked(MouseEvent evt)
                {  . . .
                }
            });
        . . .
    }
    public void mouseMoved(MouseEvent evt) {...}
    . . .
}
```

Example 8–4 is the program listing.

Example 8–4: MouseTest.java

```
import java.awt.*;
import java.awt.event.*;
import javax.swing.*;

class MousePanel extends JPanel
    implements MouseMotionListener
{  public MousePanel()
    {  addMouseListener(new MouseAdapter()
            {  public void mousePressed(MouseEvent evt)
                {  int x = evt.getX();
                    int y = evt.getY();
                    current = find(x, y);
                    if (current < 0) // not inside a square
                        add(x, y);
                }

                public void mouseClicked(MouseEvent evt)
                {  int x = evt.getX();
                    int y = evt.getY();

                    if (evt.getClickCount() >= 2)
                    {  remove(current);
                    }
```

```
           }
        });
     addMouseMotionListener(this);
  }

  public void paintComponent(Graphics g)
  {  super.paintComponent(g);
     for (int i = 0; i < nsquares; i++)
        draw(g, i);
  }

  public int find(int x, int y)
  {  for (int i = 0; i < nsquares; i++)
        if (squares[i].x - SQUARELENGTH / 2 <= x &&
               x <= squares[i].x + SQUARELENGTH / 2
               && squares[i].y - SQUARELENGTH / 2 <= y
               && y <= squares[i].y + SQUARELENGTH / 2)
           return i;
     return -1;
  }

  public void draw(Graphics g, int i)
  {  g.drawRect(squares[i].x - SQUARELENGTH / 2,
        squares[i].y - SQUARELENGTH / 2,
        SQUARELENGTH,
        SQUARELENGTH);
  }

  public void add(int x, int y)
  {  if (nsquares < MAXNSQUARES)
     {  squares[nsquares] = new Point(x, y);
        current = nsquares;
        nsquares++;
        repaint();
     }
  }

  public void remove(int n)
  {  if (n < 0 || n >= nsquares) return;
     nsquares--;
     squares[n] = squares[nsquares];
     if (current == n) current = -1;
     repaint();
  }

  public void mouseMoved(MouseEvent evt)
  {  int x = evt.getX();
     int y = evt.getY();

     if (find(x, y) >= 0)
```

```java
         setCursor(Cursor.getPredefinedCursor
            (Cursor.CROSSHAIR_CURSOR));
      else
         setCursor(Cursor.getDefaultCursor());
   }

   public void mouseDragged(MouseEvent evt)
   {  int x = evt.getX();
      int y = evt.getY();

      if (current >= 0)
      {  Graphics g = getGraphics();
         g.setXORMode(getBackground());
         draw(g, current);
         squares[current].x = x;
         squares[current].y = y;
         draw(g, current);
         g.dispose();
      }
   }

   private static final int SQUARELENGTH = 10;
   private static final int MAXNSQUARES = 100;
   private Point[] squares = new Point[MAXNSQUARES];
   private int nsquares = 0;
   private int current = -1;
}

class MouseFrame extends JFrame
{  public MouseFrame()
   {  setTitle("MouseTest");
      setSize(300, 200);
      addWindowListener(new WindowAdapter()
         {  public void windowClosing(WindowEvent e)
            {  System.exit(0);
            }
         } );

      Container contentPane = getContentPane();
      contentPane.add(new MousePanel());
   }
}

public class MouseTest
{  public static void main(String[] args)
   {  JFrame frame = new MouseFrame();
      frame.show();
   }
}
```

java.awt.event.MouseEvent

- `int getX()`
- `int getY()`
- `Point getPoint()`

  return the *x* (horizontal), *y* (vertical) coordinate, or point where the event happened, using the coordinate system of the source.

- `void translatePoint(int x, int y)`

  translates the coordinates of the event by moving x units horizontally and y units vertically.

- `int getClickCount()`

  returns the number of consecutive mouse clicks associated with this event. (The time interval for what constitutes "consecutive" is system dependent.)

java.awt.Toolkit

- `public Cursor createCustomCursor(Image image, Point hotSpot, String name)`

  creates a new custom cursor object.

Parameters:	image	the image to display when the cursor is active.
	hotSpot	the cursor's hot spot (such as the tip of an arrow or the center of cross hairs)
	name	a description of the cursor, to support special accessibility environments

java.awt.Component

- `public void setCursor(Cursor cursor)`

  sets the cursor image to one of the predefined cursors specified by the `cursor` parameter.

Separating GUI and Application Code

Up to now, we have not really used the feature of the Java event model that lets us choose an arbitrary listener for events—we generally chose this, the panel containing the user interface components, to be the listener. For simple programs, such as the demonstration programs in this chapter, this choice is certainly appropriate. However, as programs get larger, it makes a lot of sense to *separate* the responsibilities of getting user input and executing commands because it is common to have multiple ways to activate the same command. The user can choose a certain function through a menu, a keystroke, or a button on a toolbar.

The following strategy is the one we use to separate the user interface code and the application code.

1. Make an object for every command.

2. Make each command object a listener for the events that trigger it.

For example, suppose we want to add multiple interfaces to the color change application. To change the background color, you can

*   Click on one of the buttons

*   Select a color from a menu

*   Press a key (B = blue, Y = yellow, R = red)

We want each color change command to be handled in a uniform way, no matter whether it was caused by a button click, a menu selection, or a key press.

The Swing package provides a very useful mechanism to encapsulate commands and to attach them to multiple event sources: the `Action` interface. An *action* is an object that encapsulates the following:

*   A description of the command (as a text string and an optional icon)

*   Parameters that are necessary to carry out the command (such as the requested color in our example).

The `Action` interface has the following methods:

```
void actionPerformed(ActionEvent evt)
void setEnabled(boolean b)
boolean isEnabled()
void putValue(String key, Object value)
Object getValue(String key)
void addPropertyChangeListener(PropertyChangeListener listener)
void removePropertyChangeListener(PropertyChangeListener listener)
```

The first method is the familiar method in the `ActionListener` interface: in fact, the `Action` interface extends the `ActionListener` interface. Therefore, you can use an `Action` object whenever an `ActionListener` object is expected.

The next two methods let you enable or disable the action and check whether the action is currently enabled. When an action is attached to a menu or toolbar and the action is disabled, then the option is grayed out.

The `putValue` and `getValue` methods let you store and retrieve name/value pairs in the action object. There are a couple of important predefined strings, namely, `Action.NAME` and `Action.SMALL_ICON`, for storing action names and icons into an action object:

```
action.putValue(Action.NAME, "Blue");
action.putValue(Action.SMALL_ICON,
    new ImageIcon("blue-ball.gif"));
```

If the action object is added to a menu or toolbar, then the name and icon are automatically retrieved and displayed in the menu item or toolbar button.

The final two methods of the `Action` interface allow other objects, in particular menus or toolbars that trigger the action, to be notified when the properties of the action object change. For example, if a menu is added as a property change listener of an action object and the action object is subsequently disabled, then the menu is called and can gray out the action name. Property change listeners are a general construct that is a part of the "Java beans" component model. You can find out more about Java beans and their properties in Volume 2.

Note that `Action` is an *interface*, not a class. Any class implementing this interface must implement the seven methods that we just discussed. Fortunately, that is easy because a friendly soul has implemented all but the first method in a class `AbstractAction`. That class takes care of storing all name/value pairs and managing the property change listeners. All you have to add is an `actionPerformed` method.

Let's build an action object that can execute color change commands. We store the name of the command, an icon, the desired color, and the component whose color is to be changed. Just to show that it can be done either way, we will store the color in the table of name/value pairs that the `AbstractAction` class provides, and we will store the target component as an instance variable of the subclass. Here is the code for the `ColorAction` class. The constructor sets the name/value pairs, and the `actionPerformed` method carries out the color change action.

```
class ColorAction extends AbstractAction
{   public ColorAction(String name, Icon icon,
        Color c, Component comp)
    {   putValue(Action.NAME, name);
        putValue(Action.SMALL_ICON, icon);
        putValue("Color", c);
        target = comp;
    }

    public void actionPerformed(ActionEvent evt)
    {   Color c = (Color)getValue("Color");
        target.setBackground(c);
        target.repaint();
    }
```

```
        private Component target;
    }
```

Our test program creates three objects of this class, such as:

```
    Action blueAction = new ColorAction("Blue",
        new ImageIcon("blue-ball.gif"),
        Color.blue, panel);
```

Next, let's associate this action with a button. That is easy because an action object implements the `ActionListener` interface. Therefore, we can simply pass the action object to the `addActionListener` method of the button.

```
    JButton blueButton = new JButton("Blue");
    blueButton.addActionListener(blueAction);
```

It is actually more elegant to derive a new button class that associates a button with an action and retrieves the button label from the action object. And, while we are at it, we can set the button icon as well.

```
    class ActionButton extends JButton
    {   public ActionButton(Action a)
        {   setText((String)a.getValue(Action.NAME));
            Icon icon = (Icon)a.getValue(Action.SMALL_ICON);
            if (icon != null)
                setIcon(icon);
            addActionListener(a);
        }
    }
```

Now, we can simply construct the buttons out of action objects.

```
    blueButton = new ActionButton(blueAction);
```

Each button is then automatically labeled, and it automatically sends its action events to the action object.

Next, let's add the same action objects to a menu. You don't yet know how to build menus, but it is very easy to add actions to menus. The `add(Action a)` method of the `JMenu` class adds a menu item to a menu. That method retrieves the name and optional icon from the `Action` object, and it makes the `Action` object the action listener for the menu item selection. The following code should be pretty self-explanatory:

```
    JMenu m = new JMenu("Color");
    m.add(yellowAction);
    m.add(blueAction);
    m.add(redAction);
```

Next, you need to add the menu to the menu bar.

```
    JMenuBar mbar = new JMenuBar();
    mbar.add(m);
    setJMenuBar(mbar);
```

Run the sample program and look at the menu (see Figure 8–9). Note that the JMenu class automatically extracted the name and icon of the Action object, just as we did in our own ActionButton class.

![Screenshot of SeparateGUITest window showing a Color menu with Yellow, Blue, Red radio options, and Blue, Red buttons](image-placeholder)

Figure 8–9: Menu items corresponding to action objects

Finally, we want to add the action objects to keystrokes. Now we run into a technical complexity. Keystrokes are delivered to the component that has focus. Our sample application is made up of several components, namely, three buttons inside a panel. Therefore, at any time, any one of the three buttons may have focus. *Each* of the buttons would need to handle key events and listen to the Y, B, and R keys. Fortunately, there is a simpler way. Using the registerKeyboardAction, you can track keystrokes, no matter in which component they occur.

To associate actions with keystrokes, you need to generate objects of the KeyStroke class. This is a convenience class that encapsulates the description of a key. To generate a KeyStroke object, you don't call a constructor but instead use the static getKeyStroke method of the KeyStroke class. You specify the virtual key code and the flags (such as SHIFT and CONTROL key combinations):

```
KeyStroke bKey = KeyStroke.getKeyStroke(VK_B, 0);
```

The registerKeyboardAction takes three commands: an ActionListener object, a KeyStroke object, and a flag to indicate under what condition to invoke the action. The three possible values for the flag are:

flag	invoke action when key stroke occurs
WHEN_FOCUSED	in this component
WHEN_IN_FOCUSED_WINDOW	anywhere in the window containing this component
WHEN_ANCESTOR_OF_FOCUSED_COMPONENT	anywhere in a subcomponent contained in this component

For example,

```
panel.registerKeyboardAction(blueAction, bKey,
   JComponent.WHEN_IN_FOCUSED_WINDOW);
```

Now, blueAction is associated with a third user interface action, namely, the pressing of the B key. You handle the other key assignments in the same way. Example 8–5 shows the complete code.

Example 8–5: SeparateGUITest.java

```
import java.awt.*;
import java.awt.event.*;
import javax.swing.*;

class ColorAction extends AbstractAction
{  public ColorAction(String name, Icon icon,
      Color c, Component comp)
   {  putValue(Action.NAME, name);
      putValue(Action.SMALL_ICON, icon);
      putValue("Color", c);
      target = comp;
   }

   public void actionPerformed(ActionEvent evt)
   {  Color c = (Color)getValue("Color");
      target.setBackground(c);
      target.repaint();
   }

   private Component target;
}

class ActionButton extends JButton
{  public ActionButton(Action a)
   {  setText((String)a.getValue(Action.NAME));
      Icon icon = (Icon)a.getValue(Action.SMALL_ICON);
      if (icon != null)
         setIcon(icon);
      addActionListener(a);
   }
}

class SeparateGUIFrame extends JFrame
{  public SeparateGUIFrame()
   {  setTitle("SeparateGUITest");
      setSize(300, 200);
      addWindowListener(new WindowAdapter()
         {  public void windowClosing(WindowEvent e)
            {  System.exit(0);
```

```
         }
      } );


      JPanel panel = new JPanel();

      Action blueAction = new ColorAction("Blue",
         new ImageIcon("blue-ball.gif"),
         Color.blue, panel);
      Action yellowAction = new ColorAction("Yellow",
         new ImageIcon("yellow-ball.gif"),
         Color.yellow, panel);
      Action redAction = new ColorAction("Red",
         new ImageIcon("red-ball.gif"),
         Color.red, panel);

      panel.add(new ActionButton(yellowAction));
      panel.add(new ActionButton(blueAction));
      panel.add(new ActionButton(redAction));

      panel.registerKeyboardAction(yellowAction,
         KeyStroke.getKeyStroke(KeyEvent.VK_Y, 0),
         JComponent.WHEN_IN_FOCUSED_WINDOW);
      panel.registerKeyboardAction(blueAction,
         KeyStroke.getKeyStroke(KeyEvent.VK_B, 0),
         JComponent.WHEN_IN_FOCUSED_WINDOW);
      panel.registerKeyboardAction(redAction,
         KeyStroke.getKeyStroke(KeyEvent.VK_R, 0),
         JComponent.WHEN_IN_FOCUSED_WINDOW);

      Container contentPane = getContentPane();
      contentPane.add(panel);

      JMenu m = new JMenu("Color");
      m.add(yellowAction);
      m.add(blueAction);
      m.add(redAction);
      JMenuBar mbar = new JMenuBar();
      mbar.add(m);
      setJMenuBar(mbar);
   }
}

public class SeparateGUITest
{  public static void main(String[] args)
   {  JFrame frame = new SeparateGUIFrame();
      frame.show();
   }
}
```

`javax.swing.Action`

- `void setEnabled(boolean b)`

  enables or disables this action. User interface elements may query this status and disable themselves if the associated action is disabled.

- `boolean isEnabled()`

  returns `true` if this action is enabled.

- `void putValue(String key, Object value)`

  places a name/value pair inside the action object.

  Parameters: key   the name of the feature to store with the action object. This can be any string, but four names have predefined meanings:

Name	Value
`Action.NAME`	the action name, to be displayed in UI components
`Action.SMALL_ICON`	the action icon, to be displayed in UI components
`Action.SHORT_DESCRIPTION`	a short description, for example, for a tool tip hint
`Action.LONG_DESCRIPTION`	a longer description for on-line help

  value   the object associated with the name.

- `Object getValue(String key)`

  returns the value of a stored name/value pair.

`javax.swing.JMenu`

- `JMenuItem add(Action a)`

  adds a menu item to the menu that invokes the action a when selected; returns the added menu item.

`javax.swing.KeyStroke`

- `static KeyStroke getKeyStroke(int keyCode, int modifiers)`
- `static KeyStroke getKeyStroke(int keyCode, int modifiers, boolean onRelease)`

  creates a `KeyStroke` object that encapsulates a key stroke.

  Parameters: keyCode   the virtual key code

`modifiers`	any combination of `InputEvent.SHIFT_MASK`, `InputEvent.CONTROL_MASK`, `InputEvent.ALT_MASK`, `InputEvent.META_MASK`
`onRelease`	`true` if the keystroke is to be recognized when the key is released

`javax.swing.JComponent`

- `void registerKeyboardAction(ActionListener a, KeyStroke k, int flag)`

causes an action to be invoked when a keystroke occurs.

Parameters:	`a`	the action to invoke
	`k`	the keystroke that causes the action
	`flag`	a condition on the keyboard focus to trigger the action, one of:

Name	Value
`WHEN_FOCUSED`	in this component
`WHEN_IN_FOCUSED_WINDOW`	anywhere in the window containing this component
`WHEN_ANCESTOR_OF_FOCUSED_COMPONENT`	anywhere in a subcomponent contained in this component

Multicasting

In the preceding section, we had several event sources report to the same event listener. In this section, we will do the opposite. All AWT event sources support a *multicast* model for listeners. This means that the same event can be sent to more than one listener object. Multicasting is useful if an event is *potentially* of interest to many parties. Simply add multiple listeners to an event source to give all registered listeners a chance to react to the events.

CAUTION: According to Sun, "The API makes no guarantees about the order in which the events are delivered to a set of registered listeners for a given event on a given source." In particular, a listener should not consume the event—consumption is meaningless when the delivery order is random. (See the section entitled "Consuming Events" in this chapter for details on event consumption.)

Here we will show a simple application of multicasting. We will have a frame that can spawn multiple windows with the New button. And, it can close all windows with the Close all button—see Figure 8–10.

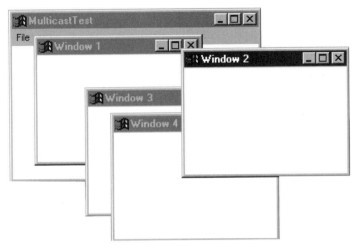

Figure 8–10: All windows listen to the Close all command

The listener to the New button is the panel containing the buttons—it makes the new child windows. But the Close all menu item has *multiple listeners*—each child window is added to the set of listeners. When that button is clicked, all windows are notified and close themselves. Example 8–6 shows the source code.

Example 8–6: MulticastTest.java

```
import java.awt.*;
import java.awt.event.*;
import javax.swing.*;

class MulticastPanel extends JPanel
    implements ActionListener
{   public MulticastPanel()
    {   JButton newButton = new JButton("New");
        add(newButton);
        newButton.addActionListener(this);

        closeAllButton = new JButton("Close all");
        add(closeAllButton);
    }

    public void actionPerformed(ActionEvent evt)
    {   // handles New button
        SimpleFrame f = new SimpleFrame();
        counter++;
        f.setTitle("Window " + counter);
```

```
        f.setSize(200, 150);
        f.setLocation(30 * counter, 30 * counter);
        f.show();
        closeAllButton.addActionListener(f);
     }

     private int counter = 0;
     private JButton closeAllButton;
}

class MulticastFrame extends JFrame
{  public MulticastFrame()
   {  setTitle("MulticastTest");
      setSize(300, 200);
      addWindowListener(new WindowAdapter()
         {  public void windowClosing(WindowEvent e)
            {  System.exit(0);
            }
         } );

      Container contentPane = getContentPane();
      contentPane.add(new MulticastPanel());
   }
}

public class MulticastTest
{  public static void main(String[] args)
   {  JFrame frame = new MulticastFrame();
      frame.show();
   }
}

class SimpleFrame extends JFrame
   implements ActionListener
{  public void actionPerformed(ActionEvent evt)
   {  // handles Close all button
      dispose();
   }
}
```

Advanced Event Handling

In this section, we show you various advanced event handling techniques that bypass or augment the regular event handling mechanism. You'll see techniques for:

- Consuming events

- Implementing secondary event loops

- Adding custom events

Keep in mind that these are all advanced techniques. You should be careful when you use these techniques in your own code—interfering with the normal event delivery can cause subtle problems in your application.

Consuming Events

Occasionally, you will want to capture an event so that it is not passed on to a user interface component. Here is a very common example. Suppose you want to write a text input field that accepts only numbers. Start out with a regular text field. (Text fields are covered in detail in Chapter 9). Simply listen to all key events and *consume* all events that don't correspond to digit keys.

```
textField.addKeyListener(new KeyAdapter()
    {  public void keyTyped(KeyEvent evt)
        {  char ch = evt.getKeyChar();
            if (ch < '0' || ch > '9') // not a digit
                evt.consume();
        }
    });
```

The result is that as far as the text field is concerned, the "key typed" event never happened if the user typed a wrong key.

Only input events (that is, mouse and keyboard events) can be consumed.

NOTE: Actually, you need to work harder to create a text field that is suitable for editing numbers. See Chapter 9 for details.

`java.awt.event.InputEvent`

- `void consume()`

  consumes a low-level event and thereby prevents it from being sent to a user interface component.

- `boolean isConsumed()`

  returns `true` if the event was consumed.

The Event Queue

When the operating system generates an event in response to a user action such as a mouse click, the part of the AWT that communicates with the operating system receives the operating-system-level event and turns it into an AWT event. The AWT then deposits the event into an *event queue*. The part of the AWT that dispatches events to listeners:

- Fetches events from the event queue
- Locates the listener object for that event
- Invokes the appropriate listener procedure for that event

An event queue is important for performance reasons. Events that occur frequently (such as mouse moves) or that are slow to carry out (such as painting) can be *combined* in the queue. If the program has not managed to extract mouse move or paint events and a new event is inserted, then the AWT can combine it with the existing event to make a single, new event. For example, we can have the new mouse position update the old one, or a new paint event can contain a request to repaint the combined areas of the old paint events.

Occasionally, it is useful to manipulate the event queue directly. For example, you can remove events from the queue, thereby bypassing how events would normally be delivered. Or, you can add new events into the queue, allowing a richer event handling than is possible in the basic Java event model. The example program in this section shows you how to remove events from the queue in order to bypass the normal event flow. In the section on custom events that follows, we show you how to insert custom event objects into the queue; these events will then be delivered in the usual way without requiring you to do any more work.

NOTE: Inserting or removing events is an advanced technique. If performed improperly or maliciously, it can wreak havoc with an application. For that reason, applets—the Java applications that are downloaded from foreign computers and run inside your browser—are not allowed access to the system event queue.

You obtain an object representing the event queue by using the method call

```
EventQueue evtq
   = Toolkit.getDefaultToolkit().getSystemEventQueue();
```

You insert a new event into the event queue with the `postEvent` method:

```
evtq.postEvent(new ActionEvent(this,
   ActionEvent.ACTION_PERFORMED, "Blue"));
```

You remove an event with the `getNextEvent` method. The `peekEvent` method returns the next event in the queue, but it does not remove it.

Let us put manipulating the event queue to work by implementing a *secondary event loop*. In a secondary event loop, you are interested only in a particular event and you must manually remove all the events until you find the one you need.

Using a secondary event loop allows you to force the user to do certain actions sequentially. For example, suppose you want to have a drawing program where the user clicks on two points sequentially in order to draw a line. If you use a secondary event loop when you prompt the user to click the mouse, the user cannot wander off and use scrollbars or menus because you can throw away all mouse activity that are not mouse clicks.

This turns out to be a major pain to implement in an event-driven style. In a purely event-driven program, we would have one method that prompts the user to click on the first point. A separate method, namely, the mouse listener, would be activated with every mouse click. The listener would need to keep track of whether the event that it is processing is a part of the line-drawing sequence or not. Then, if it decides that it is part of the line-drawing operation, it needs to decide if it is the first or the second click. This process is tedious. Instead, we want to write a method, called `getClick`, that waits until it has a mouse click from the user and returns the point that was clicked. Once we have such a method, it is straightforward to prompt the user to specify a line:

```
displayPrompt("Please click on a point");
Point p = getClick();
displayPrompt("Please click on another point");
Point q = getClick();
g.drawLine(p.x, p.y, q.x, q.y);
```

The `getClick` method requires the use of a secondary event loop. That loop grabs events until it finds a mouse click.

Note that the mouse coordinates are relative to the *frame*, not the panel. To translate them into the panel coordinates, we must find the location of the panel within the frame. The `getLocation` method of the `Component` class returns the position of the top left corner of a component inside its parent container. However, the parent of our panel is not yet the frame but is the content pane, which itself is contained in another panel, called the root pane. That panel is finally contained in the frame. Thus, we have to adjust the mouse coordinates by the location of the root pane within its parent.

Here is the event loop, together with the code to adjust the mouse coordinates:

```
while (true)
{   AWTEvent evt = eq.getNextEvent();
    if (evt.getID() == MouseEvent.MOUSE_CLICKED)
    {   MouseEvent mevt = (MouseEvent)evt;
        Point p = mevt.getPoint();
        Point top = getRootPane().getLocation();
        p.x -= top.x;
        p.y -= top.y;
        return p;
    }
}
```

Example 8–7 shows the complete source code for this application.

Example 8–7: EventQueueTest.java

```
import java.awt.*;
import java.awt.event.*;
import javax.swing.*;

class EventQueuePanel extends JPanel
```

```
      implements ActionListener
{   EventQueuePanel()
    {   JButton button = new JButton("Draw line");
        add(button);
        button.addActionListener(this);
    }

    public void actionPerformed(ActionEvent evt)
    {   Graphics g = getGraphics();

        displayPrompt(g, "Please click on a point");
        Point p = getClick();
        g.drawOval(p.x - 2, p.y - 2, 4, 4);
        displayPrompt(g, "Please click on another point");
        Point q = getClick();
        g.drawOval(q.x - 2, q.y - 2, 4, 4);
        g.drawLine(p.x, p.y, q.x, q.y);
        displayPrompt(g, "Done!");
        g.dispose();
    }

    public void displayPrompt(Graphics g, String s)
    {   y += 20;
        g.drawString(s, 0, y);
    }

    public Point getClick()
    {   EventQueue eq
            = Toolkit.getDefaultToolkit()
                .getSystemEventQueue();
        while (true)
        {   try
            {   AWTEvent evt = eq.getNextEvent();
                if (evt.getID() == MouseEvent.MOUSE_PRESSED)
                {   MouseEvent mevt = (MouseEvent)evt;
                    Point p = mevt.getPoint();
                    Point top = getRootPane().getLocation();
                    p.x -= top.x;
                    p.y -= top.y;
                    return p;
                }
            }
            catch(InterruptedException e)
            {}
        }
    }

    private int y = 60;
}

class EventQueueFrame extends JFrame
{   public EventQueueFrame()
    {   setTitle("EventQueueTest");
```

```
        setSize(300, 200);
        addWindowListener(new WindowAdapter()
            {  public void windowClosing(WindowEvent e)
                {  System.exit(0);
                }
            } );

        Container contentPane = getContentPane();
        contentPane.add(new EventQueuePanel());
    }
}

public class EventQueueTest
{  public static void main(String[] args)
    {  Frame frame = new EventQueueFrame();
        frame.show();
    }
}
```

`java.awt.EventQueue`

- `AWTEvent peekEvent()`

  returns a reference to the `AWTEvent` object that describes the next event.

- `AWTEvent getNextEvent()`

  returns a reference to the `AWTEvent` object that describes the next event and removes it from the queue.

- `void postEvent(AWTEvent anEvent)`

  places the event on the event queue.

  Parameters: anEvent   the event you want to post

Adding Custom Events

In the last section of this chapter, we will do some fairly sophisticated programming. We want to show you how to build a *custom event type* that you can insert into the AWT event queue and then have it dispatched to a listener, just like regular AWT events. For the example in this section, we will implement a timer. The timer sends an event to its listener whenever a certain time interval has elapsed. For this event, we make a new event type that we call `TimerEvent`. The associated listener will have one method, called `timeElapsed`.

Using a timer is simple. Construct a timer object and specify the interval (in milliseconds) in the constructor. Then, add a listener. The listener will be notified whenever the time interval has elapsed. Here is how you can put the timer to work:

```
public class CustomEventPanel extends JPanel
    implements TimerListener
{  public CustomEventPanel()
```

```
{   Timer t = new Timer(1000);
        // deliver timer clicks every 1000 milliseconds
    t.addTimerListener(this);
        // notify the timeElapsed method of this class
}

public void timeElapsed(TimerEvent evt)
{   . . .
        // this code is executed every 1000 milliseconds
}
. . .
}
```

As you can see, this timer has a "look and feel" that is similar to that of the other AWT events. In particular, Windows programmers will be very comfortable with this approach because Windows uses the event queue to deliver timer notifications.

NOTE: The Swing package has its own `Timer` class, which is slightly different from ours. The Swing timer does not introduce a new event type but instead sends action events to the listener. More importantly, the Swing timer does not smuggle its events inside the AWT queue but keeps its own separate queue for timer events. We are implementing our own class to show you how to add new event types to the AWT, not to build a better timer. If you need a timer in your own code, you should simply use the Swing timer, not ours.

Now, let us see how to implement a custom event. We start with the needed listener interface.

```
public interface TimerListener extends EventListener
{   public void timeElapsed(TimerEvent evt);
}
```

Any class that uses our timer events for timer notifications must implement this interface. The `TimerEvent` class is pretty simple:

*   It extends the `AWTEvent` superclass since all events in the AWT event queue must have type `AWTEvent`.

*   The constructor for the timer event receives the object that is the source of the event (that is, the timer object).

We also need to give an *event ID number* to the superclass. It does not matter what positive integer we choose, as long as we stay outside the range that the AWT uses for its own events.

How to find an unused ID? To quote Sun: "Programs should choose event ID values which are greater than the integer constant: `java.awt.AWTEvent.RESERVED_ID_MAX`."

```
class TimerEvent extends AWTEvent
{   public TimerEvent(Timer t) { super(t, TIMER_EVENT); }
    public static final int TIMER_EVENT =
        AWTEvent.RESERVED_ID_MAX   + 5555;
}
```

Finally, we need to implement the `Timer` class itself. The AWT event mechanism requires that event sources extend the class `Component`. Normally, components are user interface elements that are placed inside a window. We will simply take the attitude that a timer is an invisible component as it is, for example, in Visual Basic.

To write the code that constructs the interval that the timer "ticks," we need to use threads. (Threads are discussed in the second volume of this book, so you will need to take the thread handling code on faith for now.) Whenever the specified time interval has elapsed, we make a new timer event and insert it into the event queue. Here's the code for this, with the pieces that are needed to post the event in bold:

```
class Timer extends Component implements Runnable
{   public Timer(int i)
    {   interval = i;
        Thread t = new Thread(this);
        t.start();
    }

    public void run()
    {   while (true)
        {   try { Thread.sleep(interval); }
            catch(InterruptedException e) {}

            EventQueue evtq
                = Toolkit.getDefaultToolkit().getSystemEventQueue();
            TimerEvent te = new TimerEvent(this);
            evtq.postEvent(te);
        }
    }
    . . .
    private int interval;
}
```

After this code is processed, we know that Java has inserted our custom timer events into the queue. Event delivery is not automatic however, so our custom timer event will not be sent to anyone without additional code.

How do we make sure our custom event is sent to interested parties? The answer is that is the responsibility of the *component* to:

- Manage the listeners for the events that it generates

- Dispatch the events to the listeners that are registered for them

For the purpose of this sample we implement only a single listener. The `addTimerListener` method remembers the object that wants to listen to the timer events. Java calls the `processEvent` method whenever the AWT removes an event from the queue whose source was the timer. If the event is a timer event and we added a listener for it, then Java invokes its `timeElapsed` method.

```
class Timer extends Component implements Runnable
{  . . .
   public void addTimerListener(TimerListener l)
   {  listener = l;
   }

   public void processEvent(AWTEvent evt)
   {  if (evt instanceof TimerEvent)
      {  if (listener != null)
            listener.timeElapsed((TimerEvent)evt);
      }
      else super.processEvent(evt);
   }

   private TimerListener listener;
}
```

NOTE: For an industrial-strength timer component, one would need to support multi-casting and listener removal as well. The `Timer` class in the `javax.swing` package supports these operations, but we omit them from this example for simplicity.

As it turns out, there is one more (undocumented) problem. The AWT code that removes events from the queue and dispatches them to the event source will deliver them only if it is convinced that the container supports the new event model. One way to convince it is to call the `enableEvents` method in the `Component` class. This method takes a parameter that gives a mask for the AWT events we want to enable for this component. We don't care about AWT events at all since we are only interested in our custom timer event, so we pass a mask of 0. This happens in the constructor of the `Timer` object.

Example 8–8 shows the complete source code of a sample program that draws a rectangle whose size increases every 1,000 milliseconds (see Figure 8–11). As you can see, it is possible to add custom events to the AWT mechanism using relatively little code.

Figure 8–11: Using custom timer events to draw a growing rectangle

Example 8–8: CustomEventTest.java

```
import java.awt.*;
import java.util.*;
import java.awt.event.*;
import javax.swing.*;

class CustomEventPanel extends JPanel
    implements TimerListener
{   public CustomEventPanel()
    {   Timer t = new Timer(1000);
        t.addTimerListener(this);
    }

    public void timeElapsed(TimerEvent evt)
    {   Graphics g = getGraphics();
        g.fillRect(0, 0, ticks, 10);
        ticks++;
        g.dispose();
    }

    private int ticks = 0;
}

interface TimerListener extends EventListener
{   public void timeElapsed(TimerEvent evt);
}

class Timer extends Component implements Runnable
{   public Timer(int i)
    {   interval = i;
        Thread t = new Thread(this);
        t.start();
        evtq = Toolkit.getDefaultToolkit()
            .getSystemEventQueue();
        enableEvents(0);
    }

    public void addTimerListener(TimerListener l)
    {   listener = l;
    }

    public void run()
    {   while (true)
        {   try { Thread.sleep(interval); }
            catch(InterruptedException e) {}
            TimerEvent te = new TimerEvent(this);
            evtq.postEvent(te);
        }
    }

    public void processEvent(AWTEvent evt)
```

```
{   if (evt instanceof TimerEvent)
    {   if (listener != null)
            listener.timeElapsed((TimerEvent)evt);
    }
    else super.processEvent(evt);
}

    private int interval;
    private TimerListener listener;
    private static EventQueue evtq;
}

class TimerEvent extends AWTEvent
{   public TimerEvent(Timer t) { super(t, TIMER_EVENT); }
    public static final int TIMER_EVENT
        = AWTEvent.RESERVED_ID_MAX  + 5555;
}

class CustomEventFrame extends JFrame
{   public CustomEventFrame()
    {   setTitle("CustomEventTest");
        setSize(300, 50);
        addWindowListener(new WindowAdapter()
            {   public void windowClosing(WindowEvent e)
                {   System.exit(0);
                }
            } );

        Container contentPane = getContentPane();
        contentPane.add(new CustomEventPanel());
    }
}

public class CustomEventTest
{   public static void main(String[] args)
    {   JFrame frame = new CustomEventFrame();
        frame.show();
    }
}
```

---

java.awt.Component

- void enableEvents(long maskForEvents)

  enables the component to insert events into the event queue even when there is no listener for a particular event type.

  Parameters: maskForEvents   a mask of event types to enable, made up of constants, such as ACTION_EVENT_MASK, that are defined in the AWTEvent class.

Chapter 9

User Interface Components With Swing

The last chapter was primarily designed to show you how to use the event model in Java. In the process you did take the first steps toward learning how to build a graphical user interface. This chapter shows you the most important tools you'll need to build more full-featured graphical user interfaces.

We'll start out with a tour of the architectural underpinnings of Swing. Knowing what goes on "under the hood" is important to understanding how to use some of the more advanced components effectively. We'll then show you how to use the most common user interface components in Swing such as text boxes, list boxes, menus, and dialog boxes. Next, you will learn how to use the nifty layout manager features of Java to arrange these components in a window, regardless of the look and feel of a particular user interface. Finally, you'll see how to implement menus and dialog boxes in Swing.

This chapter covers all Swing components that have a counterpart in the AWT. These are the essential user interface components that you will need most frequently. We will cover advanced Swing components in Volume 2. For an even more comprehensive look into all details of the Swing framework, we recommend the book *Core Java Foundation Classes* by Kim Topley (Prentice-Hall 1998).

The Model-View-Controller Design Pattern

As promised, we start this chapter with a section describing the architecture of Swing components. Before we explain just what the title of this section means, let's step back for a minute and think about the pieces that make up a user interface component such as a button, a check box, a text field, or a sophisticated tree control. Every component has three characteristics:

- its *contents*, such as the state of a button (pushed in or not), or the text in a text field
- its *visual appearance* (color, size, and so on)
- its *behavior* (reaction to events)

Even a seemingly simple component such as a button exhibits some moderately complex interaction between these characteristics. Obviously, the visual appearance of a button depends on the look and feel. A Metal button looks different from a Windows button or a Motif button. And, the appearance depends on the button state: when a button is pushed in, it needs to be redrawn to look different. The state depends on the events that the button receives. When the user depresses the mouse inside the button, the button is pushed in.

Of course, when you use a button in your programs, you simply consider it as a *button*, and you don't think too much about the inner workings and characteristics. That, after all, is the job of the programmer who implemented the button. However, those programmers that implement buttons are motivated to think a little harder about them. After all, they have to implement buttons, and all other user interface components, so that they work well no matter what look and feel is installed.

To do this, the Swing designers turned to a well-known *design pattern*: the *model-view-controller* pattern. This pattern, like many other design patterns, goes back to one of the principles of object-oriented design that we mentioned way back in Chapter 5: don't make one object responsible for too much. Don't have a single button class do everything. Instead, have the look and feel of the component associated with one object and store the contents in *another* object. The model-view-controller (MVC) design pattern teaches how to accomplish this. Implement three separate classes:

- The *model*, which stores the contents
- The *view*, which displays the contents
- The *controller*, which handles user input

The pattern specifies precisely how these three objects interact. The model stores the contents and has *no user interface*. For a button, the content is pretty trivial—it is just a small set of flags that tells whether the button is currently pushed in or out, whether it is active or inactive, and so on. For a text field, the content is a bit more interesting. It is a string object that holds the current text. This is *not the same* as the view of the content—if the content is larger than the text field, the user sees only a portion of the text displayed (see Figure 9–1).

model   `"The quick brown fox jumped over the lazy dog"`

view   `brown |fox jump`

Figure 9–1: Model and view in a text field

The model must implement methods to change the contents and to discover what the contents are. For example, a text model has methods to add or remove characters in the current text and to return the current text as a string. Again, keep in mind that the model is completely abstract. It has no particular visual representation. It is the job of a view to draw the data that is stored in the model.

> NOTE: The term "model" is perhaps unfortunate because we often think of a model as a representation of an abstract concept. Car and airplane designers build models to simulate real cars and planes. But that analogy really leads you astray when thinking about the model-view-controller pattern. In the design pattern, the model stores the complete contents, and the view gives a (complete or incomplete) visual representation of the contents. A better analogy might be the model that poses for an artist. It is up to the artist to look at the model and create a view. Depending on the artist, that view might be a formal portrait, an impressionist painting, or a cubist drawing that shows the limbs in strange contortions.

One of the advantages of the model-view-controller pattern is that a model can have multiple views, each showing a different part or aspect of the full contents. For example, an HTML editor can offer two *simultaneous* views of the same contents: a WYSIWYG view and a "raw tag" view (see Figure 9–2). When the model

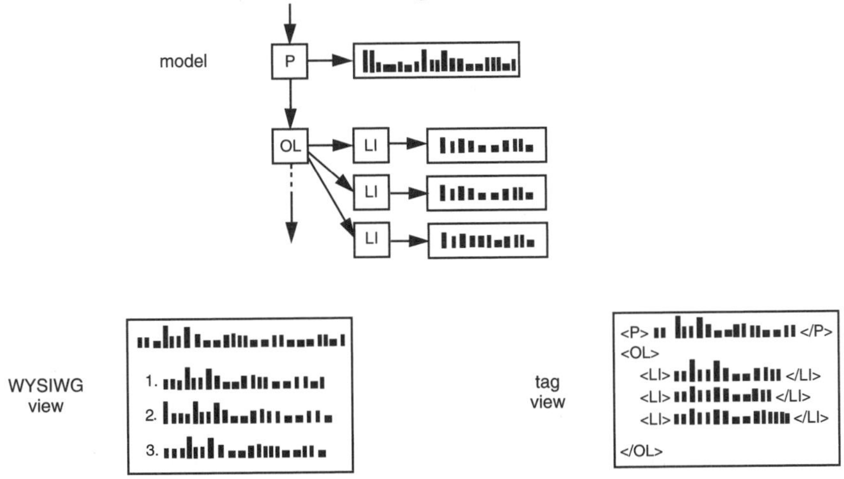

model

WYSIWYG view

tag view

Figure 9–2: Two separate views of the same model

is updated through the controller of one of the views, it tells both attached views about the change. When the views are notified, they refresh themselves automatically. Of course, for a simple user interface component such as a button, you won't have multiple views of the same model.

The controller handles the user input events such as mouse clicks and keystrokes. It then decides whether to translate these events into changes in the model or the view. For example, if the user hits a character key in a text box, the controller calls the "insert character" command of the model. The model then tells the view to update itself. The view never knows why the text changed. But if the user hits a cursor key, then the controller may tell the view to scroll. Scrolling the view has no effect on the underlying text, so the model never knows that this event happened.

Figure 9–3 shows the interactions between model, view, and controller objects.

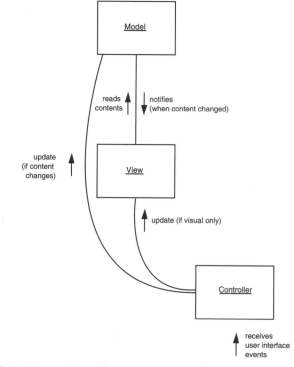

Figure 9–3: Interactions between model, view, and controller objects

Design Patterns

When solving a problem, you don't usually figure out a solution from first principles. Instead, you are likely to be guided by past experience, or you may ask other experts for advice on what has worked for them. Design patterns are a method for presenting this expertise in a structured way.

In recent years, software engineers have begun to assemble catalogs of such patterns. The pioneers in this area were inspired by the architectural design patterns of the architect Christopher Alexander. In his book *The Timeless Way of Building* (Oxford University Press 1979), Alexander gives a catalog of patterns for designing public and private living spaces. Here is a typical example:

Window Place

Everybody loves window seats, bay windows, and big windows with low sills and comfortable chairs drawn up to them...A room which does not have a place like this seldom allows you to feel comfortable or perfectly at ease...

If the room contains no window which is a "place," a person in the room will be torn between two forces:

1. He wants to sit down and be comfortable.
2. He is drawn toward the light.

Obviously, if the comfortable places—those places in the room where you most want to sit—are away from the windows, there is no way of overcoming this conflict...

Therefore: In every room where you spend any length of time during the day, make at least one window into a "window place."

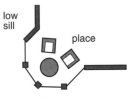

Figure 9–4: A window place

Each pattern in Alexander's catalog, as well as those in the catalogs of software patterns, follows a particular format. The pattern first describes a *context*, a situation that gives rise to a design problem. Then, the *problem* is explained, usually as a set of conflicting *forces*. Finally, the *solution* shows a configuration that balances these forces.

In the "window place" pattern, the context is a room in which you spend any length of time during the day. The conflicting forces are that you want to sit down and be comfortable and that you are drawn to the light. The solution is to make a "window place."

In the model-view-controller pattern, the context is a user interface system that presents information and receives user input. There are several forces. There may be multiple visual representations of the same data that need to be updated together. The visual representation may change, for example, to accommodate

---

various look-and-feel standards. The interaction mechanisms may change, for example, to support voice commands. The solution is to distribute responsibilities into three separate interacting components: the model, view, and controller.

Of course, the model-view-controller pattern is more complex than the "window place" pattern, and it needs to teach in some detail how to make this distribution of responsibilities work.

You will find a formal description of the model-view-controller pattern, as well as numerous other useful software patterns, in the seminal book of the pattern movement, *Design Patterns—Elements of Reusable Object-Oriented Software*, by Erich Gamma et al., Addison-Wesley 1995. We also highly recommend the excellent book *A System of Patterns* by Frank Buschmann et al., John Wiley & Sons 1996, which we find less seminal and more approachable.

The model-view-controller pattern is not the only pattern used in the design of Java. For example, the AWT event handling mechanism follows the "listener" pattern.

One important aspect of design patterns is that they become part of the culture. Programmers all over the world know what you mean when you talk about the model-view-controller pattern or the "listener" pattern. Thus, patterns become an efficient way of talking about design problems.

As a programmer using Swing components, you generally don't need to think about the model-view-controller architecture. Each user interface has a wrapper class (such as `JButton` or `JTextField`) that stores the model and the view. When you want to inquire about the contents (for example, the text in a text field), the wrapper class asks the model and returns the answer to you. When you want to change the view (for example, move the caret position in a text field), the wrapper class forwards that request to the view. However, there are occasions where the wrapper class doesn't work hard enough on forwarding commands. Then, you have to ask it to retrieve the model and work directly with the model. (You don't have to work directly with the view—that is the job of the look-and-feel code.)

Besides being "the right thing to do," the model-view-controller pattern was attractive for the Swing designers because it allowed them to implement pluggable look and feel. The model of a button or text field is independent of the look-and-feel. But of course the visual representation is completely dependent on the user interface design of a particular look and feel. The controller can vary as well. For example, in a voice-controlled device, the controller must cope with an entirely different set of events than in a standard computer with a keyboard and a mouse. By separating out the underlying model from the user interface, the Swing designers are able to reuse the code for the models and even to switch user interfaces in a running program.

Of course, patterns are only intended as guidance, not as religion. Not every pattern is applicable in all situations. For example, you may find it difficult to follow the "window places" pattern (see the sidebar on design patterns) to rearrange your cubicle. Similarly, the Swing designers found that the harsh reality of pluggable look-and-feel implementation does not always allow for a neat realization of the model-view-controller pattern. Models are easy to separate, and each user interface component has a model class. But, the responsibilities of the view and controller are not always clearly separated and are distributed over a number of different classes. Of course, as a user of these classes, you won't be concerned about this. In fact, as we pointed out before, you often won't have to worry about the models either—you can just use the component wrapper classes.

A Model-View-Controller Analysis of Swing Buttons

You already learned how to use buttons in the previous chapter, without having to worry about the controller, model, or view for them. Still, buttons are about the simplest user interface elements, so they are a good place to become comfortable with the model-view-controller pattern. You will encounter similar kinds of classes and interfaces for the more sophisticated Swing components.

For most components, the model is implemented by an interface whose name ends in `Model`. Thus, there is an interface called `ButtonModel` whose implementation classes define the state of the various kinds of buttons. Actually, buttons aren't all that complicated, and there is a single class, called `DefaultButtonModel`, that implements this interface.

You can get a sense of what sort of data is maintained by a button model by looking at the methods of the `ButtonModel` interface. Table 9–1 shows the accessor methods.

Table 9–1: The accessor methods of the `ButtonModel` interface

`getActionCommand()`	the action command string associated with this button
`getMnemonic()`	the keyboard mnemonic for this button
`isArmed()`	`true` if the button was pressed and the mouse is still over the button.
`isEnabled()`	`true` if the button is selectable
`isPressed()`	`true` if the button was pressed but the mouse button hasn't yet been released.
`isRollover()`	`true` if the mouse is over the button
`isSelected()`	`true` if the button has been toggled on (used for check boxes and radio buttons)

Each `JButton` object stores a button model object, which you can retrieve.

```
JButton button = new JButton("Blue");
ButtonModel model = button.getModel();
```

In practice, you won't care—the minutiae of the button state are only of interest to the view that draws it. And the important information—such as whether a button is enabled—is available from the `JButton` class. (The `JButton` then asks its model, of course, to retrieve that information.)

Have another look at the `ButtonModel` interface to see what *isn't* there. The model does *not* store the button label or icon. There is no way to find out what's on the face of a button just by looking at its model. (Actually, as you will see in the section on radio button groups, that purity of design is the source of some grief for the programmer.)

It is also worth noting that the *same* model (namely, `DefaultButtonModel`) is used for push buttons, radio buttons, check boxes, and even menu items. Of course, each of these button types has different views and controllers. When using the Metal look and feel, the `JButton` uses a class called `BasicButtonUI` for the view and a class called `ButtonUIListener` as controller. In general, each Swing component has an associated view object that ends in `UI`. But, not all Swing components have dedicated controller objects.

So, having given you this short introduction to what is going on under the hood in a `JButton`, you may be wondering just what is a `JButtton` really? It is simply a wrapper class inheriting from `JComponent` that holds the `DefaultButtonModel` object, some view data (such as the button label and icon), and a `DefaultButtonUI` object that is responsible for the button view.

An Introduction to Layout Management

Before we go on to discussing individual Swing components, such as text fields and radio buttons, we need to briefly cover how to arrange these components inside a frame. Since the JDK has no form designer like those in VB or Delphi, you need to write code to position (lay out) the user interface components where you want them to be.

Of course, if you have a Java-enabled development environment, it will probably have a layout tool that automates some or all of these tasks. Nevertheless, it is important to know exactly what goes on "under the hood" since even the best of these tools will usually require hand-tweaking in order to get a professional look and feel.

Let's start by reviewing the program from the last chapter that used buttons to change the background color of a frame (see Figure 9–5).

Figure 9–5: A panel with three buttons

Let us quickly recall how we built this program:

1. We defined the look of each button by setting the label string in the constructor, for example:

    ```
    JButton yellowButton = new JButton("Yellow")
    ```

2. We then added the individual buttons to a panel, for example, with:

    ```
    add(yellowButton);
    ```

3. Then, we added the needed event handlers, for example:

    ```
    yellowButton.addActionListener(this);
    ```

What happens if we add more buttons? Figure 9–6 shows what happens when you add six buttons to the panel. As you can see, they are centered in a row, and when there isn't any more room, then a new row is started.

Figure 9–6: A panel with six buttons managed by a flow layout

Moreover, the buttons stay centered in the panel, even when the user resizes the frame (see Figure 9–7).

Figure 9–7: Changing the panel size rearranges the buttons automatically

Java has a very elegant concept to enable this dynamic layout: all components in a container are managed by a *layout manager*. In our example, the buttons are managed by the *flow layout manager*, the default layout manager for a panel.

The flow layout manager lines the components horizontally until there is no more room and then starts a new row of components.

You can choose how you want to arrange the components in each row. The default is to center them in the container. The other choices are to align them to the left or to the right of the container. To use one of these alignments, specify LEFT or RIGHT in the constructor of the FlowLayout object.

```
setLayout(new FlowLayout(FlowLayout.LEFT));
```

When the user resizes the container, the layout manager automatically reflows the components to fill the available space.

> NOTE: Normally, you just let the flow layout manager control the vertical and horizontal gaps between the components. You can, however, force a specific horizontal or vertical gap by using another version of the flow layout constructor. (See the API notes.)

`java.awt.Container`

- `setLayout(LayoutManager m)`

  sets the layout manager for this container.

- `void add(Component c)`

  adds a component to this container under the control of the current layout manager.

`java.awt.FlowLayout`

- `FlowLayout(int align)`

  constructs a new `FlowLayout` with the specified alignment.

  Parameters: `align`   one of LEFT, CENTER, or RIGHT

- `FlowLayout(int align, int hgap, int vgap)`

  constructs a new `FlowLayout` with the specified alignment and the specified horizontal and vertical gaps between components.

  Parameters: `align`   one of LEFT, CENTER, or RIGHT

  `hgap`   the horizontal gap to use in pixels (negative values force an overlap)

  `vgap`   the vertical gap to use in pixels (negative values force an overlap

Border Layout

Java comes with several layout managers, and you can also make your own layout managers: we will cover all of them later on in this chapter. However, to enable us to give you more interesting examples right away, we need to briefly describe another layout manager called the *border layout manager*. This is the default layout manager of the content pane of every `JFrame`. Unlike the flow layout manager, which completely controls the position of each component, the border layout manager lets you choose where you want to place each component. You can choose to place the component in the center, north, south, east, or west of the frame (see Figure 9–8).

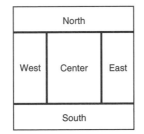

Figure 9–8: Border layout

For example:

```
class MyPanel extends JPanel
{   setLayout(new BorderLayout());
    .  .  .
    add(yellowButton, "South");
}
```

The edge components are laid out first, and the remaining available space is occupied by the center. When the container is resized, the thickness of the edge components is unchanged, but the center component changes its size. You add components by specifying a string that says in what area the object should be placed. You can specify "North", "South", "East", "West", or "Center". (The strings are case sensitive.) Not all of the positions need to be occupied. If you don't supply any string, "Center" is assumed.

Unlike the flow layout, the border layout grows all components to fill the available space. (The flow layout leaves each component at its preferred size.)

As with flow layouts, if you want to specify a gap between the regions, you can do so in the constructor for the BorderLayout.

By default, the content pane of a JFrame has a border layout. Up to now, we never took advantage of this—we simply added panels into the default (center) area. But you can add components into the other areas as well:

```
Container contentPane = getContentPane();
contentPane.add(yellowButton, "South"));
```

java.awt.Container

- void add(Component c, Object constraints)

    adds a component to this container.

    Parameters: c   the component to add

                constraints an identifier understood by the layout manager

java.awt.BorderLayout

- BorderLayout(int hgap, int vgap)

    constructs a new BorderLayout with the specified horizontal and vertical gaps between components.

    Parameters: hgap   the horizontal gap to use in pixels (negative values force an overlap)

                vgap   the vertical gap to use in pixels (negative values force an overlap)

Panels

A BorderLayout is not very useful by itself. Figure 9–9 shows what happens when you use the code snippet above. The button has grown to fill the entire southern region of the frame. And, if you were to add another button to the southern region, it would also just displace the first button.

One common method to overcome this problem is to use additional *panels*. Panels act as (smaller) containers for interface elements and can themselves be arranged inside a larger panel under the control of a layout manager. For example, you can have one panel in the southern area for the buttons and another in the center for text. By nesting panels and using a mixture of border layouts and flow layouts, you can achieve fairly precise positioning of components. This approach to layout is certainly enough for prototyping, and it is the approach that we will use for the example programs in the first part of this chapter. See the section on the `GridBagLayout` later in this chapter for the most precise way to position components.

Figure 9–9: A single button managed by a border layout

VB NOTE: Think of a panel as corresponding to a picture box without a boundary—it is invisible to the user but still functions as a container.

For example, look at Figure 9–10. The three buttons at the bottom of the screen are all contained in a panel. The panel is put into the "south" end of the frame.

Figure 9–10: A panel placed at the south end of the frame

So, suppose you want to add a panel with three buttons as in Figure 9–10. As you might expect, you first create a new instance of a `JPanel` object before you add the individual buttons to it. The default layout manager for a panel is a `FlowLayout`, which is a good choice for this situation. Finally, you add the individual buttons, using the `add` method you have seen before. Since you are adding buttons to a panel and haven't changed the default layout manager, the position of the buttons is under the control of the `FlowLayout` manager. This means the buttons stay centered within the panel and they do not expand to fill the entire area of the panel. Here's a code fragment that adds a panel containing three buttons in the south end of a container.

```
Container contentPane = getContentPane();
JPanel panel = new JPanel();
panel.add(yellowButton);
panel.add(blueButton);
panel.add(redButton);
contentPane.add(panel, "South");
```

NOTE: The panel boundaries are not visible to the user. Panels are just an organizing mechanism for the user interface designer.

As you just saw, the `JPanel` class uses a `FlowLayout` as the default layout manager. As you know, you can use the `setLayout` method to set the layout manager to something other than the default for the container. For a `JPanel` (but not for all other containers), you can also supply the layout manager object in the constructor.

`javax.swing.JPanel`

*   `JPanel(LayoutManager m)`

    sets the layout manager for the panel.

Text Input

We are finally ready to start introducing the Swing user interface components. We'll start with components that let a user input and edit text. In Java, two components are used to get text input: *text fields* and *text areas.* The difference between them is that a text field can accept only one line of text and a text area can accept multiple lines of text. The classes are called `JTextField` for single-line input and `JTextArea` for multiple lines of text.

Both of these classes inherit from a class called `JTextComponent`. You will not be able to construct a `JTextComponent` yourself since it is an abstract class. On the other hand, as is so often the case in Java, when you go searching through the API documentation, you may find that the methods you are looking for are actually in the parent class `JTextComponent` rather than in the derived class. For example, as the API notes that follow indicate, the methods that get or set the text in a text field or text area or the methods used to determine if (or to set whether) a text component can be edited by the user are actually methods in `JTextComponent`.

`javax.swing.JTextComponent`

- `void setText(String t)`

  changes the text of a text component.

  Parameters: t   the new text

- `String getText()`

  returns the text contained in this text component.

- `void setEditable(boolean b)`

  determines whether the user can edit the contents of the `JTextComponent`.

Text Fields

The usual way to add a text field to a window is to add it to a panel or other container—just as you would a button:

```
JPanel panel = new JPanel();
JTextField textField = new JTextField("Default input", 20);
panel.add(textField);
```

This code adds a text field and initializes the text field by placing the string `"Default input"` inside it. The second parameter of this constructor sets the width. In this case, the width is 20 "columns." Unfortunately, a column is a rather imprecise measurement. One column is the expected width of one character in the font you are using for the text. The idea is that if you expect the inputs to be *n* characters or less, you are supposed to specify *n* as the column width. In practice, this measurement doesn't work out too well, and you should add 1 or 2 to the maximum input length to be on the safe side. Also, keep in mind that the number of columns is only a hint to the AWT that gives the *preferred* size. If the layout manager needs to grow or shrink the text field, it can adjust its size. The column width that you set in the `JTextField` constructor is not an upper limit on the number of characters the user can enter. The user can still type in longer strings, but the input scrolls when the text exceeds the length of the field, which is irritating. If you need to reset the number of columns at run time, you can do that with the `setColumns` method.

TIP: After changing the size of a text box with the `setColumns` method, you need to call the `validate` method of the surrounding container.

```
textField.setColumns(10);
validate();
```

The `validate` method recomputes the size and layout of all components in a container. After you use the `validate` method, the layout manager repaints the container and the changed size of the text field will be visible.

In general, you want to let the user add text (or edit the existing text) in a text field. For this, quite often text fields start out blank. To make a blank text field, just leave out the string as a parameter for the JTextField constructor:

```
JTextField textField = new JTextField(20);
```

You can change the contents of the text field at any time with the setText method from the TextComponent parent class mentioned in the previous section. For example:

```
textField.setText("12");
```

And, as was also mentioned in the previous section, you can find out what the user typed by calling the getText method. This method returns the exact text that the user typed. To trim any extraneous spaces from the data in a text field, apply the trim method to the return value of getText:

```
String text = textField.getText().trim();
```

To change the font in which the user text appears, use the setFont method.

Let us put a few text fields to work. Figure 9–11 shows the running application. The program shows a clock, and there are two text fields for entering the hours and minutes. Whenever the contents of the text fields change, the clock is updated.

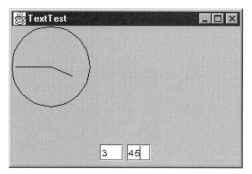

Figure 9–11: Text field example

To track every change in the text field requires a bit of an effort. First of all, note that it is not a good idea to monitor keystrokes. Some keystrokes (such as the arrow keys) don't change the text. And, depending on the look and feel, there may be mouse actions that result in text changes. As you saw in the beginning of this chapter, the Swing text field is implemented in a rather general way: the string that you see in the text field is just a visible manifestation (the *view*) of an underlying data structure (the *model*). Of course, for a humble text field, there is no great difference between the two. The view is a displayed string, and the model is a string object. But, the same architecture is used in more advanced editing components to present formatted text, with fonts, paragraphs, and other attributes, that is internally represented by a more complex data structure. The model for all text components is described by the Document interface, which covers both plain text and formatted text (such as HTML). The point is that you can ask the *document* (and not the text component) to notify you whenever the data has changed, by installing a *document listener*:

```
textField.getDocument().addDocumentListener(listener);
```

When the text has changed, one of the following three methods is called:

```
void insertUpdate(DocumentEvent e)
void removeUpdate(DocumentEvent e)
void changedUpdate(DocumentEvent e)
```

The first two methods are called when characters have been inserted or removed. The third method is not called at all for text fields. For more complex document types, it would be called when some other change, such as a change in formatting, has occurred. Unfortunately, there is no single callback to tell you that the text has changed—usually you don't care so much how it has changed. And, there is no adapter class either. Thus, your document listener must implement all three methods. Here is what we do in our sample program:

```
class TextTestFrame extends JFrame
    implements DocumentListener
{   . . .
    public void insertUpdate(DocumentEvent e)
    {   setClock();
    }
    public void removeUpdate(DocumentEvent e)
    {   setClock();
    }
    public void changedUpdate(DocumentEvent e)
    {
    }
}
```

The setClock method uses the getText method to obtain the current user input strings from the text fields. Unfortunately, that is what we get: strings. We need to convert the strings to integers, using the familiar, if cumbersome, incantation

```
int hours = Integer.parseInt(hourField.getText().trim());
int minutes = Integer.parseInt(minuteField.getText().trim());
```

But, this code won't work right when the user types a noninteger string, such as "two", into the text field or even leaves the field blank. Try it out: the terminal window will display an ugly error message complaining about a java.lang.NumberFormatException.

We will tackle the issue of validating input in the next section.

In this example, we did not analyze the DocumentEvent object at all. We simply reprocessed the changed string. That was a good thing, because it is surprisingly difficult to do anything useful with the document event object. Unlike the events that we discussed in Chapter 8, such as `ActionEvent`, `DocumentEvent` is not a class, but an interface. And, the particular objects sent out by text fields, while conforming to the `DocumentEvent` interface, do not even belong to a subclass of `EventObject`. In particular, there is no `getSource` method to tell you which user interface component produced the event.

You can get the document that has been modified:

```
public void insertUpdate(DocumentEvent e)
{   Document d = e.getDocument();
    .  .  .
}
```

What is the document? It depends. `Document` is an interface that describes the structure of an editable object—something as simple as a string for text fields or something considerably more complex for an HTML editor component. Although you can't obtain a reference to the text field from the document reference, you can still find out the new text of the document:

```
Document d = e.getDocument();
int length = d.getLength();
String text = null;
try
{   text = d.getText(0, length);
}
catch(BadLocationException ex) {}
```

But, you still have no way of knowing to which text field the changed text belongs. Therefore, you either need to install separate listeners for each text field or, as we have done in Example 9–1, simply retrieve the text from all text fields whenever one of them changes.

NOTE: Instead of listening to document events, you can also add an action event listener to a text field. The action listener is notified whenever the user hits the ENTER key. We don't recommend this approach since users don't always remember to hit ENTER when they are done entering data. If you use an action listener, you should also install a focus listener so that you can track when the user leaves the text field.

Example 9–1: TextTest.java

```
import java.awt.*;
import java.awt.event.*;
import javax.swing.*;
import javax.swing.event.*;

class TextTestFrame extends JFrame
    implements DocumentListener
{   public TextTestFrame()
```

```java
    {  setTitle("TextTest");
       setSize(300, 200);
       addWindowListener(new WindowAdapter()
       {  public void windowClosing(WindowEvent e)
          {   System.exit(0);
          }
       } );

       Container contentPane = getContentPane();

       JPanel p = new JPanel();
       hourField = new JTextField("12", 3);
       p.add(hourField);
       hourField.getDocument().addDocumentListener(this);

       minuteField = new JTextField("00", 3);
       p.add(minuteField);
       minuteField.getDocument().addDocumentListener(this);

       contentPane.add(p, "South");
       clock = new ClockPanel();
       contentPane.add(clock, "Center");
    }

    public void insertUpdate(DocumentEvent e)
    {  setClock();
    }
    public void removeUpdate(DocumentEvent e)
    {  setClock();
    }
    public void changedUpdate(DocumentEvent e)
    {
    }

    public void setClock()
    {  int hours
          = Integer.parseInt(hourField.getText().trim());
       int minutes
          = Integer.parseInt(minuteField.getText().trim());
       clock.setTime(hours, minutes);
    }

    private JTextField hourField;
    private JTextField minuteField;
    private ClockPanel clock;
}

class ClockPanel extends JPanel
{  public void paintComponent(Graphics g)
   {  super.paintComponent(g);
```

```
        g.drawOval(0, 0, 100, 100);
        double hourAngle
            = 2 * Math.PI * (minutes - 3 * 60) / (12 * 60);
        double minuteAngle
            = 2 * Math.PI * (minutes - 15) / 60;
        g.drawLine(50, 50,
            50 + (int)(30 * Math.cos(hourAngle)),
            50 + (int)(30 * Math.sin(hourAngle)));
        g.drawLine(50, 50,
            50 + (int)(45 * Math.cos(minuteAngle)),
            50 + (int)(45 * Math.sin(minuteAngle)));
    }

    public void setTime(int h, int m)
    {   minutes = h * 60 + m;
        repaint();
    }

    private int minutes = 0;
}


public class TextTest
{   public static void main(String[] args)
    {   JFrame frame = new TextTestFrame();
        frame.show();
    }
}
```

 `java.awt.Component`

- `void validate()`

recomputes the size of a component or the size and layout of the components in a container.

 `javax.swing.JTextField`

- `JTextField(int cols)`

constructs an empty `JTextField` with a specified number of columns.

Parameters: cols   the number of columns in the field

- `JTextField(String text, int cols)`

constructs a new `JTextField` with an initial string and the specified number of columns.

Parameters: text   the text to display

                cols   the number of columns

- `void setColumns(int cols)`

  tells the text field the number of columns it should use.

  Parameters: `cols`   the number of columns

`javax.swing.text.Document`

- `int getLength()`

  returns the number of characters currently in the document.

- `String getText(int offset, int length)`

  returns the text contained within the given portion of the document.

  Parameters: `offset`   the start of the text

  `length`   the length of the desired string

- `void addDocumentListener(DocumentListener listener)`

  registers the listener to be notified when the document changes.

`javax.swing.event.DocumentEvent`

- `Document getDocument()`

  gets the document that is the source of the event.

`javax.swing.event.DocumentListener`

- `void changedUpdate(DocumentEvent e)`

  is called whenever an attribute or set of attributes changed.

- `void insertUpdate(DocumentEvent e)`

  is called whenever there was an insert into the document.

- `void removeUpdate(DocumentEvent e)`

  is called whenever a portion of the document has been removed.

Input Validation

The problems mentioned in the last section are commonplace—if you have a place
to enter information, you will need to check that the input makes sense before
you work with it. In our example, we need to make sure that the user types in a
number. That is, the user is allowed to enter only digits "0" ... "9" and a minus sign
"–". The minus sign, if present at all, must be the *first* symbol of the input string. In
this section, we will develop a class, `IntTextField`, that extends the `JTextField`
class and enforces these rules. The technique discussed in this section is somewhat
advanced—feel free to skip this section if you have no interest in input validation.
If you use a professional development environment, you will likely find a

validating text component on the toolbar of your layout editor. But, if you want to find out how to implement such a component from scratch, read on.

On the surface, input validation sounds simple. We can install a key listener to the text field, and then *consume* all key events that aren't digits or a minus sign. (See Chapter 8 for consuming events.) Unfortunately, this simple approach, although commonly recommended as a method for input validation, does not work well in practice. First, not every combination of the valid input characters is a valid number. For example, `--3` and `3-3` aren't valid, even though they are made up from valid input characters. But, more importantly, there are other ways of changing the text that don't involve typing character keys. Depending on the look and feel, certain key combinations can be used to cut, copy, and paste text. For example, in the Metal look and feel, the CTRL+V key combination pastes the contents of the paste buffer into the text field. That is, we also need to monitor that the user doesn't paste in an invalid character. Clearly, trying to filter keystrokes to ensure that the content of the text field is always valid begins to look like a real chore.

Fortunately, there is another way that takes advantage of the model-view-controller architecture of the Swing text components. Recall that in the model-view-controller architecture, the controller collects the input events and translates them into commands. For example, whenever the controller processes a command that causes text to be inserted into the document, it calls the `Document.insertString` method, telling it to insert a string at the position of the caret. (The caret is the vertical bar that indicates the current editing position.) The string to be inserted can be either a single character or the contents of the paste buffer.

This is the key to solving our validation problem. The `TextField` stores its text in a `PlainDocument`, a class that implements the `Document` interface and stores a single string. We will supply a different document type that we call `IntTextDocument`. Our new class extends the `PlainDocument` class and overrides the `insertString` method. The `insertString` method of the subclass will refuse to insert any string that would produce an illegal result, that is, not a valid integer, in the document.

In the `insertString` method of the `IntTextDocument` class, we first compute the string that would result from inserting the new string at the caret position. Then, we check whether that string would be a valid integer by calling the `Integer.parseInt` method. If the string is valid, we call `super.insertString` and permit the `PlainDocument.insertString` method to insert the string to the document text. If the new string is not a valid integer, then the `Integer.parseInt` method throws an exception and we do not insert the string. Here is the source code for the `IntTextDocument` subclass and its `insertString` method. (At this point, do not worry too much about the mechanics of exception handling. We will get to that in Chapter 11.)

```
class IntTextDocument extends PlainDocument
{   public void insertString(int offs, String str,
        AttributeSet a)
        throws BadLocationException
    {   if (str == null) return;
        String oldString = getText(0, getLength());
        String newString = oldString.substring(0, offs)
            + str + oldString.substring(offs);
        try
        {   Integer.parseInt(newString + "0");
            super.insertString(offs, str, a);
        }
        catch(NumberFormatException e)
        {
        }
    }
}
```

Next, we define an `IntTextField` class that extends the `JTextField` class. Its `createDefaultModel` method creates an `IntTextDocument` instead of a `PlainDocument`.

```
class IntTextField extends JTextField
{   public IntTextField(int defval, int size)
    {   super("" + defval, size);
    }

    protected Document createDefaultModel()
    {   return new IntTextDocument();
    }
    . . .
}
```

Finally, there is another subtle point that you often run into when performing data validation. You cannot exclude all editing commands that lead to invalid entries. Sometimes, the only way to get to a valid string is to start with an invalid one. Consider the steps necessary to type the number -3. First, the user starts out with an empty field, which of course is not a valid number. Then, the user types a minus sign, resulting in a string "-", again, not a valid number. Finally, when the user adds a digit, the string becomes valid. The `insertString` method above accepts those strings—it appends a "0" to the string to be tested, thus turning both the empty string and the string "-" into legal numbers. The `IntTextField` supplies an `isValid` method to test whether the current field contents are valid.

In addition to the `insertString` and `isValid` methods, our `IntTextField` class supplies a convenience method, `getValue`, that returns the contents of the field, already converted into an integer. Before calling `getValue`, you should call `isValid` to check that the value is correct.

VB NOTE: Although quite a bit more complicated than the equivalent of setting KeyAscii to 0 in a key event procedure, the preceding code *is* the equivalent in Java to this common task. This means you will need to use similar code when porting your VB code over to Java.

Example 9–2 shows how to put the `IntTextField` class to use. This program runs much better than the one in the preceding example. Since no illegal strings can be entered, no exceptions are thrown.

NOTE: If the character the user enters is not one of the allowable ones, some user interface designs insist that the computer beep at the user in response to an illegal keypress. This is certainly not something that we would recommend, but you can do this in Java with the beep method of the `Toolkit` class:

```
Toolkit.getDefaultToolkit().beep();
```

Example 9–2: ValidationTest.java

```java
import java.awt.*;
import java.awt.event.*;
import javax.swing.*;
import javax.swing.event.*;
import javax.swing.text.*;

class ValidationTestFrame extends JFrame
    implements DocumentListener
{  public ValidationTestFrame()
   {   setTitle("ValidationTest");
       setSize(300, 200);
       addWindowListener(new WindowAdapter()
       {   public void windowClosing(WindowEvent e)
           {   System.exit(0);
           }
       } );

       Container contentPane = getContentPane();

       JPanel p = new JPanel();
       hourField = new IntTextField(12, 3);
       p.add(hourField);
       hourField.getDocument().addDocumentListener(this);

       minuteField = new IntTextField(0, 3);
       p.add(minuteField);
       minuteField.getDocument().addDocumentListener(this);

       contentPane.add(p, "South");
```

```java
      clock = new ClockPanel();
      contentPane.add(clock, "Center");
   }

   public void insertUpdate(DocumentEvent e)
   {  setClock();
   }
   public void removeUpdate(DocumentEvent e)
   {  setClock();
   }
   public void changedUpdate(DocumentEvent e)
   {
   }

   public void setClock()
   {  if (hourField.isValid() && minuteField.isValid())
      {  int hours = hourField.getValue();
         int minutes = minuteField.getValue();
         clock.setTime(hours, minutes);
      }
   }

   private IntTextField hourField;
   private IntTextField minuteField;
   private ClockPanel clock;
}

class ClockPanel extends JPanel
{  public void paintComponent(Graphics g)
   {  super.paintComponent(g);
      g.drawOval(0, 0, 100, 100);
      double hourAngle
         = 2 * Math.PI * (minutes - 3 * 60) / (12 * 60);
      double minuteAngle
         = 2 * Math.PI * (minutes - 15) / 60;
      g.drawLine(50, 50,
         50 + (int)(30 * Math.cos(hourAngle)),
         50 + (int)(30 * Math.sin(hourAngle)));
      g.drawLine(50, 50,
         50 + (int)(45 * Math.cos(minuteAngle)),
         50 + (int)(45 * Math.sin(minuteAngle)));
   }

   public void setTime(int h, int m)
   {  minutes = h * 60 + m;
      repaint();
   }

   public void tick()
   {  minutes++;
      repaint();
   }
```

```
      private int minutes = 0;
}

public class ValidationTest
{  public static void main(String[] args)
   {  JFrame frame = new ValidationTestFrame();
      frame.show();
   }
}

class IntTextDocument extends PlainDocument
{  public void insertString(int offs, String str,
      AttributeSet a)
      throws BadLocationException
   {  if (str == null) return;
      String oldString = getText(0, getLength());
      String newString = oldString.substring(0, offs)
         + str + oldString.substring(offs);
      try
      {  Integer.parseInt(newString + "0");
         super.insertString(offs, str, a);
      }
      catch(NumberFormatException e)
      {
      }
   }
}

class IntTextField extends JTextField
{  public IntTextField(int defval, int size)
   {  super("" + defval, size);
   }

   protected Document createDefaultModel()
   {  return new IntTextDocument();
   }

   public boolean isValid()
   {  try
      {  Integer.parseInt(getText());
         return true;
      }
      catch(NumberFormatException e)
      {  return false;
      }
   }

   public int getValue()
   {  try
      {  return Integer.parseInt(getText());
      }
```

```
        catch(NumberFormatException e)
        {   return 0;
        }
    }
}
```

`javax.swing.text.JTextComponent`

- `int getCaretPosition()`

  returns the position of the current insertion point (which is indicated by the insertion caret).

- `void setCaretPosition(int pos)`

  sets the insertion point (which is the position of the insertion caret).

`javax.swing.text.Document`

- `void insertString(int offset, String str)`

  inserts a string into the document. Does nothing with null or empty strings.

  Parameters: `offset`   the offset into the document

  　　　　　　　`str`   the string to insert

- `void remove(int offset, int len)`

  removes a portion of the document.

  Parameters: `offset`   the offset into the document

  　　　　　　　`len`   the number of characters to remove

`javax.swing.JTextField`

- `Document createDefaultModel()`

  creates the model to be used (an instance of `PlainDocument`). Override to return a different model.

Password Fields

Password fields are a special kind of text fields. To avoid nosy bystanders being able to glance at a password, the characters that the user entered are not actually displayed. Instead, each typed character is represented by an *echo character*, typically an asterisk (*). The Swing set supplies a `JPasswordField` class that implements such a text field.

The password field is another example of the power of the model-view-controller architecture pattern. The password field uses the same model to store the data as a regular text field, but its view has been changed to display all characters as echo characters.

`javax.swing.JPasswordField`

- `JPasswordField(String text, int columns)`

  constructs a new password field.

  Parameters: `text`   the text to be displayed, `null` if none

                 `columns`   the number of columns

- `void setEchoChar(char echo)`

  sets the echo character for this password field. This is advisory; a particular look and feel may insist on its own choice of echo character. A value of 0 resets the echo character to the default.

  Parameters: `echo`   the echo character to display instead of the text characters

- `char[] getPassword()`

  returns the text contained in this password field. For stronger security, you should overwrite the contents of the returned array after use. (The password is not returned as a `String` because a string would stay in the virtual machine until it is garbage-collected.)

Text Areas

Sometimes, you need to collect user input that is more than one line long. As mentioned earlier, you use the `JTextArea` component for this collection. When you place a text area component in your program, a user can enter any number of lines of text, using the ENTER key to separate them. Each line ends with a `'\n'` as far as Java is concerned. If you need to break up what the user enters into separate lines, you can use the `StringTokenizer` class (see Chapter 12). Figure 9–12 shows a text area at work.

In the constructor for the `JTextArea` component, you specify the number of rows and columns for the text area. For example:

```
textArea = new JTextArea(8, 40); // 8 lines of 40 columns each
getContentPane().add(textArea);
```

where the columns parameter works as before—and you still need to add a few more columns for safety's sake. Also, as before, the user is not restricted to the number of rows and columns; the text simply scrolls when the user inputs too much. You can also use the `setColumns` method to change the number of columns and the `setRows` method to change the number of rows. These numbers only indicate the preferred size—the layout manager can still grow or shrink the text area.

If there is more text than the text area can display, then the remaining text is simply clipped. You can avoid clipping long lines by turning on line-wrapping:

```
textArea.setLineWrap(true); // long lines are wrapped
```

Figure 9-12: A text area

This wrapping is a visual effect only; the text in the document is not changed—no '\n' characters are inserted into the text.

In Swing, a text area does not have scroll bars. If you want scroll bars, you have to insert the text area inside a *scroll pane*. Then, insert the scroll pane inside the content pane.

```
textArea = new JTextArea(8, 40);
JScrollPane scrollPane = new JScrollPane(textArea);
getContentPane().add(scrollPane, "Center");
```

The scroll pane now manages the view of the text area. Scroll bars automatically appear if there is more text than the text area can display, and they vanish again if text is deleted and the remaining text fits inside the area. The scrolling is handled internally in the scroll pane—your program does not need to process scroll events. This is a general mechanism that you will encounter many times when working with Swing—to add scroll bars to a component, put them inside a scroll pane.

Example 9-3 is the complete code for the text area demo. This program simply lets you edit text in a text area. Click on "Insert" to insert a sentence at the end of the text. Click the "Wrap" and "No wrap" buttons to turn line-wrapping on and off. Of course, you can simply use the keyboard to edit the text in the text area. Note how you can highlight a section of text, and how you can cut, copy, and paste with the CTRL+X, CTRL+C and CTRL+V keys. (Keyboard shortcuts are specific to the look and feel. These particular key combinations work for the Metal, Windows and Mac look and feel.)

NOTE: The JTextArea component displays plain text only, without special fonts or formatting. To display formatted text (such as HTML or RTF), you can use the JEditorPane and JTextPane classes. These classes are discussed in Volume 2.

Example 9–3: TextAreaTest.java

```java
import java.awt.*;
import java.awt.event.*;
import javax.swing.*;

class TextAreaFrame extends JFrame
    implements ActionListener
{  public TextAreaFrame()
   {  JPanel p = new JPanel();

      insertButton = new JButton("Insert");
      p.add(insertButton);
      insertButton.addActionListener(this);

      wrapButton = new JButton("Wrap");
      p.add(wrapButton);
      wrapButton.addActionListener(this);

      noWrapButton = new JButton("No wrap");
      p.add(noWrapButton);
      noWrapButton.addActionListener(this);

      getContentPane().add(p, "South");

      textArea = new JTextArea(8, 40);
      scrollPane = new JScrollPane(textArea);
      getContentPane().add(scrollPane, "Center");

      setTitle("TextAreaTest");
      setSize(300, 300);
      addWindowListener(new WindowAdapter()
      {  public void windowClosing(WindowEvent e)
         {  System.exit(0);
         }
      } );
   }

   public void actionPerformed(ActionEvent evt)
   {  Object source = evt.getSource();
      if (source == insertButton)
         textArea.append
         ("The quick brown fox jumps over the lazy dog. ");
      else if (source == wrapButton)
      {  textArea.setLineWrap(true);
         scrollPane.validate();
      }
      else if (source == noWrapButton)
      {  textArea.setLineWrap(false);
         scrollPane.validate();
      }
```

```
        }

    private JButton insertButton;
    private JButton wrapButton;
    private JButton noWrapButton;
    private JTextArea textArea;
    private JScrollPane scrollPane;
}

public class TextAreaTest {
    public static void main(String[] args)
    {   JFrame f = new TextAreaFrame();
        f.show();
    }
}
```

`javax.swing.JTextArea`

- `JTextArea(int rows, int cols)`

  constructs a new text area.

  Parameters: `rows`   the number of rows

                  `cols`   the number of columns

- `JTextArea(String text, int rows, int cols)`

  constructs a new text area with an initial text.

  Parameters: `text`   the initial text

                  `rows`   the number of rows

                  `cols`   the number of columns

- `void setColumns(int cols)`

  tells the text area the preferred number of columns it should use.

  Parameters: `cols`   the number of columns

- `void setRows(int rows)`

  tells the text area the preferred number of rows it should use.

  Parameters: `rows`   the number of rows

- `void append(String newText)`

  appends the given text to the end of the text already in the text area.

  Parameters: `newText`   the text to append

- `void setLineWrap(boolean wrap)`

  turns line-wrapping on or off.

  Parameters: `wrap`   `true` if lines should be wrapped

- void setWrapStyleWord(boolean word)

  If word is true, then long lines are wrapped at word boundaries. If it is false, then long lines are broken without taking word boundaries into account.

- void setTabSize(int c)

  sets tab stops every c columns. Note that the tabs aren't converted to spaces, but they cause alignment with the next tab stop.

  Parameters: c   the number of columns for a tab stop

javax.swing.JScrollPane

- JScrollPane(Component c)

  creates a scroll pane that displays the contents of the specified component. Scroll bars are supplied when the component is larger than the view.

  Parameters: c   the component to scroll

Labels and Labeling Components

Labels are components that hold one line of plain text. They have no decorations (for example, no boundaries). They also do not react to user input. You can use a label to identify components. For example, unlike buttons, text components have no label to identify them. To label a component that does not itself come with an identifier:

- Construct a JLabel component with the correct text.

- Place it close enough to the component you want to identify so that the user can see that the label identifies the correct component.

The constructor for a JLabel lets you specify the initial text or icon and, optionally, the alignment of the contents. You use constants from the SwingConstants interface to specify alignment. That interface defines a number of useful constants such as LEFT, RIGHT, CENTER, NORTH, EAST, and so on. The JLabel class is one of several Swing classes that implements this interface. Therefore, you can specify a left-aligned label either as:

```
JLabel label = new JLabel("Text", SwingConstants.LEFT);
```

or

```
JLabel label = new JLabel("Text", JLabel.LEFT);
```

The setText and setIcon methods let you set the text and icon of the label at run time.

Labels can be positioned inside a container like any other component. This means you can use the techniques you have seen before to place labels where you need them. For example, if you look at Figure 9–13, you can see how one of the text fields is preceded by a label with the text "with".

The quick brown fox jumped over the lazy dog.

| Replace | dog | with | dachshund |

Figure 9–13: Testing text editing

`javax.swing.JLabel`

- `JLabel(String text)`

  constructs a label with left-aligned text.

  Parameters: `text`   the text in the label

- `JLabel(Icon icon)`

  constructs a label with a left-aligned icon.

  Parameters: `icon`   the icon in the label

- `JLabel(String text, int align)`

  Parameters: `text`   the text in the label

                  `align`   one of `SwingConstants.LEFT`, `SwingConstants.CENTER`, or `SwingConstants.RIGHT`

- `JLabel(String text, Icon icon, int align)`

  constructs a label with both text and an icon. The icon is to the left of the text.

  Parameters: `text`   the text in the label

                  `icon`   the icon in the label

                  `align`   one of `SwingConstants.LEFT`, `SwingConstants.CENTER`, or `SwingConstants.RIGHT`

- `void setText(String text)`

  Parameters: `text`   the text in the label

- `void setIcon(Icon icon)`

  Parameters: `icon`   the icon in the label

Selecting Text

The text field and text area classes inherit methods from the `JTextComponent` superclass to select (highlight) the text contained in the component. They can also check which text is currently selected.

First, there is the `selectAll()` method, which highlights all the text in the field. You would use this method when presenting users with an input that they either will want to use exactly as provided or that they won't want to use at all. In the latter case, they can just type their own input, and the first keystroke replaces the selection.

The `select` method selects a part of the text. The arguments of `select` are the same as for `substring`: the first index is the start of the substring; the last is one more than the end. For example, `t.select(10, 15)` selects the tenth to fourteenth characters in the text control. End-of-line markers count as one character.

The `getSelectionStart` and `getSelectionEnd` methods return the current selection, and `getSelectedText` returns the highlighted text. How users highlight text is system dependent. In Windows, you can use the mouse or the standard SHIFT + arrow keys.

javax.swing.text.JTextComponent

- `void selectAll()`
  selects all text in the component.
- `void select(int selStart, int selEnd)`
  selects a range of text in the component.
  Parameters: `selStart`   the first position to select
                 `selEnd`   one past the last position to select
- `int getSelectionStart()`
  returns the first position of the selected text.
- `int getSelectionEnd()`
  returns one past the last position of the selected text.
- `String getSelectedText()`
  returns the selected text.

Editing Text

The `JTextArea` class contains a number of methods to modify the contents of a text area. You can append text at the end, insert text in the middle, and replace text. To delete text, simply replace the text to be deleted with an empty string. Example 9–4 shows how to implement a simple find-and-replace feature. In the program illustrated in Figure 9–13, each time you click on the Replace button, the first match of the text in the first field is replaced by the text in the second field. This is not a very realistic application, but you could use this feature to correct spelling or typing errors in URLs.

Example 9–4: TextEditTest.Java

```java
import java.awt.*;
import java.awt.event.*;
import javax.swing.*;

class TextEditFrame extends JFrame
{  public TextEditFrame()
   {  setTitle("TextEditTest");
      setSize(500, 300);
      addWindowListener(new WindowAdapter()
      {  public void windowClosing(WindowEvent e)
         {  System.exit(0);
         }
      } );

      Container contentPane = getContentPane();

      JPanel panel = new JPanel();

      JButton replaceButton = new JButton("Replace");
      panel.add(replaceButton);
      replaceButton.addActionListener(new ActionListener()
         {  public void actionPerformed(ActionEvent evt)
            {  String f = from.getText();
               int n = textArea.getText().indexOf(f);
               if (n >= 0 && f.length() > 0)
                  textArea.replaceRange(to.getText(), n,
                     n + f.length());
            }
         });

      from = new JTextField(8);
      panel.add(from);

      panel.add(new JLabel("with"));

      to = new JTextField(8);
      panel.add(to);

      textArea = new JTextArea(8, 40);
      scrollPane = new JScrollPane(textArea);

      contentPane.add(panel, "South");
      contentPane.add(scrollPane, "Center");
   }

   private JScrollPane scrollPane;
   private JTextArea textArea;
   private JTextField from, to;
```

```
}

public class TextEditTest {
    public static void main(String[] args)
    {  JFrame f = new TextEditFrame();
       f.show();
    }
}
```

javax.swing.JTextArea

- void insert(String str, int pos)

  inserts a string into the text area.

Parameters:	str	the text to insert
	pos	the position at which to insert (0 = first position; newlines count as one character)

- void replaceRange(String str, int start, int end)

  replaces a range of text with another string.

Parameters:	str	the new text
	start	the start position of the text to be replaced
	end	one past the end position of the text to be replaced

Making Choices

You now know how to collect text input from users, but there are many occasions where you would rather give users a finite set of choices rather than have them enter the data in a text component. Using a set of buttons or a list of items tells your users what choices they have. (It also saves you from the trouble of error checking.) In this section, you will learn how to program check boxes, radio buttons, and lists of choices.

Check Boxes

If you just want to collect a "yes" or "no" input, use a check box component. Check boxes automatically come with labels that identify them. The user usually checks the box by clicking inside it and turns off the check mark by clicking inside the box again. (The user can also press the space bar when the focus is at the box.) Figure 9–14 shows a simple program with two check boxes, one to turn on or off the "italic" attributes of a font and the other for boldface. Note that the first check box has focus, as indicated by the rectangle around the label. Each time the user clicks one of the check boxes, we refresh the screen, using the new font attributes.

Check boxes need a label next to them to identify their purpose. You give the label text in the constructor. To factor out repetitive code in the constructor, we wrote a small helper procedure that makes the check box, adds it to the panel, and adds the listener.

```
public CheckBoxFrame()
{   JPanel p = new JPanel();
    bold = addCheckBox(p, "Bold");
    italic = addCheckBox(p, "Italic");
    add(p, "South");
    . . .

}

JCheckBox addCheckBox(JPanel p, String name)
{   JCheckbox c = new JCheckBox(name);
    c.addActionListener(this);
    p.add(c);
    return c;
}
```

Figure 9–14: Check boxes

You use the `setSelected` method to turn a check box on or off. For example,

```
bold.setSelected(true);
```

When the user clicks on a check box, this triggers an action event. As always, we trap the event in the `actionPerformed` method. The `isSelected` method then retrieves the current state of each check box. It is `false` if unchecked; `true` if checked.

Here is the event handler for the font application. When the state of either check box changes, the code retrieves the current states of both check boxes and then notifies the panel of the new font attributes to use.

```
public void actionPerformed(ActionEvent evt)
{   int m = (bold.isSelected() ? Font.BOLD : 0)
        + (italic.isSelected() ? Font.ITALIC : 0);
    panel.setFont(m);
}
```

Example 9–5 is the complete program listing for the check box example.

> NOTE: In AWT, the equivalent component to a JCheckBox is called a Checkbox (with a lowercase "b"). It generates *item events*, not action events.

Example 9–5: CheckBoxTest.java

```java
import java.awt.*;
import java.awt.event.*;
import javax.swing.*;

class CheckBoxFrame extends JFrame
    implements ActionListener
{   public CheckBoxFrame()
    {   setTitle("CheckBoxTest");
        setSize(300, 200);
        addWindowListener(new WindowAdapter()
            {   public void windowClosing(WindowEvent e)
                {   System.exit(0);
                }
            } );

        JPanel p = new JPanel();
        bold = addCheckBox(p, "Bold");
        italic = addCheckBox(p, "Italic");
        getContentPane().add(p, "South");
        panel = new CheckBoxPanel();
        getContentPane().add(panel, "Center");
    }

    public JCheckBox addCheckBox(JPanel p, String name)
    {   JCheckBox c = new JCheckBox(name);
        c.addActionListener(this);
        p.add(c);
        return c;
    }

    public void actionPerformed(ActionEvent evt)
    {   int m = (bold.isSelected() ? Font.BOLD : 0)
            + (italic.isSelected() ? Font.ITALIC : 0);
        panel.setFont(m);
    }

    private CheckBoxPanel panel;
    private JCheckBox bold;
    private JCheckBox italic;
}

class CheckBoxPanel extends JPanel
{   public CheckBoxPanel()
    {   setFont(Font.PLAIN);
    }
```

```
    public void setFont(int m)
    {   setFont(new Font("SansSerif", m, 12));
        repaint();
    }

    public void paintComponent(Graphics g)
    {   super.paintComponent(g);
        g.drawString
            ("The quick brown fox jumps over the lazy dog.",
                0, 50);
    }
}

public class CheckBoxTest
{   public static void main(String[] args)
    {   JFrame frame = new CheckBoxFrame();
        frame.show();
    }
}
```

---

javax.swing.JCheckBox

- JCheckBox(String label)

  Parameters: label   the label on the check box

- JCheckBox(String label, boolean state)

  Parameters: label   the label on the check box

               state   the initial state of the check box

- JCheckBox(String label, Icon icon)

  constructs a check box that is initially unselected.

  Parameters: label   the label on the check box

               icon   the icon on the check box

- boolean isSelected ()

  returns the state of the check box.

- void setSelected(boolean state)

  sets the check box to a new state.

Radio Buttons

In the previous example, the user could check either, both, or none of the two check boxes. In many cases, we want to require the user to check only one of several boxes. When another box is checked, the previous box is automatically unchecked. Such a group of boxes is often called a *radio button group* because the buttons work like the station selector buttons on a radio. When you push in one button, the previously depressed button pops out. Figure 9–15 shows a typical example. We allow the user to select a font size among the choices—Small, Medium, Large, and Extra large—but, of course, we will allow the user to select only one size at a time.

Implementing radio button groups is easy in Swing. You construct one object of type `ButtonGroup` for every group of buttons. Then, you add objects of type `JRadioButton` to the button group. The button group object is responsible for turning off the previously set button when a new button is clicked.

```
smallButton = new JRadioButton("Small", false);
mediumButton = new JRadioButton("Medium", true);
. . .
ButtonGroup group = new ButtonGroup();
group.add(smallButton);
group.add(mediumButton);
. . .
```

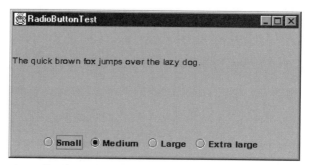

Figure 9–15: A radio button group

The second argument of the constructor is `true` for the button that should be checked initially; `false` for all others. Note that the button group controls only the *behavior* of the buttons; if you want to group the buttons together for layout purposes, you also need to add them to a container such as a `JPanel`.

If you look again at Figures 9–14 and 9–15, you will note that the appearance of the radio buttons is different from check boxes. Check boxes are square and contain a check mark when selected. Radio buttons are round and contain a dot when selected.

The event notification mechanism is simple for a radio button group. When the user checks a radio button, the radio button generates an action event.

```
public void actionPerformed(ActionEvent evt)
{   Object source = evt.getSource();
    if(source == smallButton)
        panel.setSize(8);
    else if (source == mediumButton)
        panel.setSize(12);
    . . .
}
```

As with check boxes, you can always use the `isSelected` method to find out whether a particular radio button is selected. But, if you have a group of radio buttons, you know that only one of them is selected, and it would be nice to be able to quickly find out which one, without having to query all the buttons in the group. Since the `ButtonGroup` object knows which button is selected, it would be convenient if it could give us a reference to the selected button. Indeed, the `ButtonGroup` class has a `getSelection` method, but that method doesn't return the radio button that is selected. Instead, it returns a `ButtonModel` reference to the model attached to the button. As is typical for models, there is no easy way to find the view object to which the model belongs, since in general there may be multiple view objects viewing one model object. Oddly enough, none of the `ButtonModel` methods are very helpful. The `ButtonModel` interface inherits a method `getSelectedObjects` from the `ItemSelectable` interface that, rather uselessly, returns `null`. The only hope remains the `getActionCommand` method of the `ButtonModel` class. Interestingly enough, by default, the action command of a radio button is its text label, but the action command of its model is null. (This may well be an oversight by the Swing Implementors.) However, if you explicitly set an action command with the `setActionCommand` method for all radio buttons, then both the radio buttons and their models get the same action commands. Then, you can use

```
buttonGroup.getSelection().getActionCommand()
```

to find out the action command of the currently selected radio button in a group. We use this technique in the `BorderTest` program in Example 9–7.

Example 9–6 is the complete program for font size selection that puts a set of radio buttons to work.

Example 9–6: RadioButtonTest.java

```
import java.awt.*;
import java.awt.event.*;
import javax.swing.*;

class RadioButtonFrame extends JFrame
    implements ActionListener
{   public RadioButtonFrame()
    {   setTitle("RadioButtonTest");
        setSize(400, 200);
        addWindowListener(new WindowAdapter()
        {   public void windowClosing(WindowEvent e)
            {   System.exit(0);
            }
        } );

        JPanel buttonPanel = new JPanel();
        ButtonGroup group = new ButtonGroup();
        smallButton =
            addRadioButton(buttonPanel, group, "Small", false);
```

```
        mediumButton =
            addRadioButton(buttonPanel, group, "Medium", true);
        largeButton =
            addRadioButton(buttonPanel, group, "Large", false);
        xlargeButton =
            addRadioButton(buttonPanel, group, "Extra large",
            false);
        getContentPane().add(buttonPanel, "South");
        panel = new RadioButtonTestPanel();
        getContentPane().add(panel, "Center");
    }

    public JRadioButton addRadioButton(JPanel buttonPanel,
        ButtonGroup g, String buttonName, boolean v)
    {   JRadioButton button = new JRadioButton(buttonName, v);
        button.addActionListener(this);
        g.add(button);
        buttonPanel.add(button);
        return button;
    }

    public void actionPerformed(ActionEvent evt)
    {   Object source = evt.getSource();
        if(source == smallButton)
            panel.setSize(8);
        else if (source == mediumButton)
            panel.setSize(12);
        else if (source == largeButton)
            panel.setSize(14);
        else if (source == xlargeButton)
            panel.setSize(18);
    }

    private RadioButtonTestPanel panel;
    private JRadioButton smallButton;
    private JRadioButton mediumButton;
    private JRadioButton largeButton;
    private JRadioButton xlargeButton;
}

class RadioButtonTestPanel extends JPanel
{   public RadioButtonTestPanel()
    {   setSize(12);
    }

    public void setSize(int p)
    {   setFont(new Font("SansSerif", Font.PLAIN, p));
        repaint();
    }

    public void paintComponent(Graphics g)
    {   super.paintComponent(g);
```

```
        g.drawString
            ("The quick brown fox jumps over the lazy dog.",
            0, 50);
    }
}

public class RadioButtonTest
{   public static void main(String[] args)
    {   JFrame frame = new RadioButtonFrame();
        frame.show();
    }
}
```

javax.swing.JRadioButton

- JRadioButton(String label, boolean state)

    Parameters: label   the label on the check box

                   state   the initial state of the check box

- JRadioButton(String label, Icon icon)

    constructs a radio button that is initially unselected.

    Parameters: label   the label on the radio button

                   icon   the icon on the radio button

javax.swing.ButtonGroup

- void add(AbstractButton b)

    adds the button to the group.

- ButtonModel getSelection()

    returns the button model of the selected button.

javax.swing.ButtonModel

- String getActionCommand()

    returns the action command for this button model.

javax.swing.AbstractButton

- void setActionCommand(String s)

    sets the action command for this button and its model.

Borders

If you have multiple groups of radio buttons in a window, you will want to visually indicate which buttons are grouped together. The Swing set provides a set

of useful *borders* for this purpose. You can apply a border to any component that extends JComponent. The most common usage is to place a border around a panel and fill that panel with other user interface elements such as radio buttons.

There are quite a few borders to choose from, but you follow the same steps for all of them.

1. Call a static method of the BorderFactory to create a border. You can choose among the following styles (see Figure 9–16):
   - Lowered bevel
   - Raised bevel
   - Etched
   - Line
   - Matte
   - Empty (just to create some blank space around the component)

2. If you like, add a title to your border by passing your border to BorderFactory.createTitledBorder.

3. If you really want to go all out, combine several borders with a call to BorderFactory.createCompoundBorder.

4. Add the resulting border to your component by calling the setBorder method of the JComponent class.

For example, here is how you add an etched border with a title to a panel:

```
Border etched = BorderFactory.createEtchedBorder()
Border titled = BorderFactory.createTitledBorder(etched,
   "A Title");
panel.setBorder(titled);
```

Run the program in Example 9–7 to get an idea what the various borders look like.

The various borders have different options for setting border widths and colors. See the API notes for details. True border enthusiasts will appreciate that there is also a SoftBevelBorder class for beveled borders with round corners. These borders can be constructed only by using one of the class constructors—there is no BorderFactory method for them.

![BorderTest window showing Border types radio buttons: Lowered bevel, Raised bevel (selected), Etched, Line, Matte, Empty]

Figure 9–16: Testing border types

Example 9–7: BorderTest.java

```java
import java.awt.*;
import java.awt.event.*;
import javax.swing.*;
import javax.swing.border.*;

class BorderFrame extends JFrame
    implements ActionListener
{  public BorderFrame()
    {  JPanel buttonPanel = new JPanel();
        group = new ButtonGroup();
        addRadioButton(buttonPanel, group, "Lowered bevel",
            true);
        addRadioButton(buttonPanel, group, "Raised bevel",
            false);
        addRadioButton(buttonPanel, group, "Etched",
            false);
        addRadioButton(buttonPanel, group, "Line",
            false);
        addRadioButton(buttonPanel, group, "Matte",
            false);
        addRadioButton(buttonPanel, group, "Empty",
            false);

        Border etched = BorderFactory.createEtchedBorder();
        Border titled = BorderFactory.createTitledBorder
            (etched, "Border types");
        buttonPanel.setBorder(titled);

        getContentPane().add(buttonPanel, "South");

        setDemoPanel();

        setTitle("BorderTest");
        setSize(600, 200);
        addWindowListener(new WindowAdapter()
        {  public void windowClosing(WindowEvent e)
            {  System.exit(0);
            }
        } );
    }

    public void addRadioButton(JPanel buttonPanel,
        ButtonGroup g, String buttonName, boolean v)
    {  JRadioButton button = new JRadioButton(buttonName, v);
        button.addActionListener(this);
        g.add(button);
        buttonPanel.add(button);
        button.setActionCommand(buttonName);
    }

    public void actionPerformed(ActionEvent evt)
```

```
    {   setDemoPanel();
    }

    public void setDemoPanel()
    {   JPanel panel = new JPanel();
        Border border = null;
        String command = group.getSelection()
            .getActionCommand();
        if (command.equals("Lowered bevel"))
            border = BorderFactory.createLoweredBevelBorder();
        else if (command.equals("Raised bevel"))
            border = BorderFactory.createRaisedBevelBorder();
        else if (command.equals("Etched"))
            border = BorderFactory.createEtchedBorder();
        else if (command.equals("Line"))
            border
                = BorderFactory.createLineBorder(Color.blue);
        else if (command.equals("Matte"))
            border = BorderFactory.createMatteBorder(10, 10,
                10, 10, Color.blue);
        else if (command.equals("Empty"))
            border = BorderFactory.createEmptyBorder();

        panel.setBorder(border);
        getContentPane().add(panel, "Center");
        validate();
    }

    private JPanel panel;
    private ButtonGroup group;
}

public class BorderTest
{   public static void main(String[] args)
    {   JFrame frame = new BorderFrame();
        frame.show();
    }
}
```

API `javax.swing.BorderFactory`

- static Border createLineBorder(Color color)
- static Border createLineBorder(Color color, int thickness)
  create a simple line border.
- static MatteBorder createMatteBorder(int top, int left, int bottom, int right, Color color)
- static MatteBorder createMatteBorder(int top, int left, int bottom, int right, Icon tileIcon)
  create a thick border that is filled with a color or a repeating icon.
- static Border createEmptyBorder()

- ```
  static Border createEmptyBorder(int top, int left, int bottom,
      int right)
  ```
  create an empty border.
- ```
  static Border createEtchedBorder()
  ```
- ```
  static Border createEtchedBorder(Color highlight, Color shadow)
  ```
  create a line border with a 3D effect.

  Parameters: highlight, shadow   colors for 3D effect
- ```
  static Border createBevelBorder(int type)
  ```
- ```
  static Border createBevelBorder(int type, Color highlight,
      Color shadow)
  ```
- ```
  static Border createLoweredBevelBorder()
  ```
- ```
  static Border createRaisedBevelBorder()
  ```
  create a border that gives the effect of a lowered or raised surface.

  Parameters: type   one of BevelBorder.LOWERED, BevelBorder.RAISED

        highlight, shadow   colors for 3D effect
- ```
  static TitledBorder createTitledBorder(String title)
  ```
- ```
  static TitledBorder createTitledBorder(Border border)
  ```
- ```
  static TitledBorder createTitledBorder(Border border,
      String title)
  ```
- ```
  static TitledBorder createTitledBorder(Border String title,
      int justification, int position)
  ```
- ```
  static TitledBorder createTitledBorder(Border border,
      String title, int justification, int position, Font font)
  ```
- ```
  static TitledBorder createTitledBorder(Border border,
      String title, int justification, int position, Font font,
      Color color)
  ```

Parameters:	title	the title string
	border	the border to decorate with the title
	justification	one of TitledBorder.LEFT, TitledBorder.CENTER, TitledBorder.RIGHT
	position	one of the TitledBorder constants ABOVE_TOP, TOP, BELOW_TOP, ABOVE_BOTTOM, BOTTOM, BELOW_BOTTOM
	font	the font for the title
	color	the color of the title
- ```
  static CompoundBorder createCompoundBorder(Border outsideBorder,
      Border insideBorder)
  ```
  combines two borders to a new border.

javax.swing.border.SoftBevelBorder

- `SoftBevelBorder(int type)`
- `SoftBevelBorder(int type, Color highlight, Color shadow)`

create a bevel border with rounded corners.

Parameters:	type	one of `BevelBorder.LOWERED`, `BevelBorder.RAISED`
	color, shadow	colors for 3D effect

javax.swing.JComponent

- `void setBorder(Border border)`

sets the border of this component.

Lists

If you have more than a handful of alternatives, radio buttons are not a good choice because they take up too much screen space. Instead, you can use a list component. Swing has a rather complex list component with many features. Of course, you can have lists of strings, but you can also have lists of arbitrary objects, with full control of how they appear. The internal architecture of the list component that makes this generality possible is rather elegant. Unfortunately, the designers at Sun felt that they needed to show off that elegance, rather than hiding it from the programmer who just wants to use the component. You will find that the list control is somewhat awkward to use for simple cases because you need to manipulate some of the machinery that makes the general cases possible. We'll walk you through the simple and most common case, a list box of strings, and then give a more complex example that shows off the flexibility of the list component.

The JList Component

The `JList` component is similar to a set of check boxes or radio buttons, except that the items are placed inside a single box and are selected by clicking on the items themselves, not on buttons. If you permit multiple selection for a list box, the user can select any combination of the items in the box.

Figure 9–17 shows an admittedly silly example. The user can select the attributes for the fox, such as "quick," "brown," "hungry," "wild," and, because we ran out of attributes, "static," "private," and "final." You can, thus, have the *static, final* fox jump over the lazy dog.

To construct this list component, you first start out with an array of strings, then pass the array to the `JList` constructor:

```
String[] words= { "quick", "brown", "hungry", "wild", ... };
JList wordList = new JList(words);
```

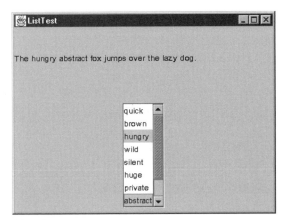

Figure 9–17: A list box

Alternatively, you can use an anonymous array:

```
JList wordList = new JList(new String[]
    {"quick", "brown", "hungry", "wild", ... });
```

List boxes do not scroll automatically. To make a list box scroll, you must insert it into a scroll pane:

```
JScrollPane scrollPane = new JScrollPane(wordList);
```

Then, you need to add the scroll pane, not the list, into the surrounding panel.

We must admit that the separation of the list display and the scrolling mechanism is elegant in theory, but it is a pain in practice. Essentially all lists that we ever encountered needed scrolling. It seems cruel to force programmers to go through hoops in the default case, just so they can appreciate that elegance.

By default, the list component displays eight items; use the `setVisibleRowCount` method to change that value:

```
wordList.setVisibleRowCount(10); // display 10 items
```

By default, a user can select multiple items. This requires some knowledge of mouse technique: To add more items to a selection, use the CTRL key while clicking on each item. To select a contiguous range of items, click on the first one, then hold down the SHIFT key and click on the last one.

You can also restrict the user to a more limited selection mode with the `setSelectionMode` method:

```
wordList.setSelectionMode
    (ListSelectionModel.SINGLE_SELECTION);
    // select one item at a time
wordList.setSelectionMode
    (ListSelectionModel.SINGLE_INTERVAL_SELECTION);
    // select one item or one range of items
```

The notification method for list boxes is not quite as easy as that for the other components. Rather than listening to action events, you need to listen to list selection events. Add a list selection listener to the list component, and implement the method

```
public void valueChanged(ListSelectionEvent evt)
```

in the listener. In our example program, the frame class is the event listener:

```
class ListFrame extends JFrame
    implements ListSelectionListener
{   public ListFrame()
    {   . . .
        JList wordList = new JList(words);
        wordList.addListSelectionListener(this);
        . . .
    }

    public void valueChanged(ListSelectionEvent evt)
    {   . . .
    }
}
```

When the user selects items, a flurry of list selection events is generated. For example, suppose the user clicks on a new item. First, when the mouse button goes down, there are two events: one that reports the deselection of the old item and one that reports the selection of the new item. These transitional events can be recognized by calling

```
evt.isAdjusting()
```

The isAdjusting method returns true if the selection is not yet final. When the mouse button goes up, there is another event, this time with isAdjusting returning false. If you are not interested in the transitional events, then you can wait for the event for which isAdjusting is false. However, if you want to give the user instant feedback as soon as the mouse button is clicked, then you need to process all events.

CAUTION: In our version of Swing, *multiple selections* (with CTRL + click) do not generate an event when the mouse button goes up. Events are only generated when the mouse button is depressed, and all reported events have isAdjusting return true. Until this bug is fixed, you cannot use the isAdjusting method in list boxes that allow multiple selections.

Once you are notified that an event has happened, you will want to find out what items are currently selected. The getSelectedValues method returns an *array of objects* containing all selected items.

VB NOTE: `getSelectedValues` works the same as the List property does in VB.

You still need to cast *each* array element to a string.

```
JList source = (JList)evt.getSource();
Object[] values = source.getSelectedValues();
for (int i = 0; i < values.length; i++)
    do something with (String)values[i];
```

CAUTION: You cannot cast the return value of `getSelectedValues` from an `Object[]` array to a `String[]` array. The return value was not created as an array of strings, but as an array of objects, each of which happens to be a string. If you want to process the return value as an array of strings, you can use the following code:

```
int length = values.length;
String[] words = new String[length];
System.arrayCopy(values, 0, words, 0, length);
```

If your list does not allow multiple selections, you can call the convenience method `getSelectedValue`. It returns the first selected value (which you know to be the only value if multiple selections are disallowed).

```
String selection = (String)source.getSelectedValue();
```

NOTE: List components do not react to double clicks with a mouse. As envisioned by the designers of Swing, you use a list to select an item, and then you need to click a button to make something happen. However, some user interfaces allow a user to double-click on a list to indicate selection of a list item *and* acceptance of an action. We don't think this is a good user interface style because it is difficult for users to discover that they are supposed to double-click. But if you do want to implement this behavior, you have to add a mouse listener to the list box, then trap the mouse event as follows:

```
public void mouseClicked(MouseEvent evt)
{   if (evt.getClickCount() == 2)
    {   JList source = (JList)evt.getSource();
        Object[] selection = source.getSelectedValues();
        doAction(selection);
    }
}
```

Example 9–8 is the listing of the program that demonstrates a list box filled with strings. Notice how the `valueChanged` method builds up the message string from the selected items.

Example 9-8: ListTest.java

```java
import java.awt.*;
import java.awt.event.*;
import javax.swing.*;
import javax.swing.event.*;

class ListFrame extends JFrame
    implements ListSelectionListener
{  public ListFrame()
   {  setTitle("ListTest");
      setSize(400,300);
      addWindowListener(new WindowAdapter()
         {  public void windowClosing(WindowEvent e)
            {  System.exit(0);
            }
         } );

      String[] words =
      {  "quick","brown","hungry","wild","silent",
         "huge","private","abstract","static","final"
      };

      JList wordList = new JList(words);
      JScrollPane scrollPane = new JScrollPane(wordList);

      JPanel p = new JPanel();
      p.add(scrollPane);
      wordList.addListSelectionListener(this);

      getContentPane().add(p, "South");
      panel = new ListTestPanel();
      getContentPane().add(panel, "Center");
   }

   public void valueChanged(ListSelectionEvent evt)
   {  JList source = (JList)evt.getSource();
      Object[] values = source.getSelectedValues();

      String text = "";
      for (int i = 0; i < values.length; i++)
      {  String word = (String)values[i];
         text += word + " ";
      }

      panel.setAttribute(text);
   }

   private ListTestPanel panel;
}

class ListTestPanel extends JPanel
```

```
{  public ListTestPanel()
   {  setAttribute("");
   }

   public void setAttribute(String w)
   {  text = "The " + w + "fox jumps over the lazy dog.";
      repaint();
   }

   public void paintComponent(Graphics g)
   {  super.paintComponent(g);
      g.drawString(text, 0, 50);
   }

   private String text;
}

public class ListTest
{  public static void main(String[] args)
   {  JFrame frame = new ListFrame();
      frame.show();
   }
```

`javax.swing.JList`

- `JList(Object[] items)`
  constructs a list that displays these items.
- `void setVisibleRowCount(int c)`
  sets the preferred number of rows in the list that can be displayed without a scroll bar.
- `void setSelectionMode(int mode)`
  determines whether single-item or multiple-item selections are allowed.
  Parameters: mode   one of `SINGLE_SELECTION`, `SINGLE_INTERVAL_SELECTION`, `MULTIPLE_INTERVAL_SELECTION`
- `void addListSelectionListener(ListSelectionListener listener)`
  add to the list a listener that's notified each time a change to the selection occurs.
- `Object[] getSelectedValues()`
  returns the selected values or an empty array if the selection is empty.
- `Object getSelectedValue()`
  returns the first selected value or `null` if the selection is empty.

`javax.swing.event.ListSelectionListener`

- `void valueChanged(ListSelectionEvent e)`
  is called whenever the list selection changes.

List Models

In the preceding section, you have seen the most common method for using a list component:

- Specify a fixed set of strings for display in the list,
- add a scrollbar,
- trap the list selection events.

In the remainder of the section on lists, we will cover more complex situations that require a bit more finesse:

- Very long lists
- Lists with changing contents
- Lists that don't contain strings

Feel free to skip to the next section if you are not yet interested in these advanced techniques.

In the first example, we constructed a JList component that held a fixed collection of strings. However, the collection of choices in a list box is not always fixed. How do we add or remove items in the list box? Somewhat surprisingly, there are no methods in the JList class to achieve this. Instead, you have to understand a little more about the internal design of the list component. As with text components, the list component uses the model-view- controller design pattern to separate the visual appearance (a column of items that are rendered in some way) from the underlying data (a collection of objects).

The JList class is responsible for the visual appearance of the data. It actually knows very little about how the data is stored—all it knows is that it can retrieve the data through some object that implements the ListModel interface:

```
public interface ListModel
{   public int getSize();
    public Object getElementAt(int i);
    public void addListDataListener(ListDataListener l);
    public void removeListDataListener(ListDataListener l);
}
```

Through this interface, the JList can get a count of elements and retrieve each one of the elements. Also, the JList object can add itself as a *list data listener*. It then gets notified if the collection of elements changes, so that it can repaint the list.

Why is this generality useful? Why doesn't the JList object simply store a vector of objects?

Note that the interface doesn't specify how the objects are stored. In particular, it doesn't force them to be stored at all! The getElementAt method is free to recompute each value whenever it is called. This is potentially useful if you want to show a very large collection without having to store the values.

Here is a somewhat silly example: we let the user choose among *all three-letter words* in a list box (see Figure 9–18).

Figure 9–18: Choosing from a very long list of selections

There are 26 {26 {26 = 17,576 three-letter combinations. Rather than storing all these combinations, we recompute them as requested when the user scrolls through them.

This turns out to be easy to implement. The tedious part, adding and removing listeners, has been done for us in the `AbstractListModel` class which we extend. We only need to supply the `getSize` and `getElementAt` methods:

```
class WordListModel extends AbstractListModel
{  public WordListModel(int n) { length = n; }
   public int getSize() { return (int)Math.pow(26, length); }
   public Object getElementAt(int n)
   {  // compute nth string
      . . .
   }
   . . .
}
```

The computation of the *n*th string is a bit technical—you'll find the details in the code listing in Example 9–9.

Now that we supplied a model, we can simply build a list that lets the user scroll through the elements supplied by the model:

```
JList wordList = new JList(new WordListModel(3));
wordList.setSelectionMode(ListSelectionModel.SINGLE_SELECTION);
JScrollPane scrollPane = new JScrollPane(wordList);
```

The point is that the strings are never *stored*. Only those strings that the user actually requests to see are generated.

There is one other setting that we must make. We must tell the list component that all items have a fixed width and height:

```
wordList.setFixedCellWidth(50);
wordList.setFixedCellHeight(15);
```

Otherwise, the list component would compute each item to measure its width and height. That would take a long time.

Example 9–9 shows the complete source code.

As a practical matter, such very long lists are rarely useful. It is extremely cumbersome for a user to scroll through a huge selection. For that reason, we believe that the list control has been completely over engineered. A selection that a user can comfortably manage on the screen is certainly small enough to be stored directly in the list component. That arrangement would have saved programmers from the pain of having to deal with the list model as a separate entity.

Example 9–9: LongListTest.java

```java
import java.awt.*;
import java.awt.event.*;
import javax.swing.*;
import javax.swing.event.*;

class WordListModel extends AbstractListModel
{  public WordListModel(int n) { length = n; }
   public int getSize()
   {  return (int)Math.pow(LAST - FIRST + 1, length);
   }
   public Object getElementAt(int n)
   {  String r = "";
      for (int i = 0; i < length; i++)
      {  char c = (char)(FIRST + n % (LAST - FIRST + 1));
         r = c + r;
         n = n / (LAST - FIRST + 1);
      }
      return r;
   }

   private int length;
   public static final char FIRST = 'a';
   public static final char LAST = 'z';
}

class LongListFrame extends JFrame
   implements ListSelectionListener
{  public LongListFrame()
   {  setTitle("LongListTest");
      setSize(400,300);
      addWindowListener(new WindowAdapter()
         {  public void windowClosing(WindowEvent e)
```

```java
            {  System.exit(0);
            }
        } );

    JList wordList = new JList(new WordListModel(3));
    wordList.setSelectionMode
        (ListSelectionModel.SINGLE_SELECTION);

    wordList.setFixedCellWidth(50);
    wordList.setFixedCellHeight(15);

    JScrollPane scrollPane = new JScrollPane(wordList);

    JPanel p = new JPanel();
    p.add(scrollPane);
    wordList.addListSelectionListener(this);

    getContentPane().add(p, "South");
    panel = new LongListPanel();
    getContentPane().add(panel, "Center");
  }

  public void  valueChanged(ListSelectionEvent evt)
  {  JList source = (JList)evt.getSource();
     String word = (String)source.getSelectedValue();
     panel.setJumper(word);
  }

  private LongListPanel panel;
}

class LongListPanel extends JPanel
{  public LongListPanel()
   {  setJumper("fox");
   }

   public void setJumper(String w)
   {  text = "The quick brown "
          + w + " jumps over the lazy dog.";
      repaint();
   }

   public void paintComponent(Graphics g)
   {  super.paintComponent(g);
      g.drawString(text, 0, 50);
   }

   private String text;
}

public class LongListTest
{  public static void main(String[] args)
```

```
  {  JFrame frame = new LongListFrame();
     frame.show();
  }
}
```

javax.swing.JList

- JList(ListModel dataModel)

  constructs a list that displays the elements in the specified model.

- void setFixedCellWidth(int width)

  if the width is greater than zero, specifies the width of every cell in the list. The default value is −1, which forces the size of each cell to be measured.

- void setFixedCellHeight(int height)

  if the height is greater than zero, specifies the height of every cell in the list. The default value is −1, which forces the size of each cell to be measured.

javax.swing.ListModel

- int getSize()

  returns the number of elements of the model.

- Object getElementAt(int index)

  returns an element of the model.

Inserting and Removing Values

You cannot directly edit the collection of list values. Instead, you must access the *model* and then add or remove elements. That, too, is easier said than done. Suppose you want to add more values to a list. You can obtain a reference to the model:

```
ListModel model = list.getModel();
```

But that does you no good—as you saw in the preceding section, the ListModel interface has no methods to insert or remove elements since, after all, the whole point of having a list model is that it need not *store* the elements.

Let's try it the other way around. One of the constructors of JList takes a vector of objects:

```
Vector values = new Vector();
values.addElement("quick");
values.addElement("brown");
  . . .
JList list = new JList(values);
```

Of course, you can now edit the vector and add or remove elements, but the list does not know that this is happening, so it cannot react to the changes. In particular, the list cannot update its view when you add the values.

Instead, you have to construct a particular model, the `DefaultListModel`, fill it with the initial values, and associate it with the list.

```
DefaultListModel model = new DefaultListModel();
model.addElement("quick");
model.addElement("brown");
. . .
JList list = new JList(model);
```

Now you can add or remove values from the `model` object. The `model` object then notifies the list of the changes, and the list repaints itself.

```
model.removeElement("quick");
model.addElement("slow");
```

The `DefaultListModel` class uses the same method names as the `Vector` class for adding and removing elements. (Unfortunately, it uses the *old* method names. The more convenient `add` and `remove` methods for inserting and removing objects haven't yet made it into the `DefaultListModel`.) In fact, the default list model uses a vector internally to store the values. It inherits the list notification mechanism from `AbstractListModel`, just as the example model class of the preceding section.

CAUTION: There are `JList` constructors that construct a list from an array or vector of objects or strings. You might think that these constructors use a `DefaultListModel` to store these values. That is not the case—the constructors build a trivial model that can access the values without any provisions for notification if the contents changes. For example, here is the code for the constructor that constructs a `JList` from a `Vector`:

```
public JList(final Vector listData)
{  this (new AbstractListModel()
    {  public int getSize() { return listData.size(); }
       public Object getElementAt(int i) { return
           listData.elementAt(i); }
    });
}
```

That means, if you change the contents of the vector after the list is constructed, then the list may show a confusing mix of old and new values until it is completely repainted. (The keyword `final` in the constructor above does not prevent you from changing the vector elsewhere—it only means that the constructor itself won't modify the value of the `listData` reference; the keyword is required because the `listData` object is used in the inner class.)

API `javax.swing.JList`

- `ListModel getModel()`

  gets the model of this list.

API `javax.swing.DefaultListModel`

- `void addElement(Object obj)`

  adds the object to the end of the model.

- `boolean removeElement(Object obj)`

  removes the first occurrence of the object from the model. Returns `true` if the object was contained in the model, `false` otherwise.

Rendering Values

So far, all lists that you saw in this chapter contained only strings. It is actually just as easy to show a list of icons—simply pass an array or vector filled with `Icon` objects. More interestingly, you can easily represent your list values with any drawing whatsoever.

While the `JList` class can display strings and icons automatically, you need to install a *list cell renderer* into the `JList` object for all custom drawing. A list cell renderer is any class that implements the following interface:

```
interface ListCellRenderer
{  Component getListCellRendererComponent(JList list,
      Object value, int index,
      boolean isSelected, boolean cellHasFocus);
}
```

If you install a list cell renderer into a list, it gets called for each list value: first, if you did not select fixed-sized cells, to measure the size of the graphical representation of the value, then to draw it. You must provide a class that returns an object of type `Component`, such that the `getPreferredSize` and paint methods of the returned object carry out these tasks as appropriate for your list values.

A simple way to do this is to create an inner class with these two methods:

```
class MyCellRenderer implements ListCellRenderer
{  public Component getListCellRendererComponent(final JList list,
      final Object value, final int index,
      final boolean isSelected, final boolean cellHasFocus)
   {  return new JPanel()
         {  public void paintComponent(Graphics g)
            {  // paint code goes here
            }
            public Dimension getPreferredSize()
            {  // size measurement code goes here
            }
         };
```

```
    }
  }
```

In Example 9–10, we display the font choices graphically by showing the actual appearance of each font (see Figure 9–19). In the paintComponent method, we display each name in its own font. We also need to make sure to match the usual colors of the look and feel of the JList class. We obtain these colors by calling the getForeground/getBackground and getSelectionForeground/getSelectionBackground methods of the JList class. In the getPreferredSize method, we need to measure the size of the string, using the techniques that you saw in Chapter 7.

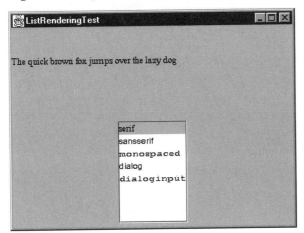

Figure 9–19: A list box with rendered cells

Here is the code for the renderer.

```
class FontCellRenderer implements ListCellRenderer
{  public Component getListCellRendererComponent(final JList list,
       final Object value, final int index,
       final boolean isSelected, final boolean cellHasFocus)
   {  return new JPanel()
         {  public void paintComponent(Graphics g);
            {  super.paintComponent(g);
               Font font = (Font)value;
               String text = font.getFamily();
               FontMetrics fm = g.getFontMetrics(font);
               g.setColor(isSelected
                  ? list.getSelectionBackground()
                  : list.getBackground());
               g.fillRect(0, 0, getWidth(), getHeight());
               g.setColor(isSelected
                  ? list.getSelectionForeground()
                  : list.getForeground());
               g.setFont(font);
```

```
            g.drawString(text, 0, fm.getAscent());
         }
         public Dimension getPreferredSize()
         {  Font font = (Font)value;
            String text = font.getFamily();
            Graphics g = getGraphics();
            FontMetrics fm = g.getFontMetrics(font);
            return new Dimension(fm.stringWidth(text),
               fm.getHeight());
         }
      };
   }
```

To install the cell renderer, simply call the setCellRenderer method:

```
fontList.setCellRenderer(new FontCellRenderer());
```

Now all list cells are drawn with the custom renderer.

There is actually a simpler method for writing custom renderers that works in many cases. If the rendered image just contains text, an icon, and possibly a change of color, then you can get by with configuring a JLabel. For example, to show the font name in its own font, we can use the following renderer:

```
class FontCellRenderer implements ListCellRenderer
{  public Component getListCellRendererComponent(JList list,
      Object value, int index, boolean isSelected,
         boolean cellHasFocus)
   {  JLabel label = new JLabel();
      Font font = (Font)value;
      label.setText(font.getFamily());
      label.setFont(font);
      label.setOpaque(true);
      label.setBackground(isSelected
         ? list.getSelectionBackground()
         : list.getBackground());
      label.setForeground(isSelected
         ? list.getSelectionForeground()
         : list.getForeground());
      return label;
   }
}
```

Note that here we don't write any paintComponent or getPreferredSize methods; the JLabel class already implements these methods to our satisfaction. All we need to do is to configure the label appropriately by setting its text, font, and color.

For added conciseness, the FontCellRenderer can even extend JLabel, configure *itself* with every call to getListCellRendererComponent, and then return this:

```
class FontCellRenderer extends JLabel implements ListCellRenderer
{  public Component getListCellRendererComponent(JList list,
        Object value, int index, boolean isSelected,
            boolean cellHasFocus)
     {   Font font = (Font)value;
        setText(font.getFamily());
        setFont(font);
        setOpaque(true);
        setBackground(isSelected
            ? list.getSelectionBackground()
            : list.getBackground());
        setForeground(isSelected
            ? list.getSelectionForeground()
            : list.getForeground());
        return this;
     }
}
```

This code is a convenient shortcut for those cases where an existing component—in this case, JLabel—already provides all functionality that is needed to render a cell value.

Example 9–10: ListRenderingTest.java

```
import java.util.*;
import java.awt.*;
import java.awt.event.*;
import javax.swing.*;
import javax.swing.event.*;

class FontCellRenderer implements ListCellRenderer
{  public Component getListCellRendererComponent
        (final JList list, final Object value,
        final int index, final boolean isSelected,
        final boolean cellHasFocus)
     {   return new JPanel()
            {  public void paintComponent(Graphics g)
                {   super.paintComponent(g);
                    Font font = (Font)value;
                    String text = font.getFamily();
                    FontMetrics fm = g.getFontMetrics(font);
                    g.setColor(isSelected
                        ? list.getSelectionBackground()
                        : list.getBackground());
                    g.fillRect(0, 0, getWidth(), getHeight());
                    g.setColor(isSelected
                        ? list.getSelectionForeground()
                        : list.getForeground());
                    g.setFont(font);
                    g.drawString(text, 0, fm.getAscent());
                }
```

```
                public Dimension getPreferredSize()
                {   Font font = (Font)value;
                    String text = font.getFamily();
                    Graphics g = getGraphics();
                    FontMetrics fm = g.getFontMetrics(font);
                    return new Dimension(fm.stringWidth(text),
                        fm.getHeight());
                }
            };
      }
}

class ListRenderingFrame extends JFrame
    implements ListSelectionListener
{   public ListRenderingFrame()
    {   setTitle("ListRenderingTest");
        setSize(400, 300);
        addWindowListener(new WindowAdapter()
            {   public void windowClosing(WindowEvent e)
                {   System.exit(0);
                }
            } );

        Vector fonts = new Vector();
        fonts.add(new Font("Serif", Font.PLAIN, 12));
        fonts.add(new Font("SansSerif", Font.PLAIN, 12));
        fonts.add(new Font("Monospaced", Font.PLAIN, 12));
        fonts.add(new Font("Dialog", Font.PLAIN, 12));
        fonts.add(new Font("DialogInput", Font.PLAIN, 12));
        JList fontList = new JList(fonts);
        fontList.setSelectionMode
            (ListSelectionModel.SINGLE_SELECTION);
        fontList.setCellRenderer(new FontCellRenderer());
        JScrollPane scrollPane = new JScrollPane(fontList);

        JPanel p = new JPanel();
        p.add(scrollPane);
        fontList.addListSelectionListener(this);

        getContentPane().add(p, "South");
        panel = new ListRenderingPanel();
        getContentPane().add(panel, "Center");
    }

    public void valueChanged(ListSelectionEvent evt)
    {   JList source = (JList)evt.getSource();
        Font font = (Font)source.getSelectedValue();
        panel.setFont(font);
    }

    private ListRenderingPanel panel;
```

```
}

class ListRenderingPanel extends JPanel
{   public ListRenderingPanel()
    {   setFont(new Font("Serif", Font.PLAIN, 12));
    }

    public void setFont(Font f)
    {   currentFont = f;
        repaint();
    }

    public void paintComponent(Graphics g)
    {   super.paintComponent(g);
        g.setFont(currentFont);
        g.drawString("The quick brown fox jumps over the lazy dog",
            0, 50);
    }

    private Font currentFont;
}

public class ListRenderingTest
{   public static void main(String[] args)
    {   JFrame frame = new ListRenderingFrame();
        frame.show();
    }
}
```

`javax.swing.JList`

- `Color getBackground()`

  returns the background color for unselected cells.

- `Color getSelectionBackground()`

  returns the background color for selected cells.

- `void setCellRenderer(ListCellRenderer cellRenderer)`

  sets the renderer that is used to paint the cells in the list.

`javax.swing.ListCellRenderer`

- `Component getListCellRendererComponent(JList list, Object item, int index, boolean isSelected, boolean hasFocus)`

  returns a component whose `paint` method will draw the cell contents. If the list cells do not have fixed size, that component must also implement `getPreferredSize`.

Parameters:	list	the list whose cell is being drawn
	item	the item to be drawn
	index	the index where the item is stored in the model
	isSelected	true if the specified cell was selected
	hasFocus	true if the specified cell has the focus

Combo Boxes

A drop-down list box is a user interface component that is similar to a list box but that takes less space. When the user clicks on the field, a list of choices drops down, and the user can then select one of them (see Figure 9–20).

Figure 9–20: A combo box

If the drop-down list box is set to be *editable*, then you can edit the current selection as if it was a text box. For that reason, this component is called a *combo box*—it combines the flexibility of an edit box with the easy selection of a list box. You call the setEditable method to make the combo box editable.

The JComboBox class implements this user interface component. Note that editing only affects the current item. It does not change the contents of the list.

You can obtain the current selection or edited text by calling the getSelectedItem method.

In the example program, the user can choose a font style from a list of styles (Serif, SansSerif, Monospaced, etc.). The user can also type in another font.

You add the choice items with the addItem method. In our program, addItem is called only in the constructor, but you can call it any time.

```
style = new JComboBox();
style.setEditable(true);
style.addItem("Serif");
style.addItem("SansSerif");
. . .
```

This method adds the string at the end of the list. You can add new items anywhere in the list with the `insertItemAt` method:

```
style.insertItemAt("Monospaced", 0); // add at the beginning
```

If you need to remove items at run time, you use the `removeItem` or `removeItemAt` method, depending on whether you supply the item to be removed or its position.

```
style.removeItem("Monospaced");
style.removeItemAt(0); // remove first item
```

There is also a `removeAllItems` method whose name says it all.

When the user selects an item from a combo box, the combo box generates an action event. However, you cannot call the `getActionCommand` method to obtain the selected string. Instead, you must call `getSource` to get a reference to the combo box that sent the event and then call the `getSelectedItem` method to retrieve the currently selected item.

```
public void actionPerformed(ActionEvent evt)
{  JComboBox source = (JComboBox)evt.getSource();
   String item = (String)source.getSelectedItem();
   panel.setStyle(item);
}
```

Example 9–11 shows the complete program.

Example 9–11: ComboBoxTest.java

```
import java.awt.*;
import java.awt.event.*;
import javax.swing.*;

class ComboBoxFrame extends JFrame
    implements ActionListener
{  public ComboBoxFrame()
   {  setTitle("ComboBoxTest");
      setSize(300,200);
      addWindowListener(new WindowAdapter()
         {  public void windowClosing(WindowEvent e)
            {  System.exit(0);
            }
         } );

      style = new JComboBox();
      style.setEditable(true);
      style.addItem("Serif");
      style.addItem("SansSerif");
      style.addItem("Monospaced");
```

```java
        style.addItem("Dialog");
        style.addItem("DialogInput");
        style.addActionListener(this);

        JPanel p = new JPanel();
        p.add(style);
        getContentPane().add(p, "South");
        panel = new ComboBoxPanel();
        getContentPane().add(panel, "Center");
    }

    public void actionPerformed(ActionEvent evt)
    {   JComboBox source = (JComboBox)evt.getSource();
        String item = (String)source.getSelectedItem();
        panel.setStyle(item);
    }

    private ComboBoxPanel panel;
    private JComboBox style;
}

class ComboBoxPanel extends JPanel
{   public ComboBoxPanel()
    {   setStyle("Serif");
    }

    public void setStyle(String s)
    {   setFont(new Font(s, Font.PLAIN, 12));
        repaint();
    }

    public void paintComponent(Graphics g)
    {   super.paintComponent(g);
        g.drawString
            ("The quick brown fox jumps over the lazy dog.",
                0, 50);
    }
}

public class ComboBoxTest
{   public static void main(String[] args)
    {   JFrame frame = new ComboBoxFrame();
        frame.show();
    }
}
```

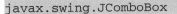

`javax.swing.JComboBox`

- `void setEditable(boolean b)`

  Parameters: b   `true` if the combo box field can be edited by the user, `false` otherwise.

- `void addItem(Object item)`

  adds an item to the item list.

- `void insertItemAt(Object item, int index)`

  inserts an item into the item list at a given index.

- `void removeItem(Object item)`

  removes an item from the item list.

- `void removeItemAt(int index)`

  removes the item at an index.

- `void removeAllItems()`

  removes all items from the item list.

- `Object getSelectedItem()`

  returns the currently selected item.

Scroll Bars

The two most common uses for scroll bars in a Java application are as follows:

- Using a scroll bar in a control as a slider. (However, the `JSlider` class is often a better choice — it has a better look and more options than a plain scroll bar. Please turn to Volume 2 for more information on the `JSlider` component.)

- Placing scroll bars at the right and at the bottom of a window to scroll through its contents. (Actually, the `JScrollPane` class that you have already seen is usually a more convenient choice for this.)

We will look briefly at both of these uses in this section.

A scroll bar has several important properties:

- *Direction.* (`Adjustable.HORIZONTAL` or `Adjustable.VERTICAL`). The direction is set in the constructor or with the `setOrientation` method. If no orientation is specified, the scroll bar is vertical.

- *Value.* This is the value corresponding to the current slider position. You can query it with the `getValue` method and set it with the `setValue` method.

- *Range.* The default range is 0–100. You can change it with the `setMinimum` and `setMaximum` methods.

- *Visible area.* If you use scroll bars to scroll through a large region, then the range is the size of the region and the visible area is the size of the scroll window. A positive visible-area value limits scrolling so that the *end* of the scroll window scrolls up to the *end* of the region that is being viewed. It also adjusts the thickness of the slider to reflect the ratio between the visible area and the scroll range. (See Figure 9–21.) If you just use a scroll bar as a slider control to specify a number, set the visible area to zero. You can set this value with the setVisibleAmount method.

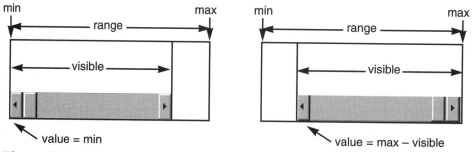

Figure 9–21: The visible area of a scroll bar

- *Unit increment.* When the user clicks on the arrow on either end of the scroll bar, the scroll bar value is changed by this amount. The default is 1. You can change it with the setUnitIncrement method.

- *Block increment.* When the user clicks on the area between the arrow and the slider, the value is changed by this amount. The default is 10. You can change it with the setBlockIncrement method.

You create a scroll bar by specifying its direction (Adjustable.HORIZONTAL or Adjustable.VERTICAL) in the constructor. You can simultaneously set the current value, visible amount, and range with the setValues method. Instead of using the setValues method, you can also use a version of the constructor for the scroll bar class that can accept the initial value, visible amount, and range.

In our first example, we use scroll bars to pick red, green, and blue values to mix and display a color value. (See Figure 9–22.) Here are two ways to initialize a scroll bar.

```
red = new JScrollBar(Adjustable.HORIZONTAL);
red.setValues(0, 0, 0, 255);
```

or

```
red = new JScrollBar(Adjustable.HORIZONTAL, 0, 0, 0, 255);
```

Figure 9–22: Scroll bars at work

When the user clicks on a scroll bar or moves the scroll bar slider to a new position, the scroll bar sends adjustment events to the listener object. Five types of adjustment events are generated by scroll bars—see Table 9–2.

Table 9–2: Adjustment event cause

UNIT_INCREMENT UNIT_DECREMENT	Generated when the user clicks on an arrow at either scroll bar end
BLOCK_INCREMENT BLOCK_DECREMENT	Generated when the user clicks between an arrow and the slider
TRACK	Generated when the user drags the slider

If evt is an adjustment event, then evt.getAdjustmentType() returns one of these values.

When processing a scroll bar event, use the getValue() method to obtain the current position of the scroll bar. As an example of this, here is the event handler for the color mixer application.

```
public void adjustmentValueChanged(AdjustmentEvent evt)
{  redLabel.setText("Red " + red.getValue());
   greenLabel.setText("Green " + green.getValue());
   blueLabel.setText("Blue " + blue.getValue());
   c.setBackground(new Color(red.getValue(),
      green.getValue(), blue.getValue()));

   c.repaint();
}
```

Example 9–12 is the complete source code for the color selection application. (The labels and scroll bars are laid out by means of a *grid layout*. We will discuss grid layouts later in this chapter.)

Example 9–12: ColorSelect.java

```java
import java.awt.*;
import java.awt.event.*;
import javax.swing.*;

public class ColorSelect extends JFrame
    implements AdjustmentListener
{  public ColorSelect()
    {  setTitle("ColorSelect");
       setSize(300, 200);
       addWindowListener(new WindowAdapter()
       {  public void windowClosing(WindowEvent e)
          {  System.exit(0);
          }
       } );

       Container contentPane = getContentPane();

       JPanel p = new JPanel();
       p.setLayout(new GridLayout(3, 2));

       p.add(redLabel = new JLabel("Red 0"));
       p.add(red = new JScrollBar(Adjustable.HORIZONTAL,
          0, 0, 0, 255));
       red.setBlockIncrement(16);
       red.addAdjustmentListener(this);

       p.add(greenLabel = new JLabel("Green 0"));
       p.add(green = new JScrollBar(Adjustable.HORIZONTAL,
          0, 0, 0, 255));
       green.setBlockIncrement(16);
       green.addAdjustmentListener(this);

       p.add(blueLabel = new JLabel("Blue 0"));
       p.add(blue = new JScrollBar(Adjustable.HORIZONTAL,
          0, 0, 0, 255));
       blue.setBlockIncrement(16);
       blue.addAdjustmentListener(this);

       contentPane.add(p, "South");

       colorPanel = new JPanel();
       colorPanel.setBackground(new Color(0, 0, 0));
       contentPane.add(colorPanel, "Center");
    }

    public void adjustmentValueChanged(AdjustmentEvent evt)
    {  redLabel.setText("Red " + red.getValue());
       greenLabel.setText("Green " + green.getValue());
       blueLabel.setText("Blue " + blue.getValue());
       colorPanel.setBackground(new Color(red.getValue(),
```

```
            green.getValue(), blue.getValue()));

      colorPanel.repaint();
   }

   public static void main(String[] args)
   {   JFrame f = new ColorSelect();
       f.show();
   }

   private JLabel redLabel;
   private JLabel greenLabel;
   private JLabel blueLabel;

   private JScrollBar red;
   private JScrollBar green;
   private JScrollBar blue;

   private JPanel colorPanel;
}
```

`javax.swing.JScrollBar`

- `JScrollBar(int orientation)`

  creates a scroll bar with range 0...100.

  Parameters: orientation   **either** HORIZONTAL **or** VERTICAL

- `JScrollBar(int orientation, int value, int visible, int`
     `minimum, int maximum)`

  Parameters: orientation   **either** HORIZONTAL **or** VERTICAL

	value	the scroll position
	visible	the visible area of the window, or 0 for a slider control
	minimum	the minimum position value of the scroll bar
	maximum	the maximum position value of the scroll bar

- `void setValue(int value)`

  Parameters: value   the new scroll position; set to the current minimum or maximum if it is outside the scroll range

- `void setValues(int value, int visible, int minimum, int maximum)`

  Parameters: value   the scroll position

	visible	the visible area of the window, or 0 for a slider control

minimum	the minimum position value of the scroll bar
maximum	the maximum position value of the scroll bar

- `void setMinimum(int value)`

  Parameters: `value`   the new minimum value

- `void setMaximum(int value)`

  Parameters: `value`   the new maximum value

- `void setVisibleAmount(int value)`

  Parameters: `value`   the new value for the visible setting

- `void setBlockIncrement(int l)`

  sets the block increment, the amount by which the scroll position changes when the user clicks between the arrows and the slider.

- `void setUnitIncrement(int l)`

  sets the unit increment, the amount by which the scroll position changes when the user clicks on the arrows at the ends of the scroll bar.

- `int getValue()`

  returns the current scroll position.

`java.awt.event.AdjustmentListener`

- `void adjustmentValueChanged(AdjustmentEvent e)`

  is called when the value of the event source has changed.

Scroll Panes

It is not all that common to use scroll bar components to collect user input. On the other hand, adding scroll bars to scroll a large area in a small window is an exceedingly common task. You can do this by hand by following these steps:

- Add scroll bars to the right and the bottom.
- Track the current scroll offset.
- Take the scroll offset into account for mouse events and painting.

As you will see in the next section, implementing scrolling in this way is instructive, but it is something of a pain. Evidently, the Swing designers agreed, and so they supply a class, `JScrollPane`, that automatically supplies scroll bars. A scroll pane is a container that has a scroll bar to the right and the bottom. You simply add the component that you want to be managed by the scroll bars. The scroll pane lets the user scroll through sections of that component by manipulating the scroll bars.

Once you add the component to a scroll pane, you write the code for the component *as if it was displayed at its full size*. The scroll pane takes care of adjusting the coordinates in mouse events and in painting. You never need to worry about scroll offsets. This is clearly a great convenience. To take advantage of this feature, simply make an object of type `JScrollPane`. Supply the component to be viewed as the first argument in the constructor.

You can specify whether you want the scroll bars to be displayed all the time or only when they are needed. The latter is the default, and it is the more useful setting. The scroll bars simply go away when the window is resized to show the full area of the component that the scroll pane manages.

For example:

```
JScrollPane sp = new JScrollPane(viewedComponent);
   // draw scroll bars as needed
```

or

```
JScrollPane sp = new JScrollPane(viewedComponent,
   ScrollPaneConstants.HORIZONTAL_SCROLLBAR_NEVER,
   ScrollPaneConstants.VERTICAL_SCROLLBAR_ALWAYS
);
```

The settings `ScrollPaneConstants.HORIZONTAL_SCROLLBAR_AS_NEEDED` and `ScrollPaneConstants.VERTICAL_SCROLLBAR_AS_NEEDED` are the defaults.

Then, add the scroll pane to the frame. For example:

```
contentPane.add(sp, "Center");
```

There is one more step that you must take in the component to be viewed. It must set a preferred size, for example, in the constructor:

```
public MyComponent()
{  setPreferredSize(new Dimension(MAX_XWIDTH, MAX_YHEIGHT));
   . . .
}
```

Alternatively, if for some reason you don't want to view the component at its preferred size, you can specify a different size to the *viewport* object that manages the scrolling activity:

```
JViewport vp = sp.getViewport();
vp.setViewSize(new Dimension(MAX_XWIDTH, MAX_YHEIGHT));
```

The viewport is the object through which you view the underlying component. The scroll bars actually move the viewport across the component, and it draws what it finds underneath (See Figure 9–23).

Example 9–12 shows the scroll pane in action. We'll reuse the mouse event test program from the previous chapter. In that program, the user clicks inside a panel to fill it with squares, drags the squares to move them, or double-clicks to erase them. We will now make the panel larger, namely 600 by 400 pixels. And, we will display it in a frame that is only 300 by 200 pixels, so we want the user to be able to scroll over the total panel.

Fortunately, it is very easy to add scroll bars to the `MousePanel` class. We only need to make a single change to the `MousePanel` code and call `setPreferredSize`. We then add the panel into a scroll pane and the scroll pane into the content pane: scrolling is now automatic. The `MousePanel` is never aware that it is being scrolled at all!

Finally, the `JScrollPane` allows you to place additional decorations around the component whose contents are scrolled. As you can see in Figure 9–23, you can add *headers* to the top and left side, opposite from the scroll bars, and you can place arbitrary components into the four corners.

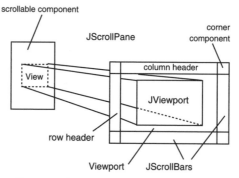

Figure 9–23: Scroll pane layout

As an example, let us place *rulers* as row and column headers. In the sample code below, you will find a simple class, `RulerPanel`, whose `paintComponent` method draws a series of ticks and tick labels, labeling the pixel positions of the component to be scrolled. Figure 9–24 shows the visual effect. The code for the tick marks is straightforward, if a little tedious, so we won't discuss it in detail.

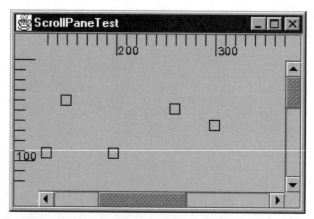

Figure 9–24: A scroll pane test program with rulers

We want to add a horizontal and vertical ruler, and of course we want them to scroll together with the component that is managed by the scroll pane. Simply create the component and call `setRowHeaderView` or `setColumnHeaderView` to install it. The row header is in vertical direction, the column header in horizontal direction. (Think of them as row or column headers in a table.) For example:

```
RulerPanel horizRulerPanel = new RulerPanel
   (SwingConstants.HORIZONTAL,
     viewedComponent.getPreferredSize().width, 25, 100, 100, 10);
sp.setColumnHeaderView(horizRulerPanel);
```

Now the scroll pane scrolls these components in sync with the viewed component.

You can use the `setCorner` method to set an arbitrary component into each of the four corners of the scroll pane (identified through constants such as `JScrollPane.UPPER_RIGHT_CORNER` rather than the standard Swing constants such as `SwingConstants.NORTH_WEST`). For example:

```
sp.setCorner(JScrollPane.UPPER_LEFT_CORNER,
   new Label(new ImageIcon("blue-ball.gif")));
```

Naturally, such gimcrackery should be avoided in practice.

Swing encourages programmers to provide keyboard alternatives for mouse actions. In our sample program, let us use the cursor keys to scroll the panel by the unit increment, and the PGUP/PGDN and CTRL+PGUP/CTRL+PGDN keys to scroll the panel by the block increment.

As you saw in Chapter 8, the easiest way to capture a keystroke in a window is with the `registerKeyboardAction` method of the `JComponent` class. This approach requires an `Action` object for each registered keystroke. Since the scrolling actions are all related, we will build a single class, `ScrollAction`, that stores the scroll pane, the direction of the scroll bar, the type (unit or block increment), and the direction (-1 for up/left, $+1$ for down/right). In the `actionPerformed` method, we obtain the appropriate `JScrollBar`, compute its new position, and call its `setValue` method:

```
class ScrollAction extends AbstractAction
{  public void actionPerformed(ActionEvent evt)
   {  JScrollBar scrollBar;
      if (orientation == JScrollBar.HORIZONTAL)
         scrollBar = scrollPane.getHorizontalScrollBar();
      else
         scrollBar = scrollPane.getVerticalScrollBar();
      if (scrollBar == null || !scrollBar.isVisible())
         return;
      int increment;
      if (type == UNIT)
         increment = scrollBar.getUnitIncrement();
      else
```

```
            increment = scrollBar.getBlockIncrement();
         scrollBar.setValue(scrollBar.getValue() +
            increment * direction);
      }
      . . .
   }
```

For each keystroke, we need to construct the appropriate `ScrollAction` object and register it with the scroll pane. For example:

```
sp.registerKeyboardAction(
   new ScrollAction(JScrollBar.HORIZONTAL, ScrollAction.UNIT, -1),
   KeyStroke.getKeyStroke(KeyEvent.VK_LEFT, 0, false),
   JComponent.WHEN_IN_FOCUSED_WINDOW);
```

That gets a little repetitive, and we supply a convenience method `register` in our `ScrollAction` class. See Example 9–13 for the full source code.

Example 9–13: ScrollPaneTest.java

```
import java.awt.*;
import java.awt.event.*;
import javax.swing.*;

class MousePanel extends JPanel
   // unchanged except for setPreferredSize
   implements MouseMotionListener
{  public MousePanel()
   {  addMouseListener(new MouseAdapter()
         {  public void mousePressed(MouseEvent evt)
            {  int x = evt.getX();
               int y = evt.getY();
               current = find(x, y);
               if (current < 0) // not inside a square
                  add(x, y);
            }

            public void mouseClicked(MouseEvent evt)
            {  int x = evt.getX();
               int y = evt.getY();

               if (evt.getClickCount() >= 2)
               {  remove(current);
               }
            }
         });
      addMouseMotionListener(this);

      setPreferredSize(new Dimension(MAX_XWIDTH,
         MAX_YHEIGHT));
   }

   public void paintComponent(Graphics g)
```

```java
{  super.paintComponent(g);
   for (int i = 0; i < nsquares; i++)
      draw(g, i);
}

public int find(int x, int y)
{  for (int i = 0; i < nsquares; i++)
      if (squares[i].x - SQUARELENGTH / 2 <= x &&
            x <= squares[i].x + SQUARELENGTH / 2
            && squares[i].y - SQUARELENGTH / 2 <= y
            && y <= squares[i].y + SQUARELENGTH / 2)
         return i;
   return -1;
}

public void draw(Graphics g, int i)
{  g.drawRect(squares[i].x - SQUARELENGTH / 2,
      squares[i].y - SQUARELENGTH / 2,
      SQUARELENGTH, SQUARELENGTH);
}

public void add(int x, int y)
{  if (nsquares < MAXNSQUARES)
   {  squares[nsquares] = new Point(x, y);
      current = nsquares;
      nsquares++;
      repaint();
   }
}

public void remove(int n)
{  if (n < 0 || n >= nsquares) return;
   nsquares--;
   squares[n] = squares[nsquares];
   if (current == n) current = -1;
   repaint();
}

public void mouseMoved(MouseEvent evt)
{  int x = evt.getX();
   int y = evt.getY();

   if (find(x, y) >= 0)
      setCursor(Cursor.getPredefinedCursor
         (Cursor.CROSSHAIR_CURSOR));
   else
      setCursor(Cursor.getDefaultCursor());
}

public void mouseDragged(MouseEvent evt)
{  int x = evt.getX();
   int y = evt.getY();
```

```
        if (current >= 0)
        {  Graphics g = getGraphics();
           g.setXORMode(getBackground());
           draw(g, current);
           squares[current].x = x;
           squares[current].y = y;
           draw(g, current);
           g.dispose();
        }
     }

     private static final int MAX_XWIDTH = 600;
     private static final int MAX_YHEIGHT = 400;
     private static final int SQUARELENGTH = 10;
     private static final int MAXNSQUARES = 100;
     private Point[] squares = new Point[MAXNSQUARES];
     private int nsquares = 0;
     private int current = -1;
  }

  class ScrollPaneFrame extends JFrame
  {  public ScrollPaneFrame()
     {  setTitle("ScrollPaneTest");
        setSize(300, 200);
        addWindowListener(new WindowAdapter()
           {  public void windowClosing(WindowEvent e)
              {  System.exit(0);
              }
           } );

        Container contentPane = getContentPane();
        Component viewedComponent = new MousePanel();
        JScrollPane sp = new JScrollPane(viewedComponent);

        RulerPanel horizRulerPanel = new RulerPanel
           (SwingConstants.HORIZONTAL,
              viewedComponent.getPreferredSize().width,
              25, 100, 100, 10);
        sp.setColumnHeaderView(horizRulerPanel);

        RulerPanel vertRulerPanel = new RulerPanel
           (SwingConstants.VERTICAL,
              25, viewedComponent.getPreferredSize().height,
              100, 100, 10);
        sp.setRowHeaderView(vertRulerPanel);
        contentPane.add(sp, "Center");

        ScrollAction.register(sp, JScrollBar.HORIZONTAL,
           ScrollAction.UNIT, -1, KeyEvent.VK_LEFT, 0);
        ScrollAction.register(sp, JScrollBar.HORIZONTAL,
           ScrollAction.UNIT, 1, KeyEvent.VK_RIGHT, 0);
        ScrollAction.register(sp, JScrollBar.VERTICAL,
```

```
            ScrollAction.UNIT, -1, KeyEvent.VK_UP, 0);
        ScrollAction.register(sp, JScrollBar.VERTICAL,
            ScrollAction.UNIT, 1, KeyEvent.VK_DOWN, 0);
        ScrollAction.register(sp, JScrollBar.HORIZONTAL,
            ScrollAction.BLOCK, -1, KeyEvent.VK_PAGE_UP,
            InputEvent.CTRL_MASK);
        ScrollAction.register(sp, JScrollBar.HORIZONTAL,
            ScrollAction.BLOCK, 1, KeyEvent.VK_PAGE_DOWN,
            InputEvent.CTRL_MASK);
        ScrollAction.register(sp, JScrollBar.VERTICAL,
            ScrollAction.BLOCK, -1, KeyEvent.VK_PAGE_UP, 0);
        ScrollAction.register(sp, JScrollBar.VERTICAL,
            ScrollAction.BLOCK, 1, KeyEvent.VK_PAGE_DOWN, 0);
    }
}

public class ScrollPaneTest
{   public static void main(String[] args)
    {   JFrame frame = new ScrollPaneFrame();
        frame.show();
    }
}

class ScrollAction extends AbstractAction
{   public ScrollAction(JScrollPane p, int orient,
        int t, int dir)
    {   scrollPane = p;
        orientation = orient;
        type = t;
        direction = dir;
    }

    public static void register(JScrollPane p, int orient,
        int t, int dir, int key, int modifier)
    {   p.registerKeyboardAction(
            new ScrollAction(p, orient, t, dir),
            KeyStroke.getKeyStroke(key, modifier, false),
            JComponent.WHEN_IN_FOCUSED_WINDOW);
    }

    public void actionPerformed(ActionEvent evt)
    {   JScrollBar scrollBar;
        if (orientation == JScrollBar.HORIZONTAL)
            scrollBar = scrollPane.getHorizontalScrollBar();
        else
            scrollBar = scrollPane.getVerticalScrollBar();
        if (scrollBar == null || !scrollBar.isVisible())
            return;
        int increment;
        if (type == UNIT)
            increment = scrollBar.getUnitIncrement();
        else
```

```
                increment = scrollBar.getBlockIncrement();
            scrollBar.setValue(scrollBar.getValue()
                +increment * direction);
        }

    private JScrollPane scrollPane;
    private int orientation; // HORIZONTAL or VERTICAL
    private int type; // UNIT or BLOCK
    private int direction; // +1 or -1

    public static final int UNIT = 1;
    public static final int BLOCK = 2;
}

class RulerPanel extends JPanel implements SwingConstants
{   public RulerPanel(int dir, int w, int h, int lbldist, int lbl,
        int subs)
    {   direction = dir;
        labelDistance = lbldist;
        label = lbl;
        subdivisions = subs;
        setPreferredSize(new Dimension(w, h));
    }

    public void paintComponent(Graphics g)
    {   super.paintComponent(g);
        Dimension d = getPreferredSize();
        if (direction == HORIZONTAL)
        {   int i = 0;
            int x = 0;
            if (subdivisions > 0)
            {   while (x < d.width)
                {   g.drawLine(x, 0, x, (d.height * 4) / 10);
                    i++;
                    x = (i * labelDistance) / subdivisions;
                }
            }
            i = 0;
            x = 0;
            while (x <= d.width)
            {   g.drawLine(x, 0, x, (d.height * 8) / 10);
                g.drawString("" + i * label, x + 2,
                    (d.height * 8) / 10);
                i++;
                x = i * labelDistance;
            }
        }
        else
        {   int i = 0;
            int y = 0;
            if (subdivisions > 0)
            {   while (y <= d.height)
```

```
            {   g.drawLine(0, y, (d.width * 4) / 10, y);
                i++;
                y = (i * labelDistance) / subdivisions;
            }
        }
        i = 0;
        y = 0;
        while (y <= d.height)
        {   g.drawLine(0, y, (d.width * 8) / 10, y);
            g.drawString("" + i * label, 2, y);
            i++;
            y = i * labelDistance;
        }
    }
}

private int direction;
private int labelDistance;
private int subdivisions;
private int label;
}
```

javax.swing.JScrollPane

- `JScrollPane(Component c)`

  creates a new scroll pane, scrolling the surface of the component c, with scroll bars only when needed.

- `ScrollPane(Component c, int horiz, int vert)`

Parameters:	c	the component to be scrolled
	horiz	one of `HORIZONTAL_SCROLLBAR_ALWAYS`, `HORIZONTAL_SCROLLBAR_AS_NEEDED`, `HORIZONTAL_SCROLLBAR_NEVER`
	vert	one of `VERTICAL_SCROLLBAR_ALWAYS`, `VERTICAL_SCROLLBAR_AS_NEEDED`, `VERTICAL_SCROLLBAR_NEVER`

- `void setRowHeaderView(Component c)`
- `void setColumnHeaderView(Component c)`

  install the component c across from the vertical or horizontal scroll bar, and scroll it together with the viewed component.

- `void setCorner(String where, Component c)`

  places a component into a corner of the scroll pane.

  | *Parameters:* | where | one of `LOWER_LEFT_CORNER`, `LOWER_RIGHT_CORNER`, `UPPER_LEFT_CORNER`, `UPPER_RIGHT_CORNER` |

Scrolling a Window

In the preceding section, you saw how to use a `JScrollPane` to scroll a panel that is larger than the frame window, so that the scroll bars can bring different parts of the larger panel into view. In this section, we will do this by hand by explicitly adding scroll bars and trapping scroll events. This will explain the mysterious "visible amount" scroll bar setting, and it will give you an idea what the `JScrollPane` class does behind the scenes. If you are not interested in the mechanics of scrolling, you can safely skip this section.

Recall the mouse event test program from the previous section. The panel has a size of 600 by 400 pixels. It is shown in a frame of only 300 by 200 pixels. We will put scroll bars into the east and south corners. The user can move the scroll bars, and we redraw the panel afterwards. Whenever we draw the window, we translate the graphics coordinates by the negatives of the scroll values. For example, if the values of the horizontal and vertical scroll bars are 200 and 100, then we want to draw the area starting at (200,100). We move the origin to (–200, –100) and repaint the entire 600-by-400-pixel image. Much of the image is clipped, but the part of the underlying image that we want to see is then shown in the window (see Figure 9–25).

Figure 9–25: A scroll bar test program

Thus, what we need to do is:

- Trap all scroll events.
- Force a redraw of the panel when an event occurs.

Here's an example of the code to do this:

```
public void adjustmentValueChanged(AdjustmentEvent evt)
{   panel.translate(horiz.getValue(), vert.getValue());
}
```

The `translate` method of our `panel` object stores the scroll offset in the fields dx and dy, then calls `repaint`.

```
public void translate(int x, int y)
{   dx = x;
    dy = y;
    repaint();
}
```

The data structure that stores the list of rectangles keeps them in *absolute coordinates,* that is, with x-values ranging from 0 to 600 and y-values ranging from 0 to 400. That is not a problem in the `paintComponent` method because we can translate the origin of the graphics context. Rectangles that don't currently fit in the window are clipped and do not get drawn.

```
public void paintComponent(Graphics g)
{   super.paintComponent(g);
    g.translate(-dx, -dy);
    g.setColor(Color.red);
    g.drawRect(0, 0, MAX_XWIDTH - 1, MAX_YHEIGHT - 1);
    g.setColor(getForeground());
    for (int i = 0; i < nsquares;i++) draw(g, i);
}
```

We also draw a red rectangle around the total area, from (0,0) to (600, 400), so that you can see how the scroll bars precisely sweep out the total area.

In the `paintComponent` method, we simply called the `translate` method to make the graphics context change the coordinates from absolute coordinates to window coordinates. In the mouse listener methods, we must carry out the opposite conversion. The mouse functions report the mouse locations in window coordinates. To test that a mouse click falls inside a square (whose coordinates are stored in absolute coordinates), we must add the scroll offset to all mouse coordinates.

```
public void mousePressed(MouseEvent evt)
{   int x = evt.getX() + dx;
    int y = evt.getY() + dy;
    current = find(x, y);
    . . .
}
```

When the window is first shown and when it is resized, we have to compute the "visible" values of the scroll bar. Since we measure the coordinates in pixels, the visible amount is the size of the panel. For example, suppose the current panel size is 280 by 180 pixels. (The visible area of the window is somewhat less than 300 by 200 because the scroll bars take some amount of space.) Now, consider the x-range of the horizontal scroll bar. When it is all the way to the left, then the *left* margin of the panel must show the absolute x-coordinate 0. When it is all the way to the right, then the *right* margin of the panel must show the absolute x-coordinate 599, the maximum x-value that we want to show. The *left* margin of the panel has then x-coordinate 599 – 280 = 319. That means the scroll range is not actually 0 ... 599, but only 0 ... 319. With the visible area set to 280, the scroll range is set correctly and the size of the slider is adjusted to reflect the proportion of the visible area to the total area.

Showing and resizing the window results in a component event. We trap the events and set the visible areas in x- and y-direction.

```
class ScrollFrame
{   public ScrollFrame()
```

```
{    . . .
     addComponentListener(new ComponentAdapter()
     {  public void componentShown(ComponentEvent evt)
        {  setVisibleAmounts();
        }
        public void componentResized(ComponentEvent evt)
        {  setVisibleAmounts();
        }
     });
  }

  public void setVisibleAmounts()
  {  Dimension d = panel.getSize();
     horiz.setVisibleAmount(d.width);
     vert.setVisibleAmount(d.height);
  }
  . . .
}
```

To demonstrate that the scroll bars *precisely* sweep out the 600 by 400 area, move them all the way to the right and the bottom. You will just see the red rectangle that delimits the total area. Then, resize the window and move the scroll bars all the way to either side. Again, they sweep out precisely the whole area of the panel. Example 9–14 is the listing of the program.

Actually, few Java programmers will want to use this method of adding scroll bars to a window. The JScrollPane container, which is discussed in the previous section, achieves the same effect with much less programming. We discussed the manual approach so that you can gain an understanding of what operations the JScrollPane class carries out under the hood.

Example 9–14: ScrollTest.java

```java
import java.awt.*;
import java.awt.event.*;
import javax.swing.*;

class MousePanel extends JPanel
   implements MouseMotionListener
{  public MousePanel()
   {  addMouseListener(new MouseAdapter()
        {  public void mousePressed(MouseEvent evt)
           {  int x = evt.getX() + dx;
              int y = evt.getY() + dy;
              current = find(x, y);
              if (current < 0) // not inside a square
              {  if (x < MAX_XWIDTH && y < MAX_YHEIGHT)
                    add(x, y);
              }
           }

           public void mouseClicked(MouseEvent evt)
```

```
            {   int x = evt.getX() + dx;
                int y = evt.getY() + dy;

                if (evt.getClickCount() >= 2)
                {   remove(current);
                }
            }
        });
    addMouseMotionListener(this);
}

public void translate(int x, int y)
{   dx = x;
    dy = y;
    repaint();
}

public void paintComponent(Graphics g)
{   super.paintComponent(g);
    g.translate(-dx, -dy);
    g.setColor(Color.red);
    g.drawRect(0, 0, MAX_XWIDTH - 1, MAX_YHEIGHT - 1);
    g.setColor(Color.black);
    for (int i = 0; i < nsquares; i++)
        draw(g, i);
}

public int find(int x, int y)
{   for (int i = 0; i < nsquares; i++)
        if (squares[i].x - SQUARELENGTH / 2 <= x &&
                x <= squares[i].x + SQUARELENGTH / 2
                && squares[i].y - SQUARELENGTH / 2 <= y
                && y <= squares[i].y + SQUARELENGTH / 2)
            return i;
    return -1;
}

public void draw(Graphics g, int i)
{   g.drawRect(squares[i].x - SQUARELENGTH / 2,
        squares[i].y - SQUARELENGTH / 2,
        SQUARELENGTH, SQUARELENGTH);
}

public void add(int x, int y)
{   if (nsquares < MAXNSQUARES)
    {   squares[nsquares] = new Point(x, y);
        current = nsquares;
        nsquares++;
        repaint();
    }
}
```

```java
    public void remove(int n)
    {   if (n < 0 || n >= nsquares) return;
        nsquares--;
        squares[n] = squares[nsquares];
        if (current == n) current = -1;
        repaint();
    }

    public void mouseMoved(MouseEvent evt)
    {   int x = evt.getX();
        int y = evt.getY();

        if (find(x, y) >= 0)
            setCursor(Cursor.getPredefinedCursor
                (Cursor.CROSSHAIR_CURSOR));
        else
            setCursor(Cursor.getDefaultCursor());
    }

    public void mouseDragged(MouseEvent evt)
    {   int x = evt.getX();
        int y = evt.getY();

        if (current >= 0)
        {   Graphics g = getGraphics();
            g.setXORMode(getBackground());
            draw(g, current);
            squares[current].x = x;
            squares[current].y = y;
            draw(g, current);
            g.dispose();
        }
    }

    private static final int SQUARELENGTH = 10;
    private static final int MAXNSQUARES = 100;
    private Point[] squares = new Point[MAXNSQUARES];
    private int nsquares = 0;
    private int current = -1;

    private int dx = 0;
    private int dy = 0;

    public static final int MAX_XWIDTH = 600;
    public static final int MAX_YHEIGHT = 400;
}

class ScrollFrame extends JFrame
    implements AdjustmentListener
{   public ScrollFrame()
    {   setTitle("ScrollTest");
        setSize(300, 200);
```

```
        addWindowListener(new WindowAdapter()
            {   public void windowClosing(WindowEvent e)
                {   System.exit(0);
                }
            } );

        Container contentPane = getContentPane();
        contentPane.add(panel = new MousePanel(), "Center");
        contentPane.add(vert = new JScrollBar
            (Adjustable.VERTICAL), "East");
        contentPane.add(horiz = new JScrollBar
            (Adjustable.HORIZONTAL), "South");
        vert.addAdjustmentListener(this);
        horiz.addAdjustmentListener(this);
        horiz.setValues(horiz.getValue(), 0, 0,
            MousePanel.MAX_XWIDTH);
        vert.setValues(vert.getValue(), 0, 0,
            MousePanel.MAX_YHEIGHT);

        addComponentListener(new ComponentAdapter()
        {   public void componentShown(ComponentEvent evt)
            {   setVisibleAmounts();
            }
            public void componentResized(ComponentEvent evt)
            {   setVisibleAmounts();
            }
        });
    }

    public void setVisibleAmounts()
    {   Dimension d = panel.getSize();
        horiz.setVisibleAmount(d.width);
        vert.setVisibleAmount(d.height);
    }

    public void adjustmentValueChanged(AdjustmentEvent evt)
    {   panel.translate(horiz.getValue(), vert.getValue());
    }

    private JScrollBar horiz;
    private JScrollBar vert;
    private MousePanel panel;
}

public class ScrollTest
{   public static void main(String[] args)
    {   JFrame frame = new ScrollFrame();
        frame.show();
    }
}
```

Sophisticated Layout Management

We have managed to lay out the user interface components of our sample applications so far by using only the border layout and flow layout. For more complex tasks, this is not going to be enough. In this section, we will give you a detailed discussion of all the layout managers that the standard Java library provides to organize components.

Windows programmers may well wonder why Java makes so much fuss about layout managers. After all, in Windows, layout management is not a big deal: First, you use a dialog editor to drag and drop your components onto the surface of the dialog, and then you use editor tools to line up components, to space them equally, to center them, and so on. If you are working on a big project, you probably don't have to worry about component layout at all—a skilled user interface designer does all this for you.

The problem with this approach is that the resulting layout must be manually updated if the size of the components changes. Why would the component size change? There are two common cases. First, a user may choose a larger font for button labels and other dialog text. If you try this out for yourself in Windows, you will find that many applications deal with this exceedingly poorly. The buttons do not grow and the larger font is simply crammed into the same space as before. The same problem can occur when translating the strings in an application to a foreign language. For example, the German word for "Cancel" is "Abbrechen." If a button has been designed with just enough room for the string "Cancel," then the German version will look broken, with a clipped command string.

Why don't Windows buttons simply grow to accommodate the labels? Because the designer of the user interface gave no instructions in which direction they should grow. After the dragging and dropping and arranging, the dialog editor merely remembers the pixel position and size of each component. It does not remember *why* the components were arranged in this fashion.

The Java layout managers are a much better approach to component layout. With a layout manager, the layout comes with instructions about the relationships between the components. This was particularly important in the original AWT, which used native user interface elements. The size of a button or list box in Motif, Windows, and the Macintosh could vary widely, and an application or applet would not know a priori on which platform it would display its user interface. To some degree, that degree of variability has gone away with Swing. If your application forces a particular look and feel, such as the Metal look and feel, then it looks identical on all platforms. However, if you let users of your application choose their favorite look and feel, then you again need to rely on the flexibility of layout managers to arrange the components.

Of course, to achieve complex layouts, you will need to have more control over the layout than the border layout and flow layout give you. In this section, we will discuss the layout managers that the standard Java library has to offer. Using a sophisticated layout manager combined with the appropriate use of multiple panels will give you complete control over how your application will look.

TIP: If none of the layout schemes fit your needs, break the surface of your window into separate panels and lay out each panel separately. Then, use another layout manager to organize the panels.

First, let's review a few basic principles. As you know, in the AWT, *components* are laid out inside *containers*. Buttons, text fields, and other user interface elements are components and can be placed inside containers. Therefore, these classes extend the class `Component`. Containers such as panels can themselves be put inside other containers. Therefore, the class `Container` derives from `Component`. Figure 9–26 shows the inheritance hierarchy for `Component`.

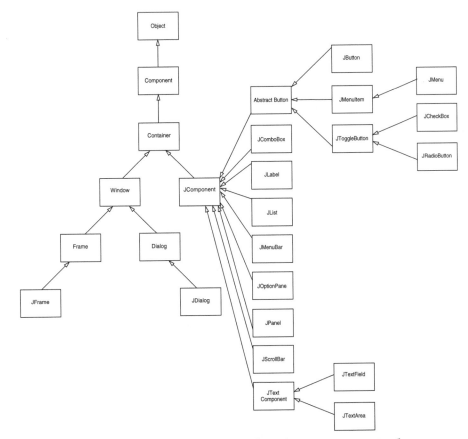

Figure 9–26: Inheritance hierarchy for the `Component` class

> NOTE: Note that some objects belong to classes extending `Component` even though they are not user interface components and cannot be inserted into containers. Top-level windows such as `JFrame` and `JApplet` cannot be contained inside another window or panel.

As you have seen, to organize the components in a container, you first specify a layout manager. For example, the statement

```
panel.setLayout(new GridLayout(4, 4));
```

will use the `GridLayout` class to lay out the panels. After you set the layout manager, you add components to the container. The `add` method of the container passes the component and any placement directions to the layout manager.

With the border layout manager, you give a string to indicate component placement:

```
panel.add(new JTextField(), "South");
```

With the grid layout that you will see shortly, you need to add components sequentially:

```
panel.add(new JCheckBox("italic"));
panel.add(new JCheckBox("bold"));
```

The grid layout is useful to arrange components in a grid, somewhat like the rows and columns of a spreadsheet. However, all rows and columns of the grid have *identical* size, which is not all that useful in practice.

To overcome the limitations of the grid layout, the AWT supplies the *grid bag layout*. It, too, lays out components in rows and columns, but the row and column sizes are flexible, and components can span multiple rows and columns. This layout manager is very flexible, but it is also very complex. The mere mention of the word "grid bag layout" has been known to strike fear in the hearts of Java programmers. Actually, in most common situations, the grid bag layout is not that hard to use, and we tell you a strategy that should make grid bag layouts relatively painless.

In an (unsuccessful) effort of designing a layout manager that would free programmers from the tyranny of the grid bag layout, the Swing designers came up with the *box layout*. The box layout simply arranges a sequence of components horizontally or vertically. When arranging components horizontally, it is similar to the flow layout; however, components do not "wrap" to a new row when one row is full. By placing a number of horizontal box layouts inside a vertical box layout (or the other way around), you can give some order to a set of components in a two-dimensional area. However, since each box is laid out independently, you cannot use box layouts to arrange neighboring components both horizontally and vertically.

The Swing set also contains an *overlay layout* that lets you place components on top of each other. This layout manager is not generally useful, and we won't discuss it.

Finally, there is a *card layout* that was used in the original AWT to produce tabbed dialogs. Since Swing has a much better tabbed dialog container (which we will discuss in Volume 2), we do not cover the card layout here.

We end the discussion of layout managers by showing you how you can bypass layout management altogether and place components manually and by showing you how you can write your own layout manager.

Grid Layout

The grid layout arranges all components in rows and columns like a spreadsheet. However, for a grid layout, cells are always the same size. The calculator program in Figure 9–27 uses a grid layout to arrange the calculator buttons. When you resize the window, the buttons grow and shrink (but always remain equal in size).

Figure 9–27: A calculator

In the constructor of the grid layout object, you specify how many rows and columns you need.

```
panel.setLayout(new GridLayout(5, 4));
```

As with the border layout and flow layout managers, you can also specify the vertical and horizontal gaps you want.

```
panel.setLayout(new GridLayout(5, 4, 3, 3));
```

The last two parameters of this constructor specify the size of the horizontal and vertical gaps (in pixels) between the components.

You add the components, starting with the first entry in the first row, then the second entry in the first row, and so on.

```
panel.add(new JButton("1"));
panel.add(new JButton("2"));
```

Example 9–15 is the source listing for the calculator program. This is a regular calculator, not the "reverse Polish" variety that is so oddly popular with Java fans.

Example 9–15: Calculator.java

```java
import java.awt.*;
import java.awt.event.*;
import javax.swing.*;

class CalculatorPanel extends JPanel
    implements ActionListener
{  public CalculatorPanel()
   {  setLayout(new BorderLayout());

      display = new JTextField("0");
      display.setEditable(false);
      add(display, "North");

      JPanel p = new JPanel();
      p.setLayout(new GridLayout(4, 4));
      String buttons = "789/456*123-0.=+";
      for (int i = 0; i < buttons.length(); i++)
         addButton(p, buttons.substring(i, i + 1));
      add(p, "Center");
   }

   private void addButton(Container c, String s)
   {  JButton b = new JButton(s);
      c.add(b);
      b.addActionListener(this);
   }

   public void actionPerformed(ActionEvent evt)
   {  String s = evt.getActionCommand();
      if ('0' <= s.charAt(0) && s.charAt(0) <= '9'
         || s.equals("."))
      {  if (start) display.setText(s);
         else display.setText(display.getText() + s);
         start = false;
      }
      else
      {  if (start)
         {  if (s.equals("-"))
            { display.setText(s); start = false; }
            else op = s;
         }
         else
         {  double x =
               Double.parseDouble(display.getText());
            calculate(x);
            op = s;
            start = true;
```

```
                }
            }
        }

    public void calculate(double n)
    {   if (op.equals("+")) arg += n;
        else if (op.equals("-")) arg -= n;
        else if (op.equals("*")) arg *= n;
        else if (op.equals("/")) arg /= n;
        else if (op.equals("=")) arg = n;
        display.setText("" + arg);
    }

    private JTextField display;
    private double arg = 0;
    private String op = "=";
    private boolean start = true;
}

class CalculatorFrame extends JFrame
{   public CalculatorFrame()
    {   setTitle("Calculator");
        setSize(200, 200);
        addWindowListener(new WindowAdapter()
            {   public void windowClosing(WindowEvent e)
                {   System.exit(0);
                }
            } );

        Container contentPane = getContentPane();
        contentPane.add(new CalculatorPanel());
    }
}

public class Calculator
{   public static void main(String[] args)
    {   JFrame frame = new CalculatorFrame();
        frame.show();
    }
}
```

Of course, few applications have as rigid a layout as the face of a calculator. In practice, small grids (usually with just one row or one column) can be useful to organize partial areas of a window. For example, if you want to have a row of buttons with identical size, then you can put the buttons inside a panel that is governed by a grid layout with a single row. (You will need to set the gap size so that the buttons have some space between them.) But, you will often find it inconvenient that each component in the grid is stretched to fill the entire cell and that all components are forced to have identical size. You can avoid these problems with the box layout that we describe next.

java.awt.GridLayout

- `GridLayout(int rows, int cols)`
  constructs a new `GridLayout`.

  | *Parameters:* | `rows` | the number of rows in the grid |
  | | `columns` | the number of columns in the grid |

- `GridLayout(int rows, int columns, int hgap, int vgap)`
  constructs a new `GridLayout` with horizontal and vertical gaps between components.

Parameters:	`rows`	the number of rows in the grid
	`columns`	the number of columns in the grid
	`hgap`	the horizontal gap to use in pixels (negative values force an overlap)
	`vgap`	the vertical gap to use in pixels (negative values force an overlap

Box Layout

The box layout lets you lay out a single row or column of components with more flexibility than the grid layout. There is even a container—the `Box` class—whose default layout manager is the `BoxLayout` (unlike the `JPanel` class whose default layout manager is the `FlowLayout`). Of course, you can also set the layout manager of a `JPanel` to the box layout, but it is simpler to just start with a `Box` container. The `Box` class also contains a number of static methods that are useful for managing box layouts.

The Box Container

To create a new container with box layout, you can simply call

```
Box b = Box.createHorizontalBox();
```

or

```
Box b = Box.createVerticalBox();
```

Then, you add components in the usual way:

```
b.add(okButton);
b.add(cancelButton);
```

In a horizontal box, the components are arranged left to right. In a vertical box, the components are arranged top to bottom. Let us look at the horizontal layout more closely. Here is in detail what the box layout manager does:

1.   It computes the height of the tallest component.
2.   It tries to grow all components vertically to that height.

3. If a component does not actually grow to that height when requested, then its y-alignment is queried by calling its `getAlignmentY` method. That method returns a floating-point number between 0 (align on top) and 1 (align on bottom). The default in the `Component` class is 0.5 (center). The value is used to align the component vertically.

4. The preferred width of each component is obtained. All preferred widths are added up.

5. If the total preferred width is less than the box width, then the components are expanded, by letting them grow, up to their maximum width. Components are then placed, from left to right, with no additional space between them. If the total preferred width is greater than the box width, the components are shrunk, potentially down to their minimum width, but no further. If the components don't all fit at their minimum width, some of them will not be shown.

For vertical layouts, the process is analogous. Figures 9–28 and 9–29 show a horizontal and vertical box, each filled with labels, text fields, and buttons. The program in Example 9–16 lets you toggle between horizontal and vertical boxes. Experiment by resizing the frame to see how the components are arranged inside the box. Note that the text fields have an "infinite" maximum width (actually, `Integer.MAX_VALUE`) that makes them fill all available horizontal space.

![BoxLayoutTest window showing Name and Password text fields with an Ok button, and radio buttons for Horizontal, Vertical, and a checkbox for Struts and Glue]

Figure 9–28: Horizontal box layout

Fillers

By default, there is no space between the components in a box layout. (Unlike the flow layout, the box layout does not have a notion of gaps between components.) To space the components out, you add invisible *fillers*. There are three kinds of fillers:

*   Struts
*   Rigid Areas
*   Glue

Figure 9–29: Vertical box layout

A strut simply adds some space between components. For example, here is how you can add five pixels of space between two buttons in a horizontal box:

```
b.add(okButton);
b.add(Box.createHorizontalStrut(5));
b.add(cancelButton);
```

You add a horizontal strut into a horizontal box, or a vertical strut into a vertical box to add space between components. You can also add a vertical strut into a horizontal box, but that does not affect the horizontal layout. Instead, it sets the minimum height of the box.

The rigid area filler is similar to a pair of struts. It separates adjacent components but also adds a height or width minimum in the other direction. For example,

```
b.add(Box.createRigidArea(new Dimension(5, 20));
```

adds an invisible area with minimum, preferred, and maximum width of 5 pixels and height of 20 pixels, and centered alignment. If added into a horizontal box, it acts like a strut of width 5 and also forces the minimum height of the box to be 20 pixels.

By adding struts, you separate adjacent components by a fixed amount. Adding glue has the opposite effect—it separates components *as much as possible*. The (invisible) glue grows as much as possible, pushing the components away from each other. (We don't know why the designers of the box layout came up with the name "glue"—"spring" would have been a more appropriate name.)

For example, here is how you space out two buttons in a box as much as possible:

```
b.add(okButton);
b.add(Box.createGlue());
b.add(cancelButton);
```

If the box contains no other components, then the okButton is moved all the way to the left and the cancelButton is moved all the way to the right.

Figure 9–30 shows a vertical box with a strut after the first text field and with glue after the second text field. The effect is to space out the two text fields

by a fixed amount and to push the Ok button all the way to the bottom of
the component.

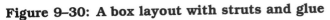

Figure 9–30: A box layout with struts and glue

Example 9–16: BoxLayoutTest.java

```
import java.awt.*;
import java.awt.event.*;
import javax.swing.*;

public class BoxLayoutTest extends JFrame
    implements ActionListener
{   public BoxLayoutTest()
    {   setTitle("BoxLayoutTest");
        setSize(300, 200);
        addWindowListener(new WindowAdapter()
        {   public void windowClosing(WindowEvent e)
            {   System.exit(0);
            }
        } );

        horizontalBox = createBox(true, false);
        verticalBox = createBox(false, false);
        horizontalStrutsAndGlueBox = createBox(true, true);
        verticalStrutsAndGlueBox = createBox(false, true);

        JPanel panel = new JPanel();
        panel.setLayout(new GridLayout(3, 1));
        ButtonGroup directionGroup = new ButtonGroup();

        horizontalButton = addRadioButton(panel,
```

```
          directionGroup, "Horizontal", true);
      verticalButton = addRadioButton(panel,
          directionGroup, "Vertical", false);
      strutsAndGlueCheckBox = addCheckBox(panel,
          "Struts and Glue");

      Container contentPane = getContentPane();
      contentPane.add(panel, "South");
      contentPane.add(horizontalBox, "Center");
      currentBox = horizontalBox;
   }

   public Box createBox(boolean horizontal,
      boolean strutsAndGlue)
   {  Box b;
      if (horizontal)
          b = Box.createHorizontalBox();
      else
          b = Box.createVerticalBox();

      b.add(new JLabel("Name"));
      b.add(new JTextField());

      if (strutsAndGlue)
          if (horizontal)
             b.add(Box.createHorizontalStrut(5));
          else
             b.add(Box.createVerticalStrut(5));

      b.add(new JLabel("Password"));
      b.add(new JTextField());

      if (strutsAndGlue)
          b.add(Box.createGlue());

      b.add(new JButton("Ok"));

      return b;
   }

   public JRadioButton addRadioButton(JPanel p,
      ButtonGroup g, String name, boolean selected)
   {  JRadioButton button
          = new JRadioButton(name, selected);
      button.addActionListener(this);
      g.add(button);
      p.add(button);
      return button;
   }

   public JCheckBox addCheckBox(JPanel p, String name)
   {  JCheckBox checkBox = new JCheckBox(name);
```

```
        checkBox.addActionListener(this);
        p.add(checkBox);
        return checkBox;
    }

    public void actionPerformed(ActionEvent evt)
    {   Container contentPane = getContentPane();
        contentPane.remove(currentBox);

        if (horizontalButton.isSelected())
        {   if (strutsAndGlueCheckBox.isSelected())
                currentBox = horizontalStrutsAndGlueBox;
            else
                currentBox = horizontalBox;
        }
        else
        {   if (strutsAndGlueCheckBox.isSelected())
                currentBox = verticalStrutsAndGlueBox;
            else
                currentBox = verticalBox;
        }

        contentPane.add(currentBox, "Center");
        contentPane.validate(); // force layout
        repaint();
    }

    public static void main(String[] args)
    {   Frame f = new BoxLayoutTest();
        f.show();
    }

    private Box horizontalBox;
    private Box verticalBox;
    private Box horizontalStrutsAndGlueBox;
    private Box verticalStrutsAndGlueBox;
    private Box currentBox;

    private JCheckBox strutsAndGlueCheckBox;
    private JRadioButton horizontalButton;
    private JRadioButton verticalButton;
}
```

`javax.swing.Box`

- `static Box createHorizontalBox()`

- `static Box createVerticalBox()`

  create a container that arranges its contents horizontally or vertically.

- `static Component createHorizontalGlue()`

- `static Component createVerticalGlue()`
- `static Component createGlue()`

  create an invisible component that can expand infinitely horizontally, vertically, or in both directions.

- `static Component createHorizontalStrut(int width)`
- `static Component createVerticalStrut(int height)`
- `static Component createRigidArea(Dimension d)`

  create an invisible component with fixed width, fixed height, or fixed width and height.

`java.awt.Component`

- `float getAlignmentX()`
- `float getAlignmentY()`

  return the alignment along the x or y axis, a value between 0 and 1. 0 denotes alignment on top or left, 0.5 is centered, 1 is aligned on bottom or right.

Grid Bag Layout

The grid bag layout is the mother of all layout managers. You can think of a grid bag layout as a grid layout without the limitations. In a grid bag layout, the rows and columns can have variable sizes. You can join adjacent cells to make room for larger components. (Many word processors, as well as HTML, have the same capability when editing tables: you start out with a grid and then can merge adjacent cells if need be.) The components need not fill the entire cell area, and you can specify their alignment within cells.

Fair warning: using grid bag layouts can be incredibly complex. The payoff is that they have the most flexibility and will work in the widest variety of situations. Keep in mind that the purpose of layout managers is to keep the arrangement of the components reasonable under different font sizes and operating systems, so it is not surprising that you need to work somewhat harder than when you design a layout just for one environment.

Consider the font selection dialog of Figure 9–31. It consists of the following components:

- A list box to specify the font style
- Two check boxes to select bold and italic
- A text field for the font size
- A label for that text box
- A text field at the bottom for the sample string

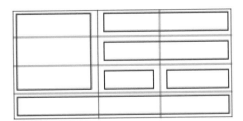

Figure 9–31: Font dialog box

Now, chop up the dialog box into a 4 × 3 grid of cells, as shown in Figure 9–32. As you can see, the list box spans three rows, each check box spans two columns, and the text field at the bottom spans three columns.

Figure 9-32: Dialog box grid used in design

To describe the layout to the grid bag manager, you must go through the following convoluted procedure.

- Create an object of type GridBagLayout. You don't tell it how many rows and columns the underlying grid has. Instead, the layout manager will try to guess it from the information you give it later.

- Set this GridBagLayout object to be the layout manager for the component.

- Create an object of type GridBagConstraints. The GridBagConstraints object will specify how the components are laid out within the grid bag.

- For *each component*, fill in the GridBagConstraints object. Then (finally), add the component with the constraints by using the call:

    ```
    add(component, constraints);
    ```

Here's an example of the code needed. (We will go over the various constraints in more detail in the sections that follow—so don't worry if you don't know what some of the constraints do.)

```
GridBagLayout layout = new GridBagLayout();
panel.setLayout(layout);
GridBagConstraints constraints = new GridBagConstraints();
```

```
constraints.weightx = 100;
constraints.weighty = 100;
constraints.gridx = 0;
constraints.gridy = 0;
constraints.gridwidth = 1;
constraints.gridheight = 3;
JList style = new JList();
panel.add(style, constraints);
```

It is obviously best to write a small helper function for this kind of repetitive code—see the listing in Example 9–14 for an example of one.

The trick is knowing how to set the state of the GridBagConstraints object. We will go over the most important constraints for using this object in the sections that follow.

The gridx, gridy, gridwidth, and gridheight *Parameters*

These constraints define where the component is located in the grid. The gridx and gridy values specify the column and row positions of the upper-left corner of the component to be added. The gridwidth and gridheight values determine how many columns and rows the component occupies.

Weight Fields

You always need to set the *weight* fields (weightx and weighty) for each area in a grid bag layout. If you set the weight to 0, then the area never grows or shrinks beyond its initial size in that direction. In the grid bag layout for Figure 9–31, we set the weighty field of the text field at the bottom to be 0. This allows the bottom field to remain a constant height when you resize the window. On the other hand, if you set the weights for all areas to 0, the container will huddle in the center of its allotted area rather than stretching to fill it.

Note that the weights don't actually give the relative sizes of the columns. They tell what proportion of the "slack" space should be allocated to each area if the container exceeds its preferred size. This isn't particularly intuitive. We recommend that you set all weights at 100. Then, run the program and see how the layout looks. Resize the dialog to see how the rows and columns adjust. If you find that a particular row or column should not grow, set the x- or y-weights of all components in it to zero. You can tinker with other weight values, but it is usually not worth the effort.

The fill *and* anchor *Parameters*

If you don't want a component to stretch out and fill the entire area, you need to set the fill field for the layout manager. You have four possibilities for this parameter: the valid values are used in the forms GridBagConstraints.NONE, GridBagConstraints.HORIZONTAL, GridBagConstraints.VERTICAL, and GridBagConstraints.BOTH.

If the component does not fill the entire area, you can specify where in the area you want it by setting the `anchor` field. The valid values are `GridBagConstraints.CENTER` (the default), `GridBagConstraints.NORTH`, `GridBagConstraints.NORTHEAST`, `GridBagConstraints.EAST`, and so on.

Padding

You can surround a component with additional blank space by setting the `insets` field of the `GridBagLayout`. Set the `left`, `top`, `right` and `bottom` values of the `Insets` object to the amount of space that you want to have around the component. This is called the *external padding*.

The `ipadx` and `ipady` values set the *internal padding*. These values are added to the minimum width and height of the component. This ensures that the component does not shrink down to its minimum size.

We have not found these settings very useful in practice.

An Alternative Method to Specify the `gridx`, `gridy`, `gridwidth`, and `gridheight` Parameters

The AWT documentation recommends that instead of setting the `gridx` and `gridy` values to absolute positions, you set them to the constant `GridBagConstraints.RELATIVE`. Then, add the components to the grid bag layout in a standardized order, going from left to right in the first row, then moving along the next row, and so on.

You still specify the number of columns and rows spanned in the `gridwidth` and `gridheight` fields. Except, if the component extends to the *last* row or column, you aren't supposed to specify the actual number, but the constant `GridBagConstraints.REMAINDER`. This tells the layout manager that the component is the last one in its row.

This scheme does seem to work. But it sounds really goofy to hide the actual placement information from the layout manager and hope that it will rediscover it.

All this sounds like a lot of trouble and complexity. But in practice, the strategy in the sidebar makes grid bag layouts relatively trouble-free.

Recipe for making a Grid Bag Layout

Step 1. Sketch out the component layout on a piece of paper.

Step 2. Find a grid such that the small components are each contained in a cell and the larger components span multiple cells.

Step 3. Label the rows and columns of your grid with 0, 1, 2, 3, ... You can now read off the `gridx`, `gridy`, `gridwidth`, and `gridheight` values.

Step 4. For each component, ask yourself whether it needs to fill its cell horizontally or vertically. If not, how do you want it aligned? This tells you the `fill` and `anchor` parameters.

Step 5. Set all weights to 100. However, if you want a particular row or column to always stay at its default size, set the `weightx` or `weighty` to 0 in all components that belong to that row or column.

Step 6. Write the code. *Carefully* double-check your settings for the `GridBagConstraints`. One wrong constraint can ruin your whole layout.

Step 7. Compile, run, and enjoy.

Example 9–17 is the complete code to implement the font dialog example.

Example 9–17: FontDialog.java

```
import java.awt.*;
import java.awt.event.*;
import javax.swing.*;
import javax.swing.event.*;

public class FontDialog extends JFrame
    implements ActionListener, ListSelectionListener
{  public FontDialog()
   {  setTitle("FontDialog");
      setSize(300, 200);
      addWindowListener(new WindowAdapter()
      {  public void windowClosing(WindowEvent e)
         {  System.exit(0);
         }
      } );

      Container contentPane = getContentPane();
      GridBagLayout gbl = new GridBagLayout();
      contentPane.setLayout(gbl);

      style = new JList(new String[]
         {  "Serif", "SansSerif", "Monospaced",
            "Dialog", "DialogInput"
         });
      style.setSelectedIndex(0);

      bold = new JCheckBox("Bold");
      italic = new JCheckBox("Italic");
      JLabel label = new JLabel("Size: ");
      size = new JTextField("10", 2);
      sample = new JTextField();
      sample.setEditable(false);

      GridBagConstraints gbc = new GridBagConstraints();
```

```java
      gbc.fill = GridBagConstraints.BOTH;
      gbc.weightx = 0;
      gbc.weighty = 100;
      add(style, gbc, 0, 0, 1, 3);
      gbc.weightx = 100;
      gbc.fill = GridBagConstraints.NONE;
      gbc.anchor = GridBagConstraints.CENTER;
      add(bold, gbc, 1, 0, 2, 1);
      add(italic, gbc, 1, 1, 2, 1);
      add(label, gbc, 1, 2, 1, 1);
      gbc.fill = GridBagConstraints.HORIZONTAL;
      add(size, gbc, 2, 2, 1, 1);
      gbc.anchor = GridBagConstraints.SOUTH;
      gbc.weighty = 0;
      add(sample, gbc, 0, 3, 4, 1);
      sample.setText("The quick brown fox");

      bold.addActionListener(this);
      italic.addActionListener(this);
      style.addListSelectionListener(this);
      size.addActionListener(this);
   }

   public void add(Component c, GridBagConstraints gbc,
      int x, int y, int w, int h)
   {  gbc.gridx = x;
      gbc.gridy = y;
      gbc.gridwidth = w;
      gbc.gridheight = h;
      getContentPane().add(c, gbc);
   }

   public void valueChanged(ListSelectionEvent evt)
   {  updateFont();
   }

   public void actionPerformed(ActionEvent evt)
   {  updateFont();
   }

   public void updateFont()
   {  Font font =
         new Font((String)style.getSelectedValue(),
            (bold.isSelected() ? Font.BOLD : 0)
               + (italic.isSelected() ? Font.ITALIC : 0),
            Integer.parseInt(size.getText()));
      sample.setFont(font);
      repaint();
   }
```

```
public static void main(String[] args)
{   Frame f = new FontDialog();
    f.show();
}

private JList style;
private JCheckBox bold;
private JCheckBox italic;
private JTextField size;
private JTextField sample;
}
```

 java.awt.GridBagConstraints

- `int gridx, gridy`

  indicates the starting column and row of cell.

- `int gridwidth, gridheight`

  indicates the column and row extent of cell.

- `double weightx, weighty`

  indicates the capacity of cell to grow.

- `int anchor`

  indicates the alignment of the component inside the cell, one of CENTER, NORTH, NORTHEAST, EAST, SOUTHEAST, SOUTH, SOUTHWEST, WEST, and NORTHWEST.

- `int fill`

  indicates the fill behavior of the component inside the cell, one of NONE, BOTH, HORIZONTAL, or VERTICAL.

- `int ipadx, ipady`

  indicates the "internal" padding around the component.

- `Insets insets`

  indicates the "external" padding along the cell boundaries.

- `GridBagConstraints(int gridx, int gridy, int gridwidth, int gridheight, double weightx, double weighty, int anchor, int fill, Insets insets, int ipadx, int ipady)`

  constructs a `GridBagConstraints` with all its fields specified in the arguments. Sun recommends that this constructor should only be used by automatic code generators since it makes your source code very hard to read.

Using No Layout Manager

There will be times when you don't want to bother with layout managers but just want to drop a component at a fixed location (sometimes called *absolute positioning.*) This is not a great idea for platform-independent applications, but there is nothing wrong with it for a quick prototype.

Here is what you do to place a component at a fixed location:

- Set the layout manager to null.
- Add the component you want to the container.
- Then specify the position and size that you want.

```
panel.setLayout(null);
JButton ok = new JButton("Ok");
panel.add(ok);
ok.setBounds(10, 10, 30, 15);
```

`java.awt.Component`

- void setBounds(int x, int y, int width, int height)

  moves and resizes a component.

  Parameters: x, y   the new top-left corner of the component
                width, height the new size of the component

Custom Layout Managers

In principle, it is possible to design your own LayoutManager class that manages components in a special way. For example, you could arrange all components in a container to form a circle (see Figure 9–33). This will almost always be a major effort and a real time sink, but as Figure 9–33 shows, the results can be quite dramatic.

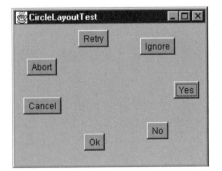

Figure 9–33: Circle layout

If you do feel you can't live without your own layout manager, here is what you do. Your own layout manager must implement the LayoutManager interface. You need to override the following five methods.

```
void addLayoutComponent(String s, Component c);
void removeLayoutComponent(Component c);
```

```
Dimension preferredLayoutSize(Container parent);
Dimension minimumLayoutSize(Container parent);
void layoutContainer(Container parent);
```

The first two functions are called when a component is added or removed. If
you don't keep any additional information about the components, you can make
them do nothing. The next two functions compute the space required for the
minimum and the preferred layout of the components. These are usually the
same quantity. The fifth function does the actual work and invokes reshape on
all components.

NOTE: The AWT has a second interface called LayoutManager2 with 10 methods to
implement rather than 5. The main point of the LayoutManager2 interface is to allow
the user to use the add method with constraints. For example, the BorderLayout
and GridBagLayout implement the LayoutManager2 interface.

Example 9–18 is a simple implementation of the CircleLayout manager,
which, amazingly and uselessly enough, lays out the components along an
ellipse inside the parent.

Example 9–18: CircleLayoutTest.java

```java
import java.awt.*;
import java.awt.event.*;
import javax.swing.*;

class CircleLayoutFrame extends JFrame
{  public CircleLayoutFrame()
   {  setTitle("CircleLayoutTest");
      setSize(300, 300);
      addWindowListener(new WindowAdapter()
      {  public void windowClosing(WindowEvent e)
         {  System.exit(0);
         }
      } );

      getContentPane().setLayout(new CircleLayout());
      getContentPane().add(new Button("Yes"));
      getContentPane().add(new Button("No"));
      getContentPane().add(new Button("Ok"));
      getContentPane().add(new Button("Cancel"));
      getContentPane().add(new Button("Abort"));
      getContentPane().add(new Button("Retry"));
      getContentPane().add(new Button("Ignore"));
   }
```

```
}

class CircleLayout implements LayoutManager
{   public void addLayoutComponent(String name,
        Component comp)
    {}

    public void removeLayoutComponent(Component comp)
    {}

    public void setSizes(Container parent)
    {   if (sizesSet) return;
        int n = parent.getComponentCount();

        preferredWidth = 0;
        preferredHeight = 0;
        minWidth = 0;
        minHeight = 0;
        maxComponentWidth = 0;
        maxComponentHeight = 0;

        for (int i = 0; i < n; i++)
        {   Component c = parent.getComponent(i);
            if (c.isVisible()) {
            Dimension d = c.getPreferredSize();
            maxComponentWidth = Math.max(maxComponentWidth,
                d.width);
            maxComponentHeight = Math.max(maxComponentWidth,
                d.height);
            preferredHeight += d.height;
            }
        }
        preferredHeight += maxComponentHeight;
        preferredWidth = 2 * maxComponentWidth;
        minHeight = preferredHeight;
        minWidth = preferredWidth;
        sizesSet = true;
    }

    public Dimension preferredLayoutSize(Container parent)
    {   Dimension dim = new Dimension(0, 0);
        setSizes(parent);
        Insets insets = parent.getInsets();
        dim.width = preferredWidth + insets.left
            + insets.right;
        dim.height = preferredHeight + insets.top
            + insets.bottom;
        return dim;
```

```
        }

        public Dimension minimumLayoutSize(Container parent)
        {   Dimension dim = new Dimension(0, 0);
            setSizes(parent);
            Insets insets = parent.getInsets();
            dim.width = minWidth + insets.left + insets.right;
            dim.height = minHeight + insets.top + insets.bottom;
            return dim;
        }

        public void layoutContainer(Container parent)
        {   Insets insets = parent.getInsets();
            int containerWidth = parent.getSize().width
                - insets.left - insets.right;
            int containerHeight = parent.getSize().height
                - insets.top - insets.bottom;
            int xradius = (containerWidth - maxComponentWidth)
                / 2;
            int yradius = (containerHeight - maxComponentHeight)
                / 2;

            setSizes(parent);
            int xcenter = insets.left + containerWidth / 2;
            int ycenter = insets.top + containerHeight / 2;

            int n = parent.getComponentCount();
            for (int i = 0; i < n; i++)
            {   Component c = parent.getComponent(i);
                if (c.isVisible())
                {   Dimension d = c.getPreferredSize();
                    double angle = 2 * Math.PI * i / n;
                    int x = xcenter
                        + (int)(Math.cos(angle) * xradius);
                    int y = ycenter
                        + (int)(Math.sin(angle) * yradius);

                    c.setBounds(x - d.width / 2, y - d.width / 2,
                        d.width, d.height);
                }
            }

        }

    private int minWidth = 0;
    private int minHeight = 0;
    private int preferredWidth = 0, preferredHeight = 0;
    private boolean sizesSet = false;
    private int maxComponentWidth = 0;
```

```
    private int maxComponentHeight = 0;
}

public class CircleLayoutTest {
    public static void main(String[] args)
    {   JFrame f = new CircleLayoutFrame();
        f.show();
    }
}
```

`java.awt.LayoutManager`

- void addLayoutComponent(String name, Component comp)

  adds a component to the layout.

  Parameters: name   an identifier for the component placement

  comp   the component to be added

- void removeLayoutComponent(Component comp)

  removes a component from the layout.

  Parameters: comp   the component to be removed

- Dimension preferredLayoutSize(Container parent)

  returns the preferred size dimensions for the container under this layout.

  Parameters: parent   the container whose components are being
  laid out

- Dimension minimumLayoutSize(Container parent)

  returns the minimum size dimensions for the container under this layout.

  Parameters: parent   the container whose components are being
  laid out

- void layoutContainer(Container parent)

  lays out the components in a container.

  Parameters: parent   the container whose components are being
  laid out

Traversal Order

When you add many components into a window, you need to give some thought to the *traversal order* (the tab index property, for VB users). When a window is first displayed, the first component in the traversal order has the keyboard focus. Each time the user presses the TAB key, the next component gains focus. (Recall that a component that has the keyboard focus can be manipulated with the keyboard. For example, a button can be "clicked" with the space bar when it has focus.) You may not personally care about using the TAB key to navigate through a set of controls, but there are plenty of users who do. Among them are the mouse haters and those who cannot use a mouse, perhaps because of a handicap or because they are navigating the user interface by voice. For that reason, you do need to know how the Swing set handles traversal order.

The Swing set attempts to traverse your components in a reasonable way, first left-to-right and then top-to-bottom. For example, in the font dialog example, the components are traversed in the following order:

1. List box

2. First check box

3. Second check box

4. First text field (the label is skipped)

5. Second text field (even though it is not editable)

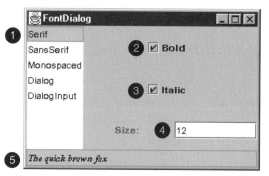

Figure 9–34: Geometric traversal order

NOTE: In the old AWT, the traversal order was determined by the order in which you inserted components into a container. In Swing, the insertion order does not matter—only the layout of the components is considered.

The situation is more complex if your container contains other containers. When the focus is given to another container, it automatically ends up with the top-left component in that container and then it traverses all other components in that container. Then, the focus is given to the component following the container.

You can use this to your advantage by grouping related elements in another container such as a panel.

Note that some components do not get focus, such as the label in the FontDialog example. In particular, all components whose isFocusTraversable method returns false cannot receive focus.

If you are not happy with the default traversal order, you have two remedies.

You can transfer the focus explicitly to a particular component, with the `requestFocus` method:

```
okButton.requestFocus();
```

This only works in reaction to a particular event. It has no permanent effect on the traversal order.

Or, you can change the traversal order with the `setNextFocusableComponent` method of the `JComponent` class. For example, suppose you want to skip from the style list directly to the size field. Then, use the command

```
style.setNextFocusableComponent(size);
```

Now the traversal order is

1. List box

2. First text field

3. First check box

4. Second check box

5. Second text field

That is, the geometric order is preserved except for the transition that you set with the `setNextFocusableComponent` method.

`java.awt.Component`

- `void requestFocus()`

    requests that this component have the input focus.

`javax.swing.JComponent`

- `void setNextFocusableComponent(Component c)`

    makes c the next component to get the focus after this one in the traversal order, overriding the default traversal order.

Menus

We started this chapter by introducing the most common components that you might want to place into a window, such as various kinds of buttons, text fields, and choice lists. You then learned how to arrange these user interface components inside their container, by using layout managers. Swing also supports another type of user-interface elements, the pull-down menus that are familiar from Windows and Motif applications. You don't need a layout manager to place menus. A *menu bar* on top of the window contains the names of the pull-down menus. Clicking on a name opens the menu containing *menu items* and *submenus*. When the user clicks on a menu item, all menus are closed and a message is sent to the program. Figure 9–35 shows a typical menu with a submenu.

Figure 9–35: A menu with a submenu

NOTE: Another popular user interface element for selecting commands is a *toolbar*. The JToolBar class implements a dockable toolbar—see Volume 2 for details.

Building Menus

Building menus is straightforward. You create a menu bar.:

```
JMenuBar menuBar = new JMenuBar();
```

A menu bar is just a component that you can add anywhere you like. Normally, you want it to appear at the top of a frame. You can add it there with the setJMenuBar method:

```
frame.setJMenuBar(menuBar);
```

For each menu, you create a menu object:

```
JMenu editMenu = new JMenu("Edit");
```

You add menu items, separators, and submenus to the menu object:

```
JMenuItem pasteItem = new JMenuItem("Paste");
editMenu.add(pasteItem);
editMenu.addSeparator();
JMenu optionsMenu = . . .; // a submenu
editMenu.add(optionsMenu);
. . .
```

You add the top-level menus to the menu bar:

```
menuBar.addMenu(editMenu);
```

When the user selects a menu, an action event is triggered. You need to install an action event listener for each menu item.

```
pasteItem.addActionListener(this);
```

Unfortunately, adding menu items and listeners is straightforward but somewhat tedious. Here is some code to build up a typical menu.

```
JMenu menu = new JMenu("Edit");
item = new JMenuItem("Cut");
item.addActionListener(this);
menu.add(item);
item = new JMenuItem("Copy");
item.addActionListener(this);
menu.add(item);
item = new JMenuItem("Paste");
item.addActionListener(this);
menu.add(item);
menuBar.add(menu);
```

We wrote a procedure called `makeMenu` that takes the drudgery out of making menus. This procedure takes three parameters. The first parameter is either a string or a menu. If it is a string, `makeMenu` makes a menu with that title. The second parameter is an array of items, each of which is a string, a menu item, or `null`. The `makeMenu` procedure makes a menu item out of each string and a separator out of each `null`, then adds all items and separators to the menu. The third parameter is the listener for the menu items. (We assume that all menu items have the same listener.) Here is a typical call to `makeMenu` that adds a menu with three items, a separator, and a submenu to the menu bar. It would take dozens of commands to build this menu structure by hand.

```
menuBar.add(makeMenu("Edit",
        new Object[]
        {   "Cut",
            "Copy",
            "Paste",
            null,
            makeMenu("Options",
                new Object[]
                {   "Insert",
                    "Overtype",
                    "Read only"
                },
                this)
        },
        this));
```

Here's the source code for the `makeMenu` procedure which can easily be added to any program that requires a sophisticated menuing system.

```
public static JMenu makeMenu(Object parent,
```

```
        Object[] items, Object target)
{   JMenu m = null;
    if (parent instanceof JMenu)
        m = (JMenu)parent;
    else if (parent instanceof String)
        m = new JMenu((String)parent);
    else
        return null;

    for (int i = 0; i < items.length; i++)
    {   if (items[i] == null)
            m.addSeparator();
        else
            m.add(makeMenuItem(items[i], target));
    }

    return m;
}

public static JMenuItem makeMenuItem(Object item, Object target)
{   JMenuItem r = null;
    if (item instanceof String)
        r = new JMenuItem((String)item);
    else if (item instanceof JMenuItem)
        r = (JMenuItem)item;
    else return null;

    if (target instanceof ActionListener)
        r.addActionListener((ActionListener)target);
    return r;
}
```

NOTE: In Windows programs, menus are generally defined in an external resource file and tied to the application with resource identifiers. It is possible to build menus programmatically, but it is not commonly done except in VB. In Java, menus are still usually built inside the program because in Java, the mechanism for dealing with external resources is far more limited than it is in Windows.

NOTE: There is a convenient method JMenu.add(String s) that adds a menu item to the end of a menu, for example:

```
editMenu.add("Paste");
```

The add method returns the created menu item, so that you can capture it and then add the listener, as follows:

```
JMenuItem pasteItem = editMenu.add("Paste");
pasteItem.addActionListener(this);
```

Reacting to Menu Events

As with buttons, you catch menu selection events in the `actionPerformed` method. You can tell that an action originated from a menu by verifying, with the `instanceof` operator, that the type of the event source is a menu item using the `instanceof` operator. To find which menu item was selected, simply call the `getActionCommand` method. Here is some sample code that does this:

```
public void actionPerformed(Event evt)
{   if (evt.getSource() instanceof JMenuItem)
        String arg = evt.getActionCommand();
        if (arg.equals("Open")) . . .
        else if (arg.equals("Save")) . . .
            . . .
    }
}
```

NOTE: In Chapter 8, you saw another method for adding menu items to a menu, using `Action` objects. You define a class that implements the `Action` interface, usually by extending the `AbstractAction` convenience class. You specify the menu item label in the constructor of the `AbstractAction` object, and you override the `actionPerformed` method to hold the menu action handler. You then call the `add(Action)` method of the `JMenu` class. A menu item is then added to the menu, and the action object becomes its listener. For example,

```
Action openAction = new AbstractAction("Open")
    {   public void actionPerformed(ActionEvent evt)
        {   // open handler goes here
        }
    };
menu.add(openAction);
```

As you saw in Chapter 8, this technique is particularly useful if you want to attach the same action to a keystroke or a button.

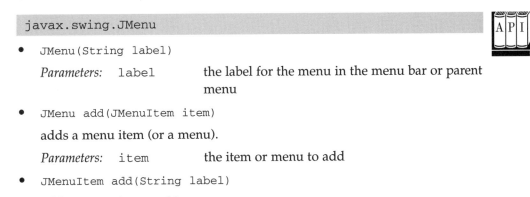

`javax.swing.JMenu`

- `JMenu(String label)`

    Parameters: `label`   the label for the menu in the menu bar or parent menu

- `JMenu add(JMenuItem item)`

    adds a menu item (or a menu).

    Parameters: `item`   the item or menu to add

- `JMenuItem add(String label)`

    adds a menu item to this menu.

Parameters: `label`   the label for the menu items

- `JMenuItem add(Action a)`

  adds a menu item and associates an action with it.

  Parameters: `a`   an action encapsulating a name, optional icon, and listener (see Chapter 8)

- `void addSeparator()`

  adds a separator line to the menu.

- `void insert(JMenuItem menu, int index)`

  adds a new menu item (or submenu) to the menu at a specific index.

  Parameters: `menu`   the menu to be added

                   `index`   where to add the item

- `void insertSeparator(int index)`

  adds a separator to the menu.

  Parameters: `index`   where to add the separator

- `void remove(int index)`

  removes a specific item from the menu.

  Parameters: `index`   the position of the item to remove

- `void remove(JMenuItem item)`

  removes a specific item from the menu.

  Parameters: `item`   the item to remove

`javax.swing.JMenuItem`

- `JMenuItem(String label)`

  Parameters: `label`   the label for this menu item

`javax.swing.JFrame`

- `void setJMenuBar(JMenuBar menubar)`

  sets the menu bar for this frame.

Icons in Menu Items

Menu items are very similar to buttons. In fact, the `JMenuItem` class extends the `AbstractButton` class. Just like buttons, menus can have just a string label, just an icon, or both. You can specify the icon either with the `JMenuItem(String, Icon)` or `JMenuItem(Icon)` constructor, or you can set it with the `setIcon` method that the `JMenuItem` class inherits from the `AbstractButton` class.

Here is an example:

```
JMenuItem cutItem = new JMenuItem("Cut", new ImageIcon("cut.gif"));
```

Figure 9–36 shows a menu with icons next to several menu items. As you can see, by default, the menu items are placed to the right of the menu text. If you prefer the icon to be placed on the left, call the `setHorizontalTextPosition` method that the `JMenuItem` class inherits from the `AbstractButton` class. For example, the call

```
cutItem.setHorizontalTextPosition(SwingConstants.RIGHT);
```

moves the menu item text to the right of the icon.

Figure 9–36: Icons in menu items

`javax.swing.JMenuItem`

- `JMenuItem(String label, Icon icon)`

  Parameters: `label`   the label for the menu item

              `icon`   the icon for the menu item

`javax.swing.AbstractButton`

- `void setHorizontalTextPosition(int pos)`

  sets the horizontal position of the text relative to the icon.

  Parameters: `pos`   `SwingConstants.RIGHT` (text is to the right of icon), `SwingConstants.LEFT` or `SwingConstants.CENTER`

Check Box and Radio Button Menu Items

Check box and *radio button* menu items display a check box or radio button next to the name (see Figure 9–37). When the user selects the menu item, the item automatically toggles between checked and unchecked.

Apart from the button decoration, you treat these menu items just as you would any others. For example, here is how you create a check box menu item.

```
JCheckBoxMenuItem readonlyItem
    = new JCheckBoxMenuItem("Read-only");
optionsMenu.add(readonlyItem);
```

The radio button menu items work just like regular radio buttons. You must add them to a button group. When one of the buttons in a group is selected, all others are automatically deselected.

```
ButtonGroup group = new ButtonGroup();
JRadioButtonMenuItem insertItem
    = new JRadioButtonMenuItem("Insert");
insertItem.setSelected(true);
JRadioButtonMenuItem overtypeItem
    = new JRadioButtonMenuItem("Overtype");
group.add(insertItem);
group.add(overtypeItem);
optionsMenu.add(insertItem);
optionsMenu.add(overtypeItem);
```

With these menu items, you don't usually want to be notified at the exact moment the user selects the item. Instead, you can simply use the `isSelected` method to test the current state of the menu item. (Of course, that means that you should keep a reference to the menu item stored in an instance variable.) Use the `setSelected` method to set the state.

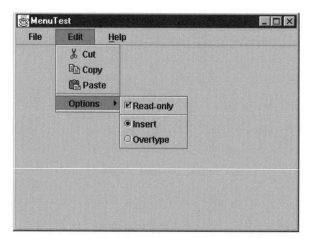

Figure 9–37: A checked menu item and menu items with radio buttons

---

`javax.swing.JCheckBoxMenuItem`

- `JCheckBoxMenuItem(String label)`

  constructs the check box menu item with the given label.

- `JCheckBoxMenuItem(String label, boolean state)`

  constructs the check box menu item with the given label and the given initial state (`true` is checked).

`javax.swing.JRadioButtonMenuItem`

- `JRadioButtonMenuItem(String label)`

  constructs the radio button menu item with the given label.

- `JRadioButtonMenuItem(String label, boolean state)`

  constructs the radio button menu item with the given label and the given initial state (`true` is checked).

`javax.swing.AbstractButton`

- `boolean isSelected()`

  returns the check state of this item (`true` is checked).

- `void setSelected(boolean state)`

  sets the check state of this item.

Pop-up Menus

A *pop-up menu* is a menu that is not attached to a menu bar but that floats somewhere (see Figure 9–38).

Figure 9–38: A pop-up menu

You create a pop-up menu similarly to the way you create a regular menu, but a pop-up menu has no title.

```
JPopupMenu popup = new JPopupMenu();
```

You then add menu items in the usual way:

```
JMenuItem item = new JMenuItem("Cut");
item.addActionListener(this);
popup.add(item);
```

Unlike the regular menu bar that is always shown at the top of the frame, you must explicitly display a pop-up menu by using the show method. You specify the parent component and the location of the pop-up, using the coordinate system of the parent. For example:

```
popup.show(panel, x, y);
```

Usually you write code to pop up a menu when the user clicks a particular mouse button, the so-called *pop-up trigger*. In Windows, the pop-up trigger is the nonprimary (usually, the right) mouse button. To pop up a menu when the user clicks the pop-up trigger:

- Install a mouse listener.

- Add code like the following to the mouse event handler:

```
public void mouseReleased(MouseEvent evt)
{  if (evt.isPopupTrigger())
       popup.show(evt.getComponent(),
           evt.getX(), evt.getY());
}
```

This code will show the pop-up menu at the mouse location where the user clicked the pop-up trigger.

> CAUTION: With our version of the JDK, the isPopupTrigger method only works correctly in the mouseReleased method, not in the mousePressed or mouseClicked method.

 `javax.swing.JPopupMenu`

- `void show(Component c, int x, int y)`

  shows the popup menu.

Parameters:	c	The component over which the popup menu is to appear
	x, y	the coordinates (in the coordinate space of c) of the top-left corner of the popup menu

497

`java.awt.event.MouseEvent`

- `boolean isPopupTrigger()`

    returns `true` if this mouse event is the pop-up-menu trigger.

Keyboard Mnemonics and Accelerators

It is a real convenience for the experienced user to select menu items by *keyboard mnemonics*. In Java, you can specify keyboard mnemonics for menu items by specifying a mnemonic letter in the menu item constructor:

```
JMenuItem cutItem = new JMenuItem("Cut", 'T');
```

The keyboard mnemonic is displayed automatically in the menu, by underlining the mnemonic letter (see Figure 9–39). For example, in the item defined in the last example, the label will be displayed as "Cut" with an underlined letter "t". When the menu is displayed, the user just needs to hit the "T" key, and the menu item is selected. (If the mnemonic letter is not part of the menu string, then typing it still selects the item, but the mnemonic is not displayed in the menu. Naturally, such invisible mnemonics are of dubious utility.)

Unfortunately, you can only supply a mnemonic letter in the constructor of a menu item, not in the constructor for a menu. Instead, to attach a mnemonic to a menu, you need to call the `setMnemonic` method:

```
JMenu helpMenu = new JMenu("Help");
helpMenu.setMnemonic('H');
```

To select a top-level menu from the menu bar, you hit ALT+ the mnemonic letter. For example, you hit ALT+H to select the Help menu from the menu bar.

Figure 9–39: Keyboard mnemonics

Keyboard mnemonics let you select a submenu or menu item from the currently open menu. In contrast, *accelerators* are keyboard shortcuts that let you select menu items without ever opening a menu. For example, many programs attach the accelerators CTRL+O and CTRL+S to the Open and Save items in the File menu. You use the `setAccelerator` method to attach an accelerator key to a menu item. The `setAccelerator` method takes an object of type `Keystroke`. For example, the following call attaches the accelerator CTRL+O to the `openItem` menu item.

```
openItem.setAccelerator(KeyStroke.getKeyStroke(KeyEvent.VK_O,
    InputEvent.CTRL_MASK));
```

When the user presses the accelerator key combination, this automatically selects the menu option and fires an action event, as if the user had selected the menu option manually.

The accelerator keys are displayed in the menu (see Figure 9–40).

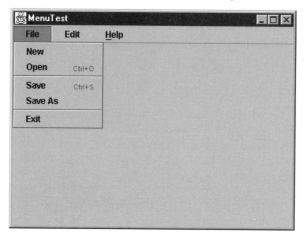

Figure 9–40: Accelerators

You can only attach accelelerators to menu items, not to menus. Accelerator keys merely accelerate menu item selection and the firing of action events. Menus do not have any action events associated with them. (One might perhaps want to accelerate the opening of a submenu, but this is not possible in Swing.)

NOTE: Under Windows, ALT+F4 closes a window. But this is not an accelerator that was programmed in Java. It is a shortcut defined by the operating system. This key combination will always trigger the `WindowClosing` event for the active window regardless of whether there is a Close item on the menu.

`javax.swing.JMenuItem`

- `JMenuItem(String label, int mnemonic)`

  Parameters: `label`   the label for this menu item

                    `mnemonic`   the mnemonic character for the item; this character will be underlined in the label

- `void setAccelerator(KeyStroke k)`

  sets the keystroke k as accelerator for this menu item. The accelerator key is displayed next to the label.

`javax.swing.AbstractButton`

- `void setMnemonic(char mnemonic)`

  sets the mnemonic character for the button. This character will be underlined in the label. (Note that `JMenuItem` and `JMenu` extend `AbstractButton`.)

  Parameters: `mnemonic`   the mnemonic character for the button

Enabling and Disabling Menu Items

Occasionally, a particular menu item should only be selected in certain contexts. For example, when a document is opened for reading only, then the Save and Save As menu items are not meaningful. Of course, we could remove those items from the menu with the `JMenu.remove` method, but users would react with some surprise to menus whose contents keeps changing. Instead, it is better to deactivate the menu items that lead to temporarily inappropriate commands. A deactivated menu item is shown in gray, and it cannot be selected (see Figure 9–41).

Figure 9–41: Disabled menu items

To enable or disable a menu item, use the `setEnabled` method:

```
saveItem.setEnabled(false);
```

There are two strategies for enabling and disabling menu items. Each time that circumstances change, you can call `setEnabled` on the relevant menu items. For example, as soon as a document has been set to read-only mode, you can locate the Save and Save As menu items and disable them. However, if you use that strategy, you may find that your code gets cluttered up with menu management in many places. A smarter strategy is not to worry about the menu item states in the remainder of the program and to set them *just before displaying the menu*. To do this, you must register a listener for the "menu selected" event. The `javax.swing.event` package defines a `MenuListener` interface with three methods:

```
void menuSelected(MenuEvent evt)
void menuDeselected(MenuEvent evt)
void menuCanceled(MenuEvent evt)
```

The `menuSelected` method is called *before* the menu is displayed. It is therefore the perfect place to disable or enable menu items. The following code shows how to disable the Save and Save As menu items whenever the Read Only check box menu item is selected:

```
public void menuSelected(MenuEvent evt)
{   saveItem.setEnabled(!readonlyItem.isSelected());
    saveAsItem.setEnabled(!readonlyItem.isSelected());
}
```

The `menuDeselected` method is called after the menu is again removed from the display. The `menuCanceled` method is called if the menu selection process is canceled, for example, by clicking with the mouse somewhere outside the menu. We are not interested in either of these two events, but there is no `MenuAdapter` class that allows us to override a single method, so we must define the latter two to do nothing.

`javax.swing.JMenuItem`

- `void setEnabled(boolean b)`

  enables or disables the menu item.

`javax.swing.event.MenuListener`

- `void menuSelected(MenuEvent e)`

  is called when the menu has been selected, before it is opened.

- `void menuDeselected(MenuEvent e)`

  is called when the menu has been deselected, after it has been closed.

- `void menuCanceled(MenuEvent e)`

  is called when the menu has been canceled, for example, by clicking outside the menu.

Example 9–19 is a sample program that generates a set of menus. It shows all the features that we saw in this section: nested menus, disabled menu items, check box and radio button menu items, a pop-up menu, and keyboard mnemonics and accelerators.

Example 9–19: MenuTest.java

```
import java.awt.*;
import java.awt.event.*;
import javax.swing.*;
import javax.swing.event.*;

public class MenuTest extends JFrame
    implements ActionListener, MenuListener
{   public MenuTest()
    {   setTitle("MenuTest");
        setSize(400, 300);
        addWindowListener(new WindowAdapter()
            {   public void windowClosing(WindowEvent e)
                {   System.exit(0);
                }
            } );

        JMenuBar mbar = new JMenuBar();
        setJMenuBar(mbar);

        // demonstrate enabled/disabled items

        JMenu fileMenu = new JMenu("File");
        fileMenu.addMenuListener(this);

        // demonstrate accelerators

        JMenuItem openItem = new JMenuItem("Open");
        openItem.setAccelerator
            (KeyStroke.getKeyStroke(KeyEvent.VK_O,
            InputEvent.CTRL_MASK));
        saveItem = new JMenuItem("Save");
        saveItem.setAccelerator
            (KeyStroke.getKeyStroke(KeyEvent.VK_S,
            InputEvent.CTRL_MASK));
        saveAsItem = new JMenuItem("Save As");

        mbar.add(makeMenu(fileMenu,
            new Object[]
            {   "New",
```

```
            openItem,
            null,
            saveItem,
            saveAsItem,
            null,
            "Exit"
        },
        this));

    // demonstrate check box and radio button menus

    readonlyItem = new JCheckBoxMenuItem("Read-only");
    ButtonGroup group = new ButtonGroup();
    JRadioButtonMenuItem insertItem
        = new JRadioButtonMenuItem("Insert");
    insertItem.setSelected(true);
    JRadioButtonMenuItem overtypeItem
        = new JRadioButtonMenuItem("Overtype");
    group.add(insertItem);
    group.add(overtypeItem);

    // demonstrate icons and nested menus

    mbar.add(makeMenu("Edit",
        new Object[]
        {   new JMenuItem("Cut",
                new ImageIcon("cut.gif")),
            new JMenuItem("Copy",
                new ImageIcon("copy.gif")),
            new JMenuItem("Paste",
                new ImageIcon("paste.gif")),
            null,
            makeMenu("Options",
                new Object[]
                {   readonlyItem,
                    null,
                    insertItem,
                    overtypeItem
                },
                this)
        },
        this));

    // demonstrate mnemonics

    JMenu helpMenu = new JMenu("Help");
    helpMenu.setMnemonic('H');

    mbar.add(makeMenu(helpMenu,
        new Object[]
        {   new JMenuItem("Index", 'I'),
```

```
              new JMenuItem("About", 'A')
        },
        this));

   // demonstrate pop-ups

   popup = makePopupMenu(
        new Object[]
        {   "Cut",
            "Copy",
            "Paste"
        },
        this);

   getContentPane().addMouseListener(new MouseAdapter()
        {   public void mouseReleased(MouseEvent evt)
            {   if (evt.isPopupTrigger())
                    popup.show(evt.getComponent(),
                        evt.getX(), evt.getY());
            }
        });
}

public void actionPerformed(ActionEvent evt)
{   String arg = evt.getActionCommand();
    System.out.println(arg);
    if(arg.equals("Exit"))
        System.exit(0);
}

public void menuSelected(MenuEvent evt)
{   saveItem.setEnabled(!readonlyItem.isSelected());
    saveAsItem.setEnabled(!readonlyItem.isSelected());
}

public void menuDeselected(MenuEvent evt)
{
}

public void menuCanceled(MenuEvent evt)
{
}

public static JMenu makeMenu(Object parent,
    Object[] items, Object target)
{   JMenu m = null;
    if (parent instanceof JMenu)
        m = (JMenu)parent;
    else if (parent instanceof String)
        m = new JMenu((String)parent);
    else
```

```
                return null;

            for (int i = 0; i < items.length; i++)
            {   if (items[i] == null)
                    m.addSeparator();
                else
                    m.add(makeMenuItem(items[i], target));
            }

            return m;
        }

        public static JMenuItem makeMenuItem(Object item,
            Object target)
        {   JMenuItem r = null;
            if (item instanceof String)
                r = new JMenuItem((String)item);
            else if (item instanceof JMenuItem)
                r = (JMenuItem)item;
            else return null;

            if (target instanceof ActionListener)
                r.addActionListener((ActionListener)target);
            return r;
        }

        public static JPopupMenu makePopupMenu
            (Object[] items, Object target)
        {   JPopupMenu m = new JPopupMenu();

            for (int i = 0; i < items.length; i++)
            {   if (items[i] == null)
                    m.addSeparator();
                else
                    m.add(makeMenuItem(items[i], target));
            }

            return m;
        }

        public static void main(String[] args)
        {   Frame f = new MenuTest();
            f.show();
        }

        private JMenuItem saveItem;
        private JMenuItem saveAsItem;
        private JCheckBoxMenuItem readonlyItem;
        private JPopupMenu popup;
}
```

Dialog Boxes

So far, all of our user interface components have appeared inside a frame window that was created in the application. This is the most common situation if you write *applets* that run inside a Web browser. But if you write applications, you usually want separate dialog boxes to pop up to give information to or get information from the user.

Just as with most windowing systems, AWT distinguishes between *modal* and *modeless* dialog boxes. A modal dialog box won't let the user interact with the remaining windows of the application until he or she deals with it. You use a modal dialog box when you need information from the user before you can proceed with execution. For example, when the user wants to read a file, a modal file dialog box is the one to pop up. The user must specify a file name before the program can begin the read operation. Only when the user closes the (modal) dialog box can the application proceed.

A modeless dialog box lets the user enter information in both the dialog box and the remainder of the application. One example of a modeless dialog is a toolbar. The toolbar can stay in place as long as needed, and the user can interact with both the application window and the toolbar as needed.

We start this section with the simplest dialogs—modal dialogs with just a single message. Swing has a convenient `JOptionPane` class that lets you put up a simple dialog without writing any special dialog box code. Next, you will see how to write more complex dialogs by implementing your own dialog windows. Finally, you will see how to transfer data from your application into a dialog and back. We conclude this section by looking at file dialogs, standard dialogs that allow a user to specify file names. File dialogs are complex, and you definitely want to be familiar with the Swing `JFileChooser` for this purpose—it would be a real challenge to write your own.

NOTE: Besides the `JFileChooser` dialog, the Swing set implements a `JColorChooser` dialog that lets a user pick a color from a spectrum of choices. We will cover this dialog in Volume 2.

Option Dialogs

The Swing set has a set of ready-made simple dialogs that suffice when you need to ask the user for a single piece of information. The `JOptionPane` has four static methods to show these simple dialogs:

`showMessageDialog`	Show a message and wait for the user to click Ok.
`showConfirmDialog`	Show a message and get a confirmation (like Ok/Cancel).

| showOptionDialog | Show a message and get a user option from a set of options. |
| showInputDialog | Show a message and get one line of user input. |

Figure 9–42 shows a typical dialog. As you can see, the dialog has the following components:

- An icon
- A message
- One or more option buttons

The input dialog has an additional field for user input. This can be a text field into which the user can type an arbitrary string, or a combo box from which the user can select one item.

The exact layout of these dialogs and the choice of icons for standard message types depend on the pluggable look and feel.

Figure 9–42: An option dialog

The icon on the left hand side depends on the *message type*. There are five message types:

```
ERROR_MESSAGE
INFORMATION_MESSAGE
WARNING_MESSAGE
QUESTION_MESSAGE
PLAIN_MESSAGE
```

The PLAIN_MESSAGE type has no icon. For each of the dialog types, there is also a method that lets you supply your own icon instead.

For each dialog type, you can specify a message. This message can be a string, an icon, a user interface component, or any other object. Here is how the message object is displayed:

String:	draw the string
Icon:	show the icon
Component:	show the component
Object[]:	Show all objects in the array, stacked on top of each other any other object: apply toString and show the resulting string

You can see these options by running the program in Example 9–20. Of course, supplying a message string is by far the most common case. Supplying a Component gives you ultimate flexibility since you can make the paintComponent method draw anything you want. Supplying an array of objects isn't all that useful since there isn't enough room in the dialog to show more than a couple of them—the dialog does not grow to accommodate all message objects.

The buttons on the bottom depend on the dialog type and the *option type*. When calling showMessageDialog and showInputDialog, you only get a standard set of buttons (Ok and Ok/Cancel, respectively). When calling showConfirmDialog, you can choose among four option types:

```
DEFAULT_OPTION
YES_NO_OPTION
YES_NO_CANCEL_OPTION
OK_CANCEL_OPTION
```

With the showOptionDialog you can specify an arbitrary set of options. You supply an array of objects for the options. Each array element is rendered as follows:

String:	make a button with the string as label
Icon:	make a button with the icon as label
Component:	show the component
any other object:	apply toString and make a button with the resulting string as label

The return values of these functions are as follows:

showMessageDialog	none
showConfirmDialog	an integer representing the chosen option
showOptionDialog	an integer representing the chosen option
showInputDialog	the string that the user supplied or selected

The showConfirmDialog and showOptionDialog return integers to indicate which button the user chose. For the option dialog, this is simply the index of the chosen option or the value CLOSED_OPTION if the user closed the dialog instead of choosing an option. For the confirmation dialog, the return value can be one of the following:

```
OK_OPTION
CANCEL_OPTION
YES_OPTION
NO_OPTION
CLOSED_OPTION
```

This all sounds like a bewildering set of choices, but in practice it is simple:

1. Choose the dialog type (message, confirmation, option or input).

2. Choose the icon (error, information, warning, question, none, or custom).

3. Choose the message (string, icon, custom component, or a stack of them).

4. For a confirmation dialog, choose the option type (default, Yes/No, Yes/No/Cancel, or Ok/Cancel).

5. For an option dialog, choose the options (strings, icons, or custom components) and the default option.

6. For an input dialog, choose between a text field and a combo box.

7. Locate the appropriate method to call in the JOptionPane API.

For example, suppose you want to show the dialog in Figure 9–42. The dialog shows a message and asks the user to confirm or cancel. Thus, it is a confirmation dialog. The icon is a warning icon. The message is a string. The option type is OK_CANCEL_OPTION. Here is the call you need to make:

```
int selection = JOptionPane.showConfirmDialog(parent,
    "Message", "Title",
    JOptionPane.OK_CANCEL_OPTION,
    JOptionPane.WARNING_MESSAGE);
if (selection == JOptionPane.OK_OPTION) . . .
```

TIP: The message string can contain newline (' \n ') characters. Such a string is displayed in multiple lines.

Figure 9–43: The OptionDialogTest program

The program in Example 9–20 lets you make these selections (see Figure 9–43). It then shows you the resulting dialog.

Example 9–20: OptionDialogTest.java

```
import java.awt.*;
import java.awt.event.*;
// import javax.swing.*;
// import javax.swing.border.*;
```

```java
import com.sun.java.swing.*;
import com.sun.java.swing.border.*;

class ButtonPanel extends JPanel
{  public ButtonPanel(String title, String[] options)
   {  setBorder(BorderFactory.createTitledBorder
         (BorderFactory.createEtchedBorder(), title));
      setLayout(new BoxLayout(this,
         BoxLayout.Y_AXIS));
      group = new ButtonGroup();

      for (int i = 0; i < options.length; i++)
      {  JRadioButton b = new JRadioButton(options[i]);
         b.setActionCommand(options[i]);
         add(b);
         group.add(b);
         b.setSelected(i == 0);
      }
   }

   String getSelection()
   {  return group.getSelection().getActionCommand();
   }

   ButtonGroup group;
}

public class OptionDialogTest extends JFrame
   implements ActionListener
{  public OptionDialogTest()
   {  setTitle("OptionDialogTest");
      setSize(600, 400);
      addWindowListener(new WindowAdapter()
      {  public void windowClosing(WindowEvent e)
         {  System.exit(0);
         }
      } );

      JPanel gridPanel = new JPanel();
      gridPanel.setLayout(new GridLayout(2, 3));

      typePanel = new ButtonPanel("Type",
         new String[]
         {  "Message",
            "Confirm",
            "Option",
            "Input"
         });

      messageTypePanel = new ButtonPanel("Message Type",
```

```
        new String[]
        {  "ERROR_MESSAGE",
           "INFORMATION_MESSAGE",
           "WARNING_MESSAGE",
           "QUESTION_MESSAGE",
           "PLAIN_MESSAGE"
        });

   messagePanel = new ButtonPanel("Message",
      new String[]
      {  "String",
         "Icon",
         "Component",
         "Other",
         "Object[]"
      });

   optionTypePanel = new ButtonPanel("Confirm",
      new String[]
      {  "DEFAULT_OPTION",
         "YES_NO_OPTION",
         "YES_NO_CANCEL_OPTION",
         "OK_CANCEL_OPTION"
      });

   optionsPanel = new ButtonPanel("Option",
      new String[]
      {  "String[]",
         "Icon[]",
         "Object[]"
      });

   inputPanel = new ButtonPanel("Input",
      new String[]
      {  "Text field",
         "Combo box"
      });

   JPanel showPanel = new JPanel();
   JButton showButton = new JButton("Show");
   showButton.addActionListener(this);
   showPanel.add(showButton);

   gridPanel.add(typePanel);
   gridPanel.add(messageTypePanel);
   gridPanel.add(messagePanel);
   gridPanel.add(optionTypePanel);
   gridPanel.add(optionsPanel);
```

```java
    gridPanel.add(inputPanel);

    Container contentPane = getContentPane();
    contentPane.add(gridPanel, "Center");
    contentPane.add(showPanel, "South");
}

public Object getMessage()
{   String s = messagePanel.getSelection();
    if (s.equals("String"))
        return messageString;
    else if (s.equals("Icon"))
        return messageIcon;
    else if (s.equals("Component"))
        return messageComponent;
    else if (s.equals("Object[]"))
        return new Object[]
        {   messageString,
            messageIcon,
            messageComponent,
            messageFont
        };
    else if (s.equals("Other"))
        return messageFont;
    else return null;
}

public Object[] getOptions()
{   String s = optionsPanel.getSelection();
    if (s.equals("String[]"))
        return new String[] { "Yellow", "Blue", "Red" };
    else if (s.equals("Icon[]"))
        return new Icon[]
        {   new ImageIcon("yellow-ball.gif"),
            new ImageIcon("blue-ball.gif"),
            new ImageIcon("red-ball.gif")
        };
    else if (s.equals("Object[]"))
        return new Object[]
        {   messageString,
            messageIcon,
            messageComponent,
            messageFont
        };
    else
        return null;
}

public int getType(ButtonPanel panel)
```

```
{  String s = panel.getSelection();
   try
   {  Class cl = JOptionPane.class;
      return cl.getField(s).getInt(cl);
   }
   catch(Exception e)
   {  return -1;
   }
}

public void actionPerformed(ActionEvent evt)
{  if (typePanel.getSelection().equals("Confirm"))
      JOptionPane.showConfirmDialog(this,
         getMessage(),
         "Title",
         getType(optionTypePanel),
         getType(messageTypePanel));
   else if (typePanel.getSelection().equals("Input"))
   {  if (inputPanel.getSelection().equals("Text field"))
      JOptionPane.showInputDialog(this,
         getMessage(),
         "Title",
         getType(messageTypePanel));
      else
         JOptionPane.showInputDialog(this,
            getMessage(),
            "Title",
            getType(messageTypePanel),
            null,
            new String[] { "Yellow", "Blue", "Red" },
            "Blue");
   }
   else if (typePanel.getSelection().equals("Message"))
      JOptionPane.showMessageDialog(this,
         getMessage(),
         "Title",
         getType(messageTypePanel));
   else if (typePanel.getSelection().equals("Option"))
      JOptionPane.showOptionDialog(this,
         getMessage(),
         "Title",
         getType(optionTypePanel),
         getType(messageTypePanel),
         null,
         getOptions(),
         getOptions()[0]);
}

public static void main(String[] args)
```

```
{   JFrame f = new OptionDialogTest();
    f.show();
}

    private ButtonPanel typePanel;
    private ButtonPanel messagePanel;
    private ButtonPanel messageTypePanel;
    private ButtonPanel optionTypePanel;
    private ButtonPanel optionsPanel;
    private ButtonPanel inputPanel;

    private String messageString = "Message";
    private Icon messageIcon
        = new ImageIcon("blue-ball.gif");
    private Font messageFont
        = new Font("Serif", Font.PLAIN, 8);
    private Component messageComponent
        = new JPanel()
            {   public void paintComponent(Graphics g)
                {   super.paintComponent(g);
                    g.setFont(messageFont);
                    g.drawString("Component", 0, 8);
                }
                public Dimension getMinimumSize()
                {   return new Dimension(12, 30);
                }
            };
}
```

`javax.swing.JOptionPane`

- static void showMessageDialog(Component parent, Object message, String title, int messageType, Icon icon)

- static void showMessageDialog(Component parent, Object message, String title, int messageType)

- static void showMessageDialog(Component parent, Object message)

- static void showInternalMessageDialog(Component parent, Object message, String title, int messageType, Icon icon)

- static void showInternalMessageDialog(Component parent, Object message, String title, int messageType)

- static void showInternalMessageDialog(Component parent, Object message)

shows a message dialog or an internal message dialog. (An internal dialog is rendered entirely within its parent frame.)

Parameters:	parent	the parent component (can be `null`)
	message	the message to show on the dialog (can be a string, icon, component, or an array of them)
	title	the string in the title bar of the dialog
	messageType	one of `ERROR_MESSAGE`, `INFORMATION_MESSAGE`, `WARNING_MESSAGE`, `QUESTION_MESSAGE`, `PLAIN_MESSAGE`
	icon	an icon to show instead of one of the standard icons

- `static int showConfirmDialog(Component parent, Object message, String title, int optionType, int messageType, Icon icon)`

- `static int showConfirmDialog(Component parent, Object message, String title, int optionType, int messageType)`

- `static int showConfirmDialog(Component parent, Object message, String title, int optionType)`

- `static int showConfirmDialog(Component parent, Object message)`

- `static int showInternalConfirmDialog(Component parent, Object message, String title, int optionType, int messageType, Icon icon)`

- `static int showInternalConfirmDialog(Component parent, Object message, String title, int optionType, int messageType)`

- `static int showInternalConfirmDialog(Component parent, Object message, String title, int optionType)`

- `static int showInternalConfirmDialog(Component parent, Object message)`

shows a confirmation dialog or an internal confirmation dialog. (An internal dialog is rendered entirely within its parent frame.) Returns the option selected by the user (one of `OK_OPTION`, `CANCEL_OPTION`, `YES_OPTION`, `NO_OPTION`), or `CLOSED_OPTION` if the user canceled the dialog.

Parameters:	parent	the parent component (can be `null`)
	message	the message to show on the dialog (can be a string, icon, component, or an array of them)
	title	the string in the title bar of the dialog
	messageType	one of `ERROR_MESSAGE`, `INFORMATION_MESSAGE`, `WARNING_MESSAGE`, `QUESTION_MESSAGE`, `PLAIN_MESSAGE`

	`optionType`	one of `DEFAULT_OPTION`, `YES_NO_OPTION`, `YES_NO_CANCEL_OPTION`, `OK_CANCEL_OPTION`
	`icon`	an icon to show instead of one of the standard icons

- `static int showOptionDialog(Component parent, Object message, String title, int optionType, int messageType, Icon icon, Object[] options, Object default)`
- `static int showInternalOptionDialog(Component parent, Object message, String title, int optionType, int messageType, Icon icon, Object[] options, Object default)`

shows an option dialog or an internal option dialog. (An internal dialog is rendered entirely within its parent frame.) Returns the index of the option selected by the user or `CLOSED_OPTION` if the user canceled the dialog.

Parameters:	`parent`	the parent component (can be `null`)
	`message`	the message to show on the dialog (can be a string, icon, component, or an array of them)
	`title`	the string in the title bar of the dialog
	`messageType`	one of `ERROR_MESSAGE`, `INFORMATION_MESSAGE`, `WARNING_MESSAGE`, `QUESTION_MESSAGE`, `PLAIN_MESSAGE`
	`optionType`	one of `DEFAULT_OPTION`, `YES_NO_OPTION`, `YES_NO_CANCEL_OPTION`, `OK_CANCEL_OPTION`
	`icon`	an icon to show instead of one of the standard icons
	`options`	an array of options (can be strings, icons, or components)
	`default`	the default option to present to the user

- `static Object showInputDialog(Component parent, Object message, String title, int messageType, Icon icon, Object[] values, Object default)`
- `static String showInputDialog(Component parent, Object message, String title, int messageType)`
- `static String showInputDialog(Component parent, Object message)`
- `static String showInputDialog(Object message)`
- `static Object showInternalInputDialog(Component parent, Object message, String title, int messageType, Icon icon, Object[] values, Object default)`

- `static String showInternalInputDialog(Component parent, Object message, String title, int messageType)`

- `static String showInternalInputDialog(Component parent, Object message)`

shows an input dialog or an internal input dialog. (An internal dialog is rendered entirely within its parent frame.) Returns the input string typed by the user, or `null` if the user canceled the dialog.

Parameters:		
	`parent`	the parent component (can be `null`)
	`message`	the message to show on the dialog (can be a string, icon, component, or an array of them)
	`title`	the string in the title bar of the dialog
	`messageType`	one of `ERROR_MESSAGE`, `INFORMATION_MESSAGE`, `WARNING_MESSAGE`, `QUESTION_MESSAGE`, `PLAIN_MESSAGE`
	`icon`	an icon to show instead of one of the standard icons
	`values`	an array of values to show in a combo box
	`default`	the default value to present to the user

Creating Dialogs

In the last section, you saw how to use the `JOptionPane` class to show a simple dialog. In this section, you will see how to create such a dialog by hand.

Figure 9–44 shows a typical modal dialog box, a program information box that is displayed when the user selects the About button.

To implement a dialog box, you derive a class from `JDialog`. This is essentially the same process as deriving the main window for an application from `JFrame`. More precisely:

1. In the constructor of your dialog box, call the constructor of the base class `JDialog`. You will need to tell it the name of the parent frame, the title of the dialog frame, and a Boolean flag to indicate if the dialog box is modal or modeless. You should supply the parent frame so that the dialog can be displayed on top of its parent, but you can also supply a `null` pointer if you don't care where the dialog is displayed.

2. Add the user interface components of the dialog box.

3. Add the event handlers.

4. Set the size for the dialog box.

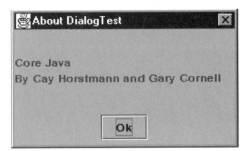

Figure 9–44: An About dialog box

Here's an example of how the code will start:

```
public AboutDialog(JFrame parent) extend JDialog
{  super(parent, "About DialogTest", true);

   Box b = Box.createVerticalBox();
   b.add(Box.createGlue());
   b.add(new JLabel("Core Java"));
   b.add(new JLabel("By Cay Horstmann and Gary Cornell"));
   b.add(Box.createGlue());
   getContentPane().add(b, "Center");

   JPanel p2 = new JPanel();
   JButton ok = new JButton("Ok");
   p2.add(ok);
   getContentPane().add(p2, "South");

   ok.addActionListener(new ActionListener()
      {  public void actionPerformed(ActionEvent evt)
         { setVisible(false); }
      } );

   setSize(250, 150);
}
```

As you can see, the constructor adds user interface elements, in this case, labels and a button. It adds a handler to the button and sets the size of the dialog.

To display the dialog box, you create a new dialog object and invoke the show method.

```
JDialog dialog = new AboutDialog(this);
dialog.show();
```

Actually, in the sample code below, we create the dialog box only once, and so we can reuse it whenever the user clicks the About button.

```
if (dialog == null) // first time
    dialog = new AboutDialog(this);
dialog.show();
```

When the user clicks on the Ok button, the dialog box should close. This is handled in the event handler of the Ok button:

```
ok.addActionListener(new ActionListener()
{  public void actionPerformed(ActionEvent evt)
   { setVisible(false); }
} );
```

When the user closes the dialog by clicking on the "close" box, then the dialog is also hidden. Just as with a JFrame, you can override this behavior with the setDefaultCloseOperation method.

Example 9–21 is the code for the About dialog box test program.

Example 9–21: DialogTest.java

```
import java.awt.*;
import java.awt.event.*;
import javax.swing.*;

class DialogFrame extends JFrame
   implements ActionListener
{  public DialogFrame()
   {  setTitle("DialogTest");
      setSize(300, 300);
      addWindowListener(new WindowAdapter()
      {  public void windowClosing(WindowEvent e)
         {  System.exit(0);
         }
      } );

      JMenuBar mbar = new JMenuBar();
      setJMenuBar(mbar);
      JMenu fileMenu = new JMenu("File");
      mbar.add(fileMenu);
      aboutItem = new JMenuItem("About");
      aboutItem.addActionListener(this);
      fileMenu.add(aboutItem);
      exitItem = new JMenuItem("Exit");
      exitItem.addActionListener(this);
      fileMenu.add(exitItem);
   }

   public void actionPerformed(ActionEvent evt)
   {  Object source = evt.getSource();
      if(source == aboutItem)
      {  if (dialog == null) // first time
            dialog = new AboutDialog(this);
         dialog.show();
      }
      else if(source == exitItem)
      {  System.exit(0);
```

```
            }
        }

    private AboutDialog dialog;
    private JMenuItem aboutItem;
    private JMenuItem exitItem;
}

class AboutDialog extends JDialog
{   public AboutDialog(JFrame parent)
    {   super(parent, "About DialogTest", true);

        Box b = Box.createVerticalBox();
        b.add(Box.createGlue());
        b.add(new JLabel("Core Java"));
        b.add(new JLabel("By Cay Horstmann and Gary Cornell"));
        b.add(Box.createGlue());
        getContentPane().add(b, "Center");

        JPanel p2 = new JPanel();
        JButton ok = new JButton("Ok");
        p2.add(ok);
        getContentPane().add(p2, "South");

        ok.addActionListener(new ActionListener()
            {   public void actionPerformed(ActionEvent evt)
                { setVisible(false); }
            } );

        setSize(250, 150);
    }
}

public class DialogTest {
    public static void main(String[] args)
    {   JFrame f = new DialogFrame();
        f.show();
    }
}
```

`javax.swing.JDialog`

- public JDialog(JFrame parent, String title, boolean modal)
  constructs a dialog. The dialog is not visible until it is explicitly shown.

Parameters:	parent	the frame that is the owner of the dialog
	title	the title of the dialog
	modal	true for modal dialogs (a modal dialog blocks input to other windows)

Data Exchange

The most common reason to put up a dialog box is to get information from the user. You have already seen how easy it is to make a dialog box object: give it initial data and then call show() to display the dialog box on the screen. Now let us see how to transfer data in and out of a dialog box.

Consider the dialog box in Figure 9–45 that could be used to obtain a user name and a password to connect to some on-line service.

Figure 9–45: Password dialog box

It is helpful to make a class that contains all data that you want to transfer out of a dialog box. We make a class ConnectInfo that holds the name and password. We initialize these data with the defaults that should be shown in the fields when the dialog box starts up. When the user finishes entering the data into the dialog box, the actual user input is put back into the transfer object. However, if the dialog was canceled or closed, we do not transfer back the data. We do all this in a showDialog method of our ConnectDialog class:

```
public boolean showDialog(ConnectInfo transfer)
{   username.setText(transfer.username);
    password.setText(transfer.password);
    ok = false; // set to true by Ok button action
    show();
    if (ok)
    {   transfer.username = username.getText();
        transfer.password = new String(password.getPassword());
    }
    return ok;
}
```

Note that the call to show() does not return until a call to setVisible(false) or dispose elsewhere in the code. (This is a welcome change in how the AWT works. In the first version of the AWT, the call to show returned immediately, *even for modal dialog boxes.* That made it extremely challenging to get the data out of the dialog box.)

There are three ways for the user to close the dialog box: through the Ok button, the Cancel button, and the windowClosing event. Each of these three events must call setVisible(false). When the user clicks the Ok button, the ok variable must be set to `true` to indicate that the values in the dialog are to be accepted and that they should be moved to the transfer object.

You invoke the dialog box by setting default values in the transfer object and then passing the transfer object to the `showDialog` procedure. If the procedure returned `true`, the user clicked on Ok.

```
ConnectInfo transfer = new ConnectInfo("yourname", "");
if (dialog == null) dialog = new ConnectDialog(this);
if (dialog.showDialog(transfer))
{   String uname = transfer.username;

    String pwd = transfer.password;

}
```

NOTE: Transferring data out of a *modeless* dialog is not as simple. When displaying a modeless dialog, the call to `show` does not block and the program continues running while the dialog is displayed. If the user selects items on a modeless dialog and then selects Ok, the dialog needs to send an event to some listener in the program. That is, another class must implement an appropriate listener interface and an object of that class should be registered as a listener. You can implement this by sending a custom event (see Chapter 8) or by sending a property change event (see the chapter on JavaBeans in Volume 2).

Example 9–22 is the complete code that illustrates the data flow into and out of a dialog box.

Example 9–22: DataExchangeTest.java

```java
import java.awt.*;
import java.awt.event.*;
import javax.swing.*;

public class DataExchangeTest extends JFrame
    implements ActionListener
{   public DataExchangeTest()
    {   setTitle("DataExchangeTest");
        setSize(300, 300);
        addWindowListener(new WindowAdapter()
        {   public void windowClosing(WindowEvent e)
            {   System.exit(0);
            }
        } );

        JMenuBar mbar = new JMenuBar();
        setJMenuBar(mbar);
        JMenu fileMenu = new JMenu("File");
        mbar.add(fileMenu);
        connectItem = new JMenuItem("Connect");
```

```java
            connectItem.addActionListener(this);
            fileMenu.add(connectItem);
            exitItem = new JMenuItem("Exit");
            exitItem.addActionListener(this);
            fileMenu.add(exitItem);
        }

    public void actionPerformed(ActionEvent evt)
    {   Object source = evt.getSource();
        if (source == connectItem)
        {   ConnectInfo transfer
                = new ConnectInfo("yourname", "pw");
            if (dialog == null)
                dialog = new ConnectDialog(this);
            if (dialog.showDialog(transfer))
            {   String uname = transfer.username;
                String pwd = transfer.password;
                Container contentPane = getContentPane();
                contentPane.add(new JLabel("username=" +
                    uname + ", password=" + pwd),
                    "South");
                validate();
            }
        }
        else if(source == exitItem)
            System.exit(0);
    }

    public static void main(String[] args)
    {   JFrame f = new DataExchangeTest();
        f.show();
    }

    private ConnectDialog dialog = null;
    private JMenuItem connectItem;
    private JMenuItem exitItem;
}

class ConnectInfo
{   public String username;
    public String password;
    public ConnectInfo(String u, String p)
        { username = u; password = p; }
}

class ConnectDialog extends JDialog
    implements ActionListener
{   public ConnectDialog(JFrame parent)
    {   super(parent, "Connect", true);
        Container contentPane = getContentPane();
        JPanel p1 = new JPanel();
```

```java
      p1.setLayout(new GridLayout(2, 2));
      p1.add(new JLabel("User name:"));
      p1.add(username = new JTextField(""));
      p1.add(new JLabel("Password:"));
      p1.add(password = new JPasswordField(""));
      contentPane.add("Center", p1);

      Panel p2 = new Panel();
      okButton = addButton(p2, "Ok");
      cancelButton = addButton(p2, "Cancel");
      contentPane.add("South", p2);
      setSize(240, 120);
   }

   JButton addButton(Container c, String name)
   {  JButton button = new JButton(name);
      button.addActionListener(this);
      c.add(button);
      return button;
   }

   public void actionPerformed(ActionEvent evt)
   {  Object source = evt.getSource();
      if(source == okButton)
      {  ok = true;
         setVisible(false);
      }
      else if (source == cancelButton)
         setVisible(false);
   }

   public boolean showDialog(ConnectInfo transfer)
   {  username.setText(transfer.username);
      password.setText(transfer.password);
      ok = false;
      show();
      if (ok)
      {  transfer.username = username.getText();
         transfer.password = new String(password.getPassword());
      }
      return ok;
   }

   private JTextField username;
   private JPasswordField password;
   private boolean ok;
   private JButton okButton;
   private JButton cancelButton;
}
```

File Dialogs

When you write an applet, you cannot access files on the remote user's machine. However, when you write an application, you usually want to be able to open and save files. A good file dialog box that shows files and directories and lets the user navigate the file system is hard to write, and you definitely don't want to reinvent that wheel. Fortunately, Swing provides a JFileChooser class that allows you to display a file dialog box similar to the one that most native applications use. JFileChooser dialogs are always modal. Note that the JFileChooser class is not a subclass of JDialog. Instead of calling show, you call showOpenDialog to display a dialog for opening a file or showSaveDialog to display a dialog for saving a file. The button for accepting a file is then automatically labeled Open or Save. You can also supply your own button label with the showDialog method. Figure 9–46 shows an example of the file chooser dialog box.

Open						☒
Look in:	⬥ C:\	▾	⬆	⌂	☐	▦ ▤

TextPadBeta
VSTASCAN
WINDOWS
WinZip
jdk1.2
snagit32
temp
AUTOEXEC.BAT

File name:	c:\		**Open**
Files of type:	All Files (*.*)	▾	**Cancel**

Figure 9–46: File chooser dialog box

Here are the steps needed to put up a file dialog box and recover what the user chooses from the box.

1. Make a JFileChooser object. Unlike the constructor for the JDialog class, you do not supply the parent component. This allows you to share a file chooser dialog for multiple frames.

    For example:

    ```
    JFileChooser d = new JFileChooser();
    ```

2. Set the directory by calling the setCurrentDirectory method.

    For example, use

    ```
    d.setCurrentDirectory(new File("."));
    ```

    to use the current working directory. You need to supply a File object. File objects are explained in detail in Chapter 12. All you need to know for now is that there is a constructor `File(String filename)` that turns a file or directory name into a `File` object.

3. If you have a default file name that you expect the user to choose, supply it with the `setSelectedFile` method:

    ```
    d.setSelectedFile(new File(filename));
    ```

4. To enable the user to select multiple files in the dialog, call the `setMultiSelectionEnabled` method. This is, of course, entirely optional and not all that common.

    ```
    d.setMultiSelectionEnabled(true);
    ```

5. If you want to restrict the display of files in the dialog to those of a particular type (for example, all files with extension `.gif`), then you need to set a *file filter*. We discuss this later in this section.

6. Show the dialog box by calling the `showOpenDialog` or `showSaveDialog` method. You must supply the parent component in these calls.

    ```
    int result = d.showOpenDialog(parent);
    ```

    or

    ```
    int result = d.showSaveDialog(parent);
    ```

    This call does not return until the user has accepted a file or canceled the file dialog box. The return value is `JFileChooser.APPROVE_OPTION` or `JFileChooser.CANCEL_OPTION`.

7. You get the selected file or files with the `getSelectedFile()` or `getSelectedFiles()` method. These methods return either a single `File` object or an array of `File` objects. If you just need the name of the file object, call its `getName` method. For example,

    ```
    String filename = d.getSelectedFile().getName();
    ```

For the most part, these steps are simple. The major difficulty with using a file dialog is to specify a subset of files from which the user should choose. For example, suppose the user should choose a GIF image file. Then, the file chooser should only display files with extension `.gif`. It should also give the user some kind of feedback that the displayed files are of a particular category, such as "GIF Images." But the situation can be more complex. If the user should choose a JPEG image file, then the extension can be either `.jpg` or `.jpeg`. Rather than coming up with a mechanism to codify these complexities, the designers of the file chooser supply a more elegant mechanism: to restrict the displayed files, you supply an object that implements the `javax.swing.filechooser.FileFilter` interface. The file chooser passes each file to the file filter and displays only the files that the file filter accepts.

To restrict the files shown in a dialog, you need to create an object of a class that implements the `FileFilter` interface. At the time of this writing, only one such class is supplied, the default filter that accept all files. The documentation hints at a class `ExtensionFileFilter`, to be used as follows:

```
ExtensionFileFilter filter = new ExtensionFileFilter();
filter.addExtension("jpg");
filter.addExtension("gif");
filter.setDescription("JPG & GIF Images");
```

However, no such class exists in our version of the JDK. But, it is easy to write your own file filters. You simply implement the two methods of the `FileFilter` interface:

```
public boolean accept(File f);
public String getDescription();
```

The first method tests whether a file should be accepted. The second method returns a description of the file type that can be displayed in the file chooser dialog. For example, to filter for GIF files, you might use

```
public class GifFilter extends FileFilter
{  public boolean accept(File f)
   {  return f.getName().toLowerCase().endsWith(".gif")
         || f.isDirectory();
   }
   public String getDescription()
   {  return "GIF Image";
   }
}
```

Once you have a file filter object, you use the `setFileFilter` method of the `JFileChooser` class to install it into the file chooser object:

```
d.setFileFilter(new GifFilter());
```

Of course, if you like, you can use an anonymous class:

```
d.setFileFilter(new FileFilter
   {  public boolean accept(File f)
      {  return f.getName().toLowerCase().endsWith(".gif")
            || f.isDirectory();
      }
      public String getDescription()
      {  return "GIF Image";
      }
   });
```

When you look closely at the file chooser dialog, you will notice that the file filter is contained in a choice field, which suggests that you can install multiple filters. You use the `addChoosableFileFilter` method to add additional file filters. For example, you can obtain the default file filter that accepts all files by calling the `getAcceptAllFileFilter` method. You can add this file filter as an additional choice for the user as follows:

```
d.addChoosableFileFilter(d.getAcceptAllFileFilter());
```

It is a good idea to do this in all file dialogs, just in case a user of your program needs to select a file with a non-standard extension.

> NOTE: There is an unrelated `FileFilter` interface in the `java.io` package that has a single method, `boolean accept(File f)`. It is used in the `listFiles` method of the `File` class to list files in a directory. We do not know why the designers of Swing didn't extend this interface—perhaps the Java class library has now become so complex that even the programmers at Sun are no longer aware of all the standard classes and interfaces.
>
> Note that you will need to resolve the name conflict between these two identically named interfaces if you import both the `java.io` and the `javax.swing.filechooser` package. The simplest remedy is to import `javax.swing.filechooser.FileFilter`, not `javax.swing.filechooser.*`.

Finally, you can customize the file chooser by providing special icons and file descriptions for each file that the file chooser displays. You do this by supplying an object of a class extending the `FileView` class in the `javax.swing.filechooser` package. This is definitely an advanced technique. Normally, you don't need to supply a file view—the pluggable look and feel supplies one for you. But if you want to show different icons for special file types, you can install your own file view. You need to extend the `FileView` class and implement five methods:

```
Icon getIcon(File f);
String getName(File f);
String getDescription(File f);
String getTypeDescription(File f);
Boolean isTraversable(File f);
```

Then you use the `setFileView` method to install your file view into the file chooser.

The file chooser calls your methods for each file or directory that it wants to display. If your method returns `null` for the icon, name, or description, the file chooser then consults the default file view of the look and feel. That is good because it means you only need to deal with the file types for which you want to do something different.

The file chooser calls the `isTraversable` method to decide whether to open a directory when a user clicks on it. Note that this method returns a `Boolean` object, not a `boolean` value! This seems weird, but it is actually convenient—if you aren't interested in deviating from the default file view, just return `null`. The file chooser will then consult the default file view. In other words, the method returns a `Boolean` to give you the choice between three options: true (`Boolean.TRUE`), false (`Boolean.FALSE`) and don't care (`null`).

Here is a simple example of a file view. It returns a coffee icon for files with extension `.java`, and does nothing special for all other files.

```
class CoffeeIconFileView extends javax.swing.filechooser.FileView
{  public Icon getIcon(File f)
   {  if (f.getName().toLowerCase().endsWith(".java"))
         return new ImageIcon("coffee.gif");
```

```
        else
            return null;
    }
    public String getDescription(File f) { return null; }
    public String getName(File f) { return null; }
    public String getTypeDescription(File f) { return null; }
    public Boolean isTraversable(File f) { return null; }
}
```

You install this file view into your file chooser with the `setFileView` method:

```
chooser.setFileView(new CoffeeIconFileView());
```

The file chooser will then show the coffee icon next to all Java files and use the default file view to show all other files.

You can find a more useful `ExampleFileView` class in the `demo/jfc/FileChooserDemo` directory of the JDK. That class lets you associate icons and descriptions with arbitrary extensions.

 `javax.swing.JFileChooser`

- `JFileChooser()`

  creates a file chooser dialog box that can be used for multiple frames.

- `void setCurrentDirectory(File dir)`

  sets the initial directory for the file dialog box.

- `setSelectedFile(File file)`
- `setSelectedFiles(File[] file)`

  set the default file choice for the file dialog box.

- `void setMultiSelectionEnabled(boolean b)`

  sets or clears multiple selection mode.

- `int showOpenDialog(Component parent)`
- `int showSaveDialog(Component parent)`

  show a "File open" or "File save" dialog. Return APPROVE_OPTION or CANCEL_OPTION.

- `File getFile()`
- `File[] getFiles()`

  get the file or files that the user selected (or return `null` if the user didn't select any file).

- `void setFileFilter(javax.swing.filechooser.FileFilter filter)`

  sets the file mask for the file dialog box. All files for which `filter.accept` returns `true` will be displayed.

- `void setFileView(FileView view)`

  sets a file view to provide information about the files that the file chooser displays.

`javax.swing.filechooser.FileFilter`

- `boolean accept(File f)`

  returns `true` if the file chooser should display this file.

- `String getDescription()`

  returns a description of this file filter, for example `"Image files (*.gif,*.jpeg)"`.

`javax.swing.filechooser.FileView`

- `String getName(File f)`

  returns the name of the file `f`, or `null`. Normally, this method simply returns `f.getName()`.

- `String getDescription(File f)`

  returns a humanly readable description of the file `f`, or `null`. For example, if `f` is an HTML document, this method might return its title.

- `String getTypeDescription(File f)`

  returns a humanly readable description of the type of the file `f`, or `null`. For example, if `f` is an HTML document, this method might return a string `"Hypertext document"`.

- `Icon getIcon(File f)`

  returns an icon for the file `f`, or `null`. For example, if `f` is a JPEG file, this method might return a thumbnail icon.

- `Boolean isTraversable(File f)`

  returns `Boolean.TRUE` if `f` is a directory that the user can open. This method might return `false` if a directory is conceptually a compound document. Like all `FileView` methods, this method can return `null` to indicate that the file chooser should consult the default view instead.

Chapter 10

Applets

- ▼ APPLET BASICS
- ▼ THE APPLET HTML TAGS
- ▼ PASSING INFORMATION TO APPLETS
- ▼ MULTIMEDIA
- ▼ THE APPLET CONTEXT
- ▼ IT'S AN APPLET. IT'S AN APPLICATION. IT'S BOTH!

At this point, you should be comfortable with using most of the features of Java's *language,* and you had a pretty thorough introduction to basic graphics programming in Java. We hope that you agree with us that Java is a nice (if not perfect), general-purpose OOP language and the Swing user interface libraries are flexible and useful. Having said all this, a rapidly improving dialect of C++ with a limited (if rapidly growing) set of platform-independent class libraries for graphics development is not why there was (and to some extent still is) so much hype surrounding Java. The unbelievable hype during the first few years of Java's life (as was mentioned in Chapter 1) stems from Java's ability to "activate the Internet." The point is that you can create a special kind of Java program (usually called an *applet*) that a Java-enabled browser can download from the Net and then run. This chapter shows you how to write basic applets. Full-featured applets depend on the programmer's mastery of Java's networking abilities along with its ability to handle multiple threads. These advanced topics will be covered in Volume 2.

Nowadays, of course, since modern browsers support Dynamic HTML and scripting (and XML-enabled browsers are on the horizon), browsers can do far more than they could when Java first came out. Still, since applets are written in a full-fledged programming language, they potentially have more power than any foreseeable combination of HTML, XML, and scripting will ever have.

Applet Basics

Before Java, you used HTML (the hypertext markup language) to describe the layout of a Web page. HTML is simply a vehicle to indicate elements of a hypertext page. For example, `<TITLE>` indicates the title of the page, and any text that follows this tag becomes the title of the page. You indicate the end of the title with the `</TITLE>` tag. (This is one of the general rules for tags: a slash followed by the name of the element indicates the end of the element.)

The basic idea of how to use applets in a Web page is simple: the HTML page must tell the browser which applets to load and then where to put each applet on the Web page. As you might expect, the HTML Java tag needed to use a Java applet must tell Java-enabled browsers the following:

- The name of the class files
- The location of the class files
- How the applet sits on the Web page (size, location, and so on)

> NOTE: The original way to embed a Java applet was via an `<APPLET>` tag with parameters that gave the information listed above. The W3 consortium has suggested people switch to the more versatile `<OBJECT>` tag, and the older `<APPLET>` tag is deprecated in the HTML 4.0 specification. The most modern browsers will recognize both tags, but you should keep in mind that older browsers do not. We will cover the basics of using these tags a little later in this chapter.

The browser then retrieves the class files from the Net (or from a directory on the user's machine) and automatically runs the applet, using its Java Virtual Machine.

In addition to the applet itself, the Web page can contain all the other HTML elements you have seen in use on Web pages: multiple fonts, bulleted lists, graphics, links, and so on. Applets are just one part of the hypertext page. It is always worth keeping in mind that Java is *not* a tool for designing HTML pages; it is a tool for *bringing them to life*. This is not to say that the GUI design elements in a Java applet are not important, but they must work with (and, in fact, are subservient to) the underlying HTML design of the Web page.

> NOTE: We do not cover general HTML tags at all; we assume that you know—or are working with someone who knows—the basics of HTML. Only a few special HTML tags are needed for Java applets. We do, of course, cover those later in this chapter. As for learning HTML, there are dozens of HTML books at your local bookstore. One that covers what you need and will not insult your intelligence is *HTML: The Definitive Guide, 3rd edition* by C. Musciano and B. Kennedy from O'Reilly.

When applets were first developed, you had to use Sun's HotJava browser to view Web pages that contain applets. Naturally, few users were willing to use a separate browser just to enjoy a new Web feature. Java applets became really popular when Netscape included a Java Virtual Machine in its browser. Internet Explorer soon followed suit. Unfortunately, the browser manufacturers have not kept up with Java. Both Netscape and Internet Explorer do a good job with Java 1.0, and their newest versions can handle most of Java 1.1.

But, we can't stress enough that there have always been and will probably continue to be annoying limitations and incompatibilities. For example, Microsoft will likely never implement certain parts of Java that it feels are particularly competitive with its own technology. Netscape has basically gone out of the virtual machine business. As we write this, Netscape has indicated that they will start offering a convenient way for users to specify their own virtual machine, but the currently shipping version of the Navigator browser does not have this feature. All this makes it difficult to deploy an applet that uses modern Java features and that can still be viewed by different browsers.

To overcome this problem, Sun released a tool called the "Java Plug-In" (originally known as the "Activator"). Using the various extension mechanisms of Internet Explorer or Navigator, it seamlessly plugs into both Netscape and Internet Explorer and allows both browsers to execute Java applets by using an external Java run-time environment that Sun supplies. Their version of the virtual machine will presumably always be up-to-date, thus ensuring that you can always take advantage of the latest and greatest features of Java.

Once you install the Java plug-in, you can switch to different versions of the Java Virtual Machine. To run the applets in this book, you need to install the plug-in and select the JDK 1.2 virtual machine (see Figure 10–1).

![Java Plug-in Properties dialog showing Basic, Advanced, Proxies tabs. Java Run Time Environment set to JRE 1.2 in C:\Program Files\JavaSoft\JRE\1.2, with Path field, Enable Just In Time Compiler checked, JIT path symcjit, Debug Settings with Enable Debug unchecked, Debug Port 2 502, and Apply/Reset buttons.]

Figure 10–1: Selecting the Java Virtual Machine in the Java Plug-In

Admittedly, if you are designing Web pages for a wide audience, it is probably unreasonable to ask the visitors to your Web page to install the plug-in, which is a fairly hefty (if one-time) download. If you agree that all this is unreasonable, then you need to design applets that can work with the Java Virtual Machines that are built into Netscape and Internet Explorer. In this case, you really have to use only Java 1.0 features and to keep the applet as simple as possible. But frankly, if your applet is that simple, you can probably do entirely without it—use JavaScript for program logic, use forms for data entry, and use animated GIF files for animations.

If you roll out more sophisticated Java programs, you should ask yourself whether there is any benefit from using the Web browser to deliver your programs. If not, then you can simply deliver Java applications that your users run on their local machines. You still have all benefits of Java, such as platform independence and easy database and network access. Of course, there are advantages to Web deployment. For a user, it is often easier to locate an application on the Web than on the local file system. (This is particularly true for applications that aren't used every day.) For an administrator, it is easier to maintain and update an application on the Web than to push out bug fixes and improvements to lots of client desktops.

Thus, among the most successful Java programs are corporate *intranet* applications that interface with corporate databases. For example, many companies have put expense reimbursement calculators, benefit tracking tools, schedule and vacation planners, purchase order requests, and so on, on their corporate intranet. These programs are relatively small, need to interface with databases, need more flexibility than Web forms can easily handle, and need to be customized to the operations of a particular company. Applets are perfect delivery vehicles for these programs, and since the user population is constrained, there is no problem with distributing the Java Plug-In.

We recommend that you choose one of the following two options for your Web applications:

1. Use the Java Plug-In to deliver Java applets if you are on an intranet. This gives you maximum control over the Java platform, fewer portability headaches, and the ability to use the most advanced Java features. Of course, you must then manage the deployment of the plug-in.

2. If you are not on an intranet, don't use applets. Use scripting for validation; use animated GIFs for animation; use forms and server-side processing (whether they are traditional CGI scripts, Java servlets, or server-side scripting languages) for data entry.

There is a third possibility. You can write applets that use Java 1.1 together with Swing. Java 1.1 is supported by modern versions of both major browsers, and you can provide a Swing set JAR file as part of your applet. We'll show you how to do this later in this chapter, but be forewarned: the Swing set is a very hefty (and recurring) download, certainly unacceptable over a dialup line.

A Simple Applet

For tradition's sake, let's modify the `NotHelloWorld` program from Chapter 7 to be an applet. Before we do that, we want to point out that from a programming point of view an applet isn't very strange. An applet is simply a Java class that (ultimately) extends the `java.applet.Applet` class. Note that although the `applet` package is not part of the AWT package, an applet is an AWT component, as the inheritance chain shown in Figure 10–2 illustrates. In this book, we will use the Swing set to implement applets. All of our applets will extend the `JApplet` class, the superclass for Swing applets. As you can see in Figure 10–2, `JApplet` is an immediate subclass of the ordinary `Applet` class

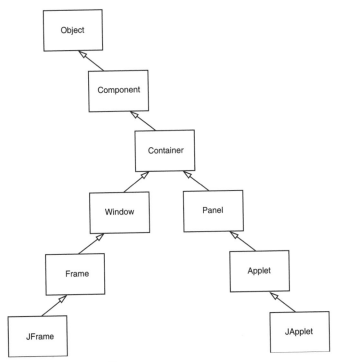

Figure 10–2: Inheritance diagram

NOTE: If your applet contains Swing components, you must extend the `JApplet` class. Swing components inside a plain `Applet` don't paint correctly.

This inheritance chain has some obvious but still useful consequences. For example, since applets are AWT components, event handling in applets is done exactly as you saw in Chapter 8.

Example 10–1 shows the code for an applet version of "Not Hello World."

Example 10–1: NotHelloWorldApplet.java

```
import java.awt.*;
import java.awt.event.*;
import javax.swing.*;

class NotHelloWorldPanel extends JPanel
{  public void paintComponent(Graphics g)
   {  super.paintComponent(g);
      g.drawString("Not a Hello, World applet", 75, 100);
   }
}

public class NotHelloWorldApplet extends JApplet
{  public void init()
   {  Container contentPane = getContentPane();
      contentPane.add(new NotHelloWorldPanel());
   }
}
```

Notice how similar this is to the corresponding program from Chapter 7. However, because the applet lives inside a Web page, there is no need to specify a method for exiting the applet.

Next, to make an applet that will work from a Web page that corresponds to this code, you need at a minimum:

- To compile this .java file into class files
- To create an HTML file that tells the browser which file to load and how to size the applet.

It is customary (but not necessary) to give the HTML file the same name as that of the applet class inside. So, following this tradition, we will call the file NotHelloWorldApplet.html.

Unfortunately, unlike the various ways of indicating an applet on a page that will be run by the browser's virtual machine (a simple <APPLET> or <OBJECT> tag with a few parameters), the HTML tags you need to use your applet with the Java Plug-In are rather cumbersome. They also need associated script code in order to determine the ambient browser. Rather than creating the tags and script code by hand, it is best to run an HTML converter tool (see Figure 10–3) that Sun supplies for this purpose.

Figure 10–3: The Java Plug-In HTML converter

That converter tool translates a simple HTML file containing the traditional
APPLET tag into the complex HTML file that is required to invoke the Java Plug-
In from various browsers. To use the converter, simply supply the name of the
HTML file or files with the simple APPLET tag and select the appropriate con-
version template. For this book, we selected "Extended (Standard + All
Browsers/Platforms)".

For example, for the NotHelloWorldApplet.html we started with the following simple HTML file:

```
<APPLET CODE="NotHelloWorldApplet.class" WIDTH=300 HEIGHT=300>
</APPLET>
```

The result of the conversion is shown in Example 10–2. We will explain these
APPLET HTML tags later in this chapter.

Example 10–2: NotHelloWorldApplet.html

```
<!--"CONVERTED_APPLET"-->
<!-- CONVERTER VERSION 1.0 -->
<SCRIPT LANGUAGE="JavaScript"><!--
    var _info = navigator.userAgent; var _ns = false;
    var _ie = (_info.indexOf("MSIE") > 0 && _info.indexOf("Win")
> 0 && _info.indexOf("Windows 3.1") < 0);
//--></SCRIPT>
<COMMENT><SCRIPT LANGUAGE="JavaScript1.1"><!--
    var _ns = (navigator.appName.indexOf("Netscape") >= 0 &&
((_info.indexOf("Win") > 0 && _info.indexOf("Win16") < 0 &&
```

```
java.lang.System.getProperty("os.version").indexOf("3.5") < 0) ||
(_info.indexOf("Sun") > 0) || (_info.indexOf("Linux") > 0)));
//--></SCRIPT></COMMENT>

<SCRIPT LANGUAGE="JavaScript"><!--
    if (_ie == true) document.writeln('<OBJECT
classid="clsid:8AD9C840-044E-11D1-B3E9-00805F499D93" WIDTH = 300
HEIGHT = 300  codebase="http://java.sun.com/products/plugin
/1.1.1/jinstall-111-win32.cab#Version=1,1,1,0"><NOEMBED><XMP>');
    else if (_ns == true) document.writeln('<EMBED type=
"application/x-java-applet;version=1.1" java_CODE =
"NotHelloWorldApplet.class" WIDTH = 300 HEIGHT = 300
pluginspage="http://java.sun.com/products/plugin/1.1.1/plugin-
install.html"><NOEMBED><XMP>');
//--></SCRIPT>
<APPLET CODE = "NotHelloWorldApplet.class" WIDTH = 300 HEIGHT =
300 ></XMP>
<PARAM NAME = CODE VALUE = "NotHelloWorldApplet.class" >

<PARAM NAME="type" VALUE="application/x-java-applet;version=1.1">

</APPLET>

</NOEMBED></EMBED></OBJECT>


<!--
<APPLET  CODE = "NotHelloWorldApplet.class" WIDTH = 300 HEIGHT =
300 >

</APPLET>
-->
<!--"END_CONVERTED_APPLET"-->
```

Testing Applets

OK, you have the HTML file and the compiled class file and you want to test your work. First, the JDK comes with a stand-alone *applet viewer* program that allows you to test your applets in a limited way. For Solaris and Windows, this program is simply called `appletviewer`. You will have to check if a version is supplied with the JDK on other platforms and what its name is. You can find it in the `bin` directory below the `jdk` directory.

To use Sun's applet viewer in our example, enter

```
appletviewer NotHelloWorldApplet.html
```

at the command line. (The command line for the applet viewer program is the name of the HTML file, not the class file.) Figure 10–4 shows the applet viewer, displaying this applet.

Figure 10–4: Viewing an applet in the applet viewer

TIP: If you are using our customized version of TextPad, then you can get a first glimpse at your applet by compiling and running the source code from within the editor. If you do this, the editor invokes a (rather weird) batch file that:
1. Tests that the source file contains the string `Applet`.
2. Creates a file and puts in the minimum number of HTML tags needed to be able to run your code as an applet (the size of the applet is fixed at 300 by 200 pixels).
3. Saves the file with an HTM extension (so it will not overwrite any of your .html files).
4. Invokes Sun's applet viewer on this file.
Close the applet viewer when you have finished testing your applet. This method gives you a quick and dirty way to test your applets without creating a full-blown HTML page.

The applet viewer is good for the first stage of testing, but at some point you need to run your applets in a browser to see them in the same way a user might use them. In particular, the applet viewer program shows you only the applet, not the surrounding HTML text. If an HTML file contains multiple applets, the applet viewer pops up multiple windows. Also, the applet viewer does not enforce applet security rules in the same way that a browser does.

Therefore, you should test your applet inside a browser. Simply load the HTML file into the browser. Provided that the Java Plug-In was installed correctly, the applet will be displayed (see Figure 10–5). If the Java Plug-In was not installed, your browser should walk you through the steps of fetching and installing it.

Figure 10–5: Viewing an applet in a browser

 TIP: Testing applets with the Java Plug-In is a bit of a pain because you need to run your HTML files through the converter. If you use a current version of Netscape with full Java 1.1 support, you can save yourself a bit of trouble, provided that your applets don't require any Java 2 features beyond Swing. (None of the applets in this chapter do.) Grab the Swing add-on to Java 1.1 from the `java.sun.com` Web page and place the file `swing.jar` into the `Netscape\Communicator\Program\Java\Classes` directory. Then, Netscape is able to load applets that use the Swing set. You just need to supply a simple HTML file with an `APPLET` tag. No conversion to `OBJECT` or `EMBED` tags is necessary.

Security Basics

Because applets are designed to be loaded from a remote site and then executed locally, security becomes vital. If a user enables Java on the browser, the browser will download all the applet code on the Web page and execute it immediately. The user never gets a chance to confirm or to stop individual applets from running. For this reason, applets (unlike applications) are restricted in what they can do. The *applet security manager* throws a `SecurityException` whenever an applet attempts to violate one of the access rules. (See Volume 2 for more on security managers.)

What *can* applets do on all platforms? They can show images and play sounds, get keystrokes and mouse clicks from the user, and send user input back to the host from which they were loaded. That is enough functionality to show facts and figures or to get user input for placing an order. But applets playing in the "sandbox" cannot alter the user's system or spy on it. In this chapter, we will look only at applets that run "inside the sandbox."

In particular, on most browsers, when running in the sandbox:

- Applets can *never* run any local executable program.

- Applets cannot communicate with any host other than the server from which they were downloaded; that server is called the *originating host*.

- Applets cannot read or write to the local computer's file system.

- Applets cannot find any information about the local computer, except for the Java version used; the name and version of the operating system; and the characters used to separate files (for instance, / or \), paths (such as : or ;), and lines (such as \n or \r\n). In particular, applets cannot find out the user's name, e-mail address, and so on.

- All windows that an applet pops up carry a warning message.

All this is possible only because applets are *interpreted* by the Java Virtual Machine and not directly executed by the CPU on the user's computer. Because the interpreter checks all critical instructions and program areas, a hostile (or poorly written) applet will almost certainly not be able to crash the computer, overwrite system memory, or change the privileges granted by the operating system. Table 10–1 shows what Java applets can do when they are run in the sandbox, as well as what stand-alone Java applications can do under the default security manager.

Table 10–1: Java program capabilities

	BR	AV	JA
Read local file	no	yes	yes
Write local file	no	yes	yes
Get file information	no	yes	yes
Delete file	no	no	yes
Run another program	no	yes	yes
Read the user.name property	no	yes	yes
Connect to network port on server	yes	yes	yes
Connect to network port on other host	no	yes	yes
Load Java library	no	yes	yes
Call exit	no	yes	yes
Create a pop-up window	with warning	yes	yes

BR = Browser, using the default applet security model

AV = Applet viewer

JA = Java running an application (not an applet) with no security manager

These restrictions are too strong for some situations. For example, on a corporate intranet, you can certainly imagine an applet wanting to access local files. To allow for different levels of security under different situations, you can use *signed applets*. A signed applet carries with it a secure "certificate" that will indicate where the applet came from. With a signed applet then, you can be certain where the applet originates and you can choose to give it additional rights. (We will cover signing in Volume 2.)

The point is that if you trust the signer of the applet you can tell the browser to give the applet more privileges. You can, for example, give applets in your corporate intranet a higher level of trust than those from www.hacker.com. The configurable Java security model allows the continuum of privilege levels you need. You can give completely trusted applets the same privilege levels as local applications. Programs from vendors that are known to be somewhat flaky can be given access to some, but not all, privileges. Unknown applets can be restricted to the sandbox.

To sum up, Java has three separate mechanisms for enforcing security:

1. Program code is interpreted by the Java Virtual Machine, not executed directly.

2. A security manager checks all sensitive operations in the Java run-time library.

3. Applets can be signed to identify their origin.

NOTE: In contrast, the security model of the ActiveX technology by Microsoft relies solely on the third option. If you want to run an ActiveX control at all, you must trust it completely. That model works fine when you deal with a small number of trusted suppliers, but it simply does not scale up to the World Wide Web. If you use Internet Explorer, you will see the ActiveX mechanism at work. You'll need to accept Sun's certificate to install the plug-in on Internet Explorer. The certificate tells you that the code came from Sun. It doesn't tell you anything about the quality of the code. Once you accept the installation, the program runs without any further security checks.

Converting Applications to Applets

It is easy to convert a graphical Java application (that is, an application that uses the AWT and that you can start with the `java` command-line interpreter) into an applet that you can embed in a Web page. Essentially, all of the user interface code can stay the same.

Here are the specific steps for converting an application to an applet.

1. Make an HTML page with the appropriate tag to load the applet code.

2. Eliminate the `main` method in the application. Usually, `main` contains code to make a new frame object. With applets, that task is automatically taken care of by the browser, since it makes an object of the class specified in the HTML page.

3. Replace the `JFrame` class with a `JApplet` class. Make this class `public`. Otherwise, the applet cannot be loaded.

4. Remove the call to `setSize`; for applets, sizing is done with the `WIDTH` and `HEIGHT` parameters in the actual HTML file. Remove the call to `addWindowListener`. An applet cannot be closed; it terminates when the browser exits. If the application calls `setTitle`, eliminate the call to the method. Applets cannot have title bars. (You can, of course, title the Web page itself, using the `<TITLE>` HTML tag.)

5. Replace the constructor with a method called `init`. When the browser creates an object of the applet class, it calls the `init()` method. This change is only necessary if you use the `getParameter` method to read parameters that affect the applet layout. You cannot call `getParameter` from the constructor. (We will discuss applet parameters later in this chapter.)

As an example of this transformation, we will change the calculator application from Chapter 7 into an applet. In Figure 10–6, you can see how it looks, sitting inside a Web page.

Figure 10–6: A calculator applet

Example 10–3 shows the HTML page. Note that there is some text in addition to the applet tags.

Example 10–3: Calculator.html (before processing with the HTML converter)

```html
<HTML>
<TITLE>A Calculator</TITLE>
<BODY>
Here is a calculator, just in case you can't find yours.
<APPLET CODE="CalculatorApplet.class" WIDTH=180 HEIGHT=180>
</APPLET>
</BODY>
</HTML>
```

Example 10–4 is the code for the applet. We eliminated the class with the `main` method, changed the panel class to an applet class, and removed the calls to `setTitle`, `setSize`, and `addWindowListener` from the constructor. Note that the panel class did not change at all.

Example 10–4: CalculatorApplet.java

```java
import java.awt.*;
import java.awt.event.*;
```

```java
import javax.swing.*;

class CalculatorPanel extends JPanel
    implements ActionListener
{  public CalculatorPanel()
   {  setLayout(new BorderLayout());

      display = new JTextField("0");
      display.setEditable(false);
      add(display, "North");

      JPanel p = new JPanel();
      p.setLayout(new GridLayout(4, 4));
      String buttons = "789/456*123-0.=+";
      for (int i = 0; i < buttons.length(); i++)
         addButton(p, buttons.substring(i, i + 1));
      add(p, "Center");
   }

   private void addButton(Container c, String s)
   {  JButton b = new JButton(s);
      c.add(b);
      b.addActionListener(this);
   }

   public void actionPerformed(ActionEvent evt)
   {  String s = evt.getActionCommand();
      if ('0' <= s.charAt(0) && s.charAt(0) <= '9'
         || s.equals("."))
      {  if (start) display.setText(s);
         else display.setText(display.getText() + s);
         start = false;
      }
      else
      {  if (start)
         {  if (s.equals("-"))
            { display.setText(s); start = false; }
            else op = s;
         }
         else
         {  calculate(Double.parseDouble(display.getText()));
            op = s;
            start = true;
         }
      }
   }

   public void calculate(double n)
   {  if (op.equals("+")) arg += n;
      else if (op.equals("-")) arg -= n;
      else if (op.equals("*")) arg *= n;
      else if (op.equals("/")) arg /= n;
```

```
        else if (op.equals("=")) arg = n;
        display.setText("" + arg);
    }

    private JTextField display;
    private double arg = 0;
    private String op = "=";
    private boolean start = true;
}

public class CalculatorApplet extends JApplet
{   public void init()
    {   Container contentPane = getContentPane();
        contentPane.add(new CalculatorPanel());
    }
}
```

java.applet.Applet

- `void init()`

  is called when the applet is first loaded. Override this method and place all initialization code here.

- `void setSize(int width, int height)`

  requests that the applet be resized. This would be a great method if it worked on Web pages; unfortunately, it does not work in current browsers because it interferes with their page-layout mechanisms. But it does work in the applet viewer, and perhaps future browsers will support it and reflow the page when the applet size changes.

Life Cycle of an Applet

Four methods in the `Applet` class give you the framework on which you build any serious applet: `init()`, `start()`, `stop()`, `destroy()`. What follows is a short description of these methods, when these methods are called, and what code you should place into them.

`init()`

This method is used for whatever initializations are needed for your applet. This works much like a constructor—it is automatically called by the system when Java launches the applet for the first time. Common actions in an applet include processing PARAM values and adding user interface components.

Applets can have a default constructor, but it is customary to perform all initialization in the `init` method instead of the default constructor.

`start()`

This method is automatically called *after* Java calls the `init` method. It is also called whenever the user returns to the page containing the applet after having gone off to other pages. This means that the `start` method can be called repeatedly, unlike the `init` method. For this reason, put the code that you want executed only once in the `init` method, rather than in the `start` method. The `start` method is where you usually restart a thread for your applet, for example, to resume an animation. If your applet does nothing that needs to be suspended when the user leaves the current Web page, you do not need to implement this method (or the `stop` method).

`stop()`

This method is automatically called when the user moves off the page on which the applet sits. It can, therefore, be called repeatedly in the same applet. Its purpose is to give you a chance to stop a time-consuming activity from slowing down the system when the user is not paying attention to the applet. You should not call this method directly. If your applet does not perform animation, play audio files, or perform calculations in a thread, you do not usually need to use this method.

`destroy()`

Java guarantees to call this method when the browser shuts down normally. Since applets are meant to live on an HTML page, you do not need to worry about destroying the panel. This will happen automatically when the browser shuts down. What you *do* need to put in the `destroy` method is the code for reclaiming any non-memory-dependent resources such as graphics contexts that you may have consumed. Of course, Java calls the `stop` method before calling the `destroy` method if the applet is still active.

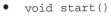

`java.applet.Applet`

- `void start()`

  overrides this method for code that needs to be executed *every time* the user visits the browser page containing this applet. A typical action is to reactivate a thread.

- `void stop()`

  overrides this method for code that needs to be executed *every time* the user leaves the browser page containing this applet. A typical action is to suspend a thread.

- `void destroy()`

  overrides this method for code that needs to be executed when the user exits the browser. A typical action is to call `destroy` on system objects.

The Applet HTML Tags and Attributes

Unfortunately, the HTML tags that will be created by the Java Plug-In are quite confusing because each applet can be specified in *three ways* and Sun's converter needs to deal with all the possibilities:

1. The EMBED tag that is understood by Netscape Navigator
2. The OBJECT tag that is understood by Internet Explorer and the latest versions of Navigator
3. The APPLET tag that is understood by the applet viewer and the HotJava browser.

Even worse, the syntax for applet properties is slightly different for each of these three tags.

We'll first focus on the APPLET tag, although it is deprecated in the latest versions of the W3 HTML specification. This is because Sun's applet viewer and Plug-In HTML translator don't yet understand the newer OBJECT tag.

In its most basic form, an example for using the APPLET tag looks like this:

```
<APPLET CODE="NotHelloWorldApplet.class" WIDTH=100 HEIGHT=100>
```

As you have seen, the CODE tag gives the name of the class file and must include the .class extension; the WIDTH and HEIGHT tags size the window that will hold the applet. Both are measured in pixels. You also need a matching </APPLET> tag that marks the end of the HTML tagging needed for an applet. These tags are required. If any are missing, the browser cannot load your applet.

All of this information would usually be embedded in an HTML page that, at the very least, might look like this:

```
<HTML>
<HEAD>
<TITLE>NotHelloWorldApplet</TITLE>
</HEAD>
<BODY>
The next line of text is displayed through
the auspices of Java:
<APPLET CODE="NotHelloWorldApplet.class" WIDTH=100 HEIGHT=100>
Any text here appears in non-Java enabled browsers only.
</APPLET>
</BODY>
</HTML>
```

NOTE: According to the HTML specification, the HTML tags such as <APPLET> can be in upper- or lowercase. Case is relevant in identifying the name of the applet class. The letter case may be significant in other items enclosed in quotes, such as names of JAR files, if the Web server file system is case sensitive.

What follows are short discussions of the various attributes that you can (or must) use following the APPLET tag in order to position your applet. For those familiar with HTML, many of these attributes are similar to those used with the <IMG> tag for image placement on a Web page.

Applet Attributes for Positioning

WIDTH, HEIGHT

These attributes are required and give the width and height of the applet, as measured in pixels. In the applet viewer, this is the initial size of the applet. You can resize any window that the applet viewer creates. In a browser, you *cannot* resize the applet. You will need to make a good guess about how much space your applet requires to show up well for all users.

ALIGN

This attribute specifies the alignment of the applet. There are two basic choices. The applet can be a block with text flowing around it, or the applet can be *inline*, floating inside a line of text as if it were an oversized text character. The first two values (LEFT and RIGHT) make the text flow around the applet. The others make the applet flow with the text.

The choices are described in Table 10–2.

Figure 10–7 shows all alignment options for an applet that floats with the surrounding text. The vertical bar at the beginning of each line is an image. Since the image is taller than the text, you can see the difference between alignment with the top or bottom of the line and the top or bottom of the text.

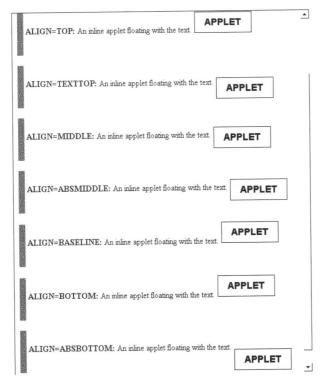

Figure 10–7: Applet alignment

Table 10–2: Applet positioning tags

Attribute	What It Does
LEFT	Places the applet at the left margin of the page. Text that follows on the page goes in the space to the right of the applet.
RIGHT	Places the applet at the right margin of the page. Text that follows on the page goes in the space to the left of the applet.
BOTTOM	Places the bottom of the applet at the bottom of the text in the current line.
TOP	Places the top of the applet with the top of the current line.
TEXTTOP	Places the top of the applet with the top of the text in the current line.
MIDDLE	Places the middle of the applet with the baseline of the current line.
ABSMIDDLE	Places the middle of the applet with the middle of the current line.
BASELINE	Places the bottom of the applet with the baseline of the current line.
ABSBOTTOM	Places the bottom of the applet with the bottom of the current line.
VSPACE, HSPACE	These optional attributes specify the number of pixels above and below the applet (VSPACE) and on each side of the applet (HSPACE).

Applet Attributes for Code

The following applet attributes tell the browser how to locate the applet code; here are short descriptions of them.

CODE

This attribute gives the name of the applet's class (or compiled) file. This name is taken relative to where the current page was located. This could be either a local directory or a Net URL. You cannot use absolute path names here. Either the CODE or the OBJECT attribute is required.

CODEBASE

This optional attribute tells the browser that your class files are found below the directory indicated in the CODEBASE tag. For example, if an applet called CalculatorApplet.class is in the directory MyApplets and the MyApplets directory is *below* the location of the Web page, you would use:

```
<APPLET CODE="CalculatorApplet.class" CODEBASE="MyApplets" WIDTH=100
    HEIGHT=150>
```

ARCHIVE

This optional attribute lists the Java archive file or files that contain classes and other resources for the applet. (See the section on JAR files later in this chapter for more on Java archive files.) These files are fetched from the Web server before the applet is loaded. This technique speeds up the loading process significantly since only one HTTP request is necessary to load a JAR file that contains many smaller files. The JAR files are separated by commas. For example:

```
<APPLET CODE="CalculatorApplet.class"
    ARCHIVE="CalculatorClasses.jar,corejava/CoreJavaClasses.jar"
    WIDTH=100 HEIGHT=150>
```

TIP: This tag has one very important application. If you have an applet that uses the Swing set but does not otherwise require any Java 2 features, you can deploy it in Java 1.1-compatible browsers (such as the current versions of Netscape and Internet Explorer) by supplying a JAR file that contains all Swing classes. You can obtain the appropriate JAR file by downloading the Swing supplement to Java 1.1 from the `java.sun.com` Web site. You must then package your applet inside a JAR file and load it together with the Swing JAR file. Then, supply an `ARCHIVE` parameter that looks like this:

```
<APPLET CODE="CalculatorApplet.class"
    ARCHIVE="CalculatorAppletClasses.jar,swing.jar"
    WIDTH=100 HEIGHT=150>
```

The file `swing.jar` is about 1 Mbyte, which is a pretty hefty download. So, you may not want to do this in a situation where some users might use a dialup line to access your Web page. Of course, the plug-In download is even larger, but it only needs to be done once. The JAR file is downloaded every time.

OBJECT

As another way to specify the applet class file, you can specify the name of a file that contains the serialized applet object, but browsers vary in support of this attribute. You will definitely need to use the plug-in if you want to use this feature. (An object is *serialized* when you write all its data fields to a file. We will discuss serialization in Chapter 12.) The object is deserialized from the file in order to return it to its previous state. When you use this tag, the `init` method is *not* called, but the applet's `start` method is called. Before serializing an applet object, you should call its `stop` method. This feature is useful for implementing a persistent browser that automatically reloads its applets and has them return to the same state that they were in when the browser was closed. This is a specialized feature, not normally encountered by Web page designers.

Either `CODE` or `OBJECT` must be present in every `APPLET` tag. For example,

```
<APPLET OBJECT="CalculatorApplet.object" WIDTH=100 HEIGHT=150>
```

NAME

Scripters will want to give the applet a NAME attribute that they can use to refer to the applet when scripting. Both Netscape and Internet Explorer let you call methods of an applet on a page through JavaScript. This is not a book on JavaScript, so we only give you a brief idea of the code that is required to call Java code from JavaScript.

> NOTE: JavaScript is a scripting language that can be used inside Web pages, invented by Netscape and originally called LiveScript. It has little to do with Java, except for some similarity in syntax. It was a marketing move to call it JavaScript. A subset (with the catchy name of ECMAScript) is standardized as ECMA-262. But, to nobody's surprise, Netscape and Microsoft support incompatible extensions of that standard in their browsers. For more information on JavaScript, we recommend the book *JavaScript: The Definitive Guide* by David Flanagan, published by O'Reilly & Associates.

To access an applet from JavaScript, you first have to give it a name.

```
<APPLET CODE="CalculatorApplet.class"
    WIDTH=100 HEIGHT=150
    NAME="calc">
</APPLET>
```

You can then refer to the object as `document.applets.`*appletname*. For example,

```
var calcApplet = document.applets.calc;
```

Through the magic of the integration between Java and JavaScript that both Netscape and Internet Explorer provide, you can call applet methods:

```
calcApplet.clear();
```

(Our calculator applet doesn't have a `clear` method; we just want to show you the syntax.)

The NAME attribute is also essential when you want two applets on the same page to communicate with each other directly. You specify a name for each current applet instance. You pass this string to the `getApplet` method of the `AppletContext` class. We will discuss this mechanism, called *inter-applet communication*, later in this chapter.

Applet Attributes for Java-Challenged Viewers

If a Web page containing an APPLET tag is viewed by a browser that is not aware of Java applets, then the browser ignores the unknown APPLET and PARAM tags. All text between the <APPLET> and </APPLET> tags is displayed by the browser. Conversely, Java-aware browsers do not display any text between the <APPLET> and </APPLET> tags. You can display messages inside these tags for those poor folks that use a prehistoric browser. For example,

```
<APPLET CODE="CalculatorApplet.class" WIDTH=100 HEIGHT=150>
If your browser could show Java, you would see
a calculator here>
</APPLET>
```

Of course, nowadays most browsers know about Java, but Java may be deactivated, perhaps by the user or by a paranoid system administrator. You can then use the ALT attribute to display a message to these unfortunate souls.

```
<APPLET CODE="CalculatorApplet.class" WIDTH=100 HEIGHT=150
ALT="If your browser could show Java, you would see
a calculator here">
```

The OBJECT Tag

The OBJECT tag is part of the HTML 4.0 standard and the W3 consortium suggests that people use it instead of the APPLET tag. There are 35 different attributes to the OBJECT tag, most of which (such as ONKEYDOWN) are only relevant to people writing Dynamic HTML. The various positioning tags such as ALIGN and HEIGHT works exactly as they did for the APPLET tag. The key attribute in the OBJECT tag for your Java applets is the CLASSID attribute. This attribute specifies the location of the object. Of course, OBJECT tags can load different kinds of objects, such as Java applets or ActiveX components like the plug-in itself. In the CODETYPE attribute, you specify the nature of the object. For example, Java applets have a code type of application/java. Here is an OBJECT tag to load a Java applet:

```
<OBJECT
    CODETYPE="application/java"
    CLASSID="java:CalculatorApplet.class"
    WIDTH=100 HEIGHT=150>
```

Note that the CLASSID attribute can be followed by a CODEBASE attribute that works exactly as it did with the APPLET tag.

You can use the OBJECT tag to load applets into the current versions of Netscape and Internet Explorer, but the applet viewer and the Plug-In HTML converter do not understand the OBJECT tag for applets.

Java Plug-In Tags

The Java Plug-In is loaded as a Netscape plug-in or an ActiveX control, via the EMBED or OBJECT tag. For example, the equivalent of the tag

```
<APPLET
    CODE="CalculatorApplet.class"
    CODEBASE="MyApplets"
    WIDTH=100
    HEIGHT=150>
<PARAM NAME="Font" VALUE="Helvetica">
</APPLET>
```

in Netscape Navigator is

```
<EMBED TYPE="application/x-java-applet;version=1.1"
    PLUGINSPAGE="http://java.sun.com/products/plugin/1.1
        /plugin-install.html"
    CODE="CalculatorApplet.class"
    CODEBASE="MyApplets"
    WIDTH=100
    HEIGHT=150>
<PARAM NAME="Font" VALUE="Helvetica">
</EMBED>
```

The equivalent tag in Internet Explorer is

```
<OBJECT CLASSID="clsid:8AD9C840-044E-11D1-B3E9-00805F499D93"
    CODEBASE="http://java.sun.com/products/plugin/1.1
        /jinstall-11-win32.cab#Version=1,1,0,0"
    WIDTH=100
    HEIGHT=150>
<PARAM NAME="TYPE" VALUE="application/x-java-applet;
    version=1.1">
<PARAM NAME="CODE" VALUE="CalculatorApplet.class">
<PARAM NAME="CODEBASE" VALUE="MyApplets">
<PARAM NAME="Font" VALUE="Helvetica">
</OBJECT>
```

Here are the details of the tag conversions if you insist on doing it by hand.

It is easy to convert from the APPLET tag to the EMBED tag: just change APPLET to EMBED and add the TYPE and PLUGINSPAGE attributes.

Converting from the APPLET tag to the OBJECT tag is more complex. You need to add the CLASSID and CODEBASE attributes and add a PARAM tag with name TYPE . (The CLASSID is always the same number; it is the globally unique ActiveX ID of the Java Plug-In.) Keep all attributes, except the ones listed in Table 10–3 that need to be converted to PARAM tags. If they conflict with existing PARAM tags, you can optionally use the prefix JAVA_ for the parameter names; for example,

```
<PARAM NAME="JAVA_CODE" VALUE="CalculatorApplet.class">
```

As you can see, the differences between these tags are purely cosmetic. In practice, it is best to use the plug-in HTML converter or some other script to produce the HTML code automatically.

The plug-in HTML converter also adds glue code that automatically selects the tags that match the browser. It either uses JavaScript or an incredibly convoluted sequence of tags that are selectively ignored by different browsers. For more information on this sordid topic, have a look at the HTML converter documentation.

Table 10–3: Translating between **APPLET** and **OBJECT** attributes

APPLET	OBJECT
`ALT=...`	N/A
`ARCHIVE=...`	`<PARAM NAME="ARCHIVE" VALUE=...>`
`CODE=...`	`<PARAM NAME="CODE" VALUE=...>`
`CODEBASE=...`	`<PARAM NAME="CODEBASE" VALUE=...>`
`OBJECT=...`	`<PARAM NAME="OBJECT" VALUE=...>`

Passing Information to Applets

Just as applications can use command-line information, applets can use parameters that are embedded in the HTML file. This is done via the HTML tag called PARAM along with attributes that you define. For example, suppose you want to let the Web page determine the style of the font to use in your applet. You could use the following HTML tags:

```
<APPLET CODE="FontParamApplet.class" WIDTH=200, HEIGHT=200>
<PARAM NAME=font VALUE="Helvetica">
</APPLET>
```

You then pick up the value of the parameter, using the getParameter method of the Applet class, as in the following example:

```
public class FontParamApplet extends JApplet
{   public void init()
    {   String fontName = getParameter("font");
    }  . . .
       . . .
}
```

NOTE: You can call the getParameter method only in the init method of the applet, *not* in the constructor. When the applet constructor is executed, the parameters are not yet prepared. Since the layout of most nontrivial applets is determined by parameters, we recommend that you don't supply constructors to applets. Simply place all initialization code into the init method.

Parameters are always returned as strings. You need to convert the string to a numeric type if that is what is called for. You do this in the standard way by using the appropriate method, such as parseInt of the Integer class.

For example, if we wanted to add a size parameter for the font, then the HTML code might look like this:

```
<APPLET CODE="FontParamApplet.class" WIDTH=200 HEIGHT=200>
<PARAM NAME=font VALUE="Helvetica">
<PARAM NAME=size VALUE="24">
</APPLET>
```

The following source code shows how to read the integer parameter.

```
public class FontParamApplet extends JApplet
{   public void init()
    {   String fontName = getParameter("font");
        int fontSize = Integer.parseInt(getParameter("size"));
        . . .
    }
}
```

NOTE: The strings used when you define the parameters via the PARAM tag and those used in the getParameter method must match exactly. In particular, both are case sensitive.

In addition to ensuring that the parameters match in your code, you should find out whether or not the `size` parameter was left out. You do this with a simple test for `null`. For example:

```
int fontsize;
String sizeString = getParameter("size");
if (sizeString == null) fontSize = 12;
else fontSize = Integer.parseInt(sizeString);
```

Here is a useful applet that uses parameters extensively. The applet draws a bar chart, shown in Figure 10–8.

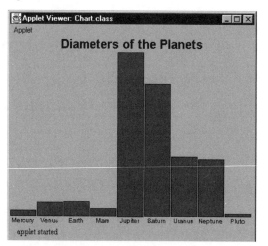

Figure 10–8: A chart applet

The applet takes the labels and the heights of the bars from the PARAM values in the HTML file. Here is what the HTML file for Figure 10–8 looks like:

```
<APPLET CODE="Chart.class" WIDTH=400 HEIGHT=300>
<PARAM NAME="title" VALUE="Diameters of the Planets">
<PARAM NAME="values" VALUE="9">
<PARAM NAME="name_1" VALUE="Mercury">
<PARAM NAME="name_2" VALUE="Venus">
<PARAM NAME="name_3" VALUE="Earth">
<PARAM NAME="name_4" VALUE="Mars">
<PARAM NAME="name_5" VALUE="Jupiter">
<PARAM NAME="name_6" VALUE="Saturn">
<PARAM NAME="name_7" VALUE="Uranus">
<PARAM NAME="name_8" VALUE="Neptune">
<PARAM NAME="name_9" VALUE="Pluto">
<PARAM NAME="value_1" VALUE="3100">
<PARAM NAME="value_2" VALUE="7500">
<PARAM NAME="value_3" VALUE="8000">
<PARAM NAME="value_4" VALUE="4200">
<PARAM NAME="value_5" VALUE="88000">
<PARAM NAME="value_6" VALUE="71000">
<PARAM NAME="value_7" VALUE="32000">
<PARAM NAME="value_8" VALUE="30600">
<PARAM NAME="value_9" VALUE="1430">
</APPLET>
```

You could have set up an array of strings and an array of numbers in the applet, but there are two advantages to using the PARAM mechanism instead. You can have multiple copies of the same applet on your Web page, showing different graphs: just put two APPLET tags with different sets of parameters on the page. And you can change the data that you want to chart. Admittedly, the diameters of the planets will stay the same for quite some time, but suppose your Web page contains a chart of weekly sales data. It is easy to update the Web page because it is plain text. Editing and recompiling a Java file on a weekly basis is more tedious.

In fact, there are commercial Java beans that do a lot fancier graphs than the one in our chart applet. If you buy one, you can drop it into your Web page and feed it parameters without ever needing to know how the applet renders the graphs.

Example 10–5 is the source code of our chart applet. Note that the init method reads the parameters, and the paintComponent method draws the chart.

Example 10–5: Chart.java

```
import java.awt.*;
import javax.swing.*;

class ChartPanel extends JPanel
```

```
{  public ChartPanel(double[] v, String[] n, String t)
   {  names = n;
      values = v;
      title = t;
   }

   public void paintComponent(Graphics g)
   {  super.paintComponent(g);
      if (values == null || values.length == 0) return;
      int i;
      double minValue = 0;
      double maxValue = 0;
      for (i = 0; i < values.length; i++)
      {  if (minValue > values[i]) minValue = values[i];
         if (maxValue < values[i]) maxValue = values[i];
      }

      Dimension d = getSize();
      int clientWidth = d.width;
      int clientHeight = d.height;
      int barWidth = clientWidth / values.length;

      Font titleFont
         = new Font("SansSerif", Font.BOLD, 20);
      FontMetrics titleFontMetrics
         = g.getFontMetrics(titleFont);
      Font labelFont
         = new Font("SansSerif", Font.PLAIN, 10);
      FontMetrics labelFontMetrics
         = g.getFontMetrics(labelFont);

      int titleWidth
         = titleFontMetrics.stringWidth(title);
      int y = titleFontMetrics.getAscent();
      int x = (clientWidth - titleWidth) / 2;
      g.setFont(titleFont);
      g.drawString(title, x, y);

      int top = titleFontMetrics.getHeight();
      int bottom = labelFontMetrics.getHeight();
      if (maxValue == minValue) return;
      double scale = (clientHeight - top - bottom)
         / (maxValue - minValue);
      y = clientHeight - labelFontMetrics.getDescent();
      g.setFont(labelFont);

      for (i = 0; i < values.length; i++)
      {  int x1 = i * barWidth + 1;
```

```
            int y1 = top;
            int height = (int)(values[i] * scale);
            if (values[i] >= 0)
                y1 += (int)((maxValue - values[i]) * scale);
            else
            {  y1 += (int)(maxValue * scale);
                height = -height;
            }

            g.setColor(Color.red);
            g.fillRect(x1, y1, barWidth - 2, height);
            g.setColor(Color.black);
            g.drawRect(x1, y1, barWidth - 2, height);
            int labelWidth
                = labelFontMetrics.stringWidth(names[i]);
            x = i * barWidth + (barWidth - labelWidth) / 2;
            g.drawString(names[i], x, y);
        }
    }

    private double[] values;
    private String[] names;
    private String title;
}

public class Chart extends JApplet
{  public void init()
    {  String v = getParameter("values");
        if (v == null) return;
        int n = Integer.parseInt(v);
        double[] values = new double[n];
        String[] names = new String[n];
        int i;
        for (i = 0; i < n; i++)
        {  values[i] = Double.parseDouble
                (getParameter("value_" + (i + 1)));
            names[i] = getParameter("name_" + (i + 1));
        }

        Container contentPane = getContentPane();
        contentPane.add(new ChartPanel(values, names,
            getParameter("title")));
    }
}
```

API `java.applet.Applet`

- `public String getParameter(String name)`

  gets a parameter defined with a PARAM directive in the Web page loading the applet. The string is case sensitive.

- `public String getAppletInfo()`

  is a method that many applet authors override to return a string that contains information about the author, version, and copyright of the current applet. You need to create this information by overriding this method in your applet class.

- `public String[][] getParameterInfo()`

  is a method that many applet authors override to return an array of PARAM tag options that this applet supports. Each row contains three entries: the name, the type, and a description of the parameter. Here is an example:

  ```
  "fps",    "1-10",    "frames per second"
  "repeat", "boolean", "repeat image loop?"
  "images", "url",     "directory containing images"
  ```

Pop-Up Windows in Applets

An applet sits embedded in a Web page, in a frame of a size that is fixed by the WIDTH and HEIGHT values in the applet tags of the HTML page. This can be quite limiting. Many programmers wonder whether they can have a pop-up window to make better use of the available space. It is, indeed, possible to create a pop-up frame. Here is a simple applet with a single button labeled Calculator. When you click on the button, a calculator pops up in a separate window.

The pop-up is easy to do. We simply use the `Calculator` class from Chapter 7. Recall that it is derived from JFrame, so we add the necessary code to create a new calculator object, as indicated by the bold line of the following code.

```
public class PopupCalculatorApplet extends JApplet
   implements ActionListener
{  public void init()
   {  Button calcButton = new Button("Calculator");
      calcButton.addActionListener(this);
      getContentPane().add(calcButton);
   }
   public void actionPerformed(ActionEvent evt)
   {  if (calc.isVisible()) calc.setVisible(false);
      else calc.show();
   }

   private JFrame calc = new CalculatorFrame();
}
```

When you click on the calculator button, the dialog box pops up and floats over the Web page. When you click on the button again, the calculator goes away.

There is, however, a catch that you need to know about before you put this applet on your Web page. To see how the calculator looks to a potential user, load the Web page from a browser, not the applet viewer. The calculator will be surrounded by a border with an ominous warning message (see Figure 10–9).

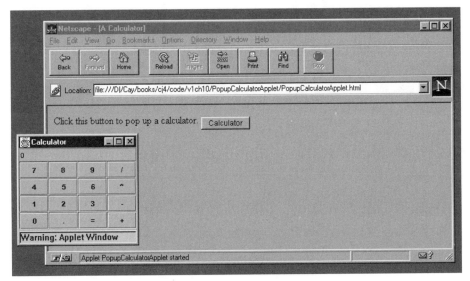

Figure 10–9: A pop-up window inside a browser

This message is a security feature of all Web browsers. The browser wants to make sure that your applet does not launch a window that the user might mistake for a local application. The fear is that an unsuspecting user could visit a Web page, which automatically launches the applets on it, and mistakenly type in a password or credit card number, which the applet would send back to its host.

To avoid any possibility of shenanigans like this, all pop-up windows launched by an applet bear a label such as "Untrusted Java Applet," "Unauthenticated Java Applet," or "Warning: Applet Window". That label is likely to be so scary to most users that you may want to avoid launching any external frames from your applet.

If your browser supports signed applets, you can configure it to omit the warning message for pop-up windows that are spawned by signed applets.

Multimedia

Applets can handle both images and audio. As we write this, images must be in GIF or JPEG form, audio files in AU, AIFF, WAV or MIDI. Animated GIFs are ok, and the animation is displayed. Usually the files containing this information are specified as URL, so we take URLs up first.

URLs

A URL is really nothing more than a description of a resource on the Internet. For example, `"http://java.sun.com/index.html"` tells the browser to use the hypertext transfer protocol on the file `index.html` located at `java.sun.com`. Java has the class URL that encapsulates URLs. The simplest way to make a URL is to give a string to the URL constructor:

```
URL u = new URL("http://java.sun.com/index.html");
```

This is called an *absolute* URL because we specify the entire resource name. Another useful URL constructor is a *relative* URL.

```
URL data = new URL(u, "data/planets.dat");
```

This specifies the file `planets.dat`, located in the `data` subdirectory of the URL `u`.

Both constructors make sure that you have used the correct syntax for a URL. If you haven't, they cause a run-time error, a so-called `MalformedURLException`. Up to now, you have been able to ignore most run-time errors, but this error is one the compiler will not let you ignore. You must tell the compiler that you are prepared for the error condition. The relevant code is as follows:

```
try
{   String s = "http://java.sun.com/index.html";
    URL u = new URL(s);
    . . .
}
catch(MalformedURLException e)
{   // deal with error
    System.out.println("Error " + e);
}
```

We will discuss this syntax for dealing with exceptions in detail in Chapter 12. For now, if you see code like this in one of our code samples, just gloss over the `try` and `catch` keywords.

A common way of obtaining a URL is to ask an applet where it came from, in particular,

- What is the URL of the page that is calling it?

- What is the URL of the applet itself?

To find the former, use the `getDocumentBase` method; to find the latter, use `getCodeBase`. You do not need to place these calls in a `try` block.

Obtaining Multimedia Files

You can retrieve images and audio files with the `getImage` and `getAudioClip` methods. For example:

```
Image cat = getImage(getDocumentBase(), "images/cat.gif");
AudioClip meow = getAudioClip(getDocumentBase(),
    "audio/meow.au");
```

Here, we use the `getDocumentBase` method that returns the URL from which your applet is loaded. The second argument to the URL constructor specifies where the image or audio clip is located, relative to the base document. (Applets do not need to go through a `Toolkit` object in order to get an image.)

NOTE: The images and audio clips must be located on the same server that hosts the applet code. For security reasons, applets cannot access any files on another server ("applets can only phone home").

Once you have the images and audio clips, what can you do with them? You saw in Chapter 7 how to display a single image. In the multithreading chapter of Volume 2, you will see how to play an animation sequence composed of multiple images. To play an audio clip, simply invoke its `play` method.

You can also call `play` without first loading the audio clip.

```
play(getDocumentBase(), "audio/meow.au");
```

However, to show an image, you must first load it.

For faster downloading, multimedia objects can be stored in JAR files (see the section below). The `getImage` and `getAudioClip/play` methods automatically search the JAR files of the applet. If the image or audio file is contained in a JAR file, it is loaded immediately. Otherwise, the browser requests it from the Web server.

`java.net.URL`

* `URL(String name)`

    creates a URL object from a string describing an absolute URL.

* `URL(URL base, String name)`

    creates a relative URL object. If the string `name` describes an absolute URL, then the `base` URL is ignored. Otherwise, it is interpreted as a relative directory from the `base` URL.

A P I `java.applet.Applet`

- `public URL getDocumentBase()`

  gets the URL for the page that contains the applet.

- `public URL getCodeBase()`

  gets the URL of the applet code itself.

- `void play(URL url)`

- `void play(URL url, String name)`

  The first form plays an audio file specified by the URL. The second form uses the string to provide a path relative to the URL in the first argument. Nothing happens if the audio clip cannot be found.

- `AudioClip getAudioClip(URL url)`

- `AudioClip getAudioClip(URL url, String name)`

  gets an audio clip, given a URL. The second form uses the string to provide a path relative to the URL in the first argument. The methods return `null` if the audio clip cannot be found.

- `Image getImage(URL url)`

- `Image getImage(URL url, String name)`

  gets an image, given a URL. These methods always return an image object immediately, even if the image does not exist. The actual image data is loaded when the image is first displayed. See Chapter 7 for details on image acquisition.

The Applet Context

An applet runs inside a browser or the applet viewer. An applet can ask the browser to do things for it, for example, fetch an audio clip, show a short message in the status line, or show a different Web page. The ambient browser can carry out these requests, or it can ignore them. For example, if an applet running inside the applet viewer asks the applet viewer program to show a Web page, nothing happens.

To communicate with the browser, an applet calls the `getAppletContext` method. That method returns an object that implements an interface of type `AppletContext`. You can think of the concrete implementation of the `AppletContext` interface as a communication path between the applet and the ambient browser. In addition to `getAudioClip` and `getImage`, the `AppletContext` interface contains four useful methods, which we discuss in the next few sections.

Inter-Applet Communication

A Web page can contain more than one applet. If a Web page contains multiple applets from the same CODEBASE, they can communicate with each other. Naturally, this is an advanced technique that you probably will not need very often.

If you give NAME tags to each applet in the HTML file, you can use the getApplet(String) method of the AppletContext interface to get a reference to the applet. For example, if your HTML file contains the tag

```
<APPLET CODE="Chart.class" WIDTH=100 HEIGHT=100 NAME="Chart1">
```

then the call

```
Applet chart1 = getAppletContext().getApplet("Chart1");
```

gives you a reference to the applet. What can you do with the reference? Provided you give the Chart class a method to accept new data and redraw the chart, you can call this method by making the appropriate cast.

```
((Chart)chart1).setData(3, "Earth", 9000);
```

You can also list all applets on a Web page, whether or not they have a NAME tag. The getApplets method returns a so-called *enumeration object*. (You will learn more about enumeration objects in Volume 2.) Here is a loop that prints the class names of all applets on the current page.

```
Enumeration e = getAppletContext().getApplets();
while (e.hasMoreElements())
{  Object a = e.nextElement();
   System.out.println(a.getClass().getName());
}
```

An applet cannot communicate with an applet on a different Web page.

Displaying Items in the Browser

You have access to two areas of the ambient browsers: the status line and the Web page display area. Both use methods of the AppletContext class.

You can display a string in the status line at the bottom of the browser with the showStatus message, for example,

```
showStatus("Loading data . . . please wait");
```

TIP: In our experience, showStatus is of limited use. The browser is also using the status line, and, more often than not, it will overwrite your precious message with chatter like "Applet running." Use the status line for fluff messages like "loading data . . . please wait," but not for something that the user cannot afford to miss.

You can tell the browser to show a different Web page with the showDocument method. There are several ways to do this. The simplest is with a call to showDocument with one argument, the URL you want to show.

```
URL u = new URL("http://java.sun.com");
getAppletContext().showDocument(u);
```

The problem with this call is that it opens the new Web page in the same window as your current page, thereby displacing your applet. To return to your applet, the user must select Back.

You can tell the browser to show the applet in another window by giving a second parameter in the call to showDocument. The second argument is a string. If it is the special string "_blank", the browser opens a new window with the document, instead of displacing the current document. More importantly, if you take advantage of the frame feature in HTML, you can split a browser window into multiple frames, each of which has a name. You can put your applet into one frame and have it show documents in other frames. We will show you an example of doing this in the next section.

Table 10–4 shows all possible arguments to showDocument.

Table 10–4: showDocument arguments

Second argument to showDocument	Location
"_self" or none	Show the document in the current frame.
"_parent"	Show the document in the parent container.
"_top"	Show the document in the topmost frame.
"_blank"	Show in new, unnamed, top-level window.
any other string	Show in the frame with that name. If no frame with that name exists, open a new window and give it that name.

java.applet.Applet

- public AppletContext getAppletContext()

  gives you a handle to the applet's browser environment. On most browsers, you can use this information to control the browser in which the applet is running.

- void showStatus(String msg)

  shows the string specified in the status line of the browser.

- `Image getImage(URL url)`

  returns an image object that encapsulates the image specified by the URL. If the image does not exist, this method immediately returns `null`. Otherwise, a separate thread is launched to load the image. See Chapter 7 for details on image acquisition.

- `AudioClip getAudioClip(URL url)`

  returns an `AudioClip` object, which stores the sound file specified by the URL. Use the `play` method to actually play the file.

`java.applet.AppletContext`

- `Enumeration getApplets()`

  returns an enumeration (see Volume 2) of all the applets in the same context, that is, the same Web page.

- `Applet getApplet(String name)`

  returns the applet in the current context with the given name; returns `null` if none exists. Only the current Web page is searched.

- `void showDocument(URL url)`
- `void showDocument(URL url, String target)`

  show a new Web page in a frame in the browser. In the first form, the new page displaces the current page. The second form uses the string to identify the target frame. The target string can be one of the following: `"_self"` (show in current frame, equivalent to the first form of the method), `"_parent"` (show in parent frame), `"_top"` (show in topmost frame), and `"_blank"` (show in new, unnamed, top-level window). Or, the target string can be the name of a frame.

NOTE: Sun's applet viewer does not show Web pages. The showDocument command is ignored in the applet viewer.

A Bookmark Applet

This applet takes advantage of the frame feature in HTML 3.2 or later. We divide the screen vertically into two frames. The left frame contains a Java applet that shows a list of bookmarks. When you double-click on any of the bookmarks in the list, the applet then goes to the corresponding Web page and displays it on the right (see Figure 10–10).

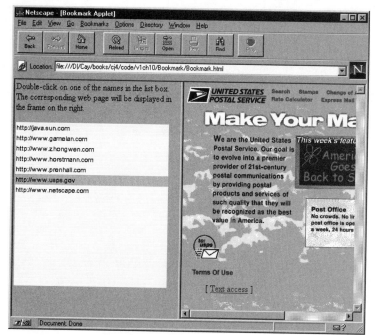

Figure 10–10: A bookmark applet

Example 10–6 shows the HTML file that defines the frames.

Example 10–6: Bookmark.html

```
<HTML>
<HEAD>
<TITLE>Bookmark Applet</TITLE>
</HEAD>
<FRAMESET COLS="320,*">
<FRAME NAME="left" SRC="Left.html"
   MARGINHEIGHT=2 MARGINWIDTH=2
   SCROLLING="no" NORESIZE>
<FRAME NAME="right" SRC="Right.html"
   MARGINHEIGHT=2 MARGINWIDTH=2
   SCROLLING="yes" NORESIZE>
</FRAMESET>
</HTML>
```

We will not go over the exact syntax elements. What is important is that each frame has two essential features: a name (given by the NAME tag) and a URL (given by the SRC tag). We could not think of any good names for the frames, so we simply named them "left" and "right".

The left frame (Example 10–7) loads a file that we called Left.html, which loads the applet into the left frame. It simply specifies the applets and the bookmarks. You can customize this file for your own Web page by changing the bookmarks.

Example 10–7: Left.html (before processing with the HTML converter)

```
<HTML>
<TITLE>A Bookmark Applet</TITLE>
<BODY>
Double-click on one of the names in the list box.
The corresponding web page
will be displayed in the frame on the right.
<P>
<APPLET CODE="Bookmark.class" WIDTH=290 HEIGHT=300>
<PARAM NAME=link_1 VALUE="http://java.sun.com">
<PARAM NAME=link_2 VALUE="http://www.gamelan.com">
<PARAM NAME=link_3 VALUE="http://www.zhongwen.com">
<PARAM NAME=link_4 VALUE="http://www.horstmann.com">
<PARAM NAME=link_5 VALUE="http://www.prenhall.com">
<PARAM NAME=link_6 VALUE="http://www.usps.gov">
<PARAM NAME=link_7 VALUE="http://www.netscape.com">
</APPLET>
</BODY>
</HTML>
```

The right frame (Example 10–8) loads a dummy file that we called Right.html. (Netscape did not approve when we left the right frame blank, so we gave it a dummy file for starters.)

Example 10–8: Right.html

```
<HTML>
<TITLE>
Web pages will be displayed here.
</TITLE>
<BODY>
Double-click on one of the names in the list box to the left.
The web page will be displayed here.
</BODY>
</HTML>
```

The code for the bookmark applet that is given in Example 10–9 is simple. It reads the values of the parameters link_1, link_2, and so on, into the list box. When you double-click on one of the items in the list box, the showDocument method displays that page in the right frame.

Example 10–9: Bookmark.java

```java
import java.awt.*;
import java.applet.*;
import java.util.*;
import java.net.*;
import javax.swing.*;
import javax.swing.event.*;

public class Bookmark extends JApplet
    implements ListSelectionListener
{   public void init()
    {   int i = 1;
        String s;
        Vector v = new Vector();
        while ((s = getParameter("link_" + i)) != null)
        {   v.add(s);
            i++;
        }
        JList links = new JList(v);
        Container contentPane = getContentPane();
        contentPane.add(links);
        links.addListSelectionListener(this);
    }

    public void valueChanged(ListSelectionEvent evt)
    {   if (evt.getValueIsAdjusting()) return;
        JList source = (JList)evt.getSource();
        String arg = (String)source.getSelectedValue();
        try
        {   AppletContext context = getAppletContext();
            URL u = new URL(arg);
            context.showDocument(u, "right");
        } catch(Exception e)
        {   showStatus("Error " + e);
        }
    }
}
```

JAR Files

The calculator applet from this chapter uses two classes: `CalculatorApplet` and `CalculatorPanel`. You know that the applet tag references the class file that contains the class derived from `JApplet`:

```
<APPLET CODE="CalculatorApplet.class" WIDTH=100 HEIGHT=150>
```

When the browser reads this line, it makes a connection to the Web server and fetches the file `CalculatorApplet.class`. The *class loader* of the Java interpreter that is built into the browser then loads the `CalculatorApplet` class from that file. During the loading process, the class loader must *resolve* the other classes used in this class. After doing so, it then knows it needs one more class to run the applet. The browser, therefore, makes an additional connection to the Web server. Most applets consist of more than two classes, and the Web browser must make many connections, one for each class file. Loading such an applet over a slow network connection can take many minutes.

NOTE: It is important to remember that the reason for this long loading time is not the size of the class files—they are quite small—rather it is because of the *considerable* overhead involved in establishing a connection to the Web server. If you need to make dozens of separate connections, you will wait a long, long time.

Java now supports an improved method for loading class files, which allows you to package all the needed class files into a single file. This file can then be downloaded with a *single* HTTP request to the server. Files that archive Java class files are called Java ARchive, or JAR, files. JAR files can contain both class files and other file types such as image and sound files. JAR files can also be compressed, using the familiar ZIP compression format, as defined by PKWARE. You should definitely take advantage of JAR files once your audience has browsers that can deal with them.

You use the `jar` tool to make JAR files. (In the default installation, it's in the `\jdk\bin` directory.) The most common command, to make a new JAR file, uses the following syntax:

```
jar cf JARFileName File1 File2 . . .
```

For example,

```
jar cf CalculatorClasses.jar *.java icon.gif
```

In general, the `jar` command has the format

```
jar options File1 File2 . . .
```

Table 10–5 lists all the options for the `jar` program. They are similar to the options of the UNIX `tar` command.

Table 10–5: `jar` program options

Option	Description
c	Creates a new or empty archive and adds files to it. If any of the specified file names are a directory, then the `jar` program processes them recursively.
t	Displays the table of contents.
x	Extracts files. If you supply one or more file names, only those files are extracted. Otherwise, all files are extracted.
f	Specifies the JAR file name as the second command-line argument. If this parameter is missing, then `jar` will write the result to standard output (when creating a JAR file) or read it from standard input (when extracting or tabulating a JAR file).
v	Generates verbose output.
m	Adds a *manifest* to the JAR file. A manifest is a description of the archive contents and origin. Every archive has a default manifest, but you can supply your own if you want to authenticate the contents of the archive. We will discuss this in the security chapter of Volume 2.
0	Stores without ZIP compression.
M	Does not create a manifest file for the entries.

Once you have a JAR file, you need to reference it in the `APPLET` tag, as in the following example.

```
<APPLET CODE="CalculatorApplet.class"
    ARCHIVE="CalculatorClasses.jar"
    WIDTH=100 HEIGHT=150>
```

Note that the `CODE` attribute must still be present. The `CODE` attribute tells the browser the name of the applet. The `ARCHIVE` is merely another source where the applet class and other files may be located, in addition to the Web server. Whenever a class, image, or sound file is needed, a JAR-aware browser searches the JAR files in the `ARCHIVE` list first. Only if the file is not contained in the archive will it be fetched from the Web server.

Resources

Classes that are used in both applets and applications often use associated data files, such as

* Image and sound files

- Text files with message strings and button labels
- Files with binary data, for example, to describe the layout of a map

In Java, such an associated file is called a *resource*.

> NOTE: In Windows, the term "resource" has a more specialized meaning. Windows resources also consist of images, button labels, and so on, but they are attached to the executable file and accessed by a standard programming interface. In contrast, Java resources are stored as separate files, not as part of class files. And it is up to each class to access and interpret the resource data.

For example, consider a class `AboutPanel` that displays a message such as the one in Figure 10–11.

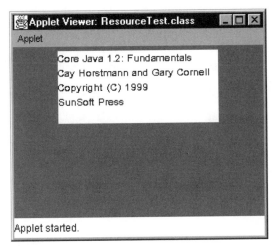

Figure 10–11: Displaying a resource from a JAR file

Of course, the book title and copyright year in the panel will change for the next edition of the book. To make it easy to track this change, we want to put the text inside a file and not hardcode it as a string in the dialog class.

Suppose we want to place the `about.txt` file always in the same location as the class file `AboutPanel.class`. The problem is that a class file can be in one of many locations:

- In the local file system, relative to the class path
- In a JAR file
- On a Web server

The class loader knows how to search all relevant locations until it has located the class file, but we would need to manually repeat this search process to locate the associated resource file. The resource loading feature automates this task. To load a resource, do the following:

1. Get the `Class` object of the class that has a resource, for example, `AboutPanel.class`.

2. Call `getResource(name)` to get the resource file as a URL.

3. If the resource is an image or audio file, read it directly with the `getImage` or `getAudioClip` method.

4. Otherwise, use the `openStream` method on the URL to read in the data in the file. (See Chapter 12 for more on streams.)

The point is that the class loader remembers the location where it loaded the class, and then it can search for the associated resource in the same location.

For example, to read in the file `about.txt`, you can use the following commands:

```
URL url = AboutPanel.class.getResource("about.txt");
InputStream in = url.openStream();
```

Because this combination is so common, there is a convenient shortcut method: `getResourceAsStream` returns an `InputStream`, not a URL.

```
InputStream in
    = AboutPanel.class.getResourceAsStream("about.txt");
```

To read from this stream, you will need to know how to process input (see Chapter 12 for details). In the sample program, we read the stream a line at a time with the following instructions:

```
BufferedReader br = new BufferedReader(new
    InputStreamReader(in));
String line;
while ((line = br.readLine()) != null)
    process line;
```

On the CD-ROM, you will find a JAR file that contains all class files for this example and the resource file `about.txt`. This demonstrates that the applet locates the resource file in the same location as the class file, namely, inside the JAR file.

TIP: As you saw in the preceding section, you can place image and audio files inside a JAR file and simply access them with the `getImage` and `getAudioClip` methods—these methods automatically search JAR files. But, to load other files from a JAR file, you need the `getResourceAsStream` method.

Instead of placing a resource file inside the same directory as the class file, you can place it in a subdirectory. You can use a hierarchical resource name such as

```
data/text/about.txt
```

This is a relative resource name, and it is interpreted relative to the package of the class that is loading the resource. Note that you must always use the / separator, regardless of the directory separator on the system that actually stores the resource files. For example, on Windows, the resource loader automatically translates / to \ separators.

A resource name starting with a / is called an absolute resource name. It is located by Java in the same way that a class inside a package would be located. For example, a resource

```
/corejava/title.txt
```

is located in the `corejava` directory (which may be a subdirectory of the class path, inside a JAR file, or on the Web server).

Automating the loading of files is all that the resource loading feature does. There are no standard methods for interpreting the contents of a resource file. Each applet must have its own way of interpreting the contents of its resource files.

Another common application of resources is the internationalization of applets and applications. Language-dependent strings, such as messages and user interface labels, are stored in resource files, with one file for each language. The *internationalization API*, which is discussed in Volume 2, supports a standard method for organizing and accessing these localization files.

Example 10–10 is the HTML source for testing a resource; Example 10–11 is the Java code.

Example 10–10: ResourceTest.html

```
<APPLET CODE="ResourceTest.class"
    WIDTH=300 HEIGHT=200
    ARCHIVE="ResourceTest.jar">
</APPLET>
```

Example 10–11: ResourceTest.java

```
import java.io.*;
import java.awt.*;
import java.awt.event.*;
import java.applet.*;
import javax.swing.*;

public class ResourceTest extends JApplet
{  public void init()
   {  Container contentPane = getContentPane();
      contentPane.add(new AboutPanel());
   }
```

```
}

class AboutPanel extends JPanel
{   public AboutPanel()
    {   JTextArea ta = new JTextArea();
        add(ta);

        try
        {   InputStream in = AboutPanel.class.
                getResourceAsStream("about.txt");
            BufferedReader br = new BufferedReader(new
                InputStreamReader(in));
            String line;
            while ((line = br.readLine()) != null)
                ta.append(line + "\n");
        } catch(IOException e) {}
    }
}
```

java.lang.Class

- URL getResource(String name)

- InputStream getResourceAsStream(String name)

    find the resource in the same place as the class and then return a URL or
    input stream you can use for loading the resource. The methods return null
    if the resource isn't found and so do not throw an exception for an I/O error.

    Parameters: name   the resource name

It's an Applet. It's an Application. It's Both!

Quite a few years ago, a "Saturday Night Live" skit poking fun at a television
commercial showed a couple arguing about a white, gelatinous substance. The
husband said, "It's a dessert topping." The wife said, "It's a floor wax." And the
announcer concluded triumphantly, "It's both!"

Well, in this section, we will show you how to write a Java program that is *both*
an applet and an application. That is, you can load the program with the applet
viewer or a browser, or you can start it from the command line with the java
interpreter. We are not sure how often this comes up—we found it interesting
that this could be done at all and thought you would, too.

The screen shots in Figures 10–12 and 10–13 show the *same* program, launched
from the command line as an application and viewed inside the applet viewer
as an applet.

Let us see how this can be done. Every class file has exactly one public class.
In order for the applet viewer to launch it, that class must derive from

Figure 10–12: The calculator as an application

Figure 10–13: The calculator as an applet

Applet. In order for Java to start the application, it must have a static main method. So far, we have

```
class MyAppletApplication extends JApplet
{  public void init() { . . . }
   . . .
   static public void main(String[] args) { . . . }
}
```

What can we put into main? Normally, we make an object of the class and invoke show on it. But this case is not so simple. You cannot show a naked applet. The applet must be placed inside a frame. And once it is inside the frame, its init method needs to be called.

To provide a frame, we create the class AppletFrame, like this:

```
public class AppletFrame extends JFrame
{  AppletFrame(Applet a, int x, int y)
   {  setTitle(a.getClass().getName());
      setSize(x, y);
      addWindowListener(new WindowAdapter()
```

```
                     {   public void windowClosing(WindowEvent e)
                         {   System.exit(0);
                         }
                     } );
                Container contentPane = getContentPane();
                contentPane.add(a);
                a.init();
                show();
                a.start();
            }
            . . .
    }
```

The constructor of the frame puts the applet (which derives from Component) inside the frame, calls the init function, calls show (to show the frame), and then starts the applet. The frame also supplies a handler to close the program when the user closes the window.

In the main method of the applet/application, we make a new frame of this kind. In this example, we just reuse the calculator.

```
class MyAppletApplication extends JApplet
{   . . .
    public static void main(String args[])
    {   new AppletFrame(new MyAppletApplication(), 620, 400);
    }
}
```

There is one catch. If the program is started with the Java interpreter and not the applet viewer, and it calls getAppletContext, it gets a null pointer because it has not been launched inside a browser. This causes a run-time crash whenever we have code like

```
getAppletContext().showStatus(message);
```

While we do not want to write a full-fledged browser, we do need to supply the bare minimum to make calls like this work. The call displays no message, but at least it will not crash the program. It turns out that all we need to do is implement two interfaces: AppletStub and AppletContext.

You have already seen applet contexts in action. They are responsible for fetching images and audio files and for displaying Web pages. They can, however, politely refuse, and this is what our applet context will do. The major purpose of the AppletStub interface is to locate the applet context. Every applet has an applet stub (set with the setStub method of the Applet class).

In our case, AppletFrame implements both AppletStub and AppletContext. We supply the bare minimum functionality that is necessary to implement these two interfaces.

```
public class AppletFrame extends JFrame
    implements AppletStub, AppletContext
{   . . .

    // AppletStub methods
    public boolean isActive() { return true; }
    public URL getDocumentBase() { return null; }
    public URL getCodeBase() { return null; }
    public String getParameter(String name) { return ""; }
    public AppletContext getAppletContext() { return this; }
    public void appletResize(int width, int height) {}

    // AppletContext methods
    public AudioClip getAudioClip(URL url) { return null; }
    public Image getImage(URL url) { return null; }
    public Applet getApplet(String name) { return null; }
    public Enumeration getApplets() { return null; }
    public void showDocument(URL url) {}
    public void showDocument(URL url, String target) {}
    public void showStatus(String status) {}
}
```

NOTE: When you compile this file, you will get a warning that `java.awt.Window` also has a method called `isActive` that has package visibility. Since this class is not in the same package as the `Window` class, it cannot override the `Window.isActive` method. That is fine with us—we want to supply a new `isActive` method for the `AppletStub` interface. And, interestingly enough, it is entirely legal to add a new method with the same signature to the subclass. Whenever the object is accessed through a `Window` reference inside the `java.awt` package, the package-visible `Window.isActive` method is called. But whenever the object is accessed through an `AppletFrame` or `AppletStub` reference, the `AppletFrame.isActive` method is called.

Next, the constructor of the frame class calls `setStub` on the applet to make itself its stub.

```
public class AppletFrame extends JFrame
    implements AppletStub, AppletContext
{   AppletFrame(Applet a, int x, int y)
    {   setTitle(a.getClass().getName());
        setSize(x, y);
        addWindowListener(new WindowAdapter()
            {   public void windowClosing(WindowEvent e)
                {   System.exit(0);
                }
            } );
        Container contentPane = getContentPane();
        contentPane.add(a);
```

```
            a.setStub(this);
            a.init();
            show();
            a.start();
        }
        . . .
    }
```

One final twist is possible. Suppose we want to use the calculator as an applet and application simultaneously. Rather than moving the methods of the `CalculatorApplet` class into the `CalculatorAppletApplication` class, we will just use inheritance. Here is the code for the class that does this.

```
public class CalculatorAppletApplication extends CalculatorApplet
{  public static void main(String args[])
    {  new AppletFrame(new CalculatorApplet(), 100, 150);
    }
}
```

You can do this with any applet, not just with the calculator applet. All you need to do is derive a class `MyAppletApplication` from your applet class and pass a new `MyApplet()` object to the `AppletFrame` in the `main` method. The result is a class that is both an applet and an application.

Examples 10–12 and 10–13 list the code.

Example 10–12: AppletFrame.java

```
import java.awt.*;
import java.awt.event.*;
import java.applet.*;
import java.net.*;
import java.util.*;
import javax.swing.*;

public class AppletFrame extends JFrame
    implements AppletStub, AppletContext
{  AppletFrame(Applet a, int x, int y)
    {  setTitle(a.getClass().getName());
        setSize(x, y);
        addWindowListener(new WindowAdapter()
            {  public void windowClosing(WindowEvent e)
                {  System.exit(0);
                }
            } );
        Container contentPane = getContentPane();
        contentPane.add(a);
        a.setStub(this);
        a.init();
```

```
        show();
        a.start();
    }

    // AppletStub methods
    public boolean isActive() { return true; }
    public URL getDocumentBase() { return null; }
    public URL getCodeBase() { return null; }
    public String getParameter(String name) { return ""; }
    public AppletContext getAppletContext() { return this; }
    public void appletResize(int width, int height) {}

    // AppletContext methods
    public AudioClip getAudioClip(URL url) { return null; }
    public Image getImage(URL url) { return null; }
    public Applet getApplet(String name) { return null; }
    public Enumeration getApplets() { return null; }
    public void showDocument(URL url) {}
    public void showDocument(URL url, String target) {}
    public void showStatus(String status) {}
}
```

Example 10–13: CalculatorAppletApplication.java

```
public class CalculatorAppletApplication
    extends CalculatorApplet
// It's an applet. It's an application. It's BOTH!
{ public static void main(String[] args)
    { new AppletFrame(new CalculatorApplet(), 180, 180);
    }
}
```

Chapter 11

Exceptions and Debugging

- ▼ DEALING WITH ERRORS
- ▼ CATCHING EXCEPTIONS
- ▼ SOME TIPS ON USING EXCEPTIONS
- ▼ DEBUGGING TECHNIQUES
- ▼ USING THE JDB DEBUGGER

In a perfect world, users would never enter data in the wrong form, files they choose to open would always exist, and code would never have bugs. So far, we have mostly presented code as though we lived in this kind of perfect world. It is now time to turn to the mechanisms Java has for dealing with the real world of bad data and buggy code.

Encountering errors is unpleasant. If a user loses all the work he or she did during a program session because of a programming mistake or some external circumstance, that user may forever turn away from your program. At the very least, you must:

- Notify the user of an error
- Save all work
- Allow users to gracefully exit the program

For exceptional situations, such as bad input data with the potential to bomb the program, Java uses a form of error-trapping called, naturally enough,

583

exception handling. Exception handling in Java is similar to that in C++ or Delphi. It is far more flexible than the On Error GoTo syntax used in VB. The first part of this chapter covers Java's exceptions.

The second part of this chapter concerns finding bugs in your code before they cause exceptions at run time. Unfortunately, if you just use the JDK, then bug detection is just as it was back in the dark ages. We give you some tips and a few tools to ease the pain. Then, we explain how to use the command-line debugger as a tool of last resort. For the serious Java developer, products such as Sun's Java WorkShop, Symantec's Café, and Inprise's JBuilder have quite useful debuggers that alone can make the products well worth their cost.

Dealing with Errors

Suppose an error occurs while a Java program is running. The error might be caused by a file containing wrong information, a flaky network connection, or (we hate to mention it) use of an invalid array index or an attempt to use an object reference that hasn't yet been assigned to an object. Users expect that programs will act sensibly when errors happen. If an operation cannot be completed because of an error, the program ought to either:

• Return to a safe state and enable the user to execute other commands

or

• Allow the user to save all his or her work and terminate the program gracefully

This may not be easy to do: the code that detects (or even causes) the error condition is usually far removed from the code that can roll back the data to a safe state, or the code that can save the user's work and exit cheerfully. The mission of error-handling is to transfer control from where the error occurred to an error-handler that can deal with the situation. To handle exceptional situations in your program, you must take into account the errors and problems that may occur. What sorts of problems do you need to consider?

User input errors. In addition to the inevitable typos, some users like to blaze their own trail instead of following directions. Suppose, for example, that a user asks to connect to a URL that is syntactically wrong. Your code should check the syntax, but suppose it does not. Then, the network package will complain.

Device errors. Hardware does not always do what you want it to. The printer may be off. A web page may be temporarily unavailable. Devices will often fail in the middle of a task. For example, a printer may run out of paper in the middle of a printout.

Physical limitations. Disks can fill up; you run out of available memory.

Code errors. A method may not perform correctly. For example, it could deliver wrong answers or use other methods incorrectly. Computing an invalid array index, trying to find a nonexistent entry in a hash table, and trying to pop an empty stack are all examples of a method's responding to code errors.

The traditional reaction to an error in a method is to return a special error code that the calling method analyzes. For example, methods that read information back from files often return a –1 end-of-file value marker rather than a standard character. This can be an efficient method for dealing with many exceptional conditions, and for certain I/O operations, Java does return null if the operation wasn't successful. (In Chapter 10, you saw an example of this with the getParameter method of the Applet class.) Unfortunately, it is not always possible to return an error code. There may be no obvious way of distinguishing valid and invalid data. A method returning an integer cannot simply return –1 to denote the error—the value –1 might be a perfectly valid result.

Moreover, it is hardly in keeping with the ideas behind object-oriented programming to return a number as a mark of an error condition.

Instead, as we mentioned back in Chapter 5, Java allows every method an alternate exit path if it is unable to complete its task in the normal way. In this situation, the method does not return a value. Instead, it *throws* an object that encapsulates the error information. Note that the method exits immediately; it does not return its normal (or any) value. Moreover, Java doesn't activate the code that called the method; instead, the exception-handling mechanism begins its search for an *exception handler* that can deal with this particular error condition.

Exceptions have their own syntax and are part of a special inheritance hierarchy. We take up the syntax first and then give a few hints on how to use this language feature effectively.

The Classification of Exceptions

In Java, an exception object is always an instance of a class derived from Throwable. In particular, as you will soon see, you can create your own exception classes, if the ones built into Java do not suit your needs.

Figure 11–1 is a simplified diagram of the exception hierarchy in Java.

Notice that all exceptions descend from Throwable, but the hierarchy immediately splits into two branches: Error and Exception.

The Error hierarchy describes internal errors and resource exhaustion inside the Java run-time system. You should not throw an object of this type. There is little you can do if such an internal error occurs, beyond notifying the user and trying to terminate the program gracefully. These situations are quite rare.

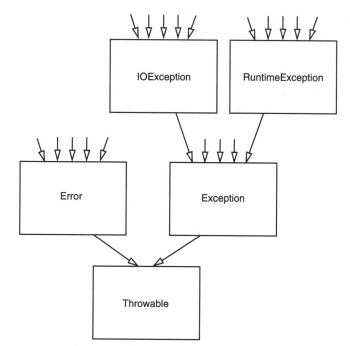

Figure 11–1: Exception hierarchy in Java

When doing Java programming, you focus on the `Exception` hierarchy. The `Exception` hierarchy also splits into two branches: exceptions that derive from `RuntimeException` and those that do not. The general rule is this:

- A `RuntimeException` happens because you made a programming error. Any other exception occurs because a bad thing, such as an I/O error, happened to your otherwise good program.

Exceptions that inherit from `RuntimeException` include such problems as:

- A bad cast
- An out-of-bounds array access
- A null pointer access

Exceptions that do not inherit from `RuntimeException` include:

- Trying to read past the end of a file
- Trying to open a malformed URL
- Trying to find a `Class` object for a string that does not denote an existing class

The rule "If it is a `RuntimeException`, it was your fault" works pretty well. You could have avoided that `ArrayIndexOutOfBoundsException` by testing the array index against the array bounds. The `NullPointerException` would not have happened had you checked whether or not the variable was `null` before using it.

How about a malformed URL? Isn't it also possible to find out whether it is "malformed" before using it? Well, different browsers can handle different kinds of URLs. For example, Netscape can deal with a `mailto:` URL, whereas the applet viewer cannot. Thus, the notion of "malformed" depends on the environment, not just on your code.

NOTE: The name `RuntimeException` is somewhat confusing. Of course, all of the errors we are discussing occur at run time.

C++ NOTE: If you are familiar with the (much more limited) exception hierarchy of the ANSI C++ library, you will be really confused at this point. C++ has two fundamental exception classes, `runtime_error` and `logic_error`. The `logic_error` class is the equivalent of Java's `RuntimeException` and also denotes logical errors in the program. The `runtime_error` class is the base class for exceptions caused by unpredictable problems. It is equivalent to exceptions in Java that are *not* of type `RuntimeException`.

Advertising the Exceptions That a Method Throws

A Java method can throw an exception if it encounters a situation it cannot handle. The idea is simple: a method will not only tell the Java compiler what values it can return, *it is also going to tell the compiler what can go wrong.* For example, code that attempts to read from a file knows that the file might not exist or that it might be empty. The code that tries to process the information in a file therefore will need to notify the compiler that it can throw some sort of `IOException`.

The place where you advertise that your method can throw an exception is in the header of the method; the header changes to reflect the exceptions the method can throw. For example, here is the header for a method in Java's `BufferedReader` class that is supposed to read a line of text from a stream, such as a file or network connection. (See Chapter 12 for more on streams.)

```
public String readLine() throws IOException
```

The header indicates this method returns a string, but it *also* has the capacity to go wrong in a special way—by throwing an `IOException`. If this sad state should come to pass, the method will not return a string but instead will throw an object of the `IOException` class. If it does, then the run-time system will begin to search for an exception handler that knows how to deal with `IOException` objects.

When you write your own methods, you don't have to advertise every possible throwable object that your method might actually throw. To understand when (and what) you have to advertise in the `throws` clause of the methods you write, keep in mind that an exception is thrown in any of the following four situations:

- You call a method that throws an exception, for example, the `readLine` method of the `BufferedReader` class.

- You detect an error and throw an exception with the `throw` statement (we cover the `throw` statement in the next section).

- You make a programming error, such as `a[-1] = 0`.

- An internal error occurs in Java.

If either of the first two scenarios occurs, you must tell the people who will use your method that using your method may cause an exception to be thrown.

Why? Any method that throws an exception is a potential death trap. If no handler catches the exception, the program terminates. (Programmers using your code do not generally like to have their programs end unexpectedly as a result of using your ever-so-carefully crafted code.)

As with Java methods that are part of the supplied classes, you declare that your method may throw an exception with an *exception specification* in the method header.

```
class Animation
{   . .

    public Image loadImage(String s) throws IOException
    {   . . .
    }
}
```

If a method must deal with more than one exception, you must indicate all exceptions in the header. Separate them by a comma as in the following example:

```
class Animation
{   . . .
    public Image loadImage(String s)
        throws EOFException, MalformedURLException
    {   . . .
    }
}
```

However, you do not need to advertise internal Java errors, that is, exceptions inheriting from `Error`. Any code could potentially throw those exceptions, and they are entirely beyond your control.

Similarly, you should not advertise exceptions inheriting from `RuntimeException`.

```
class Animation
{   . . .
```

```
    void drawImage(int i)
        throws ArrayIndexOutOfBoundsException // NO!!!
    {   . . .
    }
}
```

These run-time errors are completely under your control. If you are so concerned about array index errors, you should spend the time needed to fix them instead of advertising the possibility that they can happen.

The Java Language Specification calls any exception that derives from the class `Error` or the class `RuntimeException` an *unchecked* exception. All other exceptions are called *checked* exceptions. This is useful terminology that we will also adopt. It is the checked exceptions that are the ones you should deal with, either by handling them (see below) or advertising that they may be propagated. Unchecked exceptions are either beyond your control (`Error`) or result from conditions that you should not have allowed in the first place (`RuntimeException`).

The Java rule for exception specifications is simple:

A method must declare all the checked exceptions it throws.

If your method fails to do this, the Java compiler will issue an error message.

CAUTION: If you override a method from a superclass in your subclass, the subclass method cannot throw more checked exceptions than the superclass method that you replace. (It can throw fewer, if it likes.) In particular, if the superclass method throws no checked exception at all, neither can the subclass. For example, if you override `JComponent.paintComponent`, your `paintComponent` method may not throw any checked exceptions, since the superclass method doesn't throw any.

When a method in a class declares that it throws an exception that is an instance of a particular class, then it may throw an exception of that class or of any of its subclasses. For example, the `readLine` method of the `BufferedReader` class says that it throws an `IOException`. We do not know what kind of `IOException`. It could be a plain `IOException` or an object of one of the various child classes, such as `EOFException`.

C++ NOTE: The `throws` specifier is the same as the `throw` specifier in C++, with one important difference. In C++, `throw` specifiers are enforced at *run time*, not at compile time. That is, the C++ compiler pays no attention to exception specifications. But if an exception is thrown in a function that is not part of the `throw` list, then the `unexpected` function is called, and, by default, the program terminates.

Also, in C++, a function may throw any exception if no `throw` specification is given. In Java, a method without a `throws` specifier may not throw any checked exception at all.

How to Throw an Exception

Let us suppose something terrible has happened in your code. You have a method, readData, that is reading in a file whose header promised

```
Content-length: 1024
```

But, you get an end of file after 733 characters. You decide this situation is so abnormal that you want to throw an exception.

You need to decide what exception type to throw. Some kind of IOException would be a good choice. Perusing the tree.html file in the Java API documentation, you find an EOFException with the description "Signals that an EOF has been reached unexpectedly during input." Perfect. Here is how you throw it:

```
throw new EOFException();
```

or, if you prefer,

```
EOFException e = new EOFException();
throw e;
```

Here is how it all fits together:

```
String readData(BufferedReader in) throws EOFException
{   . . .
    while (. . .)
    {   if (ch == -1) // EOF encountered
        {   if (n < len)
                throw new EOFException();
        }
        . . .
    }
    return s;
}
```

The EOFException has a second constructor that takes a string argument. You can put this to good use by describing the exceptional condition more carefully.

```
String gripe = "Content-length: " + len + " Received: " + n;
throw new EOFException(gripe);
```

As you can see, throwing an exception is easy if one of the existing exception classes works for you. In this case:

1. Find an appropriate exception class.

2. Make an object of that class.

3. Throw it.

Once a method throws an exception, the method does not return to its caller. This means that you do not have to worry about cooking up a default return value or an error code.

C++ NOTE: Throwing an exception is the same in C++ and in Java, with one small exception. In Java, you can throw only objects of child classes of `Throwable`. In C++, you can throw values of any type.

Creating Exception Classes

Your code may run into a problem that is not adequately described by any of the standard exception classes. In this case, it is easy enough to create your own exception class. Just derive it from `Exception` or from a child class of `Exception` such as `IOException`. It is customary to give both a default constructor and a constructor that contains a detailed message. (The `toString` method of the `Throwable` base class prints out that detailed message, which is handy for debugging.)

```
class FileFormatException extends IOException
{   public FileFormatException() {}
    public FileFormatException(String gripe)
    {   super(gripe);
    }
}
```

Now you are ready to throw your very own exception type.

```
String readData(BufferedReader in) throws FileFormatException
{   . . .
    while (. . .)
    {   if (ch == -1) // EOF encountered
        {   if (n < len)
                throw new FileFormatException();
        }
        . . .
    }
    return s;
}
```

`java.lang.Throwable`

- `Throwable()`

  constructs a new `Throwable` object with no detailed message.

- `Throwable(String message)`

  constructs a new `Throwable` object with the specified detailed message. By convention, all derived exception classes support both a default constructor and a constructor with a detailed message.

- `String getMessage()`

  gets the detailed message of the `Throwable` object.

Catching Exceptions

You now know how to throw an exception. It is pretty easy. You throw it and you forget it. Of course, some code has to catch the exception. Catching exceptions requires more planning.

If an exception occurs that is not caught anywhere in a nongraphical application, the program will terminate and print a message to the console giving the type of the exception and a stack trace. A graphics program (both an applet and an application), prints the same error message, but the program goes back to its user interface processing loop. (When you are debugging a graphically based program, it is a good idea to keep the Console available on the screen and not minimized.)

To catch an exception, you set up a `try`/`catch` block. The simplest form of the `try` block is as follows:

```
try
{   code
    more code
    more code
}
catch(ExceptionType e)
{   handler for this type
}
```

If any of the code inside the `try` block throws an exception of the class specified in the `catch` clause, then,

1.   The program skips the remainder of the code in the `try` block.

2.   The program executes the handler code inside the `catch` clause.

If none of the code inside the `try` block throws an exception, then the program skips the `catch` clause.

If any of the code in a method throws an exception of a type other than the one named in the `catch` clause, this method exits immediately. (Hopefully, one of its callers has already coded a `catch` clause for that type.)

To show this at work, here is some code in our `Console` class from our corejava package.

```
public static String readLine()
{   int ch;
    String r = "";
    boolean done = false;
    while (!done)
    {   try
```

```
        {   ch = System.in.read();
            if (ch < 0 || (char)ch == '\n')
                done = true;
            else
                r = r + (char) ch;
        }
        catch(IOException e)
        {   done = true;
        }
    }
    return r;
}
```

Notice that most of the code in the `try` clause is straightforward: it accumulates characters until we encounter the end of the line or the end of the file. As you can see by looking at the Java API, there is the possibility that the `read` method will throw an `IOException`. In that case, the entire `if` statement is skipped and we set `done` to `true` in the `catch` clause. We figured that if there is a problem with the input, the caller does not want to know about it and wants to use only the characters that we have accumulated so far. For the `Console` class, that seems like a reasonable way to deal with this exception. What other choice do you have?

Often, the best choice is to do nothing at all. If an error occurs in the `read` method, let the caller of the `readLine` method worry about it! If we take that approach, then we have to advertise the fact that the method may throw an `IOException`.

```
public static String readLine()
    throws IOException
{   int ch;
    String r = "";
    boolean done = false;
    while (!done)
    {   ch = System.in.read();
        if (ch < 0 || (char)ch == '\n')
            done = true;
        else
            r = r + (char) ch;
    }
    return r;
}
```

Remember, the compiler strictly enforces the `throws` specifiers. If you call a method that throws a checked exception, you must either handle it or pass it on.

Which of the two is better? As a general rule, you should catch those exceptions that you know how to handle and propagate those that you do not know how to handle. When you propagate an exception, you must add a `throws` modifier to alert the caller that an exception may be thrown.

Look at the Java API documentation to see what methods throw which exceptions. Then, decide whether you should handle them or add them to the `throws` list. There is nothing embarrassing about the latter choice. It is better to direct an exception to a competent handler than to squelch it.

Please keep in mind that there is one exception to this rule, as we mentioned earlier.

If you are writing a method that overrides a superclass method that throws no exceptions (such as `paintComponent` in `JComponent`), then you *must* catch each checked exception in the method's code. You are not allowed to add more `throws` specifiers to a subclass method than are present in the superclass method.

TIP: Don't be shy about throwing or propagating exceptions to signal problems that you can't handle properly. On the other hand, your fellow programmers will hate you if you write methods that throw exceptions unnecessarily and that they must handle or pass on. If you can do something intelligent about an exceptional condition, then you should not use the sledgehammer of an exception.

C++ NOTE: Catching exceptions is almost the same in Java and in C++. Strictly speaking, the analog of

```
catch(Exception e) // Java
```

is

```
catch(Exception& e) // C++
```

There is no analog to the C++ `catch(...)`. This is not needed in Java because all exceptions derive from a common base class.

Catching Multiple Exceptions

You can catch multiple exception types in a `try` block and handle each type differently. You use a separate `catch` clause for each type as in the following example:

```
try
{   code that might
    throw exceptions
}
catch(MalformedURLException e1)
{   // emergency action for malformed URLs
}
catch(UnknownHostException e2)
{   // emergency action for unknown hosts
}
catch(IOException e3)
{   // emergency action for all other I/O problems
}
```

The exception object (e1, e2, e3) may contain information about the nature of the exception. To find out more about the object, try

```
e3.getMessage()
```

to get the detailed error message (if there is one), or

```
e3.getClass().getName()
```

to get the actual type of the exception object.

Rethrowing Exceptions

Occasionally, you need to catch an exception without addressing the root cause of it. This need typically occurs when you have to do some local cleanup but can't fully resolve the problem. You then want to take your emergency action and again call throw to send the exception back up the calling chain. You can see a typical example of this in the following code.

```
Graphics g = image.getGraphics();
try
{   code that might
    throw exceptions
}   catch(MalformedURLException e)
{   g.dispose();
    throw e;
}
```

The above code shows one of the most common reasons for having to rethrow an exception that you have caught. If you do not dispose of the graphics context object in the catch clause, it will *never* be disposed of. (Of course, its finalize method might dispose of it, but that can take a long time.)

On the other hand, the underlying cause, the malformed URL exception, *has not disappeared.* You still want to report it to the authorities, who presumably know how to deal with such an exception. (See the next section for a more elegant way to achieve the same result.)

You can also throw a different exception than the one you catch.

```
try
{   acme.util.Widget a = new acme.util.Widget();
    a.load(s);
    a.paint(g);
}
catch(RuntimeException e)
{   // sheesh—another ACME error
    throw new Exception("ACME error");
}
```

The `finally` *Clause*

When your code throws an exception, it stops processing the remaining code in your method and exits the method. This is a problem if the method has acquired some local resource that only it knows about and if that resource must be cleaned up. One solution is to catch and rethrow all exceptions. But this solution is tedious because you need to clean up the resource allocation in two places, in the normal code and in the exception code.

Java has a better solution, the `finally` clause:

```
Graphics g = image.getGraphics();
try
{   code that might
    throw exceptions
}
catch(IOException e)
{   done = true;
}
finally
{   g.dispose();
}
```

This program executes the code in the `finally` clause whether or not an exception was caught. This means, in the example code above, the program will dispose of the graphics context *under all circumstances.*

Let us look at the three possible situations where the program will execute the `finally` clause.

1. The code throws no exceptions. In this event, the program first executes all the code in the `try` block. Then, it executes the code in the `finally` clause and then executes the first line after the `try` block.

2. The code throws an exception that is caught in a `catch` clause, in our case, an `IOException`. For this, the program executes all code in the `try` block, up to the point at which the exception was thrown. The remaining code in the `try` block is skipped. Then, the program executes the code in the matching `catch` clause, then the code in the `finally` clause, and then exits the method.

    If the `catch` clause does not throw an exception, then the program executes the first line after the `try` block. If it does, then the exception is thrown back to the caller of this method.

3. The code throws an exception that is not caught in any `catch` clause. For this, the program executes all code in the `try` block until the exception is thrown. The remaining code in the `try` block is skipped. Then, the code in the `finally` clause is executed, and the exception is thrown back to the caller of this method.

You can use the `finally` clause without a `catch` clause. For example, consider the following `try` statement:

```
Graphics g = image.getGraphics();
try
{   code that might
    throw exceptions
}
finally
{   g.dispose();
}
```

The `g.dispose()` command in the `finally` clause is executed whether or not an exception is encountered in the `try` block. Of course, if an exception is encountered, it is rethrown and must be caught in another `catch` clause.

C++ NOTE: There is one fundamental difference between C++ and Java with regard to exception-handling. Java has no destructors; thus, there is no stack unwinding as in C++. This means that the Java programmer must manually place code to reclaim resources in `finally` blocks. Of course, since Java does garbage collection, there are far fewer resources that require manual deallocation.

A Final Look at Java Error- and Exception-Handling

Example 11–1 deliberately generates a number of different errors and catches various exceptions (see Figure 11–2).

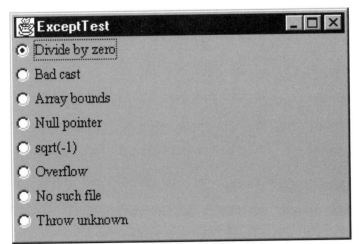

Figure 11-2: A program that generates exceptions

Try it out. Click on the buttons and see what exceptions are thrown.

As you know, a programmer error such as a bad array index throws a
RuntimeException. An attempt to open a nonexistent file triggers an
IOException. The program catches RuntimeException objects, then
general Exception objects.

```java
try
{   // various bad things
}
catch(RuntimeException e)
{   System.out.println("Caught RuntimeException: " + e);
}
catch(Exception e)
{   System.out.println("Caught Exception: " + e);
}
```

You can see which exception you caused in the console window. If you click on
the "Throw Unknown" button, an UnknownError object is thrown. This is not a
child class of Exception, so our program does not catch it. Instead, the user
interface code prints an error message and a stack trace to the console.

> NOTE: As you can see when you run the program in Example 11–1, not all the bad
> things you can do in Java throw exceptions. Floating-point divides by zero, overflows,
> and math errors do not throw any exceptions at all. (Interger division by 0 throws an
> ArithmeticException.)

Example 11–1: ExceptTest.java

```java
import java.awt.*;
import java.awt.event.*;
import javax.swing.*;
import java.io.*;

public class ExceptTest extends JFrame
    implements ActionListener
{   public ExceptTest()
    {   JPanel p = new JPanel();;
        ButtonGroup g = new ButtonGroup();
        p.setLayout(new GridLayout(8, 1));
        divideByZeroButton
            = addRadioButton("Divide by zero", g, p);
        badCastButton = addRadioButton("Bad cast", g, p);
        arrayBoundsButton
            = addRadioButton("Array bounds", g, p);
        nullPointerButton
            = addRadioButton("Null pointer", g, p);
        negSqrtButton = addRadioButton("sqrt(-1)", g, p);
        overflowButton = addRadioButton("Overflow", g, p);
        noSuchFileButton
```

```
        = addRadioButton("No such file", g, p);
     throwUnknownButton
        = addRadioButton("Throw unknown", g, p);
     getContentPane().add(p);
   }

   private JRadioButton
     addRadioButton(String s, ButtonGroup g, JPanel p)
   {  JRadioButton button = new JRadioButton(s, false);
      button.addActionListener(this);
      g.add(button);
      p.add(button);
      return button;
   }

   public void actionPerformed(ActionEvent evt)
   {  try
      {  Object source = evt.getSource();
         if (source == divideByZeroButton)
         {  a[1] = a[2] / (a[3] - a[3]);
         }
         else if (source == badCastButton)
         {  f = (Frame)evt.getSource();
         }
         else if (source == arrayBoundsButton)
         {  a[1] = a[10];
         }
         else if (source == nullPointerButton)
         {  f = null;
            f.setSize(200, 200);
         }
         else if (source == negSqrtButton)
         {  a[1] = Math.sqrt(-1);
         }
         else if (source == overflowButton)
         {  a[1] = 1000 * 1000 * 1000 * 1000;
            int n = (int)a[1];
         }
         else if (source == noSuchFileButton)
         {  FileInputStream is
               = new FileInputStream("No such file");
         }
         else if (source == throwUnknownButton)
         {  throw new UnknownError();
         }
      }
      catch(RuntimeException e)
      {  System.out.println("Caught RuntimeException: " + e);
      }
      catch(Exception e)
      {  System.out.println("Caught Exception: " + e);
      }
   }
```

```
public static void main(String[] args)
{   JFrame frame = new ExceptTest();
    frame.setSize(150, 200);
    frame.addWindowListener(new WindowAdapter()
        {   public void windowClosing(WindowEvent e)
            { System.exit(0); }
        } );

    frame.show();
}

private double[] a = new double[10];
private Frame f = null;
private JRadioButton divideByZeroButton;
private JRadioButton badCastButton;
private JRadioButton arrayBoundsButton;
private JRadioButton nullPointerButton;
private JRadioButton negSqrtButton;
private JRadioButton overflowButton;
private JRadioButton noSuchFileButton;
private JRadioButton throwUnknownButton;
}
```

Some Tips on Using Exceptions

There is a tendency to overuse exceptions. After all, who wants to go to the trouble to write methods that parse input before using it when exception-handling makes it so easy? Instead of parsing a URL when the user enters it, just send it off to a method that catches a `MalformedURLException`. Saves time, saves trouble. Wrong! While having an exception handler costs nothing, the actual handling of an exception will almost always cost a lot of time. Misusing exceptions can therefore slow your code down dramatically. Here are four tips on using exceptions.

1.   *Exception-handling is not supposed to replace a simple test.*

As an example of this, we wrote some code that uses the built-in `Stack` class. The code in Example 11–2 tries 1,000,000 times to pop an empty stack. It first does this by finding out whether or not the stack is empty.

```
if (!s.empty()) s.pop();
```

Next, we tell it to pop the stack no matter what. Then, we catch the `EmptyStackException` that tells us that we should not have done that.

```
try()
{   s.pop();
}
catch(EmptyStackException e)
{
}
```

On our test machine, we got the timing data in Table 11–1.

Table 11–1: Timing data

Test	Throw/Catch
990 milliseconds	18020 milliseconds

As you can see, it took roughly 18 times longer to catch an exception than it does to perform a simple test. The moral is: Use exceptions for exceptional circumstances only.

2. *Do not micromanage exceptions.*

Many people wrap every statement in a separate `try` block.

```
istream is;
Stack s;

for (i = 0; i < 100; i++)
{  try
   {    n = s.pop();
   }
   catch (EmptyStackException s)
   {    // stack was empty
   }
   try
   {    out.writeInt(n);
   }
   catch (IOException e)
   {    // problem writing to file
   }
}
```

This approach blows up your code dramatically. Think about the task that you want the code to accomplish. Here we want to pop 100 numbers off a stack and save them to a file. (Never mind why—it is just a toy example.) There is nothing we can do if a problem rears its ugly head. If the stack is empty, it will not become occupied. If there is an error in the file, the error will not magically go away. It therefore makes sense to wrap the *entire task* in a `try` block. If any one operation fails, you can then abandon the task.

```
try
{  for (i = 0; i < 100; i++)
   {  n = s.pop();
      out.writeInt(n);
   }
}
catch (IOException e)
```

```
{ // problem writing to file
}
catch (EmptyStackException s)
{ // stack was empty
}
```

This looks much cleaner. It fulfills one of the promises of exception-handling, to *separate* normal processing from error-handling.

3.   *Do not squelch exceptions.*

In Java, there is the tremendous temptation to shut up exceptions. You write a method that calls a method that might throw an exception once a century. The compiler whines because you have not declared the exception in the `throws` list of your method. You do not want to put it in the `throws` list because then the compiler will whine about all the methods that call your method. So you just shut it up:

```
Image loadImage(String s)
{   try
    {   lots of code
    }
    catch(Exception e)
    {} // so there
}
```

Now your code will compile without a hitch. It will run fine, except when an exception occurs. Then, the exception will be silently ignored. If you believe that exceptions are at all important, you need to make some effort to handle them right.

4.   *Propagating exceptions is not a sign of shame.*

Many programmers feel compelled to catch all exceptions that are thrown. If they call a method that throws an exception, such as the `FileInputStream` constructor or the `readLine` method, they instinctively catch the exception that may be generated. Often, it is actually better to *propagate* the exception instead of catching it:

```
void readStuff(String name) throws IOException
{   FileInputStream in = new FileInputStream(name);
    . . .
}
```

Higher-level methods are often better equipped to inform the user of errors or to abandon unsuccessful commands.

Example 11-2: ExceptionalTest.java

```
import java.util.*;

class ExceptionalTest
{   public static void main(String[] args)
```

```
{   int i = 0;
    int ntry = 1000000;
    Stack s = new Stack();
    long s1;
    long s2;
    System.out.println("Testing for empty stack");
    s1 = new Date().getTime();
    for (i = 0; i <= ntry; i++)
        if (!s.empty()) s.pop();
    s2 = new Date().getTime();
    System.out.println((s2 - s1) + " milliseconds");

    System.out.println("Catching EmptyStackException");
    s1 = new Date().getTime();
    for (i = 0; i <= ntry; i++)
    {   try
        {   s.pop();
        }
        catch(EmptyStackException e)
        {
        }
    }
    s2 = new Date().getTime();
    System.out.println((s2 - s1) + " milliseconds");
}
}
```

Debugging Techniques

Suppose you wrote your program and made it bulletproof by catching and properly handling all exceptions. Then you run it, and it does not work right. Now
what? (If you never have this problem, you can skip the remainder of this chapter.)

Of course, it is best if you have a convenient and powerful debugger. Debuggers
are available as a part of professional development environments such as Inprise
JBuilder, Java WorkShop or Supercede's Java product. However, if you use a
new version of Java that is not yet supported by development environments or
if you are on a budget or work on an unusual platform, you will need to do a
great deal of debugging by the time-honored method of inserting print statements into your code.

Useful Tricks for Debugging

Here are some tips for efficient debugging if you have to do it all yourself.

1.   You can print the value of any variable with code like this:

```
System.out.println("x = " + x);
```

If x is a number, it is converted to its string equivalent. If x is an object,
then Java calls its toString method. Most of the classes in the Java library

are very conscientious about overriding the `toString` method to give you useful information about the class. This is a real boon for debugging. You should make the same effort in your classes.

2. To get the state of the current object, print the state of the `this` object.

```
System.out.println("Entering loadImage. this = " + this);
```

This code calls the `toString` method of the current class, and you get a printout of all instance fields. Of course, this approach works best when the `toString` method in this class does a conscientious job and reports the values of all data fields.

3. Recall that we gave you the code for a generic `toString` method in Chapter 5—we used the reflection feature to enumerate and print all data fields. Here is an even shorter version of that code.

```
public String toString()
{   java.util.Hashtable h = new java.util.Hashtable();
    Class cls = getClass();
    Field[] f = cls.getDeclaredFields();
    try
    {   AccessibleObject.setAccessible(fields, true);
        for (int i = 0; i < f.length; i++)
            h.put(f[i].getName(), f[i].get(this));
    }
    catch (SecurityException e) {}
    catch (IllegalAccessException e) {}

    if (cls.getSuperclass().getSuperclass() != null)
        h.put("super", super.toString());
    return cls.getName() + h;
}
```

The code uses the reflection mechanism to enumerate all fields. It puts the pairs (field name, field value) into a hash table. It then uses the `toString` method of the `Hashtable` class to print out the names and values. The only drawback is that the (name, value) pairs are listed in random order.

Here is a typical printout:

```
Employee{hireDay=Day[1996,12,1], salary=35000.0,
    name=Harry Hacker}
```

4. You can get a stack trace from any exception object with the `printStackTrace` method in the `Throwable` class. The following code catches any exception, prints the exception object and the stack trace, and rethrows the exception so it can find its intended handler.

```
try
{  . . .
}
catch(Throwable t)
{  t.printStackTrace();
   throw t;
}
```

5. You don't even need to catch an exception to generate a stack trace. Simply insert the statement

```
new Throwable().printStackTrace();
```

anywhere into your code to get a stack trace.

Normally, the stack trace is displayed on `System.out`. You can send it to a file with the `void printStackTrace(PrintWriter s)` method. Or, if you want to display the stack trace in a window, here is how you can capture it into a string:

```
StringWriter out = new StringWriter();
new Throwable().printStackTrace(new PrintWriter(out));
String trace = out.toString();
```

(See Chapter 12 for the `PrintWriter` and `StringWriter` classes.)

6. If you ever looked at a Swing window and wondered how its designer managed to get all the components to line up so nicely, you can spy on the contents. Hit CTRL+SHIFT+F1, and you get a printout of all components in the hierarchy:

```
FontDialog[frame0,0,0,300x200,layout=java.awt.BorderLayout,...
    javax.swing.JRootPane[,4,23,292x173,layout=javax.swing.JRootPane$RootLayout,...
      javax.swing.JPanel[null.glassPane,0,0,292x173,hidden,layout=java.awt.FlowLayout,...
      javax.swing.JLayeredPane[null.layeredPane,0,0,292x173,...
        javax.swing.JPanel[null.contentPane,0,0,292x173,layout=java.awt.GridBagLayout,...
          javax.swing.JList[,0,0,73x152,alignmentX=null,alignmentY=null,...
            javax.swing.CellRendererPane[,0,0,0x0,hidden]
              javax.swing.DefaultListCellRenderer$UIResource[,-73,-19,0x0,...
          javax.swing.JCheckBox[,157,13,50x25,layout=javax.swing.OverlayLayout,...
          javax.swing.JCheckBox[,156,65,52x25,layout=javax.swing.OverlayLayout,...
          javax.swing.JLabel[,114,119,30x17,alignmentX=0.0,alignmentY=null,...
          javax.swing.JTextField[,186,117,105x21,alignmentX=null,alignmentY=null,...
          javax.swing.JTextField[,0,152,291x21,alignmentX=null,alignmentY=null,...
```

Actually, there will be two identical copies of the printout—one when you depress the F1 key, one when you release it. To capture the typically lengthy output, run your program from the command line as

```
java MyProgram > output.txt
```

Then press the key combination, close the program and look for the printout inside the file `output.txt`.

7. If you design your own custom Swing component, and it doesn't seem to be displayed correctly, you'll really love the *Swing graphics debugger*. And

even if you don't write your own component classes, it is instructive and fun to see exactly how the contents of a component is drawn. To turn on debugging for a Swing component, use the `setDebugGraphicsOptions` method of the `JComponent` class. The following options are available:

`DebugGraphics.FLASH_OPTION`	Flashes each line, rectangle and text in red before drawing it
`DebugGraphics.LOG_OPTION`	Prints a message for each drawing operation
`DebugGraphics.BUFFERED_OPTION`	Displays the operations that are performed on the offscreen buffer
`DebugGraphics.NONE_OPTION`	Turns graphics debugging off

We have found that for the flash option to work, you must disable "double buffering", the strategy used by Swing to reduce flicker when updating a window. The magic incantation for turning on the flash option is:

```
RepaintManager.currentManager(getRootPane())
    .setDoubleBufferingEnabled(false);
((JComponent)getContentPane())
    .setDebugGraphicsOptions(DebugGraphics.FLASH_OPTION);
```

Simply place these lines at the end of your frame constructor. When the program runs, you will see the content pane filled in slow motion. Or, for more localized debugging, just call setDebugGraphicsOptions for a single component. Control freaks can set the duration, count, and color of the flashes—see the online documentation of the DebugGraphics class for details.

8. One seemingly little-known but very useful trick is that you can put a separate `main` method in each public class. Inside it, you can put a unit test stub that lets you test the class in isolation. Make a few objects, call all methods, and check that each of them does the right thing. You can leave all these `main` methods in place and call the Java interpreter separately on each of the files to run the tests. When you run an applet, none of these `main` methods are ever called. When you run an application, Java calls only the `main` method of the startup class. All others are ignored. (For example, look at our `Format.java` file in the `corejava` directory. It has a `main` method that tests the formatting extensively.)

Assertions

It often happens that your code relies on the fact that some of your variables have certain values. For example, object references are supposed to be initialized, and integer indexes are supposed to be within certain limits. It is a good idea to occasionally check these assumptions. If the assumptions turn out to be incorrect, you can throw an exception. Here is a typical example:

```
public void f(int[] a, int i)
{   if (!(a != null && i >= 0 && i < a.length))
        throw new IllegalArgumentError("Assertion failed");
    . . .
}
```

Such checks are usually called *assertions*. We want to assert that some condition is true before continuing. To make the code easier to read, it is helpful to use a static method check:

```
public void f(int[] a, int i)
{   Assertion.check(a != null && i >= 0 && i < a.length);
    . . .
}

public class Assertion
{   public static void check(boolean condition)
    {   if (!condition)
            throw new IllegalArgumentError("Assertion failed");
    }
}
```

Assertions are strictly a debugging tool. We don't ever expect the condition to be false, and if it is, we are happy to be notified and to have the program terminate. Once the program has been debugged and is deployed, all assertions should go away, since checking the conditions increases the running time and code size.

The question is how to remove the assertion code. Of course, you can manually remove all assertions, but that is tedious. And, of course, if the release version did not turn out to be quite as perfect as you thought, you might have to stick them all back in to help in the next round of debugging. The "official" solution to this problem is to use a static final variable that is set to true during debugging and to false when the program is deployed:

```
public void f(int[] a, int i)
{   if (debug) // a static final variable
        Assertion.check(a != null && i >= 0 && i < a.length);
    . . .
}
```

If debug is false, then the compiler realizes that the call to Assertion.check can never happen and it does not generate any code for it. Of course, you have to remember to flip the debug flag and recompile whenever you switch between the debug and release versions. This is still somewhat tedious, and there is an even better way.

We simply put the test into a separate class and then *not ship the code for that class with the release version!* Of course, the easiest way to generate a simple new class is as an anonymous inner class:

```
public void f(final int[] a, final int i)
{  if (debug) // a boolean variable, not necessarily static final
      new Assertion()
      {  {  check(a != null && i >= 0 && i < a.length);
         }
      };
   . . .
}
```

As so often with inner class code, this code snippet looks exceedingly mysterious. The statement

```
new Assertion() { . . . };
```

creates an object of an anonymous class that inherits from `Assertion`. That anonymous class has no methods, just a single constructor. The constructor is written as an initialization block (see Chapter 4) since we cannot give names to constructors of anonymous classes.

```
new Assertion() { { check(. . .) } };
```

When the `debug` variable is `true`, then the compiler loads the inner class and constructs an assertion object. The constructor calls the static `check` method of the `Assertion` class and tests the condition. (Because local class code can only refer to `final` variables of the ambient block, the parameters of `f` had to be declared `final`.) However, if `debug` is `false`, then the inner class is not even loaded. That means the inner class code need not be shipped with the release version of the program!

C++ NOTE: This assertion facility is not as convenient as the one offered by C and C++. The C `assert` macro causes the tested expression to be printed out when the assertion fails. And by defining the NDEBUG macro and recompiling, you not only turn off assertions, they do not generate any code. Both of these capabilities are possible because `assert` is a feature of the *preprocessor*. Java has no preprocessor, and hence it is not possible to play tricks with macros. However, in Java you can use dynamic linking to conditionally activate code, which is ultimately a more elegant mechanism.

`java.lang.Throwable`

• `void printStackTrace()`

prints the `Throwable` and the stack trace.

Trapping AWT Events

When you write a fancy user interface in Java, you need to know what events AWT sends to what components. Unfortunately, the AWT documentation is somewhat sketchy in this regard. For example, suppose you want to show hints in the status line when the user moves the mouse over different parts of the screen. AWT does generate mouse and focus events that you may be able to trap.

We give you a useful `MessageCracker` class to spy on these events. It prints out a text description of the event, cracking the event codes and printing only those fields of the `Event` structure that are relevant to a particular event. See Figure 11–3 for a display of the cracked messages. (Look in the terminal window.)

To spy on messages, you need only add one line of code to your frame class constructor or the `init` method of your applet.

```
public class MyFrame extends JFrame
{  public MyFrame()
   {  // add components
      new MessageCracker().add(this);
   }
   . . .
}
```

This prints out a textual description of all events, except for mouse motion events. (You would not want to see a flood of events every time you move the mouse.) Example 11–3 shows you how a class might use the `MessageCracker` class.

Example 11–3: MessageCrackerTest.java

```
import java.awt.*;
import java.awt.event.*;
import javax.swing.*;

public class MessageCrackerTest extends JFrame
{  public MessageCrackerTest()
   {  setTitle("MessageCrackerTest");
      setSize(400, 400);
      addWindowListener(new WindowAdapter()
         {  public void windowClosing(WindowEvent e)
            {  System.exit(0);
            }
         } );

      JPanel p = new JPanel();
      p.setLayout(new BorderLayout());
      p.add(new JButton("Test"), "South");
      p.add(new JScrollBar(), "East");
```

```
        p.add(new JScrollBar(), "East");
        getContentPane().add(p);

        new MessageCracker().add(this);
    }

    public static void main(String[] args)
    {   JFrame f = new MessageCrackerTest();
        f.show();
    }
}
```

Figure 11–3 : The `MessageCracker` **class at work**

Example 11–4 is the actual `MessageCracker` class. The idea behind the class is easy even if the implementation is a bit tedious.

1. The class directly implements every possible listener interface by implementing each of the required event handlers to simply print out the event. (You can add more interfaces to this list, for example, if you want to listen to Swing events.)

2. When you add a component, then the `addListener` method is called for each of the interfaces that the `MessageCracker` class implements. Furthermore, if the component is a container, then listeners are also added to all subcomponents.

3. The `addListener` is called with two parameters: the component on whose events we want to spy and a `Class` object representing a listener interface. The method uses the reflection mechanism to find out if the component has

this as the listener. That is, the various message handling methods of the
MessageCracker object are called whenever an event occurs. (Recall that
all these methods simply print out the event.)

This program is a good example of the power of the reflection mechanism.
We don't have to hardwire the fact that the JButton class has a method
addActionListener whereas a JScrollBar has a method
addAdjustmentListener. The reflection mechanism discovers these
facts for us.

Example 11–4: MessageCracker.java

```java
import java.awt.*;
import java.awt.event.*;
import java.lang.reflect.*;

public class MessageCracker
    implements MouseListener, ComponentListener,
    FocusListener, KeyListener, ContainerListener,
    WindowListener, TextListener, AdjustmentListener,
    ActionListener, ItemListener
{   public void add(Component c)
    {   Class[] interfaces = getClass().getInterfaces();

        for (int i = 0; i < interfaces.length; i++)
        {   addListener(c, interfaces[i]);
        }

        if (c instanceof Container)
        {   Component[] a = ((Container)c).getComponents();
            for (int i = 0; i < a.length; i++)
            add(a[i]);
        }
    }

    public void addListener(Component c, Class iface)
    {   /* strip off package name from interface */
        String name = iface.getName();
        name = name.substring(name.lastIndexOf('.') + 1);
        /* name is an XXXListener
            find out whether c supports a method
            addXXXListener(XXXListener)
        */
        try
        {   Method listenerAddMethod
            = c.getClass().getMethod("add" + name,
                new Class[] { iface });
            listenerAddMethod.invoke(c, new Object[] { this });
        }
        catch(Exception e) {}
```

```
        /* lots of things can go wrong in the getMethod and
           invoke calls; in that case, we simply don't add
           the listener
        */
   }

   public void mouseClicked(MouseEvent e)
   {  System.out.println(e);
   }
   public void mouseEntered(MouseEvent e)
   {  System.out.println(e);
   }
   public void mouseExited(MouseEvent e)
   {  System.out.println(e);
   }
   public void mousePressed(MouseEvent e)
   {  System.out.println(e);
   }
   public void mouseReleased(MouseEvent e)
   {  System.out.println(e);
   }

   public void componentHidden(ComponentEvent e)
   {  System.out.println(e);
   }
   public void componentMoved(ComponentEvent e)
   {  System.out.println(e);
   }
   public void componentResized(ComponentEvent e)
   {  System.out.println(e);
   }
   public void componentShown(ComponentEvent e)
   {  System.out.println(e);
   }

   public void focusGained(FocusEvent e)
   {  System.out.println(e);
   }
   public void focusLost(FocusEvent e)
   {  System.out.println(e);
   }

   public void keyPressed(KeyEvent e)
   {  System.out.println(e);
   }
   public void keyReleased(KeyEvent e)
   {  System.out.println(e);
   }
   public void keyTyped(KeyEvent e)
   {  System.out.println(e);
   }
```

```
    public void windowActivated(WindowEvent e)
    {   System.out.println(e);
    }
    public void windowClosed(WindowEvent e)
    {   System.out.println(e);
    }
    public void windowClosing(WindowEvent e)
    {   System.out.println(e);
    }
    public void windowDeactivated(WindowEvent e)
    {   System.out.println(e);
    }
    public void windowDeiconified(WindowEvent e)
    {   System.out.println(e);
    }
    public void windowIconified(WindowEvent e)
    {   System.out.println(e);
    }
    public void windowOpened(WindowEvent e)
    {   System.out.println(e);
    }

    public void componentAdded(ContainerEvent e)
    {   System.out.println(e);
    }
    public void componentRemoved(ContainerEvent e)
    {   System.out.println(e);
    }

    public void textValueChanged(TextEvent e)
    {   System.out.println(e);
    }

    public void adjustmentValueChanged(AdjustmentEvent e)
    {   System.out.println(e);
    }

    public void actionPerformed(ActionEvent e)
    {   System.out.println(e);
    }

    public void itemStateChanged(ItemEvent e)
    {   System.out.println(e);
    }
}
```

Displaying Debug Messages in Graphics Programs

If you run an applet inside a browser, you may not be able to see any messages that are sent to `System.out`. We expect that most browsers will have some sort of Java Console window. (Check the help system for your browser.) For example, Netscape

Navigator has one, as does Internet Explorer 4. If you use the Java Plug-in, check the Show Java Console box in the configuration panel (see Figure 11–4).

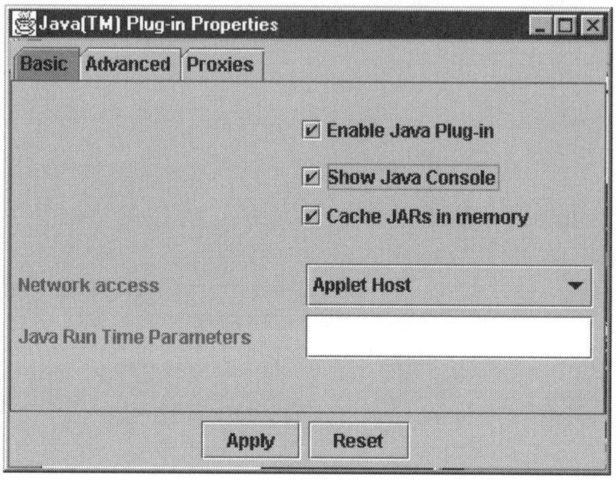

Figure 11–4: Activating the Java Console in the Java Plug-in

You can see an example of this in Figure 11–5. This window displays all the strings sent to `System.out`. In some browsers, the Java Console window has a set of scroll bars, so you can retrieve messages that have scrolled off the window, a definite advantage over the DOS shell window in which the `System.out` output normally appears.

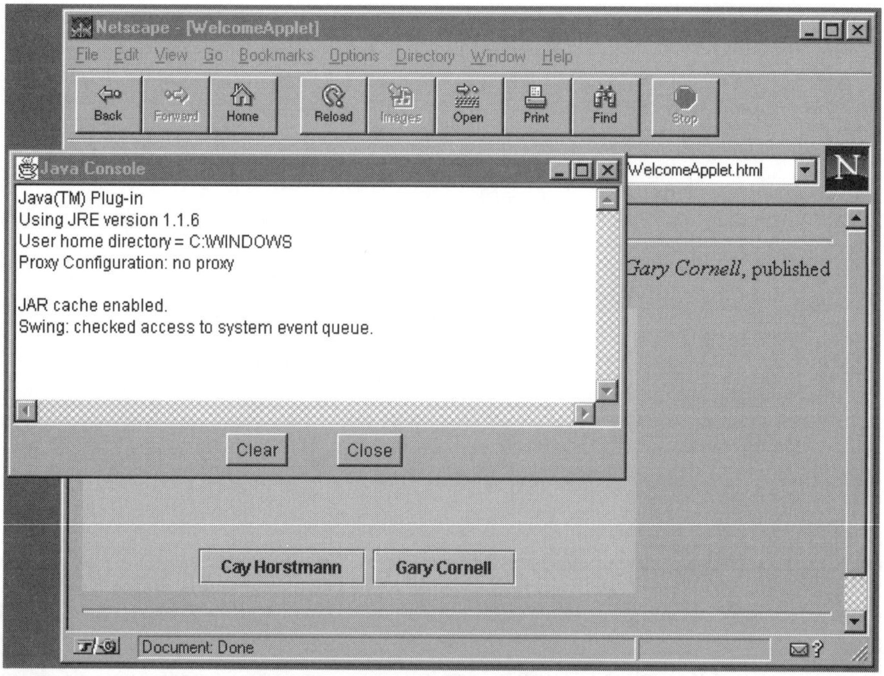

Figure 11–5: The Java Console in a browser

This is a nice feature, and we give you a similar window class so you can enjoy the same benefit of seeing your debugging messages in a window when debugging an applet in an environment that does not have a Java Console. Figure 11–6 shows our `DebugWinTest` class in action.

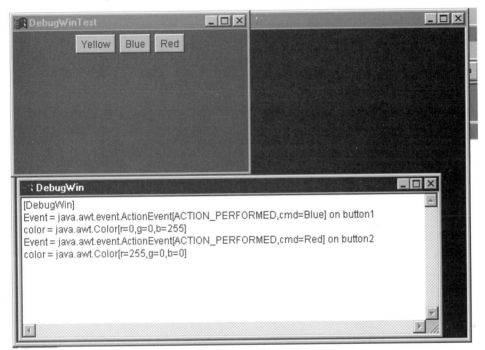

Figure 11–6: The debug window

The class is easy to use. You make a variable of type `DebugWin` in your `JFrame` or `JApplet` class and use the `print` method to print an object in the window. Here is an example of debugging code to spy on an action event.

```
class MyFrame extends JFrame
      implements ActionListener
{   . . .
   public void actionPerformed(ActionEvent evt)
   {  dw.print("Event = " + evt);
      . . .
   }
      . . .
   private DebugWin dw = new DebugWin();
}
```

Example 11–5 lists the code for the `DebugWin` class. As you can see, the class is very simple. Messages are displayed in a `JTextArea` inside a `JScrollPane`. The `print` method simply appends each message to the end of the text in the text area.

Example 11–5: DebugWin.java

```java
import java.awt.*;
import java.awt.event.*;
import javax.swing.*;

class DebugWin extends JFrame
{  public void print(Object ob)
   {  output.append("\n" + ob);
   }

   public DebugWin()
   {  setTitle("DebugWin");
      output.setEditable(false);
      output.setText("[DebugWin]");
      getContentPane().add(new JScrollPane(output), "Center");
      setSize(300, 200);
      setLocation(200, 200);
      addWindowListener(new WindowAdapter() { public void
         windowClosing(WindowEvent e)
         { setVisible(false); } } );
      show();
   }

   private JTextArea output = new JTextArea();
}
```

Using the JDB Debugger

Debugging with print statements is not one of life's more joyful experiences. You constantly find yourself adding and removing the statements, then recompiling the program. Using a debugger is better because a debugger runs your program in full motion until it reaches a breakpoint, and then you can look at everything that interests you.

The JDK includes JDB, an extremely rudimentary command-line debugger. Its user interface is so minimal that you will not want to use it except as a last resort. It really is more a proof of concept than a useable tool. We, nevertheless, give a brief introduction because there are situations in which it is better than no debugger at all. Of course, many Java programming environments have far more convenient debuggers. The main principles of all debuggers are the same, and you may want to use the example in this section to learn to use the debugger in your environment instead of JDB.

Have a look at a deliberately corrupted version of the ButtonTest (Figure 11–7) program from Chapter 7.

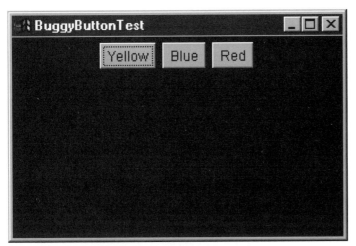

Figure 11–7: The buggy button application

When you click in Example 11–6 on any of the buttons, the background changes to black. Look at the source code—it is supposed to set the background color to the color specified by the button name.

Example 11–6: BuggyButtonTest.java

```
import java.awt.*;
import java.awt.event.*;
import javax.swing.*;

public class BuggyButtonTest extends JFrame
    implements ActionListener
{   public BuggyButtonTest()
    {   pane = new JPanel();

        JButton yellowButton = new JButton("Yellow");
        pane.add(yellowButton);
        yellowButton.addActionListener(this);

        JButton blueButton = new JButton("Blue");
        pane.add(blueButton);
        blueButton.addActionListener(this);

        JButton redButton = new JButton("Red");
        pane.add(redButton);
        redButton.addActionListener(this);

        Container contentPane = getContentPane();
```

```
        contentPane.add(pane);
    }

    public void actionPerformed(ActionEvent evt)
    {   String arg = evt.getActionCommand();
        Color color = Color.black;
        if (arg.equals("yellow")) color = Color.yellow;
        else if (arg.equals("blue")) color = Color.blue;
        else if (arg.equals("red")) color = Color.red;
        pane.setBackground(color);
        repaint();
    }

    public static void main(String[] args)
    {   JFrame f = new BuggyButtonTest();
        f.addWindowListener(new WindowAdapter()
            {   public void windowClosing(WindowEvent e)
                { System.exit(0); }
            } );
        f.setSize(400, 400);
        f.show();
    }

    private JPanel pane;
}
```

In a program this short, you may be able to find the bug just by reading the source code. Let us pretend that this was so complicated a program that reading the source code is not practical. Here is how you can run the debugger to locate the error.

To use JDB, you must first compile your program with the -g option, for example:

```
javac -g BuggyButtonTest.java
```

When you compile with this option, the compiler adds the names of local variables and other debugging information into the class files. Then you launch the debugger:

```
jdb BuggyButtonTest
```

Once you launch the debugger, you will see a display that looks something like this:

```
Initializing jdb...
0x139f3c8:class(BuggyButtonTest)
>
```

The > prompt indicates the debugger is waiting for a command. Table 11–2 shows all the debugger commands. Items enclosed in [...] are optional, and the suffix(s) means that you can supply one or more arguments separated by spaces.

Table 11–2: Debugging commands

`threads [`*`threadgroup`*`]`	lists threads
`thread `*`thread_id`*	sets default thread
`suspend [`*`thread_id(s)`*`]`	suspends threads (default: `all`)
`resume [`*`thread_id(s)`*`]`	resumes threads (default: `all`)
`where [`*`thread_id`*`] `**`or`**` all`	dumps a thread's stack
`wherei [`*`thread_id`*`] `**`or`**` all`	dumps a thread's stack and program counter info
`threadgroups`	lists threadgroups
`threadgroup `*`name`*	sets current threadgroup
`print `*`name(s)`*	prints object or field
`dump `*`name(s)`*	prints all object information
`locals`	prints all current local variables
`classes`	lists currently known classes
`methods `*`class`*	lists a class's methods
`stop in `*`class.method`*	sets a breakpoint in a method
`stop at `*`class:line`*	sets a breakpoint at a line
`up [`*`n`*`]`	moves up a thread's stack
`down [`*`n`*`]`	moves down a thread's stack
`clear `*`class:line`*	clears a breakpoint
`step`	executes the current line, stepping inside calls
`stepi`	executes the current instruction
`step up`	executes until the end of the current method
`next`	executes the current line, stepping over calls
`cont`	continues execution from breakpoint
`catch `*`class`*	breaks for the specified exception
`ignore `*`class`*	ignores the specified exception
`list [`*`line`*`]`	prints source code
`use [`*`path`*`]`	displays or changes the source path
`memory`	reports memory usage
`gc`	frees unused objects
`load `*`class`*	loads Java class to be debugged
`run [`*`class`* `[`*`args`*`]]`	starts execution of a loaded Java class
`!!`	repeats last command
`help (or ?)`	lists commands
`exit (or quit)`	exits debugger

We will cover only the most useful JDB commands in this section. The basic idea, though, is simple: you set one or more breakpoints, then run the program. When the program reaches one of the breakpoints you set, it stops. Then, you can inspect the values of the local variables to see if they are what they are supposed to be.

To set a breakpoint, use the

```
stop in class.method
```

or

```
stop at class:line
```

command.

For example, let us set a breakpoint in the `actionPerformed` method of BuggyButtonTest. To do this, enter:

```
stop in BuggyButtonTest.actionPerformed
```

Now we want to run the program up to the breakpoint, so enter:

```
run
```

The program will run, but the breakpoint won't be hit until Java starts processing code in the `actionPerformed` method. For this, click on the Yellow button. The debugger breaks at the *start* of the `actionPerformed` method. You'll see:

```
Breakpoint hit: BuggyButtonTest.actionPerformed
(BuggyButtonTest:32)
```

Because the debugger does not give you a window with the current source line showing, it is easy to lose track of where you are; the `list` command lets you find out where you are. While the program is stopped after you enter `list`, the debugger will show you the current line and a couple of the lines above and below it. You also see the line numbers. For example:

```
28                      setContentPane(pane);
29              }
30
31              public void actionPerformed(ActionEvent evt)
32      =>      {  String arg = evt.getActionCommand();
33                 Color color = Color.black;
34                 if (arg.equals("yellow")) color = Color.yellow;
35                 else if (arg.equals("blue")) color =
                       Color.blue;
36                 else if (arg.equals("red")) color = Color.red;
```

Type `locals` to see all local variables. For example:

```
Method arguments:
Local variables:
   this = BuggyButtonTest[frame0,0,0,400x400,
layout=java.awt.BorderLayout,resizable,title=]
   evt = java.awt.event.ActionEvent[ACTION_PERFORMED,
cmd=Yellow] on java.awt.swing.JButton[,97,5,71x25,
layout=java.awt.swing.OverlayLayout]
```

For more detail, use:

```
dump variable
```

For example,

```
dump evt
```

displays all instance fields of the `evt` variable.

```
evt = (java.awt.event.ActionEvent)0xc8 {
    protected transient Object source =
        (java.awt.swing.JButton)0xcc
    protected boolean consumed = true
    protected int id = 1001
    private transient long data = 0
    int modifiers = 0
    String actionCommand = Yellow
}
```

There are two basic commands to single-step through a program. The `step` command steps into every method call. Unfortunately, it easily becomes confused between threads. (Volume 2 covers threads.) We found it safer to use the `next` command, which goes to the next line without stepping inside any further method calls. Type `next` three times and then type `list` to see where you are:

The program stops in line 35.

```
31              public void actionPerformed(ActionEvent evt)
32              {   String arg = evt.getActionCommand();
33                  Color color = Color.black;
34                  if (arg.equals("yellow")) color = Color.yellow;
35       =>         else if (arg.equals("blue")) color = Color.blue;
36                  else if (arg.equals("red")) color = Color.red;
37                  pane.setBackground(color);
38                  repaint();
39              }
```

That is not what should have happened. It was supposed to set the `color` variable to yellow and then go to the `setBackground` command.

Now we can see what happened. The value of `arg` was `"Yellow"`, with an uppercase Y, but the comparison tested

```
    if (arg.equals("yellow"))
```

with a lowercase y. Mystery solved.

To quit the debugger, type:

```
    quit
```

As you can see from this example, the debugger can be used to find an error, but only with a lot of work. Setting breakpoints in an `actionPerformed` method or another event-handler works pretty well to find out why an event-handler wasn't triggered, for example. Remember to use `list` and `locals` whenever you are confused about where you are. Get a better debugger for serious debugging work.

Chapter 12

Streams and Files

- ▼ STREAMS
- ▼ THE COMPLETE STREAM ZOO
- ▼ ZIP FILE STREAMS
- ▼ PUTTING STREAMS TO USE
- ▼ OBJECT STREAMS
- ▼ FILE MANAGEMENT

Applets are not normally allowed to work with files on the user's system. Applications, of course, need to do this a lot. In this chapter, we cover the methods for handling files and directories as well as the methods for actually writing and reading back information to and from files. This chapter also shows you the object serialization mechanism that lets you store objects as easily as you can store text or numeric data.

Streams

Input/output techniques are not particularly exciting, but without the ability to read and write data, your applications and (occasionally) applets are severely limited. This chapter is about how to get input from any source of data that can send out a sequence of bytes and how to send output to any destination that can receive a sequence of bytes. These sources and destinations of byte sequences can be—and often are—files, but they can also be network connections and even blocks of memory. There is a nice payback to keeping this generality in mind: for example, information stored in files and information retrieved from a network connection is handled in *essentially the same way*. (See Volume 2 for programming with networks.) Of course, while data is always *ultimately* stored in a series of bytes, it is often more convenient to think of it as having some higher-level structure such as being a sequence of characters or objects. We cover Java higher-level input/output facilities as well.

In Java, an object from which we can read a sequence of bytes is called an *input stream*. An object to which we can write a sequence of bytes is called an *output stream*. These are implemented in the abstract classes InputStream and OutputStream. Since byte-oriented streams are inconvenient for processing information stored in Unicode (recall that Unicode uses two bytes per character), there is a separate hierarchy of classes for processing Unicode characters that inherit from the abstract Reader and Writer superclasses. These classes have read and write operations that are based on 2-byte Unicode characters rather than on single-byte characters.

You saw abstract classes in Chapter 5. Recall that the point of an abstract class is to provide a mechanism for factoring out the common behavior of classes to a higher level. This leads to cleaner code and makes the inheritance tree easier to understand. The same game is at work with input and output in Java.

As you will soon see, Java derives from these four abstract classes a zoo of concrete classes: you can visit almost any conceivable input/output creature in this zoo.

Reading and Writing Bytes

The InputStream class has an abstract method:

```
public abstract int read() throws IOException
```

This method reads one byte and returns the byte that was read, or –1 if it encounters the end of the input source. The designer of a concrete input stream class overrides this method in order to provide useful functionality. For example, in the FileInputStream class, this method reads one byte from a file. System.in is a predefined object of a subclass of InputStream that allows you to read information from the keyboard.

The InputStream class also has nonabstract methods to read an array of bytes or to skip a number of bytes. These methods call the abstract read method, so that subclasses need to override only one method.

Similarly, the OutputStream class defines the abstract method

```
public abstract void write(int b) throws IOException
```

which writes one byte to an output location.

Both the read and write methods can *block* a thread until the byte is actually read or written. This means that if the stream cannot immediately be read from or written to (usually because of a busy network connection), Java suspends the thread containing this call. This gives other threads the chance to do useful work while the method is waiting for the stream to again become available. (We discuss threads in depth in Volume 2.)

The `available` method lets you check the number of bytes that are currently available for reading. This means a fragment like the following is unlikely to ever block:

```
int bytesAvailable = System.in.available();
if (bytesAvailable > 0)
{   byte[] data = new byte[bytesAvailable];
    System.in.read(data);
}
```

When you have finished reading or writing to a stream, close it, using the appropriately named `close` method, because streams use operating system resources that are in limited supply. If an application opens many streams without closing them, system resources may become depleted. Closing an output stream also *flushes* the buffer used for the output stream: any characters that were temporarily placed in a buffer so that they could be delivered as a larger packet are sent off. In particular, if you do not close a file, the last packet of bytes may never be delivered. You can also manually flush the output with the `flush` method.

Even if a stream class provides concrete methods to work with the raw `read` and `write` functions, Java programmers seldom use them because programs rarely need to read and write streams of bytes. The data that you are interested in probably contain numbers, strings, and objects.

Java gives you many stream classes derived from the basic `InputStream` and `OutputStream` classes that let you work with data in the forms that you usually use rather than at the low, byte level.

`java.io.InputStream`

- `abstract int read()`

    reads a byte of data and returns the byte read. The `read` method returns a −1 at the end of the stream.

- `int read(byte[] b)`

    reads into an array of bytes and returns the number of bytes read. As before, the `read` method returns a −1 at the end of the stream. Reads at most `b.length` bytes.

- `int read(byte[] b, int off, int len)`

    reads into an array of bytes. The `read` method returns the actual number of bytes read, or −1 at the end of the stream.

Parameters:	b	the array into which the data is read
	off	the offset into b where the first bytes should be placed
	len	the maximum number of bytes to read

- `long skip(long n)`

skips n bytes in the input stream. It returns the actual number of bytes skipped (which may be less than n if the end of the stream was encountered).

- `int available()`

returns the number of bytes available without blocking. (Recall that blocking means that the current thread loses its turn.)

- `void close()`

closes the input stream.

- `void mark(int readlimit)`

puts a marker at the current position in the input stream. (Not all streams support this feature.) If more than `readlimit` bytes have been read from the input stream, then the stream is allowed to forget the marker.

- `void reset()`

returns to the last marker. Subsequent calls to `read` reread the bytes. If there is no current marker, then the stream is not reset.

- `boolean markSupported()`

returns `true` if the stream supports marking.

 java.io.OutputStream

- `public abstract void write(int b)`

writes a byte of data.

- `public void write(byte[] b)`

writes all bytes in the array b.

- `public void write(byte[] b, int off, int len)`

Parameters:	b	the array from which to write the data
	off	the offset into b to the first byte that will be written
	len	the number of bytes to write

- `public void close()`

flushes and closes the output stream.

- `public void flush()`

flushes the output stream, that is, sends any buffered data to its destination.

The Complete Stream Zoo

Unlike C, which gets by just fine with a single type FILE*, or VB, which has three file types, Java has a whole zoo of more than 60 (!) different stream types (see Figures 12–1 and 12–2). Library designers claim that there is a good reason to give users a wide choice of stream types: it is supposed to reduce programming errors. For example, in C, some people think it is a common mistake to send output to a file that was open only for reading. (Well, it is not that common, actually.) Naturally, if you do this, the output is ignored at run time. In Java and C++, the compiler catches that kind of mistake because an InputStream (Java) or istream (C++) has no methods for output.

(We would argue that, in C++ and even more so in Java, the main tool that the stream interface designers have against programming errors is intimidation. The sheer complexity of the stream libraries keeps programmers on their toes.)

C++ NOTE: ANSI C++ gives you more stream types than you want, such as istream, ostream, iostream, ifstream, ofstream, fstream, wistream, wifstream, istrstream, and so on (18 classes in all). But Java really goes overboard with streams and gives you the separate classes for selecting buffering, lookahead, random access, text formatting, or binary data.

Let us divide the animals in the stream class zoo by how they are used. Four abstract classes are at the base of the zoo: InputStream, OutputStream, Reader, and Writer. You do not make objects of these types, but other methods can return them. For example, as you saw in Chapter 10, the URL class has the method openStream that returns an InputStream. You then use this InputStream object to read from the URL. As we mentioned before, the InputStream and OutputStream classes let you read and write only individual bytes and arrays of bytes; they have no methods to read and write strings and numbers. You need more-capable child classes for this. For example, DataInputStream and DataOutputStream let you read and write all the basic Java types.

For Unicode text, on the other hand, as we mentioned before, you use classes that descend from Reader and Writer. The basic methods of the Reader and Writer classes are similar to the ones for InputStream and OutputStream.

```
public abstract int read() throws IOException
public abstract void write(int b) throws IOException
```

They work just as the comparable methods do in the InputStream and OutputStream classes except, of course, the read method returns either a Unicode character (as an integer between 0 and 65535) or –1 when you have reached the end of the file.

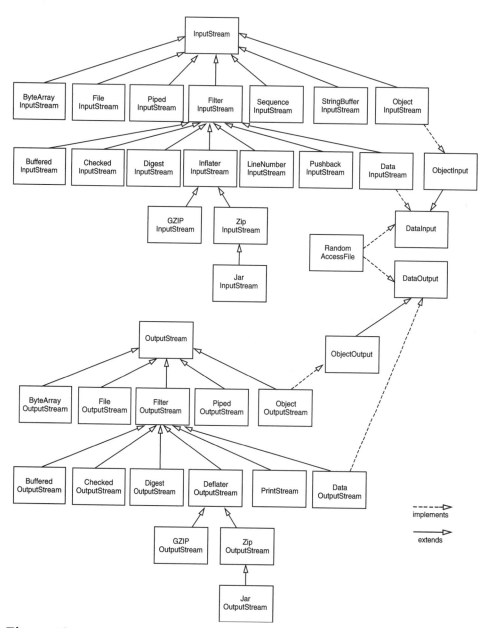

Figure 12–1: Input and Output stream hierarchy

Finally, there are streams that do useful stuff, for example, the `ZipInputStream` and `ZipOutputStream` that let you read and write files in the familiar ZIP compression format.

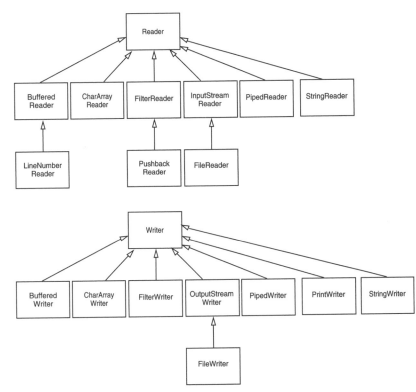

Figure 12–2: Reader and Writer hierarchy

Layering Stream Filters

`FileInputStream` and `FileOutputStream` give you input and output streams attached to a disk file. You give the file name or full pathname of the file in the constructor. For example,

```
FileInputStream fin = new FileInputStream("employee.dat");
```

looks in the current directory for a file named `"employee.dat"`.

CAUTION: Since the backslash character is the escape character in Java strings, be sure to use `\\` for Windows-style pathnames (`"C:\\Windows\\win.ini"`). In Windows, you can also use a single forward slash (`"C:/Windows/win.ini"`) since most Windows file handling system calls will interpret forward slashes as file separators. However, this is not recommended—the behavior of the Windows system functions is subject to change, and on other operating systems, the file separator may yet be different. Instead, for portable programs, you should use the correct file separator character. It is stored in the constant string `File.separator`.

You can also use a `File` object (see the end of the chapter for more on file objects):

```
File f = new File("employee.dat");
FileInputStream fin = new FileInputStream(f);
```

Like the abstract `InputStream` and `OutputStream` classes, these classes only support reading and writing on the byte level. That is, we can only read bytes and byte arrays from the object `fin`.

```
byte b = fin.read();
```

TIP: Since all the classes in `java.io` interpret relative pathnames as starting with the user's current working directory, you may want to know this directory. You can get at this information via a call to `System.getProperty("user.dir")`.

As you will see in the next section, if we just had a `DataInputStream`, then we could read numeric types:

```
DataInputStream din = . . .;
double s = din.readDouble();
```

But just as the `FileInputStream` has no methods to read numeric types, the `DataInputStream` has no method to get data from a file.

Java uses a clever mechanism to separate two kinds of responsibilities. Some streams (such as the `FileInputStream` and the input stream returned by the `openStream` method of the URL class) can retrieve bytes from files and other more exotic locations. Other streams (such as the `DataInputStream` and the `PrintWriter`) can assemble bytes into more useful data types. The Java programmer has to combine the two into what are often called *filtered streams* by feeding an existing stream to the constructor of another stream. For example, to be able to read numbers from a file, first create a `FileInputStream` and then pass it to the constructor of a `DataInputStream`.

```
FileInputStream fin = new FileInputStream("employee.dat");
DataInputStream din = new DataInputStream(fin);
double s = din.readDouble();
```

It is important to keep in mind that the data input stream that we created with the above code does not correspond to a new disk file. The newly created stream *still* accesses the data from the file attached to the file input stream, but the point is that it now has a more capable interface.

If you look at Figure 12–1 again, you can see the classes `FilterInputStream` and `FilterOutputStream`. You combine their child classes into a new filtered stream to construct the streams you want. For example, by default, streams are not buffered. That is, every call to read contacts the operating system to ask it to dole out yet another byte. If you want buffering *and* data input for a file named `employee.dat` in the current directory, you need to use the following rather monstrous sequence of constructors:

```
DataInputStream din = new DataInputStream
    (new BufferedInputStream
        (new FileInputStream("employee.dat")));
```

Notice that we put the `DataInputStream` *last* in the chain of constructors because we want to use the `DataInputStream` methods, and we want *them* to use the buffered `read` method. Regardless of the ugliness of the above code, it is necessary: you must be prepared to continue layering stream constructors until you have access to the functionality you want.

For example, sometimes you'll need to keep track of the intermediate streams when chaining them together. For example, when reading input, you often need to peek at the next byte to see if it is the value that you expect. Java provides the `PushbackInputStream` for this purpose.

```
PushbackInputStream pbin = new PushbackInputStream
    (new BufferedInputStream
        (new FileInputStream("employee.dat")));
```

Now you can speculatively read the next byte

```
int b = pbin.read();
```

and throw it back if it isn't what you wanted.

```
if (b != '<') pbin.unread(b);
```

But reading and unreading are the *only* methods that apply to the pushback input stream. If you want to look ahead and also read numbers, then you need both a pushback input stream and a data input stream reference.

```
DataInputStream din = new DataInputStream
    (pbin = new PushbackInputStream
        (new BufferedInputStream
        (new FileInputStream("employee.dat"))));
```

Of course, in the stream libraries of other programming languages, niceties such as buffering and lookahead are automatically taken care of, so it is a bit of a hassle in Java that one has to resort to layering stream filters in these cases. But the ability to mix and match filter classes to construct truly useful sequences of streams does give you an immense amount of flexibility. For example, you can read numbers from a compressed ZIP file by using the following sequence of streams (see Figure 12–3).

```
ZipInputStream zin
    = new ZipInputStream(new FileInputStream("employee.zip"));
DataInputStream din = new DataInputStream(zin);
```

Figure 12–3: A sequence of filtered streams

(See the section on "ZIP file streams" later on in this chapter for more on Java's ability to handle ZIP files.)

All in all, apart from the rather monstrous constructors that are needed to layer streams, the ability to mix and match streams is a very useful feature of Java!

java.io.FileInputStream

- `FileInputStream(String name)`

  creates a new file input stream, using the file whose pathname is specified by the `name` string.

- `FileInputStream(File f)`

  creates a new file input stream, using the information encapsulated in the `File` object. (The `File` class is described at the end of this chapter.)

java.io.FileOutputStream

- `FileOutputStream(String name)`

  creates a new file output stream specified by the `name` string. Pathnames that are not absolute are resolved relative to the current working directory. *Caution:* automatically deletes any existing file with that name.

- `FileOutputStream(String name, boolean append)`

  creates a new file output stream specified by the `name` string. Pathnames that are not absolute are resolved relative to the current working directory. If the `append` parameter is `true`, then data is added at the end of the file. An existing file with the same name will not be deleted.

- `FileOutputStream(File f)`

  creates a new file output stream using the information encapsulated in the `File` object. (The `File` class is described at the end of this chapter.) *Caution:* automatically deletes any existing file with that name.

java.io.BufferedInputStream

- `BufferedInputStream(InputStream in)`

  creates a new buffered stream with a default buffer size. A buffered input stream reads characters from a stream without causing a device access every time. When the buffer is empty, a new block of data is read into the buffer.

- `BufferedInputStream(InputStream in, int n)`

  creates a new buffered stream with a user-defined buffer size.

`java.io.BufferedOutputStream`

- `BufferedOutputStream(OutputStream out)`

    creates a new buffered stream with a default buffer size. A buffered output stream collects characters to be written without causing a device access every time. When the buffer fills up, or when the stream is flushed, the data is written.

- `BufferedOutputStream(OutputStream out, int n)`

    creates a new buffered stream with a user-defined buffer size.

`java.io.PushbackInputStream`

- `PushbackInputStream(InputStream in)`

    constructs a stream with one-character lookahead.

- `PushbackInputStream(InputStream in, int size)`

    constructs a stream with a pushback buffer of specified size.

- `void unread(int ch)`

    pushes back a character, which is retrieved again by the next call to read. You can push back only one character at a time.

    Parameters: ch   the character to be read again

Data Streams

You often need to write the result of a computation or read one back. The data streams support methods for reading back all of the basic Java types. To write a number, character, Boolean value, or string, use one of the following methods of the `DataOutput` interface:

```
writeChars
writeInt
writeShort
writeLong
writeFloat
writeDouble
writeChar
writeBoolean
writeUTF
```

For example, `writeInt` always writes an integer as a 4-byte binary quantity regardless of the number of digits, and `writeDouble` always writes a `double` as an 8-byte binary quantity. The resulting output is not humanly readable but the space needed will be the same for each data type, and reading it back in will be faster. (See the section on the `PrintWriter` class later in this chapter for how to output numbers as human readable text.)

> NOTE: There are two different methods of storing integers and floating-point numbers in memory, depending on the platform you are using. Suppose, for example, you are working with a 4-byte quantity, like an `int` or a `float`. This can be stored in such a way that the first of the 4 bytes in memory holds the most significant byte (MSB) of the value, the so-called *big-endian* method, or it can hold the least significant byte (LSB) first, which is called, naturally enough, the *little-endian* method. For example, the SPARC uses big-endian; the Pentium, little-endian. This can lead to problems. For example, when saving a file using C or C++, the data is saved *exactly* as the processor stores it. That makes it challenging to move even the simplest data files from one platform to another. In Java, all values are written in the big-endian fashion, regardless of the processor. That makes Java data files platform independent.

The `writeUTF` method writes string data using Unicode Text Format (UTF). UTF format is as follows. A 7-bit ASCII value (that is, a 16-bit Unicode character with the top 9 bits zero) is written as one byte:

$0a_6a_5a_4a_3a_2a_1a_0$

A 16-bit Unicode character with the top 5 bits zero is written as a 2-byte sequence:

$110a_{10}a_9a_8a_7a_6 \quad 10a_5a_4a_3a_2a_1a_0$

(The top zero bits are not stored.)

All other Unicode characters are written as 3-byte sequences:

$1110a_{15}a_{14}a_{13}a_{12} \quad 10a_{11}a_{10}a_9a_8a_7a_6 \quad 10a_5a_4a_3a_2a_1a_0$

This is a useful format for text consisting mostly of ASCII characters because ASCII characters still take only a single byte. On the other hand, it is not a good format for Asiatic languages, for which you are better off directly writing sequences of double-byte Unicode characters. Use the `writeChars` method for that purpose.

Note that the top bits of a UTF byte determine the nature of the byte in the encoding scheme.

`0xxxxxxx`	:	ASCII
`10xxxxxx`	:	Second or third byte
`110xxxxx`	:	First byte of 2-byte sequence
`1110xxxx`	:	First byte of 3-byte sequence

To read the data back in, use the following methods:

`readInt`	`readDouble`
`readShort`	`readChar`
`readLong`	`readBoolean`
`readFloat`	`readUTF`

> NOTE: The binary data format is compact and platform independent. Except for the UTF strings, it is also suited to random access. The major drawback is that binary files are not readable by humans.

`java.io.DataInput`

- `boolean readBoolean()`

  reads in a Boolean value.

- `byte readByte()`

  reads an 8-bit byte.

- `char readChar()`

  reads a 16-bit Unicode character.

- `double readDouble()`

  reads a 64-bit double.

- `float readFloat()`

  reads a 32-bit float.

- `void readFully(byte[] b)`

  reads bytes, blocking until all bytes are read.

  Parameters: b   the buffer into which the data is read

- `void readFully(byte[] b, int off, int len)`

  reads bytes, blocking until all bytes are read.

  Parameters: b   the buffer into which the data is read

                   off   the start offset of the data

                   len   the maximum number of bytes read

- `int readInt()`

  reads a 32-bit integer.

- `String readLine()`

  reads in a line that has been terminated by a \n, \r, \r\n, or EOF. Returns a string containing all bytes in the line converted to Unicode characters.

- `long readLong()`

  reads a 64-bit long integer.

- `short readShort()`

  reads a 16-bit short integer.

- `String readUTF()`

  reads a string of characters in UTF format.

- `int skipBytes(int n)`

  skips bytes, blocking until all bytes are skipped.

  Parameters: n   the number of bytes to be skipped

java.io.DataOutput

- `void writeBoolean(boolean b)`

  writes a Boolean value.

- `void writeByte(byte b)`

  writes an 8-bit byte.

- `void writeChar(char c)`

  writes a 16-bit Unicode character.

- `void writeChars(String s)`

  writes all characters in the string.

- `void writeDouble(double d)`

  writes a 64-bit double.

- `void writeFloat(float f)`

  writes a 32-bit float.

- `void writeInt(int i)`

  writes a 32-bit integer.

- `void writeLong(long l)`

  writes a 64-bit long integer.

- `void writeShort(short s)`

  writes a 16-bit short integer.

- `void writeUTF(String s)`

  writes a string of characters in UTF format.

Random-Access File Streams

The RandomAccessFile stream class lets you find or write data anywhere in a file. It implements both the DataInput and DataOutput interfaces. Disk files are random access, but streams of data from a network are not. You open a random-access file either for reading only or for both reading and writing. You specify the option by using the string "r" (for read access) or "rw" (for read/write access) as the second argument in the constructor.

```
RandomAccessFile in = new RandomAccessFile("employee.dat", "r");
RandomAccessFile inOut
   = new RandomAccessFile("employee.dat", "rw");
```

When you open an existing file as a RandomAccessFile, it does not get deleted.

A random-access file also has a *file pointer* setting that comes with it. The file pointer always indicates the position of the next record that will be read or written. The seek method sets the file pointer to an arbitrary byte position within the file. The argument to seek is a long integer between zero and the length of the file in bytes.

The getFilePointer method returns the current position of the file pointer.

To read from a random-access file, you use the same methods—such as readInt and readUTF—as for DataInputStream objects. That is no accident. These methods are actually defined in the DataInput interface that both DataInputStream and RandomAccessFile implement.

Similarly, to write a random-access file, you use the same writeInt and writeUTF methods as in the DataOutputStream class. These methods are defined in the DataOutput interface that is common to both classes.

The advantage of having the RandomAccessFile class implement both DataInput and DataOutput is that this lets you use or write methods whose argument types are the DataInput and DataOutput *interfaces*.

```
class Employee
{   . . .
    read(DataInput in) { . . . }
    write(DataOutput out) { . . . }
}
```

Note that the read method can handle either a DataInputStream or a RandomAccessFile object because both of these classes implement the DataInput interface. The same is true for the write method.

java.io.RandomAccessFile

- RandomAccessFile(String name, String mode)

  Parameters: name   system-dependent file name

                             mode   "r" for reading only, or "rw" for reading and writing

- RandomAccessFile(File file, String mode)

  Parameters: file   a File object encapsulating a system-dependent file name. (The File class is described at the end of this chapter.)

                             mode   "r" for reading only, or "rw" for reading and writing

- long getFilePointer()

  returns the current location of the file pointer.

- void seek(long pos)

  sets the file pointer to pos bytes from the beginning of the file.

- public long length()

  returns the length of the file in bytes.

Text Streams

In the last section, we discussed *binary* input and output. While binary I/O is fast and efficient, it is not easily readable by humans. In this section, we will focus on *text* I/O. For example, if the integer 1234 is saved in binary, it is written as the sequence of bytes 00 00 04 D2 (in hexadecimal notation). In text format, it is saved as the string "1234".

Unfortunately, doing this in Java requires a bit of work. Since, as you know, Java uses Unicode characters. That is, the character encoding for the string "1234" really is 00 31 00 32 00 33 00 34 (in hex). However, at the present time most environments where your Java programs will run use their own character encoding. This may be a single-byte, a double-byte, or a variable-byte scheme. For example, under Windows, the string would need to be written in ASCII, as 31 32 33 34, without the extra zero bytes. If the Unicode encoding were written into a text file, then it would be quite unlikely that the resulting file will be humanly readable with the tools of the host environment. To overcome this problem, as we mentioned before, Java now has a set of stream filters that bridges the gap between Unicode-encoded text and the character encoding used by the local operating system. All of these classes descend from the abstract Reader and Writer classes, and the names are reminiscent of the ones used for binary data.

For example, the `InputStreamReader` class turns an input stream that contains bytes in a particular character encoding into a reader that emits Unicode characters. Similarly, the `OutputStreamWriter` class turns a stream of Unicode characters into a stream of bytes in a particular character encoding.

For example, here is how you make an input reader that reads keystrokes from the console and automatically converts them to Unicode.

```
InputStreamReader in = new InputStreamReader(System.in);
```

This input stream reader assumes the normal character encoding used by the host system. For example, under Windows, it uses the ISO 8859-1 encoding (also known as ISO Latin-1 or, among Windows programmers, as "ANSI code"). You can choose a different encoding by specifying it in the constructor for the `InputStreamReader`. This takes the form

```
InputStreamReader(InputStream, String)
```

where the string describes the encoding scheme that you want to use. For example,

```
InputStreamReader in = new InputStreamReader(new
    FileInputStream("kremlin.dat"), "8859_5");
```

Table 12–1 lists the currently supported encoding schemes.

Table 12–1: Character encodings

8859_1	ISO Latin-1
8859_2	ISO Latin-2
8859_3	ISO Latin-3
8859_5	ISO Latin/Cyrillic
8859_6	ISO Latin/Arabic
8859_7	ISO Latin/Greek
8859_8	ISO Latin/Hebrew
8859_9	ISO Latin-5
Big5	Big5, Traditional Chinese
CNS11643	CNS 11643, Traditional Chinese
Cp037	USA, Canada (Bilingual, French), Netherlands, Portugal, Brazil, Australia
Cp1006	IBM AIX Pakistan (Urdu)
Cp1025	IBM Multilingual Cyrillic: Bulgaria, Bosnia, Herzegovina, Macedonia (FYR)
Cp1026	IBM Latin-5, Turkey
Cp1046	IBM Open Edition US EBCDIC
Cp1097	IBM Iran (Farsi)/Persian
Cp1098	IBM Iran (Farsi)/Persian (PC)
Cp1112	IBM Latvia, Lithuania
Cp1122	IBM Estonia
Cp1123	IBM Ukraine
Cp1124	IBM AIX Ukraine
Cp1250	Windows Eastern Europe / Latin-2
Cp1251	Windows Cyrillic
Cp1252	Windows Western Europe / Latin-1
Cp1253	Windows Greek
Cp1254	Windows Turkish

Cp1255	Windows Hebrew
Cp1256	Windows Arabic
Cp1257	Windows Baltic
Cp1258	Windows Vietnamese
Cp1381	IBM OS/2, DOS People's Republic of China (PRC)
Cp1383	IBM AIX People's Republic of China (PRC)
Cp273	IBM Austria, Germany
Cp277	IBM Denmark, Norway
Cp278	IBM Finland, Sweden
Cp280	IBM Italy
Cp284	IBM Catalan/Spain, Spanish Latin America
Cp285	IBM United Kingdom, Ireland
Cp297	IBM France
Cp33722	IBM-eucJP - Japanese, superset of 5050
Cp420	IBM Arabic
Cp424	IBM Hebrew
Cp437	PC Original
Cp500	EBCDIC 500V1
Cp737	PC Greek
Cp775	PC Baltic
Cp838	IBM Thailand extended SBCS
Cp850	PC Latin-1
Cp852	PC Latin-2
Cp855	PC Cyrillic
Cp857	PC Turkish
Cp860	PC Portuguese
Cp861	PC Icelandic
Cp862	PC Hebrew
Cp863	PC Canadian French
Cp864	PC Arabic
Cp865	PC Nordic
Cp866	PC Russian
Cp869	PC Modern Greek
Cp871	IBM Iceland
Cp874	Windows Thai
Cp875	IBM Greek
Cp918	IBM Pakistan (Urdu)
Cp921	IBM Latvia, Lithuania (AIX, DOS)
Cp922	IBM Estonia (AIX, DOS)
Cp930	Japanese Katakana-Kanji mixed with 4370 UDC, superset of 5026
Cp933	Korean Mixed with 1880 UDC, superset of 5029
Cp935	Simplified Chinese Host mixed with 1880 UDC, superset of 5031
Cp937	Traditional Chinese Host mixed with 6204 UDC, superset of 5033
Cp939	Japanese Latin Kanji mixed with 4370 UDC, superset of 5035
Cp942	Japanese (OS/2), superset of 932
Cp948	OS/2 Chinese (Taiwan), superset of 938
Cp949	PC Korean
Cp950	PC Chinese (Hong Kong, Taiwan)
Cp964	AIX Chinese (Taiwan)
Cp970	AIX Korean

EUCJIS	Japanese EUC
GB2312	GB2312, EUC encoding, Simplified Chinese
GBK	GBK, Simplified Chinese
ISO2022CN	ISO 2022 CN, Chinese
ISO2022CN_CNS	CNS 11643 in ISO-2022-CN form, T. Chinese
ISO2022CN_GB	GB 2312 in ISO-2022-CN form, S. Chinese
ISO2022KR	ISO 2022 KR, Korean
JIS	JIS
JIS0208	JIS 0208, Japanese
KOI8_R	KOI8-R, Russian
KSC5601	KS C 5601, Korean
MS874	Windows Thai
MacArabic	Macintosh Arabic
MacCentralEurope	Macintosh Latin-2
MacCroatian	Macintosh Croatian
MacCyrillic	Macintosh Cyrillic
MacDingbat	Macintosh Dingbat
MacGreek	Macintosh Greek
MacHebrew	Macintosh Hebrew
MacIceland	Macintosh Icelandic
MacRoman	Macintosh Roman
MacRomania	Macintosh Romania
MacSymbol	Macintosh Symbol
MacThai	Macintosh Thai
MacTurkish	Macintosh Turkish
MacUkraine	Macintosh Ukraine
SJIS	PC and Windows Japanese
UTF8	Standard UTF-8

Of course, there are many Unicode characters that cannot be represented by these encoding schemes. If those characters are part of the stream, they are displayed by a ? in the output.

Because it is so common to want to attach a reader or writer to a file, there is a pair of convenience classes, `FileReader` and `FileWriter`, for this purpose. For example, the writer definition

```
FileWriter out = new FileWriter("output.txt");
```

is equivalent to

```
OutputStreamWriter out = new OutputStreamWriter(new
    FileOutputStream("output.txt"));
```

Writing Text Output

For text output, you want to use a `PrintWriter`. A print writer can print strings and numbers in text format. Just as a `DataOutputStream` has useful output methods but no destination, a `PrintWriter` must be combined with a destination writer.

```
PrintWriter out = new PrintWriter(new
    FileWriter("employee.txt"));
```

You can also combine a print writer with a destination (output) stream.

```
PrintWriter out = new PrintWriter(new
    FileOutputStream("employee.txt"));
```

The `PrintWriter(OutputStream)` constructor automatically adds an `OutputStreamWriter` to convert Unicode characters to bytes in the stream.

To write to a print writer, you use the same `print` and `println` methods that you used with `System.out`. You can use these methods to print numbers (`int`, `short`, `long`, `float`, `double`), characters, Boolean values, strings, and objects.

> NOTE: Java veterans probably wonder whatever happened to the `PrintStream` class and to `System.out`. In Java 1.0, the `PrintStream` class simply truncated all Unicode characters to ASCII characters by dropping the top byte. Conversely, the `readLine` method of the `DataInputStream` turned ASCII to Unicode by setting the top byte to 0. Clearly, that was not a clean or portable approach, and it was fixed with the introduction of readers and writers in Java 1.1. For compatibility with existing code, `System.in`, `System.out`, and `System.err` are still streams, not readers and writers. But now the `PrintStream` class internally converts Unicode characters to the default host encoding in the same way as the `PrintWriter`. Objects of type `PrintStream` act exactly like print writers when you use the `print` and `println` methods, but unlike print writers, they allow you to send raw bytes to them with the `write(int)` and `write(byte[])` methods.

For example, consider this code:

```
String name = "Harry Hacker";
double salary = 75000;
out.print(name);
out.print(' ');
out.println(salary);
```

This writes the characters

```
Harry Hacker 75000
```

to the stream `out`. The characters are then converted to bytes and end up in the file `employee.txt`.

The `println` method automatically adds the correct end-of-line character for the target system (`"\r\n"` on Windows, `"\n"` on Unix, `"\r"` on Macs) to the line. This is the string obtained by the call `System.getProperty("line.separator")`.

If the writer is set to *autoflush mode*, then all characters in the buffer are sent to their destination whenever `println` is called. (Print writers are always buffered.) By default, autoflushing is *not* enabled. You can enable or disable autoflushing by using the `PrintWriter(Writer, boolean)` constructor and passing the appropriate Boolean as the second argument.

```
PrintWriter out = new PrintWriter(new
    FileWriter("employee.txt"), true); // autoflush
```

The print methods don't throw exceptions. You can call the `checkError` method to see if something went wrong with the stream.

NOTE: You cannot write raw bytes to a `PrintWriter`. Print writers are designed for text output only.

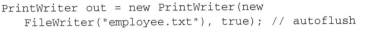

- `PrintWriter(Writer out)`

  creates a new `PrintWriter`, without automatic line flushing.

  Parameters: out   a character-output writer

- `PrintWriter(Writer out, boolean autoFlush)`

  creates a new `PrintWriter`.

  Parameters: out   a character-output writer

  autoFlush   if true, the `println()` methods will flush the output buffer

- `PrintWriter(OutputStream out)`

  creates a new `PrintWriter`, without automatic line flushing, from an existing `OutputStream` by automatically creating the necessary intermediate `OutputStreamWriter`.

  Parameters: out   an output stream

- `PrintWriter(OutputStream out, boolean autoFlush)`

  also creates a new `PrintWriter` from an existing `OutputStream` but allows you to determine whether the writer autoflushes or not.

  Parameters: out   an output stream

  autoFlush   if true, the `println()` methods will flush the output buffer

- `void print(Object obj)`

  prints an object by printing the string resulting from `toString`.

  Parameters: obj   the object to be printed

- `void print(String s)`

  prints a Unicode string.

- `void println(String s)`

  prints a string followed by a line terminator. Flushes the stream if the stream is in autoflush mode.

- `void print(char[] s)`

  prints an array of Unicode characters.

- `void print(char c)`

  prints a Unicode character.

- `void print(int i)`

  prints an integer in text format.

- `void print(long l)`

  prints a long integer in text format.

- `void print(float f)`

  prints a floating-point number in text format.

- `void print(double d)`

  prints a double-precision floating-point number in text format.

- `void print(boolean b)`

  prints a Boolean value in text format.

- `boolean checkError()`

  returns `true` if a formatting or output error occurred. Once the stream has encountered an error, it is tainted and all calls to `checkError` return `true`.

Reading Text Input

As you know:

- To write data in binary format, you use a `DataOutputStream`.
- To write in text format, you use a `PrintWriter`.

Therefore, you might expect that there is an analog to the `DataInputStream` that lets you read data in text format. Unfortunately, Java does not provide such a class. (That is why we wrote our own `Console` class for use in the beginning chapters.) The only game in town for processing text input is the `BufferedReader` method—it has a method, `readLine`, that lets you read a line of text. You need to combine a buffered reader with an input source.

```
BufferedReader in = new BufferedReader(new
    FileReader("employee.txt"));
```

The `readLine` method returns `null` when no more input is available. A typical input loop, therefore, looks like this:

```
String s;
while ((s = in.readLine()) != null)
{   do something with s;
}
```

The `FileReader` class already converts bytes to Unicode characters. For other input sources, you need to use the `InputStreamReader`—unlike the `PrintWriter`, the `InputStreamReader` has no automatic convenience method to bridge the gap between bytes and Unicode characters.

```
BufferedReader in2 = new BufferedReader(new
    InputStreamReader(System.in));
BufferedReader in3 = new BufferedReader(new
    InputStreamReader(url.openStream()));
```

To read numbers from text input, you need to read a string first and then convert it.

```
String s = in.readLine();
double x = Double.parseDouble(s);
```

That works if there is a single number on each line. Otherwise, you must work harder and break up the input string, for example, by using the `StringTokenizer` utility class. We will see an example of this later in this chapter.

TIP: Java has `StringReader` and `StringWriter` classes that allow you to treat a string as if it were a data stream. This can be quite convenient if you want to use the same code to parse both strings and data from a stream.

ZIP File Streams

ZIP files are archives that store one or more files in (usually) compressed format. Java 1.1 can handle both GZIP and ZIP format. (See RFC 1950, RFC 1951, and RFC 1952, for example at `http://www.faqs.org/rfcs`.) In this section we concentrate on the more familiar (but somewhat more complicated) ZIP format and leave the GZIP classes to you if you need them. (They work in much the same way.)

NOTE: The classes for handling ZIP files are in `java.util.zip` and not in `java.io`, so remember to add the necessary `import` statement. Although not part of `java.io`, the GZIP and ZIP classes do subclass `java.io.FilterInputStream` and `java.io.FilterOutputStream`. The `java.util.zip` packages also contain classes for computing CRC checksums. (CRC stands for cyclic redundancy check and is a method to generate a hashlike code that the receiver of a file can use to check the integrity of data transmission.)

Each ZIP file has a header with information such as the name of the file and the compression method that was used. In Java, you use a `ZipInputStream` to read a ZIP file by layering the `ZipInputStream` constructor onto a `FileInputStream`. You then need to look at the individual entries in the archive. The `getNextEntry` method returns an object of type `ZipEntry` that describes the entry. The `read` method of the `ZipInputStream` is modified to return –1, not at the end of the ZIP file but at the end of the current entry. You must then call `closeEntry` to read the next entry. Here is a typical code sequence to read through a ZIP file:

```
ZipInputStream zin = new ZipInputStream
    (new FileInputStream(zipname));
ZipEntry entry;
while ((entry = zin.getNextEntry()) != null)
{   analyze entry;
    read the contents of zin;
    zin.closeEntry();
}
zin.close();
```

To read the contents of a ZIP entry, you will probably not want to use the raw `read` method; usually, you will use the methods of a more competent stream filter. For example, to read a text file inside a ZIP file, you can use the following loop:

```
BufferedReader in = new BufferedReader
    (new InputStreamReader(zin));
String s;
while ((s = in.readLine()) != null)
    do something with s;
```

The program in Example 12–1 lets you open a ZIP file. It then displays the files stored in the ZIP archive in the list box at the top of the screen. If you double-click on one of the files, the contents of the file are displayed in the text area, as shown in Figure 12–4.

Example 12–1: ZipTest.java

```
import java.awt.*;
import java.awt.event.*;
import java.io.*;
import java.util.*;
import java.util.zip.*;
import javax.swing.*;

public class ZipTest extends JFrame
    implements ActionListener
{   public ZipTest()
    {   setTitle("ZipTest");
```

```
    setSize(300, 400);

    JMenuBar mbar = new JMenuBar();
    JMenu m = new JMenu("File");
    openItem = new JMenuItem("Open");
    openItem.addActionListener(this);
    m.add(openItem);
    exitItem = new JMenuItem("Exit");
    exitItem.addActionListener(this);
    m.add(exitItem);
    mbar.add(m);

    fileList.addActionListener(this);

    Container contentPane = getContentPane();
    contentPane.add(mbar, "North");
    contentPane.add(fileList, "South");
    contentPane.add(fileText, "Center");
}

public void actionPerformed(ActionEvent evt)
{   Object source = evt.getSource();
    if (source == openItem)
    {   JFileChooser chooser = new JFileChooser();
        chooser.setCurrentDirectory(new File("."));
        chooser.setFileFilter(new
            javax.swing.filechooser.FileFilter()
            {   public boolean accept(File f)
                {   return f.getName().toLowerCase()
                        .endsWith(".zip");
                }
                public String getDescription()
                { return "ZIP Files"; }
            });

        int r = chooser.showOpenDialog(this);
        if (r == JFileChooser.APPROVE_OPTION)
        {   zipname = chooser.getSelectedFile().getPath();
            scanZipFile();
        }
    }
    else if (source == exitItem) System.exit(0);
    else if (source == fileList)
        loadZipFile((String)fileList.getSelectedItem());
}

public void scanZipFile()
```

```
    {   fileList.removeAllItems();
        try
        {   ZipInputStream zin = new ZipInputStream(new
                FileInputStream(zipname));
            ZipEntry entry;
            while ((entry = zin.getNextEntry()) != null)
            {   fileList.addItem(entry.getName());
                zin.closeEntry();
            }
            zin.close();
        }
        catch(IOException e) {}
    }

    public void loadZipFile(String name)
    {   try
        {   ZipInputStream zin = new ZipInputStream(new
                FileInputStream(zipname));
            ZipEntry entry;
            fileText.setText("");
            while ((entry = zin.getNextEntry()) != null)
            {   if (entry.getName().equals(name))
                {   BufferedReader in = new BufferedReader(new
                        InputStreamReader(zin));
                    String s;
                    while ((s = in.readLine()) != null)
                        fileText.append(s + "\n");
                }
                zin.closeEntry();
            }
            zin.close();
        }
        catch(IOException e) {}
    }

    public static void main(String[] args)
    {   Frame f = new ZipTest();
        f.show();
    }

    private JComboBox fileList = new JComboBox();
    private JTextArea fileText = new JTextArea();
    private JMenuItem openItem;
    private JMenuItem exitItem;
    private String zipname;
}
```

Figure 12–4: The ZipTest program

> NOTE: The ZIP input stream throws a `ZipException` when there is an error in reading a ZIP file. Normally this error occurs when the ZIP file is corrupted.

To write a ZIP file, you open a `ZipOutputStream` by layering it onto a `FileOutputStream`. For each entry that you want to place into the ZIP file, you create a `ZipEntry` object. You pass the file name to the `ZipEntry` constructor; it sets the other parameters such as file date and decompression method automatically. You can override these settings if you like. Then, you call the `putNextEntry` method of the `ZipOutputStream` to begin writing a new file. Send the file data to the ZIP stream, and when you are done, call `closeEntry`. Repeat for all the files you want to store. Here is a code skeleton:

```
FileOutputStream fout = new FileOutputStream("test.zip");
ZipOutputStream zout = new ZipOutputStream(fout);
for all files
{   ZipEntry ze = new ZipEntry(file name);
    zout.putNextEntry(zout);
    send data to ze;
    zout.closeEntry();
}
zout.close();
```

NOTE: JAR files (which were discussed in Chapter 10) are simply ZIP files with another entry, the so-called manifest. You use the `JarInputStream` and `JarOutputStream` classes to read and write the manifest entry.

ZIP streams are a good example of the power of the stream abstraction. Both the source and the destination of the ZIP data are completely flexible. You layer the most convenient reader stream onto the ZIP file stream to read the data that is stored in compressed form, and that reader doesn't even realize that the data is being decompressed as it is being requested. And the source of the bytes in ZIP formats need not be a file—the ZIP data can come from a network connection. In fact, the JAR files that we discussed in Chapter 10 are ZIP-formatted files. Whenever the class loader of an applet reads a JAR file, it reads and decompresses data from the network.

java.util.zip.ZipInputStream

- `ZipInputStream(InputStream in)`

  This constructor creates a `ZipInputStream` that allows you to inflate data from the given `InputStream`.

  Parameters: in   the underlying input stream

- `ZipEntry getNextEntry()`

  returns a `ZipEntry` object for the next entry or `null` if there are no more entries.

- `void closeEntry()`

  closes the current open entry in the ZIP file. You can then read the next entry by using `getNextEntry()`.

java.util.zip.ZipOutputStream

- `ZipOutputStream(OutputStream out)`

  This constructor creates a `ZipOutputStream` that you use to write compressed data to the specified `OutputStream`.

  Parameters: out   the underlying output stream

- `void putNextEntry(ZipEntry ze)`

  writes the information in the given `ZipEntry` to the stream and positions the stream for the data. The data can then be written to the stream by `write()`.

  Parameters: ze   the new entry

- `void closeEntry()`

  closes the currently open entry in the ZIP file. Use `putNextEntry()` to start the next entry.

- void setLevel(int level)

  sets the default compression level of subsequent DEFLATED entries. The default value is Deflater.DEFAULT_COMPRESSION. Throws an IllegalArgumentException if the level is not valid.

  Parameters: level   a compression level, from 0 (NO_COMPRESSION) to 9 (BEST_COMPRESSION)

- void setMethod(int method)

  sets the default compression method for this ZipOutputStream for any entries that do not specify a method.

  Parameters: method   the compression method, either DEFLATED or STORED

java.util.zip.ZipEntry

- ZipEntry(String name)

  Parameters: name   the name of the entry

- long getCrc()

  returns the CRC32 checksum value for this ZipEntry.

- String getName()

  returns the name of this entry.

- long getSize()

  returns the uncompressed size of this entry, or −1 if the uncompressed size is not known.

- boolean isDirectory()

  returns a Boolean that indicates whether or not this entry is a directory.

- void setMethod(int method)

  Parameters: method   the compression method for the entry; must be either DEFLATED or STORED

- void setSize(long size)

  sets the size of this entry. Only required if the compression method is STORED.

  Parameters: size   the uncompressed size of this entry

- void setCrc(long crc)

  sets the CRC32 checksum of this entry. Use the CRC32 class to compute this checksum. Only required if the compression method is STORED.

  Parameters: crc   the checksum of this entry

`java.util.zip.ZipFile`

- `ZipFile(String name)`

  this constructor creates a `ZipFile` for reading from the given string.

  Parameters: name   a string that contains the pathname of the file

- `ZipFile(File file)`

  this constructor creates a `ZipFile` for reading from the given `File` object.

  Parameters: file   the file to read; the `File` class is described at the end of this chapter

- `Enumeration entries()`

  returns an `Enumeration` object that enumerates the `ZipEntry` objects that describe the entries of the `ZipFile`.

- `ZipEntry getEntry(String name)`

  returns the entry corresponding to the given name, or `null` if there is no such entry.

  Parameters: name   the entry name

- `InputStream getInputStream(ZipEntry ze)`

  returns an `InputStream` for the given entry.

  Parameters: ze   a `ZipEntry` in the ZIP file

- `String getName()`

  returns the path of this ZIP file.

Putting Streams to Use

In the next four sections, we will show you how to put some of the creatures in the stream zoo to good use. For these examples, we will assume you are working with the `Employee` class and some of its derived classes, such as `Manager`. (See Chapters 4 and 5 for more on these example classes.) We will consider four separate scenarios for saving an array of employee records to a file and then reading them back into memory.

1. Saving data of the same type (`Employee`) in text format
2. Saving data of the same type in binary format
3. Saving and restoring polymorphic data (a mixture of `Employee` and `Manager` objects)
4. Saving and restoring data containing embedded references (managers with pointers to other employees)

Writing Delimited Output

In this section, you will learn how to store an array of `Employee` records in the time-honored *delimited* format. This means that each record is stored in a separate line. Instance fields are separated from each other by delimiters. We use a vertical bar (|) as our delimiter. (A colon (:) is another popular choice. Part of the fun is that everyone uses a different delimiter.) Naturally, we punt on the issue of what might happen if a | actually occurred in one of the strings we save.

NOTE: Especially on Unix systems, an amazing number of files are stored in exactly this format. We have seen entire employee databases with thousands of records in this format, queried with nothing more than the Unix `awk`, `sort`, and `join` utilities. (In the PC world, where excellent database programs are available at low cost, this kind of ad hoc storage is much less common.)

Here is a sample set of records:

```
Harry Hacker|35500|1989|10|1
Carl Cracker|75000|1987|12|15
Tony Tester|38000|1990|3|15
```

Writing records is simple. Since we write to a text file, we use the `PrintWriter` class. We simply write all fields, followed by either a | or, for the last field, a \n. Finally, in keeping with the idea that we want the *class* to be responsible for responding to messages, we add a method, `writeData`, to our `Employee` class.

```
public void writeData(PrintWriter os) throws IOException
{  os.println(name + "|"
      + salary + "|"
      + hireDay.getYear() + "|"
      + hireDay.getMonth() + "|"
      + hireDay.getDay());
}
```

To read records, we read in a line at a time and separate the fields. This is the topic of the next section, in which we use a utility class supplied with Java to make our job easier.

String Tokenizers and Delimited Text

When reading a line of input, we get a single long string. We want to split it into individual strings. This means finding the | delimiters and then separating out the individual pieces, that is, the sequence of characters up to the next delimiter. (These are usually called *tokens*.) The `StringTokenizer` class in `java.util` is designed for exactly this purpose. It gives you an easy way to break up a large string that contains delimited text. The idea is that a string tokenizer object attaches to a string. When you construct the tokenizer object, you specify which characters are the delimiters. For example, we need to use

```
StringTokenizer t = new StringTokenizer(line, "|");
```

You can specify multiple delimiters in the string. For example, to set up a string tokenizer that would let you search for any delimiter in the set

```
" \t\n\r"
```

use the following:

```
StringTokenizer t = new StringTokenizer(line, " \t\n\r");
```

(Notice that this means that any white space marks off the tokens.)

NOTE: These four delimiters are used as the defaults if you construct a string tokenizer like this:

```
StringTokenizer t = new StringTokenizer(line);
```

Once you have constructed a string tokenizer, you can use its methods to quickly extract the tokens from the string. The `nextToken` method returns the next unread token. The `hasMoreTokens` method returns `true` if more tokens are available.

NOTE: In our case, we know how many tokens we have in every line of input. In general, you have to be a bit more careful: call `hasMoreTokens` before calling `nextToken` because the `nextToken` method throws an exception when no more tokens are available.

A P I `java.util.StringTokenizer`

* `StringTokenizer(String str, String delim)`

    Parameters: str   the input string from which tokens are read

                 delim   a string containing delimiter characters (any character in this string is a delimiter)

* `StringTokenizer(String str)`

    constructs a string tokenizer with the default delimiter set `" \t\n\r"`.

* `boolean hasMoreTokens()`

    returns `true` if more tokens exist.

* `String nextToken()`

    returns the next token; throws a `NoSuchElementException` if there are no more tokens.

- ```
  String nextToken(String delim)
  ```

  returns the next token after switching to the new delimiter set. The new delimiter set is subsequently used.

- ```
  int countTokens()
  ```

  returns the number of tokens still in the string.

Reading Delimited Input

Reading in an `Employee` record is simple. We simply read in a line of input with the `readLine` method of the `BufferedReader` class. Here is the code needed to read one record into a string.

```
BufferedReader in
    = new BufferedReader(new FileReader("employee.dat"));
. . .
String line = in.readLine();
```

Next, we need to extract the individual tokens. When we do this, we end up with *strings*, so we need to convert them to numbers.

Just as with the `writeData` method, we add a `readData` method of the `Employee` class. When you call

```
e.readData(in);
```

this method overwrites the previous contents of e. Note that the method may throw an `IOException` if the `readLine` method throws that exception. There is nothing this method can do if an `IOException` occurs, so we just let it propagate up the call chain.

Here is the code for this method:

```
public void readData(BufferedReader is) throws IOException
{   String s = is.readLine();
    StringTokenizer t = new StringTokenizer(s, "|");
    name = t.nextToken();
    salary = Double.parseDouble(t.nextToken());
    int y = Integer.parseInt(t.nextToken());
    int m = Integer.parseInt(t.nextToken());
    int d = Integer.parseInt(t.nextToken());
    hireDay = new Day(y, m, d);
}
```

Finally, in the code for a program that tests these methods, the static method

```
void writeData(Employee[] e, PrintWriter out)
```

first writes the length of the array, then writes each record. The static method

```
Employee[] readData(BufferedReader in)
```

first reads in the length of the array, then reads in each record, as illustrated in Example 12–2.

Example 12–2: DataFileTest.java

```java
import java.io.*;
import java.util.*;
import corejava.*;

public class DataFileTest
{  static void writeData(Employee[] e, PrintWriter out)
      throws IOException
   {  out.println(e.length);
      int i;
      for (i = 0; i < e.length; i++)
         e[i].writeData(out);
   }

   static Employee[] readData(BufferedReader in)
      throws IOException
   {  int n = Integer.parseInt(in.readLine());
      Employee[] e = new Employee[n];
      int i;
      for (i = 0; i < n; i++)
      {  e[i] = new Employee();
         e[i].readData(in);
      }
      return e;
   }


   public static void main(String[] args)
   {  Employee[] staff = new Employee[3];

      staff[0] = new Employee("Harry Hacker", 35500,
         new Day(1989,10,1));
      staff[1] = new Employee("Carl Cracker", 75000,
         new Day(1987,12,15));
      staff[2] = new Employee("Tony Tester", 38000,
         new Day(1990,3,15));
      int i;
      for (i = 0; i < staff.length; i++)
         staff[i].raiseSalary(5.25);

      try
      {  PrintWriter out = new PrintWriter(new
            FileWriter("employee.dat"));
         writeData(staff, out);
         out.close();
      }
```

```
        catch(IOException e)
        {   System.out.print("Error: " + e);
            System.exit(1);
        }

        try
        {   BufferedReader in = new BufferedReader(new
                FileReader("employee.dat"));
            Employee[] e = readData(in);
            for (i = 0; i < e.length; i++) e[i].print();
            in.close();
        }
        catch(IOException e)
        {   System.out.print("Error: " + e);
            System.exit(1);
        }
    }
}


class Employee
{   public Employee(String n, double s, Day d)
    {   name = n;
        salary = s;
        hireDay = d;
    }
    public Employee() {}
    public void print()
    {   System.out.println(name + " " + salary
            + " " + hireYear());
    }
    public void raiseSalary(double byPercent)
    {   salary *= 1 + byPercent / 100;
    }
    public int hireYear()
    {   return hireDay.getYear();
    }
    public void writeData(PrintWriter out) throws IOException
    {   out.println(name + "|"
            + salary + "|"
            + hireDay.getYear() + "|"
            + hireDay.getMonth() + "|"
            + hireDay.getDay());
    }

    public void readData(BufferedReader in) throws IOException
    {   String s = in.readLine();
```

```
    StringTokenizer t = new StringTokenizer(s, "|");
    name = t.nextToken();
    salary = Double.parseDouble(t.nextToken());
    int y = Integer.parseInt(t.nextToken());
    int m = Integer.parseInt(t.nextToken());
    int d = Integer.parseInt(t.nextToken());
    hireDay = new Day(y, m, d);
  }

  private String name;
  private double salary;
  private Day hireDay;
}
```

Random-Access Streams

If you have a large number of employee records of variable length, the storage technique used in the preceding section suffers from one limitation: it is not possible to read a record in the middle of the file without first reading all records that come before it. In this section, we will make all records the same length. This lets us implement a random-access method of reading back the information using the RandomAccessFile streams that you saw earlier—we can use this to get at any record in the same amount of time.

We will store the numbers in the instance fields in our classes in a binary format. This is done with the writeInt and writeDouble methods of the DataOutput interface. (As we mentioned earlier, this is the common interface of the DataOutputStream and the RandomAccessFile classes.)

However, since the size of each record must remain constant, we need to make all the strings the same size when we save them. The variable-size UTF format does not do this, and the rest of the Java library provides no convenient means of accomplishing this. We need to write a bit of code to implement two helper methods to make the strings the same size. We will call the methods writeFixedString and readFixedString. These methods read and write Unicode strings that always have the same length.

The writeFixedString method takes the parameter size. Then, it writes the specified number of characters, starting at the beginning of the string. (If there are too few characters the method pads the string, using characters whose Unicode values are zero.) Here is the code for the writeFixedString method:

```
static void writeFixedString
    (String s, int size, DataOutput out)
    throws IOException
{   int i;
    for (i = 0; i < size; i++)
    {   char ch = 0;
```

```
        if (i < s.length()) ch = s.charAt(i);
        out.writeChar(ch);
    }
}
```

The `readFixedString` method reads characters from the input stream until it has consumed `size` characters or until it encounters a character with Unicode 0. Then, it should skip past the remaining zero characters in the input field.

For added efficiency, this method uses the `StringBuffer` class to read in a string. A `StringBuffer` is an auxiliary class that lets you preallocate a memory block of a given length. In our case, we know that the string is, at most, `size` bytes long. We make a string buffer in which we reserve `size` characters. Then we append the characters as we read them in.

> NOTE: Using the `StringBuffer` class in this way is more efficient than reading in characters and appending them to an existing string. Every time you append characters to a string, the string object needs to find new memory to hold the larger string: this is time consuming. Appending even more characters means the string needs to be relocated again and again. Using the `StringBuffer` class avoids this problem.

Once the string buffer holds the desired string, we need to convert it to an actual `String` object. This is done with the `String(StringBuffer b)` constructor or the `StringBuffer.toString()` method. These methods do not copy the characters from the string buffer to the string. Instead, they *freeze* the buffer contents. If you later call a method that makes a modification to the `StringBuffer` object, the buffer object first gets a new copy of the characters and then modifies those. The string object keeps the frozen contents.

```
static String readFixedString(int size, DataInput in)
    throws IOException
{   StringBuffer b = new StringBuffer(size);
    int i = 0;
    boolean more = true;
    while (more && i < size)
    {   char ch = in.readChar();
        i++;
        if (ch == 0) more = false;
        else b.append(ch);
    }
    in.skipBytes(2 * (size - i));
    return b.toString();
}
```

> NOTE: These two functions are packaged inside the `DataIO` helper class.

To write a fixed-size record, we simply write all fields in binary.

```
public void writeData(DataOutput out) throws IOException
{   DataIO.writeFixedString(name, NAME_SIZE, out);
    out.writeDouble(salary);
    out.writeInt(hireDay.getYear());
    out.writeInt(hireDay.getMonth());
    out.writeInt(hireDay.getDay());
}
```

Reading the data back is just as simple.

```
public void readData(DataInput in) throws IOException
{   name = DataIO.readFixedString(NAME_SIZE, in);
    salary = in.readDouble();
    int y = in.readInt();
    int m = in.readInt();
    int d = in.readInt();
    hireDay = new Day(y, m, d);
}
```

In our example, each employee record is 100 bytes long because we specified that the name field would always be written using 40 characters. This gives us a breakdown as indicated in the following:

40 characters = 80 bytes for the name

1 `double` = 8 bytes

3 `int` = 12 bytes

As an example, suppose you want to position the file pointer to the third record. You can use the following version of the `seek` method:

```
long int n = 3;
int RECORD_SIZE = 100;
in.seek((n - 1) * RECORD_SIZE);
```

Then you can read a record:

```
Employee e = new Employee();
e.readData(in);
```

If you want to modify the record and then save it back into the same location, remember to set the file pointer back to the beginning of the record:

```
in.seek((n - 1) * RECORD.SIZE);
    // again
e.writeData(in);
```

To determine the total number of bytes in a file, use the `length` method. The total number of records is the length divided by the size of each record.

```
long int nbytes = in.length(); // length in bytes
int nrecords = (int)(nbytes / RECORD_SIZE);
```

The test program shown in Example 12–3 writes three records into a data file and then reads them from the file in reverse order. To do this efficiently requires random access—we need to get at the third record first.

Example 12–3: RandomFileTest.java

```
import java.io.*;
import corejava.*;

public class RandomFileTest
{  public static void main(String[] args)
   {  Employee[] staff = new Employee[3];

      staff[0] = new Employee("Harry Hacker", 35000,
         new Day(1989,10,1));
      staff[1] = new Employee("Carl Cracker", 75000,
         new Day(1987,12,15));
      staff[2] = new Employee("Tony Tester", 38000,
         new Day(1990,3,15));
      int i;
      try
      {  DataOutputStream out = new DataOutputStream(new
            FileOutputStream("employee.dat"));
         for (i = 0; i < staff.length; i++)
            staff[i].writeData(out);
         out.close();
      }
      catch(IOException e)
      {  System.out.print("Error: " + e);
         System.exit(1);
      }

      try
      {  RandomAccessFile in
            = new RandomAccessFile("employee.dat", "r");
         int n = (int)(in.length() / Employee.RECORD_SIZE);
         Employee[] newStaff = new Employee[n];

         for (i = n - 1; i >= 0; i--)
         {  newStaff[i] = new Employee();
            in.seek(i * Employee.RECORD_SIZE);
            newStaff[i].readData(in);
         }
         for (i = 0; i < newStaff.length; i++)
            newStaff[i].print();
      }
      catch(IOException e)
      {  System.out.print("Error: " + e);
         System.exit(1);
      }
```

```
      }
   }

class Employee
{  public Employee(String n, double s, Day d)
   {  name = n;
      salary = s;
      hireDay = d;
   }
   public Employee() {}
   public void print()
   {  System.out.println(name + " " + salary
         + " " + hireYear());
   }
   public void raiseSalary(double byPercent)
   {  salary *= 1 + byPercent / 100;
   }
   public int hireYear()
   {  return hireDay.getYear();
   }
   public void writeData(DataOutput out) throws IOException
   {  DataIO.writeFixedString(name, NAME_SIZE, out);
      out.writeDouble(salary);
      out.writeInt(hireDay.getYear());
      out.writeInt(hireDay.getMonth());
      out.writeInt(hireDay.getDay());
   }

   public void readData(DataInput in) throws IOException
   {  name = DataIO.readFixedString(NAME_SIZE, in);
      salary = in.readDouble();
      int y = in.readInt();
      int m = in.readInt();
      int d = in.readInt();
      hireDay = new Day(y, m, d);
   }

   public static final int NAME_SIZE = 40;
   public static final int RECORD_SIZE
      = 2 * NAME_SIZE + 8 + 4 + 4 + 4;

   private String name;
   private double salary;
   private Day hireDay;
}

class DataIO
{  public static String readFixedString(int size,
      DataInput in) throws IOException
   {  StringBuffer b = new StringBuffer(size);
```

```
    int i = 0;
    boolean more = true;
    while (more && i < size)
    {   char ch = in.readChar();
        i++;
        if (ch == 0) more = false;
        else b.append(ch);
    }
    in.skipBytes(2 * (size - i));
    return b.toString();
}

public static void writeFixedString(String s, int size,
    DataOutput out) throws IOException
{   int i;
    for (i = 0; i < size; i++)
    {   char ch = 0;
        if (i < s.length()) ch = s.charAt(i);
        out.writeChar(ch);
    }
}
}
```

java.lang.StringBuffer

- `StringBuffer()`

  constructs an empty string buffer.

- `StringBuffer(int length)`

  constructs an empty string buffer with the initial capacity `length`.

- `StringBuffer(String str)`

  constructs a string buffer with the initial contents `str`.

- `int length()`

  returns the number of characters of the buffer.

- `int capacity()`

  returns the current capacity, that is, the number of characters that can be contained in the buffer before it must be relocated.

- `void ensureCapacity(int m)`

  enlarges the buffer if the capacity is fewer than `m` characters.

- `void setLength(int n)`

  if `n` is less than the current length, characters at the end of the string are discarded. If `n` is larger than the current length, the buffer is padded with `'\0'` characters.

- `char charAt(int i)`

  returns the i'th character (i is between 0 and `length()`-1); throws a `StringIndexOutOfBoundsException` if the index is invalid.

- `void getChars(int from, int to, char[] a, int offset)`

  copies characters from the string buffer into an array.

Parameters:	from	the first character to copy
	to	the first character not to copy
	a	the array to copy into
	offset	the first position in a to copy into

- `void setCharAt(int i, char ch)`

  sets the i'th character to ch.

- `StringBuffer append(String str)`

  appends a string to the end of this buffer (the buffer may be relocated as a result); returns `this`.

- `StringBuffer append(char c)`

  appends a character to the end of this buffer (the buffer may be relocated as a result); returns `this`.

- `StringBuffer insert(int offset, String str)`

  inserts a string at position `offset` into this buffer (the buffer may be relocated as a result); returns `this`.

- `StringBuffer insert(int offset, char c)`

  inserts a character at position `offset` into this buffer (the buffer may be relocated as a result); returns `this`.

- `String toString()`

  returns a string pointing to the same data as the buffer contents. (No copy is made.)

`java.lang.String`

- `String(StringBuffer buffer)`

  makes a string pointing to the same data as the buffer contents. (No copy is made.)

Object Streams

Using a fixed-length record format is a good choice if you need to store data of the same type. However, objects that you create in an object-oriented program are rarely all of the same type. For example, you may have an array called `staff` that is nominally an array of `Employee` records but contains objects that are actually instances of a child class such as `Manager`.

If we want to save files that contain this kind of information, we must first save the type of each object and then the data that defines the current state of the object. When we read this information back from a file, we must

- Read the object type
- Create a blank object of that type
- Fill it with the data that we stored in the file

It is entirely possible (if very tedious) to do this by hand, and in the first edition of this book we did exactly this. However, Sun Microsystems developed a powerful mechanism that allows this to be done with much less effort. As you will soon see, this mechanism, called *object serialization*, almost completely automates what was previously a very tedious process. (You will see later in this chapter where the term "serialization" comes from.)

Storing Objects of Variable Type

To save object data, you first need to open an `ObjectOutputStream` object:

```
ObjectOutputStream out = new ObjectOutputStream(new
    FileOutputStream("employee.dat"));
```

Now, to save an object, you simply use the `writeObject` method of the `ObjectOutputStream` class as in the following fragment:

```
Employee harry = new Employee("Harry Hacker",
    35000, new Day(1989, 10, 1));
Manager carl = new Manager("Carl Cracker",
    75000, new Day(1987, 12, 15));
out.writeObject(harry);
out.writeObject(carl);
```

To read the objects back in, first get an `ObjectInputStream` object:

```
ObjectInputStream in = new ObjectInputStream(new
    FileInputStream("employee.dat"));
```

Then, retrieve the objects in the same order in which they were written, using the `readObject` method.

```
Employee e1 = (Employee)in.readObject();
Employee e2 = (Employee)in.readObject();
```

When reading back objects, you must carefully keep track of the number of objects that were saved, their order, and their types. Each call to `readObject` reads in another object of the type `Object`. You, therefore, will need to cast it to its correct type.

If you don't need the exact type or you don't remember it, then you can cast it to any superclass or even leave it as type `Object`. For example, e2 is an `Employee` object variable even though it actually refers to a `Manager` object. If you need to dynamically query the type of the object, you can use the `getClass` method that we described in Chapter 5.

You can write and read only *objects* with the `writeObject`/`readObject` methods, not numbers. To write and read numbers, you use methods such as `writeInt`/`readInt` or `writeDouble`/`readDouble`. (The object stream classes implement the `DataInput`/`DataOutput` interfaces.) Of course, numbers inside objects (such as the salary field of an `Employee` object) are saved and restored automatically. Recall that, in Java, strings and arrays are objects and can, therefore, be restored with the `writeObject`/`readObject` methods.

There is, however, one change you need to make to any class that you want to save and restore in an object stream. The class must implement the `Serializable` interface:

```
class Employee implements Serializable { . . .}
```

The `Serializable` interface has no methods, so you don't need to change your classes in any way. In this regard, it is similar to the `Cloneable` interface that we also discussed in Chapter 5. However, to make a class cloneable, you still had to override the `clone` method of the `Object` class. To make a class serializable, you do not need to do *anything* else. Why aren't all classes serializable by default? We will discuss this in the section "Security."

Example 12–4 is a test program that writes an array containing two employees and one manager to disk and then restores it. Writing an array is done with a single operation:

```
Employee[] staff = new Employee[3];
. . .
out.writeObject(staff);
```

Similarly, reading in the result is done with a single operation. However, we must apply a cast to the return value of the `readObject` method:

```
Employee[] newStaff = (Employee[])in.readObject();
```

Once the information is restored, we give each employee a 100% raise, not because we are feeling generous, but because you can then easily distinguish employee and manager objects by their different `raiseSalary` actions. This should convince you that we did restore the correct types.

Example 12–4: ObjectFileTest.java

```
import java.io.*;
import corejava.*;

class ObjectFileTest
{ public static void main(String[] args)
```

```
  {  try
     {  Employee[] staff = new Employee[3];

        staff[0] = new Employee("Harry Hacker", 35000,
           new Day(1989,10,1));
        staff[1] = new Manager("Carl Cracker", 75000,
           new Day(1987,12,15));
        staff[2] = new Employee("Tony Tester", 38000,
           new Day(1990,3,15));

        ObjectOutputStream out = new ObjectOutputStream(new
           FileOutputStream("employee.dat"));
        out.writeObject(staff);
        out.close();

        ObjectInputStream in =  new
           ObjectInputStream(new FileInputStream("employee.dat"));
        Employee[] newStaff = (Employee[])in.readObject();

        int i;
        for (i = 0; i < newStaff.length; i++)
           newStaff[i].raiseSalary(100);
        for (i = 0; i < newStaff.length; i++)
           newStaff[i].print();
     }
     catch(Exception e)
     {  System.out.print("Error: " + e);
        System.exit(1);
     }
  }
}

class Employee implements Serializable
{  public Employee(String n, double s, Day d)
   {  name = n;
      salary = s;
      hireDay = d;
   }

   public Employee() {}

   public void print()
   {  System.out.println(name + " " + salary
         + " " + hireYear());
   }

   public void raiseSalary(double byPercent)
   {  salary *= 1 + byPercent / 100;
   }

   public int hireYear()
```

```
    {  return hireDay.getYear();
    }

    private String name;
    private double salary;
    private Day hireDay;
}

class Manager extends Employee
{   public Manager(String n, double s, Day d)
    {   super(n, s, d);
        secretaryName = "";
    }

    public Manager() {}

    public void raiseSalary(double byPercent)
    {   // add 1/2% bonus for every year of service
        Day today = new Day();
        double bonus = 0.5 * (today.getYear() - hireYear());
        super.raiseSalary(byPercent + bonus);
    }

    public void setSecretaryName(String n)
    {   secretaryName = n;
    }

    public String getSecretaryName()
    {   return secretaryName;
    }

    private String secretaryName;
}
```

java.io.ObjectOutputStream

- `ObjectOutputStream(OutputStream out)`

  creates an `ObjectOutputStream` so that you can write objects to the specified `OutputStream`.

- `void writeObject(Object obj)`

  writes the specified object to the `ObjectOutputStream`. The class of the object, the signature of the class, and the values of any field not marked as `transient` are written, as well as the nonstatic fields of all of its superclasses.

`java.io.ObjectInputStream`

- `ObjectInputStream(InputStream is)`

  creates an `ObjectInputStream` to read back object information from the specified `InputStream`.

- `Object readObject()`

  reads an object from the `ObjectInputStream`. In particular, this reads back the class of the object, the signature of the class, and the values of the nontransient and nonstatic fields of the class and all of its superclasses. It does deserializing to allow multiple object references to be recovered.

Object Serialization File Format

Object serialization saves object data in a particular file format. Of course, you can use the `writeObject`/`readObject` methods without having to know the exact sequence of bytes that represents objects in a file. Nonetheless, we found studying the data format to be extremely helpful for gaining insight into the object streaming process. We did this by looking at hex dumps of various saved object files. However, the details are somewhat technical, so feel free to skip this section if you are not interested in the implementation.

Every file begins with the 2-byte "magic number"

    AC ED

followed by the version number of the object serialization format, which is currently

    00 05

(We will be using hexadecimal numbers throughout this section to denote bytes.) Then, it contains a sequence of objects, in the order that they were saved.

String objects are saved as

    74   2-byte length   characters

For example, the string "Harry" is saved as

    74   00 05   H a r r y

The Unicode characters of the string are saved in UTF format.

When an object is saved, the class of that object must be saved as well. The class description contains

1. The name of the class

2. The *serial version unique ID*, which is a fingerprint of the data field types and method signatures

3. A set of flags describing the serialization method

4. A description of the data fields

Java gets the fingerprint by:

- First, ordering descriptions of the class, superclass, interfaces, field types, and method signatures in a canonical way

- Then, applying the so-called Secure Hash Algorithm (SHA) to that data

SHA is a very fast algorithm that gives a "fingerprint" to a larger block of information. This fingerprint is always a 20-byte data packet, regardless of the size of the original data. It is created by a clever sequence of bit operations on the data that makes it essentially 100 percent certain that the fingerprint will change if the information is altered in any way. SHA is a U.S. standard, recommended by the National Institute for Science and Technology (NIST). (For more details on SHA, see, for example, *Network and Internetwork Security*, by William Stallings [Prentice Hall].) However, Java uses only the first 8 bytes of the SHA code as a class fingerprint. It is still very likely that the class fingerprint will change if the data fields or methods change in any way.

Java can then check the class fingerprint in order to protect us from the following scenario: An object is saved to a disk file. Later, the designer of the class makes a change, for example, by removing a data field. Then, the old disk file is read in again. Now the data layout on the disk no longer matches the data layout in memory. If the data were read back in its old form, it could corrupt memory. Java takes great care to make such memory corruption close to impossible. Hence, it checks, using the fingerprint, that the class definition has not changed when restoring an object. It does this by comparing the fingerprint on disk with the fingerprint of the current class.

NOTE: Technically, as long as the data layout of a class has not changed, it ought to be safe to read objects back in. But Java is conservative and checks that the methods have not changed either. (After all, the methods describe the meaning of the stored data.) Of course, in practice, classes do evolve, and it may be necessary for a program to read in older versions of objects. We will discuss this in the section "Versioning."

Here is how a class identifier is stored:

72
2-byte length of class name
class name
8-byte fingerprint
1-byte flag
2-byte count of data field descriptors

data field descriptors

78 (end marker)

superclass type (70 if none)

The flag byte is composed of three bit masks, defined in

```
java.io.ObjectStreamConstants:
static final byte SC_WRITE_METHOD = 1;
    // class has writeObject method that writes additional data
static final byte SC_SERIALIZABLE = 2;
    // class implements Serializable interface
static final byte SC_EXTERNALIZABLE = 4;
    // class implements Externalizable interface
```

We will discuss the `Externalizable` interface later in this chapter; for now, all our example classes will implement the `Serializable` interface and will have a flag value of 02.

Each data field descriptor has the format

1-byte type code

2-byte length of field name

field name

class name (if field is an object)

The type code is one of the following:

```
B       byte
C       char
D       double
F       float
I       int
J       long
L       object
S       short
Z       Boolean
[       array
```

When the type code is L, the field name is followed by the field type. Class and field name strings do not start with the string code 74, but field types do. Field types use a slightly different encoding of their names, namely, the format used by native methods. (See Volume 2 for native methods.)

For example, the day field of the `Day` class is encoded as

```
I 00 03 d a y
```

Here is the complete class descriptor of the Day class:

```
72
00 0C c o r e j a v a . D a y
EE A7 E7 DE BE 67 25 7B
02
00 03
I 00 03 d a y
I 00 05 m o n t h
I 00 04 y e a r
78
70
```

These descriptors are fairly long. If the *same* class descriptor is needed again in the file, then an abbreviated form is used:

71   4-byte serial number

The serial number refers to the previous explicit class descriptor. We will discuss the numbering scheme later.

An object is stored as

73   class descriptor   object data

For example, here is how a Day object is stored:

```
73                     new object
72 . . . 70            new class descriptor
00 00 00 01            integer 1
00 00 00 0A            integer 10
00 00 07 C5            integer 1989
```

As you can see, the data file contains enough information to restore the Day object.

Arrays are saved in the following format:

75   class descriptor   4-byte number of entries   entries

The array class name in the class descriptor is in the same format as that used by native methods (which is slightly different from the class name used by class names in other class descriptors). In this format, class names start with an L and end with a semicolon.

For example, here is an array of two Day objects.

75	array
72	class descriptor
00 0F	length
[L c o r e j a v a / D a y ;	class name
FE F8 AC 6C 78 06 C7 36 02	fingerprint and flag

00 00	no data fields
78	end marker
70	no superclass
00 00 00 02	number of entries
73	new object
72 . . . 70	new class
00 00 00 01	integer 1
00 00 00 0A	integer 10
00 00 07 C5	integer 1989
73	new object
71 00 7E 00 02	existing class + serial number
00 00 00 0F	integer 15
00 00 00 0C	integer 12
00 00 07 C3	integer 1987

Note that the fingerprint for an array of Day objects is different from a fingerprint of the Day class itself.

Of course, studying these codes can be about as exciting as reading the average phone book. But it is still instructive to know that the object stream contains a detailed description of all the objects that it contains, with sufficient detail to allow reconstruction of both objects and arrays of objects.

The Problem of Saving Object References

We now know how to save objects that contain numbers, strings, or other simple objects (like the Day object in the Employee class). However, there is one important situation that we still need to consider. What happens when one object is shared by several objects as part of its state?

To illustrate the problem, let us make a slight modification to the Manager class. Rather than storing the name of the secretary, save a reference to a secretary object, which is an object of type Employee. (It would make sense to derive a class Secretary from Employee for this purpose, but we will not do that here.)

```
class Manager extends Employee
{  // previous code remains the same
   private Employee secretary;
}
```

This is a better approach to designing a realistic Manager class than simply using the name of the secretary—the Employee record for the secretary can now be accessed without the need to search the staff array.

Having done this, you must keep in mind that the Manager object now contains a *reference* to the Employee object that describes the secretary, *not* a separate copy of the object.

In particular, two managers can share the same secretary, as is the case in Figure 12–5 and the following code:

```
harry = new Employee("Harry Hacker", . . .);
Manager carl = new Manager("Carl Cracker", . . .);
carl.setSecretary(harry);
Manager tony = new Manager("Tony Tester", . . .);
tony.setSecretary(harry);
```

Now, suppose we write the employee data to disk. What we *don't* want is that the Manager saves its information according to the following logic:

- Save employee data

- Save secretary data

Then, the data for harry would be saved *three times*. When reloaded, the objects would have the configuration shown in Figure 12–6.

This is not what we want. Suppose the secretary gets a raise. We would not want to hunt for all other copies of that object and apply the raise as well. We want to save and restore only *one copy* of the secretary. To do this, we must copy and restore the original references to the objects. In other words, we want the object layout on disk to be exactly like the object layout in memory. This is called *persistence* in object-oriented circles.

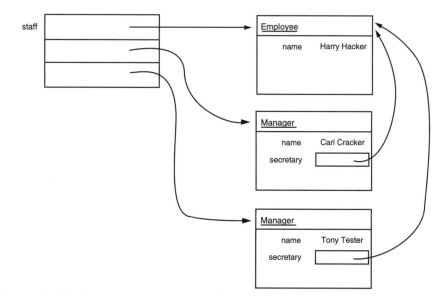

Figure 12–5: Two managers can share a mutual employee

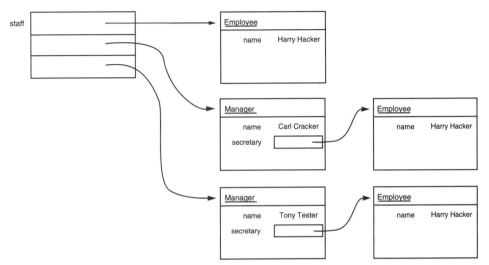

Figure 12–6: Here, Harry is saved three times

Of course, we cannot save and restore the memory addresses for the secretary objects. When an object is reloaded, it will likely occupy a completely different memory address than it originally did.

Instead, Java uses a *serialization* approach. Hence, the name *object serialization* for this new mechanism. Here is the algorithm:

• All objects that are saved to disk are given a serial number (1, 2, 3, and so on, as shown in Figure 2–7).

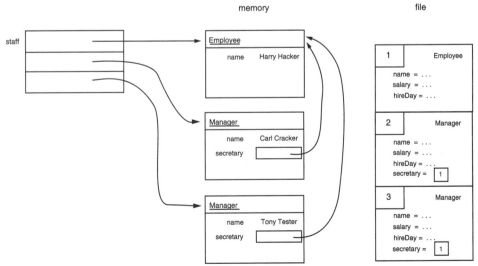

Figure 12–7: An example of object serialization

- When saving an object to disk, find out if the same object has already been stored.

- If it has been stored previously, just write "same as previously saved object with serial number *x*". If not, store all its data.

When reading back the objects, simply reverse the procedure. For each object that you load, note its sequence number and remember where you put it in memory. When you encounter the tag "same as previously saved object with serial number *x*", you look up where you put the object with serial number *x* and set the object reference to that memory address.

Note that the objects need not be saved in any particular order. Figure 12–8 shows what happens when a manager occurs first in the staff array.

All of this sounds confusing, and it is. Fortunately, when object streams are used, the process is also *completely automatic*. Object streams assign the serial numbers and keep track of duplicate objects. The exact numbering scheme is slightly different from that used in the figures—see the next section.

NOTE: In this chapter, we use serialization to save a collection of objects to a disk file and retrieve it exactly as we stored it. Another very important application is the transmittal of a collection of objects across a network connection to another computer. Just as raw memory addresses are meaningless in a file, they are also meaningless when communicating with a different processor. Since serialization replaces memory addresses with serial numbers, it permits the transport of object collections from one machine to another. We will study that use of serialization when discussing remote method invocation in Volume 2.

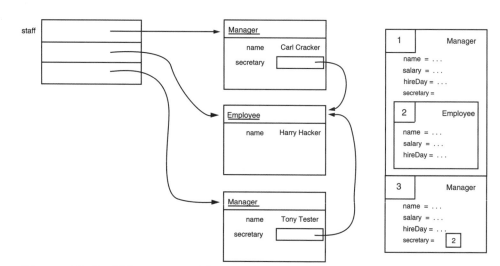

Figure 12–8: Objects saved in random order

Example 12–5 is a program that saves and reloads a network of employee and manager objects (some of which share the same employee as a secretary). Note that the secretary object is unique after reloading—when staff[0] gets a raise, that is reflected in the secretary fields of the managers.

Example 12–5: ObjectRefTest.java

```java
import java.io.*;
import java.util.*;
import corejava.*;

class ObjectRefTest
{  public static void main(String[] args)
   {  try
      {
          Employee[] staff = new Employee[3];

          Employee harry = new Employee("Harry Hacker", 35000,
              new Day(1989,10,1));
          staff[0] = harry;
          staff[1] = new Manager("Carl Cracker", 75000,
              new Day(1987,12,15), harry);
          staff[2] = new Manager("Tony Tester", 38000,
              new Day(1990,3,15), harry);

          ObjectOutputStream out = new ObjectOutputStream(new
              FileOutputStream("employee.dat"));
          out.writeObject(staff);
          out.close();

          ObjectInputStream in =  new
              ObjectInputStream(new
                  FileInputStream("employee.dat"));
          Employee[] newStaff = (Employee[])in.readObject();

          for (int i = 0; i < newStaff.length; i++)
              newStaff[i].raiseSalary(100);
          for (int i = 0; i < newStaff.length; i++)
              newStaff[i].print();
      }
      catch(Exception e)
      {  e.printStackTrace();
          System.exit(1);
      }
   }
}

class Employee implements Serializable
{  public Employee(String n, double s, Day d)
   {  name = n;
```

```
        salary = s;
        hireDay = d;
    }

    public Employee() {}

    public void raiseSalary(double byPercent)
    {   salary *= 1 + byPercent / 100;
    }

    public int hireYear()
    {   return hireDay.getYear();
    }

    public void print()
    {   System.out.println(name + " " + salary
            + " " + hireYear());
    }

    private String name;
    private double salary;
    private Day hireDay;
}

class Manager extends Employee
{   public Manager(String n, double s, Day d, Employee e)
    {   super(n, s, d);
        secretary = e;
    }

    public Manager() {}

    public void raiseSalary(double byPercent)
    {   // add 1/2% bonus for every year of service
        Day today = new Day();
        double bonus = 0.5 * (today.getYear() - hireYear());
        super.raiseSalary(byPercent + bonus);
    }

    public void print()
    {   super.print();
        System.out.print("Secretary: ");
        if (secretary != null) secretary.print();
    }

    private Employee secretary;
}
```

Output Format for Object References

This section continues the discussion of the output format of object streams. If you skipped the discussion before, you should skip this section as well.

All objects (including arrays and strings) and all class descriptors are given serial numbers as they are saved in the output file. This process is referred to as *serialization* because every saved object is assigned a serial number. (The count starts at 00 7E 00 00.)

We already saw that a full class descriptor for any given class occurs only once. Subsequent descriptors refer to it. For example, in our previous example, the second reference to the Day class in the array of days was coded as

```
71 00 7E 00 02
```

The same mechanism is used for objects. If a reference to a previously saved object is written, it is saved in exactly the same way, that is, 71 followed by the serial number. It is always clear from the context whether the particular serial reference denotes a class descriptor or an object.

Finally, a null reference is stored as

```
70
```

Here is the commented output of the ObjectRefTest program of the preceding section. If you like, run the program, look at a hex dump of its data file employee.dat, and compare it with the commented listing. The important lines toward the end of the output (in bold) show the reference to a previously saved object.

AC ED 00 05	file header
75	array staff (serial #1)
72	new class Employee[] (serial #0)
00 0B	length
[L E m p l o y e e ;	class name
FC BF 36 11 C5 91 11 C7 02	fingerprint and flags
00 00	number of data fields
78	end marker
70	no superclass
00 00 00 03	number of entries
73	new object harry (serial #5)
72	new class Employee (serial #2)
00 08	length
E m p l o y e e	class name
3E BB 06 E1 38 0F 90 C9 02	fingerprint and flags
00 03	number of data fields
D 00 06 salary	
L 00 07 hireDay	
74 00 0E Lcorejava/Day;	(serial #3)
L 00 04 name	
74 00 12 Ljava/lang/String;	(serial #4)
78	end marker
70	no superclass

40 E1 17 00 00 00 00 00	8-byte `double` salary
73	new object `harry.hireDay` (serial #7)
72	new class `Day` (serial #6)
00 0C	length
c o r e j a v a . D a y	
EE A7 E7 DE BE 67 25 1B 02	fingerprint and flags
00 03	3 data fields
I 00 03 day	
I 00 05 month	
I 00 04 year	
78	end marker
70	no superclass
00 00 00 01	3 integers `day`, `month`, `year`
00 00 00 0A	
00 00 07 C5	
74	string (serial #8)
00 0C	length
H a r r y H a c k e r	
73	new object `staff[1]` (serial #11)
72	new class `Manager` (serial #9)
00 07	length
M a n a g e r	class name
B1 C5 48 6B 95 EE BE C2 02	fingerprint and flags
00 01	1 data field
L 00 09 secretary	
74 00 0A Employee;	(serial #10)
78	end marker
71 00 7E 00 02	**existing base class Employee—** use serial #2
40 F2 4F 80 00 00 00 00	8-byte `double` salary
73	new object `staff[1].hireDay` (serial #12)
71 00 7E 00 06	**existing class Day—use serial #6**
00 00 00 0F	3 integers `day`, `month`, `year`
00 00 00 0C	
00 00 07 C3	
74	string (serial #13)
00 0C	length
C a r l C r a c k e r	
71 00 7E 00 05	**existing object harry—use** serial #5
73	new object `staff[2]` (serial #14)
71 00 7E 00 09	**existing class Manager— use**

	serial #9
`40 E2 8E 00 00 00 00 00`	8-byte `double` salary
`73`	new object `staff[2].hireDay`
	(serial #15)
`71 00 7E 00 06`	**existing class Day**—use serial #6
`00 00 00 0F`	3 integers day, month, year
`00 00 00 03`	
`00 00 07 C6`	
`74`	string (serial #16)
`00 0B`	length
`T o n y    T e s t e r`	
`71 00 7E 00 05`	**existing object harry**—use
	serial #5

It is usually not important to know the exact file format (unless you are trying to create an evil effect by modifying the data—see the next section). What you should remember is this:

- The object stream output contains the types and data fields of all objects.
- Each object is assigned a serial number.
- Repeated occurrences of the same object are stored as references to that serial number.

Security

Even if you only glanced at the file format description of the preceding section, it should become obvious that a knowledgeable hacker can exploit this information and modify an object file so that invalid objects will be read in when you reload the file.

Consider, for example, the `Day` class in the `corejava` package. That class has been carefully designed so that all of its constructors check that the day, month, and year fields never represent an invalid date. For example, if you try to build a `new Day(1996, 2, 31)`, no object is created and an `IllegalArgumentException` is thrown instead.

However, this safety guarantee can be subverted through serialization. When a `Day` object is read in from an object stream, it is possible—either through a device error or through malice—that the stream contains an invalid date. There is nothing that the serialization mechanism can do in this case—it has no understanding of the constraints that define a legal date.

For that reason, Java's serialization mechanism provides a way for individual classes to add validation or any other desired action instead of the default behavior. A serializable class can define methods with the signature

```
private void readObject(ObjectInputStream in)
    throws IOException, ClassNotFoundException;
```

```
private void writeObject(ObjectOutputStream out)
    throws IOException;
```

Then, the data fields are no longer automatically serialized, and these methods are called instead.

For example, let us add validation to the Day class. We don't need to change the writing of Day objects, so we won't implement the writeObject method.

In the readObject method, we first need to read the object state that was written by the default write method, by calling the defaultReadObject method. This is a special method of the ObjectInputStream class that can only be called from within a readObject method of a serializable class.

```
class Day
{   .  .  .
    private void readObject(ObjectInputStream in)
        throws IOException, ClassNotFoundException
    {  in.defaultReadObject();
        if (!isValid()) throw new IOException("Invalid date");
    }
}
```

The isValid method checks whether the day, month, and year fields represent a valid date. That is the same method that we use in the Day constructor to check the constructor arguments. If the date is not valid (for example, because someone modified the data file), then we throw an exception.

NOTE: Another way of protecting serialized data from tampering is authentication. As you will see in Volume 2, a stream can save a *message digest* (such as the SHA fingerprint) to detect any corruption of the stream data.

Classes can also write additional information to the output stream by defining a writeObject method that first calls defaultWriteObject and then writes other data. Of course, the readObject method must then read the saved data—otherwise, the stream state will be out of sync with the object. Also, the writeObject and readObject can completely bypass the default storage of the object data by simply *not* calling the defaultWriteObject and defaultReadObject methods.

In any case, the readObject and writeObject methods only need to save and load their data fields. They should not concern themselves with superclass data or any other class information.

Rather than letting the serialization mechanism save and restore object data, a class can define its own mechanism. To do this, a class must implement the Externalizable interface. This in turn requires it to define two methods:

```
public void readExternal(ObjectInputStream in)
    throws IOException, ClassNotFoundException;
public void writeExternal(ObjectOutputStream out)
    throws IOException;
```

Unlike the `readObject` and `writeObject` methods that were described in the preceding section, these methods will be fully responsible for saving and restoring the entire object, *including the superclass data*. The serialization mechanism merely records the class of the object in the stream. When reading an externalizable object, the object stream creates an object with the default constructor and then calls the `readExternal` method.

CAUTION: Unlike the `readObject` and `writeObject` methods, which are private and can only be called by the serialization mechanism, the `readExternal` and `writeExternal` methods are *public*. In particular, `readExternal` potentially permits modification of the state of an existing object.

Finally, certain data members should never be serialized, for example, integer values that store file handles or handles of windows that are only meaningful to native methods. Such information is guaranteed to be useless when you reload an object at a later time or transport it to a different machine. In fact, improper values for such fields can actually cause native methods to crash. Java has an easy mechanism to prevent such fields from ever being serialized. Mark them with the keyword `transient`. Transient fields are always skipped when objects are serialized.

As you saw, by default all non-`static`, non-`transient` fields of an object are serialized. If for whatever reason you aren't happy about this mechanism, you can turn off this default selection of serialized fields and instead nominate any other values for serialization. You do this by specifying an array of `ObjectStreamField` objects, each of which gives the name and type of a value. You must define a `private static final` array and call it `serialPersistentFields`. This is not a common thing to do, and we don't want to dwell on the details. We'll walk through a simple example, but you need to refer to the API documentation for more information.

Suppose you want to save the state of a `Day` object not by saving the `day`, `month`, and `year` fields, but instead by saving the single number

```
10000 * year + 100 * month + day
```

For example, February 28, 1996 would be saved as the number `19960228`. We'll call this value `date`. You tell the `Day` class that its serialized form consists of a single field, `date`, of type `long`:

```
class Day
{   . . .
    private static final ObjectStreamField[]
        serialPersistentFields =
    {   new ObjectStreamField("date", long.class),
    };
}
```

Now you need to take over the streaming of this class. In the `writeObject` method, you retrieve the set of fields for the object with the `putFields` method. (This method returns an object that encapsulates the field set--it's type is the inner class `ObjectOutputStream.PutField`). You then set the value of the date field, and finally you write the field set to the stream:

```
private void writeObject(ObjectOutputStream out)
    throws IOException
{   ObjectOutputStream.PutField fields = out.putFields();
    fields.put("date", year * 10000L + month * 100 + day);
    out.writeFields();
}
```

To read the object back, you override the `readObject` method. First read in all the fields with the `readFields` method. Then you retrieve the value of each field with one of the overloaded `get` methods of the inner class `ObjectInputStream.GetField`. The first argument of the get method is the name of the field. The second value is the default, to be used when the field is not present. (This could happen if the version of the object on the stream is different than the current version of the class.) You have to be careful about the *type* of the default value--the type is used to pick between overloaded methods

```
int get(String name, int defval);
long get(String name, long defval);
float get(String name, float defval);
double get(String name, double defval);
char get(String name, char defval);
short get(String name, short defval);
. . .
```

If the default value is zero, you must supply a zero of the appropriate type:

```
0
0L
0.0F
0.0
'\0'
(short)0
. . .
```

Here is the `readObject` method for our modified Day class. It reads the date value and splits it up into day, month, and year.

```
private void readObject(ObjectInputStream in)
    throws IOException, ClassNotFoundException
{   ObjectInputStream.GetField fields = in.readFields();
    long date = fields.get("date", 0L);
    day = (int)(date % 100);
    month = (int)((date / 100) % 100);
    year = (int)(date / 10000);
}
```

Couldn't we just have used the `writeExternal`/`readExternal` mechanism instead? There is a slight difference—by using serial fields, the stream contains the name and type of the `date` value, not just raw bytes. Thus, the stream can still do type checking and versioning when reading the object back in.

Beyond the possibility of data corruption, there is another potentially worrisome security aspect to serialization. Any code that can access a reference to a serializable object can

- Write that object to a stream
- Then study the stream contents

and thereby know the values of all the data fields in the objects, *even the private ones*. After all, the serialization mechanism automatically saves all private data. Fortunately, this knowledge cannot be used to *modify* data. The `readObject` method does not overwrite an existing object but always creates a new object. Nevertheless, if you need to keep certain information safe from inspection via the serialization mechanism, you should take one of the following three steps:

1. Don't make the class serializable.

2. Mark the sensitive data fields as `transient`.

3. Do not use the default mechanism for saving and restoring objects. Instead, define `readObject`/`writeObject` or `readExternal`/`writeExternal` to encrypt the data.

Versioning

In the past sections, we showed you how to save relatively small collections of objects via an object stream. But those were just demonstration programs. With object streams, it helps to think big. Suppose you write a program that lets the user produce a document. This document contains paragraphs of text, tables, graphs, and so on. You can stream out the entire document object with a single call to `writeObject`:

```
out.writeObject(doc);
```

The paragraph, table, and graph objects are automatically streamed out as well. One user of your program can then give the output file to another user who also has a copy of your program, and that program loads the entire document with a single call to `readObject`:

```
doc = (Document)in.readObject();
```

This is very useful, but your program will inevitably change, and you will release a version 1.1. Can version 1.1 read the old files? Can the users who still use 1.0 read the files that the new version is now producing? Clearly, it would be desirable if object files could cope with the evolution of classes.

At first glance it seems that this would not be possible. When a class definition changes in any way, then its SHA fingerprint also changes, and you know that object streams will refuse to read in objects with different fingerprints. However, a class can indicate that it is *compatible* with an earlier version of itself. To do this, you must first obtain the fingerprint of the *earlier* version of the class. You use the stand-alone `serialver` program that is part of the JDK to obtain this number. For example, running

```
serialver corejava.Day
```

prints out

```
corejava.Day:    static final long serialVersionUID =
 -1249775427708836485L;
```

If you start the `serialver` program with the `-show` option, then the program brings up a graphical dialog box (see Figure 12–9).

Figure 12–9: The graphical version of the serialver program

All *later* versions of the class must define the `serialVersionUID` constant to the same fingerprint as the original.

```
class Day // version 1.1
{   . . .
    static final long serialVersionUID
        = -1249775427708836485L;
}
```

When a class has a static data member named `serialVersionUID`, it will not compute the fingerprint manually but instead will use that value.

Once that static data member has been placed inside a class, the serialization system is now willing to read in different versions of objects of that class.

If only the methods of the class change, then there is no problem with reading the new object data. However, if data fields change, then you may have problems. For example, the old file object may have more or fewer data fields than the one in the program, or the types of the data fields may be different. In that case, the object stream makes an effort to convert the stream object to the current version of the class.

The object stream compares the data fields of the current version of the class with the data fields of the version in the stream. Of course, the object stream considers only the nontransient and nonstatic data fields. If two fields have matching names but different types, then the object stream makes no effort to convert one type to the other—the objects are incompatible. If the object in the stream has data fields that are not present in the current version, then the object stream ignores the additional data. If the current version has data fields that are not present in the streamed object, the added fields are set to their default (null for objects, zero for numbers).

Here is an example. Suppose we have saved a number of employee records on disk, using the original version (1.0) of the class. Now we change the Employee class to version 2.0 by adding a data field called department. Figure 12–10 shows what happens when a 1.0 object is read into a program that uses 2.0 objects. The department field is set to null. Figure 12–11 shows the opposite scenario: a program using 1.0 objects reads a 2.0 object. The additional department field is ignored.

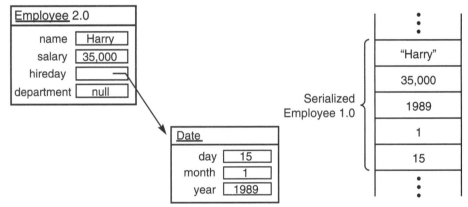

Figure 12–10: Reading an object with fewer data fields

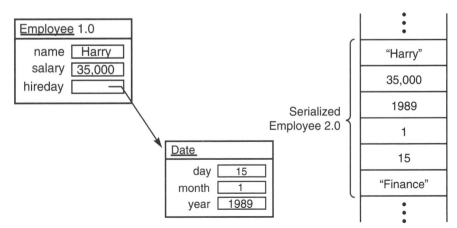

Figure 12–11: Reading an object with more data fields

Is this process safe? It depends. Dropping a data field seems harmless—the recipient still has all the data that it knew how to manipulate. Setting a data field to `null` may not be so safe. Many classes work hard to initialize all data fields in all constructors to non-`null` values, so that the methods don't have to be prepared to handle `null` data. It is up to the class designer to implement additional code in the `readObject` method to fix version incompatibilities or to make sure the methods are robust enough to handle `null` data.

Using serialization for cloning

There is one other amusing (and, occasionally, very useful) use for the new serialization mechanism: it gives you an easy way to clone an object *provided* the class is serializable. (Recall from Chapter 5 that you need to do a bit of work in order to allow an object to be cloned.) As the following example program shows, to get `clone` for free, simply derive from the `SerialCloneable` class, and you are done.

```
import java.io.*;
import corejava.*;

public class SerialCloneTest
{  public static void main(String[] args)
    {   Employee harry = new Employee("Harry Hacker", 35000,
            new Day(1989,10,1));
        Employee harry2 = (Employee)harry.clone();
        harry.raiseSalary(100);
        harry.print();
        harry2.print();
    }
}

class SerialCloneable implements Cloneable, Serializable
{  public Object clone()
    {   try
        {   ByteArrayOutputStream bout = new
                ByteArrayOutputStream();
            ObjectOutputStream out = new ObjectOutputStream(bout);
            out.writeObject(this);
            out.close();
            ByteArrayInputStream bin = new
                ByteArrayInputStream(bout.toByteArray());
            ObjectInputStream in = new ObjectInputStream(bin);
            Object ret = in.readObject();
            in.close();
            return ret;
        }   catch(Exception e)
        {   return null;
        }
    }
```

```
}

class Employee extends SerialCloneable
{   public Employee(String n, double s, Day d)
    {   name = n;
        salary = s;
        hireDay = d;
    }
    public Employee() {}

    public void print()
    {   System.out.println(name + " " + salary + " " +
            hireYear());
    }

    public void raiseSalary(double byPercent)
    {   salary *= 1 + byPercent / 100;
    }

    public int hireYear()
    {   return hireDay.getYear();
    }

    private String name;
    private double salary;
    private Day hireDay;
}
```

You should be aware that this method, although clever and occasionally necessary, will usually be much slower than a clone method that explicitly constructs a new object and copies or clones the data fields (as you saw in Chapter 6).

File Management

You have learned how to read and write data from a file. However, there is more to file management than reading and writing. The File class encapsulates the functionality that you will need to work with the file system on the user's machine. For example, you use the File class to find out when a file was last modified or to remove or rename the file. In other words, the stream classes are concerned with the contents of the file, whereas the File class is concerned with the storage of the file on a disk.

NOTE: As is so often the case in Java, the File class takes the least common denominator approach. For example, under Windows, you can find out (or set) the read-only flag for a file, but while you can find out if it is a hidden file, you can't hide it without using a native method (see Volume 2).

The simplest constructor for a `File` object takes a (full) file name. If you don't supply a pathname, then Java uses the current directory. For example:

```
File foo = new File("test.txt");
```

gives you a file object with this name in the current directory. (The current directory is the directory in which the program is running.) A call to this constructor *does not create a file with this name if it doesn't exist*. Actually, creating a file from a `File` object is done with one of the stream class constructors or the `createNewFile` method in the `File` class. The `createNewFile` method only creates a file if no file with that name exists, and it returns a `boolean` to tell you whether it was successful.

On the other hand, once you have a `File` object, the `exists` method in the `File` class tells you whether a file exists with that name. For example, the following trial program would almost certainly print "false" on anyone's machine, and yet it can print out a pathname to this nonexistent file.

```
import java.io.*;

public class Test
{   public static void main(String args[])
    {   File foo = new File("sajkdfshds");
        System.out.println(foo.getAbsolutePath());
        System.out.println(foo.exists());
    }
}
```

There are two other constructors for `File` objects:

```
File(String path, String name)
```

which creates a `File` object with the given name in the directory specified by the `path` parameter. (If the `path` parameter is `null`, this constructor then creates a `File` object, using the current directory.)

Finally, you can use an existing `File` object in the constructor:

```
File(File dir, String name)
```

where the `File` object represents a directory and, as before, if `dir` is `null`, the constructor creates a `File` object in the current directory.

Somewhat confusingly, a `File` object can represent either a file or a directory (perhaps because the operating system that the Java designers were most familiar with happens to implement directories as files). You use the `isDirectory` and `isFile` methods to tell you whether the file object represents a file or a directory. This is surprising—in an object-oriented system, one might have expected a separate `Directory` class, perhaps extending the `File` class.

To make an object representing a directory, you simply supply the directory name in the `File` constructor:

```
File tempDir = new File(File.separator + "temp");
```

If this directory does not yet exist, you can create it with the `mkdir` method:

```
tempDir.mkdir();
```

If a file object represents a directory, use `list()` to get an array of the file names in that directory. The program in Example 12–6 uses all these methods to print out the directory substructure of whatever path is entered on the command line. (It would be easy enough to change this program into a utility class that returns a vector of the subdirectories for further processing.)

Example 12–6: FindDirectories.java

```java
import java.io.*;

public class FindDirectories
{   public static void main(String args[])
    {   if (args.length == 0) args = new String[] { ".." };

        try
        {   File pathName = new File(args[0]);
            String[] fileNames = pathName.list();

            for (int i = 0; i < fileNames.length; i++)
            {   File tf = new File(pathName.getPath(),
                    fileNames[i]);
                if (tf.isDirectory())
                {   System.out.println(tf.getCanonicalPath());
                    main(new String [] { tf.getPath() });
                }
            }
        }
        catch(IOException e)
        {   System.out.println("Error: " + e);
        }
    }
}
```

Rather than listing all files in a directory, you can use a `FileNameFilter` object as a parameter to the `list` method to narrow down the list. These objects are simply instances of a class that satisfies the `FilenameFilter` interface.

All a class needs to do to implement the `FilenameFilter` interface is define a method called `accept()`. Here is an example of a simple `FilenameFilter` class that allows only files with a specified extension:

```java
import java.io.*;
public class ExtensionFilter implements FilenameFilter
{   private String extension;
    public ExtensionFilter(String ext)
    {   extension = "." + ext;
    }
```

```
      public boolean accept(File dir, String name)
      {  return name.endsWith(extension);
      }
   }
```

When writing portable programs, it is a challenge to specify file names with sub-directories. As we mentioned earlier, it turns out that you can use a forward slash (the Unix separator) as the directory separator in Windows as well, but other operating systems might not permit this, so we don't recommend using a forward slash.

CAUTION: If you do use forward slashes as a directory separator in Windows when constructing a `File` object, the `getAbsolutePath` method returns a file name that contains forward slashes, which will look strange to Windows users. Instead, use the `getCanonicalPath` method—it replaces the forward slashes with backslashes.

It is much better to use the information about the current directory separator that the `File` class stores in a static instance field called `separator`. (In a Windows environment, this is a backslash (\); in a Unix environment, it is a forward slash (/)). For example:

```
   File foo = new File("Documents" + File.separator + "data.txt")
```

Of course, if you use the second alternate version of the `File` constructor,

```
   File foo = new File("Documents", "data.txt")
```

then Java will supply the correct separator.

The API notes that follow give you what we think are the most important remaining methods of the `File` class; their use should be straightforward.

`java.io.File`

- `boolean canRead()`

  indicates whether the file can be read by the current application.

- `boolean canWrite()`

  indicates whether the file is writable or read-only.

- `static boolean createTempFile(String prefix, String suffix)`
  `static boolean createTempFile(String prefix, String suffix,`
  `    File directory)`

  creates a temporary file in the system's default temp directory or the given directory, using the given prefix and suffix to generate the temporary name.

Parameters: prefix   a prefix string that is at least three characters long.

             suffix   an optional suffix. If null, .tmp is used.

             directory   the directory in which the file is created. If it is null, the file is created in the current working directory.

- boolean delete()

tries to delete the file; returns true if the file was deleted; false otherwise.

- void deleteOnExit()

requests that the file be deleted when the VM shuts down.

- boolean exists()

true if the file or directory exists; false otherwise.

- String getAbsolutePath()

returns a string that contains the absolute pathname. Tip: Use getCanonicalPath instead.

- File getCanonicalFile()

returns a File object that contains the canonical pathname for the file. In particular, redundant " . " directories are removed, the correct directory separator is used, and the capitalization preferred by the underlying file system is obtained.

- String getCanonicalPath()

returns a string that contains the canonical pathname. In particular, redundant " . " directories are removed, the correct directory separator is used, and the capitalization preferred by the underlying file system is obtained.

- String getName()

returns a string that contains the file name of the File object (does not include path information).

- String getParent()

returns a string that contains the parent directory of the file, or null if you are at the root.

- File getParentFile()

returns a File object for the parent directory of the file, or null if you are at the root or this File object does not represent a directory.

- String getPath()

returns a string that contains the pathname of the file.

- `boolean isDirectory()`

  returns `true` if the `File` represents a directory; `false` otherwise.

- `boolean isFile()`

  returns `true` if the `File` object represents a file as opposed to a directory or a device.

- `boolean isHidden()`

  returns `true` if the `File` object represents a hidden file or directory.

- `long lastModified()`

  returns the time the file was last modified, or 0 if the file does not exist.

- `long length()`

  returns the length of the file in bytes, or 0 if the file does not exist.

- `String[] list()`

  returns an array of strings that contain the names of the files and directories contained by this `File` object, or `null` if this `File` was not representing a directory.

- `String[] list(FilenameFilter filter)`

  returns an array of the names of the files and directories contained by this `File` that satisfy the filter, or `null` if none exist.

  Parameters: `filter`   the `FilenameFilter` object to use

- `File[] listFiles()`

  returns an array of `File` objects corresponding to the files and directories contained by this `File` object, or `null` if this `File` was not representing a directory.

- `File[] listFiles(FilenameFilter filter)`

  returns an array of `File` objects for the files and directories contained by this `File` that satisfy the filter, or `null` if none exist.

  Parameters: `filter`   the `FilenameFilter` object to use

- `File[] listRoots()`

  returns an array of `File` objects corresponding to all the available file roots. (For example, on a Windows system, you get you the `File` objects representing the installed drives (both local drives and mapped network drives). On a Unix system, you simply get "`/`".)

- `boolean createNewFile()`

  makes a subdirectory whose name is given by the `File` object. Returns `true` if the directory was successfully created; `false` otherwise.

- `boolean mkdir()`

  makes a subdirectory whose name is given by the `File` object. Returns `true` if the directory was successfully created; `false` otherwise.

- `boolean mkdirs()`

  unlike `mkdir`, creates the parent directories if necessary. Returns `false` if any of the necessary directories could not be created.

- `boolean renameTo(File dest)`

  returns `true` if the name was changed; `false` otherwise.

  Parameters: `dest`   a `File` object that specifies the new name

- `boolean setLastModified(long time)`

  sets the last modified time of the file. Returns `true` if successful, `false` otherwise.

  Parameters: `long`   a long integer representing the number of milliseconds since the epoch (Midnight January 1, 1970).

- `boolean setReadOnly()`

  sets the file to be read-only. Returns `true` if successful, `false` otherwise.

- `URL toURL()`

  converts the `File` object to a file URL.

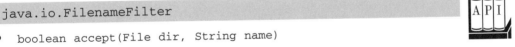

`java.io.FilenameFilter`

- `boolean accept(File dir, String name)`

  returns `true` if the file matches the filter criterion.

  Parameters: `dir`   a `File` object representing the directory that contains the file

                  `name`   the name of the file

Appendix I

Java Keywords

Keyword	Meaning	See Chapter
abstract	an abstract class or method	5
boolean	the Boolean type	3
break	breaks out of a `switch` or loop	3
byte	the 8-bit integer type	3
case	a case of a `switch`	3
catch	the clause of a `try` block catching an exception	11
char	the Unicode character type	3
class	defines a class type	4
const	not used	
continue	continues at the end of a loop	3
default	the default clause of a `switch`	3
do	the top of a `do/while` loop	3
double	the double-precision floating-number type	3
else	the `else` clause of an `if` statement	3
extends	defines the parent class of a class	4
final	a constant, or a class or method that cannot be overridden	5
finally	the part of a `try` block that is always executed	11
float	the single-precision floating-point type	3
for	a loop type	3
goto	not used	
if	a conditional statement	3
implements	defines the interface(s) that a class implements	6
import	imports a package	4
instanceof	tests if an object is an instance of a class	5

`int`	the 32-bit integer type	3
`interface`	an abstract type with methods that a class can implement	6
`long`	the 64-bit long integer type	3
`native`	a method implemented by the host system (see Volume 2)	
`new`	allocates a new object or array	3
`null`	a null reference	3
`package`	a package of classes	4
`private`	a feature that is accessible only by methods of this class	4
`protected`	a feature that is accessible only by methods of this class, its children, and other classes in the same package	5
`public`	a feature that is accessible by methods of all classes	4
`return`	returns from a method	3
`short`	the 16-bit integer type	3
`static`	a feature that is unique to its class, not to objects of its class	3
`super`	the superclass object or constructor	4
`switch`	a selection statement	3
`synchronized`	a method that is atomic to a thread (see Volume 2)	
`this`	the implicit argument of a method, or a constructor of this class	4
`throw`	throws an exception	12
`throws`	the exceptions that a method can throw	11
`transient`	marks data that should not be persistent	12
`try`	a block of code that traps exceptions	11
`void`	denotes a method that returns no value	3
`volatile`	not used	
`while`	a loop	3

Appendix **II**

The **javadoc** Utility

The javadoc utility parses source files for classes, methods, and /** . . . */ comments. It produces an HTML file in the same format as the API documentation. In fact, the API documentation is the javadoc output of the Java source files.

If you add comments that start with the special delimiter /** to your source code, you too can produce professional-looking documentation easily. This is a very nice scheme because it lets you keep your code and documentation in one place. Traditional documentation efforts suffered from the problem that the code and comments diverged over time. But since the documentation comments are in the same file as the source code, it is an easy matter to update both and run javadoc again.

We used the /** comments and javadoc on the files in our corejava package. Point your Web browser to \CoreJavaBook\api\index.html, and you will see the corejava documentation in a format that looks startlingly familiar.

How to Insert Comments

The javadoc utility extracts information for every

- package;
- public class;
- public interface;
- public or protected method;
- public or protected variable or constant.

You can (and should) supply a comment for each of these features.

Each comment is placed immediately *above* the feature it describes. A comment starts with a /** and ends with a */.

Each /** . . . */ documentation comment contains *free-form text* followed by *tags*. A tag starts with a @, such as @author or @param.

The *first sentence* of the free-form text should be a *summary statement*. The javadoc utility automatically generates summary pages that extract these sentences.

In the free-form text, you can use HTML modifiers such as `<i>...</i>` for italics, `<tt>...</tt>` for a monospaced "typewriter" font, `<b>...</b>` bold for bold, and even `<img ...>` to include an image. You should, however, stay away from heading `<h1>` or rules `<hr>` since they interfere with the formatting of the document.

General Comments

The following tags can be used in all documentation comments.

> `@since` *text*

This tag makes a "since" entry. The *text* can be any description of the version that introduced this feature.

> `@deprecated` *text*

This tag adds a comment that the class, method, or variable should no longer be used. The *text* should suggest a replacement. For example, `@deprecated Use <tt>setVisible(true)</tt>`.

You can use hyperlinks to other relevant parts of the `javadoc` documentation, or to external documents, with the `@see` and `@link` tags.

> `@see` *link*

This tags adds a hyperlink in the "See also" section. It can be used both with classes and methods. Here, *link* can be one of the following:

- `package.class#feature    label`
- `<a href="...">label</a>`
- `"text"`

The first case is the most useful. You supply the name of a class, method, or variable, and `javadoc` inserts a hyperlink to the documentation. For example, `@see corejava.Console#readInt(java.lang.String)` makes a link to the `readInt(String)` method in the `corejava.Console` class. You can omit the name of the package or both the package and class name. Then, the feature will be located in the current package or class.

Note that you must use a #, not a period, to separate the class from the method or variable name. The Java compiler itself is highly skilled in guessing the various meanings of the period character, as separator between packages, sub-packages, classes, inner classes, and methods and variables. But, the `javadoc` utility isn't quite as clever, and you have to help it along.

If the `@see` tag is followed by a `<` character, then you need to specify a hyperlink. You can link to any URL you like. For example, `@see <a href="www.horstmann.com/corejava.html">The Core Java home page</a>`.

In each of these cases, you can specify an optional *label* that will appear as the link anchor. If you omit the label, then the user will see the target code name or URL as the anchor.

If the `@see` tag is followed by a `"` character, then the text is displayed in the "see also" section. For example, `@see "Core Java 1.2 volume 2"`.

You can add multiple `@see` tags for one feature, but you must keep them all together.

If you like, you can place hyperlinks to other classes or methods anywhere into any of your comments. You insert a special tag of the form `{@link package.class#feature label}` anywhere into a comment. The feature description follows the same rules as for the `@see` tag.

Class and Interface Comments

The class comment must be placed *after* any `import` statements, directly before the `class` definition.

The following tags are supported.

`@author` *name*

This tag makes an "author" entry. There can be multiple author tags, but they must all be together.

`@version` *text*

This tag makes a "version" entry. The *text* can be any description of the current version.

Here is an example of a class comment:

```
/**
    A class for formatting numbers that follows <tt>printf</tt>
    conventions. All options of the C <tt>printf</tt> function are
    supported.

    @version 1.01 15 Feb 1996
    @author Cay Horstmann
    @see "Kernighan and Ritchie, The C Programming Language,
        2nd ed."
*/
```

Method Comments

Each method comment must immediately precede the signature of the method that it describes. In addition to the general-purpose tags, you can use the following tags:

@param *variable description*

This tag adds an entry to the "parameters" section of the current method. The description can span multiple lines and can use HTML tags. All @param tags for one method must be kept together.

@return *description*

This tag adds a "Returns" section to the current method. The description can span multiple lines and can use HTML tags.

@throws *class description*

This tag adds an entry to the "Throws" section of the current method. A hyperlink is automatically created. The description can span multiple lines and can use HTML tags. All @throws tags for one method must be kept together.

Here is an example of a method comment:

```
/**
    Formats a double into a string (like <tt>sprintf</tt> in C)

    @param x the number to format
    @return the formatted string
    @throws IllegalArgumentException if bad argument
*/
```

Serialization Comments

As of Java 1.2, there are three new tags to document object serialization. (See Chapter 12 for more information on object serialization and object streams.) As we write this, these tags are not yet fully supported.

@serial *text*

You are supposed to use this tag for *all* fields that are not static or transient in all classes that implement the Serializable interface, provided they don't override the default serialization mechanism. This sounds like a lot of trouble, but it is supposed to make you think twice about whether each field can be safely serialized. We suspect that this requirement is going to be dropped once everyone realizes just how onerous it is. The optional text is supposed to contain a description of the legal values of the field. With the version of javadoc that we used for testing, you get a warning if you omit the @serial comment from a serializable field.

@serialField *name type text*

Use this tag for all fields that are listed in the `serialPersistentFields` array of a class that does override the default serialization mechanism. (See Chapter 12 for information on this alternate serialization mechanism).

@serialData *text*

Use this tag to describe additional data that is written by the `writeObject` or `writeExternal` method. (See Chapter 12 for information on these methods.) Place it with the documentation of the method that writes or reads the data.

Package and Overview Comments

You place class, method, and variable comments directly into the Java source files, delimited by `/**` . . . `*/` documentation comments. However, to generate package comments, you need to add a file named `package.html` in each package directory. All text between the tags `<BODY>...</BODY>` is extracted.

You can also supply an overview comment for all source files. Place it in a file called `overview.html`, located in the parent directory that contains all the source files. All text between the tags `<BODY>...</BODY>` is extracted. This comment is displayed when the user selects "Overview" from the navigation bar.

How to Extract Comments

Here, *docDirectory* is the name of the directory you want the HTML files to go to. Follow these steps:

1. Move to the directory that contains the source files you want to document. If you have nested packages to document, such as `com.corejava`, you must be in the directory that contains the subdirectory `com`. (This is the directory that contains the `overview.html` file, if you supplied one.)

2. Run the command

    ```
    javadoc -d docDirectory nameOfPackage
    ```

    for a single package. Or run

    ```
    javadoc -d docDirectory nameOfPackage1 nameOfPackage2...
    ```

    to document multiple packages.

The `javadoc` program can be fine-tuned by numerous command-line options. For example, you can use the `-author` and `-version` options to include the `@author` and `@version` tags in the documentation. (By default, they are omitted.) We refer you to the online documentation of the `javadoc` utility.

If you require further customization, for example, to produce documentation in a format other than HTML, then you can supply your own *doclet* to generate the output in any form you desire. Clearly, this is a specialized need, and we refer you to the online documentation for details on doclets.

Appendix III

Installing the CD-ROM

Contents of the CD-ROM

The CD-ROM has the following directory structure:

```
corejava
windows
solaris
```

Other operating systems may be added.

The `corejava` directory contains the sample files for both volumes of Core Java. The `windows` directory contains the Java development kit (JDK) for Windows 95/NT and a number of useful shareware programs. The `solaris` directory contains the JDK for the Solaris operating system.

NOTE: If you do not have a CD-Rom drive, you can download all materials from the Net. Look for them at the following URLs:

JDK	`java.sun.com`
Sample programs	`www.phptr.com/corejava`
Winzip	`www.winzip.com`
TextPad	`www.textpad.com`
HexWorkshop	`www.bpsoft.com`
Together/J	`www.oi.com`

Installation Directions

Install the JDK

You can skip this step if you already have a Java development environment installed that supports the most current version of Java.

1. On the CD-ROM locate the subdirectory that matches your operating system.

2.   You will find an installation file for the JDK in a format that is appropriate for your operating system, accompanied by installation instructions. For example, for Windows, this will be an `.exe` file.

3.   Install the JDK files onto your computer, following the procedure that is appropriate for your operating system. We recommend that you place the files inside a directory `jdk`. If you have an older version of the JDK, completely remove it before installing the newer version.

NOTE: If the JDK is installed by a setup program, the setup program usually offers a different default for each version of the JDK, such as `jdk1.2.3`. We recommend that you change the directory to `jdk`. However, if you are a Java enthusiast who enjoys collecting different versions of the JDK, go ahead and accept the default.

4.   Add the `jdk\bin` directory to the `PATH`. For example, under Windows 95, place the following line at the *end* of your `AUTOEXEC.BAT` file:

```
SET PATH=c:\jdk\bin;%PATH%
```

NOTE: If you installed the JDK into another directory such as `jdk1.2.3`, then you need to set the path to `jdk1.2.3\bin`. You need to modify the other instructions as well. We won't mention this again.

5.   Check whether there is a separate installation for other Java tools, such as the Bean Development Kit (BDK), the Java Plug-in, or the Plug-in HTML converter, for your operating system on the CD. If so, install these tools as needed.

6.   Install the documentation (which is contained in a separate archive). We also recommend that you unpack the source code (which is contained in the file `src.jar` in the `jdk` directory).

TIP: Sun Microsystems frequently releases updates to the JDK. You should check the Java web site `http://java.sun.com` to see whether a newer version of the JDK is available. In that case, we recommend that you download and install the JDK from the Web instead of the CD.

Install Trial Software

Skip this step if you do not use Windows 95/98 or NT.

We include a number of trial programs on the CD-ROM that you may find useful, including

- WinZip, our favorite ZIP tool. You can use it to uncompress files in the ZIP, JAR, and TAR formats.

- TextPad, our favorite ASCII text editor for Windows. This version of TextPad is enhanced to compile and run Java programs. (Look in the Tools menu for the commands.)

- HexWorkshop, our favorite hex editor. In Volume 2, we show you how to use HexWorkshop to snoop inside class files.

There may be other software that we think might be of interest; have a look at the windows directory.

To install the software, locate the installation files in the subdirectory of the windows directory (such as windows\winzip or windows\textpad) and run the setup program in that subdirectory.

Install the Core Java Example Files

The CD-ROM contains the source code for all example programs in the book. All files are packed inside a single ZIP archive, corejava.zip.

If you have a ZIP utility such as WinZip (which is supplied on the CD-ROM), you can use it to unzip the files. Otherwise, you need to first install the JDK, as previously described. The JDK program jar can uncompress ZIP files.

Here are the steps to install the Core Java example files:

1. Uncompress the corejava.zip file into the CoreJavaBook directory. You can use WinZip, another ZIP utility, or the jar program that is part of the JDK. If you use jar, do the following:

   - Make sure the JDK is installed.

   - Make a directory CoreJavaBook.

   - Copy the corejava.zip file to that directory.

   - Change to that directory.

   - Execute the command

     ```
     jar xvf corejava.zip
     ```

2. Add an environment variable CLASSPATH. This environment must contain

   - the current directory (.)

   - CoreJavaBook (the directory into which you installed the Core Java examples)

   For example, under Windows, you add the following line to your AUTOEXEC.BAT file:

   ```
   SET CLASSPATH=.;c:\CoreJavaBook
   ```

   If you use the C shell under Unix, place the following command in your .cshrc file.

   ```
   setenv CLASSPATH .:$home/CoreJavaBook
   ```

NOTE: Many integrated Java development environments have their own methods for setting the class path. If you use such a product, find out how to tell it to search the `CoreJavaBook` directory for class files. Consult the documentation of your environment and contact the vendor for assistance if necessary.

The example files are organized as follows:

```
CoreJavaBook
    corejava
    docs
    v1ch2
        Welcome
        WelcomeApplet
        ImageViewer
    v1ch3
        FirstSample
        LotteryOdds
        LotteryDrawing
        Mortgage
        MortgageLoop
        Retirement
        SquareRoot
    . . .
    v2ch1
    . . .
```

There is a separate directory for each chapter of this book. Each of these directories has separate subdirectories for example files. For instance, `CoreJavaBook\ch2\ImageViewer` contains the source code and sample images for the image viewer application. (There is no source code for Volume 1, Chapter 1.)

 NOTE: The `corejava` directory contains a number of useful Java classes we wrote to supplement missing features in the standard Java library. These files are needed for many examples in the book. It is crucial that your `CLASSPATH` environment variable is set to include the `CoreJavaBook` directory so that the programs can find our files, such as `CoreJavaBook\corejava\Format.class` and `CoreJavaBook\corejava\Day.class`.

The `api` directory contains the documentation for the classes in the `corejava` directory. Point your Web browser to `CoreJavaBook\api\index.html` for a summary of the utility classes that we supply. Click on the links to get more information about each class.

Testing the Installation

Testing the JDK

Go to the `CoreJavaBook\v1ch2\Welcome` directory. Then, enter the following commands:

```
javac Welcome.java
java Welcome
```

Or, if you use an integrated development environment, load the file `Welcome.java`, then compile and run the program. There should be no warning or error messages during compilation.

When the program runs, it should write a welcome message in the console window.

Testing the Core Java Utility Package

Go to the `CoreJavaBook\v1ch3\LotteryOdds` directory. Then, enter the following commands:

```
javac LotteryOdds.java
java LotteryOdds
```

You should be prompted for two numbers. Enter 6 and 49, and the program will tell you the odds of winning the jackpot in a "choose 6 numbers from 49" lottery. Good luck!

If the program fails to compile or to run, you did not set the class path correctly.

Testing Swing Set Support

Go to the `CoreJavaBook\v1ch7\NotHelloWorld` directory. Then, enter the following commands:

```
javac NotHelloWorld.java
java NotHelloWorld
```

Or, if you use an integrated development environment, load the file `NotHelloWorld.java`, then compile and run the program. There should be no warning or error messages during compilation. If the program does not compile, your development environment does not support the Swing Set user interface components.

When the program runs, it should pop up a window with a silly message.

By now, you may be feeling like the person who buys a gas grill, only to find that it is actually a gas grill assembly kit, not a ready-to-use grill. There is a reason, after all, why this is called the Java development *kit*. Undoubtedly, all this confusion will end once integrated development environments support the most up-to-date versions of Java.

Troubleshooting

Here are some troubleshooting hints in case the installation was not successful.

PATH *and* CLASSPATH

The single, most common problem we encountered with Java is an incorrect PATH or CLASSPATH environment variable. Check the following:

1. The \jdk\bin directory must be on PATH.

2. The CoreJavaBook directory must be on the CLASSPATH for all programs that import the corejava package.

3. With some versions of the JDK, the current directory (that is, the . directory) must be on CLASSPATH.

Double-check these settings and reboot your computer if you run into trouble.

TIP: Be careful *not to put spaces into the* SET CLASSPATH *statement.* In particular, there should be no spaces around the equal sign in the statement

```
SET CLASSPATH=.;c:\CoreJavaBook
```

Memory Problems

If you have only 16 Mbytes of memory, you may get "insufficient memory" errors from the Java compiler. In that case, close memory hogs like Netscape and Microsoft Exchange. If you have less than 16 Mbytes of memory, you will probably be unable to compile large programs.

NOTE: Only the compiler and applet viewer pig out on memory. Once you compile an application, you should have no trouble running it with the Java interpreter or a browser, even with less than 16 Mbytes of memory.

Case Sensitivity

Java is case sensitive. HTML is sometimes case sensitive. DOS is not case sensitive. This caused us no end of grief, especially since Java can give very bizarre error messages when it messes up because of a spelling error. Always check file names, parameter names, class names, keywords, and so on for capitalization.

Browsers

You need to install the Java Plug-in to use your Web browser to view the applets that are supplied with this book. If you do not want to install the Java Plug-in, simply use the applet viewer.

About Other Platforms

The setup that we described assumes that your platform has a command-line interface and a way for setting environment variables. That is the case for Windows, Unix, and OS/2, but it is not the case for the Macintosh. Read the information supplied by Sun Microsystems or the vendor of your development environment, and modify the installation instructions accordingly.

Updates and Bug Fixes

The CD-ROM contains several hundred files, and some of them are bound to have minor glitches and inconsistencies. We keep a list of frequently asked questions, a list of typographical errors, and bug fixes on the Web. (The main Web page for the book is `http://www.horstmann.com/corejava.html`.) We very much welcome any reports of typographical errors, example program bugs, and suggestions for improvement.

Before contacting us, please consider the following:

1. Please check the FAQ and list of bug reports on the Core Java Web page before mailing us. We get many duplicate queries and bug reports.

2. Please, no requests for handholding. Many readers have successfully compiled and executed the programs on the CD-ROM. If you have problems, there is an overwhelming likelihood that the problem is on your end, not because of a flaw with the CD-ROM contents. On the other hand, if we goofed and there is a serious problem with the CD-ROM, then there is an overwhelming chance that hundreds of readers complained to us already and that you will find a resolution on the FAQ.

3. We want to support and improve the Core Java book and example files, but we cannot help you with problems with the Java compiler, your development environment, or the trial programs on the CD-ROM. Please contact the product vendor for assistance in those cases. If the product vendor does not supply contact information, then that means that the trial product is *completely unsupported*.

4. Finally, when contacting us, please use e-mail only. Please don't be disappointed if we don't answer every query or if we don't get back to you immediately. We do read all e-mail and consider your input to make future editions of this book clearer and more informative.

Index

6. **Termination.** This Agreement is effective until terminated. You may terminate this Agreement at any time by destroying all copies of Software. This Agreement will terminate immediately without notice from Sun if you fail to comply with any provision of this Agreement. Upon termination, you must destroy all copies of Software.

7. **Export Regulations.** All Software and technical data delivered under this Agreement are subject to U.S. export control laws and may be subject to export or import regulations in other countries. You agree to comply strictly with all such laws and regulations and acknowledge that you have the responsibility to obtain such licenses to export, re-export, or import as may be required after delivery to you.

8. **U.S. Government Restricted Rights.** Use, duplication, or disclosure by the U.S. Government is subject to restrictions set forth in this Agreement and as provided in DFARS 227.7202-1(a) and 227.7202-3(a) (1995), DFARS 252.227-7013(c)(1)(ii) (Oct 1988), FAR 12.212(a)(1995), FAR 52.227-19 (June 1987), or FAR 52.227-14 (ALT III) (June 1987), as applicable.

9. **Governing Law.** Any action related to this Agreement will be governed by California law and controlling U.S. federal law. No choice of law rules of any jurisdiction will apply.

10. **Severability.** If any provision of this Agreement is held to be unenforceable, this Agreement will remain in effect with the provision omitted, unless omission of the provision would frustrate the intent of the parties, in which case this Agreement will immediately terminate.

11. **Integration.** This Agreement is the entire agreement between you and Sun relating to its subject matter. It supersedes all prior or contemporaneous oral or written communications, proposals, representations and warranties and prevails over any conflicting or additional terms of any quote, order, acknowledgment, or other communication between the parties relating to its subject matter during the term of this Agreement. No modification of this Agreement will be binding, unless in writing and signed by an authorized representative of each party.

For inquiries please contact: Sun Microsystems, Inc., 901 San Antonio Road, Palo Alto, California 94303

JAVA™ DEVELOPMENT KIT VERSION 1.2
SUPPLEMENTAL LICENSE TERMS

These supplemental terms ("Supplement") add to the terms of the Binary Code License Agreement ("Agreement"). Capitalized terms not defined herein shall have the same meanings ascribed to them in the Agreement. The Supplement terms shall supersede any inconsistent or conflicting terms in the Agreement.

1. Limited License Grant. Sun grants to you a non-exclusive, non-transferable limited license to use the Software without fee for evaluation of the Software and for development of Java™ applets and applications provided that you: (i) may not re-distribute the Software in whole or in part, either separately or included with a product. (ii) may not create, or authorize your licensees to create additional classes, interfaces, or subpackages that are contained in the "java" or "sun" packages or similar as specified by Sun in any class file naming convention; and (iii) agree to the extent Programs are developed which utilize the Windows 95/98 style graphical user interface or components contained therein, such applets or applications may only be developed to run on a Windows 95/98 or Windows NT platform. Refer to the Java Runtime Environment Version 1.2 binary code license (http://java.sun.com/products/JDK/1.2/index.html) for the availability of runtime code which may be distributed with Java applets and applications.

2. Java Platform Interface. In the event that Licensee creates an additional API(s) which: (i) extends the functionality of a Java Environment; and, (ii) is exposed to third party software developers for the purpose of developing additional software which invokes such additional API, Licensee must promptly publish broadly an accurate specification for such API for free use by all developers.

3. Trademarks and Logos. This Agreement does not authorize Licensee to use any Sun name, trademark or logo. Licensee acknowledges as between it and Sun that Sun owns the Java trademark and all Java-related trademarks, logos and icons including the Coffee Cup and Duke ("Java Marks") and agrees to comply with the Java Trademark Guidelines at http://java.sun.com/trademarks.html.

4. High Risk Activities. Notwithstanding Section 2, with respect to high risk activities, the following language shall apply: the Software is not designed or intended for use in on-line control of aircraft, air traffic, aircraft navigation or aircraft communications; or in the design, construction, operation or maintenance of any nuclear facility. Sun disclaims any express or implied warranty of fitness for such uses.

5. Source Code. Software may contain source code that is provided solely for reference purposes pursuant to the terms of this Agreement.

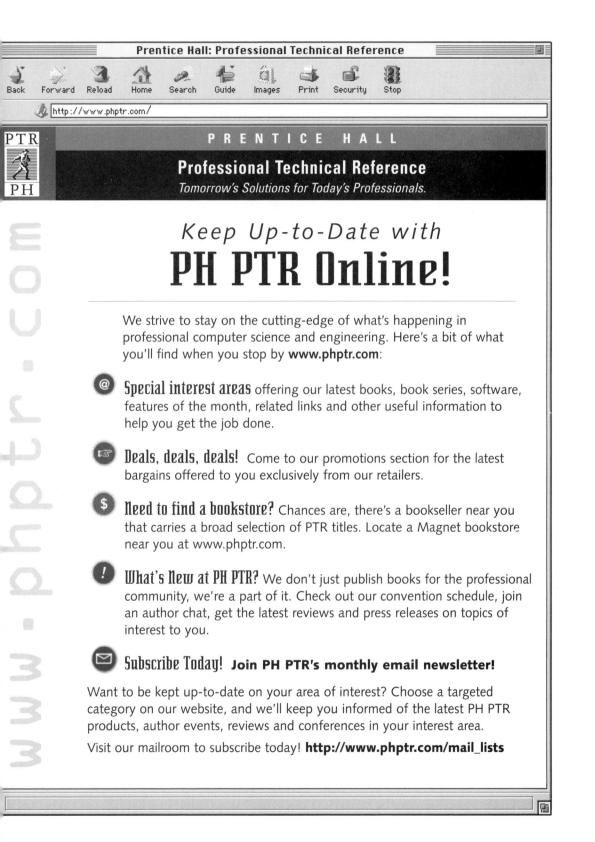

ABOUT THE CD

Please note: Because the final version of the JDK 1.2 was not available at press time, this CD does NOT include a copy of the JDK. To obtain the most current version of the JDK, go to `http://java.sun.com` and follow the instructions provided for downloading and installing the JDK. Use of the JDK is subject to the Binary Code License terms and conditions on page 738.

The *Core Java 1.2, Vol. I CD* is a standard ISO-9660 disc formatted with RockRidge and Joliet extensions. The software on this CD requires Solaris 2.x, Windows 95, or Windows NT. Windows 3.1 is not supported. This CD contains source code for the example programs in the book, as well as a number of useful shareware programs. The files are organized as follows:

`CoreJava`	This directory contains the *Core Java* example files. All of the files are packed inside a single ZIP archive named `corejava.zip` that can be unpacked with WinZip or the jar program that is part of the JDK.
`Solaris`	This directory contains a version of the Java Plug-in HTML Converter utility for Solaris.
`Windows`	This directory contains a number of useful Windows utilities and shareware programs described below.
`Hexwrkshp`	This directory contains an evaluation copy of Hex Workshop, a hex file and disk editor. Unzip the file `hw32v22.zip` and double click on `setup.exe` to launch the installation program.
`Htmlconverter`	This directory contains a version of the Java Plug-in HTML Converter utility for Windows.
`SourceAgain`	This directory contains Source Again 1.1 Personal, a decompiler for Java class files. Unzip the file `srcagain.zip` and then open the file `Readme.html` for further instructions.
`Textpad`	This directory contains an evaluation copy of TextPad 3.2.5, an ASCII text editor enhanced to compile and run Java programs. Double click on the file `tpe32325.exe` to launch the installation program.
`Together_J`	This directory contains a trial version of Together/J, Object International's UML modeler. Unzip the file `tg352w.zip` and double click on `Setup.exe` to launch the installation program.
`Winzip`	This directory contains WinZip 7.0, an archive utility that you can use to uncompress files in the ZIP, JAR, and TAR formats. To launch the installation program, double click on the file `winzip70.exe`.

Technical Support

Prentice Hall does not offer technical support for this software. If there is a problem with the media, however, you may obtain a replacement CD by emailing a description of the problem. Send your email to:

`disc_exchange@prenhall.com`